# Introduction to
# CRIMINOLOGY

Fourth Edition

# Introduction to
# CRIMINOLOGY

## Hugh D. Barlow

Southern Illinois University, Edwardsville

Scott, Foresman and Company

Glenview, Illinois   Boston   London

**Library of Congress Cataloging in Publication Data**

Barlow, Hugh D.
  Introduction to criminology.

  Includes bibliographical references and index.
  1. Crime and criminals.   2. Criminal justice,
Administration of.   I. Title.
HV6025.B29 1987     364'.0973     86-27225
ISBN 0-673-39564-2

ISBN 0-673-39564-2

345678910-RRC-908988

## Text Acknowledgments

The author gratefully acknowledges permission to quote material from the following sources.

James Boyd, excerpt from "The Ritual of Wiggle: From Ruin to Reelection." Reprinted with permission from *The Washington Monthly.* Copyright 1970 by The Washington Monthly Co., 1711 Connecticut Avenue, N.W., Washington, D.C. 20009.

Robert L. Burgess and Ronald L. Akers, from "A Differential Association Reinforcement Theory of Criminal Behavior," adaptation of Table 1. Copyright © 1966 by The Society for the Study of Social Problems. Reprinted from *Social Problems*, 14, 2, Fall 1966, pp. 128–147, by permission

Donald R. Cressey, abridged from pp. x–xi, 163–164, 175–178, 248, 250, and 251–252 in *Theft of the Nation.* Copyright © 1969 by Donald R. Cressey. Reprinted by permission of Harper & Row, Publishers, Inc.

Delbert S. Elliott and Suzanne S. Ageton, "Reconciling Race and Class Differences in Self-Reported and Official Estimates of Delinquency," *American Sociological Review,* vol. 45, pp. 108–109 (1980). Reprinted by permission.

Cyrus Gordon, from *Hammurabi's Code.* Copyright © 1957 by Cyrus Gordon. Reprinted by permission.

Francis A. J. Ianni, *Black Mafia: Ethnic Succession in Organized Crime.* Copyright © 1974 by Francis A. J. Ianni. Reprinted by permission of Simon & Schuster, Inc.

James A. Inciardi, excerpts from *Careers in Crime,* © 1975 Rand McNally College Publishing Company, Chicago. Reprinted by permission.

Carl B. Klockars, reprinted with permission of The Free Press, a Division of Macmillan, Inc., from *The Professional Fence* by Carl B. Klockars. Copyright © 1974 by Carl B. Klockars.

Burton M. Leiser, reprinted with permission of Macmillan Publishing Company from *Liberty, Justice and Morals* by Burton M. Leiser. Copyright © 1973 by Burton M. Leiser.

Peter Letkemann, *Crime as Work,* © 1973. Reprinted by permission of Prentice-Hall, Inc., Englewood Cliffs, New Jersey.

Continued text and photograph acknowledgments appear on page 504

To my children:
Alison, Melissa, and Colin

# Preface

In the ten years since going to press with the first edition of *Introduction to Criminology,* much has happened in the field. Among theoretical developments we have seen the rise of opportunity, rationality, and situational perspectives, as well as growing interest in the contributions of sociobiology. Research methodologies have changed, too, with the development of data banks and the continued refinement of statistical techniques and computer modelling. Cohort studies begun decades ago are providing new and exciting information on many important topics. Finally, public policy and practice have undergone significant changes, among them the rise of determinate sentencing and the implementation of victim compensation and restitution.

Crime itself has changed, primarily as a result of different opportunities, but also because authorities have exercised their power to create—or remove—criminal labels. Even crimes that were conventionally identified as victimless ten years ago are under reevaluation. A case in point is prostitution. Not only have many women's groups been active in drawing attention to the victimizing aspects of prostitution, but the spread of AIDS has become a major issue in the debate.

This fourth edition of the text keeps students abreast of these and other developments. Criminological theory is given expanded coverage, especially in chapters 2 and 3, but also elsewhere in the text. The discussion of violence has been entirely reworked, and a new chapter on sexual violence immediately follows Chapter 5 on homicide and assault. Chapter 9, on occupational crime, has been thoroughly updated, with more attention paid to current theory. A new Chapter 11 combines the topics of prostitution and drugs, treating both as public-order crimes; new material includes descriptive accounts of the daily lives of inner-city heroin addicts that highlight some of the prevailing myths about heroin addiction. Chapter 13, on the judicial process, now includes discussions of selective incapacitation and more on the prosecution and sentencing of felony offenders. There are many other lesser changes throughout the text, and of course all data and statistics have been updated whenever possible.

Once again I am indebted to various colleagues and graduate assistants for their help with this revision. The arduous work of updating statistics fell largely on the shoulders of Paula Rayney and Cindy Brueggenjohann. Ms. Brueggenjohann, together with Marlien Pennekamp, Deborah Ariosto, and Rose-Marie Johnson, also helped with modernization of the reference format, which turned out to be a major undertaking. I am particularly grateful to Ms. Pennekamp for her word processing skills. Brian Sullivan helped at various stages of the project in important ways, Rose-Marie Johnson took on additional work when I most needed assistance, and Mark Brueggenjohann developed the negatives for my photographs on very short notice. I would also like to give special thanks to Annice Barlow for her help with the indexes. Professors Robert Mendelsohn, South Dakota State University; Jay Corzine, University of Nebraska; Joan Neff Gurney, University of Richmond; and James DeFronzo, The University of Connecticut helped give direction to the revision. I would especially like to thank Professor Jay Corzine for his detailed and helpful critique of the previous edition. Needless to say, any errors and oversights in this fourth edition are mine.

My wife Lynne and son Colin have been a never-ending source of love and support, and my daughters Alison and Melissa, though far away, have a special place in my heart. I dedicate this edition to my family, and to all students embarking on a study of criminology.

H. D. B.

# Contents

## PART II   Crimes and Criminal Offenders

## PART III Doing Something About Crime

## 12. Policing Society    355

Introduction to
**CRIMINOLOGY**

# PART I

# Criminology: Theory and Method

# CHAPTER 1

# Crime, Criminal Law, and Criminals

Few people would contest the assertion that there is a crime problem in America. This does not mean, however, that everyone agrees on exactly what the problem is — or, for that matter, its solution. Consider these findings on crime and criminals in America:

Nearly two million wives are abused by their husbands each year.

Six men are arrested for every woman apprehended.

Thousands of schoolchildren around the country occasionally stay at home because they are afraid of violence at school.

The risk of being prosecuted for computer-related crime is about 1 in 22,000.

The ratio of male to female prisoners is over twenty to one.

Nearly two million American children are at risk of being physically abused by another family member.

In some states, over three-quarters of convicted felons receive probation as part or all of their sentence.

The United States has the highest homicide rate of any industrialized democracy.

Around 75 percent of American adults favor stricter gun control.

For Americans as a whole, the chance of being victimized by rape, robbery, or assault is once in fifty years; for blacks living in large cities, the chance is once per year.

Around 30 percent of American households are directly victimized by crime every year.

Elderly Americans are the *least* likely victims of violent crime.

Over 10 percent of robbery and burglary victims suffer severe emotional aftereffects.

The list could go on. These are just a few of the findings that are reflected in people's perceptions of the crime problem. Naturally, people tend to regard crimes that affect them as the most important ones. Some react to the extensive involvement of young people in crime, others to the rapid rise and high cost of occupational crimes like computer theft and the leniency with which the criminal justice system deals with white-collar offenders. Many people fear they will be victims of violent crime — with good reason if they are poor, young, and black. Some view the real crime problem as the breakdown of order in the nation's schools, where early delinquencies could perhaps be prevented. Others are incensed by the extensiveness of child abuse, including sexual assaults by other family members. Some people assert that crime is largely a problem of males overplaying their masculinity and prizing strength and aggression. Still others see the rising crime rate as the failure of the judicial system.

An area of concern to many officials is the habitual offender who makes crime a career. Whereas most people implicated in crimes are amateurs and opportunists, it has become evident that the bulk of robberies, burglaries, and other "street" crimes are committed by a relatively small number of repeat offenders. The suggestion that some criminals may commit hundreds of thousands of crimes during their careers seems a bit farfetched, but offenders who commit three or four hundred crimes a year are certainly not unusual. They are considered the major target of law enforcement efforts in many jurisdictions.

If different people see the problem of crime differently, it is also true that they often define *crime* in different ways. What exactly is a crime? Some people define crime to include acts that harm innocent victims, and others include so-called victimless behaviors — use of illicit drugs, prostitution, and homosexual acts between consenting adults. Yet others favor a broad conception: crimes, they say, are acts that violate "society's" rules. Criminologists tend to be more precise, but this does not mean there is complete agreement on a single definition.

# Defining Crime

Let us consider first what is commonly called the "legal" or "legalistic" definition of crime. It generally goes something like this: *Crime is a human act that violates the criminal law.*

This definition has two important components. First, crime involves *behavior:* Someone has to perform some act. Second, this behavior is identified in terms of a body of *Law*. According to that law, a number of specific criteria must normally be met for an act to be considered a crime and the perpetrator a criminal. First, there must be *conduct* (mere thoughts, no matter how terrible, are not crimes). Second, the conduct must constitute a *social harm,* that is, be injurious to the state (or "the people"). Third, the conduct must be *prohibited by law*. Fourth, the conduct must be performed *voluntarily*. Fifth, the conduct usually must be performed *intentionally* (the issue here is criminal intent, expressed in the concept of *mens rea,* meaning guilty mind); however, unintentional acts of negligence or omission may qualify as crimes in some cases. Sixth, the harm must be *causally related* to the conduct; that is, the act must produce the harm. Finally, the conduct must be *punishable by law* (in fact, the punishment must be specified in advance of the conduct).

## ARGUMENTS FOR AND AGAINST THE LEGALISTIC DEFINITION

Over the years, scholars have debated the pros and cons of the legalistic definition. Among those who favor this definition are Jerome Michael and Mortimer Adler (1933:2), who assert that the legalistic definition is "the only possible definition of crime." In their view the definition is precise and identifies the heart of the subject, namely, its relation to law. Three other common observations are (1) the legalistic definition recognizes a common thread binding instances of human conduct (they are legally identified as criminal); (2) the word *crime* is reserved for a class of acts to which stigma is attached by virtue of their illegality — to alter the definition to include other types of rule-breaking behavior would needlessly broaden the scope of this stigmatization; and (3) this definition identifies clear-cut boundaries for criminology, which distinguish it from the study of other areas of nonconformity and "deviance."

Taking an alternative position, Thorsten Sellin (1938) has argued for a more universally applicable definition that would encompass any violation of what he calls "conduct norms." Noting that legal rules are only a part of the more general body of social norms regulating behavior and that laws tend to vary over time and space, Sellin suggests that the legal criterion invoked in definitions of crime is at best artificial and arbitrary and at worst ignores other socially significant actions that conflict with the "general social interest." In Sellin's view, criminologists should study not just illegal acts, but any and all conduct that violates group norms.

Other critics have questioned the emphasis on social harm. In his discussion of criminal law, Jerome Hall (1960:14–26) observes that the notion of social harm is central to legal conceptions of crime. But what about acts that are harmful yet not identified in law as crimes — smoking cigarettes in public and other forms of pollution, for example. Should they not also be treated as crimes?

Some criminologists take issue with the legalistic definition more for what it implies than for its substance. This is an important issue, because definitions have implications for the kinds of questions we ask. When we define crime as violation of criminal law, our efforts to understand and explain crime are inevitably drawn to such questions as "Why do people violate the law?" and "What can be done about the violation?" Attention is thus drawn away from such questions as "Why are the laws what they are?" "How did they come about?" "Who created them?" and "What purposes do they serve?" The law side of the coin is considered primarily as a formal cause of crime — it "creates" crime by identifying acts that violate it — and not as an integral part of the crime picture that in itself needs to be explained. By treating law as a given, we may fall into the trap of mysticizing the concept of law: The law is the law; who is to question its existence? If our definition of crime leads us in this direction, some scholars argue, our understanding of crime will never be complete.

## MODIFICATIONS OF THE LEGALISTIC DEFINITION

Some authors have suggested modifications of the traditional legalistic definition. Walter Reckless (1950:8), for example, suggests that we should limit our attention to those illegal acts that have been reported to the police:

> To the question: What constitutes crime? the modern criminologist must answer that crime exists when a violation of the criminal code is reported. Otherwise,

the phenomenon is a non-reported violation, and we are not sure philosophically whether a non-reported violation is a phenomenon at all. A star might fall in the heavens, but if no one saw it and reported it and got confirmation from others who saw it, then the star did not fall in fact. So the fact of crime is the reporting of a violation of a criminal code. Anything else is not a crime in fact.

Other authors limit crime even more, namely, to those acts for which an offender has been caught, tried, and punished (Korn and McCorkle, 1957). In effect they are saying that the significance of crime as a legal phenomenon lies not so much in the idea that an act happens to violate the law but, rather, in the quality the act takes on when the machinery of law acts upon it. Some laws on the books, for example, are never enforced; in these cases it makes little sense to treat the illegal act as a crime. On paper the act is a crime; but as part of social experience it is not. As Roscoe Pound (1923) noted many years ago, *law in action* is the appropriate focus for those interested in the reality of law. Law in action involves the activities of those who create and enforce criminal law.

**The Labeling Perspective: Crime As Status**   Definitions that refer to those who administer the law emphasize the idea that crimes are distinguished from other acts precisely because they have been defined as crimes by those in a position to react to them (Quinney, 1970a:5–6). The activities of those who administer the criminal law lead to the imposition of the label *crime* on a behavior, at which point the behavior in question becomes part of the crime scene. Although those who create the law do, in fact, impose labels on behavior, the social significance of a given act is in the reactions it calls forth.

The idea that crimes are identifiable in terms of the reactions to them is not new. Emile Durkheim (1964:70), one of the fathers of sociology, noted that a crime is "every act which, in any degree whatever, invokes against its author the characteristic reaction we term punishment." Speaking on the more general topic of deviance, Howard Becker (1963:9) has observed that

> . . . deviance is *not* a quality of the act the person commits, but rather a consequence of the application by others of rules and sanctions to an "offender." The deviant is one to whom the label has been successfully applied; deviant behavior is behavior that people so label.

Pursuing this reasoning, what makes behavior distinctive is the kinds of reactions it calls forth. The distinctive thing about *criminal* behavior is that the behavior in question has been labeled crime (Hartjen, 1974:5–8).

When labeled crime, behavior is transformed into criminal behavior, and the actor may be transformed into a criminal. This transformation is called *criminalization*. The opposite process — when the label *criminal* is removed from an action, event, or person — is called *decriminalization*. For those who favor the *labeling perspective*, as it is often called, why and how the transformation occurs is crucial to an understanding of crime. In their view, how people perceive the actions of others, and what they do about it, should be central issues in criminology.

It happens that the acquisition of criminal status is rarely determined solely by what a person does, and sometimes people escape criminal labeling despite doing criminal things.

A well-known study by William Chambliss (1973) illustrates these points. Chambliss observed the experiences of two small-town juvenile gangs whose members regularly engaged in delinquent acts. However, only the members of one gang — the "Roughnecks" — were considered delinquent by officials and repeatedly arrested. The other gang — the "Saints" — largely escaped criminal labeling, and no members were ever arrested. A major distinction between the two gangs was that the Roughnecks were children from lower-class families, and the Saints came from respectable, upper-middle-class homes.

The labeling perspective views crime as *status* rather than as behavior. But who ascribes this status to acts? Certainly, in the broadest sense, we all do. Based on our experiences, our knowledge, and our feelings about things, our perceptions may lead us to define certain actions as crimes. This category of crime can be called "natural" crime, to distinguish it from "legal" crime (Quinney, 1970:7–8).

If we define crime as legal status, then we treat acts as crimes only when they are so labeled by those who create and administer the criminal law. We are once again reminded that criminal law plays an important part in the determination of crime, but here it is clearly more than a "formal" cause of crime. Apart from anything else, criminal law *in action* sets the conditions under which labels can be applied, and it restricts, in theory if not always in practice, the range of behaviors that will be defined as crime.

Viewed in this way, crime actually has five distinct meanings. The five levels of meaning depend on the stage in the legal process that we are considering. Legislatures and other agencies, whose job it is to *create* legal definitions of behavior, provide us with formulations of criminal law. These formulations identify acts that violate them and that therefore are crimes. But those who *enforce* the criminal law also define crime. The act of arrest applies the crime label at another stage of the legal process. Persons who are not arrested escape the imposition of the label crime at this and any subsequent stages. Although in terms of the first stage their behavior might be a crime, it is not a crime at the arrest stage, since no arrest is made.

In the *prosecution* and *conviction* stages, specific interpretations of conduct are again made within the framework of criminal law. The personal and social ramifications of labeling at these stages may be different from those at earlier stages. Finally, we can identify a fifth stage when *punishment* is meted out. Conduct reaching this stage may be said to constitute crime at all levels of meaning.

Bearing these conceptual distinctions in mind, we can now define crime:

*Crime is a label that is attached to human conduct by those who create and administer the criminal law.*

It is important to stress that the creation of criminal labels is often noncontroversial. In other words, there is general agreement among members of society that particular acts should be designated as crimes. This agreement or consensus even extends to attitudes toward the relative seriousness of crimes.

In the early 1960s, for example, Thorsten Sellin and Marvin Wolfgang (1964) asked samples of judges, police, and university students to rate the seriousness of 141 offenses. They found much agreement. A later survey of adults in Baltimore (Rossi et al., 1974) again found much consensus on a similar list of illegal acts. But, this study did find a prominent difference among white and black respondents: blacks rated violence among family and friends lower in seriousness than did whites. Thus, although there may be general agreement on crime seriousness, subgroups of the population may not share the general attitude toward particular crimes.

The most recent, and by far the most extensive, study confirms these earlier findings (Wolfgang et al., 1985). A total of 204 crimes were rated by a national sample of sixty thousand respondents (though no one person rated more than 25 offenses). Some of the specific crimes and their seriousness scores are shown in the box on pages 10–11. Overall, there was broad consensus. Violent crimes were rated more serious than were property offenses, and drug dealing was taken seriously, as was virtually any offense that had the potential for harming or killing more than one person. The study showed also that people evaluate crimes according to their consequences for the victims, and not surprisingly, respondents who had been victims of crime tended to assign higher seriousness scores than did others. Whites tended generally to assign higher scores than did minority groups.

A word of caution is appropriate with respect to these studies. It appears that consensus on seriousness is affected by the particular rating tasks given to subjects, by how consensus itself is measured, and by the particular offense under consideration (see Miethe 1982; Cullen et al., 1985). Of special significance is that most studies show relatively high levels of consistency in the ratings (the rank ordering of offenses tends to be similar), but much lower levels of agreement (i.e., concurrence on the absolute scores given to an offense). More work is clearly needed to sort out substance from method.

## Social Control and Law

We have seen that crime and law are intertwined. Now is an appropriate time to look more closely at law in general, and criminal law in particular. As a type of law, criminal law is generally regarded as a relatively recent development. Although no specific date of origin can be identified, criminal law in

## SERIOUSNESS SCORES FROM THE NATIONAL SURVEY OF CRIME SEVERITY

### Highest Scores

**72.1** A person plants a bomb in a public building. The bomb explodes and 20 people are killed.

**52.8** A man forcibly rapes a woman. As a result of physical injuries, she dies.

**47.8** A parent beats his young child with his fists. As a result, the child dies.

**43.2** A person robs a victim at gunpoint. The victim struggles and is shot to death.

**39.2** A man stabs his wife. As a result, she dies.

**39.1** A factory knowingly gets rid of its waste in a way that pollutes the water supply of a city. As a result, 20 people die.

**35.7** A person stabs a victim to death.

**35.6** A person intentionally injures a victim. As a result, the victim dies.

**33.8** A person runs a narcotics ring.

**33.0** A person plants a bomb in a public building. The bomb explodes and one person is injured but no medical treatment is required.

**32.7** An armed person skyjacks an airplane and holds the crew and passengers hostage until a ransom is paid.

**30.0** A man forcibly rapes a woman. Her physical injuries require hospitalization.

**27.9** A woman stabs her husband. As a result, he dies.

### Lowest Scores

**0.2** A person under 16 years old plays hooky from school.

**0.3** A person is a vagrant. That is, he has no home and no visible means of support.

**0.5** A person takes part in a dice game in an alley.

**0.6** A person trespasses in the backyard of a private home.

**0.7** A person under 16 years old breaks a curfew law by being out on the street after the hour permitted by law.

**0.8** A person is drunk in public.

**0.8** A person knowingly trespasses in a railroad yard.

**0.8** A person under 16 years old runs away from home.

**0.9** A person under 16 years old is reported to police by his parents as an offender because they are unable to control him.

**1.1** A person under 16 years old illegally has a bottle of wine.

the Western world developed from already existing systems of law some two thousand years ago and began to take shape in the later years of the Roman Empire. Before tracing the development of criminal law, let us examine the nature of law in general.

In any social group, efforts are made to ensure that members behave predictably and in accordance with the expectations and evaluations of others. These efforts are at the heart of *social control,* and their success is thought to be indispensable to orderly group life. It is difficult to imagine how group life could endure if members simply acted impulsively or in continued violation of the expectations of others.

Social control appears in different guises. It may appear in facial expressions, gestures, language, threats, gossip, ridicule, or ostracism. It may take the form of written rules backed by force, or it may consist largely of unwritten rules passed on by word of mouth, by example, or, even unconsciously, with little more than social disapproval of nonconformity. Sometimes conformity is promoted through the use of rewards ("positive sanctions"), sometimes through the use of penalties ("negative sanctions"). The effect of all these measures may be to create a sense of guilt and shame, which become internal controls.

## Some Other Scores

1.3 Two persons willingly engage in a homosexual act.

1.4 A person has some marijuana for his own use.

1.6 A person breaks into a parking meter and steals $10 worth of nickels.

1.6 A person is a customer in a house of prostitution.

2.1 A person engages in prostitution.

2.2 A person steals $10 worth of merchandise from the counter of a department store.

3.1 A person breaks into a home and steals $100.

3.6 A person knowingly passes a bad check.

6.2 An employee embezzles $1,000 from his employer.

6.7 A person, using force, robs a victim of $10. The victim is hurt and requires treatment by a doctor, but not hospitalization.

7.4 A person illegally gets monthly welfare checks.

7.9 A teenage boy beats his father with his fists. The father requires hospitalization.

9.0 A person, armed with a lead pipe, robs a victim of $1,000. No physical harm occurs.

9.2 Several large companies illegally fix the retail prices of their products.

10.3 A person operates a store where he knowingly sells stolen property.

10.5 A person smuggles marijuana into the country for sale.

12.0 A police officer takes a bribe not to interfere with an illegal gambling operation.

13.9 A legislator takes a bribe from a company to vote for a law favoring the company.

14.6 A person, using force, robs a victim of $10. The victim is hurt and requires hospitalization.

16.4 A person attempts to kill a victim with a gun. The gun misfires, and the victim escapes injury.

17.7 An employer orders one of his employees to commit a crime.

18.3 A man beats his wife with his fists. She requires hospitalization.

20.6 A person sells heroin to others for resale.

21.7 A person pays another person to commit a serious crime.

SOURCE: Wolfgang, Marvin E., Robert M. Figlio, Paul E. Tracy, and Simon I. Singer (1985), The National Survey of Crime Severity. Washington, D.C.: U.S. Department of Justice, pp. vi–x.

*Law* is a type of social control. It is an example of what we call *formal* social control, described here by F. James Davis (1962:43):

> Formal social control is characterized by (1) explicit rules of conduct, (2) planned use of sanctions to support the rules, and (3) designated officials to interpret and enforce the rules, and often to make them.

A classic definition of law was written by German sociologist Max Weber (1954:2):

> An order will be called *law* if it is externally guaranteed by the probability that coercion (physical or psychological), to bring about conformity or avenge violation, will be applied by a *staff* of people holding themselves specially ready for that purpose.

Weber contends that law has three essential features, which, taken together, distinguish it from other normative orders such as *custom* and *convention*. First, regardless of whether an individual wants to obey rules or does so out of habit, pressures to conform must be *external*, in the form of actions or threats of action by others. Second, these external actions or threats are specific: they involve coercion or force. Third, those who carry out the coercive threats are persons whose official role is enforcing the law. When this staff or administrative body is part of an agency of political authority, Weber defines it as "state" law.

Customs and conventions differ from law because they do not involve one or more of these features. Customs are rules *of* conduct that people follow "without thinking," or as Weber put it, with "unreflective imitation." These customary rules of conduct are called *usages,* and there is no sense of "oughtness," or obligation, about them. On the other hand, conventions are rules *for* conduct, and they do involve a question of obligation. Pressures to conform are brought to bear on rule breakers, and these usually involve some form of disapproval. However, unlike law, a conventional order "lacks specialized personnel for the implementation of coercive power" (Weber, 1954:27).

Some prominent scholars adhere to the essentials of Weber's definition of law but take issue with two major points. First, it is pointed out that by emphasizing coercion Weber ignored other, possibly more important considerations that influence people to conform to obligatory rules. For example, the authoritative character of legal rules may produce a special kind of obligation not dependent on the use or threat of force (Selznick, 1968). H. L. A. Hart (in Gibbs, 1968:431–432) writes that coercion is only one guarantee of conformity and in fact is less important as a characteristic of law than subjective evaluations on the basis of which individuals " 'apply' the rules themselves to themselves."

Weber appears to have been quite aware of this issue. People, he said, obey laws for a variety of reasons — sometimes because of an emotional commitment to them, sometimes through fear of disapproval, sometimes because it is in their interests to do so, and sometimes simply out of habit. Many laws are obeyed because we feel it is our duty to obey them, and this feeling seems to articulate a special kind of obligation that is built into authority relations. But Weber makes it clear that the question of why people obey obligatory rules is really irrelevant to a definition of law. The existence of a coercive apparatus in no way precludes the possibility that noncoercive pressures are more important in guaranteeing obedience. Most important in distinguishing legal systems from other methods of social control is that coercion is available and may be used by an authorized staff to ensure conformity or avenge violation.

The second objection is over the special staff. Some critics claim that Weber's definition unnecessarily restricts use of the term *law* when making cross-cultural and historical comparisons. Rather than use the word *staff,* which implies an organized administrative apparatus that may not exist in certain nonliterate and primitive societies, some suggest using a less restrictive term. Jack P. Gibbs (1966:29) offers "special status"; E. Adamson Hoebel (1954:28) mentions persons possessing "a socially authorized third party." Law in America, of course, provides for specific "officers" to administer and enforce it, and its very creation is the task of appointed and elected officials operating within the framework of an established political system. Still, we should bear these suggestions in mind when studying societies other than our own.

## Criminal Law

Criminal law is a specific type of law. Sutherland and Cressey (1974:4) write:

> The criminal law . . . is defined conventionally as a body of specific rules regarding human conduct which have been promulgated by political authority, which apply uniformly to all members of the classes to which the rules refer, and which are enforced by punishment administered by the state.

This definition identifies four critical features of criminal law: *politicality, penal sanction, specificity,* and *uniformity.* Briefly stated, *politicality* invokes the notion of political authority. Generally, it means that we include in criminal law only those rules created and enforced by authorized agents of the state.

*Penal sanction* "refers to the notion that violators will be punished or at least threatened with punishment by the state." *Specificity* points at the specific rather than general character of rules: "The criminal law . . . generally gives a strict definition of a specific act." *Uniformity* refers to the applicability of criminal laws and the way they are used. Such laws apply to all persons to whom they are relevant and must be applied without regard for personal status or prestige.

Sutherland and Cressey acknowledge the difficulties of applying this definition in the real world. Criminal law in action rarely seems to come up to this ideal characterization, and some of the distinctions are essentially arbitrary or ambiguous. Rather than retain the definition simply because it is conventional, some authors have taken steps to improve it.

In his definition of criminal law, Richard Quinney (1970a:16) leaves out any reference to uniformity. In his view, criminal law is not considered uniformly applicable by those who create and administer it, nor is it applied uniformly. Thus, it is somewhat pointless and misleading to include uniformity in the definition. Quinney also disagrees with the inclusion of penal sanction, pointing out that although criminal law contains provisions for the use of punitive sanctions, actual enforcement practices are quite another thing.

For our purposes, criminal law *encompasses specialized rules, created by those with the authority and power to do so, which contain provisions for punishments to be administered in the name of the group, community, or society.* Further, unlike tort or civil law, which requires that the victim make a complaint, *these rules may be enforced without the invitation or implied consent of the victim* (Gibbs, 1966:33).

# Origins and Development of Criminal Law

Much of what we know about the origins and development of criminal law has come through the efforts of legal historians and cultural anthropologists. Classic historical works such as *Ancient Law* by Sir Henry Sumner Maine (1905) and *The Growth of Criminal Law in Ancient Greece* by George Calhoun (1927) provide us with important interpretative accounts of early law. Twentieth-century anthropologists have added to the store of knowledge by drawing attention to rule making, rule breaking, and rule enforcement in primitive societies. Works by A. R. Radcliffe-Brown (1948), Bronislaw Malinowski (1926), E. Adamson Hoebel (1941), and E. E. Evans-Pritchard (1940) are among the best known.

## THE DECLINE OF PRIMITIVE LAW

It is generally agreed that "primitive law" — the system of rules and obligations in preliterate and semiliterate societies — represents the foundation on which modern legal systems were built. Primitive law contains three important features: (1) acts that injured or wronged others were considered "private wrongs," that is, injuries to particular individuals rather than the group or tribe as a whole (exceptions to this were acts deemed harmful to the entire community, for example, aiding an enemy or witchcraft); (2) the injured party or family typically took personal action against the wrongdoer, a kind of self-help justice; (3) this self-help justice usually amounted to retaliation in kind. Blood feuds were not uncommon under this system of primitive justice.

Strongly entrenched customs and traditions, the relative autonomy of the family, homogeneity of the population and its activities, and other features of primitive life were undermined as technological progress and a growing division of labor moved society toward the modern era. Growing differences in wealth, prestige, and power found consolidation in new patterns of authority and decision making. The rise of chieftains and kings set the stage for the centralization of political authority, the establishment of territorial domain, and the emergence of sovereign authority and the civil state. The handling of disputes slowly moved out of the hands of the family and into the hands of the sovereign and, subsequently, the state. So, too, the creation of legal rules became the prerogative of central authority.

These changes did not happen overnight. Criminal law as we know it today is a product of centuries of change. The earliest known code of written law dates back to the twenty-first century B.C. This is the code of Ur-Nammu, the Sumerian king who founded the Third Dynasty of Ur. The famous Code of Hammurapi (sometimes spelled Hammurabi) was discovered in 1901 in Susa, near the Persian Gulf. This code dates from around 1650 B.C. Other ancient codes of law include the Twelve Tables of Rome, the Mosaic code, the laws of ancient Greece, and the laws of Tacitus. All these codes show strong ties with the self-help justice typical of more primitive eras. As Maine

(1905:341–342) noted, early penal law was primarily the law of torts (or private wrongs). The Twelve Tables treated theft, assault, and violent robbery as *delicta* (private wrongs) along with trespass, libel, and slander. The person, not the state or the public, was the injured party.

The maturing legal systems of ancient Greece and Rome moved steadily toward the formulation of offenses against the state (public wrongs, or *crimena*) and the establishment of machinery for administration and enforcement. According to Maine, the legislative establishment of permanent criminal tribunals around the first century B.C. represented a crucial step in the emergence of true criminal law.

One of the most interesting features of these early codes is the number of activities they cover. The Code of Hammurapi is particularly wide ranging. The laws covered such diverse areas as kidnapping, unsolved crimes, price fixing, rights of military personnel, the sale of liquor, marriage and the family, inheritance, and slavery (Gordon, 1957). The contents of these early codes suggest four important observations: (1) most laws are products of prevailing social, political, and economic conditions; (2) some laws articulate long-established customs and traditions and can be thought of as formal restatements of existing mores; (3) some laws reflect efforts to regulate and coordinate increasingly complex social relations and activities; and (4) some laws display prevailing ethical and moral standards and show close ties to religious ideas and sentiments.

## MALA PROHIBITA AND MALA IN SE

There has been much legal debate concerning the connection between law and morality. In the minds of many people, law is based on ethical beliefs, and criminal codes are a sort of catalogue of sins. But others have argued that there is much in our criminal codes that bears no obvious connection with ethics or morality. In what sense, for example, are laws prohibiting certain forms of drug use or certain kinds of business activities matters of sin?

Laws were once indistinguishable from the general code governing social conduct. As primitive societies became more complex, law and justice were identified as concepts that regulated the moral aspects of social conduct. Even the extensive legal codes of Greece and Rome fused morality with law. And in some languages, Hungarian for example, the word for *crime* means not only an act that is illegal but also one that is evil or sinful (Schafer, 1969). In time criminal codes expanded and laws were passed to regulate activities in business, politics, the family, social services, and even our intimate private lives. The connection between law and morality became less clear, and people categorized crimes as *mala prohibita* — meaning evil because they are forbidden — or *mala in se* — meaning evil in themselves. *Mala prohibita* crimes include drug offenses, traffic violations, and embezzlement; examples of *mala in se* crimes, acts that are inherently evil, include incest, murder, arson, and robbery.

## INTERESTS AND THE DEVELOPMENT OF LAW

As we have learned more about the history of criminal law, particularly by analyzing past legal decisions, another important facet of its development has received growing attention. This is the role that *interests* play in the creation, content, and enforcement of legal rules.

One of the first systematic discussions of interests in the formulation of law was by Roscoe Pound. According to Pound (1943:39), law helps to adjust and harmonize conflicting individual and group interests:

> Looked at functionally, the law is an attempt to satisfy, to reconcile, to harmonize, to adjust these overlapping and often conflicting claims and demands, either through securing them directly and immediately, or through securing certain individual interests, or through delimitations or compromises of individual interests, so as to give effect to the greatest total of interests, or to the interests that weigh the most in our civilization, with the least sacrifice of the scheme of interests as a whole.

Pound's view suggests that the laws of heterogeneous and pluralistic societies are best understood as efforts at *social compromise,* with the maintenance of social order and harmony a priority.

The interest theory of sociological jurisprudence offered by Pound has been attacked in recent years for its emphasis on compromise and harmony and for its suggestion that there will be consensus where important social interests are concerned. According to Richard Quinney (1970b:35),

> society is characterized by diversity, conflict, coercion, and change, rather than by consensus and stability. Second, law is a *result* of the operation of interests, rather than an instrument that functions outside of particular interests. Though law may control interests, it is in the first place created by interests. Third, law incorporates the interests of specific persons and groups; it is seldom the product of the whole society. Law is made by men, representing special interests, who have the power to translate their interests into public policy. Unlike the pluralistic conception of politics, law does not represent a compromise of the diverse interests in society, but supports some interests at the expense of others.

Quinney seems to be saying that all criminal laws reflect special interests and the exercise of power in support of them. But in what sense are laws prohibiting murder or incest special interest laws? As we saw earlier, there is much public consensus that these acts are serious offenses. And what of laws that may not be in the interests of those who create legal policy, such as those prohibiting influence peddling and political corruption?

Though agreeing that there is a connection between conflict, power, and criminal law, we should again note the distinction between *mala in se* and *mala prohibita* crimes. Conflict between interests and the exercise of power are more relevant to the latter. (This will become evident when we discuss the historical development of certain offenses.) In addition, conflict between interests and the exercise of power in defense of special interests are important when applying criminal labels to people. Historically, those low in status, social prestige, or power have usually found themselves labeled criminals the most often and punished the most severely for their crimes. Many early legal codes contained special provisions specifying different reactions according to distinctions of status. The more powerful were the more privileged. Finally, conflict and power help explain why some activities are not crimes. This is especially evident in matters relating to business and government.

This last point can be illustrated by a controversy over the conflicting interests of a multinational corporation and Third World mothers. Some years ago the Nestlé Company launched an international campaign to promote its infant formula. Ads proclaiming "Give your baby love and Lactogen" were used to promote the product in less developed countries, where families are typically large. However, the promotion discouraged mothers from breast feeding and encouraged practices that were more expensive, irreversible, and, because of contaminated water supplies, less healthful. Many babies became ill, and some died. But Nestlé had committed no crime, nor were any sanctions imposed on the company. In effect, the law both here and abroad protected the company, and had it not been for the publicity surrounding the efforts of social activists in England and America, the company doubtless would have continued its legal but ultimately victimizing practices (see Post and Baer, 1978).

John Hagan (1982a) argues that the advantages enjoyed by corporations in matters of crime also extend to situations in which corporations are the victims of crime. He concludes: "The form and content of criminal justice in modern capitalistic societies supports and legitimates the use of criminal law for the protection of corporate property against individuals. That is . . . the modern criminal justice system better serves corporate than individual interests" (p. 1019). These issues are examined in detail in Chapter 9, but you will come across them from time to time throughout the text.

## Anglo-American Criminal Law

Criminal law in the United States draws mainly from Greek, Mosaic, and Roman law via English law. The common law of England can be traced to the reign of Henry II (1154–1189). For centuries English law had been a system of tribal justice, the primitive law of private wrongs and self-help retaliation. As feudalism took hold in the eighth and ninth centuries, Anglo-Saxon society underwent important changes. The family lost its autonomy; kings and kingdoms emerged; and the blood feud was replaced by a system of material compensation (usually money), directed by individuals with special status — by king, lord, or bishop. Equally important, political unification was under way, as territorial acquisitions of the new kings transformed a patchwork of small kin-dominated domains into fewer, larger kingdoms. With the Norman conquest of 1066 complete political unification was but a short step away.

The Normans centralized their administrative machinery, including that concerned with law. During the reign of Henry II, new legal procedures emerged, including a court of "common law". Those with complaints against others could bring them to traveling courts, and justice dispensed there became a body of "precedent" to guide future judgments. But most important, during this period certain acts were identified as offenses against king and country ("Breaches of the King's Peace"), and with them the curtain was raised on modern criminal law (see Jeffery, 1957).

By the time the Puritans arrived in New England, criminal law was firmly established in England, and the new colonists imported its essential features virtually intact. Not only was the machinery of imposition and enforcement similar to that in the mother country, but the laws themselves departed little from those found in England (see Pound, 1951; K. Erickson, 1966). By the time the Declaration of Independence was signed, changes in law and the legal system were already taking place. Over the next two hundred years both substantive and procedural features of the criminal law were slowly "Americanized."

The distinction between *procedural* and *substantive* criminal law draws attention to two basic issues in law: (1) how the authorities handle matters of law and deal with law violators — the question of procedure, and (2) the content of the specific rules making up the body of criminal law — the question of substance. The rules embodied in American criminal law, substantive and procedural, come from four sources: (1) federal and state constitutions; (2) decisions by courts (common law or case law), including decisions of precedent and Supreme Court rulings; (3) administrative regulations — those policy decisions employed by agencies on the federal, state, and local levels as they carry out their legal duties; and (4) statutory enactments by legislatures.

Procedural rules govern the way we officially handle matters of criminal law. They are applicable at all stages of the legal process. They govern the different groups handling offenses and offenders — the police, the prosecution and defense, the courts, and those who administer punishment. They shape the administration of criminal justice and help determine whether given acts and individuals will be officially identified as criminal, how offenders will be "processed," and what will happen to them if they are found guilty of a crime. Procedural aspects of criminal law are vital to the study of crime, criminals, and legal sanctions. They set the tone for the process of criminalization and provide us with insights into criminal law in action.

We have defined crime and criminal law, but who is the "criminal"? Paul Tappan (1947) used this question to draw attention to the fact that criminologists disagree on whom they have in mind when they speak of the criminal.

Differences of opinion over the definition of the criminal mirror some of the disputes over the definition of crime. Some scholars identify criminals in terms of strict legal considerations, and others emphasize the antisocial character of their behavior or their involvement in the skills, techniques, attitudes, and life-styles of repetitive law violators.

From the standpoint of criminal law, a criminal is an individual who is legally capable of conduct that violates the law and who can be shown to have actually and intentionally engaged in that conduct. If it cannot be demonstrated that the person committed the illegal act or that he or she was capable of committing it — for example, by meeting requirements of age and mental condition — or that the act was intentional (or the result of negligence), then the person is not legally a criminal. The box on pages 20–21 shows some of the defenses against conviction of a crime. Emphasizing the legalistic view, Tappan suggests "only those are criminal who have been adjudicated as such by the courts."

A conception of the criminal more in keeping with our definition of crime would stress that even though people are ostensibly innocent of crime until proven guilty, those suspected of violating the law are treated in a special way by the machinery of justice. People who are investigated by the police, people who are arrested, people who end up in court, and people who are convicted and punished all are in fact treated as if they belonged to the same category, that of the law violator. The moment that the machinery of criminal law bears down on anyone, that person is singled out for special consideration. Accordingly, we can define the criminal as *a person whose conduct has been labeled a crime by those who create and administer the criminal law*.

The criminal label can be applied at different stages in the legal process, from the point at which criminal conduct is created in law to the point at which punishment ends. In addition, the label often stays with people long after they have paid the official price for their behavior. Criminal labels stigmatize. When friends or associates know a person has been labeled criminal by agencies of law, and react punitively because of this knowledge, then to all intents and purposes that person's social identity becomes that of a criminal.

You may be wondering: Why emphasize the activities of those who enforce the law when surely a person is a criminal because of something he or she does, not because of something the enforcers do? If we take this latter position, we underemphasize the social dimension of human existence; we fail to take into account the extent to which the attitudes, knowledge, ideas, and actions of others give meaning to an individual's behavior. The idea of

## DEFENSES AGAINST CRIMINAL CHARGES

**Self-Defense:** Use of force is deemed justifiable when one can establish that one feared for one's life, could not reasonably escape the situation, and was not the initiator of aggressive actions. The belief that one must use deadly force to prevent harm to self need only be *reasonable* given the circumstances.

**Defense of Others:** Most states permit use of deadly force if the person doing so reasonably believed that another's life was in danger and could reasonably take no other course of action to protect that person.

**Defense of Property:** Most states allow a person to use force to prevent the commission of a felony, to arrest a person who has committed a felony involving property, or to prevent forcible entry into one's residence. However, *deadly* force may not generally be used unless the property owner reasonably fears for his or her life.

**Time Limitations:** Statutes of limitation exist for most offenses (an exception being murder), and they specify a time limit during which criminal responsibility lasts for different offenses. A person accused after the time limit runs out is no longer held criminally responsible.

**Duress:** Duress is a defense *if* the defendant, through no personal fault, is put in fear for his or her life or the life of another. Most states require that the threat seem of greater magnitude than the crime itself.

A similar defense is that of *necessity,* in which some natural peril "forces" a person to commit a crime (for example, to break into someone else's house or property in order to escape being swept away in a flood).

**Absence of Intent by Mistake:** Absence of Intent is a defense when, for example, someone mistakenly believes he is the owner of a piece of property and removes it for his own use.

**Entrapment:** Entrapment is a defense if it is shown that a law enforcement agent posing as a participant in a crime convinced the defendant to commit the crime when he or she would not normally have done so.

**Involuntary Act:** An example of this defense is a person doing injury to another while sleepwalking, hypnotized, or in a state of near unconsciousness.

---

the "criminal" is created by people. It is something we impute to another's behavior. That person's behavior is not criminal until we say it is by our words and deeds. On its own, the physical act that a person performs is only that, a physical act. Even its meaning to the actor is dependent on previous experiences and the course of learning as a social being.

It seems, then, that we are partly what we do and partly what others do to us. We are criminal not simply because we break the law, but because those who make official judgments about our behavior decide to treat us as criminal and act on that decision. Remember, discretion is involved in applying the criminal label, and power and social position can influence the decision. If you are young, black, poor, less well educated, or live in the inner-city slums, you are more susceptible than others are to having the status of criminal assigned to you. In America people with these characteristics turn up in crime statistics more often than we would expect on the basis of their numbers in the total population. Why? In part because the police concentrate their energies in areas of towns and cities where such people are likely to be found. Also because the actions of legal agencies are inherently political actions and stem from decision making and the exercise of power as part of the political process. Low-status people are generally excluded from the political process and are in effect without voice in the creation and enforce-

**Involuntary Intoxication:** A person who is intoxicated or drugged at the hands of another without permission or by trick or deceit will normally not be held criminally responsible for any offense committed while intoxicated or drugged.

**Victim Consent:** A defense of consent may be accepted when the victim of a crime in fact gave consent to it voluntarily. This defense is rarely used and surfaces mostly in sex-related cases.

**Alibi:** An alibi is a witness-supported defense based on the claim that the defendant was not present at the scene of the crime during the time it was carried out.

**Insanity:** Insanity is a defense when it can be shown that the defendant lacks the mental capacity for criminal responsibility or suffers from some mental illnesses that render the defendant insane or of unsound mind. Three prevalent tests for insanity are

1. The "Wild Beast" test. To claim innocence under this rule the defendant must have been acting more or less like a "raving maniac," to have had no more knowledge of what he or she was doing than a wild beast.

2. The McNaghten Rule. It must be competently shown that the defendant did not know what he or she was doing or he or she did not know that it was wrong.

3. Irresistible Impulse test. This adds an element of mental impulse to the traditional McNaghten Rule; defendants may be declared innocent if irresistible impulses render them incapable of choosing between right or wrong.

**Accident:** Accident is a defense when there is not such negligence in the commission or omission of an act that defendant could be held criminally culpable. An example would be death caused when a pedestrian falls in the path of a car that could not stop in time. The driver would not be held criminally responsible unless other damaging factors (intoxication, driving recklessly) were present.

Further details on these defenses may be found in the following sources: Holten, Gary N. and Melvin E. Jones (1982), The System of Criminal Justice, 2nd ed. (Boston: Little, Brown); Kerper, Hazel B. and Jerold H. Israel (1979), Introduction to the Criminal Justice System, 2nd ed. (St. Paul: West Publishing).

---

ment of criminal law. As relatively powerless members of society, they are more susceptible to actions that identify their behavior as "deviant."

If criminals are identified strictly on the basis of their actions, then most of us are probably criminals. Whether we take home office supplies, lie a little on our tax returns, have sexual intercourse out of wedlock, drink alcohol while under age, open another's mail, gamble, put slugs in vending machines, engage in some kind of fraudulent activity, or commit murder, robbery, assault, or arson may matter little according to the letter of the law. It matters a great deal from the standpoint of social experience, however, for the criminal label will be applied in the last four situations far more often than in the others. Ultimately, the decision to apply the label is wholly in the hands of those who create and administer the criminal law.

This may suggest that we need only study the creation and application of criminal definitions in order to grasp the "real" crime scene. But what about those actions and people who escape societal reactions and remain secret as far as the law is concerned? Should these be ignored in criminology? The answer is no. Our definitions of *crime* and *criminal* do not exclude the rule-creation and application processes, but neither do they lead us to ignore the behavioral elements in crime. The criminologist who focuses only on crime as status and on the people to whom the label has been applied looks at

merely a part of the crime scene. Crime is also behavior in the sense that it constitutes a human activity. The criminologist is therefore interested in explaining the occurrence of that behavior. Why do people kill? Why are some people more likely to be killed than others? How is the behavior we call crime distributed throughout the population? Is criminal activity random, or does it follow a pattern? If patterned in a certain way, why? Questions such as these are compatible with our definitions.

# CHAPTER 2

# Theories of Crime, I: Foundations of Modern Criminology

Criminology is a relatively young field of study, dating back roughly a hundred years. Many criminologists today receive their academic training in the social sciences, often taking degrees in sociology. The pioneers in the new field, however, were trained in other disciplines. Cesare Lombroso (1835–1909) was a physician and surgeon; Raffaele Garofalo (1852–1934) was a professor of law and a magistrate; Enrico Ferri (1856–1929) was a criminal lawyer and member of the Italian parliament; and Gustav Aschaffenburg (1866–1944) was a psychiatrist, as was William Healy (1869–1965), one of the American pioneers.

Criminology gained its place in American academe between 1920 and 1940. During these years textbooks covering the developing field began to appear. These books were primarily the work of sociologists, the most important being that of Edwin Sutherland (1934). Today, people from a wide variety of disciplines continue to make important contributions to the field. And criminology has also benefited from the knowledge and insights of those with little or no academic training but plenty of experience with some aspect of the crime scene.

## What is Criminology?

Today, criminology is an established field of study, but this does not mean that criminologists agree on a definition of the field. Those authors of criminology texts who do offer a definition (not all do) rarely offer the same one. True, most textbooks depict criminology as the *scientific study of crime as a social phenomenon,* but in more detailed explication differences usually emerge.

Though it is comforting to believe that science can be divorced from values or prejudices, this is simply not true. Values enter scientific activity at many points because human beings subscribe to values and to the assumptions and beliefs accompanying them. In criminology, as in other fields, values and beliefs affect the decisions made about what to investigate, what questions to ask, and what to do with the knowledge acquired. We see the impact of values, also, in how criminologists conceptualize their field and its subject matter. The differences of opinion over the definition of crime and criminals reflect in part the intrusion of values.

This is not wrong, but it warns us not to expect consensus when we seek definitions of criminology. About the only thing on which criminologists do agree is that criminology today is vastly different from what it was one hundred, fifty, or even twenty-five years ago. And it is different in large part because different values have been expressed in the work criminologists have done and in the questions they have asked.

# Conservative, Liberal-Cynical, and Radical Criminology

Don C. Gibbons and Peter Garabedian (1974) discuss the competing value-perspectives that have shaped criminology over the years. They identify three major perspectives: conservative, liberal-cynical, and radical (sometimes called "critical"). Further illustrations of these perspectives are presented in Chapter 16, along with a discussion of the ideology underlying criminal justice policy.

Conservative criminology gained ascendancy in America with the writings of the American pioneers in sociological criminology. It incorporates the following ideas: (1) criminal law is not challenged but, rather, is interpreted as the codification of prevailing moral precepts; (2) in accordance with this view, criminals are looked upon as morally defective; (3) the questions appropriate for the criminologist to study include "How are morally defective persons produced?" and "How can society better protect itself against criminals?"; (4) when dealing with etiological questions conservative criminologists advocate a multifactor approach, emphasizing a combination of personality and biological and environmental factors; and (5) conservative criminology tends to have "faith in the ultimate perfectability of the police and criminal justice machinery" (Gibbons and Garabedian, 1974:52).

Liberal-cynical criminology emerged along with the more sophisticated sociological analyses of crime that began to appear during the 1940s and early 1950s. Because liberal-cynical criminology has dominated the field over the past thirty years, we might also call it "mainstream" criminology.

Early liberal criminology retained the emphasis on offenders and their behavior and attempted to explain crime in terms of either social structure or social process (rarely both). There are three major versions of liberal criminology. *Control* theory states that crime and delinquency result "when an individual's bond to society is weak or broken" (Hirschi, 1971:16). When this occurs, conformity to social rules is undermined, and a decline in social control follows, allowing more room for individual deviance. *Strain* theory suggests that when people find they cannot achieve valued goals through conventional (i.e., legitimate) means, they experience stress and frustration, which in turn may lead to rule-violating behavior. Delinquency and crime are seen as normal adaptations to conditions of discontinuity between means and ends (Sykes, 1972).

The third version of liberal criminology, *cultural transmission* theory, draws attention to the manner in which people become criminal as they interact with their immediate social environment. This type of theory asserts that delinquency and crime represent *conformity*, but conformity to definitions that are deviant when viewed from the standpoint of the dominant culture. A useful way of looking at this version of liberal criminology is simply to say that "lawbreaking is the result of ordinary learning processes occurring within a crimogenic culture" (Gibbons and Garabedian, 1974:53).

Some liberal criminologists have moved toward an emphasis on crime as *status* and on the processes of making and enforcing criminal laws (e.g., Turk, 1969; Hills, 1971; Chambliss, 1975a). According to this view, society is characterized by conflict, and criminality is the product of power differentials and the struggle to defend group and individual interests. Society's criminals are those who lack power and are unsuccessful in the struggle to defend their interests — lower-class people, blacks, the young, the poor, and other minorities. Criminal law and its enforcement are products of institutionalized power differentials and reflect the ability of some groups to criminalize those who deviate from the standards the powerful support.

Gibbons and Garabedian (1974:55) find the cynical aspect of liberal criminology most often in discussions of the criminal justice system and correctional institutions:

> The sociologist brings to the analysis of these structures the inside dopester's awareness that social organizations are often "screwed up." That is, he knows about all kinds of complex organizations that operate in ways quite different from those sketched in organizational charts or manuals of procedure. This growing sophistication of criminological analysis has been paralleled by a marked decline in the criminologist's faith in the perfectability of the legal-correctional machinery.

The cynical criticism focuses on the failure of police and courts to live up to ideals of justice, the lack of real efforts to treat and rehabilitate offenders, and the failure of juvenile justice both to follow the basic rules of due process and to achieve its long-standing goals of individualized treatment and child care.

The liberal-cynical criminologist is skeptical of the perfectability of crime control efforts and locates crimogenic forces in the basic structure and institutions of society but still retains a belief in the continued viability of American society in its present form. In radical (or critical) criminology such a belief is absent. Further, the radical criminologist rejects the liberal reformism that, it is claimed, "has helped to create probation and parole, the juvenile court system, reformatories and halfway houses, the indeterminate sentence, adjustment and diagnostic centers, public defenders, youth service bureaus," all of which "have served to strengthen the power of the State over the poor, Third World communities and youth" (Platt, 1974:3). Radical criminologists view crime and the criminal as manifestations of the exploitative character of monopoly capitalism. Unless the present political-economic structure of American capitalistic society is changed, they argue, criminality as we know it today will remain, and the legal machinery will continue to undermine the interests of the people while serving those of the economic-political elite.

As we look more closely at past and present theory in criminology, it will be apparent that all three perspectives have made important contributions to understanding crime. And they are continuing to do so in the 1980s.

## Early Criminology

The birth of criminology is usually traced to nineteenth-century Europe. By the latter half of that century the scientific revolution was well under way. The armchair philosophizing that for centuries had dominated learned discourse was replaced by the logic and methodology of objective, empirical science. Observation, measurement, and experimentation became the basic tools of the scientific method, and their use in the study of human behavior and social phenomena heralded the development of disciplines we now take for granted — biology, anthropology, psychiatry, psychology, sociology, and statistics. Europe, if not yet the world, had entered the age of positivism, and crime became one of the phenomena newly placed under the microscope of science.

### THE RISE OF POSITIVISM

Actually, the notion that crime could be studied objectively through the methods of science had received support early in the nineteenth century in the works of André Michel Guerry (1833) and Adolphe Quetelet (1835) who studied variations in rates of crime and delinquency. These authors linked crime to other social, demographic, and ecological variables. As Leon Radzinowicz (1966:35) has observed, "for the first time in history crime became thought of as a social fact moulded by the very environment of which it was an integral part." This was an important break with the classical theorists, who viewed criminal behavior as stemming from the exercise of free will and a rational pursuit of pleasure (see Chapter 3). But equally important, Guerry and Quetelet demonstrated that tools of scientific analysis could be used productively to study crime.

The major impetus to the rise of positivistic criminology was provided by Charles Darwin's work on animal evolution. Darwin's interpreters argued that human behavior is largely determined by our place on the evolutionary scale and our constant battle with others for survival. The impact of these factors on an individual was considered to be a matter for empirical investigation; but in any case, behavior was to be understood as a consequence of forces largely beyond individual control.

### THE SEARCH FOR THE CRIMINAL TYPE

Influenced by the scientific revolution and the theory of evolution, positivistic criminology took shape in the hands of Cesare Lombroso (1911). A physician attached first to the army and later to prisons and asylums, Lombroso examined thousands of individuals, many of whom came before him precisely because they were "deviants." Profoundly influenced by the evolutionary doctrine, Lombroso searched for physiological evidence that would provide the link between human behavior, especially its deviant forms, and biological forces.

In 1870 Lombroso found what he took to be evidence of *atavism* (that is, a biological throwback to a more primitive evolutionary state) in the criminals he was studying. This led him to claim a major discovery, that some persons are born criminals and can be identified by certain physical stigmata or anomalies. Among the stigmata Lombroso observed were an asymmetrical cranium, a receding chin, a low forehead, too many fingers, a sparse beard, low sensitivity to pain, large ears, protruding lips, and peculiarities of the eye. The presence of five or more of these stigmata was taken as evidence of a personality predisposed to criminal behavior.

But the born criminal was not the only type of criminal that Lombroso identified, nor did he argue that crime was solely the result of biological forces. He distinguished other categories of criminals, including *insane criminals* (idiots, imbeciles, alcoholics, and others exhibiting degeneracy), *criminaloids* (who had less pronounced physical stigmata and biological degeneracy but were drawn into occasional crime by situational or environmental factors), and *criminals by passion* (who were neither atavistic nor products of degeneracy but were drawn into crime by love, politics, offended honor, or other emotional pressures). The core of his theory was biological, but Lombroso recognized the importance of precipitating situational and environmental factors. He mentioned poverty, emigration, food prices, police corruption, and the changing nature of the law as among the nonbiological determinants of criminal conduct (Wolfgang, 1961:207). It was not, however, until one of his followers, Enrico Ferri, undertook his own studies of criminals that the impact of environmental forces received serious attention in positivistic criminology (see Sellin, 1937).

Notwithstanding considerable and sometimes bitter criticism of his research methods and his conclusions, Lombroso's ideas had a tremendous impact on the emerging field of criminology. One of the most telling results of his work was the impetus it gave to further research on the individual criminal offender. For more than fifty years scholars concentrated their efforts on the criminal in attempting to formulate detailed classifications of criminals and to distinguish them from noncriminals.

Many felt strongly that such research would identify traits and characteristics peculiar to criminals. The American anthropologist Earnest A. Hooton (1939) studied 13,873 male criminals from ten different states, as well as 3,023 assorted civilians, and claimed to have demonstrated the organic inferiority of criminals. Hooton did see environmental factors as precipitating influences, but he clung to the idea of an underlying connection between physical types and criminal behavior. He also claimed that physical type is linked to type of criminal behavior: thin, tall men tend to commit murder and robbery; short, heavy men are prone to commit sex and assaultive crimes; and small men commit theft and burglary.

Researchers between 1880 and 1940 piled up what they claimed to be hard evidence of a causal link between criminal behavior and heredity. As Elmer Johnson (1974:206–207) notes, belief in biological inheritance of crime has been based on one of two assumptions: (1) that the criminal act itself is inherited, that is, biological structure is somehow connected with behavior; or (2) that "the inheritance of crime is viewed as a propensity, tendency, or mental predisposition which is part of the physical endowment." Studies reflecting these views were conducted on identical twins, on the so-called feebleminded, on body types, on glandular secretions, and on a host of constitutional variables. And in recent years, research on chromosomal abnormality (for example, the so-called XYY pattern, found in a number of prisoners) has been offered as further support for the link between heredity and criminal behavior (see Sarbin and Miller, 1970; Fox, 1971; Hood, 1973).

## BIOSOCIAL VIEWS

The search for biological correlates of criminality largely disappeared during the 1950s and 1960s, as criminology came more and more under the influence of sociological perspectives. In the last decade or so, however, there has been a rebirth of interest in constitutional factors in crime, the latest example of which is a monumental review by James Q. Wilson and Richard Herrnstein (1985).

Wilson and Herrnstein take a *biosocial* approach, believing that certain constitutional factors, some of which are genetic, predispose individuals to engage in antisocial behavior through their impact on decision making. However, these predispositions are also influenced by environmental forces, including the person's own personality. Neither biology alone nor environment alone is sufficient to explain why some individuals commit crime and others do not, and why some individuals commit crimes often and others rarely. Crime is explained by some — as yet unknown — combination of biological and environmental factors. However, the authors take care to point out that "there is no 'crime gene' and so there is no 'born criminal. . . .' " (1985:69). Their position is summarized as follows (1985:103):

> The existence of biological predispositions means that circumstances that activate criminal behavior in one person will not do so in another, that social forces cannot deter criminal behavior in 100 percent of the population, and that the distribution of crime within and across societies may, to some extent, reflect underlying distributions of constitutional factors. . . . [C]rime cannot be understood without taking into account individual predispositions and their biological roots.

Wilson and Herrnstein infer the existence of constitutional influences from two observations. First is the widespread finding that "street" crimes such as murder, robbery, and burglary are committed disproportionately by people who are young, male, black, and of lower intelligence. The most striking differences in criminality are observed for sex: men are up to fifty times as likely as women are to commit crimes (p. 460). And second is the large body of research suggesting something constitutionally distinctive about "the average offender," for example, that he is more muscular than other people are and is more likely to have biological parents who are themselves criminals.

Studies of genetic factors in crime have largely focused on twins and adopted children. Wilson and Herrnstein (1985:69–103) review much of this work. In twin studies, the theory is that if there is a genetic component in crime, it should show up when identical twins (monozygotic, born of the same egg) raised in the same environment are compared with fraternal twins (dyzygotic, from two separately fertilized eggs) raised in the same environment. Much of the research has been conducted in Scandinavia (Christiansen, 1977a, 1977b). In general, if one identical twin has committed crimes, the other is more likely also to have a criminal record. This finding does not hold for fraternal twins. An American study based on self-reported crime (see Chapter 4) among Ohio twins also found greater criminal "concordance" in monozygotic twins (Rowe and Osgood, 1984).

Adoption studies consider the relative contributions of biology and environment by comparing the criminality of children with the criminality of both their biological and adoptive parents. If genetics has an influence despite the environment, we should expect to see more criminality among adopted children whose natural parents were criminal but whose adoptive parents were not, and less criminality among adopted children whose biological parents were not criminals but whose adoptive parents were. Sarnoff Mednick and colleagues (1984) report on 14,427 male and female children adopted in Denmark between 1924 and 1947. The findings showed that the criminality of biological parents was more significant than was the criminality of adoptive parents and also that biological parents with three or more convictions were three times as likely to produce an adopted son with multiple convictions than was a biological parent with no criminal record.

Both twin and adoptive studies have methodological problems. The biggest difficulty with twin studies lies in separating out environmental effects, for the behavior of others may accentuate the similarities among identical twins and the differences between fraternal twins. In adoptive studies, children are not placed randomly with adoptive parents, nor always at birth, nor can it be ascertained whether the adoptive parents treated the children differently because they were adopted. All these factors muddy the waters. In any case, with current technology, the genetic contribution can only be inferred, not demonstrated directly in either type of study.

How are constitutional factors thought to influence criminal behavior? Wilson and Herrnstein are cautious on this point, as well they might be, since many of the findings they review can be explained by other theories. However, their answer seems to be in the impact of constitutional factors on what people considered rewarding, on their ability (or desire) to consider future — as opposed to immediate — rewards and punishments, and on their ability to develop internal, moral constraints — "the bite of conscience." Aggressive drives, hence needs, are dominant in males; younger and less intelligent people are more inclined to be impulsive, to want rewards now rather than later; and the cognitive skills relevant to the development of conscience grow with age and relate positively to intelligence. Individuals who are aggressive, impulsive, opportunistic, and less constrained by conscience are at the greatest risk of committing crimes.

More will be said about Wilson's and Herrnstein's theory of criminal behavior in Chapter 3. It is mentioned here both because it is a theory of individual differences and because it uses biological factors to explain crime. Although the authors do not say it categorically, the two constitutional factors that appear to place individuals at greatest risk of criminality are aggressive temperament and intelligence. We shall discuss aggression in Chapters 5 and 6.

**Intelligence and Race**   Much of the work on intelligence and crime has concluded that boys with lower aptitudes are more likely to be involved in delinquency and crime, as reported by the police or by their own admission (see Hirschi and Hindelang, 1977). Some scholars believe as much as 80 percent of intelligence is inherited. When blacks score lower on intelligence tests than whites, as they consistently do on the average, it is easy to conclude that blacks are less intelligent because they are black (Jensen, 1969). When we then observe that blacks are overrepresented in almost every statistic on serious crime, especially violent offenses (Hindelang, 1978; Hindelang et al., 1979), it is also easy to conclude that differences in criminality between blacks and whites are the result of genetic differences in intelligence or aptitude.

Wilson and Herrnstein (1985:470–472) qualify this view, however, pointing out that intelligence varies among blacks (and whites) much more than it does between the two races and that it is by no means established that those *group* differences are biologically caused. Environmental differences — neighborhood, upbringing, economic conditions, schools, nutrition, and so forth — might well account for most of the difference in intelligence between blacks and whites. Whether dealing with individual or group differences, however, the unresolved factual issue for the biosocial perspective is to establish how constitutional and environmental factors come together to influence crime rates.

We are a long way from categorical answers to the intelligence-race-criminality puzzle. Thomas Bernard (in Vold, 1979:97) is correct in cautioning that "low intelligence" will probably not get much mileage as an explanation of crime in general: "It does not account for fluctuations in crime rates in the population at large or within a specific group, and it fails to take into account white collar crime, organized crime (particularly its leadership), and political crime — all of which require considerable intellectual ability."

**Psychogenic Approaches**  The psychogenic approach to criminality emphasises the links between criminal behavior and mental states, especially mental disease, mental disorders and pathologies, and emotional problems. Early evidence of such a connection came from research on personality defects and disorders in delinquents, on mental disease in prisoners, on parent–child interactions, on the psychopathic and sociopathic personalities, and on the subconscious (or unconscious) repression of drives and desires (see Vold and Bernard, 1986). More recent epidemiological studies suggest that the amount of mental disorder among offenders and the amount of offending among the mentally disordered is larger than for the general population (Monahan and Steadman, 1983).

During the late 1970s, the work of Samuel Yochelson and Stanton Samenow (1976, 1977) was received with much fanfare. *The Criminal Personality* records the authors' research at St. Elizabeth's Hospital in Washington, D.C., over more than a decade. Their goal was to change the behavior of 240 criminals, mostly hard-core adult offenders. Their work is noteworthy because it breaks with traditional psychiatry and because it advocates the position that criminal behavior is a manifestation of the offender's exercise of free will, rather than of environmental influence:

> It is not the environment that turns a man into a criminal. Rather, it is a series of choices that he makes starting at a very early age. . . . There is a continuity in his thinking and action regardless of setting. . . . Crime does not come to him; he goes to it. . . . He seeks out other delinquents. . . . By the time he is apprehended, he has more than likely committed hundreds, if not thousands, of offenses. . . . The excitement that is involved [in crime] is what is important. . . . (Yochelson and Samenow, 1976:247)

Throughout their account, Yochelson and Samenow stress the calculating, hedonistic personality of their subjects. In this they remind us of the classical school of criminological thought, as seen in the works of Beccaria and Bentham (see Chapters 3 and 14). The authors firmly believe that crime can be deterred, but whereas conventional views of deterrence stress the use of external threats and sanctions (such as stiff penalties, rigorously applied), Yochelson and Samenow favor the development of internal deterrents to crime: deter the person from *thinking* in criminal ways, and you will reduce the likelihood of that person *acting* in criminal ways.

Although we cannot give a detailed account of Yochelson and Samenow's thesis here, we should nevertheless be alerted to some major problems with their work. Bernard (in Vold, 1979:155) has criticized their methodology:

> The assertion is made that criminals think in a certain way, and this statement is supported with several examples to illustrate it. That format has no scientific

validity, since literally any statement can be made in a similar way. One can say: "All criminals come from bad home environments — for example, Joe's father beat him and his mother drank. . . ." and so on. No terms are operationally defined, no indication is given as to how it was ascertained that all these thinking patterns were present in all the 240 subjects involved in the experiment, or why it is thought that these traits, which are found in a highly selected population . . . would be found in the general population of criminals.

Even more alarming, the authors repeatedly assert that crime is a consequence of the way criminals think, but they do not say how that thinking arises in the first place. Since environmental influences are apparently ruled out, one is tempted to believe that it must be something in the criminal's biological makeup. But the authors are not clear on this important point.

Some difficulties and problems are common to much of the biogenic and psychogenic research. On the conceptual level, vagueness and ambiguity are common place. Even when concepts have been defined with care, problems have plagued the effort to move from the theoretical to the empirical level. In psychogenic research, concepts such as intelligence, psychopathy, sociopathy, feeblemindedness, and drives have been bandied about, even though experts disagree on how to define them, let alone measure them. Another conceptual problem is that crime has received a restrictive, behavioristic conception, and little attention has been paid to its relativity or the manner in which it is created. The underlying assumption seems to be that something constant and inherent in behavior distinguishes the criminal from the noncriminal. Also, some authors have tended to wish away the interaction between environmental forces and the biological or psychological. Their thinking has been shaped by a belief in the existence of a single, basic cause of crime, or else they have conveniently sidestepped the problem of separating one realm of etiological influence from another.

In a recent survey of research on genetics and criminal behavior, Lee Ellis (1982) shows that this sort of narrow-minded thinking is not necessary and is actually counterproductive when explaining criminal behavior. He proposes a model in which the environment and genetics interact in a dynamic fashion and then influence behavior through their joint effect on *neurochemical* factors:

The approach . . . leads first to the conclusion that only neurochemical factors control *any* behavior in a direct sense, including that which happens to be defined as criminal. Second, the approach assumes that only by way of their joint influences upon the nervous system does either genetics *or* environment have any relevance whatsoever to behavior. Finally, according to the perspective, the effects of genetics and environment continue throughout the life of an organism, so that past behavior constantly feeds back to affect subsequent environmental parameters, but always within certain genetic constraints.

Criticisms of the methodological strategies used in biogenic and psychogenic research have been many. Experimental research has often lacked the essential control group without which the impact of variable manipulation cannot be properly assessed. When control groups have been used, they have been either too small or unrepresentative of the population as a whole. The problem of unrepresentativeness has also plagued much of the research trying to identify traits or characteristics of offenders based on samples of prisoners or juvenile delinquents. Such samples are rarely, if ever, representative of all offenders to which the research relates. Further, it is not always clear precisely how some samples were produced, and many scholars have succumbed to temptation and generalized on the basis of evidence drawn from extremely small samples.

Some critics take exception to an entire field of criminological research on methodological grounds, as in the case of psychoanalysis. George Vold (1958:125) has written: "A methodology under which only the patient knows the 'facts' of the case, and only the analyst understands the meaning of those 'facts' as revealed to him by the patient, does not lend itself to external, third-person, impersonal verification or to generalizations beyond the limits of any particular case." For those who believe that crime can and should be the object of verifiable scientific analysis, such a criticism is a devastating indictment of the psychoanalytical approach, and it leads them to reject the approach and its findings.

## Multifactor Approaches

A long-standing criticism of the early biogenic and psychogenic approaches to crime has been that much of the work centered on the search for a single factor (or single set of like factors) that could be shown to account for all criminal behavior. Thus, biological degeneracy, or feeblemindedness, or psychopathy was held up as the single cause of crime. Yet if feeblemindedness, or poverty, or broken homes, or race were the only cause of crime, the other factors could not also be.

The multifactor approach in criminology grew out of the discrepancies and arguments attending the single-factor tradition of the early days. The underlying assumption was that crime is the product of many factors — biological, psychological, social — and that different crimes will be the result of different combinations of factors. Hence the "proper" approach in criminology is an eclectic one emphasizing the identification and analysis of multiple factors. The multifactor approach gained its momentum from the research efforts of William Healy, the English scholar Cyril Burt, and Sheldon and Eleanor Glueck.

Healy (1915) engaged in a five-year study of nearly one thousand delinquency cases brought before juvenile court authorities. He was interested solely in the identification of any "causal factor" present among his subjects. The result was a list of 138 distinct delinquency factors, most of which were psychological, though some were biological or social-environmental. Clearly influenced by Healy's work, Burt (1925) pursued a similar investigation in England, and he found no less than 170 distinct delinquency factors, which he classified into nine major categories. For their part, the Gluecks published a series of studies focusing on sociocultural, biological, and psychological factors in a search for correlates of delinquency. In their best-known work, *Unraveling Juvenile Delinquency,* the Gluecks (1950) matched five hundred "delinquents" with five hundred "nondelinquents" on a number of dimensions, including residence, age, and general intelligence. They then looked for delinquency factors in an extensive analysis of social background, home life, physical characteristics, intellectual ability, psychiatric states, emotion, and temperament. They concluded that although a host of different factors show statistical associations with delinquency, the major causes of delinquency are problems in the home (parental separation or prolonged absence, parental drunkenness and other physical or mental ailments, poor home management, lack of child supervision, or little show of affection toward child or children).

## CRITICISMS OF THE MULTIFACTOR APPROACH

The multifactor approach has not gone without criticism. The most frequent criticisms were catalogued by Albert K. Cohen (1951). First, advocates of the approach have tended to eschew the search for integrated theories of criminality, arguing that such efforts are futile, given the many factors associated with crime. By the same token, they have rejected as too narrow and particularistic the explanations afforded by their colleagues. Cohen believes they have confused explanation *by means of a single theory* with single-factor explanations. A list of factors associated with crime does not explain crime; nor does a single theory necessarily explain crime in terms of a single factor. Theories are concerned with *variables* (aspects or characteristics of things that vary with respect to other aspects or characteristics), and a single theory usually incorporates a number of different variables. To explain crime we need theories, which consist of logically related statements asserting particular relationships among a number of variables.

Second, Cohen objected to a major assumption of the multifactor approach, namely, that factors have intrinsic crime-producing qualities. Factors found statistically associated with crime are often asserted to cause crime or to be one cause among others. Each factor is presumed to carry a fixed amount of crimogenic power. But, argues Cohen, not only do factors have no intrinsic crime-producing qualities, they should not be confused with causes. Causal power cannot be assumed on the basis of a discovery that a certain factor, or combination of factors, shows a statistical association with crime.

Finally, Cohen observed that many multifactor studies have run afoul of the "evil causes evil" fallacy. The fallacious notion is that evil consequences (crime) must have evil precedents (biological pathologies, low IQ, pathological mental states, sordid living conditions).

## ECOLOGICAL PERSPECTIVES

Sociological investigations of crime and delinquency factors have given considerable attention to the so-called sins of cities (Moore, 1964:905). Much of the work focusing on crime-producing features of city environments has come out of the specialty known as *human ecology*, which is the study of the relationship between human beings and the physical and social space they occupy. Ecological studies of crime came into their own during the early twentieth century and were especially prominent at the University of Chicago. But even before that time, interest in criminal ecology had been growing, spurred on by the research of Quetelet and Guerry and two monumental nineteenth-century English works — Henry Mayhew's *London Labour and the London Poor* and Charles Booth's *Life and Labour of the People of London*.

Led by Robert E. Park and E. W. Burgess, sociologists at the University of Chicago published a series of studies uncovering numerous environmental correlates of crime and delinquency (e.g., Anderson, 1923; Shaw, 1931; Shaw and McKay, 1942). The label "delinquency (or delinquent) areas" was introduced and applied to those areas of Chicago displaying the highest delinquency rates. Upon examination, these areas were found to be close to the central business district and to be areas of population transition. They were characterized by slum conditions, overcrowding, mobility and migration, physical deterioration, concentrations of black and foreign-born residents, concentrated poverty, lack of home ownership, lack of locally supported community organizations, and concentrations of unskilled and unemployed workers. Later work showed that these areas also had high rates of school truancy, young-adult crime, infant mortality, tuberculosis, and mental disorder. Research findings from other cities — for example, Boston, Cincinnati, and Philadelphia — supported the earlier claims that crime and delinquency-producing factors were inherent in communities experiencing population transition and social disorganization (Shaw and McKay, 1942; Morris, 1958). Clifford Shaw (1931:387), the major figure in delinquency area studies, summarized the process of delinquency concentration:

> In the process of city growth, the neighborhood organizations, cultural institutions and social standards in practically all of the areas adjacent to the central business district and the major industrial centers are subject to rapid change and disorganization. The gradual invasion of these areas by industry and commerce, the continuous movement of the older residents out of the area and the influx of newer groups, the confusion of many divergent cultural standards,

the economic insecurity of the families, all combine to render difficult the development of a stable and efficient neighborhood organization for the education and control of the child and the suppression of lawlessness.

*Environmental*

# Social Structural Theories of Crime and Delinquency

Human ecologists look at the impact of social and physical environments on the behavior of individuals and groups. In broader terms, their work is part of sociologists' continuing interest in the impact of *social structure* — the organization of social relationships and group interactions — on behavior.

Theories of crime and delinquency emphasizing social structure treat crime as normal rather than abnormal or pathological. By *normal,* sociologists mean that something is a characteristic feature of social life. The idea that crime is normal was first developed by Emile Durkheim (1964:65–66), the nineteenth-century French sociologist:

> Crime is present not only in the majority of societies of one particular species but in all societies of all types. There is no society that is not confronted with the problem of criminality. Its form changes; the acts thus characterized are not the same everywhere; but, everywhere and always, there have been men who have behaved in such a way as to draw upon themselves penal repression. . . . There is . . . no phenomenon that presents more indisputably all the symptoms of normality, since it appears closely connected with the conditions of all collective life.

If crime is normal, why is it not distributed evenly throughout society? This is the basic question underlying social structural theories of crime.

## STRAIN THEORIES

In *Suicide* (1952), Durkheim used the term *anomie* (sometimes spelled *anomy*) to refer to a social condition in which "normlessness" prevails, that is, in which the system of regulations and restraint has broken down so that individuals suffer a loss of external guidance and control in their goal-seeking endeavors. The structure regulating social relationships is disrupted, and social cohesion and solidarity are weakened. According to Durkheim, anomie is most likely during periods of rapid social change, when traditional norms have not been effective in regulating human conduct, but new modes have not yet been accepted.

Robert K. Merton (1938, 1957) extended and elaborated on Durkheim's notion of anomie, making it the central feature of a *strain* theory of crime. In Merton's view, pressures are exerted on some segments of society to engage in crime, and these pressures relate directly to structural arrangements conducive to a state of anomie. Merton argues that all social structures establish institutionalized means for the attainment of culturally supported goals. These means and goals, however, are not always in a state of harmony or integration. In some societies there may be much stress on goals and little concern with the prescribed means for achieving them; in others there may be a ritualistic concern with the means to achieve goals but little emphasis on the goals themselves. In between these polar situations are varying states of means–goals integration.

Looking at American society — and we should note that he was writing in the 1930s — Merton argues that a state of anomie exists because goals receive structural emphasis, but the means to achieve them do not. He describes America as a society with an inordinate emphasis on success goals, represented mainly by the possession and consumption of goods and services that are held up as achievable by all. Not all segments of society, however, have the same access to these goals, for the institutionalized means are not distributed evenly throughout the population. Rather, structural arrangements are such that certain segments of the population — especially blacks, the lower classes, and the poor — are routinely denied access to legitimate means of achievement. The accepted routes to success — a good education, the "right" background, promotions, managerial and other skilled jobs — typically are not the routes open to such people.

What happens? In Merton's view, a number of "modes of adaptation" are possible. One is *conformity,* or acceptance of the prevailing state of affairs. A second is *innovation,* in which the goals are accepted and the means are rejected and alternatives are substituted in their place. A third is *ritualism,* in which socially approved means are given particular emphasis and cultural goals more or less rejected. A fourth is *retreatism,* a rejection of both culturally supported goals and institutionalized means. Finally there is *rebellion,* a rejection of means and ends coupled with the substitution of new means and goals — in other words, an attempt to introduce a new social order.

Merton offers his category of innovation in support of the argued link between anomie and crime (mostly property crime). The innovator, in rejecting institutionalized means and substituting alternatives, is likely to find that the new means are illegal ones, and the actions, crimes. Innovation is thus the key mode of adaptation in Merton's theory of anomie and crime, and he uses it to explain the high crime rates among lower-class, poor segments of the population. Their disadvantaged status coupled with the high cultural priority given to pecuniary success as a dominant goal for all make high rates of crime a "normal outcome" for those segments of the American population.

**Crime and Unemployment** Unemployment is a routine hardship for many lower-class people and indeed is a major factor accounting for their low social status. Not surprisingly, unemployment is often considered one of the factors leading to crimes of theft and violence. Sometimes the arguments are typical of strain theories — unemployed people cannot successfully compete for scarce resources; they cannot take advantage of opportunities; and their frustration leads to crime. At other times the argument encompasses elements of utilitarian theory (to be discussed in Chapter 3): unemployed people have less to lose and more to gain by committing crime.

The research findings on unemployment and crime have been mixed. Whenever a study is published purporting to show a positive relationship between unemployment and crime (e.g., Berk et al., 1980; Calvin, 1981), another comes out showing a negative relationship or no relationship at all (e.g., Orsagh, 1980). Part of the problem is that the various studies do not use the same kinds of measures and/or data. Another difficulty is that unemployment is only one aspect of economic conditions, and at times other aspects (for example, general prosperity, extent of welfare benefits, training opportunities) may exacerbate or reduce the impact of unemployment, thus affecting the relationship with crime.

It has also been observed that much of the existing theory and research on unemployment and crime has used a *unidirectional* perspective (Thornberry and Christenson, 1984). Unemployment is seen as a cause of crime, when in fact the relationship may be reciprocal; that is, crime may also cause unemployment. For example, a person who invests in crime might suffer in the legitimate job market or might find that the gains from crime outweigh the expected gains from employment. Thornberry and Christenson point out that the reciprocal view is not incompatible with strain theory or other prominent perspectives; it is merely unexplored.

Using a 10 percent sample of 9,945 males born in Philadelphia in 1945 for whom arrest records have been maintained through age 30, Thornberry and Christenson found strong support for a reciprocal model. In this particular case, unemployment appeared to have an immediate effect on criminal activity, and criminal activity had a longer-range effect on unemployment. As further work is undertaken, we should move closer to understanding the links between unemployment and crime.

## LOWER-CLASS CRIMINALITY

Ecological studies of crime and Merton's theory of anomie and deviance made much of the high rates of crime officially observed among the lower classes. From 1940 to 1960, lower-class criminality received considerable sociological attention, and a number of theories were advanced purporting to explain the high crime rates. Most of these theories retained a social structural emphasis, though they differed in some important specifics.

**Delinquent Subcultures or Cultural Deviancy**   A number of theories during this period focused on what is called the "delinquent subculture." Any heterogeneous society is likely to have a parent or dominant culture and a number of different subcultures. The *dominant culture* consists of the beliefs, attitudes, symbols, ways of behaving, meanings, ideas, values, and norms shared by those who regularly make up the membership of a society. *Subcultures* differ from the dominant culture and consist of the beliefs and values shared by members of identifiable subgroups of the society. The differences between a subculture and the parent culture and among subcultures themselves are a function of differences in life experiences and social conditions.

According to Cloward and Ohlin (1960:7), a *delinquent subculture* "is one in which certain forms of delinquent activity are essential for the performance of the dominant roles supported by the subculture. It is the central position accorded to specifically delinquent activity that distinguishes the delinquent subculture from other deviant subcultures." In terms of the subculture's norms, values, and expectations, delinquent activity is supported as right and proper and assumes a central place in the life-style of the membership.

Based on research with lower-class delinquent gangs, a number of authors have offered subcultural theories of delinquency. Albert K. Cohen (1955), for example, suggests that high rates of lower-class delinquency reflect a basic conflict between lower-class youth subculture and the dominant middle-class culture. The delinquent subculture arises as a reaction to the dominant culture that effectively discriminates against lower-class members of society. Exhorted in school and elsewhere to strive for middle-class goals and behave according to middle-class values (be orderly, clean, responsible, ambitious, and so forth), lower-class youths find that their socialization experiences have not prepared them for the challenge. They become "status frustrated" as a result of their inability to meet middle-class standards and goals and in reaction turn to delinquent activities and form delinquency-centered groups as an alternative to status, autonomy, and control. The resulting delinquency is characterized by Cohen as *nonutilitarian* (they steal, for example, "for the hell of it"), *malicious* (they derive "enjoyment in the discomfort of others"), and *negativistic* (they take pride in doing things precisely because they are wrong by middle-class standards).

An alternative theory of delinquency was offered by Richard A. Cloward and Lloyd E. Ohlin (1960). In *Delinquency and Opportunity,* these authors begin with the theories of Durkheim and Merton and argue that there are "marked discrepancies between culturally induced aspirations . . . and the possibilities for achieving them by legitimate means" for certain segments of the population, especially the youth of the lower classes. This condition produces pressures toward the formation of delinquent subcultures:

Our hypothesis can be summarized as follows: The disparity between what lower class youth are led to want and what is actually available to them is the source of a major problem of adjustment. Adolescents who have formed delinquent subcultures, we suggest, have internalized an emphasis upon conventional goals. Faced with limitations on legitimate avenues of access to these goals, and unable to revise their aspirations downward, they experience intense frustrations; the exploration of nonconformist alternatives may be the result (p. 86).

Cloward and Ohlin find three major kinds of delinquent subcultures in which the bulk of delinquents participate. *Criminal subcultures* — characterized by illegal money-making activities and often providing a stepping-stone toward adult criminal careers — tend to arise in those lower-class slum areas with relatively stable accommodative relationships between adult carriers of conventional and criminal values and with relatively well-organized age hierarchies of criminal involvement. The latter condition provides the young with criminal role models and encourages their recruitment into instrumental crime; the former condition is illustrated by established adult roles such as "fixer" and "fence" and helps encourage and facilitate involvement in illegal money-making activities as the appropriate alternative route to success goals.

The *conflict subculture,* dominated by gang fighting and acts of violence, arises in disorganized slum areas with weak social controls, an absence of institutionalized channels to success goals, either legitimate or illegitimate, and a predominance of personal failure. Violence is a route to status besides being a release for pent-up frustrations.

The *retreatist subculture,* marked by the prevalence of drug use and addiction, emerges as an adaptation for some lower-class youths when they have failed in both the criminal or conflict subcultures or have failed to take good advantage of either the legitimate or illegitimate opportunity structures. Members of this subculture disengage from the competitive struggle for success goals.

**Lower-Class Life and "Focal Concerns"** Focusing primarily on youthful gangs, Walter Miller (1958) argues that lower-class cultural prescriptions and expectations encourage delinquent behavior. Developing in response to structural patterns such as material and social deprivation or female-led households, lower-class culture emphasizes certain issues or themes. These themes then come to command widespread attention, and a high degree of emotional commitment is attached to them. These "focal concerns" include "toughness," "trouble" (a concern to avoid entanglements with the authorities), "smartness" (being able to con, or outwit, others; being able to hustle), "autonomy" (remaining free from domination or control by other people), and "excitement" (avoiding routine and monotony; getting kicks).

Some of the activities shaped by these focal concerns are delinquent, for the law, reflecting the dominant standards of middle-class society, has defined them as such. But even when given a choice, the individual finds the "deviant" activity more attractive because reference-group norms and peer-group pressures point to it as a means of acquiring prestige, status, and respect.

These theories purport to show a relationship between the organization or structure of society and the behavior of people. The almost exclusive focus on lower-class delinquency obviously limits the scope of the theories, and no author claims to have advanced a theory of crime or delinquency that is applicable to all types of crime and all types of offenders in all situations. Yet by emphasizing lower-class criminality as the focus for criminological theory, they encourage those who persist in viewing crime as a lower-class phenomenon. In addition, these theorists have not concerned themselves with the problematic nature of crime or delinquency but have chosen instead to accept the objective existence of crime and to assume that crimes differ inherently from noncrimes. These theories make conflicting claims, and no single theory has received uncontested empirical support. The value of these theories lies in their identification of some of the routes to delinquency (as behavior) and in their efforts to relate social structure to patterns of human conduct. That they have also served to shift the emphasis in criminology away from the individual offender and the idea that he or she is somehow abnormal or defective is also important.

## Social Process Theories

A common observation regarding social structural theories is that they fail to explain why some of those exposed to a particular "crime-producing" structure are not criminals or delinquents and why some of those not so exposed do commit crimes or delinquent acts. Criminologists who view crime from a *social process* perspective try to answer those questions.

Social process theories are concerned with how individuals acquire temporary or permanent attributes. In criminology, social process theories attempt to describe and explain the processes by which individuals become criminals. They deal with the links between an individual's immediate social world and that person's motivations, perceptions, self-conceptions, attitudes, and behavior. An underlying assumption is that criminal behavior can be analyzed within the same theoretical framework as noncriminal behavior. A common theme in many social process theories is that like any other kind of social behavior, criminal behavior is learned; accordingly, they emphasize the manner in which learning takes place and the factors thought to affect the content of learning.

### DIFFERENTIAL ASSOCIATION

In the 1939 edition of *Principles of Criminology,* Edwin H. Sutherland introduced the *theory of differential association.* According to this theory, which has remained unchanged but for some slight modifications made in 1947, criminal behavior patterns are acquired through processes of interaction and communication, just as are other behavior patterns. The principle of differential association accounts for the behavior pattern acquired through these processes. Individuals acquire criminal behavior patterns because they are exposed to situations in which the learning of definitions favorable to lawbreaking outweighs the learning of definitions unfavorable to lawbreaking. The theory as a whole consists of the following nine statements or propositions (Sutherland and Cressey, 1974:75–77):

1. Criminal behavior is learned.
2. Criminal behavior is learned in interaction with other persons in a process of communication.
3. The principal part of the learning of criminal behavior occurs within intimate personal groups.
4. When criminal behavior is learned, the learning includes (a) techniques of committing the crime, which are sometimes very complicated, sometimes very simple; and (b) the specific direction of motives, drives, rationalizations, and attitudes.
5. The specific direction of motives and drives is learned from definitions of the legal codes as favorable or unfavorable.
6. A person becomes delinquent because of an excess of definitions favorable to violation of law [the principle of differential association].
7. Differential association may vary in frequency, duration, priority, and intensity.
8. The process of learning criminal behavior by association with criminal and anticriminal patterns involves all of the mechanisms that are involved in any other learning.
9. While criminal behavior is an expression of general needs and values, it is not explained by those general needs and values, since noncriminal behavior is an expression of the same needs and values.

Two important observations should be made about this theory. First, the theory of differential association purports to explain noncriminal as well as criminal behavior. That is, noncriminal behavior emerges because of an excess of definitions unfavorable to law violation. Second, the theory can be used to explain variations in crime rates as well as individual criminality. Although the theory focuses on how individuals come to engage in criminal behavior, a compatible explanation of variations in crime rates is possible. Accordingly, high crime rates are predicted for areas and groups having a social organization with extensive exposure to definitions favorable to law violation and with a high probability that such definitions will be learned by a significant portion of the population.

It is fair to say that the theory of differential association is one of the most influential contributions to modern criminology. Yet few theories have been subjected to more extensive criticism. The points of contention have been many, ranging from objections to words and individual propositions to the theory as a whole. Among the major criticisms are (1) the language of the theory is imprecise; (2) major concepts, such as "definitions favorable to law violation," cannot be measured; (3) because they cannot be measured, the theory cannot be tested; (4) the theory does not take into account personality traits, personality factors, or psychological variables in criminal behavior;

and (5) the theory does not explain the "differential response" patterns that emerge when different individuals are exposed to the same situation.

C. Ray Jeffery (1959) has raised other questions concerning differential association theory. For example, if criminality is learned, it must first exist, and so what accounts for that first criminal act? How are crimes of passion to be explained? How do we account for criminal behavior in people who have had no prior contact with criminals or their attitudes?

**Modifications of Differential Association Theory** Daniel Glaser (1956) proposed that Sutherland's theory be reconceptualized to place greater emphasis on the identification processes that go on in all forms of interaction between an individual and the environment (including himself or herself). The term *differential identification* refers to the core process in Glaser's scheme. "A person," he argues, "pursues criminal behavior to the extent that he identifies himself with real or imaginary persons from whose perspective his criminal behavior seems acceptable" (1956:440). During the course of interaction, the individual selects persons with whom to identify, and these serve as behavior models. But this selection also occurs in contexts other than the immediate groups to which an individual belongs. Hence Glaser acknowledges what Sutherland did not: the possibility that portrayal of criminal roles in mass media is linked with the adoption of criminal behavior patterns. The theory of differential identification considers relevant any and all features of a person's world to the extent that they affect with whom he or she identifies.

Among the notable efforts to rework Sutherland's theory of differential association is the contribution of Robert Burgess and Ronald Akers (1966). These authors attempted a restatement of the theory based on a body of modern learning theory, asserting that behavior is learned through a process called *operant conditioning*. According to this view, social actions are repeated (or not repeated) as a consequence of their association in the actor's mind with punishing or rewarding experiences. If the response has been punished in the past, the tendency will be not to repeat the particular behavior; if, however, the response has been rewarded, the behavior in question has been *reinforced* and will tend to be repeated. The notion of reinforcement is central, then, to the explanation of the learning of social behavior. Applied to criminal behavior, the operant conditioning–reinforcement theory advanced by Burgess and Akers asserts that people engage in crime because it has been more highly reinforced in the past than has other behavior. That some people become criminals and others do not they explain by noting that all people do not go through the same socialization process, during which the reinforcement of criminal and other social behavior occurs, nor are they exposed to the same nonsocial situations of reinforcement. (For a complete statement of the Burgess and Akers theory, see the box on p. 45.)

Attempts have been made to test Sutherland's original theory — which is

## THE DIFFERENTIAL ASSOCIATION—REINFORCEMENT THEORY OF CRIMINAL BEHAVIOR

1. Criminal behavior is learned according to the principles of operant conditioning.
2. Criminal behavior is learned both in nonsocial situations that are reinforcing or discriminative and through that social interaction in which the behavior of other persons is reinforcing or discriminative for criminal behavior.
3. The principal part of the learning of criminal behavior occurs in those groups that comprise the individual's major source of reinforcement.
4. The learning of criminal behavior, including specific techniques, attitudes, and avoidance procedures, is a function of the effective and available reinforcers, and the existing reinforcement contingencies.
5. The specific class of behaviors that are learned and their frequency of occurrence are a function of the reinforcers that are effective and available, and the rules and norms by which these reinforcers are applied.
6. Criminal behavior is a function of norms that are discriminative for criminal behavior, the learning of which takes place when such behavior is more highly reinforced than noncriminal behavior is.
7. The strength of criminal behavior is a direct function of the amount, frequency, and probability of its reinforcement.

SOURCE: Burgess, Robert L. and Ronald L. Akers (1966), A differential association-reinforcement theory of criminal behavior. Social Problems 14:128–147. Adapted from Table 1, p. 146, and reprinted by permission of the Society for the Study of Social Problems and the authors.

no easy venture — but both the methods and the results have been inconsistent. What support has been shown for the theory has not been strong. D. A. Andrews (1980:448–462) claims that part of the problem stems from the lack of controlled experiments in which group influences on definitions favorable or unfavorable to law violation might be evaluated. Andrews presents a seven-year series of experimental studies in correctional settings showing that highly cohesive groups tend to exert considerable influence on law definitions, regardless of their direction. He claims his work shows impressive support for differential association and calls for further experiments in diverse settings.

For the differential association–reinforcement theory of Burgess and Akers, the results have generally shown more promise. In addition, whereas Sutherland is primarily concerned with the acquisition of behavior, Burgess and Akers deal with both acquisition and maintenance. Consider the opiate user. According to the differential association–reinforcement theory, individuals *become* drug users because the reinforcing effects of the drug itself combine with social reinforcements such as peer group approval. They *continue* as users for the same reasons; however, if addiction occurs, use will be further reinforced because it allows the addict to avoid the distress of withdrawal. When addicts succeed in breaking their physiological dependence on the drug, however, they may yet *relapse* into its use because reinforcements gained through association with others are once again combined with the reinforcing effects — the "jolt," "kick," euphoria — of the drug. And so the cycle continues (Akers et al., 1968).

## SELF-CONCEPT IN CRIMINOLOGY

The theories reviewed in the preceding section share a common emphasis in that they draw attention to socialization processes. Learning, communication, and interaction are key elements in socialization, and it is through these mechanisms that individuals acquire the personal organization, or personality, that marks them as human beings. Personal organization consists of many things, including motivations, ideas and beliefs, perceptions, feelings about things, preferences, attitudes, values, self-control and inhibitions, and an awareness or sense of self.

In dealing with the question "Why do people behave the way they do?" psychologists, social psychologists, and sociologists have long asserted a connection between personality and behavior. Although their perspective on the connection is shaped in part by their particular discipline, scholars in these fields have generally agreed that a sense of self, or self-concept, is an element in personal organization deserving serious attention in efforts to explain behavior. In criminology, interest in self-concept gained momentum during the 1950s and remains strong today.

One of the major contributors to theory and research linking self-concept with delinquent and criminal behavior has been Walter Reckless. Reckless believes that the individual confronted by choices of action feels a variety of "pulls" and "pushes." The pulls are environmental factors — such as adverse living conditions, poverty, lack of legitimate opportunities, abundance of illegitimate opportunities, or family problems — that serve to pull the individual away from the norms and values of the dominant society. The pushes take the form of internal pressures — hostility, biopsychological impairments, aggressiveness, drives, or wishes — that may also divert the individual away from actions supported by dominant values and norms.

But not all people faced with the same pulls and pushes become delinquent or criminal. To explain why some do not, Reckless advances the idea of *containment*. According to Reckless (1973:55–56), there are two kinds of containment, inner and outer:

> Inner containment consists mainly of self components, such as self-control, good self-concept, ego strength, well-developed superego, high frustration tolerance, high resistance to diversions, high sense of responsibility, goal orientation, ability to find substitute satisfactions, tension-reducing rationalizations, and so on. These are the inner regulators.
>
> Outer containment represents the structural buffer in the person's immediate social world which is able to hold him within bounds. It consists of such items as a presentation of a consistent moral front to the person, institutional reinforcement of his norms, goals, and expectations, the existence of a reasonable set of social expectations, effective supervision and discipline (social controls), provisions for reasonable scope of activity (including limits and responsibilities) as well as for alternatives and safety-valves, opportunity for acceptance, identity, and belongingness. Such structural ingredients help the family and other supportive groups contain the individual.

In Reckless's view, the inner control system, primarily self-concept, provides a person with the strongest defense against delinquency involvement. Commenting on the results of a follow-up study of white schoolboys in high-delinquency areas in Columbus, Ohio, Reckless and Simon Dinitz (1967:517) observe:

> In our quest to discover what insulates a boy against delinquency in a high delinquency area, we believe we have some tangible evidence that a good self-concept, undoubtedly a product of favorable socialization, veers slum boys away from delinquency, while a poor self-concept, a product of unfavorable socialization, gives the slum boy no resistance to deviancy, delinquent companions, or delinquent subculture. We feel that components of the self strength, such as a favorable concept of self, act as an inner buffer or inner containment against deviancy, distraction, lure, and pressures.

The work of Reckless and his associates has not gone without criticism (see Schwartz and Tangri, 1965). Interest in self-concept and its connection with criminality, however, has remained very much alive in some circles. One interesting theoretical contribution bearing on self-concept comes from David Matza and Gresham Sykes. Matza (1964) argues that individuals are rarely committed to or compelled to perform delinquent or criminal behavior. Rather, they drift into and out of it, retaining a commitment neither to convention nor to crime.

In Matza's view, delinquents are never totally immune to the demands for conformity made by the dominant social order. At most they are merely flexible in their commitment to them. In a joint publication, Sykes and Matza (1957) argue that if delinquents do form subcultures in opposition to dominant society, they are surprisingly weak in their commitment to them. They show guilt and shame, though one would expect none; they "frequently" accord respect and admiration to the "really honest" person and to law-abiding people in their immediate social environment; and they often draw a sharp line between appropriate victims and those who are not fair game; all of which suggests that "the virtue of delinquency is far from unquestioned." In terms of the dominant normative order, the delinquent appears to be both conforming and nonconforming.

Sykes and Matza believe that in order to practice nonconformity delinquents must somehow handle the demands for conformity to which they accord at least some recognition. In the view of these authors, delinquents handle those demands by neutralizing them in advance of violating them. That is, they redefine their contemplated action, putting it in the category of "acceptable" if not "right" behavior. The authors identify five "techniques of neutralization" that facilitate the juvenile's drift into delinquency: (1) *denial of responsibility* ("alcohol causes me to do it; I am helpless"); (2) *denial of injury* ("my action won't hurt anyone"); (3) *denial of the victim* ("so-and-so deserves it"); (4) *condemnation of the condemners* ("those who condemn me are worse than I am"); and (5) *appeal to higher loyalties* ("my friends come first, so I must do it"). Yet Sykes and Matza caution us:

> Techniques of neutralization may not be powerful enough to fully shield the individual from the force of his own internalized values and the reactions of conforming others, for as we have pointed out, juvenile delinquents often appear to suffer from feelings of guilt and shame when called into account for their deviant behavior. And some delinquents may be so isolated from the world of conformity that techniques of neutralization need not be called into play. Nonetheless, we would argue that techniques of neutralization are critical in lessening the effectiveness of social controls and that they lie behind a large share of delinquent behavior (1957:669–670).

Empirical evaluations of the neutralization hypothesis are few and far between. This is partly explained by the difficulty of establishing what happens cognitively *before* a law violation occurs. Almost all research has looked at rationalizations after the fact, and this provides at best only inferential evidence.

In any case, the evidence is not very supportive. Yet the absence of neutralizations does not mean they might not have operated at some time in the mind of an offender. Hirschi (1971:208) suggests that neutralizations might arise *after* earlier transgressions and act as rationalizations for later ones, perhaps contributing to a "hardening" process that leads to a commitment to deviance.

William Minor (1980:103–120) has suggested that neutralization may be necessary only for certain offenders. Neutralization, he writes, "should only be necessary when a potential offender has both a strong desire to commit an offense and a strong belief that to do so would violate his personal morality. . . . If one's morality is *not* constraining, however, then neutralization or rationalization is simply unnecessary."

## HIRSCHI'S CONTROL THEORY

Like Matza and others, control theorists emphasize the episodic character of much crime and delinquency, but unlike their colleagues they build in no assumptions about what motivates people to commit deviance. In the words of Steven Box (1981:122), "They assume that human beings are born free to break the law and will refrain from doing so only if special circumstances exist." The most prominent version of control theory is that of Travis Hirschi (1971:16–34). According to Hirschi, these special circumstances exist when the individual's bond to conventional, or moral, society is strong.

As originally conceived, Hirschi's theory posits that this bond is based on four elements: *attachment, commitment, belief,* and *involvement. Attachment* refers to the individual's affective involvement with conventional others, including sensitivity to his or her thoughts, feelings, and desires. When that attachment is weakened, the individual is free to deviate. *Commitment* is the "rational" component in conformity. It refers to the weighing of the costs and risks of deviance in light of that person's investment, or "stake," in conformity. "When or whenever he considers deviant behavior, he must consider the costs of this deviant behavior, the risks he runs of losing the investment he has made in conventional behavior" (Hirschi, 1971:20). The weaker the commitment to conformity, the lower the costs of deviance; hence the freer one is to deviate. (For more on rationality, see Chapter 3.)

*Belief* Hirschi posits as "a common value system within the society or group whose norms are being violated." But individuals differ in the *strength* of their belief in the moral validity of these social rules. If for some reason these beliefs are weakened, the individual will be freer to deviate. By including *involvement,* Hirschi suggests that deviance is in part a matter of opportunities to deviate. He argues that the more one is involved in conventional things, the less one has the opportunity to do deviant things. This is one of the weakest parts of the theory, as Hirschi himself discovered in his research with over four thousand California junior high and high school students, because opportunities for criminal or delinquent activities increase along with opportunities for noncriminal activities (see Chapter 3).

Both the clarity of its exposition and the many research findings supporting it have given Hirschi's control theory a prominent place in criminology. But a recent study by Robert Agnew (1985) suggests that its utility as an explanation of youth crime may have been exaggerated. Whereas other studies have found that 25 to 50 percent of the variance in delinquency can be accounted for by such social bond variables as parental attachment, school grades, and commitment, only 1 to 2 percent of the variance was explained by these variables in Agnew's study of delinquency in a national sample of 1,886 male youths interviewed first in the tenth grade and again at the end of the eleventh grade. Agnew found delinquency involvement to be remarkably stable over the two-year period, with the delinquency measured in the tenth grade accounting for 65 to 68 percent of the delinquency measured later. Agnew speculates that as children grow older, the importance of the bonds discussed by Hirschi may diminish, but he does not rule out that they may be important among younger children.

One final comment on this prominent theory is in order. Some criminologists contend that control theory ignores the criminal activity of career offenders, as well as the crimes of people in positions of economic and political power (e.g., Box, 1981; Hagan, 1985). John Hagan, in particular, suggests that the "upperworld" individual is actually freed by conventional society to engage in "indiscretions" because these are not viewed as especially disreputable, much less criminal. Such a person may thus exhibit strong social bonds to conventional society *and* considerable involvement in illegal activities. Hagan (1985:171) argues that "expanding the attention of control theory to upperworld crime and deviance will serve to correct a limitation in its previous application."

## The Labeling Process and Its Impact

Up to this point, we have focused on crime and delinquency as behavior and on people who commit crimes and the distinctions between them and those who do not. The questions "What causes or influences criminal behavior?" and "What factors are associated with committing crime or becoming crimi-

The labeling process begins early in life as significant others — parents, teachers, peers — react to a child's behavior. The labels that contribute to a deviant or delinquent self-image often remain with the individual throughout his or her life.

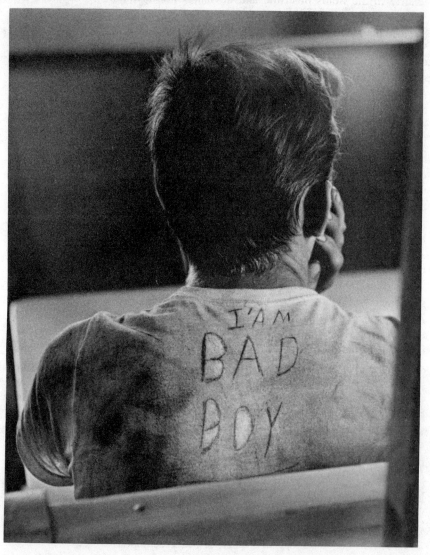

nals?" are underlying concerns in the work we reviewed. However, the conception of crime and the criminal that underlies such questions is not the only one that has been recognized. Instead of viewing crime simply as illegal behavior and the criminal as one who engages in it, some criminologists draw attention to the labeling behavior of those in a position to react to the existence and actions of others. Crime is a label attached to behavior, and the criminal is one whose behavior has been labeled crime. Crime is thus problematic and a question of social definitions. Nothing intrinsic in behavior makes it a crime.

Labeling theory, or the societal reactions approach, gained immense popularity in the fields of crime and deviance during the 1960s. Sociologists Howard Becker (1963), Kai Erickson (1962), and John Kitsuse (1962) helped develop interest in it. Labeling theory ranks today as a major perspective in sociology. In its applications to the crime scene, labeling theory has been used to explain why individuals continue to engage in activities that others define as criminal, why individuals become career criminals, why the official data on crime and criminals look the way they do, why crime waves occur, why law enforcement is patterned the way it is, why criminal stereotypes emerge and persist, and why some groups in society are more likely to be punished, and punished more severely, than others.

## LABELING AND "SECONDARY DEVIATION"

Though labeling theory gained popularity during the 1960s, precedents for it were established by the important contributions of Frank Tannenbaum (1938) and Edwin Lemert (1951, 1972). Forty years ago, Tannenbaum pointed out that society's efforts at social control may actually help create precisely what those efforts are meant to suppress: crime. By labeling individuals as "delinquents" or "criminals" and by reacting to them in a punitive way, Tannenbaum argued, the community encourages those individuals to redefine themselves in accordance with the community's definition. A change in self-identification (or self-concept) may occur, so that individuals "become" what others say they are. As Tannenbaum (pp. 17–18) described the process:

> From the community's point of view, the individual who used to do bad and mischievous things has now become a bad and unredeemable human being. From the individual's point of view there has taken place a similar change. He has gone slowly from a sense of grievance and injustice, of being unduly mistreated and punished, to a recognition that the definition of him as a human being is different from that of other boys in his neighborhood, his school, street, community. This recognition on his part becomes a process of self-identification and integration with the group which shares his activities. It becomes, in part, a process of rationalization; in part, a simple response to a specialized type of stimulus. The young delinquent becomes bad because he is defined as bad and because he is not believed if he is good. There is a persistent demand for consistency in character. The community cannot deal with people whom it cannot define. Reputation is this sort of public definition.

Even if the individual acts in ways normally defined as good, his or her goodness will not be believed. Once stigmatized, he or she finds it extremely difficult to get rid of the label "delinquent" or "criminal." As Erickson (1966:17) notes in *Wayward Puritans,* "The common feeling that deviant persons never really change . . . may derive from a faulty premise; but the feeling is expressed so frequently and with such conviction that it eventually creates the facts which later 'prove' it to be correct."

Societal reaction to crime and delinquency helps turn individuals away from an image of themselves as basically "straight" and respectable and toward an image of themselves as deviant. In discussing the impact of the labeling process, Lemert (1951, 1972) uses the term *secondary deviation* to refer to the norm-violating behavior associated with the individual's acquired status as a deviant and his or her ultimate acceptance of it. Lemert thinks secondary deviation emerges from a process of reaction and adjustment to the punishing and stigmatizing actions of significant others, such as schoolteachers, parents, and law enforcement officials. Although initially the individuals engage for a short time in deviant acts that they regard as incompatible with their true selves (suggesting the need for the techniques of neutralization discussed earlier), they eventually come to accept their new identities as deviants and are well on the road toward a career in deviance. Lemert (1951:77) pictures the process:

> The sequence of interaction leading to secondary deviation is roughly as follows: (1) primary deviation [initial acts of deviance prompted by any number of reasons]; (2) social penalties; (3) further primary deviation; (4) stronger penalties and rejections; (5) further deviation, perhaps with hostilities and resentments beginning to focus upon those doing the penalizing; (6) crisis reached in the tolerance quotient, expressed in formal action by the community stigmatizing of the deviant; (7) strengthening of the deviant conduct as a reaction to the stigmatizing and penalties; (8) ultimate acceptance of deviant social status and efforts at adjustment on the basis of the associated role.

Whether an individual moves from primary to secondary deviation depends greatly on the degree to which others' disapproval finds expression in concrete acts of punishment and stigmatization. In another article, Lemert (1974:457) notes: "While communication of invidious definitions of persons or groups and the public expression of disapproval were included [in earlier discussions] as part of the societal reaction, the important point was made that these had to be validated in order to be sociologically meaningful. Validation was conceived as isolation, segregation, penalties, supervision, or some kind of organized treatment."

In one attack on labeling theory, Charles Wellford (1975:342) argues that many of its key assumptions are not supported by the bulk of available evidence. In addition, he asserts that the averred connection between punitive reactions, changes in self-concept, and secondary deviation is "a simplistic view of behavior causation, one that stresses the explanation of intellectual as opposed to behavioral characteristics of the subject." According to Wellford, the claim that changes in self-concept produce changes in behavior has yet to be demonstrated. He prefers to view behavior as situationally determined and, citing research on prisonization (see Chapter 15), argues that crime may well occur quite independently of the actor's self-concept. Wellford's viewpoint is yet to be substantiated, however.

## CONFLICT, AUTHORITY, AND POWER

A common observation regarding societal reactions to crime is that certain individuals and groups are more likely to suffer the ignominy of being stigmatized as criminals and to be subjected to punitive sanctions than others are. As a general rule, those lacking wealth, prestige, and political influence are more likely to be labeled criminal, to be convicted of criminal offenses, and to be punished by incarceration. By the same token, those *victims* of crime who lack wealth, prestige, and political influence are less likely than others are to receive justice at the hands of the authorities (for an example, see the discussion of historical developments in criminal theft on pp. 206–207).

These observations remind us that crime cannot be divorced from the basic social, political, legal, economic, and historical arrangements that characterize a society, nor from the values or behavior that characterize its members. But also, a comprehensive grasp of the crime scene requires that we go beyond such questions as "Why do people commit crimes?" Questions of equal importance are "Why have certain activities been designated crimes and others not?" "Why are certain segments of the population more likely than others are to suffer criminal labeling and stigmatization?" and "Why are official reactions to crime patterned in a particular way?"

The *conflict perspective* in criminology has sought answers to questions like these and in doing so has enlarged our understanding of the crime scene. Proponents of the perspective differ on specific issues, but their work shares a common interest in the consequences of group differences in power and influence and the conflicts that arise as groups seek to fulfill their interests. Charles McCaghy (1976:89) points out:

> Basic to any conflict perspective is the assumption that whichever groups can exert the greatest influence on the legislative and the enforcement processes are most assured that their interests will be protected. What is illegal depends upon the outcome of struggles between concerned parties. Who is treated as criminal depends upon the bureaucratic interpretation of both law and behavior.

Austin Turk (1966, 1969) developed one of the most promising theoretical treatments of crime and criminalization from the conflict point of view. He begins by rejecting the conception of crime as behavior, arguing instead that criminality is a *status* acquired during the course of interaction between norm creators, interpreters, and enforcers (lawmakers, police, prosecution, judges, and others in positions of legal authority) and the general public. He then constructs a theory to explain and predict *criminalization,* the acquisition of criminal status. In Turk's (1969:53) view, criminology needs a theory stating "the conditions under which cultural and social differences between authorities and subjects will probably result in conflict, the conditions under which criminalization will probably occur in the course of conflict, and the conditions under which the degree of deprivation associated with becoming a criminal will probably be greater or lesser."

Turk argues that conflict between groups is most likely when what people say ought to be (cultural norms) corresponds to a high degree with what they actually do (social norms) for both authorities and subjects regarding a particular activity. For example, if the authorities hold that the use of marijuana is wrong and abstain from its use themselves, but a group of subjects holds that the the use of marijuana is acceptable and consume it themselves, then conflict is likely, for there is no room for compromise. In such a case, Turk argues, the authorities are likely to resort to coercion in order to get their way. Conflict is least likely when neither authorities nor subjects display high congruence between what they think should be and how they actually behave. In such cases the particular issue provokes little or no conflict, for it is more symbolic than anything else, and both sides leave plenty of room for modifications and adjustments.

Other factors affecting the probability of conflict include the degree to which those having an illegal attribute or engaging in an illegal act are organized, and their degree of sophistication. Sophistication here means "knowledge of patterns in the behavior of others which is used in attempts to manipulate them" (Turk, 1969:58). Conflict is more probable, Turk argues, the less organized and sophisticated the norm resisters are.

Turk says that the probability of criminalization depends on power differences between authorities and subjects and on the realism of moves (the tactical skills employed by the opposing parties) in the conflict. The probability of criminalization is greater the more power differences there are that favor enforcers over norm resisters and the less realistic are the moves adopted by the latter. Any move is likely to be unrealistic that (1) increases the visibility of the attribute or behavior perceived as offensive by the norm enforcers; (2) draws attention to additional offensive attributes or violates an even more significant norm of the authorities; (3) increases consensus among the various levels of enforcers by, for example, turning opposition to a particular rule into an attack on "the whole system"; or (4) increases the power difference in favor of the enforcers (Turk, 1969:72).

In addition to the theory itself, Turk suggests what kinds of data are relevant to empirical tests and submits some of his own findings in tentative support of some of the theory's predictions. The theory still awaits careful test and evaluation, but it must be counted as a significant contribution to the efforts to unravel the puzzles of criminality. If nothing else, Turk's effort represents one of the best examples of theory construction in criminology and has alerted us to some of the critical issues that serious students of crime must confront in their efforts to comprehend variations in criminality. Foremost among these issues is the nature of the relationships among those who create, interpret, and enforce legal norms and those who are subject to their decisions and actions. Crime has no objective reality apart from the meanings attached to it, and criminality is an expression of those meanings and the actions that give them life. Turk has reminded us that criminality is a product of social interaction; as such, its patterns and variations reflect those that characterize relations among the people who come in contact with one another as authorities and subjects.

## Summary

Early criminological theories stressed behavioral dimensions of crime and couched explanations in terms of individual differences. Criminals were presumed to be somehow different from other people and were thought by many to be morally defective. The criminal, it was argued, must be a product of some sort of biological or psychic degeneracy.

As sociological interest in crime grew, the search for causes led to investigation of the social environment. Although at first there was still much interest in the individual as the unit of analysis, the emphasis slowly shifted to the impact of social conditions. Although the multifactor approach supported a search for crime-producing factors in the realm of biology and psychology, the die was cast: from the 1930s on, sociology dominated the study of crime.

In sociological criminology, the question "Why do people commit crimes?" was answered first by looking at the impact of social structure on group life. Theories linking anomic conditions to crime gained considerable attention, as did those linking delinquent subcultures with certain characteristics of urban ecology. Yet as these views were gaining prominence, Edwin Sutherland offered an alternative, a social process theory, which argued that like any other social behavior, crime is learned through interaction in intimate social groups. Sparked by Sutherland's differential association theory, an interest developed in the processes by which individuals become criminals.

The social structural and early social process theories shared in common the view that crime is normal rather than pathological. The criminal, furthermore, is not morally defective but is, instead, much like anyone else. The fact that some segments of society have higher crime rates than do others reflects different social experiences and conditions, not a tendency toward "sickness" or "moral defectiveness." These perspectives also shared the long-standing view that there *is* something called crime, which is different in substance from noncrime and can be studied objectively.

Later social process theorists rejected this view, treating crime as problematic instead. The so-called labeling theorists took the view that crime is nothing more than a label attached to conduct and people and that what need to be explained are variations in labeling behavior. Crime was thought of as a status applied to behavior, not as a particular kind of act. Accordingly, the processes of making and enforcing criminal laws received central attention from labeling theorists. The imposition of criminal labels explains why there are criminals, and the fact that some groups display higher rates of criminality than others is explained largely in terms of social conflict. The conflict theories of the 1960s drew attention away from crime as behavior and toward the activities of those in positions of power and authority. They also revived the interest in social structure and helped prepare the way for the radical-critical theories of the 1970s.

# CHAPTER 3

# Theories of Crime, II: Radical, Situational, and Rationality Perspectives

During the 1970s three significant developments occurred in criminological theory: First, there was the rise of radical-critical theory, which focused attention on the relationship between crime and the political economy of capitalist society. Second, a revival of what has come to be known as "classical" criminology emerged. Dating from the eighteenth century, this approach stresses the rationality of criminal behavior and views criminals as those who wilfully choose to commit crimes when they see the gains outweighing the costs. Third, the 1970s saw the development of a "situational" perspective on crime, and followers of this approach visualize crime as an event reflecting the convergence in time and space of offenders, opportunities, and inducements.

## Radical-Critical Criminology

Conflict theorists writing in the 1960s and early 1970s sought to explain why some people and activities have a greater chance of being labeled criminal than others do. Their theories emphasized the conflicts that arise when interests clash and the roles that power and authority play in legislative and enforcement processes that result in the imposition of criminal labels.

Radical-critical theorists have gone further, however, casting conflicts of interest and criminal labeling within a general theory of political economy having roots in the theories of Karl Marx.

### THE MARXIAN HERITAGE

Although Karl Marx said little about crime, radical criminology recognizes a substantial debt to this nineteenth-century scholar. The substance and the intent of Marx's work have had considerable influence on those writers who identify themselves with radical criminology. His ideas about the nature of humanity, the nature of society, social relations under capitalism, and the nature of social change provide a framework for the analysis of crime. His desire to strip away the myths and "false consciousness" created and fostered by those in power has become a major component of the radical perspective (Taylor, Walton, and Young, 1975).

Marx's social theory provides some of the themes and ideas that hold an important place in critical criminology. First is Marx's view that the mode of economic production — the manner in which the production of goods and services is organized — determines in large part the organization of social relations, that is, the structure of individual and group interaction. Under a capitalistic mode of production, social relations are structured differently than under the mode of production found in feudal societies. Accordingly, to "know" society we must first understand how the forces of material production are organized.

In addition, Marx believed that those who own and control the means of production are in a position to control the lives of others. They have the power, for they are the ones who control the most basic of socially meaningful human activities: work. But more than this, Marx asserted that this ruling class also controls the formulation and implementation of moral and legal norms, and even ideas. As he put it in *The German Ideology* (1947:39): "The ideas of the ruling class are in every epoch the ruling ideas. . . . The class which has the means of material production at its disposal, has control at the same time over the means of mental production."

Marx identified two great classes in advanced capitalistic societies — the *bourgeoisie,* owners of the means of production (capital), and the *proletariat,* sellers of their ability to work. Inevitably, the interests of these two classes conflict, for capitalism places them in a relationship of asymmetrical exchange and exploitation. From the standpoint of the bourgeoisie, survival and growth depend on success in the competition for scarce resources and the drive for maximization of profits. For the proletariat, survival depends on the ability to sell themselves as workers. But since the ruling class controls production, it also controls work. The worker is thus a pawn in the game of competition and profit maximization that the bourgeoisie inevitably must play. Relations between the two classes are marked by the bourgeoisie's exploitation of the worker, just as the chess player exploits pawns in the effort to beat an opponent.

This relationship affects law — and by extension, crime. Legal rules and the relations they support flow from the "material conditions of life," that is, the conditions produced by relations of production (Marx, 1971:20). When the economic structure of society changes, law and crime change. Since the dominant class controls the instruments of law creation and implementation, legal rules and enforcement practices are shaped by, and supportive of, the interests of that class. Yet, as Marx and Engels point out, the image of law presented to the masses depicts law as the "will of the people." This "juridical illusion" is fostered by the ruling class as part of the effort to undermine the formation of sentiments of opposition and resistance (1947:58–62).

Some authors point out that Marx's method, more than anything else, helped shape contemporary radical criminology. It is a critical method in the sense that it encourages the attempt not only to know the "real" reality but also to think negatively. As Richard Quinney (1979:17–18) describes it:

A critical mode of inquiry is a radical philosophy — one that goes to the roots of our lives, to the foundations and the fundamentals, to the essentials of consciousness. In rooting out presuppositions we are able to assess every actual and possible experience. The operation is one of demystification, removing the myths created by the official reality. Conventional experience is revealed as a reification of the social order, exposing the underside of official reality. . . .

A critical philosophy lets us break with the ideology of the age, for built into critical thinking is the ability to think negatively. This *dialectical* form of thought, by being able to entertain an alternative, allows us to question current experience and better understand what exists. Instead of merely looking for an objective reality, we are interested in negating the established order, which will make us better able to understand what we experience. By applying this dialectic in our thought we can comprehend and surpass the present.

Important to Marx's critical thought was his refusal to separate people from society. People are social products and cannot be understood apart from society. But people are also products of history, for society is shaped by the past as well as the present. In the view of Marx and the radical criminologists, social relations must be examined in their historical context.

## WILLEM BONGER ON CRIME AND ECONOMIC CONDITIONS

Though Marx said little about crime in particular, Willem Bonger sought to apply various of Marx's theoretical arguments to crime in capitalistic societies. In *Criminality and Economic Conditions* (published in English in 1916), Bonger observed that capitalistic societies appear to have considerably more crime than do precapitalistic societies. Furthermore, while capitalism developed, crime rates increased steadily. Bonger's underlying concern was to account for change in people. He considered people to be products of their social environment, "which is determined in its turn by the mode of production" (1969:33).

Under capitalism, Bonger argued, the characteristic trait of humans is self-interest (egoism). Given the emphasis on profit maximization and competition, and the fact that social relations are class structured and geared to economic exchange, capitalistic societies spawn intra- and interclass conflicts as individuals seek to survive and prosper. Interclass conflict is one-sided, however, since those who own and control the means of production are in a position to coerce and exploit their less fortunate neighbors. Criminal law, as one instrument of coercion, is used by the ruling class to protect its position and interests. Criminal law "is principally constituted according to the will of" the dominant class, and "hardly any act is punished if it does not injure the interests of the dominant class" (pp. 379–380). Behavior threatening the interests of the ruling class is designated as criminal.

Since social relations are geared to competition, profit seeking, and the exercise of power, considerations of mutual support and reciprocity are subordinated to egoistic tendencies. These tendencies lead, in Bonger's view, to a weakening of altruistic sentiment and internal restraint. Both the bourgeoisie and proletariat become prone to crime. The working class is subject to further demoralization, however, because of its inferior exchange position and its exploitation at the hands of the ruling class. As Bonger describes it: "Long working hours and monotonous labor brutalize those who are forced into them; bad housing conditions contribute also to debase the moral sense, as do the uncertainty of existence, and finally absolute poverty, the frequent consequence of sickness and unemployment" (1969:195).

In Bonger's view, economic conditions that induce egoism, coupled with a system of law creation and enforcement controlled by the capitalist class, account for (1) higher crime rates in capitalistic societies than in other societies, (2) crime rates increasing with industrialization, and (3) official crime as predominantly a working-class phenomenon.

Bonger's analysis has a number of major weaknesses. First, he sees a direct causal link between economic conditions and all crime. He does admit the possibility that some criminal acts may be due to psychic disturbance and degeneracy in the individual, but he ends by relating these to underlying economic causes. Second, his use of arrest data in the major part of his analysis is questionable. More than anything else these data reflect the behavior of social control agencies, not those who commit crimes. While appropriate for analyses of the implementation and enforcement of criminal law, Bonger uses arrest data as well to demonstrate the egoism of individuals who have acted antisocially by committing crimes. Third, the important precipitating variable in his scheme, egoism, is not itself measured but is inferred from the existence of what it presumes to explain, namely, crime. Apparently, where there is crime there is egoism, for where there is egoism there is crime. This gets us nowhere. Even if we accept the proposed link between egoism and crime, we must remember that crimes may be entirely unselfishly motivated: how would we categorize the mother who shoplifts under the pressure of family hunger?

These criticisms leave Bonger's theory in jeopardy. Even so, he must be credited with making an important attempt to apply Marxian theory to criminality and with drawing the attention of criminologists to social conflict, class struggles, power, interests, economic conditions, and exploitation as possible determinants of crime.

## RADICAL CRIMINOLOGY TODAY

In America, the 1970s saw the first systematic statements on crime from the perspective of radical criminology. The views of David M. Gordon and Richard Quinney illustrate two versions of the perspective.

According to David Gordon (1971, 1973), most crime is a rational response to the structure of institutions, including the legal, found in capitalistic societies. Crime is "a means of survival in a society within which survival is never assured" (1971:59). Gordon finds three types of crime in America as the best examples of this rationality: ghetto crime, organized crime, and corporate, or white-collar, crime. These types offer a chance at survival, status, or respect in a society geared to competitive forms of social interaction and characterized by substantial inequalities in the distribution of social resources, wealth, political power, and so on.

Involvement in different types of crime is explained by class position. Those in the upper socioeconomic classes have access to jobs where paper transactions, lots of money, and unobtrusive communication are important features. Illegal opportunities are manifest in the many forms of white-collar crime. Those in the lower classes, especially those who are "raised in poverty," do not have easy access to money and nonviolent means to manipulate it. Accordingly, illegal activities tend to be the sort that involve taking things by force or physical stealth.

Gordon sees duality in American justice in that the state tends to ignore certain kinds of crime — most notably corporate and white-collar crimes — whereas it concerns itself "incessantly" with crimes among the poor. According to Gordon, we can understand this duality only if we view the state through the radical perspective. First of all, government in a capitalistic society exists primarily to serve the interests of the capitalist class, and preservation of the system itself is the priority. So long as power and profits are not undermined, the offenses that tend in general to harm members of other classes receive little interest. Second, even though offenses of the poor tend to harm others who are poor, they are collectively viewed as a threat to the stability of the system and the interests of the ruling class. Furthermore, an aggressive lower class is a dangerous class, and the spread of ghetto crime (conveniently identified with blacks) to other parts of the nation's cities heightens the fears of the affluent classes who are in a position to influence policy. Gordon's critical approach provides a framework for explaining both the status of criminality and the behavior of the criminal (see also Spitzer, 1975).

Richard Quinney (1975) has written a more detailed radical theory of crime. Dealing with the problem of crime in America, Quinney urges us to recognize the links between the nature of our society, its criminal laws, conceptions of crime, and crime control practices. Quinney sets down six propositions that make up a critical-Marxian theory, which, he argues, strips away the "official reality" of crime and uncovers what he calls the "social reality of crime." The social reality of crime is a reality constructed out of conflict and the exercise of power and consists of the meanings people attach to events and activities as they interact with others. The theory's propositions are

1. *The Official Definition of Crime:* Crime as a legal definition of human conduct is created by agents of the dominant class in a politically organized society.
2. *Formulating Definitions of Crime:* Definitions of crime are composed of behaviors that conflict with the interests of the dominant class.
3. *Applying Definitions of Crime:* Definitions of crime are applied by the class that has the power to shape the enforcement and administration of criminal law.
4. *How Behavior Patterns Develop in Relation to Definitions of Crime:* Behavior patterns are structured in relation to definitions of crime, and within this context people engage in actions that have relative probabilities of being defined as criminal.
5. *Constructing an Ideology of Crime:* An ideology of crime is constructed and diffused by the dominant class to secure its hegemony.

6. *Constructing the Social Reality of Crime:* The social reality of crime is constructed by the formulation and application of definitions of crime, the development of behavior patterns in relation to these definitions, and the construction of an ideology of crime. (Quinney, 1975:37–41)

Proposition 1 is a definition, and proposition 6 a composite of the first five propositions; accordingly, Quinney identifies the body of his theory in the four middle propositions.

Quinney calls these propositions a theory, but a careful reading leaves unclear precisely what they explain. Furthermore, the theory offers no specific predictions about variations in either crime or crime control. Such deficiencies are not peculiar to Quinney's work, nor are they found only among those who subscribe to the radical perspective. However, they certainly do not help us formulate a critical theory that will "demystify" our understanding of crime.

The radical perspective is not a unified approach, nor are its diverse views adequately summarized in this brief discussion of Gordon's and Quinney's works. Vigorous debate has ensued within the radical camp itself. One major point of controversy concerns the perspective's relationship to Marxism. Radicals are not in agreement as to how Marx's theories should be applied to crime, and some have criticized their colleagues for a shallow and selective reading of Marx (Greenberg, 1981:11–13).

Major differences among radical criminologists have been outlined by Robert Bohm (1982). Briefly stated, some of these are as follows:

**1.** Some radicals see the state and its apparatus of law as manipulated by and serving the parochial interests of individual members of the ruling class; others see them as determined by impersonal forces within capitalism, for example, the "market."

**2.** Some radicals believe that the ruling class has intentionally pulled the wool over the eyes of the populace as to the true sources of domination and power; others believe that the mystification of domination results from the ideology of free enterprise that inheres in the capitalistic mode of production itself.

**3.** For some radicals, the solution of the crime problem in capitalist societies lies in the replacement of capitalism with socialism; for others socialism is no answer at all.

## CRITICISMS OF RADICAL CRIMINOLOGY

Radical criminology has stirred up considerable debate, which tells us that the perspective is something to be reckoned with. Interestingly, a criticism lodged against some proponents of the new criminology is that they have failed to allow for differences in studying crime. In a symposium reviewing an English contribution to radical criminology, Paul Rock (1973:595) observed: "*The New Criminology's* master vision makes no provisions for a division of intellectual labor. It does not recognize the possibility that the study of deviancy is not always enhanced by the imposition of one grand scheme upon all its subordinate projects." Although proponents of the new perspective are quick to condemn mainstream liberal criminology for its intellectual domination of the field, their own position seems to advocate replacing one kind of domination with another.

Some radical criminologists would have us believe that some criminals are "real" and presumably that some are not real. According to the Union of Radical Criminologists, "the real criminals govern this society [America] and are protected by its laws (Quinney, 1975:593). Who are these people? Does this mean that "real" criminals are only to be found in America? It is unlikely that the answer to the second question would be yes. But the first question cannot be answered easily, and it is an especially important one, for the answer should tell us who are the appropriate objects of criminological interest for the union. Sometimes the image conjured up is one of a small group of powerful individuals in constant touch with one another who determine the destinies of the rest of us. At other times the image suggests a category of people broad enough to include almost everybody. But beyond this, what makes this category of people "real" criminals? The answer to this remains in doubt.

Does this mean we should not consider the new radical criminology a significant contribution to the field? Not at all. It means, partly, that the radicals have important problems to iron out. None of the criticisms mentioned is a fatal flaw. As a matter of fact, we must credit the radical perspective with bringing to the forefront issues deserving careful consideration and constant reappraisal. One of these is the utility of alternative theoretical perspectives in improving our understanding of the crime scene. The interest in Marxian theory encourages serious criminologists to familiarize themselves with its potentialities in the study of crime. The radical criminologist asks us to look at crime in new ways and suggests how we might do so, making a challenge to established ideas that ought not to be ignored. David Greenberg (1981:17) believes that one of the major contributions of the radical perspective lies in its emphasis on analyzing crime in terms of the character of society as a whole. By contrast, in nonradical criminology:

> The society itself rarely appears. The possibility that *its* organization — its way of producing and distributing material goods, and of organizing its political and legal institutions, for example — might have major implications for the amount and kinds of crime present in society, as well as for the character of its crime control apparatus, is not even considered.

Learning decays unless new ideas are forthcoming. That these ideas sometimes conflict with strongly held beliefs does not make them any less important. The same is true of the information gathered by those whose perspectives depart from our own. Radical criminology, concerned with the exercise of power in defense of ruling interests, has brought forth facts about the crime scene that otherwise might not have been supplied in a systematic way. Such information adds to our store of knowledge when it is not ignored or set aside on ideological grounds.

## FUTURE TRENDS

The status of radical criminology among the competing theoretical orientations of the field seems less secure today than it was at the beginning of the 1970s. This is not surprising, for that decade began at a time of social and political unrest. The radical vision offered hope of relief for those feeling the exploitation and oppression (real and imagined) of monopoly capitalism. With the end of American involvement in Vietnam and with the demise of the Nixon era, things quieted down considerably. Inflation, high oil prices, and crime in the streets eventually replaced the counterculture, political repression, and the Vietnam war as issues of pressing concern to most Americans. A law-and-order reaction to the rebellion of the 1960s set in, not just among so-called middle Americans, but also on college campuses and in the inner cities. The appeal of radical theory has to some extent been undermined by these changes.

The radicalization of criminological thinking may itself have sparked a counterreaction on the part of those in a position to affect the discipline:

> As criminology has radicalized and politicized, authorities and those in positions of power have reinforced their own commitments to the status quo, convinced themselves of the limited practical contributions of research, and solidified their resistance to self-exposure. By announcing its assumptions regarding the role of social agencies, the new criminology has precipitated an already serious crisis of confidence in the discipline's ability to deal fairly with the problem of crime and criminality. Politicalization has met with counter-politicalization (Friday, 1977:166).

In addition, there were claims in academic circles that both labeling theory and critical criminology had been leading theory and research too far away from the criminal. We know a tremendous amount about the social control apparatus and its personnel, Stanton Wheeler (1976) has claimed, but we know little more about the criminal offender now than we knew twenty-five years ago. Others have questioned whether the newer brands of criminology offer hope of a better explanation of crime and criminality than can be expected from more traditional approaches (Pelfrey, 1979).

## Situational and Rationality Perspectives

Whereas the radical-critical theorists helped resurrect the nineteenth-century writings of Marx and gave them new application, an even older body of ideas has seen a revival in recent years: the so-called *classical* perspective, with roots in eighteenth-century utilitarianism and an emphasis on volition and rationality. But that is not all: the past decade has also witnessed a quite different development in criminology, one that proposes a new way of looking at crime. Crime is visualized not simply as behavior or status but as an *event* arising from the timely interaction of offenders, opportunities, and inducements. According to this view, there are many elements in crime, and it takes the "right" situation to bring it forth. Crime is much more than something a person does.

Both the revival of classical views and the emphasis on situational elements in crime came about because doubts had emerged about the efficacy of prevailing strategies of crime prevention. The steady rise in the rates of major crimes since the early 1960s was seen by many as evidence of failure. Some blamed the positivistic theories underlying rehabilitation and other programs designed to manipulate offenders or to reduce their exposure to crimogenic influences. Criminals, they felt, were much more in command of their actions than the positivists believed. Make the choice of committing crime less attractive, the critics suggested, by increasing the amount and risks of punishment. Not surprisingly, *deterrence* became one of the hottest issues of the 1970s (see Chapters 14 and 15).

The emphasis on deterrence was countered in other quarters by proposals for an alternative strategy, one that sought to reduce crime by manipulating the *opportunities* for its occurrence. Steering locks were introduced in automobiles, street lamps made brighter, private security forces beefed up, home burglar-alarm systems sold everywhere, surveillance devices planted in subways, banks, stores, and apartment buildings, new gun-control laws proposed, and all sorts of environmental modifications envisioned. The idea was that criminal events could be prevented if opportunities and situational inducements were removed.

Also important to shaping the situational and rationality perspectives were the contributions of economists and urban geographers. The idea that criminal events take shape in an ecological context is certainly not new (see p. 36), but geographers brought a new vigor and sophistication to the spatial analysis of crime. They used cartographic techniques to develop maps of urban areas showing places of greatest risk and providing insights into the movement of offenders in relation to the spatial distribution of criminal opportunities. For their part, economists developed models of criminal behavior based on the premise that individuals weigh costs and benefits when contemplating crime and will choose activities that maximize benefits while minimizing costs.

At the heart of the situational approach to crime is the idea that certain situations promote the occurrence of criminal events and others tend to inhibit them. Much of the literature focuses on the nature and distribution of criminal opportunities. Central to the classical perspective are the issues of *volition* (or free will), *rationality,* and *utility* (or benefit).

Crime is not an event until it has occurred, for an event *is* an occurrence or happening. The situational approach looks at crimes that have occurred and asks what things came together to make them happen.

## BASIC ELEMENTS OF CRIMINAL EVENTS

Crimes differ in so many ways that any attempt to identify the basic elements that all criminal events share would be doomed from the start. A criminal event need not even have an offender present as it occurs, for crimes may occur after the perpetrator is long gone or even dead. Bombings and arson, various forms of extortion, many forms of consumer fraud, and a host of other offenses are consummated when the criminal is somewhere else. The point is not as trivial as it may seem: detection, prosecution, conviction, and punishment all rely on tying the suspect to the event.

Some criminal events have no victim, or at least no one who sees himself or herself as a victim. Some criminal events occur more or less at a *point* in time; others occur over a *period* of time, and sometimes a lengthy one at that. Strange as it may seem, some criminal events occur only in the presence of police officers, as in resisting arrest and police brutality.

An effort is under way to identify the basic elements in different types of crime. The crimes that the public fears most are *predatory* crimes, defined as "illegal acts where someone definitely and intentionally takes or damages the person or property of another" (Glaser, 1971:4). Robbery, burglary, rape, auto theft, embezzlement, shoplifting, hijacking, and arson are examples of predatory crimes. According to Lawrence Cohen and Marcus Felson (1979), predatory criminal events contain the following minimal elements: (1) motivated offenders, (2) suitable targets, and (3) the absence of capable guardians. If any one of these elements is lacking, a predatory criminal event will not occur. No mention is made of capable offenders, those able to consummate a criminal act, to "pull it off" (though they may later get caught). Much crime is in fact not pulled off, making the distinction between completed and uncompleted crime quite significant. Indeed, the law has long recognized the distinction, treating attempted crimes less severely. From the situational point of view, the distinction is interesting because it prompts us to compare attempted and completed crimes in order to establish exactly how they differ and which elements in the events account for the outcomes. This is discussed in Chapter 5 in relation to murder and assault.

## CRIME AND OPPORTUNITY

If there is a basic element in all events, criminal or otherwise, it is opportunity. An opportunity makes an event possible; a criminal opportunity makes a criminal event possible. One cannot drive a car without having the opportunity to do so, and that depends first on the invention of the automobile. One cannot rob a bank without the opportunity to do so, and that rests first on the existence of banks. Put simply, the presence of automobiles provides the opportunity for driving (and for auto theft), and the presence of banks provides the opportunity for bank robbery (or for shopping by check).

The existence of automobiles and banks provides both criminal and noncriminal opportunities. This is important for two reasons. First, no event is criminal until those who create and administer the criminal law say it is. Accordingly, two otherwise similar societies may have different criminal opportunities simply because the authorities in one have labeled more (or different) events as crimes. Second, the opportunities for crime are tied to the opportunities for noncrime.

The computer further illustrates these points. No one could use computers before they were invented; once invented, however, the opportunity existed for their use. Suppose that at some point someone observed that computers could be used to someone else's disadvantage — to steal or falsify information, to invade privacy, and so forth. The possibility of computer crime is born as soon as laws are enacted to regulate the use of computers, and some of these laws assess criminal penalties for violations. Three hypothetical societies could thus have the following differences:

Society "A" No computers, hence no computer use either criminal or noncriminal.
Society "B" Computers, hence the opportunity for computer use, but no designation of use as criminal, hence no possibility of computer crime.
Society "C" Computers, hence the opportunity for computer use, plus designation of "X" types of use as criminal, hence the opportunity for computer crime.

Other things being equal, where would we look for computer crime? The answer is, of course, that we would look for computer crime in society "C."

In this illustration, we see that opportunities for crime are linked to opportunities for noncrime. This is always the case, and the reason is simple: an act that is possible remains so whether or not it is defined as criminal.

## SOCIAL CHANGE AND CRIMINAL OPPORTUNITIES

Something else worth noting in the computer illustration is the relationship between technology and criminal opportunities. As knowledge grows and technology advances, so do the ways of doing old things and the number of new things there are to do. *Both* noncriminal and criminal opportunities grow as the range of what is possible expands. This is probably what the nineteenth-century Italian scholar Francesco Poletti had in mind when he observed that the more honest activity there is the more dishonest activity there will be. Of course, this would be true even if there were no fundamental changes in the criminal law.

To illustrate, consider what many Americans now take for granted: electronic fund transfer (EFT). Little more than ten years ago this computer-based service was known and used only by banks and the larger corporations; now, the automatic teller machine (ATM) is familiar to most urbanites and is even found on university campuses. People with personal computers may also take advantage of home banking services, another version of EFT.

But with the development and spread of EFT services has come the potential for criminal abuse. The U.S. Justice Department now recognizes four generic types of ATM abuse or fraud (Bureau of Justice Statistics, 1984a):

**1.** Unauthorized use of access devices, as when someone steals an access card or uses one without the permission of the authorized holder. Many people make this abuse easier by writing down the secret personal identification number and keeping it with their card. Individual ATM frauds of this sort can involve thousands of dollars.

**2.** Fraud by a legitimate cardholder. For example, a person makes an authorized withdrawal and then denies any knowledge of it, claiming some unauthorized person must have done it and demanding that the bank "refund" the money.

**3.** Insider manipulation, as when a bank employee steals directly from the machine, intercepts a card mailed to a customer, or creates a fictitious account by manipulating the host computer.

**4.** Physical attack. The automated teller machines often hold considerable amounts of cash and thus become targets of attempts to break them open, or customers using the machines become the target of robbery attempts after they have withdrawn money.

Criminologists on both sides of the Atlantic have noted the relationship between crime and social change, arguing that the general growth of crime over the past hundred and fifty years is largely accounted for by increased criminal opportunities (e.g., Shelley, 1980; Sparks, 1980; Mack, 1975). In one American study of the relationship Leroy Gould (1969) argued that the significant rise in property crime rates from 1930 to 1969 was mainly attributable to the growing abundance of property. On a different plane, studies of American increases in homicide rates have attributed much of the rise in violent death rates to the increase in opportunities for murder provided by the growing availability and use of firearms (see Chapter 5).

In an analysis of the relationship between social change and criminal opportunities, Mary McIntosh (1971) writes that changes in English society not only increased the opportunities for property crime but also changed the nature of those opportunities. This resulted in a shift from what she calls "craft crime" to "project crime." Craft crime developed during Elizabethan times as cities grew and a growing number of people carried cash and valuables on their person. The thief could steal small amounts from many victims and with practice could master a variety of skilled techniques. Picking pockets, shoplifting, and various gambling cheats and con games were major types of craft crime.

Project crime emerged as a by-product of industrialization, becoming an important form of thievery around the beginning of the nineteenth century. Project crime is similar to what American criminologist Werner Einstadter (1969) has called the "planned operation," a high-risk crime for high stakes. It arises in response to the opportunity to steal large amounts from relatively small numbers of commercial victims — banks and other businesses — who go to greater lengths to protect their property and in doing so develop new methods of protection which the thief must then overcome. Innovations on the part of potential victims result in counter-innovations on the part of thieves, and so it goes on. Project crimes of necessity involve considerable skill, planning, and organization. One does not hijack a Brinks armored car alone or on the spur of the moment.

## The Routine Activity Approach

Change sooner or later affects all social institutions as well as the physical environment in which people live, work, and play. The growth of cities, the smashing of the atom, the conquest of near space, the invention of the assembly line, the end of piracy, the discovery of penicillin, the defeat of Nazi Germany, the migration from southern states to northern states and back again, the growth of service industries — all have affected our daily lives in one way or another. Though the extent of its influence varies, social change inevitably affects the way we organize our activities in pursuit of goals.

The relationship among change, opportunities, and criminal events has been explored in a series of studies by Lawrence Cohen and his colleagues (Cohen et al., 1980, 1981). Cohen calls his work a "routine activity approach." By *routine activity* Cohen means any recurrent, prevalent activity that provides for basic individual and collective needs. Work is a routine activity, but so are sex, child rearing, eating, going to the movies, and vacationing. Much crime is also routine activity.

Cohen's position is that changes in noncriminal routine activities affect criminal opportunities by affecting the convergence in time and space of those elements necessary for a criminal event to occur. Cohen focuses on robbery, murder, burglary, and other "direct contact" predatory crimes, but there is no reason the approach should not be applicable to other kinds of criminal events. Cohen's basic proposition is that "the probability that a violation will occur at any specific time and place . . . is . . . . a function of the convergence of likely offenders and suitable targets in the absence of capable guardians" (Cohen and Felson, 1979:590).

Cohen examines this proposition for both society and individuals. At the societal level he looks at changing predatory crime rates in America from 1947 to 1974 (and later to 1977) and finds that they can be largely accounted for by the dispersion of routine activities away from the household. Increased participation in work, play, and family activities away from the home increases the likelihood that suitable targets will come into contact with motivated offenders while in the absence of capable guardians. To put it another way, when fewer people stay at home, more household property is less well protected, and when more people are out and about after dark or alone (as they are when they spend more and more time away from the home), more people are less well protected.

Looking at the risks of being a victim in criminal events such as robbery, rape, and assault, Cohen finds that these risks are greatest for people away from home or alone. A study of the risk of being robbed showed, as predicted, that the risks were highest for those people more likely to be out and about than sheltered in home or work situations. The risk of being robbed while alone, Cohen found, was ten times greater than the risk of being robbed when accompanied by one or more others (Cohen et al., 1981:649).

**Dangerous Places**  Routine activities are carried on in all sorts of different places, and some places are more dangerous than others. The risks of crime vary in part because places differ in the extent to which they afford effective guardianship of life and property. A place where there are few opportunities for people to observe what is going on, where anonymity is characteristic, and where people who may not belong can come and go with ease lacks what Oscar Newman (1972) called *defensible space*. Such a place is crime prone.

Newman developed the idea of defensible space in a study of public housing projects in New York. He discovered that the annual rates for such serious crimes as robbery increased with the height of the building, from 8.3 per thousand people in three-story buildings to 20.2 per thousand in buildings sixteen stories or higher. In addition, he found that more than half of the crime in high-rise buildings occurred in poorly monitored communal areas with easy access. He concluded that building design influenced the opportunities for crime by affecting the residents' surveillance and control of semipublic places.

Despite criticisms of Newman's approach (S. Wilson, 1980; Booth, 1981), the idea of defensible space has continued to draw attention, and Newman himself has spent considerable energy researching his thesis. It now appears clear that the design of the built environment can and does influence the occurrence of criminal events, but that influence is affected by such factors as the age composition of the resident or user population (more young people, more crime), by the family composition of households (more single-parent households, more crime), and by the size and density of resident and surrounding populations (more people in a given space, more crime) (Pyle, 1976).

There seems to be growing consensus that the value of defensible space as an explanatory variable is lessened by its almost exclusive emphasis on the design features of the built environment. Undoubtedly, considerable interaction takes place between the physical and social features of environments. Summarizing his analysis of serious crimes in all residential city blocks in Cleveland and San Diego in 1970, Dennis Roncek (1981:88) writes: "the most dangerous city blocks are relatively large in population and area with high concentrations of primary individuals [single-member households] and apartment housing. These blocks also tend to be in heavily populated surroundings." Among the most important factors influencing crime risk were anonymity and those environmental features affecting population movement, contacts, and interaction.

## Access to Criminal Opportunities

The routine activity approach is a promising perspective on the relationship between criminal events and the everyday behavior of individuals and populations. For direct-contact, predatory property crimes, the perspective correctly predicts that young people are more likely to be victims and offenders than old people are, poorer people more likely than rich people, men than women, the unemployed than the employed, the active than the inactive, the single-adult household than the multiadult household, and the urban than the rural. It also correctly predicts that small but valuable pieces of property — stereos, car radios, portable TVs — and property left unguarded will most often be the targets of predatory property crime.

But one thing that proponents of the routine activity approach have not discussed in detail is the manner in which organization of routine activities influences the range of criminal events in which motivated offenders participate. This is a question of access to criminal opportunities as well as their composition. It concerns the likelihood that potential offenders can take advantage of available criminal opportunities.

Neither criminal opportunities nor access to them are distributed evenly in time and space *or* throughout a population. Obviously, the opportunities for motor vehicle theft are greater where there are more cars, but getting at those cars, especially the most appealing ones, is not as easy for some motivated thieves as for others. The opportunities for shoplifting are greater where there are more stores, larger stores and stores with open displays, but these stores may be clustered only in certain areas of town. The opportunities to pilfer at work expand as more people work and as places of work grow larger and more impersonal; but only the employed can pilfer, and some employees can pilfer much more valuable things than others do. At a different level of occupational crime, there is more opportunity for embezzlement as financial operations expand, but only for those in positions of financial trust. The opportunities for executive crime — price fixing, bribery and kickbacks, corporate frauds, and other deceptions — increase as corporations grow in number and size and as service industries expand, but relatively few citizens are in a position to take advantage of them.

**Opportunities and Female Crime**  A popular explanation of the recent growth in female crime is couched in terms of opportunities (Adler, 1975). Women, the argument goes, are more exposed to the opportunities for crime than they used to be. More women are working; more women are free to move about, less tied to the home; more women are taking on family-centered responsibilities that have traditionally been the domain of males; and more women are going their own way, choosing whom to work for, how to spend their time. All this has meant more autonomy and greater freedom from the constraints of traditional female roles (Simon, 1975).

Though few dispute the growing freedom of women, some disagree over just how much the access to opportunities for crime has broadened for women. Most recent commentary argues that female crime has really not changed its colors — it is still largely nonviolent, mostly petty, and linked to conventional female roles. If accessible opportunities have expanded they have done so in relation to mundane activities that do not require (or provide) special skills and resources (Smart, 1979; Leonard, 1982). Women who are criminally motivated do what men do: they take advantage of the opportunities that are available and readily accessible in the situations in which they routinely find themselves. When the situations men and women routinely find themselves in are similar, we should expect to find, other things being equal, that their rates of crime are similar. It remains to be seen how much of the difference in male and female crime rates can be accounted for by situational factors and how much by differences in inclination and motivation. The question not adequately answered is why female crime rates are so much lower than male rates. It is likely that differences in criminal opportunities and other situational factors cannot entirely account for the gap (Leonard, 1982:42).

## RESOURCES FOR CRIME

Access to criminal opportunities is governed by available resources. Other things being equal, the greater an individual's or population's resources, the greater the range of accessible criminal activities. Some crimes require special skills (safe cracking, counterfeiting, con games); some crimes require special equipment or devices (computer crime, record pirating, bombing, heroin production); some crimes require special planning or organization (embezzlement, numbers running, prostitution); some require lots of money (importation of heroin, large-scale gambling, loan sharking) or lots of muscle (extortion, hijacking, racketeering, terrorism); some crimes require special prestige or social position (bribery, corporate crime, police corruption, the "fix," welfare fraud); and some crimes require "connections" (drug dealing, fencing).

In an analysis of fraud in economic transactions, Graeme Newman and colleagues (1981) show how opportunities for fraud vary considerably and how the extent and type of fraud committed depends on the offender's access to positions of authority, communications media, technology, and mass markets. They also point out how personal skills involving manipulation of people, use of status, management abilities, and technical expertise facilitate the practice of fraud.

The routine activities most likely to improve access to criminal opportunities are those related to work. Work has much to do with shaping experiences, and through it people gain access to the resources and skills that they can channel in criminal or noncriminal directions. The importance of work is stressed by Gibbs and Short (1974), who argue that there will be a wider range of criminal activities in populations with a wider range of occupations. Their analysis of arrests and occupations for different age groups in the United States confirmed this prediction.

Access to criminal opportunities influences not only which criminal events are more, or less, likely to occur, but also the range of criminal events for an individual or population. Other things being equal, criminal events occur more often when they involve relatively few resources. However, the range of criminal events is narrower the fewer the available resources. Those who are poor, unemployed, or otherwise disadvantaged in the competition for resources are restricted in their access to criminal opportunities just as they are in their access to noncriminal opportunities. Wanting to act in a certain way is not the same as being able to do so.

## Crime and Rationality

The routine activity approach examines how "the spatio-temporal organization of social activities helps people to translate their criminal inclinations into action" (Cohen and Felson, 1979:589). Criminal motivations are treated as given: It is not necessary to know why people decide to commit crimes in order to understand why some situations are more crime prone than others. However, the routine activity approach does rest on an assumption about how offenders act, at least in the case of predatory property crime: they engage in "rational choice behavior" (Cohen, Felson, and Land, 1980:98). To say that behavior is rational means that it is *purposive* (conscious and goal oriented) and that it has been selected as the most *reasonable* (efficient, economical) means of attaining a given end. Since there are usually many different ways of doing something, rational action implies making choices, and the reasonable choice is made on the basis of a comparison of alternatives. However, Hirschi (1985) correctly warns against assuming that rational choice theories require that individuals carefully plan and execute their crimes or use sophisticated techniques. All that is assumed is some minimal level of planning or foresight for the act to occur.

## "CLASSICAL CRIMINOLOGY"

According to the theories of Cesare Beccaria and Jeremy Bentham in the late eighteenth century, criminals are free, rational, and hedonistic. They choose among alternative courses of action according to the benefits believed to accrue from them; they avoid behavior they expect will bring pain unless, of course, the pleasure outweighs the pain and the gain is greater than that associated with alternative courses of action. Since they exercise free will in choosing among alternatives, they are responsible for their behavior.

**The Economic Model of Crime** A modern formulation of the classical view of crime has been advanced by economists, among them Gary Becker (1968), one of the first to publish work in this vein. Many quite complicated models have been developed, but they all share certain ideas. First, the approach "is predicated on the assumption that individuals choose to commit crimes" (Warren, 1978:439). Second, individuals are assumed to make the same choice of action when confronted by the same alternatives. This is rationality as economists use the term, and choice is guided by maximization of satisfactions, or "utility."

Each activity available to an individual is evaluated according to its utility; in the case of illegal acts it is an expected utility weighed against the probability of being caught and convicted and against the monetary equivalent of being punished if convicted. When the expected utility of a criminal act is greater than the utility of a noncriminal alternative, the economic model predicts selection of the crime.

The classical and economic models of criminal behavior assume, then, that crime follows from some sort of calculation in which the perceived rewards, costs, and risks of alternative actions are compared. They assume, also, that choice is exercised in a rational, if not totally free, manner.

Neither of these assumptions sits well with those social scientists who hold the view that people are "pulled" or "pushed" into crime by forces beyond their control. But one need not take an either-or position in the debate. It is likely, in fact, that people are pulled or pushed toward crime, but in the last analysis choose to commit crime from among alternatives that include noncriminal actions. The choice completes what biological, cultural, or economic factors began. And once the individual chooses to commit a crime, external factors may again enter the picture as situational influences encouraging or inhibiting completion of the crime, or the choice of one type of crime (say, robbery) instead of another (say, burglary).

**The Wilson–Herrnstein Theory** A recent addition to the growing literature on rationality and criminal decision making is found in the work of Wilson and Herrnstein (1985). Their theory is about the "forces that control individual behavior" (p. 42) and combines behavioral, biological, and environmental factors to explain why some people commit "serious" street crimes and others do not.

An underlying assumption of the theory is that when individuals are faced with choices of action, they evaluate them according to their consequences and will prefer those with the highest anticipated ratio of rewards to costs. To the extent that individuals act on this basis, their behavior is rational, and therefore, both stealing and bestiality can be rational. Wilson and Herrnstein believe that individuals can choose to commit or not commit a crime, and for any given level of internal restraint (the "bite of conscience"), they will select crime over noncrime whenever the reward–cost ratio is greater for the crime than for the noncrime.

What any given individual considers rewarding (or costly) is part human nature (i.e., it satisfies such primary drives as hunger and sex) and part learned. These rewards may be material or nonmaterial, certain or uncertain, and immediate or delayed. The evaluation of any particular action will be influenced by how well a person handles uncertainty and delay, which Wilson and Herrnstein believe is influenced by nature, temperament, and social environment. Aggressive individuals, for example, are inclined to be more impulsive and less able to delay gratification, a trait characteristic also of youth. The rewards of noncrime are often delayed, whereas the rewards of crime generally precede their costs and will therefore be preferred by less mature and more impulsive individuals. Finally, there is the important question of equity: crime may be preferred to noncrime if it is perceived to correct an imbalance in distributive justice. Such an imbalance occurs when people feel that in comparison to them, others get more than they deserve on the basis of their contribution.

The Wilson–Herrnstein theory is new and will be controversial partly because of their claim that the theory is general enough to encompass most sociological theories of criminal behavior (1985:63–66), partly because it is used to justify conservative crime control policies (pp. 528–529), and, perhaps most of all, because it links criminal behavior to constitutional factors, as we noted in Chapter 2. On the other hand, Wilson and Herrnstein have explored some new avenues and some old ones in a way that merits serious study.

A major criticism of their approach is its focus on "serious" street crime — murder, theft, rape — to the exclusion of other forms of criminality. A general theory of crime that explains only a small range of behaviors is not so general, and in any case it is certainly not established that embezzlers, con artists, organized criminals, fences, and pilferers are constitutionally different from noncriminals, or for that matter, from other criminals. It is also curious that despite their declared focus on serious street crime, the voluminous research that Wilson and Herrnstein bring to bear on their theory often does not make that distinction. Finally, the Wilson–Herrnstein approach manifests the ideology of conservative criminology in its thinly veiled search for the criminal type. This will not sit well with many of their academic colleagues (for additional criticisms, see Gibbs, 1985).

## THE SPATIAL ANALYSIS OF CRIME

We get a further feel for the workings of rationality and the constraints under which choices are made when we look at the recent work by geographers. Geographers are teaching us a lot about where criminal events occur and about the movement of criminal offenders to and from the sites of crime. Coupled with studies of target selection, this work offers new insights into the links between criminal opportunities, routine activities, and criminal decision making. Most of this important work has focused on criminal events occurring in urban areas.

Routine activities can be viewed from a spatial perspective. Brantingham and Brantingham (1981:35) write: "one of the striking things about criminals is that most of them behave as ordinary people most of the time." In being "ordinary" the individual grows familiar with certain parts of the city — the route to work, the immediate neighborhood, the local shopping center, the entertainment district, the areas where friends and relatives live, and so on. These areas constitute a person's "awareness," or "action" space — they are the familiar environment, the parts of the city a person knows.

Choices are influenced by knowledge. Regardless of where the best criminal opportunities actually are located, motivated offenders will tend to take advantage of or seek out those opportunities in places with which they are familiar. Studies of the distance between crime site and offender's place of residence show that this rarely exceeds two miles (McIver, 1981). In addition, there is evidence of what geographers call "distance decay": the amount of criminal activity decreases as one moves farther from the offender's home base.

Needless to say, motivated offenders living in places with few criminal opportunities have a problem. They must either forego some or all crime or else move outside the boundaries of their awareness space. Doing the latter increases the risks and costs of crime because (1) the motivated offenders are unfamiliar with the territory and, therefore, its targets and guardians; (2) they will use up more of their resources in getting there, in getting their bearings, and in getting back; and (3) they are more likely to be pegged as strangers, and therefore watched more closely, by those who do "belong" there.

The problem is exacerbated for potential offenders who lack the resources for criminal opportunities that do exist in unfamiliar places or who stand out because of some characteristic that cannot easily be hidden, such as race or sex. In their fascinating study of crime in Oklahoma City, Carter and Hill (1979) discovered that black offenders had to forego areas they designated as having "easy marks" in favor of areas with which they were "highly familiar." For white offenders, easy marks and familiarity had roughly equal strength in predicting target-area preference. Further investigation showed that black offenders had a much more restricted image of the city than whites, who routinely moved around more freely.

A study of St. Louis crime patterns by one of the pioneers in work on opportunities and crime further substantiates the importance of familiarity as a factor in black crime. Sarah Boggs (1964) found that black homicides, assaults, and residential burglaries were committed most often in the neighborhoods in which the offenders lived.

Those motivated offenders with access to criminal opportunities in areas outside their activity space may be "pulled" toward those areas when the opportunities are especially abundant (as in "red light" districts) or the anticipated rewards from particular jobs are especially high. The rationality model predicts the selection of those areas that maximize utility, and even high-risk areas may be selected when the expected returns significantly outweigh those from safer areas.

## ABLE CRIMINALS

Some criminals reduce the risk and increase the likelihood of successful completion of a crime through planning, organization, and skill. This is the rationalist's answer to overcoming risks when the anticipated rewards are compelling, and it has the added benefit of increasing the future rewards from crime by increasing the feasibility of taking on more difficult but more lucrative crimes. As with noncriminal activities, the development of methods to overcome one set of obstacles usually helps in the solution of new problems.

Relatively few criminal events appear to have involved much planning or organization (Erez, 1980). Most crimes are unskilled, petty violations, and they occur more or less spontaneously, often in association with alcohol. Alcohol and other situational factors (a dare by peers, an argument, an unlocked car door, the presence of a weapon, a tempting victim) account for the impulsiveness of much crime.

There is, nonetheless, a hard core of repeat offenders who engage in serious crimes and are responsible for a large proportion of the street crimes that come to the attention of authorities. For some of these offenders, crime is a means of livelihood, and they make more money at crime than they could earn in the kind of legal work usually open to them. These are the "able criminals" — experienced, often skilled, connected, and informed (Mack, 1964). They seek out opportunities even if that means charting new waters. The bulk of major property crime in England appears to have been committed by such offenders. In the United States, most predatory crime seems to be committed by a core of relatively young but experienced offenders, many with a history of heavy drug use.

A recent study of California prison inmates estimated that a typical group of one hundred inmates convicted of robbery would have committed 490 armed robberies, 310 assaults, 720 burglaries, 70 auto thefts, 100 forgeries, and 3,400 drug sales in one year of street freedom. It seems, too, that the more mobile offenders committed the greater number of crimes. Yet once again there is evidence of activity constraints working more strongly in the case of black than white offenders. Peterson, Braiker, and Polich (1980:ix) found that although blacks were overrepresented in the California prison population, "they reported committing the least number of different types of crime and reported the lowest rates for the crimes they committed." This finding held even after age, prior record, drug use, and various psychological factors were taken into account. Either the black or white inmates might be lying to the interviewers, but it is quite likely the differences in fact reflect the effects of lower resources and restricted mobility on the ability of black offenders to take advantage of criminal opportunities.

## Rationality in the Selection of Crime Target

The rationality model predicts that individuals weigh the expected rewards, costs, and risks of alternative actions and choose those actions that maximize their satisfactions. If the model has merit, it should show in the selection of targets by criminally motivated individuals. What little research has been done has been mainly confined to predatory property offenders. This fits the prevalent view that property offenders are more likely to act rationally than other criminals are, a view that stems from the idea that property crime is *instrumental* crime, done for another purpose, rather than *expressive* crime, done for its own sake. However, other types of crime also involve rationality, if only to the extent that they hardly ever happen in front of a police officer.

One of the best examples of recent research is Thomas Reppetto's (1974) study of residential burglary and robbery. In interviews with offenders, Reppetto confirmed that target preferences existed and were taken into account by his subjects in contemplating a crime. Burglars looked for unoccupied single-family dwellings (call them *risk* factors) with easy access (a *low skill* factor), which appeared affluent (a *reward* factor), and which were located in neighborhoods where offenders felt they "fit in" (another *risk* factor). Young and black burglars appeared most concerned about risk factors; older burglars chose affluence as the first consideration in selecting a target. Robbers, by the way, tended to select lone victims who were outside their residence and could be hustled inside quickly (risk probably being the main factor). This American study shows some support, then, for the view that criminally motivated individuals weigh rewards and risks in their selection of targets.

**Residential Burglary in England**  Two studies of house burglary in England also lend limited support to the rationality model. Walsh's (1980) study of Exeter burglars found that although relatively few offenders admitted doing much preplanning or "casing" of targets, most burglars were very concerned about being seen or about entering occupied houses. Walsh constructed a "decision tree" showing the typical selection considerations of his burglars (see Figure 3.1, pp. 80–81). The tree shows that both architectural and social factors are weighed when assessing the suitability of a target.

**Figure 3.1** Decision making for motivated burglars*

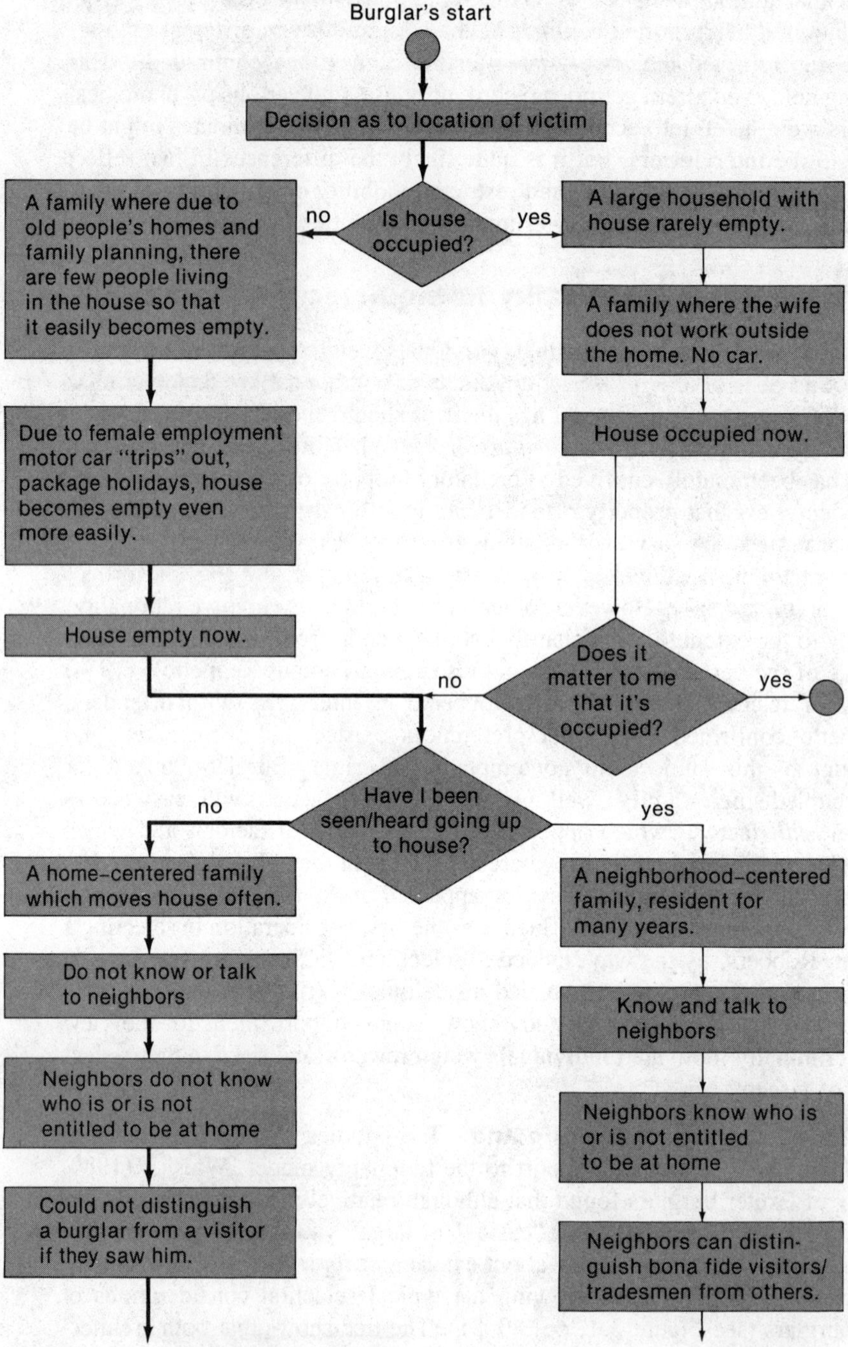

Burglar's start

Decision as to location of victim

Is house occupied?

— no → A family where due to old people's homes and family planning, there are few people living in the house so that it easily becomes empty.

— yes → A large household with house rarely empty.

A family where the wife does not work outside the home. No car.

House occupied now.

Due to female employment motor car "trips" out, package holidays, house becomes empty even more easily.

House empty now.

Does it matter to me that it's occupied?

— no

— yes

Have I been seen/heard going up to house?

— no → A home-centered family which moves house often.

Do not know or talk to neighbors

Neighbors do not know who is or is not entitled to be at home

Could not distinguish a burglar from a visitor if they saw him.

— yes → A neighborhood-centered family, resident for many years.

Know and talk to neighbors

Neighbors know who is or is not entitled to be at home

Neighbors can distinguish bona fide visitors/tradesmen from others.

*The pathway most commonly used is marked ————

SOURCE: Dermot Walsh, from *Break-ins: Burglary from Private Houses.*(London: Constable, 1980), pp. 144–45. Reprinted with permission of Constable Publishers.

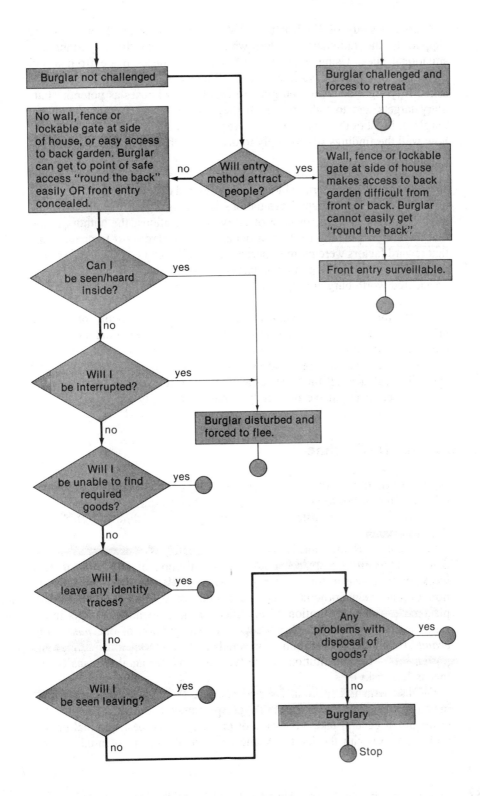

A second study of English burglars is more detailed and lends further support to the rationality model, while pointing out the importance of situational cues. Using videotapes of thirty-six houses made from a van traveling slowly along various streets, Bennett and Wright (1981, 1984) asked fifty-eight convicted burglars to evaluate the houses as potential burglary targets and to indicate which they would select if contemplating a burglary. Most of these burglars were very experienced, so there is no saying how well the findings would apply to occasional thieves or to newcomers to burglary.

Although there was considerable variation in target choice, the burglars strongly agreed about certain blocks of houses and over one or two individual houses. When they grouped evaluations according to whether the burglars mentioned risk, reward, or ease of entry considerations, the authors found that the burglars mentioned risk of being seen or heard most frequently and that reward factors were more important than skill factors only when given as reasons *not* to select a particular target. It seems that a house that is not considered worth burglarizing is not worth it regardless of how easy it might be to get in.

These studies do not investigate actual criminal behavior, only what offenders say about it. For that reason they give only inferential support for the rationality model. Bennett and Wright (1981:16) also point out that situational cues about ease of access and neighbor surveillance may not be carefully evaluated all the time, especially when thieves are "desperate for money, feeling impulsive or bloody-minded, or simply too lazy."

## Displacement of Crime

Whenever motivated offenders decide not to commit a crime at a certain place or time or not to choose a certain target or victim but choose another place, time, or victim instead, the substitution is sometimes referred to as *displacement*.

Geographers Hakim and Rengert (1981) identify five types of displacement: (1) *temporal* displacement — the substitution of one time of day, week, or even season for another; (2) *spatial* displacement — the substitution of one neighborhood, area, or region for another; (3) *target* displacement — the substitution of an easier (or more rewarding) target in the same area; (4) *tactical* displacement — the substitution of one *modus operandi* (method of operation) for another; and (5) *type of crime* displacement — the substitution of one type of crime for another (usually one that is less risky).

Displacement is important for two reasons. First, its occurrence is predicted by situational and rationality perspectives. The idea, again, is that criminals in general take advantage of or seek out the best criminal opportunities, those with the least risk and cost and the most potential reward.

When opportunities change, the offender's behavior changes — assuming rationality and some freedom of choice.

Second, displacement is important because it is one of the potential costs of crime prevention efforts. For example, when criminal opportunities are reduced in one place by increased efforts by the police, the net result may be an increase in crime in another place, as criminally motivated individuals seek out opportunities in "safer" areas. Thus, one community's benefit from reduced crime may be another's loss from increased crime.

## DOES DISPLACEMENT OCCUR?

Research on displacement is still in its infancy and findings must therefore be considered tentative. Measuring criminal substitution behavior as it occurs is extremely difficult, for obvious reasons. One would need to show that a given criminal event occurred as it did and that some other criminal event did not occur because the offender changed his or her mind. Criminologists end up inferring displacement from studies of spatial or temporal changes in the volume of crime or by asking offenders if and when they have made substitutions in their past behavior. Neither method is entirely satisfactory. Most studies are further limited in their findings because they focus only on spatial or temporal displacement.

In reviewing some of the American evidence, John McIver (1981:32) suggests that spatial displacement is probably quite limited "because criminals prefer to operate in known territory." Still, four studies of the effects of local police enforcement changes on neighboring communities did find significant "spillover" of crime into those communities. However, displacement occurred with property crime but not with crimes of violence. The latter are often impulsive and spur-of-the-moment and occur in the course of routine activities around the home and the local bar. Therefore much violence is relatively impervious to displacement pressures.

Studies in England tentatively confirm the existence of displacement effects for some crimes. When steering locks were introduced in British cars in the mid-seventies, the rates of auto crime did not drop significantly. Many thieves merely turned their attention to the abundant older cars that did not have steering locks. In addition, Riley (1980) argued that determined thieves could quickly learn methods for overcoming the devices, and so displacement might be restricted in any case to amateur and opportunistic thieves.

A massive car-locking publicity campaign in 1977 apparently had little effect on people's car-locking behavior, but it did seem to affect the behavior of car thieves, for daytime thefts went down appreciably while nighttime thefts rose — a temporal displacement. Thieves apparently reacted to all the publicity, fearing, perhaps, greater public surveillance. These English findings might be taken as evidence that criminally motivated individuals are more concerned with risks of being seen than with the difficulty of the criminal action itself. If correct, this would complement findings on target selection (Burrows and Heal, 1980).

A third British study looked at the impact of installing closed-circuit television in some of the subway stations in London (Mayhew et al., 1979). Generally, stations with the highest traffic had experienced larger numbers of robberies and other thefts because there were more criminal opportunities. But once the televisions were installed, the level of thefts dropped fourfold, whereas robberies remained about the same. However, during the test period of three years, the numbers of robberies at subway stations without televisions increased dramatically. Though by no means conclusive, the finding suggests an offense-specific spatial displacement.

British criminologists appear skeptical that many offenders actually substitute new crimes for old when criminal opportunities are reduced. Income tax evaders, shoplifters, and employee thieves will not become burglars, con artists, and robbers. Some professional criminals, they believe, respond to reduced opportunities by increasing their skills and directing their energies toward the most lucrative targets. They become better criminals, perhaps, but they may also become more dangerous. This happened with the tactical displacement in bank theft from safe cracking to over-the-counter robbery to robbery of cash in transit (Ball, Chester, and Perrott, 1978).

And finally, some authors see the possibility of societal-level crime displacement as a result of large-scale changes in criminal opportunities:

> Opportunities for one sort of offense might be greatly reduced but only at the expense of creating an entirely new set of criminal opportunities for a different group of people. For instance, the movement to a "checkless" society in which financial transactions are largely computerized would greatly reduce the scope for petty pilfering but would create opportunities for theft of a very different order — large-scale computer crime (Hough et al., 1980:12)

## Opportunity and Rationality Theories Reviewed

If there is a message in all of this, it is surely that crime cannot properly be understood apart from the nature and distribution of opportunities for its occurrence. We began with a discussion of criminal events in relation to both criminal and noncriminal opportunities. That led to the routine activity approach, a promising framework for the analysis of some forms of crime. We saw, too, that some places are more dangerous than others, though the design of the physical environment cannot by itself account for the danger.

Underlying the opportunity theory that informs the routine activity approach is the assumption that criminally motivated people engage in rational choice behavior, especially when they are motivated to commit predatory property crimes. This assumption operates in conjunction with classical and economic models of criminal behavior. In recognition that neither the availability nor the accessibility of criminal opportunities are distributed evenly among people or places, theorists argue that choice is not exercised freely but within constraints resulting from conditions largely beyond anyone's control. On the other hand, because of the uneven distribution of criminal opportunities, some motivated criminals have a better shot at some types of crime than others.

Geographers have shown us that criminal events tend to cluster where the opportunities are, but sometimes the "best" opportunities must be forgone because they are in places where the risks of being caught or the costs of getting there are too high. Unfamiliar places seem to inhibit potential offenders, especially those who are younger or less experienced or feel that they would draw attention to themselves by being there. Displacement, one of the potential costs of crime prevention efforts, implies the evaluation of risks and rewards prior to committing property crime. It shows us how changes in criminal opportunities combine with evaluation of risks, rewards, and costs to move criminal events from one time or place to another or to change their nature.

The rational view of crime assumes that offenders contemplate a crime before doing it, and this probably precludes the impulsive, spur-of-the-moment actions of many offenders. But it is one thing to commit an impulsive crime and another to commit an "expressive" crime, which is an end in itself. Though the rationality model has been applied most often to property crime (see Holzman, 1982), this is too narrow a view. Rape, child molesting, prostitution, homosexual encounters, drug use, and myriad other expressive offenses display elements of rationality in choice of victim and manner of execution.

## Summary

One of the important things to observe about criminological theory is that few modern attempts have been made to develop a general theory, one that purports to explain all, or even most, crime. Recognizing that crime is both varied *and* the legal creation of authorities, many theorists have narrowed their sights, hoping to explain variations in particular types of crime or aspects of criminality. Criminologists must now evaluate just how well existing theories account for what is happening in the crime scene.

The perspectives discussed in this chapter are not presented as replacements for the theories and perspectives reviewed in Chapter 2. Instead, they constitute different ways of looking at crime and raise alternative questions. Radical-critical criminology, an outgrowth of the conflict perspective, has adopted a largely Marxian view of social relations in capitalist societies. Such societies are seen as exploitative and crime as both an aspect and a result of exploitation in the service of ruling-class interests. The opportunity-rationality perspective starts with criminally motivated individuals and then tries to account for the hows, wheres, and whens of criminal events. Figure 3.2 illustrates some of the connections emphasized by the perspective and shows how potential crime situations can turn into actual criminal events.

**Figure 3.2** Crime as an Event

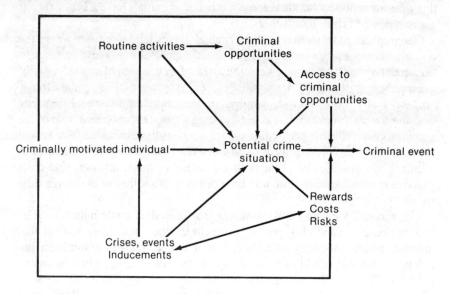

The emphasis on crime as an event is seen by some criminologists as a fitting counterweight to the "dispositional bias" that has characterized the bulk of criminological theory (Hough et al., 1980).

Obviously, we have not yet reached the point at which we can hold any single theory to be the explanation of crime, nor are we likely to. One reason is that people do not agree on what constitutes crime, the phenomenon to be explained. We only achieve an incomplete grasp of the crime scene when we treat crime as behavior *or* status *or* an event. To understand crime we must ask not only why certain people and activities are labeled criminal, but also why people engage in those activities and how it is that criminal events occur and take on the characteristics that they do.

With this in mind, some of the theoretical perspectives we have reviewed may not be as incompatible as they appear. Travis Hirschi (1985) suggests, for example, that control theory is compatible with rationality theory. Control theory specifies the kinds of things that come into play — attachment, commitment, belief, and involvement — when actors evaluate the benefits of alternative courses of action. "In pure control theory," he asserts, "it is assumed that all people are capable of crime if the price is right . . ." (p. 6). The major distinction Hirschi finds between control and rationality theories is that the former is a theory about criminality, which he defines as the relative propensity to engage in criminal acts, whereas the latter is a theory about crime, which is the criminal event itself. As suggested earlier, many of the theories in criminology are complementary, and pursuit of this idea may hold the best hope for a complete understanding of our subject.

# CHAPTER 4

# Getting a Line on Crime: The Production and Use of Data

Most authors of criminology texts make a special point of warning readers about the many pitfalls encountered in the compilation and use of data on crime. These warnings usually contain strong words about the inadequacies of crime statistics. Here are some typical remarks:

> The statistics about crime and delinquency are probably the most unreliable and most difficult of all social statistics (Sutherland and Cressey, 1974:25).

> Crime statistics are among the most unreliable and questionable social facts (Gibbons, 1973:100).

> Crime statistics contain numerous labyrinths to trap the incautious, even when presented with the purest of intentions (Bloch and Geis, 1970:111–112).

These warnings refer to the data compiled and reported by administrators of criminal law. Unquestionably, for some purposes, official statistics are woefully inadequate, if not downright useless. To understand the meaning and limitations of crime data we must first know something about how the data are produced.

## Producing Crime Data

People create crime and people produce information about it. The production of data on crime and criminals begins when an evaluation by someone results in the label "crime" being attached to a piece of behavior. This label may have no legal meaning, for people do not always know the precise legal definitions of crimes. Nevertheless, when the label "crime" is attached to an activity, then the activity is criminal for the person making the evaluation.

Sometimes an activity escapes the scrutiny of others and remains known only to the actor. When this happens, the activity in question must be regarded as unknown and unknowable; it can never become part of the data on crime. In other words, to become part of a potential body of data on crime, an activity must be labeled "criminal," or at least "possibly criminal," by someone other than the actor.

### PRODUCING OFFICIAL DATA: AN ILLUSTRATION

Suppose that 1,000 actions occur in an hour. Of these actions, only 900 are ever known to anyone other than the person responsible for them. These 900 actions become eligible for evaluation by others; the other 100 are "lost." When the 900 known activities are evaluated by someone, there are three possibilities: (1) the actions are labeled "noncrimes"; (2) they are labeled "crimes"; or (3) they are labeled "possible crimes." This does not mean that people go around calling things "noncrimes" or "possible crimes" in the real world. The three possibilities are merely categories into which we can divide evaluations. By implication, when a person does not think of an activity as a crime or a possible crime, it is a noncrime.

Imagine that of 900 known actions, 800 are evaluated as "noncrimes." As with the 100 activities that were lost, these are never going to appear in the data on crime. Now we have 100 activities left. At this point we come to an important question: who does the labeling? If the evaluator is also an administrator of criminal law (a police officer, lawyer, or judge), the label "crime" will take on new significance. It is now an official label, and the behavior in question becomes part of the official data on crime. By the same token, when an administrator of criminal law applies the label "criminal" to a person, that action produces part of the official data on criminals.

Not all activities or people considered criminal by members of the general public will be so labeled by officials. Sometimes this is because they are not criminal according to legal definitions. But the reasons may have nothing to do with strict legal rules. For example, discretion is an important facet of police work, and sometimes the exercise of police discretion results in the criminal label's not being applied, even when existing legal definitions call for it. When this happens, these acts or people do not appear as part of the official record on crime, but they do remain part of a potential pool of data on crime. They comprise, along with other acts and people that have been labeled criminal by someone, the unofficial data on crime and criminals. (In a moment we shall discuss how this seemingly lost information on crime can be recovered by the criminologist.)

To become part of the *official* data on crime, activities must be known to legal officials and must be appropriately labeled by them. Activities become known to the police and hence become eligible for official labeling as crimes, in two ways. The more common way is when a member of the public notifies the police of a "crime" or "possible crime." The less common way is when the police directly witness an activity that they then label crime. This means that most actions that eventually become official crimes do so only because they have been evaluated as "crimes" or "possible crimes" by the public, who then bring them to the attention of the police. Here we see the importance of unofficial (public) evaluations and behavior in the production of official crime data.

To return to the hypothetical situation, suppose that of the 100 "crimes" or "possible crimes," 50 come to the attention of the police in one way or another. (For reasons discussed in a moment, the other 50 unofficial crimes are "lost" to the production of official crime data.) Yet not all of the 50 activities known to the police will necessarily be labeled crime; some will be screened out. Imagine that 15 of the 50 activities are screened out — as far as the police are concerned, these are "noncrimes." This leaves 35 activities, each of which has been evaluated as a crime by the police. These 35 crimes make up the pool of official data on crime; they are called, appropriately enough, "crimes known to the police." Figure 4.1 summarizes this.

The production of official data on criminals starts when activities are first labeled "crime" or "possible crime" by someone. The hypothetical illustration has 100 activities to which persons can be linked as "criminals" or

**Figure 4.1** The production of data: "Crimes known to the police"

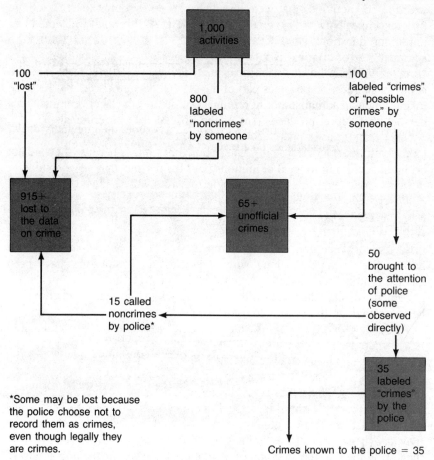

"possible criminals" by someone. However, more than one person may have committed the act in question. On the other hand, the same individual may have committed more than one "crime." If the former is generally the case, data will show more criminals than instances of criminal activity; if the latter holds, data will show fewer criminals than "crimes." This warns us not to expect a one-to-one relationship between activities and people. Even though the illustration has 100 possible crimes, 200 criminals may be involved, or then again only 50. Generally, even if every known crime were solved by the identification of those responsible, the number of "crimes" and the number of "criminals" would probably not be the same. Since the police do not solve every known crime, we usually find many more official crimes than official criminals. Accordingly, we should not expect to find the 35 "crimes known to the police" in Figure 4.1 matched with 35 "criminals known to the police."

## THE POLICE ROLE IN DATA PRODUCTION

Some of the "crimes" and "possible crimes" that come to police attention fail to make it into the official record. This is because the police may decide not to acknowledge officially an incident as a crime. This decision shapes not only the official data on crimes but also those on criminals (Black, 1970). If the police officially record an activity as a crime, the person who performed the activity will become eligible for the official label "criminal" and will be subject to scrutiny by the police, as well as others in the criminal justice system. If the activity is not officially recorded as crime, then the individual will be lost to official statistics on arrests, charges, adjudication, and sentencing.

Studies of police labeling behavior have produced some interesting findings regarding the kinds of things that influence decisions about those incidents brought to police attention. We have learned that the police respond to public pressures and are extremely sensitive to the possibility of criticism. When they feel that prevailing public sentiments call for less or more attention to specific kinds of crime, they adjust their labeling practices accordingly. One example of this occurred in England some years ago. During the 1950s and early 1960s much public and private attention was focused on the issue of homosexuality and the law. A government commission was established to look into the matter and make recommendations regarding public policy. The so-called Wolfendon report recommended the decriminalization of homosexual activity between consenting adults in private (a recommendation that has since become law). But the interesting thing is that in a ten-year period from the mid-1950s to the mid-1960s, official records of arrests for "gross indecency between males" fell off by more than 50 percent. The decline was not due to a corresponding decline in the incidence of the behavior itself but, rather, to changes in police behavior. Under the national spotlight, the police were apparently less willing to take official action than they had been in the past (Walker, 1971).

One of the major determinants of police labeling behavior is the *legal seriousness* of the offense. Looking at police actions in Boston, Chicago, and Washington, D.C., Donald Black (1970:746) discovered that "the police officially recognize proportionately more legally serious crimes than legally minor crimes." Suspected felonies were officially recorded as crimes 72 percent of the time, compared with only 53 percent of the time in the case of suspected misdemeanors. Even so, the fact that around a quarter of the suspected felonies were not officially recognized by the police leaves little doubt that factors other than seriousness come into play.

In the same study, Black discovered that the likelihood of official labeling was influenced by (1) the *demeanor* of the complainant — those more deferential toward the police were more successful in getting their complaints officially recorded; (2) the complainant's apparent *preference* for formal or informal action — those asking for formal action tended to get that action;

and (3) the *relational distance* between the suspect and the complainant — acts committed by strangers were more likely to be officially recognized as crimes than were acts committed by members of the complainant's family or by close friends or acquaintances.

In their work the police are often required to make on-the-spot evaluations of events and people. Customary departmental rules and policies together with work norms generated by the officers themselves support considerable discretion in the determination of what action to take. Studies indicate that the legal character of an activity is no guarantee that official action will be taken. An internal audit of the Chicago Police Department found that many crimes were incorrectly recorded as "unfounded" (*Chicago Sun Times,* April 28, 1983). Of 377 rape cases reviewed, 18 percent were judged to have been incorrectly labeled; of 649 robbery cases, 36.4 percent were considered incorrect; and of 708 burglaries, 46.6 percent were incorrectly called unfounded.

When we look at official arrest figures we have to remember that those arrested have not necessarily committed the act for which they were apprehended. In dealing with the complex demands of their work, "the police attempt to accomplish their job with a minimum of strain and . . . the effort leads to the selection of law violators *not* according to legal prescriptions alone" (Chambliss and Liell, 1966:317). Factors that influence the police in their decisions to arrest someone include the person's age, sex, demeanor, prior contacts with the police, and reputation and respect with the community. In sum, the official record on crime and criminals is shaped by police decisions, which in turn are influenced by factors that may have nothing to do with criminal law. Knowing how and why police decisions are made becomes one of the keys to understanding the official crime picture.

**Police-reporting Behavior** The police are besieged with thousands of calls a day, and many of these calls for assistance are not criminal complaints. Table 4.1 shows the calls received in a seven-month period by Chicago police dispatchers in 1976. The dispatchers classified only 16.2 percent as criminal complaints to which patrolling units should be sent. Even when police units were sent to the scene, the officers did not always record the event as a crime (the third column in the table). Decisions not to record complaints as crimes were less frequent with crimes such as rape, robbery, burglary, and other felony theft, but many events nevertheless failed to make it into the record books. Apparently, work load had a lot to do with the large proportion of less serious complaints that investigating officers failed to record (Maxfield et al., 1980).

**Other Considerations** One other aspect of official compilation of data on crime deserves attention. Even if we grant the impact of situational variables on police decisions, the records that become part of the official data on crime may also be affected by "in-house" decisions that have nothing to do with street contacts, complainants, and officer discretion.

The police exist and work in a political and economic environment that

**Table 4.1**  Police calls for service and verified crimes, Chicago, January through July, 1976

| POLICE DISPATCH DECISION | CALLS FOR SERVICE | | VERIFIED AND RECORDED AS CRIMES BY INVESTIGATING POLICE OFFICERS |
| --- | --- | --- | --- |
| | NUMBER | PERCENT OF TOTAL | PERCENT |
| *Classified as crimes* | | | |
| Violent crime (homicide, robbery, aggravated assault) | 23,136 | 1.6 | 72.9 |
| Property crime (burglary, larceny, motor vehicle theft) | 122,844 | 8.6 | 81.0 |
| All other crimes | 86,127 | 6.0 | 61.4 |
| *Classified as non-crimes* | | | |
| Disturbances[a] | 330,461 | 23.0 | |
| Miscellaneous | 791,865 | 55.2 | |
| Other | 81,002 | 5.6 | |
| Total | 1,435,435 | 100.0 | |

SOURCE: Adapted from Maxfield, Michael A., Dan A. Lewis, and Ron Szoc (1980), Producing official crimes: Verified crime reports as measures of police output. Social Science Quarterly 61, p. 225. Reprinted with the permission of The University of Texas Press.
a. A small but unknown percentage of disturbance calls are reclassified as assaults by investigating officers.

places demands on their behavior and decision making. Two constant pressures on any police department are financial security and bureaucratic survival and growth. Besides the fact that police departments cost money to operate, they are like other organizations in that self-perpetuation comes high on the list of priorities. In their dealings with political and business leaders, police executives strive to meet these pressures by demonstrating on the one hand that service is successful and on the other that there are continuing financial and personnel needs.

One way to demonstrate needs is to show that without certain resources the community will suffer. Suppose you are a police chief and you want additional equipment. You have been told that money is tight, and any additional funds will be allocated only on the basis of most urgent needs. How do you

## NUMBERS AND RATES

Numbers tell us how many crimes have been recorded, but they fail to take into account the size of the population in which those crimes occurred. Suppose two cities have officially recorded these numbers of crimes for 1986:

|                | City A  | City B  |
| -------------- | ------- | ------- |
| Violent crimes | 5,000   | 10,000  |
| Property crimes| 15,000  | 40,000  |
| Other crimes   | 20,000  | 50,000  |
| Total number   | 40,000  | 100,000 |

At first glance, City B has more crime than City A. If you wanted to move to one of these cities and decided to base your selection on the extent of crime, you might well choose City A over City B. But you might be making a big mistake.

Suppose you find out that the population of City A is 1 million and that of City B 2.5 million. With this information you can compute a crime *rate* that takes into account the number of people in each city. After all, if there are more people in one city than in another, you would expect more crime in the former, other things being equal.

With the population information in hand, you compute crime rates for the two cities by applying the conventional formula, which gives the number of crimes per 100,000 people:

$$\frac{\text{Number of crimes known to police} \times 100,000}{\text{population}}$$

The crime rates, then, are as follows:

| | Numbers of Crimes Per 100,000 | |
| -------------- | ------ | ------ |
| | City A | City B |
| Violent crime  | 500    | 400    |
| Property crime | 1500   | 1600   |
| Total crime    | 2000   | 2000   |

You now see that the overall crime rates are the same, but the rate for violent crime is higher in City A than City B, while the rate for property crime is lower in City A than City B. If this were all the information you had, your choice of city might well hinge on which type of crime you would rather avoid.

**Other kinds of crime rates.** Though crime rates are often expressed in terms of total population,

meet the requirement? One way is to manipulate crime and arrest data so that they look as if, instead of reducing or containing crime, your department is being swamped by it. Such manipulations can take a number of forms. Skolnick (1966) found that one of the police departments he studied would periodically manipulate the data on crimes "cleared by arrest." In America (as in some other countries) the police tally the proportion of known crimes cleared by arrest *(clearance rate)*. (For more information on the meaning of crime rates, see the box above.) "Cleared by arrest" does not mean that the person arrested has been proved guilty. Rather, the police consider a case solved for their purposes when an arrest has been made. In order to make the crime problem appear overwhelming and so demonstrate the need for patrol cars (or additional personnel), you might manipulate the clearance rate so that the *ratio of arrests to known crimes* appears lower than it actually is. For example, suppose your department had actually arrested 2,000 suspects during the year. Instead of reporting this figure you report only 1,500 arrests. If there were 10,000 reported crimes over the same period, a ratio of 1,500 to 10,000 would indicate greater difficulties in the areas of detection and arrest than would the true ratio of 2,000 to 10,000. As police chief you could achieve the same end by ordering fewer arrests in the first place, but the risks are greater with this method because it is more likely that people will catch there are other useful ways of computing them. One way is to compute rates for specific categories of population: males, females; blacks, whites; young, old; and so on. When this is done arrest data are commonly used, and the rates are computed as follows:

Race-specific arrest rates =

$$\frac{\text{number of whites (blacks) arrested} \times 100{,}000}{\text{number of whites (blacks) in population}}$$

Age-specific arrest rates =

$$\frac{\text{number of (say) 16–18-yr-olds arrested} \times 100{,}000}{\text{number of 16–18-yr-olds in population}}$$

Sex-specific arrest rates =

$$\frac{\text{number of males (females) arrested} \times 100{,}000}{\text{number of males (females) in population}}$$

Another useful way of computing crime rates is in terms of the risks of or opportunities for crime. Sarah Boggs (1964) was among the first to advocate this approach, arguing that it makes sense to express crime in terms of people or objects at risk. For example, two cities may have similar conventional rates of residential burglary but when one takes into account the number of residences rather than the number of people, the picture might look quite different. The following hypothetical data illustrate this.

|  | City A | City B |
| --- | --- | --- |
| Number of residential burglaries | 1,000 | 1,500 |
| Population of city | 100,000 | 200,000 |
| Number of residences | 30,000 | 40,000 |
| Conventional crime rate for burglary | 1,000 | 750 |
| Opportunity-based crime rate for burglary | 3,333.3 | 3,750.0 |

The two rates produce different results. The opportunity-based rate suggests that the risk of one's residence being burglarized is in fact higher in City B than City A, though the conventional rate might have led one to believe otherwise.

This rather superficial excursion into numbers and rates raises two questions about published crime statistics: (1) Are the crime data rates or absolute numbers? (2) If the crime data are rates, then are the rates expressed in terms of total population, specific population, persons or places at risk, or some other base?

on. In any case, if the politicians are interested in helping defend the community against criminals, you argue, they must pay for devices that help raise the clearance rate.

Just as the police may on occasion manipulate crime data to make their needs appear urgent, they may also manipulate the data to make their department look good. This may mean underreporting certain known offenses, as was the case in New York City in 1966 (Wolfgang, 1967). It may mean manipulation of the clearance rate so that the ratio of arrests to known crimes is higher than it actually is (Skolnick, 1966). This practice is most likely to occur, it seems, in police departments whose administrators are political appointees or elected by the public. To keep their jobs they must demonstrate progress in combating crime. By the same token, administrators may come under pressure from city and state officials who see their own jobs in jeopardy when crime gets out of hand. A little manipulation for the mayor or governor may be called for.

Unfortunately, we have no way of assessing how much false information is created in this way. With computerized techniques of data recording and dissemination, it may now be more difficult for individual departments to manipulate the records after they have been initially compiled. But even then, department officials can still order their men to "go slow" or speed up on arrests, thus providing another means to the same end. Lacking accurate ways of assessing the situation, we have to remember that what is reported by the police may be quite different from what is actually known or recorded by them.

English sociologist Dennis Chapman (1968:10–11) has enumerated some additional reasons that police underreport crime: first, much crime occurs in family and organizational settings. A good deal (perhaps most) of such crime tends not to be reported to the police in the first place, and when the police do know of possible crimes, they find it difficult to penetrate the institutional privacy of these settings. Second, the detection of crime is in part a function of the "social range of the police, who are drawn from the lower middle class and the working class and, in addition, find their social relations restricted by their occupation. . . . In general, the effectiveness of the police can be expected to decline as the social-class area of the problem is raised. . . ." Third, crimes differ in the degree to which they can be readily concealed. Crimes involving symbols and paper — embezzlement, fraud, political corruption, and the like — tend to be greatly underreported in comparison with acts of violence and other forms of theft because those crimes are less easily concealed. Fourth, police-patrolling practices coupled with middle-class concerns with privacy make it less likely that crimes in middle-class neighborhoods will be recorded. This helps explain why the official police data show a preponderance of lower-class crime.

## How We "Lose" and "Find" Crime Data

The hypothetical situation presented in the opening section of this chapter purposely emphasizes that a considerable proportion of the potential official data on crime is "lost." Some potential data are lost because those who have committed a crime were clever enough to conceal their activities from others. Some potential data are missed because people are not sufficiently observant. Although it is impossible to estimate the amount of data lost as a result of these two situations, studies indicate it is probably substantial. Evidence on "disappearing money" shows that Americans cannot account for the disappearance of billions of dollars each year. In a significant proportion of cases, the money has apparently been stolen (see Fooner, 1971).

### LOSING DATA THROUGH NONREPORTING

Much information on crime is lost because individuals simply do not bring suspicious events to the attention of police. Estimates in recent years indicate that even in regard to serious crimes such as robbery, rape, and burglary, a considerable proportion of offenses are not brought to police attention — perhaps as high as 75 percent (see Skogan, 1977). Apparently, many victims of crime do not report their experiences to the police. *Victimization rates* (the number of incidents in which persons are victims of crime per 100,000 people) are generally between two and three times the crime rates officially published for rape, burglary, robbery, and aggravated assault. The picture is different with auto theft, however. Here, official rates and victimization rates are similar. This is largely because victims must report the offense in order to collect insurance.

One might think that failure to report criminal incidents to the police results because people are generally unaware that what has happened is a crime. While this may be true in some cases, it is unlikely with such incidents as robbery, burglary, and interpersonal violence. In fact, there is ample evidence that even when a person recognizes that he or she is the victim of a crime, or a witness to one, there is no guarantee that the police will be notified. In the case of some offenses — especially shoplifting, forgery, and employee theft — the probability that they will be reported is so low that statistics make them appear infrequent when they are, in reality, among the most numerous offenses.

Why, of all people, do the victims of crime not report their victimization to the police? Two of the more common explanations given by the victims themselves are that they felt "nothing could be done anyway," or they felt that the police would not want to be bothered with their problems. Another reason often given is that the incident was a private matter, and the victim would rather keep it that way (Bureau of Justice Statistics, 1985c:8).

It is not only victims who fail to report actions they have identified as "crimes" or "possible crimes." People who witness or simply hear about a possible crime may also avoid reporting it to the police. Again the reasons vary: Some people don't want to get involved; others believe the police already know about the crime; some fear the offender will seek revenge; and others simply do not know what to do.

## FINDING DATA WITH VICTIMIZATION STUDIES

**The National Crime Survey**   Every year since 1973, the U.S. Department of Justice has sponsored a nationwide survey of sixty thousand households to find out more about the American experience with crime. Called the National Crime Survey (NCS), this program fills in some of the gaps left by official police statistics, not only because it uncovers unreported crimes, but also because it is broader in scope and can inform us about the victims of crimes and the manner in which crimes are committed.

The NCS interview begins with a series of "screening" questions that prepare the interviewer for more detailed questioning on those incidents mentioned by the respondent. The following are some of these screening questions:

*Item:* During the last 12 months, did anyone break into or somehow illegally get into your home, garage, or another building on your property?

YES _____ how many times? _____

NO _____

*Item:* Other than the incidents just mentioned, did you find a door jimmied, a lock forced, or any other signs of an *attempted* break-in?

YES _____ how many times? _____

NO _____

*Item:* During the last 12 months, did anyone take anything directly from you by using force, such as by a stickup, mugging, or threat?

YES _____ how many times? _____

NO _____

*Item:* Did anyone *try* to rob you by using force or threatening to harm you?

YES _____ how many times? _____

NO _____

*Item:* Did anyone beat you up, attack you, or hit you with something, such as a rock or bottle?

YES _____ how many times? _____

NO _____

*Item:* Were you knifed, shot at, or attacked with some other weapon by anyone at all (other than incidents already mentioned)?

YES _____ how many times? _____

NO _____

*Item:* Did anyone *try* to attack you in some other way?

YES _____ how many times? _____

NO _____

The more detailed questioning that follows is designed to pin down exactly what happened. On superficial glance an incident may look like a crime but turn out not to be one; it may look like a burglary when in fact it was "merely" vandalism. In addition, detailed questioning about the incidents can give the researcher information about the characteristics of offenses, the actions of the offender, the actions of the victim, the extent of the injury or loss, and so forth. This information can be invaluable in helping us understand the experiences of crime victims, and the nature of criminal activities themselves.

The National Crime Survey is not without its limitations. First, its findings are based solely on recall, and people's memories are not perfect. Second, people may purposely deceive interviewers, though this is a risk that carefully constructed questionnaires and properly trained investigators can help reduce. Table 4.2 shows some of the findings of this survey for three different years. Table 4.3 presents estimates of the percentage of offenses

Current fact-finding techniques only scratch the surface of child abuse and other family offenses.

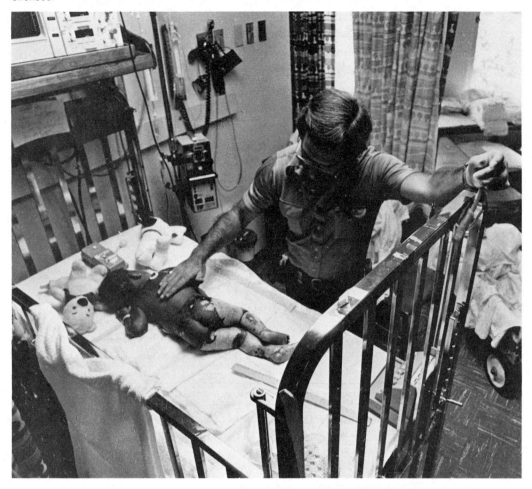

reported to the police in 1983. Included is a comparison of reporting behavior for victimizations involving strangers and nonstrangers. Offenses by strangers are, on the whole, more likely to be reported if they involve violence.

## SELF-REPORTED CRIMINALITY

In addition to victimization studies, researchers may recover lost data by asking members of the public to tell about their own involvement in criminal activities. The idea behind these "self-report" studies is to establish more reasonable estimates of the extent of criminality. The feeling has long been that official statistics give us only the tip of the iceberg. Self-report studies provide a means to uncover the remainder of the iceberg — the so-called hidden criminality.

**Table 4.2** Victimizations by type of crime, 1978, 1980, and 1982

| TYPE OF CRIME | 1978 | 1980 | 1982 |
|---|---|---|---|
| Crimes of violence (combined) | | | |
| Number | 5,941,000 | 5,974,000 | 6,459,000 |
| Rate[a] | 33.7 | 33.1 | 34.3 |
| Rape | | | |
| Number | 171,000 | 169,000 | 153,000 |
| Rate[a] | 1.0 | 0.9 | 0.8 |
| Robbery | | | |
| Number | 1,038,000 | 1,179,000 | 1,334,000 |
| Rate[a] | 5.9 | 6.5 | 7.1 |
| Aggravated assault | | | |
| Number | 1,708,000 | 1,661,000 | 1,754,000 |
| Rate[a] | 9.7 | 9.2 | 9.3 |
| Simple assault | | | |
| Number | 3,024,000 | 2,966,000 | 3,219,000 |
| Rate[a] | 17.2 | 16.4 | 17.1 |
| Crimes of theft | | | |
| Number | 17,050,000 | 14,936,000 | 15,553,000 |
| Rate[a] | 96.8 | 82.8 | 82.5 |
| Household burglary | | | |
| Number | 6,704,000 | 6,817,300 | 6,663,000 |
| Rate[a] | 86.0 | 84.2 | 78.2 |
| Motor vehicle theft | | | |
| Number | 1,365,100 | 1,354,600 | 1,377,000 |
| Rate[a] | 17.5 | 16.7 | 16.2 |

SOURCE: Bureau of Justice Statistics (1984a), Criminal victimization in the United States, 1982. Washington, D.C.: U.S. Government Printing Office.

a. Number per 1,000 population age 12 and over.
b. Number per 1,000 households.

**Table 4.3** Percentage of victimizations reported to police, 1983

| TYPE OF CRIME | RELATIONAL DISTANCE | | |
|---|---|---|---|
| | TOTAL | STRANGER | NONSTRANGER |
| Crimes of Violence | 47.2 | 48.3 | 45.5 |
| Rape | 47.0 | 48.5 | 44.9 |
| Robbery | 52.6 | 52.1 | 54.4 |
| Aggravated assault | 56.5 | 54.5 | 59.2 |
| Crimes of Theft | 26.5 | — | — |
| Purse snatching | 50.6 | 50.6 | 51.1 |
| Pocket picking | 29.2 | 29.1 | 31.6 |

SOURCE: Bureau of Justice Statistics (1985c), Criminal victimization in the United States, 1983. Washington, D.C.: U.S. Department of Justice.

The self-report technique commonly employs a questionnaire listing a variety of deviant, delinquent, and illegal activities. Respondents are asked to check if they have engaged in any of them during a specified period of time, say, the past year. Self-report studies have usually focused on adolescents because it is recognized that much crime and delinquency in this population remains hidden from official records and because representative samples are readily available for interviewing in school settings.

With adolescents as their targets, self-report questionnaires invariably include acts that would not be crimes if committed by adults (see box on pp. 102–103). Furthermore, it is now recognized that these questionnaires tap generally trivial delinquency and crime, rather than the serious street crime emphasized in official statistics (Hindelang et al., 1979). In a study by Martin Gold (1970:30) the 10 percent "most delinquent" group included a boy whose admitted delinquent activities from age 12 were as follows:

. . . he and a friend had knocked down a tent in a neighbor boy's back yard — the aftermath of an earlier mud fight.

That winter, he had shoplifted gum a few times from a neighborhood store.

On turning 13, he had begun to lie regularly about his age to cashiers at movie theaters.

In June, 1961, he had shoplifted a cartridge belt from a hardware store and later given it to a friend.

The month after, he had taken an address book from a department store.

In the summer of 1961, he and a friend had helped themselves to several beers from his friend's refrigerator.

In late August, 1961, he and another friend had twice raided an orchard not far from R's home, taking ripe pears and unripe apples and grapes. They ate the first, and threw the rest at various targets.

In September, 1961, he had lifted a hunting knife from a sporting-goods store just for something to do. "We took it back the next day, snuck it back in."

He regularly carried a hunting knife under his jacket "for protection" when he went collecting on Friday nights on his paper route.

Although most self-report studies measure less serious crime and delinquency in supposed "nondelinquent" populations, the findings nevertheless show widespread involvement in behavior that is in technical violation of the law. In most studies, more than 75 percent of those surveyed admit having committed at least one illegal act, and most admit more than one. Although self-report studies confirm the overrepresentation of males in criminal activities, they also show that females are heavily implicated in trivial criminality. What is also confirmed in these studies, for both juveniles and adults, is that a small portion of those surveyed admit committing the bulk of serious offenses. A survey of 646 California inmates (whose criminality had already been established in legal proceedings) found that one-fourth of the sample admitted committing 65 percent of the burglaries, 58 percent of the robberies, 48 percent of the drug sales, and 46 percent of the auto thefts (Peterson, Braiker, and Polich, 1980).

## SELF-REPORTED DELINQUENCY ITEMS FROM THE 1977 NATIONAL YOUTH SURVEY

[The following behavior items were designed to tap delinquent or criminal behavior as reported by interview respondents. It should be noted that the National Youth Survey items cover a more extensive list of behaviors than have most previous questionnaires. The researchers wanted a set of items that was both comprehensive and representative of the range of delinquent acts. This list of forty-seven acts may well become the standard for future self-report measures.]

### Self-Reported Delinquency and Drug-Use Items As Employed in the National Youth Survey

*How many times in the last year have you:*
1. purposely damaged or destroyed property belonging to your *parents* or other *family members*.
2. purposely damaged or destroyed property belonging to a *school*.
3. purposely damaged or destroyed *other property* that did not belong to you (not counting family or school property).
4. stolen (or tried to steal) a *motor vehicle,* such as a car or motorcycle.
5. stolen (or tried to steal) something worth more than $50.
6. knowingly bought, sold, or held stolen goods (or tried to do any of these things).
7. thrown objects (such as rocks, snowballs, or bottles) at cars or people.
8. run away from home.
9. lied about your age to gain entrance or to purchase something; for example, lying about your age to buy liquor or get into a movie.
10. carried a hidden weapon other than a plain pocket knife.
11. stolen (or tried to steal) things worth $5 or less.
12. attacked someone with the idea of seriously hurting or killing him/her.
13. been paid for having sexual relations with someone.
14. had sexual intercourse with a person of the opposite sex other than your wife/husband.
15. been involved in gang fights.
16. sold marijuana or hashish ("pot," "grass," "hash").
17. cheated on school tests.
18. hitchhiked where it was illegal to do so.
19. stolen money or other things from your *parents* or *other members of your family.*

---

Self-report studies are not without their methodological problems. Three common sources of error are (1) those who agree to answer questions may be markedly different from those who refuse, which leaves in doubt the representativeness of any sample of persons interviewed; (2) those who do take part may conceal their previous involvement in crime; or (3) they may exaggerate their participation crime — for example, by "admitting" acts they had not committed or admitting more serious crimes than they had in fact committed (Walker, 1971). Another problem relates to the wording of items in the questionnaires. Respondents can be expected to have a hard time relating their previous conduct to legal descriptions of offenses. Accordingly, the usual ploy is to phrase items in everyday language and to include examples by way of illustration. Unfortunately, the translation of legal offense categories into everyday language is not always easy, and some respondents may be left wondering whether a specific act they committed should be counted when it does not exactly fit the illustrations (Blackmore, 1974).

Despite the difficulties, most criminologists accept self-report studies as a major means of identifying the extent and nature of hidden criminality among youth. It appears on balance that a good deal of faith can be placed in the

20. hit (or threatened to hit) a *teacher* or other adult at school.
21. hit (or threatened to hit) one of your *parents.*
22. hit (or threatened to hit) other *students.*
23. been loud, rowdy, or unruly in a public place (disorderly conduct).
24. sold hard drugs, such as heroin, cocaine, and LSD.
25. taken a vehicle for a ride (drive) without the owner's permission.
26. bought or provided liquor for a minor.
27. had (or tried to have) sexual relations with persons against their will.
28. used force (strong-arm methods) to get money or things from other *students.*
29. used force (strong-arm methods) to get money or things from a *teacher* or other adult at school.
30. used force (strong-arm methods) to get money or things from *other* people (not students or teachers).
31. avoided paying for such things as movies, bus or subway rides, and food.
32. been drunk in a public place.
33. stolen (or tried to steal) things worth between $5 and $50.
34. stolen (or tried to steal) something at school, such as someone's coat from a classroom, locker, or cafeteria, or a book from the library.
35. broken into a building or vehicle (or tried to break in) to steal something or just to look around.
36. begged for money or things from strangers.
37. skipped classes without an excuse.
38. failed to return extra change that a cashier gave you by mistake.
39. been suspended from school.
40. made obscene telephone calls, such as calling someone and saying dirty things.

*How often in the last year have you used:*

41. alcoholic beverages (beer, wine, and hard liquor).
42. marijuana — hashish ("grass," "pot," "hash").
43. hallucinogens ("LSD," "Mescaline," "Peyote," "Acid").
44. amphetamines ("Uppers," "Speed," "Whites").
45. barbiturates ("Downers," "Reds").
46. heroin ("Horse," "Smack").
47. cocaine ("Coke").

SOURCE: Elliott, Delbert S. and Suzanne S. Ageton (1980), Reconciling race and class differences in self-reported and official estimates of delinquency. American Sociological Review 45:108–109. Reprinted by permission.

results of these investigations. Though it is virtually impossible to guarantee that concealment or lying will not occur, the general feeling seems to be that most of those interviewed tell the truth. Since the estimates of the proportion of crimes that go undetected and unacted upon range up to more than 90 percent for juveniles, self-report investigations are vital to finding out about youthful crime.

One place where self-report studies have not ventured is the executive suites of government and business. Self-reported crime data thus exclude illegal acts such as price fixing, corporate fraud, industrial pollution, monopolistic practices, violations of work safety laws, false advertising, computer fraud, tax avoidance, and other occupation-related activities that violate criminal laws. Aside from the difficulties of penetrating "the protective walls of secrecy behind which corporate executives conspire to commit crime," Steven Box (1981:86) observes that the omission is understandable: "It is extremely unlikely that corporate executives would complete a self-report schedule, and certainly not for the inducement of £5 ($7.00) which often gets the hands of adolescents eagerly ticking away." As Box points out, the irony is that the major purpose of self-report studies is to improve on the deficiencies of official statistics.

# The FBI Uniform Crime Reports

Certain kinds of data are clearly inappropriate for some types of research problems in criminology. You would not, for instance, go to official data sources for an accurate count of the rate of criminal behavior. Instead you might supplement official records with information compiled from the pool of unofficial data found in victimization and self-report studies. On the other hand, if you want to find out about police reactions to crime, what better place could you start than with the police themselves?

The scientific enterprise being what it is, decisions to use one data source over another are often geared not so much to the known or suspected inadequacies of available data, but to the fact of their availability. Research costs time and money, two commodities not always in good supply. This being the case, many criminologists use already available data, even though they fully realize the pitfalls in doing so. In recent years efforts have been made in the social sciences to establish and stock data banks containing a wide range of information, most of which has been acquired through the efforts of individual researchers pursuing various investigations. The University of Michigan has one such data bank. Using the information contained there, a researcher can shed light on a problem when the use of official statistics would be less satisfactory.

It remains true, nevertheless, that official, readily accessible sources of data turn up time and again in works on crime (this text included). One widely used official data source is the FBI's *Uniform Crime Reports (UCR)*, published annually by the Department of Justice. Begun over forty years ago, these reports came about in the effort to meet growing demands from many quarters that crime data be systematically collected and made accessible to those with an interest in the subject. At first, only the largest police departments sent their records to the FBI. Now, even though the program is still voluntary for police agencies, the FBI claims to receive crime information from law enforcement agencies representing more than 98 percent of the total national population.

Tables 4.4 to 4.7 and Figure 4.2 are samples of what is available in the annual *UCR*. Today the reports contain information on the number and rate of crimes reported by the police, on arrests, and on other topics ranging from crime on university campuses, to the killing of police officers, to law enforcement employment statistics. A major portion of the report deals with data on a select number of offenses — called Part I, or Index, offenses. These data are presented for the nation as a whole, for states, for standard metropolitan statistical areas (SMSAs), for cities of various sizes, for suburbs, and for rural areas.

The Part I offense list was established some years ago as an index of serious crime, the idea being that the dimensions of the crime problem could best be assessed from year to year by keeping track of certain serious offenses. (What is serious and what is not serious is a matter of conjecture;

**Figure 4.2** Crime clock, 1984

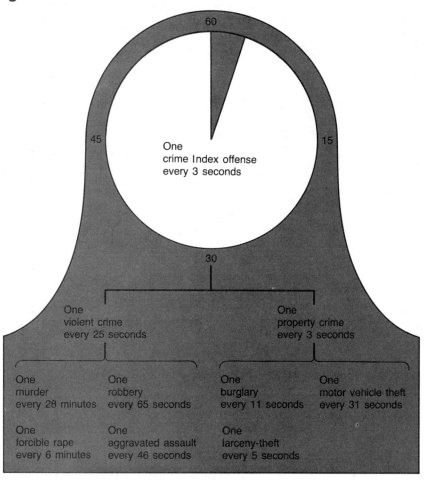

The crime clock should be viewed with care. Being the most aggregate representation of *UCR* data, it is designed to convey the annual reported crime experience by showing the relative frequency of occurrence of the Index offenses. This mode of display should not be taken to imply a regularity in the commission of the Part I offenses; rather, it represents the annual ratio of crime to fixed time intervals.

SOURCE: FBI (1985), Crime in the United States, 1984. Washington, D.C.: U.S. Government Printing Office, p. 5.

certainly, the FBI's Index should not be taken as the definitive statement.) The Index offenses are homicide (murder and nonnegligent manslaughter), forcible rape, robbery, aggravated assault, burglary, larceny-theft, and auto theft. Arson was added to the list in 1979. The Appendix, on page 501, presents the FBI definitions of all the offenses covered in its reports.

There are serious drawbacks to the *UCR*. At best the FBI data give us

**Table 4.4** Index of crime, United States, 1984

| AREA | POPULATION[a] | CRIME INDEX TOTAL | VIOLENT CRIME[b] | PROPERTY CRIME[b] | MURDER AND NON-NEGLIGENT MANSLAUGHTER | FORCIBLE RAPE | ROBBERY | AGGRAVATED ASSAULT | BURGLARY | LARCENY-THEFT | MOTOR VEHICLE THEFT |
|---|---|---|---|---|---|---|---|---|---|---|---|
| **United States Total** | **236,158,000** | **11,881,755** | **1,273,282** | **10,608,473** | **18,692** | **84,233** | **485,008** | **685,349** | **2,984,434** | **6,591,874** | **1,032,165** |
| Rate per 100,000 inhabitants | — | 5,031.3 | 539.2 | 4,492.1 | 7.9 | 35.7 | 205.4 | 290.2 | 1,263.7 | 2,791.3 | 437.1 |
| **Metropolitan Statistical Area** | **179,598,637** | | | | | | | | | | |
| Area actually reporting[c] | 97.8% | 10,127,651 | 1,136,452 | 8,991,199 | 15,645 | 72,796 | 467,285 | 580,726 | 2,521,340 | 5,524,240 | 945,619 |
| Estimated totals | 100.0% | 10,267,903 | 1,147,501 | 9,120,402 | 15,803 | 73,745 | 469,963 | 587,990 | 2,557,967 | 5,605,048 | 957,387 |
| Rate per 100,000 inhabitants | — | 5,717.1 | 638.9 | 5,078.2 | 8.8 | 41.1 | 261.7 | 327.4 | 1,424.3 | 3,120.9 | 533.1 |
| **Other Cities** | **22,798,725** | | | | | | | | | | |
| Area actually reporting[c] | 93.7% | 949,497 | 66,197 | 883,300 | 996 | 4,430 | 9,315 | 51,456 | 205,842 | 638,322 | 39,136 |
| Estimated totals | 100.0% | 1,014,766 | 71,247 | 943,519 | 1,082 | 4,759 | 9,991 | 55,415 | 220,458 | 681,244 | 41,817 |
| Rate per 100,000 inhabitants | — | 4,451.0 | 312.5 | 4,138.5 | 4.7 | 20.9 | 43.8 | 243.1 | 967.0 | 2,988.1 | 183.4 |
| **Rural Area** | **33,763,638** | | | | | | | | | | |
| Area actually reporting[c] | 90.3% | 550,748 | 49,219 | 501,529 | 1,614 | 5,158 | 4,522 | 37,925 | 189,328 | 282,246 | 29,955 |
| Estimated totals | 100.0% | 599,086 | 54,534 | 544,552 | 1,807 | 5,729 | 5,054 | 41,944 | 206,009 | 305,582 | 32,961 |
| Rate per 100,000 inhabitants | — | 1,774.4 | 161.5 | 1,612.8 | 5.4 | 17.0 | 15.0 | 124.2 | 610.2 | 905.1 | 97.6 |

SOURCE: FBI (1985). Crime in the United States, 1984. Washington, D.C.: U.S. Government Printing Office, p. 42.

[a] Populations are Bureau of the Census provisional estimates as of July 1, 1984, and are subject to change.

[b] Violent crimes are offenses of murder, forcible rape, robbery, and aggravated assault. Property crimes are offenses of burglary, larceny-theft, and motor vehicle theft. Data are not included for the property crime of arson.

[c] The percentage representing area actually reporting will not coincide with the ratio between reported and estimated crime totals, since these data represent the sum of the calculations for individual states which have varying populations, portions reporting, and crime rates.

indications of what is officially recognized as crime and reported to the FBI. In that sense the data provide us with a means of assessing the contours of some aspects of the American crime scene as seen through the eyes of the police and other official agencies. Since these contours are the ones readily given the public via the mass media, these are also the contours of the American "crime problem," as it is brought to public attention.

Those who try to use official data such as those published by the FBI face many difficulties. One problem concerns the use of official data for comparative purposes. Sooner or later most scientific research becomes comparative research. Animals, diseases, gases, rocks, stars, people, and crimes are compared along one dimension or another in the search for generalizations, laws, predictions, and explanations. Criminology is no exception. But comparative research on crime using official data is beset with difficulties.

First, the criminal law definitions of offenses vary. This is a particularly vexing problem in international comparisons, though steps have been taken to improve the situation. For example, Archer and Gartner (1984) spent ten years developing the Comparative Crime Data File (CCDF) containing information on seven offense categories, between 1900 and 1970. A total of 110 countries and 44 international cities participated in this monumental project. The difficulty is this: (1) different jurisdictions may treat different things as crimes, and so what is crime in one state or country may not be crime in another; and (2) one jurisdiction may define a particular type of crime, say auto theft, differently from another, so what they report as auto theft may not be quite the same thing.

Second, comparisons over time are especially hazardous. For one thing, the FBI's own offense classification system has not remained uniform over the years. In both 1958 and 1974, for instance, a number of definitional changes were made, rendering comparisons of figures before and after these dates rather difficult. In addition to this problem is the question of the crime rate computation itself. Rates are used for comparative purposes because they express the number of reported crimes in proportion to some base, thus making comparisons more meaningful. Population is traditionally used in the computation of rates, but accurate figures on population are notoriously difficult to get. Even census figures amount to estimates rather than true numbers. But official crime rates for many years were figured using population data from the most recent past census. Since the national census is conducted every ten years, this meant that crime rate figures for 1959, for example, were based on a population figure for 1950. Obviously, if both crime and population are on the increase but *only* crime increases are taken into account, the rates for a year like 1959 will be substantially higher than for 1950; but much of the rate increase might disappear if the corresponding population increases were taken into account.

Another difficulty is the composition or structure of the population. Suppose, for example, you are comparing two states, and you find that the crime rate in state X is higher than that in state Y. Suppose also that in state X a

**Table 4.5** Index of crime, United States, 1975–1984

| POPULATION[a] | CRIME INDEX TOTAL[b] | VIOLENT CRIME[c] | PROPERTY CRIME[c] | MURDER AND NON-NEGLIGENT MANSLAUGHTER | FORCIBLE RAPE | ROBBERY | AGGRAVATED ASSAULT | BURGLARY | LARCENY-THEFT | MOTOR VEHICLE THEFT |
|---|---|---|---|---|---|---|---|---|---|---|
| Number of offenses:[d] | | | | | | | | | | |
| 1975-213,124,000 | 11,292,400 | 1,039,710 | 10,252,700 | 20,510 | 56,090 | 470,500 | 492,620 | 3,265,300 | 5,977,700 | 1,009,600 |
| 1976-214,659,000 | 11,349,700 | 1,004,210 | 10,345,500 | 18,780 | 57,080 | 427,810 | 500,530 | 2,108,700 | 6,270,800 | 966,000 |
| 1977-216,332,000 | 10,984,500 | 1,029,580 | 9,955,000 | 19,120 | 63,500 | 412,610 | 534,350 | 3,071,500 | 5,905,700 | 977,700 |
| 1978-218,059,000 | 11,209,000 | 1,085,550 | 10,123,400 | 19,560 | 67,610 | 426,930 | 571,460 | 3,128,300 | 5,991,000 | 1,004,100 |
| 1979-220,099,000 | 12,249,500 | 1,208,030 | 11,041,500 | 21,460 | 76,390 | 480,700 | 629,480 | 3,327,700 | 6,601,000 | 1,112,800 |
| 1980-225,349,264 | 13,408,300 | 1,344,520 | 12,063,700 | 23,040 | 82,990 | 565,840 | 672,650 | 3,795,200 | 7,136,900 | 1,131,700 |
| 1981-229,146,000 | 13,423,800 | 1,361,820 | 12,061,900 | 22,520 | 82,500 | 592,910 | 663,900 | 3,779,700 | 7,194,400 | 1,087,800 |
| 1982-231,534,000 | 12,974,400 | 1,322,390 | 11,652,000 | 21,010 | 78,770 | 553,130 | 669,480 | 3,447,100 | 7,142,500 | 1,062,400 |
| 1983-233,981,000 | 12,108,600 | 1,258,090 | 10,850,500 | 19,310 | 78,920 | 506,570 | 653,290 | 3,129,900 | 6,712,800 | 1,007,900 |
| 1984-236,158,000 | 11,881,800 | 1,273,280 | 10,608,500 | 18,690 | 84,230 | 485,010 | 685,350 | 2,984,400 | 6,591,900 | 1,032,200 |
| Percent change; number of offenses: | | | | | | | | | | |
| 1984/1983 | -1.9 | +1.2 | -2.2 | -3.2 | +6.7 | -4.3 | +4.9 | -4.6 | -1.8 | +2.4 |
| 1984/1980 | -11.4 | -5.3 | -12.1 | -18.9 | +1.5 | -14.3 | +1.9 | -21.4 | -7.6 | -8.8 |
| 1984/1975 | +5.2 | +22.5 | +3.5 | -8.9 | +50.2 | +3.1 | +39.1 | -8.6 | +10.3 | +2.2 |

**Table 4.5** *(Continued)*

Rate per 100,000 inhabitants:

| Year | | | | | | | | | | |
|---|---|---|---|---|---|---|---|---|---|---|
| 1975 | 5,298.5 | 487.8 | 4,810.7 | 9.6 | 26.3 | 220.8 | 231.1 | 1,532.1 | 2,804.8 | 473.7 |
| 1976 | 5,287.3 | 467.8 | 4,819.5 | 8.8 | 26.6 | 199.3 | 233.2 | 1,448.2 | 2,921.3 | 450.0 |
| 1977 | 5,077.6 | 475.9 | 4,601.7 | 8.8 | 29.4 | 190.7 | 247.0 | 1,419.8 | 2,729.9 | 451.9 |
| 1978 | 5,140.3 | 497.8 | 4,642.5 | 9.0 | 31.0 | 195.8 | 262.1 | 1,434.6 | 2,747.4 | 460.5 |
| 1979 | 5,565.5 | 548.9 | 5,016.6 | 9.7 | 34.7 | 218.4 | 286.0 | 1,511.9 | 2,999.1 | 505.6 |
| 1980 | 5,950.0 | 596.6 | 5,353.3 | 10.2 | 36.8 | 251.1 | 298.5 | 1,684.1 | 3,167.0 | 502.2 |
| 1981 | 5,858.2 | 594.3 | 5,263.9 | 9.8 | 36.0 | 258.7 | 289.7 | 1,649.5 | 3,139.7 | 474.7 |
| 1982 | 5,603.6 | 571.1 | 5,032.5 | 9.1 | 34.0 | 238.9 | 289.2 | 1,488.8 | 3,084.8 | 458.8 |
| 1983 | 5,175.0 | 537.7 | 4,637.4 | 8.3 | 33.7 | 216.5 | 279.2 | 1,337.7 | 2,868.9 | 430.8 |
| 1984 | 5,031.3 | 539.2 | 4,492.1 | 7.9 | 35.7 | 205.4 | 290.2 | 1,263.7 | 2,791.3 | 437.1 |

Percent change; rate per 100,000 inhabitants:

| | | | | | | | | | | |
|---|---|---|---|---|---|---|---|---|---|---|
| 1984/1983 | -2.8 | +.3 | -3.1 | -4.8 | +5.9 | -5.1 | +3.9 | -5.5 | -2.7 | +1.5 |
| 1984/1980 | -15.4 | -9.6 | -16.1 | -22.5 | -3.0 | -18.2 | -2.8 | -25.0 | -11.9 | -13.0 |
| 1984/1975 | -5.0 | +10.5 | -6.6 | -17.7 | +35.7 | -7.0 | +25.6 | -17.5 | -.5 | -7.7 |

SOURCE: FBI (1985), Crime in the United States, 1984. Washington, D.C.: U.S. Government Printing Office, p. 41.

aPopulations are Bureau of the Census provisional estimates as of July 1, except April 1, 1980, preliminary census counts, and are subject to change.
bBecause or rounding, the offenses may not add to totals.
cViolent crimes are offenses of murder, forcible rape, robbery, and aggravated assault.

Property crimes are offenses of burglary, larceny-theft, and motor vehicle theft. Data are not included for the property crime of arson.
dAnnual totals for years prior to 1984 have been adjusted and may not be consistent with those in prior editions of this publication. See "Offense Estimation", pages 3 and 4 for details.
All rates were calculated on the offenses before rounding.

**Table 4.6** Total estimated arrests,[a] United States, 1984

| | |
|---|---|
| TOTAL[b] | 11,564,000 |
| Murder and nonnegligent manslaughter | 17,770 |
| Forcible rape | 36,700 |
| Robbery | 138,630 |
| Aggravated assault | 300,860 |
| Burglary | 433,600 |
| Larceny-theft | 1,291,700 |
| Motor vehicle theft | 121,200 |
| Arson | 19,000 |
| Violent crime[c] | 493,960 |
| Property crime[d] | 1,865,600 |
| Crime Index total[e] | 2,359,500 |
| Other assaults | 527,000 |
| Forgery and counterfeiting | 82,400 |
| Fraud | 270,700 |
| Embezzlement | 8,100 |
| Stolen property; buying, receiving, possessing | 123,100 |
| Vandalism | 245,900 |
| Weapons; carrying, possessing, etc. | 177,500 |
| Prostitution and commercialized vice | 112,200 |
| Sex offenses (except forcible rape and prostitution) | 97,800 |
| Drug abuse violations | 708,400 |
| Opium or cocaine and their derivatives | 181,800 |
| Marijuana | 419,400 |
| Synthetic or manufactured drugs | 19,000 |
| Other dangerous nonnarcotic drugs | 88,300 |
| Gambling | 34,700 |
| Bookmaking | 3,200 |
| Numbers and lottery | 8,800 |
| All other gambling | 22,700 |
| Offenses against family and children | 44,300 |
| Driving under the influence | 1,779,400 |
| Liquor laws | 505,500 |
| Drunkenness | 1,152,300 |
| Disorderly conduct | 665,900 |
| Vagrancy | 29,100 |
| All other offenses (except traffic) | 2,406,900 |
| Suspicion (not included in totals) | 21,300 |
| Curfew and loitering law violations | 86,600 |
| Runaways | 147,000 |

SOURCE: FBI (1985), Crime in the United States, 1984. Washington, D.C.: U.S. Government Printing Office, p. 163.

[a]Arrest totals based on all reporting agencies and estimates for unreported areas.
[b]Because or rounding, items may not add to totals.
[c]Violent crimes are offenses of murder, forcible rape, robbery, and aggravated assault.
[d]Property crimes are offenses of burglary, larceny-theft, motor vehicle theft, and arson.
[e]Includes arson.

## ARREST TABULATIONS

Arrest statistics are collected monthly from contributing law enforcement agencies. In using these arrest figures, it's important to remember that the same person may be arrested several times during one year for the same type or for different offenses. Each arrest is counted. Further, the arrest of one person may solve several crimes and in other instances two or more persons may be arrested during the solution of one crime.

Arrests are primarily a measure of law enforcement activity as it relates to crime.

Arrest data, while primarily a measure of law enforcement activity, are also a gauge of criminality when used within their limitations as must be done with all forms of criminal statistics including court and penal.

SOURCE: FBI (1985), Crime in the United States, 1984. Washington, D. C.: U.S. Government Printing Office, p. 163.

larger proportion of the population is under age 21 than in state Y. Part of the difference in rates could, then, be due to differences in the age composition of the two state populations. Unless you have accurate ways to assess population structure (and this includes racial composition, sex composition, and so forth) your comparisons lend themselves to faulty interpretations. The problem would be solved if those responsible for the publication of official crime rates provided rates specific to certain population groups, that is, age-specific rates, sex-specific rates, and so on. The FBI is now beginning to release this information as part of its Uniform Crime Reporting Program.

These are not the only difficulties facing those who do comparative research on crime. Variations and changes in data-recording technology, in police policy and practice, and in public sentiments hamper efforts to do such research and to make constructive interpretations of crime patterns and trends. Yet comparative analysis is important to criminology. We are not going to uncover the complexities of the crime scene if we cannot compare one time with another and one place with another. It is hoped, therefore, that efforts continue to be made in ironing out problems in this area.

## Official Data on the Criminal Justice System

Suppose you wanted to know how many Americans were serving time in the nation's prisons, the reasons they were there, and how long they had been there. Suppose you wanted to know about the physical, social, and health conditions in jails. Or suppose you were interested in comparing the social characteristics of those in prison with those in community-based correctional programs and those on parole and probation. Where would you look to find out?

It was not until the late sixties that authorities displayed much interest in the compilation of national data on the processing of suspects and offenders. However, the Law Enforcement Assistance Administration (LEAA) helped turn things around. With its financial backing, much research on the criminal justice system was undertaken during the 1970s. In 1970 a much-needed *National Jail Census* was conducted by the United States Bureau of the

**Table 4.7** Total Arrest Trends, Sex, 1983–1984
(8,658 agencies, 1984 estimated population 162,547,000)

| | MALES | | | | | | FEMALES | | | | | |
| | TOTAL | | | UNDER 18 | | | TOTAL | | | UNDER 18 | | |
| OFFENSE CHARGED | 1983 | 1984 | PERCENT CHANGE | 1983 | 1984 | PERCENT CHANGE | 1983 | 1984 | PERCENT CHANGE | 1983 | 1984 | PERCENT CHANGE |
|---|---|---|---|---|---|---|---|---|---|---|---|---|
| TOTAL | 6,845,124 | 6,844,155 | (a) | 1,111,882 | 1,111,692 | (a) | 1,359,602 | 1,378,565 | +1.4 | 307,102 | 316,165 | +3.0 |
| Murder and nonnegligent manslaughter | 11,305 | 10,737 | -5.0 | 886 | 836 | -5.6 | 1,731 | 1,681 | -2.9 | 109 | 96 | -11.9 |
| Forcible rape | 23,880 | 25,820 | +8.1 | 3,607 | 4,014 | +11.3 | 253 | 228 | -9.9 | 45 | 53 | +17.8 |
| Robbery | 96,897 | 91,743 | -5.3 | 26,202 | 24,135 | -7.9 | 7,836 | 7,198 | -8.1 | 1,840 | 1,654 | -10.1 |
| Aggravated assault | 179,061 | 182,925 | +2.2 | 22,896 | 23,773 | +3.8 | 27,373 | 28,334 | +3.5 | 4,506 | 4,791 | +6.3 |
| Burglary | 307,152 | 281,582 | -8.3 | 120,594 | 108,313 | -10.2 | 22,885 | 22,711 | -.8 | 8,894 | 8,524 | -4.2 |
| Larceny-theft | 662,926 | 651,251 | -1.8 | 227,666 | 229,973 | +1.0 | 285,644 | 282,069 | -1.3 | 84,361 | 84,572 | +.3 |
| Motor vehicle theft | 75,307 | 77,295 | +2.6 | 26,290 | 27,414 | +4.3 | 7,555 | 7,844 | +3.8 | 3,270 | 3,516 | +7.5 |
| Arson | 12,222 | 11,921 | -2.5 | 4,860 | 5,291 | +8.9 | 1,690 | 1,617 | -4.3 | 542 | 511 | -5.7 |
| Violent crime[b] | 311,143 | 311,225 | (a) | 53,591 | 52,758 | -1.6 | 37,193 | 37,441 | +.7 | 6,500 | 6,594 | +1.4 |
| Property crime[c] | 1,057,607 | 1,022,049 | -3.4 | 379,410 | 370,991 | -2.2 | 317,774 | 314,241 | -1.1 | 97,067 | 97,123 | +.1 |
| Crime Index total[d] | 1,368,750 | 1,333,274 | -2.6 | 433,001 | 423,749 | -2.1 | 354,967 | 351,682 | -.9 | 103,567 | 103,717 | +.1 |
| Other assaults | 294,285 | 319,017 | +8.4 | 44,984 | 47,544 | +5.7 | 51,388 | 57,384 | +11.7 | 12,822 | 14,398 | +12.3 |
| Forgery and counterfeiting | 38,915 | 38,707 | -.5 | 3,775 | 3,982 | +5.5 | 20,034 | 19,905 | -.6 | 1,853 | 1,825 | -1.5 |
| Fraud | 115,525 | 111,778 | -3.2 | 15,287 | 12,945 | -15.3 | 73,282 | 75,764 | +3.4 | 4,183 | 3,747 | -10.4 |
| Embezzlement | 3,579 | 3,554 | -.7 | 269 | 274 | +1.9 | 1,883 | 2,111 | +12.1 | 112 | 141 | +25.9 |

# Table 4.7  (Continued)

| | | | | | | | | | | | | |
|---|---|---|---|---|---|---|---|---|---|---|---|---|
| Stolen property; buying, receiving, possessing | 79,932 | 77,608 | -2.9 | 19,935 | 19,110 | -4.1 | 10,413 | 10,311 | -1.0 | 2,126 | 2,097 | -1.4 |
| Vandalism | 151,881 | 158,037 | +4.1 | 69,387 | 73,915 | +6.5 | 15,825 | 17,033 | +7.6 | 6,357 | 6,901 | +8.6 |
| Weapons; carrying, possessing, etc. | 115,918 | 116,912 | +.9 | 16,580 | 17,776 | +7.2 | 9,893 | 9,652 | -2.4 | 1,103 | 1,220 | +10.6 |
| Prostitution and commercialized vice | 24,643 | 23,583 | -4.3 | 621 | 606 | -2.4 | 65,642 | 58,582 | -10.8 | 1,498 | 1,560 | +4.1 |
| Sex offenses (except forcible rape and prostitution) | 56,460 | 65,399 | +15.8 | 9,493 | 11,648 | +22.7 | 4,452 | 4,670 | +4.9 | 618 | 831 | +34.5 |
| Drug abuse violations | 408,329 | 435,303 | +6.6 | 48,267 | 51,805 | +7.3 | 66,450 | 70,148 | +5.6 | 9,487 | 9,356 | -1.4 |
| Gambling | 24,304 | 21,138 | -13.0 | 623 | 526 | -15.6 | 3,190 | 3,293 | +3.2 | 41 | 56 | +36.6 |
| Offenses against family and children | 24,893 | 24,055 | -3.4 | 635 | 904 | +42.4 | 3,617 | 3,996 | +10.5 | 385 | 497 | +29.1 |
| Driving under the influence | 1,107,412 | 1,092,028 | -1.4 | 16,718 | 14,607 | -12.6 | 141,277 | 143,925 | +1.9 | 2,478 | 2,361 | -4.7 |
| Liquor laws | 291,081 | 289,838 | -.4 | 70,183 | 69,818 | -.5 | 56,964 | 57,096 | +.2 | 24,070 | 24,365 | +1.2 |
| Drunkenness | 800,996 | 763,142 | -4.7 | 21,489 | 18,179 | -15.4 | 75,772 | 72,171 | -4.8 | 3,935 | 3,469 | -11.8 |
| Disorderly conduct | 393,247 | 393,955 | +.2 | 57,012 | 56,223 | -1.4 | 78,144 | 82,992 | +6.2 | 12,818 | 12,829 | +.1 |
| Vagrancy | 19,986 | 18,809 | -5.9 | 1,916 | 1,531 | -20.1 | 2,425 | 2,378 | -1.9 | 320 | 359 | +12.2 |
| All other offenses (except traffic) | 1,437,181 | 1,464,198 | +1.9 | 193,900 | 192,730 | -.6 | 253,900 | 258,732 | +1.9 | 49,245 | 49,696 | +.9 |
| Suspicion (not included in totals) | 9,520 | 9,738 | +2.3 | 1,832 | 1,900 | +3.7 | 1,592 | 1,562 | -1.9 | 430 | 425 | -1.2 |
| Curfew and loitering law violations | 46,930 | 49,167 | +4.8 | 46,930 | 49,167 | +4.8 | 14,044 | 15,163 | +8.0 | 14,044 | 15,163 | +8.0 |
| Runaways | 40,877 | 44,653 | +9.2 | 40,877 | 44,653 | +9.2 | 56,040 | 61,577 | +9.9 | 56,040 | 61,577 | +9.9 |

SOURCE: FBI (1985), Crime in the United States, 1984. Washington, D.C.: U.S. Government Printing Office, p. 171.

aLess than one-tenth of 1 percent.

bViolent crimes are offenses of murder, forcible rape, robbery, and aggravated assault.

cProperty crimes are offenses of burglary, larceny-theft, motor vehicle theft, and arson.

dIncludes arson.

Census. This study covered all aspects of jail operations, including facilities, programs, inmate populations, physical conditions, and day-to-day use. Its findings were a startling revelation for those who thought that inhumane conditions were largely a thing of the past and that jails were meant to be places where the *guilty* are punished. Certainly, jails are a punitive experience for those in them; but the jail census found that of 160,863 persons being held on the census date, less than half were actually serving sentences; the remainder were awaiting trial or some kind of postconviction action. In 1982, the picture was no different: of 210,000 jail inmates, 60 percent had not been convicted of any offense (Bureau of Justice Statistics, 1983a).

The LEAA sponsored other fact-finding surveys of correctional institutions in America. In 1972 and again in 1978, more detailed surveys of the nation's jails were undertaken, and in 1974 there was a census of state prison populations. The criminologist interested in the confinement side of the legal process will find a wealth of information in these reports. Yet they are likely to be "one-shot" affairs rather than an annual event and hence are of limited value for longitudinal research.

If you want to find out about imprisonment from year to year, the United States Bureau of Prisons' National Prisoner Statistics series is a useful data source. However, these bulletins, together with a few special reports, provide only gross data on an extremely limited number of issues. Far broader in their coverage of criminal justice issues are the recent volumes compiled by the Hindelang Criminal Justice Research Center of Albany, New York. (Flanagan et al., 1982). Under grants from the Department of Justice, this center has put together the *Sourcebook of Criminal Justice Statistics* dealing with the most recent data compiled by both governmental and private agencies. It includes information on just about every aspect of the criminal justice system as well as on public attitudes toward criminal justice topics. Annual editions have been published since 1973, and let us hope that the effort will continue.

For scholars interested in keeping track of research efforts sponsored by private and public agencies, the Department of Justice maintains an information dissemination service called the National Criminal Justice Reference Service (NCJRS). This very useful source provides the public with bulletins and research monographs compiled by the Bureau of Justice Statistics (BJS), including all of the victimization studies of the National Crime Survey. You will see many references to BJS publications throughout this text. Government-sponsored research now touches on all areas of crime and justice — victimization, parole, police practices, prisons, prosecution, homicide, organized crime, rape, deterrence, burglary, juvenile justice, alternatives to prison, white-collar crime, and more.

Needless to say, not all criminological research deals with problems to which the available data apply. If you are not interested in aggregate phenomena such as crime rates or rates of imprisonment, then official data will probably be irrelevant. You certainly would not find much on the social

## A SAMPLING OF CURRENT JOURNALS DEALING WITH CRIME AND JUSTICE

American Criminal Law Review
American Journal of Sociology
American Sociological Review
British Journal of Criminology
Canadian Journal of Criminology
Corrections Today (formerly American Journal of Corrections)
Crime and Delinquency
Crime and Social Justice
Criminology: An Interdisciplinary Journal
Federal Probation

Journal of Criminal Justice
Journal of Criminal Law and Criminology
Journal of Police Science and Administration
Journal of Research in Crime and Delinquency
Judicature
Justice Quarterly
Law and Society Review
Social Problems

— plus a host of law journals and a variety of practice-oriented magazines and journals focusing on particular occupations and professions.

NOTE: Not all these journals deal only with crime-related topics.

---

organization of burglary by thumbing through the *Uniform Crime Reports*. Sometimes it is both necessary and desirable to collect your own data according to a specific research design. Scholars and practitioners recognize the need to keep abreast of developments in the field, and so they belong to professional associations such as the American Society of Criminology and the Academy of Criminal Justice Sciences. They also read the journals relevant to their interests — there are now a good many of these available (see box above). In this way they keep aware of theoretical advances, new methodologies, and new evidence.

In regard to the broad spectrum of criminological issues and problems no one kind of data will serve our needs. Criminology is a growing and changing field; new perspectives and new interests call for new methodologies, new data, new lines of inquiry. Throughout the remainder of this text you will see tradition and innovation side by side in the continuing quest for insights and explanations. If we recognize the limitations of available (usually official) data on the crime scene, if we bear in mind that they give us some information on some aspects of our subject, and if we know when *not* to use them, then we will no doubt find an important place for them in our enterprise. Certainly, we should continue to strive for systematic, routine collection and dissemination of national, state, and local crime data. Because the task is both monumental and expensive, government agencies will most likely continue to do the job for us. We do our subject an injustice if we do not know something about how crime, criminals, and criminal justice appear in their official guises. In many important respects the official crime scene *is* the crime scene.

# PART II

# Crimes and Criminal Offenders

# CHAPTER 5

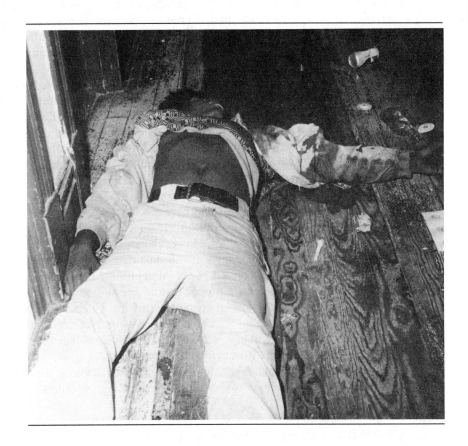

# Murder and Assault

This chapter examines criminal homicide and assault. Sexual assault, similar in many respects, is discussed in Chapter 6. The box on page 121 defines homicide and assault according to the American Law Institute's Model Penal Code.

## Violence in Historical Perspective

Most people agree that a better understanding of the present is accomplished through an awareness of the past. Certainly, violence is not unique to the twentieth century. Human history bears witness to its occurrence throughout the ages. As long as physical force remains an option in humanity's repertoire of actions, it may surface at any time.

Violence is found in primitive societies just as it is in civilized societies. Under primitive law, acts of physical aggression were typically handled privately by the injured parties or their kinfolk. Redress of grievances was often sought through bloody retaliation. If, as was sometimes the case, this violent retaliation was viewed by the original offender as an offense in itself, a bloody feud was likely to result. Feuds thus begun might last for a short time or they might last for generations. Feuds are not uncommon in some societies even today (Wolfgang and Ferracuti, 1967:280–282).

In ancient Rome, a civilized society by the standards of its day, violence was met with violence. The eye-for-an-eye conception of proper retaliation was invoked in the Twelve Tables. However, not all judicial violence was in retaliation for other violence: anyone who stole by night was subject to death at the hands of the injured party. A. W. Lintott (1968:26, 29) says "A general belief that private force was a proper instrument to execute private justice seems to have been in evidence at the time of the Twelve Tables." Also, "violence that was used to secure a man's natural or legal rights was recognized as a perfectly proper way of freeing him from undeserved restrictions." The Romans were used to violence, and the upper classes in particular placed no great value on human life. Indeed, toward the end of the Republic, bands of strong-arm thugs roamed the streets acting on orders from their upper-class retainers.

In the Middle East, the Code of Hammurapi identified various acts of violence: kidnapping children, assaulting parents, and assaults resulting in miscarriage. The punishments for these offenses varied. If someone kidnapped another's son, he was executed; if a boy struck his father, his hand was cut off; if an assailant caused a miscarriage, he was punished according to the victim's status — the higher her status, the more severe the penalty. Generally, whenever an offense injured a person of higher status than the offender, the punishment was accordingly more severe. Women were regarded as socially inferior to men, and the laws reflected this. The Code of Hammurapi (Gordon, 1957:14) reads: "If a man's wife has caused the death of her husband because of another male, they shall impale that woman on a stake."

## DEFINITIONS OF CRIMINAL VIOLENCE IN THE MODEL PENAL CODE

### Criminal Homicide

(1) A person is guilty of criminal homicide if he purposely, knowingly, recklessly, or negligently causes the death of another human being.

(2) Criminal homicide is murder, manslaughter, or negligent homicide.

**Murder:** Criminal homicide constitutes murder when (a) it is committed purposely or knowingly; or (b) it is committed recklessly under circumstances manifesting extreme indifference to the value of human life. (Such recklessness and indifference is generally assumed when the defendant is committing a felony or attempting to flee from the scene of a felony).

**Manslaughter:** Criminal homicide constitutes manslaughter when (a) it is committed recklessly, or (b) it is a homicide which otherwise would be murder except that it is committed under the influence of extreme mental or emotional disturbance for which there is reasonable explanation or excuse. The reasonableness of such explanation or excuse shall be determined from the viewpoint of a person in the actor's situation under the circumstances as he believes them to be.

**Negligent Homicide:** Criminal homicide constitutes negligent homicide when it is committed negligently.

### Aggravated Assault

A person is guilty of aggravated assault if he:

(a) attempts to cause serious bodily injury to another, or causes such injury purposely, knowingly, or recklessly under circumstances manifesting extreme indifference to the value of human life; or

(b) attempts to cause or purposely or knowingly causes bodily injury to another with a deadly weapon.

### Simple Assault

A person is guilty of assault if he

(a) attempts to cause or purposely, knowingly, or recklessly causes bodily injury to another, or

(b) negligently causes bodily injury to another with a deadly weapon, or

(c) attempts by physical menace to put another in fear of imminent serious bodily injury.

SOURCE: Excerpted from the Model Penal Code, copyright 1962 by The American Law Institute. Reprinted with the permission of The American Law Institute.

---

No such law appears to have existed for cases of a man killing his wife for the sake of another woman.

With the development of English criminal law, reactive violence slowly moved out of the hands of private individuals and into the hands of the state. Thus violence became legal and permissible in most situations only when perpetrated by the state. This was partly due to the political processes that accompanied the developing Norman grip on English society during the twelfth and thirteenth centuries. Since the Normans were in effect occupation forces and interested in consolidating their hold over the country, one of the first things on their agenda was to secure control over the routine use of force: "Private armies and bands of retainers were abolished; manorial courts were squeezed out of existence; local bodies of law were absorbed or overridden" (Wolin, 1970:30).

This did not mean a declining role for violence in everyday affairs. On the contrary, violence surfaced not merely in wars and disputes among political foes, both common events, but also in sports, from the earlier jousting matches to cock fighting, wrestling, and other pastimes; in the routine affairs of governments and the judicial system; and in the efforts of peasants and outlaws to make a living. Notwithstanding its condemnation under law, physical aggression found expression in myriad forms. We might think that the modern world is violent; but medieval England was no tranquil paradise.

## VIOLENCE IN AMERICAN HISTORY

The Puritans came to America largely to escape the violence associated with efforts to suppress their free exercise of religious preferences. Perhaps because of this, violence by New Englanders was generally a rare thing. Violence in the name of justice, however, was not. Consider what happened during the celebrated Salem witch hunts. In one year alone a score of deaths resulted from this repressive episode in criminal justice — and more were to die before the witch scare died down (Erickson, 1966:149).

Some people believe that violence is never right, that it is immoral and without justification no matter what the circumstances. Others think violence can be justified, though only under exceptional circumstances, such as for self-defense. Others contend that violence can be justified by its accomplishments: a greater good or the prevention of a greater evil (Runkle, 1976). Much of the violence that has marked America's history has been justified on the grounds that it brought about important, constructive changes in American society. The Revolutionary War, the Civil War, the Indian wars, frontier vigilante justice, and labor violence have been called examples of "positive" violence (Brown, 1969). That thousands of people were killed, maimed, orphaned, and left homeless has been played down; the ends have been used to justify the means.

During the nineteenth century, instrumental violence, that is, violence used to achieve an ulterior purpose, became a way of life in America. Riots plagued the major cities; feuds erupted in Kentucky, Virginia, West Virginia, and Texas; guerrilla bands roamed the Midwest in search of glory and fortune; outlaws plundered the frontier regions of the country, often chased by bloodthirsty posses; citizens formed groups of vigilantes to establish law and order; workers seeking the right to unionize took to the streets and were met by police and hired thugs; lynch mobs plagued the South and dealt their own brand of justice; and the mass destruction of Native Americans continued. Wherever it surfaced, conflict seemed destined to result in violence.

The ready resort to violence as a problem-solving device continued into the twentieth century. The labor movement was marked by violence as it confronted stubborn bosses and like-minded politicians. Especially violent were the clashes in the country's mining areas. In one mining strike — against the Colorado Fuel and Iron Company, from 1913 to 1914 — more than thirty men, women, and children lost their lives in the fighting between the two sides (Brown, 1969:55). The first half of the twentieth century also witnessed new forms of violence: during and after Prohibition, gangland killings became routine events in some cities, Chicago in particular; the Ku Klux Klan became a national organization and brought its hatred and prejudice to bear on blacks, Catholics, Jews, and "radical" whites in brutal beatings and killings.

The historical American experience with individual rather than group acts of violence is difficult to pin down because of the lack of national statistics regarding past levels and trends. In their report to the National Commission on the Causes and Prevention of Violence (hereafter called the National Commission), Mulvihill and Tumin argue that "there is no unequivocal evidence to suggest that recent levels and trends of violence per capita are significantly greater than in the more historical past" (Mulvihill and Tumin, with Curtis, 1969:49). Given the postrevolutionary war levels of group violence, a reasonable expectation would be that individual acts of violence were at high, not low, levels and followed an upward, not downward, trend during the nineteenth century. Mulvihill and Tumin (p. 52) conclude:

> If any general reported trend can be hypothesized, the available evidence suggests an initial high level of violence slowly rising in the late 19th century, perhaps leveling off for a period, rising to a new peak shortly after the turn of the 20th century, and then declining somewhat thereafter. The question of whether or not Americans have historically shown a propensity or impulse to acts of violence remains difficult to answer.

## Homicide and Assault: The Current Picture

Violent crime has been on the increase in America for over three decades. The National Commission found about a 47 percent increase in the official rates for murder and nonnegligent manslaughter between 1958 and 1968. Rates for aggravated assault showed even higher increases, around 100 percent. FBI data confirm that aggravated assault rates continued to rise during the 1970s, although more slowly. The most recent four-year period for which information is available shows that police rates have leveled off, with homicide rates actually decreasing (see Figure 5.1). The 23 percent decrease in murder may be partly due to the declining proportion of people under age 21, but because the rates for large cities did not decline (FBI, 1985:7) this explanation would be relevant only to rural and small city decreases.

### HOMICIDE

Official rates of murder and nonnegligent manslaughter vary around the country. New England states typically have the lowest rates, while southern states lead the country (see Table 5.1). Rates also vary by size of city. The highest rates are found in cities with over 250,000 population, and the rates tend to decline along with city size. Homicide is primarily a large-city phenomenon. However, for many years, rural rates have been slightly higher than the rates for many small- and medium-sized cities. One reason may be that the distance from and quality of medical services in rural areas render

**Figure 5.1** Trends in aggravated assault and murder, 1980–1984

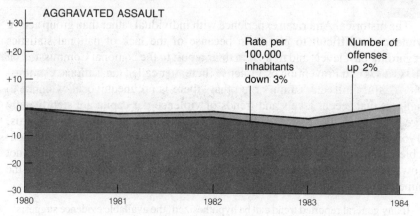

AGGRAVATED ASSAULT

Rate per 100,000 inhabitants down 3%

Number of offenses up 2%

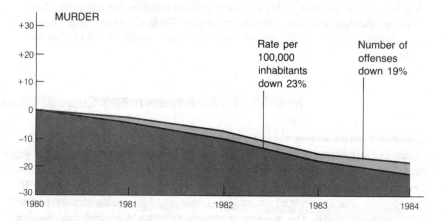

MURDER

Rate per 100,000 inhabitants down 23%

Number of offenses down 19%

SOURCE: FBI (1985), Crime in the United States, 1984. Washington, D.C.: U.S. Government Printing Office, p. 42.

assaults more likely to turn into homicides (see Doerner, 1983; Barlow, 1985).

More detailed information about official homicides is found in arrest data. Fortunately, official statistics on homicides are among the best available. Homicides rarely go unreported, and it is also rare that a suspect is not apprehended and charged with the crime. Police departments generally take great pride in their ability to solve homicides, which is made possible by the existence of a corpse and the crime's typical circumstances. Certainly, the clearance rate for homicide is markedly better than that for any other Index crime (see Figure 5.2).

More than half of the arrests for homicide occur in cities over 250,000; of all those arrested, 85 percent are males and 43 percent are under the age of 25.

**Table 5.1** U.S. Homicide Rates Per 100,000 Population, By Region, 1984

| | |
|---|---|
| NORTHEAST | 6.3 |
| *New England:* Connecticut, Maine, Massachusetts, New Hampshire, Rhode Island, Vermont | 3.2 |
| *Middle Atlantic:* New York, New Jersey, Pennsylvania | 7.3 |
| SOUTH | 10.0 |
| *South Atlantic:* Delaware, Florida, Georgia, Maryland, North Carolina, South Carolina, Virginia, West Virginia | 9.5 |
| *East South Central:* Alabama, Kentucky, Tennessee, Mississippi | 8.4 |
| *West South Central:* Oklahoma, Texas, Arkansas, Louisiana | 11.9 |
| NORTH CENTRAL | 6.0 |
| *East North Central:* Illinois, Indiana, Ohio, Michigan, Wisconsin | 6.9 |
| *West North Central:* Iowa, Kansas, Minnesota, Missouri, Nebraska, North Dakota, South Dakota | 3.7 |
| WEST | 8.4 |
| *Mountain:* Arizona, Colorado, Idaho, Montana, Nevada, New Mexico, Utah, Wyoming | 6.2 |
| *Pacific:* California, Hawaii, Oregon, Washington, Alaska | 9.2 |
| UNITED STATES RATE: homicides per 100,000 population | 7.9 |

SOURCE: FBI (1985), Crime in the United States, 1984. Washington, D.C.: U.S. Government Printing Office, pp. 44–51.

Blacks are arrested around 49 percent at the time, and 9 percent of the total are under the age of 17. According to FBI data, nearly 20 percent of those homicides on which information is available are committed in the course of another felony crime, most often rape, robbery, or burglary. In most of these cases, the arrested suspect is white.

The most common homicide situation starts when the parties to the fatal interaction are involved in an argument or altercation, often over matters that might appear relatively trivial to many people. Quarrels over money, over girl friends, in bars, and sundry other situational disputes are the precipitating circumstances. The FBI estimates that nationally around 42 percent of all known homicides follow this pattern. A recent study of eight cities found that homicides were most likely to involve acquaintances, followed by family members, then lastly, strangers (Riedel and Zahn, 1985).

The victims of homicides, national data show, are preponderantly male and usually between 20 and 30 years old. Most victims are of the same race and socioeconomic status as the offender, which most often means black and relatively poor. Most likely, the offender and victim know each other as relatives, friends, or acquaintances. Official national data suggest that a young black male living in one of the nation's larger cities has a better chance

**Figure 5.2** Crimes cleared by arrest, 1984

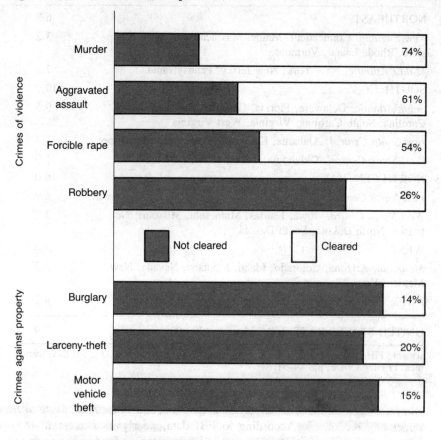

SOURCE: FBI (1985), *Crime in the United States, 1984*. Washington, D.C.: U.S. Government Printing Office, p. 153.

than anyone else of being arrested for homicide or of being the victim of one.

Table 5.2 shows the lifetime probability of being murdered in the United States. The probabilities are based on FBI statistics collected between 1978 and 1980. Clearly, the risk is not shared equally.

**Urban Studies**  Although official statistics on homicide are valuable for assessing gross patterns and trends, those who wish a more complete picture will find a number of in-depth urban studies to which they can turn. The pioneering study of homicide was conducted by Marvin Wolfgang (1958) in the mid-1950s. Wolfgang looked at homicides that had come to the attention of Philadelphia police from 1948 to 1952. He investigated a host of variables, including race, sex, age, temporal patterns, spatial patterns, motives, and offender–victim relationships.

**Table 5.2** Lifetime Probability of Being Murdered

| POPULATION GROUP | PROBABILITY |
| --- | --- |
| U.S. total | 1 chance in 153 |
| Male | 1 chance in 100 |
| Female | 1 chance in 323 |
| White total | 1 chance in 240 |
| Male | 1 chance in 164 |
| Female | 1 chance in 450 |
| Black total | 1 chance in 47 |
| Male | 1 chance in 28 |
| Female | 1 chance in 117 |

SOURCE: Adapted from FBI (1982), Crime in the United States, 1981. Washington, D.C.: U.S. Government Printing Office, p. 339.

Since the publication of Wolfgang's study, there have been quite a few other urban investigations of homicide. In America, the settings for these investigations have included Houston (Pokorny, 1965; Lundesgaarde, 1977), Dallas, Newark, and Memphis (Riedel and Zahn, 1985), Chicago (Voss and Hepburn, 1968; Block and Zimring, 1973), Detroit (Fisher, 1976), Atlanta (Munford et al., 1976; Rose and McClain, 1981), and greater Cleveland (Bensing and Schroeder, 1960). With few exceptions, these studies tend to confirm the following observations about homicide: (1) young black adult males are most likely to be identified as offenders and victims; (2) offenders and victims tend to be of low socioeconomic status and to reside in inner-city slums; (3) homicides usually occur during the late evening and early morning hours of the weekend; (4) around half of the known homicides occur in either the offender's or the victim's home; (5) homicides do not follow consistent seasonal patterns — they do not, as a prevalent myth has it, occur more often during the hot months of the year; (6) offenders and victims are usually acquainted and often live in the same immediate neighborhood; and (7) strangers are killed most often during the commission of another felony, such as robbery or burglary.

Studies in Atlanta and Chicago provide us with some interesting observations regarding trends in homicide. Three conclusions seem warranted on the basis of the evidence from these studies: (1) the homicide offender is getting younger — the proportion of offenses committed by persons under age 25 has been rising; (2) interracial homicides seem to be on the increase, though the increases are small in both Chicago and Atlanta; and (3) the proportion of homicides involving strangers has been increasing, though it still remains low relative to homicides involving friends and acquaintances.

**Guns and Murder**  Nationwide, nearly 70 percent of homicides are committed with a firearm, usually a handgun (FBI, 1985; Riedel and Zahn, 1985). This picture has remained virtually unchanged since the late sixties. When cities are compared, some exceptions to the general picture emerge: Riedel and Zahn (1985) found that in 1978, at least, knives edged out handguns as the most common homicide weapon in Newark (35.2 percent to 34.1), whereas in Memphis and Dallas over 60 percent of homicides involved handguns. Riedel and Zahn also discovered that handguns were most common in homicides involving strangers, perhaps because these homicides were more likely to occur in connection with some other offense, such as armed robbery. Around the nation, handguns are least likely to be used in family killings — but are still the most commonly used weapon. As of 1984, only eight states required handgun permits, though others required written applications and a waiting period before taking delivery.

Estimates of the number of firearms in private hands in America vary, and it is important to recognize their source. One should be wary of estimates made by people with a financial or political interest in guns. Probably no one claims to know the exact number, and so any figure must be treated as a more or less educated guess. Having said this, academic estimates for the late 1970s put the figure at 120 million, plus or minus 20 million, with handguns making up around 30 percent of the total (Wright and Rossi, 1981). A more recent estimate of the number of handguns in private hands put the figure at 65 million, roughly two for every household (*Newsweek,* October 14, 1985).

Wright and Rossi (1981) estimate that around 25 percent of private guns are kept for protection and self defense. Clearly, many Americans are fearful of their lives or property. By comparison, relatively few people actually die from a firearm — around 30,000 annually. Still, an estimated 900,000 incidents occur annually in which guns are brandished or fired, intentionally or by accident (Wright and Rossi, 1981).

One of the most troublesome issues regarding firearms in America is the growing interest in military assault guns capable of rapid fire. An estimated 620,000 such weapons are in private hands, and these include the UZI, MAC-10, and AR-15 (*Newsweek,* October 15, 1985). The lethal capability of these weapons is awesome: a MAC-10 is large caliber (.45 or 9 mm) and can fire up to 1,100 rounds per minute. It is very small, hence easily concealed, and costs less than $300. In semiautomatic form these guns may be legally owned in most states as of this writing.

Some claim that if Americans could not readily acquire guns, there would be less killing; others argue that the availability of guns has no bearing on homicide rates — that people kill, not guns. The debate on the issue is fierce and seems unlikely to be resolved in the near future. Since guns are a fact of life in America and have been a prominent possession for at least two centuries, talk of civilian disarmament generally falls on deaf ears. Powerful interest groups such as the National Rifle Association (NRA) and the highly profitable gun industry, which earns over $2 billion a year, resist more stringent controls.

Guns are clearly a factor in American homicide (Klebba, 1975; Farley, 1980), but the causal significance of their availability is disputed. Wright and Rossi (1981), for example, find no persuasive evidence that decreasing the availability of firearms would decrease homicide rates, and Wolfgang (1958:83) points out in his Philadelphia study that "few homicides due to shootings could be avoided merely if a firearm were not immediately present." But Fisher's (1976) study of homicide trends in Detroit shows a link between the increasing availability of firearms, especially handguns, and that city's rising homicide rate, and Rose and McClain (1981:100) suggest that the relatively high proportion of handgun homicides among blacks in Atlanta, regardless of the circumstances of the incident, is due to the widespread availability of handguns in the black community.

Other evidence cited in support of the connection between gun availability and homicide rates concerns regional variations in these two phenomena. George Newton and Franklin Zimring (1969:9–10) point out that known weapon ownership rates are highest in the South: 59 percent of all households owned weapons in 1968. On the other hand, only 33 percent of all households in the East owned firearms. In 1967, the official homicide rate for the South was almost 10 per 100,000 people; for the East it was just over 4 per 100,000 people.

The presence of a gun in the home or in the pocket does not mean a murder will occur. Millions of Americans own and carry guns, but relatively few kill or are killed by them. Yet the presence of a gun increases the probability that someone will die when tempers flare and somebody seeks a weapon with which to attack or defend. The gun is a *situational* factor providing an easily accessible *opportunity* for murder.

The situational importance of guns to homicide was born out in studies in Chicago and St. Louis. Both studies found not only that guns were more lethal than knives but also that some guns were more lethal than others. In Chicago (Zimring, 1972) .38 caliber handguns were twice as deadly as .22s; .32 caliber handguns were more lethal than .25s; and .25s were more lethal than .22s. The St. Louis (Barlow, 1983) study found that 47.7 percent of those victims shot by a "large-caliber" weapon (i.e., .38, .357, .44, or .45) died, versus "only" 33.3 percent of those shot with a .32 or smaller-caliber handgun. In further contrast, only 18.5 percent of victims who were knifed died.

It should be pointed out that the relative lethality of different firearms is affected by the location of the wound. In general, wounds to the head are more likely to be fatal than wounds to other parts of the body. However, Barlow's (1983) study also found that the difference in lethality between large-caliber and small-caliber handguns virtually disappeared in head-wound cases. Shoot someone in the head, and it matters little whether the gun is a .357 magnum or a .25 caliber derringer.

**Alcohol and Murder** Just as guns turn up as the weapon used in most homicides, so alcohol turns up as a situational feature in most homicides. Wolfgang, for example, found that in Philadelphia, alcohol was present in either the offender or victim or both in 63.6 percent of his 588 homicide cases. Other studies have found alcohol to be present in similar or greater proportions (Wolfgang, 1958:136). More often than not, both offender and victim had been drinking immediately before or during the fatal interaction.

Does this mean that alcohol in some way caused the subsequent killing? Most authors recognize the statistical association between presence of alcohol and homicides but do not speak of the relationship in causal terms. True, alcohol is a psychoactive drug (see p. 332), meaning that it produces mental changes in most people who consume it. The kind of changes and how extensive they are depends on numerous factors, including the quantity consumed, the consumer's physiological state, the consumer's tolerance for the drug, and whether or not he or she has just eaten. Summarizing their review of the literature, Mulvihill and Tumin (1969:648–649) conclude:

> It cannot be overemphasized that the relationship between alcohol and crime is a highly complex one. Only occasionally can one say with certainty that a violent crime would not have been committed if the offender had not been drinking. Therefore, while the relationships indicated . . . between alcohol and violent crimes are highly suggestive, they cannot, of course, be construed as causal connections. . . . It has been pointed out, however, that a causal relationship does appear to exist in many instances between alcohol and violence. For example, when a man kills his best friend over a trivial situation, drunkenness often appears as a direct factor. On the other hand, although many serious crimes may be committed by drunk persons, more often drunkenness is only one of several complicating factors. It must also be remembered that most men who drink or who are drunk *do not* commit serious crimes, and particularly do not commit homicide. . . . One must keep in mind that even if alcohol appears to be a necessary element in some instances of homicide, it is clearly not necessary for all of them. Further, it is important to bear in mind that alcohol use does not automatically or necessarily lead to violence.

In short, alcohol is best viewed as one likely precipitating factor in violence. To the extent that alcohol lowers social inhibitions and fosters in many cases a reduction of anxiety and guilt, people who are or have been drinking and are involved in some sort of dispute may find themselves acting more aggressively than otherwise would have been the case. The dispute may have erupted anyway, and the individuals concerned may well have been tempted to seek a violent solution; with the situational influence of alcohol missing, however, fear, anxiety, guilt, and social inhibitions are there to serve as constraints.

**Victim Precipitation** There is growing evidence that many homicide victims precipitate their own deaths. Many years ago Hans von Hentig underscored the importance of victim precipitation. In a landmark book, *The Criminal and His Victim* (1948), von Hentig argued that killers are often driven to murder as much by their victim's activities as by their own inclination. This is most likely to occur when those involved know each other and are attuned to each other's personality. Tensions and mutual aggravations may reach the point where both personalities see reconciliation only through violence; this can occur suddenly or develop over a long period of time. In any event, the violence is to be understood as an outcome of actions and responses by both parties and not merely those of the subsequent slayer.

A standard definition of victim precipitation is given by Wolfgang (1958:252):

> The term *victim-precipitated* is applied to those criminal homicides in which the victim is a direct, positive precipitator in the crime. The role of the victim is characterized by his having been the first in the homicide drama to use physical force directed against his subsequent slayer. The victim-precipitated cases are those in which the victim was the first to show and use a deadly weapon, to strike a blow in an altercation — in short, the first to commence the interplay of resort to physical violence.

Examples given by Wolfgang (1958:253), taken from Philadelphia police files, illustrate typical situations of victim-precipitated homicide:

> During a lover's quarrel, the male (victim) hit his mistress and threw a can of kerosene at her. She retaliated by throwing the liquid on him, and then tossed a lighted match in his direction. He died from the burns.

> A victim became incensed when his eventual slayer asked for money which the victim owed him. The victim grabbed a hatchet and started in the direction of his creditor, who pulled out a knife and stabbed him.

Estimates of the number of victim-precipitated homicides are difficult to make, because doing so requires intimate knowledge of the interaction before the killing took place. Since one party is dead, re-creation of the incident must rely on personal accounts by the killer and any witnesses who might be available. Estimates have nevertheless been made, and these range from around 25 percent of homicides to upwards of 50 percent. Evidence from Wolfgang, the National Commission, and elsewhere suggests that many victim-precipitated homicides occur when the offender and victim know each other well. In addition, victim precipitation appears to occur more often when the parties to the interaction are black and the victim is female.

## VIOLENCE AS A SITUATED TRANSACTION

No murder is exactly like another; all social situations are unique in some respect. Yet so many situations of violence look alike that the similarities have led some people to ask whether there might not be some typical dynamic characterizing the interaction that results in violence.

David Luckenbill (1977) looked at homicide incidents with just this question in mind. He found evidence of six stages in the "transaction" between the participants in various homicide situations.

In Stage I, one person insults or offends another. To onlookers the action may not seem particularly offensive, but the person to whom it is directed is angered by it. In Stage II, the offended individual sees that the insult is directed at him or her personally and not at someone else or people in general. Sometimes this clarification results from meanings assigned by onlookers or friends, sometimes it derives from the history of interactions between the parties involved, as when, say, a husband has experienced past fights with his wife and now interprets the present situation as similar.

Stage III involves decisions about reactions to the insult or affront. The offended individual may excuse the other's behavior, putting it down to his or her being drunk, or joking, or acting "crazy." If such face-saving techniques do not work or are inappropriate, the individual must retaliate or back down. Retaliation is the route taken in homicide situations and those in which someone is severely injured.

Sometimes death or injury occurs in Stage III. If not, a fourth stage may be entered, in which counterretaliation takes place. In Stage IV, the original offender continues or escalates the insulting behavior, perhaps with actual or threatened violence. In this stage, onlookers may take sides in the dispute, escalating and even directing the conflict.

In Stage V both parties are unable to back down without losing face, and weapons will be produced if they have not already appeared. In Luckenbill's study, many disputants already had guns or knives with them; others converted bottles, pool cues, and other implements to weapons or temporarily left the situation to get one. With the weapons at hand, one party either kills the other quickly, or a battle ensues with one or both eventually falling.

Throughout all this no one has given much, if any, thought to the police. The police are irrelevant to the transaction. In Stage VI the police enter the picture and become the most important element in the situation, influencing the actions of remaining (that is, live) participants. Some killers flee, some are restrained by onlookers, some are aided by friends, and some call the police themselves. The transactions of the original situation have created a new situation in which outsiders are involved and must be reckoned with.

This view of violent situations is not intended to describe all murderous encounters. However, as a depiction of the most "normal" homicide and serious assault it describes the dynamics well. Conflict, victim precipitation, face saving, retaliation and escalation, and the presence of weapons somehow conspire to produce deadly violence. That many situations also involve alcohol, drugs, or partying makes defusing the process a difficult, if not impossible, task.

## HOMICIDE ON THE INTERNATIONAL SCENE

The United States is certainly not alone in experiencing violence in interpersonal relations. True, violence among group members is rare or seemingly nonexistent in some societies — the Arapesh of New Guinea, the Lepchas of Sikkim, the Eskimos, and the Zuni Indians are examples — but this is clearly the exception to the rule.

Nevertheless, the level of violence does vary from society to society. Regardless of legal definitions, some societies do seem to be more violence prone than others are. Table 5.3 shows rates of death by violence (mainly homicides) for twenty-six countries around the world. Whereas differences in classification and reporting practices may explain some of the variation, the more sizable differences are obviously a result of other factors.

The United States ranks first among highly industrialized countries and has for many years. When compared with America, European countries generally show much lower rates, as in fact do most nations for which data are available. Over the last few years, however, some countries have shifted position relative to one another.

Homicide is most often a crime of passion: it is rarely planned and committed in cold blood. In other countries, as in America, murders tend to occur during arguments. A study of murder in Great Britain found, for instance, that more than half of the murders committed by persons not found

**Table 5.3** Homicide Rates for Selected Countries, Circa 1980[a]

| COUNTRY | RATE | COUNTRY | RATE |
|---------|------|---------|------|
| Mexico | 49.4[b] | Israel | 1.8 |
| Columbia | 30.0[b] | Hong Kong | 1.6 |
| Egypt | 26.9[b] | Italy | 1.6 |
| Philippines | 16.8[b] | Austria | 1.5 |
| Venezuela | 12.8[b] | Scotland | 1.5 |
| United States | 9.9 | W. Germany | 1.2 |
| Sweden | 8.6[b] | Spain | 1.1[b] |
| Guatemala | 7.7 | France | 1.0 |
| Finland | 6.9[b] | Japan | 1.0 |
| Canada | 6.2[b] | Greece | 0.8 |
| Denmark | 5.4[b] | Ireland | 0.7 |
| Bulgaria | 3.4 | New Zealand | 0.5 |
| Belgium | 2.4[b] | England and Wales | 0.4 |
| Australia | 1.9 | | |

SOURCE: United Nations (1983), Demographic Yearbook. New York: United Nations Publishing Service, Table 21.

a. Rates are the number of homicides per 100,000 population. They do not include auto fatalities.
b. Includes deaths due to riots and terrorism.

insane or who had not afterward committed suicide (usually a fairly high proportion of killers in that country) occurred during or as a result of a passionate, highly charged exchange with the victim (Gibson and Klein, 1969). Similar findings exist for other countries.

Needless to say, arguments do not normally result in physical assaults, let alone killings. But when they do, homicide situations around the world share some other common features. First, offenders are likely to be male, young (under 30), and of relatively low socioeconomic status. Second, they are likely to have known the victim, as a relative, friend, or acquaintance. Third, in countries with racial or ethnic heterogeneity, the offender and victim are usually of the same race or ethnic group. Fourth, many homicides appear to be victim precipitated, especially when the victim is male or the offender is female. The actions of the victim, in many cultures, are often instrumental in creating the aura of violence characteristic of homicide (Bohannan, 1960; Palmer, 1968).

## AGGRAVATED ASSAULT

Aggravated assault is not as well researched as homicide. What we know about it, however, suggests a striking resemblance to homicide. Pittman and Handy (1964), the National Commission, and other sources agree that these two offense categories are alike in many important respects. This should not surprise anyone, for the essential difference between the two is the existence of a corpse.

Those arrested for aggravated assault are disproportionately young black males who come from low socioeconomic backgrounds and reside in the inner cities of the nation's large urban centers. The victims also tend to fit this characterization. Wilbanks (1985), however, argues that black offenders are slightly more likely to commit assaults (and robberies and rapes) that are interracial, involving white victims, rather than intraracial. Most studies have focused on who is victimized by whom, and they show that whites and blacks are generally victimized by members of their own races. But Wilbanks turns the question around and asks: "Who do members of each race choose as victims?" His analysis of nationwide victimization data shows that whereas 81.9 percent of black victims were assaulted by black offenders (the usual way of looking at things), 55 percent of black offenders selected white victims. Whether this pattern holds for different regions and cities or for different time periods was not explored.

As with homicides, aggravated assaults often occur inside the home or around bars and street corners. Not surprisingly, knives are the weapons most often used (were guns the weapons most frequently used, assaults would often become homicides). As with homicide, it is estimated that quite a number of violent assaults are victim precipitated. Although accurate figures are difficult to secure — partly because aggravated assaults often escape the attention of the authorities — it seems that the victim's actions are often instrumental in generating the atmosphere of violence that makes physical assault more likely to occur. Insinuating gestures and language may be all that is needed to provoke a violent outcome in interpersonal relations (Mulvihill and Tumin, with Curtis, 1969:226).

In sum, homicides and violent assaults are much alike in many respects. This means that in all probability, satisfactory explanations of the one are also good explanations of the other. The key to unlocking the mysteries of homicide and aggravated assault lies in explaining why personal violence occurs and is patterned in certain ways.

## FAMILY VIOLENCE

Many homicides and assaults occur in family settings. If there are still doubts that violence is widespread in the American family, consider the following facts: In Detroit, 50 percent of all homicides are domestic, and Boston police receive an average of 45 calls a day — that's 16,425 a year — involving family disputes (U.S. Dept. of Justice, 1979). Nationally, an estimated 1.4 to 1.9 million children are physically abused by family members and 2 million wives are beaten by their husbands. Indeed, "a person is more likely to be hit or killed in his or her own home by another family member than anywhere else or by anyone else" (Gelles and Straus, 1979:15).

Finding out about family violence is not easy. This is partly because there is uncertainty and disagreement over what constitutes criminal violence in family settings. When does a spanking or other "disciplinary" physical action become abuse or crime? Consequently, even the most nonthreatening interviews will fail to uncover cases of family violence that respondents have not defined as such. This may explain why victimization surveys find parental abuse of children much less often reported than spousal violence. In addition, many people consider what happens within the family to be a private matter. When people are asked why they did not call the police after being attacked by another family member, this is the reason most often given (Bureau of Justice Statistics, 1984b).

The contours of family violence appear to be consistent with those of homicide and assault. Most incidents occur during arguments or other heated exchanges; offensive remarks or moves are made by one party, invoking retaliation from the other. The interaction moves inexorably toward violence, perhaps acting out an internecine drama that has occurred many times before. If weapons are used, the result will invariably be serious injury or death. Often it is the victim who first uses violence.

Women are much more likely than men to be the victims of domestic violence, and most spousal violence involves a female victimized by her husband or ex-husband. Victimization studies indicate also that participants in spousal violence are more often divorced or separated than are members of the general population, and they are most likely to be between 20 and 34 years of age.

Death is less common when the victims of violence are children. Nevertheless, the potential for serious injury is always there, finding expression in brain damage, skull and bone fractures, internal injuries, and other severe traumas. A nationwide survey of 2,143 families found that during the year preceding the survey, over 20 percent had experienced parental assaults on children, involving throwing or hitting with some object, and kicking, biting, or hitting with fists (Gelles, 1978). While this sort of violence can be found in all social classes, the weight of the evidence indicates that it is more common in families of low socioeconomic status. In general, domestic violence appears to reproduce the uneven class representation found in official statistics on homicides and assaults. It does not appear that this finding can be accounted for in differential reporting practices or police recording behavior (Gil, 1970).

Graeme Newman (1979:145–146) has enumerated some of the correlates of family violence, especially wife abuse. These include presence of alcohol; male feelings of sexual inadequacy and dependency; excessive brooding; emotional explosion or flash of anger during a dispute; social approval of "disciplining" through violence; economic failure; and previous experience as a victim of battering, usually as a child. This list includes factors that are structural, situational, and learned, suggesting that violence is complex and thus unlikely to be explained by any single cause.

## Explaining Violence

The explanation of violence has interested scholars and laypersons alike for centuries. Needless to say, many different theories have been advanced, and the search goes on. In this section we shall review some of the more prominent perspectives on violence.

### BIOSOCIAL VIEWS

Some biologists believe that humans are instinctively aggressive, basing their claim on studies of animal behavior. According to Konrad Lorenz (1971), nature gave animals an instinct for aggression for three reasons: (1) to ensure that the strongest males succeed in mating with the most desirable females, thus ensuring a kind of genetic quality control; (2) to protect the physical space, or territory, necessary for raising the young, securing food, and the like; and (3) to maintain hierarchies of dominance and through them a stable, well-policed society.

Following Lorenz and Desmond Morris — the author of *The Naked Ape* — Pierre van den Berghe (1974) believes that human behavior is not "radically discontinuous from that of other species" (p. 777), and he advocates a biosocial approach to understanding human violence. Essentially, the argument is that humans, like animals, have predispositions to violence that are innate, that is, biologically grounded. Though conclusive proof of this is still wanting, one promising indication is that aggression is a universal behavior pattern for a species: in humans, aggression has been observed everywhere, despite widely differing habitats, cultures, and technologies. The viewpoint receives additional support from the documented relationship between aggression and the male hormone testosterone, and the discovery of "aggression centers" in the brain (van den Berghe, 1974; Bailey, 1976; Wilson and Herrnstein, 1985).

Robert L. Burgess (1979) has drawn on evolutionary theory to explain variations in child abuse and family violence (for other sociobiological views of domestic violence, see Wilson and Herrnstein, 1985:253–263). Burgess argues that mature humans have two, related problems. The first is to pass on their genes through successive generations, and the second is to protect their offspring despite limited resources. The solution is for parents to invest most in those genetic offspring who show the best prospects for surviving and reproducing and least in nongenetic relatives and/or those genetic offspring who show the worst prospects of surviving and reproducing.

The problems, and their solutions will produce greater risks of abuse and neglect in families with stepchildren, in poorer families, and in those with less education, in families with many children, in single-parent families, and in families whose children have mental or physical impairments. Burgess cites studies both here and abroad that confirm these predictions. However, it should be emphasized that child abuse is not inevitable in families with these characteristics, and it is found in many families without them. As in virtually all theories of human behavior, we are dealing with the relative probabilities of certain behaviors occurring, and many factors conspire to make predictions imperfect.

As noted on page 29, the so-called **XYY** chromosomal abnormality has been advanced as an explanation of violent behavior in some people. This rare abnormality (the normal chromosomal combination in males is one X and one Y chromosome) is most likely to be found among tall white males. It has been linked to severe violence among some convicted criminals and persons who have been classified as mentally retarded or defective. However, as things stand now, many important questions remain. One has to do with the fact that the abnormality is almost unheard of in blacks, tempting Mulvihill and Tumin to ask: "Are we to believe that Negro violence cannot be accounted for by XYY chromosomes, but that white violence can?" Concluding their analysis of this and other "born violent" explanations of human violence, Mulvihill and Tumin (1969:424) observe:

Under specific circumstances, some individuals are more likely than others to become criminals or violent as a result of biological makeup. But it is never "given" in the "nature" of any individual that he will be criminal or law abiding, pacific or violent, cooperative or competitive, selfish or altruistic. All these are complex forms of social behavior, which depend upon the social and cultural milieu of the developing individual.

**Triggers and Inhibitors** To say that people have an innate predisposition toward violence does not mean they will be violent, nor does it explain different levels and types of violence. The actual display of aggression is affected by *triggers* and *inhibitors,* controls that may be innate but also may be learned or situational.

Some psychiatrists believe that humans develop internal inhibitors during early childhood. According to Sigmund Freud, the individual psyche is composed of three parts: the ego, the id, and the superego. Behavior is motivated by those drives, Freud believed, that are innate and make up the id. These are the sex drive, the aggression drive, and even the death drive. As we develop and interact with others, our superego emerges. This part of our psyche consists of social ideals and rules that are internalized through socialization. Finally, the ego strikes a balance between the demands of the id and the constraints of the superego.

The aggressive drive is expressed as violence, Freudians believe, when disturbances occur within the psyche. Mulvihill and Tumin (1969:460–461) put it this way:

> The id may overflow with violent drives: the individual hates too much, enjoys pain too much, or wants to destroy himself. Sometimes the id is just too much for the ego to control, and the individual breaks out into violent behavior. . . . Alternatively, the superego may be extremely overformed or underformed. If the superego tries to quash *all* expression of dislike or hatred, and to quell all fantasies about violence, the individual may build up a greater and greater reserve of unfulfilled desire, until he can no longer control himself. Then he becomes violent. If the superego is underdeveloped, the individual simply sees nothing wrong with violence; he will use it whenever the occasion seems to call for it. In the underdeveloped superego, we are not dealing with a "sick" man at variance with his environment; we are rather dealing with a sick environment which has encouraged violence as the "normal" mode of response.

Some psychiatrists locate the seeds of emotional disturbance, hence violence, in parent–child relationships. It is suggested, for example, that the "love bonds" between parent and child are important to regulating the aggressive drive and that destructive behavior is prevented by the formation of stable human relationships in early childhood (Chodorkoff and Baxter, 1969). By the same token, excessive physical disciplining undermines these bonds and, further, teaches youngsters that there is a place for violence in relationships with loved ones.

Although psychiatrists may have much to tell us about aggression and violence among those who are "disturbed" or "sick," their work has not proved very helpful in sorting out the reasons for variation in the level and types of violence for whole populations and societies. Indeed, some question the applicability of the psychiatric approach to even extreme forms of aggression such as murder, for, they point out, available evidence does not indicate that known violent offenders suffer from mental disorders as a rule.

Summarizing the findings of investigations into mental disorders among murderers, psychiatrist Donald Lunde argues:

> I cannot emphasize too strongly the well-established fact that mental patients, in general, are no more murderous than the population at large. While it should not be surprising to find that psychotic killers have been previously hospitalized for treatment of psychosis, *the incidence of psychosis among murderers is no greater than the incidence of psychosis in the total population*. Furthermore, the percentage of murderers among former mental patients is actually slightly *lower* than that among persons who have never been in a mental hospital. Crimes committed by the mentally ill tend to receive disproportionate publicity, which reinforces a widespread myth about mental illness and violence. (Lunde, 1970:93)

## FRUSTRATION-AGGRESSION THEORIES

The so-called frustration-aggression hypothesis was first advanced in the thirties by psychologists at Yale University. Originally, the hypothesis asserted that "the occurrence of aggressive behavior always presupposes the existence of frustration, and . . . the existence of frustration always leads to some form of aggression" (Dollard et al., 1939:1). Frustration arises whenever something interferes with an individual's attempt to reach a valued goal.

It was soon recognized that this early statement of the frustration-aggression relationship needed modification to accommodate the complexities of real life. Even though the impulse for aggression may be strong following some frustrating experience, the actual display of aggression may be inhibited by internal or external controls. Further, frustrations may be cumulative, one experience adding to another, and they may remain potent over a long period of time. It is now known that people evaluate frustrating experiences differently, according to whether they are arbitrary or unreasonable, for example. Finally, socialization teaches people how to respond to frustrations, and since the content of what is learned varies considerably from group to group and from society to society, the reactions to frustration can be expected to vary. In short, aggressive actions are not an automatic consequence of frustration, nor is the relationship between the two a simple one.

**Violence and Economic Hardship** In recent years, a variant of frustration-aggression theory has been used to explain the relatively high rates of homicide and other violent crimes among blacks. In one account (Bowman, 1980), violence is an outgrowth of the frustrations stemming from the employment-related experiences of young black males. Taking a "dual" or "split" labor-market approach, Bowman argues that blacks are disproportionately employed in the secondary sector, where the pay is low, the working conditions are inferior, and there is limited opportunity for advancement and little job security (see also Farley, 1982:225–226). According to Bowman, these stressful and frustrating conditions lead to high rates of drug and alcohol abuse and high rates of black-on-black violence.

Bowman does not adequately explain, however, whether the violence results directly from the frustrating job experiences or indirectly through the conditions and interactions associated with drug and alcohol abuse. Numerous studies of the relationship between homicide rates and economic hardship show conflicting results but, in any case, can only infer the psychological mechanisms that might be at work for any given individual (for recent work, see K. Williams, 1984).

## MODELING VIOLENCE

Many scholars believe that aggression is learned, just like any other behavior. One prominent theory is that we learn it by imitating or modeling the behavior of people we "look up to." Albert Bandura (1973) showed that the behavior of aggressive models is readily imitated by experimental subjects, whether observed in the flesh or via film. In one well-known experiment, Bandura played a film of a woman sitting on, beating, kicking, and hacking an inflatable doll. After witnessing the film, nursery school children, when placed in a room with a similar doll, duplicated the woman's behavior and also engaged in other aggressive acts.

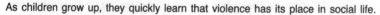
As children grow up, they quickly learn that violence has its place in social life.

Experiments such as these have established the existence of immediate imitation, but how enduring are the behaviors learned, and does each new situation have to be virtually identical with the one originally observed in order for similar behavior to occur? While the jury is still out on these questions, the evidence from work by Bandura and others (see Bailey, 1976) suggests that imitated behaviors do survive over time and that people will generalize from the initial modeling situation to other, sometimes quite dissimilar, situations.

Theories of learning through imitation are quite controversial in social psychology (see Berkowitz, 1962), but some recent support, at least for immediate imitation, was found in a study by David Phillips (1983). Phillips began with the hypothesis that portrayals of violence that are seen as rewarding, exciting, real, justified, intentional, and legitimate will elicit aggression in people exposed to them. He related the daily count of homicides from 1973 to 1978 to both television and closed-circuit portrayals of heavyweight boxing championship fights. He discovered that homicides increased immediately after the fights and peaked three days later. He also found that when white boxers lost, the killing of whites increased and that when black boxers lost, the homicides of blacks increased. In Phillips's view, the best available explanation for the findings is that "the prize fight provokes some imitative aggressive behavior which results in an increase in homicides" (1983:566).

## REWARDS FOR VIOLENCE

People tend to repeat activities for which they are rewarded and to avoid those for which they are punished. They also tend to copy others when they see the other person rewarded; in this case the reward is experienced *vicariously*. The learning that results from the application of rewards and punishments may apply to any sort of behavior.

Regrettably, perhaps, violent behavior has many rewards, and we learn about some of them quite early in life. We learn, for example, that wars and many lesser conflicts can be won through the threat or use of violence; we learn that violence can be effective as a rule-enforcing technique; and we learn, in general, that violence helps people get their way in the face of resistance. We also discover that "respectables" and those with prestige will often reward others who use violence in their interest, especially against "outsiders" and others regarded as a threat. We learn from history that violence helped make America a better place to live. Closer to everyday life, we learn in various contexts that successful use of violence often confers status, authority, and even riches.

This brief list by no means exhausts the rewards associated with violence. The point is that as we grow up we have many opportunities to learn that violence is rewarded. But we also learn that it has its costs. William Goode

(1973:162) looks at these from the standpoint of a growing boy: "A boy is punished more for using violence on a girl than on a boy, on a younger boy than on a boy his own age, on a teacher than on a stranger; more for imposing his will by violence than for defending his rights." Violence is costly, in other words, when used at the wrong time, in the wrong place, or against the wrong person. But since there are group differences of opinion and belief as to when the use of violence is wrong, the costs (and rewards) of violence in any given situation will be perceived differently by members of different groups.

## Subcultures of Violence

We have seen that lower-class, inner-city black males are found disproportionately in homicide statistics. We also know that the typical homicide involves people who know each other, who are young rather than old, and who are of the same race. For many years, the homicide rate has been highest in the South, and we know that it varies widely from country to country.

These patterns cannot be explained adequately by reference to the biological predispositions or psychic states of individuals. We also need to consider the characteristics of populations and the relationships among individuals and groups. This is where sociological criminology comes in.

One of the best theories yet advanced to account for variations in the prevalence and incidence of violence was developed by Marvin Wolfgang and Franco Ferracuti (1967) in their book *Subcultures of Violence*. In brief, their thesis is as follows: All heterogeneous societies have a dominant, or parent, culture accessible and attractive in varying degrees to its members. In America, the dominant culture is commonly referred to as white, middle-class society.

In addition to the dominant culture, such societies have various subcultures. These subcultures differ in degree, but never completely, from the dominant culture. Some are merely different — the Amish settlements, for example — and others directly oppose the parent culture — the hippies of the 1960s, for example, or the Hells Angels. The latter have been referred to as "contracultures" to emphasize the conflict between parent culture and subculture (see Vander Zanden, 1970:47–49).

Through socialization young people come to adopt, more or less, the values and life-styles of the subculture(s) to which they are exposed. If the subculture is significantly different from the dominant culture, a person's strong attachment to it may lead to his or her complete dissociation from the values, attitudes, and life-styles of the parent culture. Most people, however, are influenced by both the dominant culture and the subculture, even when the latter opposes the former. For example, many communes in the sixties failed because the participants were unable, or unwilling, to break completely from conventional American culture.

People are said to belong to a subculture of violence to the extent that aggression is expected and legitimated by the subculture in situations in which it is not supported by the dominant culture. Members of violent subcultures see violence as a significant element of their lives, an integral part of their way of life, and they make judgments regarding its proper use in interpersonal relations.

A subculture of violence is not something to which we can point, as we would a rock or tree; rather, its presence is inferred by the existence of certain attitudes, behaviors, and conditions common to a group of people. In America, a subculture or violence might be inferred to exist if we found the following:

**1.** Relatively high rates of violence — homicide, assault, child and spouse abuse, sexual violence.

**2.** Common use or threats of violence in everyday disputes among friends and intimates.

**3.** Weapons carrying and other behaviors indicating anticipation of violence.

**4.** Relatively high rates of violence among the young, whose socialization exposes them to the subculture during their formative years.

**5.** Relatively high rates of victim precipitation — if violence is a dominant theme in life, people are likely to be "keyed up" for it and ready to provoke one another.

**6.** Criminal records and other personal histories indicating the repetition of violent crime.

**7.** The persistence of the above characteristics over time: subcultures do not develop overnight, nor do they disappear at the drop of a hat.

The existence of a subculture of violence means that violence will have predictable features. Far from being senseless and random, aggression will be patterned and quite rational when viewed in light of the subcultural values, norms, and expectations governing its use. All subcultures contain cognitive and behavioral elements that together provide meaning, legitimation, and justification and help stabilize group life. Actions that may appear senseless to outsiders are not so to group members, and it is precisely because they are predictable that they endure over time.

Three real-life examples illustrate some of the features of violent subcultures listed above. The first case shows victim precipitation, weapons carrying, offender–victim acquaintance, violence in the family, and prior involvement in violence (Ward et al., 1969:881):

> The female victim was fatally stabbed to death by the defendant. . . . Both the defendant and the victim were in a bar when they exchanged some words, apparently about a mutual acquaintance. Defendant then left the bar and shortly

thereafter re-entered, having changed her clothes. . . . As the defendant walked through the bar . . . the victim hit her on the head with a beer bottle . . . and after this attack, defendant removed a paring knife from her brassiere and struck the victim an unknown number of times.

Defendant's arrest record shows four previous arrests for violent attacks. Two arrests involved fights with her husband. . . . The other arrests involved attacks on bar patrons; once she cut a man with a beer bottle and the second time she stabbed a man with a knife.

The second illustration comes from Wolfgang's (1958:188–189) study of Philadelphia homicides and shows the subcultural meanings, values, and expectations among different groups:

. . . the significance of a jostle, a slightly derogatory remark, or the appearance of a weapon in the hands of an adversary are stimuli differentially perceived and interpreted by Negroes and whites, males and females. Social expectations of response in particular types of social interaction result in differential "definitions of the situation." A male is usually expected to defend the name and honor of his mother, the virtue of womanhood . . . and to accept no derogation about his race (even from a member of his own race), his age, or his masculinity. Quick resort to physical combat as a measure of daring, courage, or defense of status appears to be a cultural expectation, especially for lower socioeconomic class males of both races.

**Gang Violence**   The juvenile gang provides the setting in which many young inner-city males explore violence. The ideals of masculinity, toughness, excitement, and reputation are stressed in gang activities. Members must show that they can take care of themselves when threatened or provoked, and much emphasis is placed on the conquest and dominance of women (an issue of great relevance to discussions of sexual violence).

The third illustration comes from a study of violent gang subcultures in Puerto Rico (Toro-Calder, 1962; see also Clinard and Abbott, 1973:59–60). Interviews with ninety-eight males serving time for violent crimes turned to the following features of gang life:

**1.** Carrying weapons, for example, machetes, knives, or firearms, is common, accepted, and expected in their group.
**2.** Fighting and other aggressive behavior are common in their social group.
**3.** Certain situations, especially related to gambling, reputation (personal and of family), and honor are defined as provoking violence.
**4.** These individuals had witnessed fights in which weapons were used and had been involved in such fights, directly or indirectly.

A two-year study of urban youth gangs in Boston by Walter Miller (1966) shows further evidence of subcultural aspects of violent crime. Assaultive behavior occurred quite frequently, though it was less common than other activities, some of which were criminal, and it was often a matter of words rather than deeds. Gang members frequently expressed violent sentiments but rarely carried them out, indicating the existence of group norms governing the actual use of force.

Seven gangs were studied intensively, and Miller found that criminal violence was committed in groups rather than by individuals. Eighty-eight incidents were observed over the two-year period, and most of the time weapons were not used; adults or women were not assaulted; and the targets were themselves gang affiliated. Contrary to the views of some other researchers (e.g., Yablonsky, 1966), the gang violence was not erratic, unpredictable, or senseless. When approved by the group, violence was used as a means to achieve prestige, honor, and recognition — a difficult concept for most middle-class adults to grasp:

> Gang members fight to secure and defend their honor as males; to secure and defend the reputation of their local area and the honor of their women; to show that an affront to their pride and dignity demands retaliation. Combat between males is a major means to achieve these ends. (Miller, 1966:112)

## REGIONAL AND INTERNATIONAL VARIATIONS IN HOMICIDE

We have already seen that homicide rates vary considerably from region to region and from country to country. The hypothesis of a subculture of violence has been used to account for such variations. Wolfgang and Ferracuti (1967) discuss the extremely high rates of homicide in Mexico and Colombia (see Table 5.3). In Mexico, nearly a quarter of a million people were arrested for homicide between 1928 and 1963, and in Colombia an even greater number of homicides were reported between 1948 and 1965. In regard to the situation in Mexico, Wolfgang and Ferracuti (1967:280) observe:

> The high rates of criminal homicide in Mexico, the convergence of such social factors as male sex, membership of the working class, and a tradition of employing physical aggression, suggest that there exist in that country subcultural areas of violence. Where the use of violence is taken for granted and homicide is a common form of death, subcultural values encouraging the use of violence can surely be assumed to be present.

The term *la violencia Colombiana* has been applied to the violence in Colombia. There, subcultural values and life-styles combine with severe economic hardship, political corruption, and oppression, to support banditry and violence among the rural population in particular (Eder, 1965:28).

It is generally agreed that subcultural pressures leading to violence are often conditioned and reinforced by aspects of the dominant culture. Subcultures do not develop in a vacuum, and it would be a mistake to lay the blame for high rates of violence at their doorstep without considering the impact of the parent culture and societal conditions in general. In regard to the high rates of violence among inner-city blacks, Mulvihill and Tumin (1969:37) point out:

. . . if the poor, young, black male is conditioned in the ways of violence by his immediate subculture, he is also under the influence of many forces in the general dominant culture. [Violence] is a pervasive theme in the mass media [that] tends to foster permissive attitudes toward violence. Much the same can be said about guns in American society. The highest gun-to-population ratio in the world, the glorification of guns in our culture, and the television and movies' display of guns by heroes surely contribute to the scope and extent of urban violence.

In addition, the experiences of black inner-city residents reflect conditions that have their roots in American history and social structure. Lack of opportunities, overcrowding, physical deterioration, poverty and unemployment, transience, extensive police surveillance, and high rates of criminal victimization are typical ghetto conditions. These are problems that have a local impact but societal underpinnings. Given the combined cultural and structural pressures that eat away at a healthy self-concept and send young blacks into the streets in combative search for fulfillment, it is perhaps surprising that there are not more murders in America.

The high rates of violence in the South have been the focus of further applications of the subcultural view. Some believe that slavery, lynchings, post–Civil War adjustments, poverty, and long-standing traditions have spawned a cultural climate supportive of interpersonal aggression (Hackney, 1969; Gastil, 1971; Reed, 1971). John Shelton Reed (1977) has enumerated some of the features of "Southernness" that may help explain the difference in homicide rates between the South and elsewhere:

1. The South maintains laws that permit an individual to assault another in certain situations.
2. Certain forms of violence are taken for granted in the South; that is, they are seen as natural.
3. Violence occurs more often than elsewhere in some situations, but less often than elsewhere in others: "The statistics show that the Southerner who can avoid both arguments and adultery is as safe as any other American, and probably safer" (Reed, 1977).
4. Violence is found among well-socialized southerners, the upright citizens.
5. Violence is more commonly found in southern music, literature, and even jokes, than in the music, literature, and jokes of other regions of the country.

The Southernness explanation of North–South differences in homicide rates has been roundly criticized (e.g., Loftin and Hill, 1974; Lizotte and Bordua, 1980) but the many tests have not produced consistent results. Some of the inconsistency is due to methodological differences, either in the nature of the data analyzed or in the methods used. Two recent studies comparing the homicide rates of SMSAs (Standard Metropolitan Statistical Areas) around the country show that regional affects persist even after taking poverty, percentage of blacks, and various other variables into account (Messner, 1983; K. Williams, 1984). Steven Messner (1983) suggests that the controversy over the southern subculture of violence will not be resolved until more sensitive measures of Southernness are used. He suggests measuring "subcultural orientations by means of the 'naturally' expressed preferences for art, literature, music, and leisure activities with predominantly violent themes" (p. 1006). Another tack is to measure Southernness by the proportion of a population born in the South. This was recently done in a study of state homicide rates, and the findings indicate that Southernness helps account for variations in both white and black homicide rates (Huff-Corzine, Corzine, and Moore, 1986).

## Societal Reactions to Violence

There is a clear duality in American values and attitudes regarding violence: it is supported, and yet it is also condemned. The popularity of contact sports and martial arts, of movies depicting slaughter and mayhem (*The Terminator* and the *Rambo* films are recent box office smashes), and the extensive ownership of firearms are cultural supports of violence. On the other hand, in both law and public opinion (see box, pp. 10–11) violent crimes are the most serious a person can commit, especially when someone is killed. Further mixed messages regarding violence are conveyed by the criminal justice system itself. What happens when people kill others, for example, depends on who the offenders and victims are. Two early studies (Johnson, 1941; Garfinkel, 1949) showed that blacks who killed other blacks were likely to receive lighter sentences than were blacks who killed whites, and whites who killed blacks were less likely to be indicted or given the death penalty than were blacks who killed whites. A study of Texas sentencing (Bullock, 1961) showed that although as a rule, blacks received stiffer sentences than whites in murder cases, they received slightly shorter sentences. Bullock noted that most black murders had black victims and suggested that local mores tolerated, and perhaps even indulged black-against-black crime.

More recent research confirms that racial prejudice may be responsible for some of the variation in official responses to homicide. Almost half of the more than three thousand people executed for murder in the United States since 1930 were black, a proportion far exceeding their representation in the general population. When given the death penalty, whites are more likely than blacks to have their sentences commuted (Wolfgang and Cohen, 1970:85–86). In a study of homicide dispositions in Harris County, Texas, Louise San Marco (1979) found that although the offender's race did not seem to affect the outcome, the race of the victim did: offenders who killed white victims, particularly females, received longer sentences.

Official reactions to violent crime are sometimes influenced by other nonlegal factors. A study of 125 "crime-specific" homicides (those occurring during the commission of another crime) found that young unemployed offenders who killed employed victims were more likely to be prosecuted than other offenders, a finding that remained true even after such legal variables as prior criminal record were taken into account (Boris, 1979). Studies of murder in Houston and St. Louis (Lundsgaarde, 1977; Barlow, 1985) show that prosecution, conviction, and sentencing all are influenced by the degree of intimacy between offender and victim. In Houston, for example, 61 percent of murderous relatives escaped any sort of legal penalty. However, even in cases of domestic violence, dispositions varied considerably, prosecutors apparently considering the extent of prior family violence and evidence of victim precipitation.

As a general rule, prosecutors pursue the cases they are most likely to win, and the fact that someone was injured or killed does not alter this strategy (Williams, 1978). The St. Louis study found that of 142 suspects arrested for murder or severe assault, 74 percent were not prosecuted or had their cases dismissed. Thirty-three offenders were eventually convicted, and the sentences they received were as follows: 1 received the death penalty, 4 got 15 to 24 years, 8 got 5 to 14 years, 8 received 4 years or less, and 5 got probation. It is noteworthy that all of the cases in this study involved either death or life-threatening injuries, and over 60 percent involved firearms (Barlow, 1985).

In general, official reactions to domestic violence tend toward leniency, complementing the view that family affairs are private matters. Even when the victims are children, there is a considerable filtering effect, with most convicted offenders avoiding jail or prison, and when imprisonment is imposed, the sentence is generally shorter than that received by other felony offenders (Bureau of Justice Statistics, 1984d). There are signs, however, that officialdom is slowly taking a more serious view of family violence. As of 1984, forty-three states have established funds for sheltering victims, require more accurate police record keeping, or authorize the courts to issue protective orders. Iowa's statute regarding spouse abuse is characteristic of the more progressive legislation in this area: "It allows the court . . . to order that the defendant grant exclusive possession of the residence to the plaintiff, that the defendant stay away from the plaintiff, and that the defendant pay a sum of money for the plaintiff's support. The statute also allows the court to issue an order determining temporary custody of minor children and establishing visitation rights" (Search Group, Inc., 1984a).

We have observed that homicide and serious assault are similar in many respects: offenders and victims tend to be young; rates are highest in large cities and in southern states; and both show the hallmarks of cultural influence, victim precipitation, and the presence of alcohol. Yet in outcome they are different: someone dies in a homicide.

In order to understand homicide, we must ask why some violent events result in death and others do not. Looking at violence as an event draws

**Figure 5.3** The violent event: elements and linkages

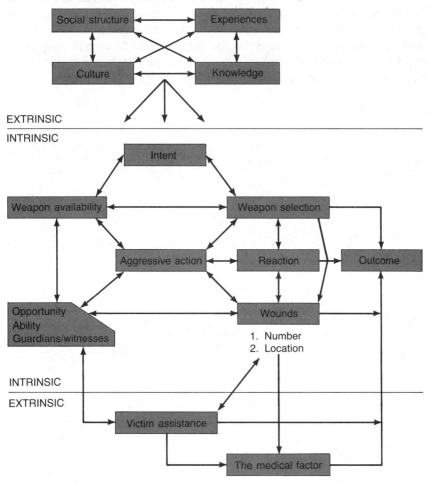

attention away from etiological factors and toward the situational elements that are intrinsic to violent encounters — victim precipitation, weapon availability and selection, witness behavior, offender–victim interaction, number and location of wounds, intent, action, and reaction, and the impact of opportunity and ability. There is also the medical factor. When victims do not immediately die, there is a chance that quality emergency medical care can be delivered in timely fashion. In the last analysis this may make the difference between a homicide and a "merely" severe assault. Figure 5.3 illustrates how the intrinsic factors in violent events are linked with one another and also with extrinsic factors that are etiological (e.g., culture, social structure, experience, knowledge) and situational (e.g., victim assistance and the medical factor). Our understanding of homicidal violence may benefit from a perspective that emphasizes outcome as well as etiology.

There is still a long way to go in understanding violence and dealing effectively with it. The material reviewed in this chapter shows that the problem has been a serious one in America and remains so. The mixed messages about violence may be the biggest obstacle to real progress. I suspect this is true of murder and assault, and I am certain it is true of sexual aggression, the topic of Chapter 6.

# CHAPTER 6

# Sexual Assault

Sexual assaults have much in common with other forms of violence, and now rape is conventionally viewed as a crime of violence rather than of sex. In this chapter we shall discuss rape as well as child molestation, different in some respects, but still a crime of coercion.

## Rape: Violence with Sex

Not long ago, rape and other sexual assaults were only mentioned in sensational news stories and discussed, if at all, in secretive whispers. Even the scientific community kept the subject at arm's length. Some believe that this collective avoidance was only partly due to the sensitive nature of the subject, that it was also due to the fact that it is women, not men, who are the usual victims of sexual assault, and that female problems are not viewed with urgency in male-dominated societies (e.g., Griffin, 1971; Brownmiller, 1975). In addition, some branches of science have largely ignored rape, thinking it the proper domain of disciplines that study behavioral disorders and mental pathologies. And finally, it had long been believed that sexual assault is a rare thing that crops up from time to time, but not often enough to merit real concern, even among women.

In recent years, however, sexual assault has become something of a *cause célèbre*. We owe this development largely to the efforts of women who have sought to dispel the myths and mystique surrounding rape and the sexual abuse of children and to help those who are its victims.

**The Popular Image of Rape**   A major contention of some feminists is that a popular image of rape has been fostered by males and sustains certain myths about rape and the rapist. This popular image, portrayed in such films as *Straw Dogs, A Clockwork Orange,* and Alfred Hitchcock's *Frenzy,* emphasizes the violence of male attackers who pop up from nowhere and vent their repressed sexual desires in the rape of unsuspecting females, who in turn do everything humanly possible to prevent their attackers from "taking" them. This image reflects and perpetuates cultural definitions emphasizing (1) male dominance and female vulnerability; (2) the idea that a woman's body, especially her vagina, is man's property, and, like any other property, can be stolen by those to whom it does not belong; (3) the view that "good" women must defend that property at almost any cost; and (4) the idea that normal males will not need to resort to force in order to acquire the sexual property represented by a woman — they learn to do it in other ways (Brownmiller, 1975; Russell, 1983).

**The Legal Conception of Rape**   Though laws dealing with the subject begin to show signs of change (see box on pp. 154–155), the popular image of rape is mirrored in legal conceptions of it. Common law traditions have long emphasized lack of victim consent, physical resistance, the use of force, actual penetration of the vagina, and offender–victim sexual unfamiliarity (Gammage and Hemphill, 1974).

Force and victim resistance are fundamental. Rape convictions are most likely to be secured when there is evidence of force by the accused and physical resistance by the victim. Physical injuries, torn clothing, and disarray at the scene of the alleged rape are just some of the things courts look for in establishing that force occurred and was met by active resistance. Under common law, the victim was expected to resist vigorously and repeatedly; modern courts, though recognizing that resistance is not a black-and-white issue, are inclined nevertheless to treat active physical resistance as an important factor in establishing that rape actually occurred. Prosecutors across the country tend to screen out cases in which evidence of force and resistance is considered weak (LEAA, 1977:30–31).

Offender–victim relationships are important also. Legal traditions are such that rape accusations are looked upon with some suspicion in cases in which there is anything more than passing acquaintance. In some states, a man who lives with a woman, even though they are not married, cannot be accused of raping her. As a general rule, a rape defendant who can show that he has had prior sexual intimacies with his accuser will have a strong point in his favor if the case gets to court.

From the time of the earliest legal codes, the true rape victim has been pictured as a sexually naive woman, usually a virgin. Indeed, the Code of Hammurapi and the ancient Jewish laws specifically distinguished between virgins and nonvirgins in their treatment of rape. According to these early codes, a married woman could not be raped, but if she were sexually assaulted by someone other than her husband, both parties would be charged with adultery, a capital offense. Furthermore, the ancient Jewish laws did not rely solely on the distinction between virgins and nonvirgins, for they ignored the virginity of those women raped within the city walls. In such cases, complicity was assumed, "for the elders reasoned that if the girl had screamed she would have been rescued (Brownmiller, 1975:20)."

The traditional view of rape has focused on penile-vaginal intercourse, but feminists have lately been successful in getting some states to change rape laws to include oral and anal sex and the use of any object to effect even the slightest degree of penetration. Russell (1983:43) comments on the traditional definition as follows:

> The focus on [penile] penetration of the vagina has often been seen as a vestige of an outdated patriarchal notion that female purity and virtue requires a vagina that has not been penetrated. According to this perspective a female who has experienced all manner of "foreplay," including oral or anal sex, whether voluntary or involuntary, may still be regarded as a virgin.

Though most jurisdictions no longer emphasize virginity as a legal issue in the determination of rape, much can still be made of the victim's character. A

## WISCONSIN RAPE AND SEXUAL ASSAULT STATUTES FROM 1858 TO 1976

### 1858

If any person shall ravish and carnally know any female of the age of ten or more, by force and against her will, he shall be punished by imprisonment in the state prison, not more than thirty years nor less than ten years; but if the female shall be proven on the trial to have been, at the time of the offense, a common prostitute, he shall be imprisoned not more than seven years nor less than one year.

### 1955

(1) Any male who has sexual intercourse with a female he knows is not his wife, by force and against her will, may be imprisoned not more than 30 years.

(2) In this section the phrase "by force and against her will" means either that her utmost resistance is overcome or prevented by physical violence or that her will to resist is overcome by threats of imminent physical violence likely to cause great bodily harm.

### 1976

(1) FIRST DEGREE SEXUAL ASSAULT
Whoever does any of the following shall be fined not more than $15,000 or imprisoned not more than 15 years or both:

(a) Has sexual contact or sexual intercourse with another person without consent of that person and causes pregnancy or great bodily harm to that person.

(b) Has sexual contact or sexual intercourse with another person without consent of that person by use or threat of use of a dangerous weapon or any article used or fashioned in a manner to lead the victim reasonably to believe it to be a dangerous weapon.

(c) Is aided or abetted by one or more other persons and has sexual contact or sexual intercourse with another person without consent of that person by use or threat of force or violence.

(d) Has sexual contact or sexual intercourse with a person 12 years or younger.

(2) SECOND DEGREE SEXUAL ASSAULT
Whoever does any of the following shall be fined not more than $10,000 or imprisoned not more than 10 years or both:

---

woman who has had premarital or extramarital sex relations, or one who is or has been a prostitute, does not fit the image of the rape victim as a chaste, morally upstanding female who reserves her body for the "rightful owner" — her present or future husband. Some rape statutes even specify that "sexually active" females cannot be raped (Ploscowe, 1951:183–184). The tide is turning, however, and, in the view of some, none too soon. The following states are among those restricting admission in court of a rape victim's prior sexual conduct: Alabama, Arkansas, Kentucky, Maryland, Massachusetts, Mississippi, New Jersey, North Carolina, Pennsylvania, Vermont, West Virginia, and Wisconsin.

**Rape in Marriage**   Recent developments in some jurisdictions have led to a significant change in the scope of their rape laws: a husband may be held liable for rape if he forces sexual intercourse on his resisting wife. This possibility has existed for some years in Norway, Sweden, and Denmark, and in many communist countries, but only recently has Anglo-Saxon jurisprudence seriously entertained the idea (Geis, 1978a). Two Australian states now prohibit marital rape — South Australia (in 1976) and New South Wales (in 1980) — and the Israeli Supreme Court in 1980 dismissed a

(a) Has sexual contact or sexual intercourse with another person without consent of that person by use or threat of force or violence.

(b) Has sexual contact or sexual intercourse with another person without consent of that person and causes injury, illness, disease or loss or impairment of a sexual or reproductive organ, or mental anguish requiring psychiatric care for the victim.

(c) Has sexual contact or sexual intercourse with a person who suffers from a mental illness or deficiency which renders that person temporarily or permanently incapable of appraising the person's conduct, and the defendant knows of such condition.

(d) Has sexual contact or sexual intercourse with a person who the defendant knows is unconscious.

(e) Has sexual contact or sexual intercourse with a person who is over the age of 12 years and under the age of 18 years without consent of that person.

(3) THIRD DEGREE SEXUAL ASSAULT

Whoever has sexual intercourse with a person without the consent of that person shall be fined not more than $5,000 or imprisoned not more than 5 years or both.

(3m) FOURTH DEGREE SEXUAL ASSAULT

Whoever has sexual contact with a person without the consent of that person shall be fined not more than $500 or imprisoned not more than one year in the county jail or both.

(4) CONSENT

"Consent" means words or overt actions by a person who is competent to give informed consent indicating a freely given agreement to have sexual intercourse or sexual contact. A person under 15 years of age is incapable of consent as matter of law. The following persons are presumed incapable of consent but the presumption may be rebutted by competent evidence, subject to the provisions of s.972.11(2):

(a) a person who is 15 to 17 years of age.

(b) a person suffering from a mental illness or defect which impairs capacity to appraise personal conduct.

(c) a person who is unconscious or for any other reason is physically unable to communicate unwillingness to an act.

SOURCE: Wisconsin Statute Book, 1858, 1955, 1976. Compiled by Laurel Stepp.

husband's appeal of his conviction for marital rape, arguing that the Talmud prohibits forced sexual intercourse between a man and his wife (Russell, 1983:336).

In America, a survey of state statutes by the National Center on Women and Family Law (Schulman, 1981) shows that most states allow for a "marital rape exemption." However, the possibility of rape in marriage is currently recognized in California, Connecticut, Delaware, Illinois, Iowa, Massachussetts, Minnesota, Nebraska, New Hampshire, New Jersey, Oregon, and Wisconsin.

The issue bears comment for two reasons. First, it represents a significant departure from legal tradition and precedent going back hundreds of years. These traditions were clearly steeped in sexism, with the wife always the loser. Matthew Hale, the seventeenth-century English jurist whose caution on rape (that it is easy to charge and difficult to defend) has guided judges and legislators, was unquestionably a misogynist, as Gilbert Geis (1978b) amply documents.

Second, the new changes reflect the influence of the feminist movement, showing yet again how important the pressure of organized interest groups has become in the realm of law. The actual extent to which women's interests are met by the rape-in-marriage developments will depend on two factors: how widespread the change becomes and whether the courts support the change in their rulings on individual cases. A test for Oregon was the much-publicized 1978 Rideout case. Greta Rideout charged her husband, John, with rape; he was subsequently acquitted. A similar case in Belgium also resulted in acquittal, though the husband was given a three-month suspended sentence for assault and battery (Shearer, 1979). We are reminded once more that there can be a marked difference between laws on the books and law in action.

## THE OFFICIAL RECORD ON RAPE

According to official police records, nearly 70 out of every 100,000 American women annually are the victims of rape. Most experts agree, however, that the true rate of victimization is far greater than this. Estimates have placed the figure at from two to ten times the official rate. This difference can be explained in large part by two things: victim reluctance to report offenses, and police labeling practices.

Among the reasons that victims fail to report their rape to the authorities are embarrassment and humiliation. Given prevailing views on the subject and considering that family and friends may be more embarrassed by the incident than the victim herself, the victim is under strong pressure to keep silent. In addition, some women do not report their experience because they would rather avoid what quite often turns out to be a harrowing time at the hands of police and courts. Some victims believe that it would do no good to report their suffering to the authorities for the simple reason that the circumstances of their rape did not fit the popular image. One rape victim recounted to me her own experience and explained that she "just knew" nothing would come of her accusation. As she described it, not only had she had prior dates with her attacker, but she had invited him into her apartment on that particular night. She offered no physical resistance when he ripped off her dress and made his intentions known, and she did not scream, even though her consent to sexual intercourse was vehemently and repeatedly withheld. It may be that in situations like these victims come to view the event as a "personal" or "private" matter. A recent survey of rape victims in twenty-six cities indicates this characterization as another reason for not reporting rape (McDermott, 1979).

As women have begun to talk more freely of rape, the manner in which rape complaints have been received by officialdom has surfaced time and again as a factor in nonreporting. In their dealings with the police, rape victims are often subjected to intense and sometimes hostile questioning quite unlike that typically experienced by the victims of burglaries, robberies, and other crimes. One victim gave this account of her experience:

> They rushed me down to the housing cops who asked me questions like "Was he your boy-friend?" "Did you know him?" Here I am, hysterical, I'm 12 years old,

Greater sensitivity in official responses to rape may encourage more rape victims to come forward, especially when the circumstances do not fit the popular image of rape.

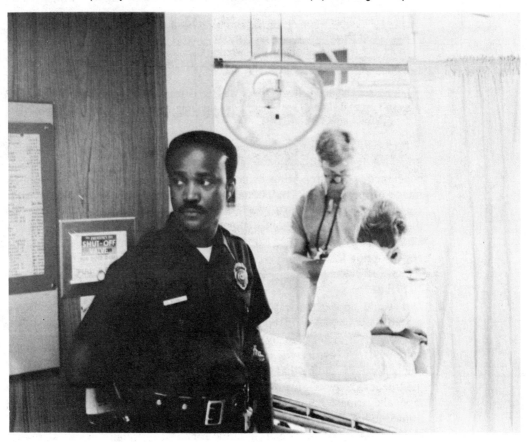

and I don't know these things even happen to people. Anyway, they took me to the precinct after that, and there, about four detectives got me in the room and asked how long was his penis — like I was supposed to measure it. Actually, they said, "How long was the *instrument?*" I thought they were referring to the knife — how was I supposed to know? *That* I could have told them 'cause I was sure enough lookin' at the knife (Brownmiller, 1975:365).

In court, rape victims are subject to the rigors of a cross-examination in which they are required to recall, in explicit detail, the humiliating and frightening encounter with the alleged rapist. Of course, rape is a serious offense in all jurisdictions, and defense attorneys quite naturally seek to discredit the testimony of victims and demonstrate that a real rape did not occur. But even so, from the standpoint of the victim who wonders whether to report her rape to the authorities and thus subject herself to this sort of humiliation, the problem is a very real one and may only be resolved by a decision to keep silent. Here are the comments of two rape victims:

> I had heard other women say that the trial is the rape. It's no exaggeration. My trial was one of the dirtiest transcripts you could read. Even though I had been warned about the defense attorney you wouldn't believe the things he asked me to describe. It was very humiliating (*Newsweek*, November 10, 1975).

> I don't understand it. It was like I was the defendant and *he* was the plaintiff. I wasn't on trial. I don't see where I did anything wrong. I screamed, I struggled. . . . (Brownmiller, 1975:373).

Important in the generation of police records on any crime is the decision to acknowledge formally that an offense has taken place. Where rape is concerned, police-reporting behavior has been congruent with the popular image of the offense. The police have generally been more likely to view rape allegations as "founded" when offender and victim are strangers, when there is physical injury, when the offense takes place in the open, when weapons have been used, when the rape did not occur on a date, when there was no prior sexual intimacy between the offender and victim, and when sexual acts other than intercourse were also inflicted on the victim (LEAA, 1977).

It would appear that rape charges are now being recorded with greater accuracy by the police. FBI data gathered during the 1970s show that forcible rape had risen faster than any other violent crime. From 1977 to 1980 a rate increase of 25 percent was recorded; however, it has leveled off somewhat since then. It could be that this increase reflected a corresponding change in the true incidence of rape. More likely it is due to more rigorous handling of rape allegations; many large police departments now have special units trained to handle such cases. More compassionate treatment of victims may be encouraging more women to come forward, especially blacks and other minority women. In its victimization survey of twenty-six American cities, the Department of Justice found that 76 percent of minority victims reported to the police, compared with only 62 percent of white victims (McDermott, 1979:45).

Victimization data on forcible rape collected by the National Crime Survey show that rates of victimization have not changed significantly since 1973 for either households or individuals. The 1982 figure for the completed or attempted rape of females aged 12 and over was 143 per 100,000. Once again, the rise in police rates may be due to more complete reporting to or by the police.

## RAPE: PEOPLE AND CIRCUMSTANCES

During the 1960s and early 1970s, information collected independently in Philadelphia (Amir, 1971), Denver (MacDonald, 1971), and Memphis (Brown, 1974), and by the National Commission on the Causes and Prevention of Violence, suggested that the popular image of rape accurately depicts only a small portion of all rape incidents. The publication of more recent research has left some of the earlier findings in doubt. Since these later studies are primarily based on victims' reports, I am tempted to favor the newer evidence over that based on official police reports (so-called police-blotter rape). It would be premature, however, to discard the earlier findings as no longer tenable, and we should remember that rape characteristics may well vary from area to area.

Before turning to the conflicting evidence, let us review the points of agreement. First, rape offenders and victims tend to be young, usually under 25. Second, offenders and victims tend to be of the same race and socioeconomic status. With some exceptions (e.g., MacDonald, 1971; Wilbanks, 1985), research shows that most rape, like most homicide, is intraracial. However, Linda Williams (1984) argues that there may well be significant *under*reporting of white rape of black females, something that has been largely ignored in the literature. Although the National Crime Survey data on 1,511,000 completed or attempted rapes from 1972 to 1983 cannot directly address Williams's point, they do show that (1) black women are as likely to report being sexually assaulted to the police as are white women, and that (2) when rape is interracial, it is more likely to involve white than black victims (Bureau of Justice Statistics, 1985c).

In absolute terms, more white women are raped than black women, and more white men rape than black men. However, the probabilities of being a victim or an offender are significantly higher for blacks than for whites — as is the case with homicide and aggravated assault. The most likely victims and offenders in rape incidents, regardless of race, come from relatively low socioeconomic neighborhoods in the nation's larger cities, again mirroring other interpersonal violence.

Third, most rapes are likely to occur in private or semiprivate locations such as homes, apartments, automobiles, or parking garages. Although initial contact between the rapist and victim often occurs outdoors or in public places like bars and theaters, the single most common location for the actual assault is inside a home, usually the victim's. Fourth, those intent on rape are more often unarmed than armed with a weapon. When they are armed, rapists tend to carry knives. The presence of a weapon significantly increases the probability that the rape attack will be completed.

Now for the points on which the evidence is conflicting or unclear. First, the earlier studies put the chances of being raped by someone known to the victim at around fifty-fifty. However, more recent victimization surveys show a different pattern. McIntyre and Myint (1979) refer to three mid-1970 studies in which rape by a stranger was more prevalent than rape by an acquaintance. The national survey of victimization in twenty-six cities found that 82 percent of rapes and attempted rapes were by strangers. And the National Crime Survey mentioned above found that stranger rapes were twice as common as were nonstranger attacks. Thus there appears to be substantial support for the popular view that rape is committed by strangers. A word of caution, however, is necessary. Many victims consider the rape incident a private matter, and it could be that considerable numbers of nonstranger rapes are not reported to survey interviewers.

Second, there seems to be some question about the extent of injury associated with rape. There is no question that the psychological trauma associated with rape victimization is severe and potentially devastating, but what about physical injuries? Amir (1971) and MacDonald (1971) found that very few women suffer severe injury and that most injuries are a result of the rape act itself. The national victimization survey looked in detail at the injury question, and McDermott (1979:36–38) concludes:

> Briefly, most rape and most attempted rape victims who were attacked were injured. Injuries included rape and attempted rape injuries, as well as additional injuries. . . . [M]ost often the additional injury was in the form of bruises, cuts, scratches, and black eyes. These survey data on injury suggest that the element of violence in rape is the physical force used to attempt and/or achieve sexual intercourse with a woman against her will. Generally, it does not appear to be violence in the form of additional, capricious beatings, stabbings, and so forth.

The popular image of rape and its legal counterpart has placed considerable emphasis on the violence of rape and the physical resistance of the victim. The impression gained from Amir's Philadelphia study was that rape victims put up token verbal resistance. The national victimization surveys, using a different categorization of resistance, established a rather different picture. Most victims took measures to protect themselves by screaming, trying to use some form of physical force against the attacker, or attempting to flee.

It is important to note that when potential victims resist a rape attack they increase the chances that the rape will not be completed, while at the same time, they increase the chances that they will be seriously injured. This resistance–injury connection points to "an important danger in the popular notion (and some statutory requirements) that a victim of an attack should resist to her utmost" (LEAA, 1977:14–15).

Third, what of the contention that rapes are not spur-of-the-moment events but are instead planned attacks? We are faced here with an awesome evidentiary problem, for the only way to be certain in any given case is to hear the truth from the offender himself. Failing this, we are left with informed speculation.

Speculation has generally held that rapes are usually not spontaneous. Some sort of planning is involved, and this seems most likely in situations involving multiple attackers. Amir (1971:143) found evidence of planning in 58 percent of single-offender rapes, in 83 percent of two-offender rapes, and in 90 percent of group rapes. The National Commission on the Observance of International Women's Year (1978) estimated that 71 percent of all rapes are planned. On the other hand, a national survey of prosecutors found that only

25 percent of the cases presented to them by police showed any evidence of premeditation (LEAA, 1977:16).

This difference may be because few of the rapes in this latter study were committed by multiple offenders. The data here, and in the national victimization surveys, show that rapists generally act alone. Yet group rapes do account for a significant minority of reported rapes, a fact that should be kept in mind in assessing the view that rape is not so much sexual as an aggressive display of male power and domination over women.

**Marital Rape**   There have been few studies of rape in marriage, probably because of a widespread belief that there is no such thing. The recent study by Diana Russell (1983) is a monumental effort worth more space than we can give it here.

Russell conducted interviews with 930 women aged 18 and over living in San Francisco. Of these women, 644 were or had been married and were the major focus of her study. Russell defined rape as forced sexual activity that involves intercourse, oral sex, anal sex, or forced digital penetration. One in seven of these women had been the victims of at least one completed or attempted rape by a husband or ex-husband; 10 percent had been the victims of both rape and other forms of physical abuse; and 15 percent had been victims of either rape or other abuse, but not both.

The characteristics of Russell's rape incidents were as follows: 84 percent involved some physical force; 9 percent were threatened with physical harm; and 5 percent were unable to give consent, because they were asleep or drugged when the attack commenced. Weapons, usually guns, were used in 17 percent of the incidents. Force was generally minimal, that is, pinning or pushing; 16 percent involved hitting, kicking, or slapping; and 19 percent, beating or slugging. Most of the completed incidents involved penile penetration: 9 percent involved anal or oral sex; 31 percent were isolated cases; but another 31 percent involved more than twenty different attacks, sometimes over a period of weeks or even over a period of more than five years. Alcohol was frequently present before or during the incidents, though Russell (1983:156–166) points out that no simple connection could be identified: sometimes it appeared to be a factor and sometimes it did not.

The demographics of Russell's marital rape cases are particularly striking in light of other research on rape. White, not black, rapists were slightly overrepresented, and husbands were equally likely to hold lower-class, middle-class, or upper-middle-class jobs. Most of the husbands had at least some college education, and fewer than 20 percent were living at or below the poverty line at the time of the first incident. The majority of rapists were between the ages of 21 and 35. These findings depart from those commonly reported for rape in general. Russell warns against generalizations, however, as her study was plagued by refusals from many of the subjects initially contacted for interviews. On the other hand, it is probable that if cases such as those described by Russell were fully represented in victimization surveys, the demographics of sexual assault would look less young, black, and lower class.

## UNDERSTANDING RAPE

Some dimensions of police-blotter rape bring to mind other forms of interpersonal violence, most notably, homicide. For example, both rape and homicide are intraracial offenses of violence usually involving lower-class urban youths, many of whom are black, who assault victims of similar status and age. Noting this, some authors have followed Amir's lead in designating rape as yet another manifestation of a lower-class subculture of violence.

The idea is that lower-class urban youths learn to adopt violence as a legitimate means to settle disputes, acquire status and recognition, and bolster self-esteem. Further, they see the use of force as an acceptable alternative to which they can turn when their goals cannot be reached by other means. If it so happens that the goal they seek is identified as a challenge to their very identity as males — to achieve it is to be a "real man" — the pressures to secure that goal are considerable, and the likelihood is greater that force will be employed when obstacles are met. Women are perceived as a challenge to manliness, not only because to "have" a woman is to be a real man, but also because it is expected that sexual advances will be met by at least some resistance, and this must be overcome. A man who cannot overcome that resistance is open to the derision of his peers, especially since prevailing definitions of womanhood include the idea that females are weak and vulnerable and should submit to men's demands.

Among lower-class males, some authors have argued, sex is treated combatively: women are perceived as beings to be conquered and dominated, and sex is one of the prizes (Ferdinand, 1968). However, the important element in lower-class male-female relationships is not so much the sexual aspect, it seems, but rather the demonstration that the male is indeed dominant and superior. A man gets what he wants from a woman precisely because he is a man. And so, as W. H. Blanchard (1959) showed in a study of gang rape, the pressures to live up to lower-class conceptions of masculinity, superiority, and toughness may find themselves resolved in the violent "taking" of a woman.

A Texas study of public opinions about rape found that black males differed sharply from whites and from black females. For example, blacks were more likely to believe that rape could be avoided if women did not provoke it, that women were curious and excited about rape, that a woman could not be raped by her husband, that most men were capable of raping, and that men were often falsely accused of committing rape (Williams and Holmes, 1981). These findings might indicate strong subcultural support for sexual violence among black males, but they remain to be confirmed in other studies.

The emphasis on rape as a behavioral manifestation of a lower-class subculture of violence has been criticized by some writers who remind us that rape statistics showing a preponderance of black lower-class offenders may not be an accurate reflection of the true rape picture. Furthermore, male aggressiveness toward females is by no means limited to one particular group of men. Thus, Charles McCaghy (1976:133) writes:

. . . [I]t is tempting simply to classify sexual assault as another instance of a subculture of interpersonal violence. But it is important to remember that the values supporting interpersonal violence have their roots in more general cultural values supporting violence as a means of solving problems. Despite the statistics, the case for assigning responsibility for sexual violence primarily to lower class, black males is not that convincing. Aggressiveness, if not open violence, by males toward females is pervasive in American society. Indeed, it may be argued that male sexual aggression in the United States has been the rule not the exception.

Diana Russell (1983:108) makes a similar argument:

The fact that Black men are greatly over-represented amongst those arrested for violent crimes is cited by some to justify their racism, by others to demonstrate the consequences of racism, either because they purportedly reveal discriminatory arrest practices, or because they show that racist oppression causes criminal behavior. What is invariably overlooked is that the factor that is most highly correlated to violent crimes is not race, nor social class, but sex. Many theories that relate crime to lack of economic well-being, as well as other deprivations, overlook the fact that Black women should then be the most over-represented group among criminals. But they are not. . . . The primary cause of violence in this country is related to notions that connect masculinity and violence, plus the power imbalance between the sexes that allows men to act out this dangerous connection.

In virtually all areas of American life — the family, work, politics, sports, education, and so on — males have traditionally found themselves in positions of power, domination, independence, and self-determination. Women, on the other hand, are expected to take subordinate positions and to acquiesce to the decisions and demands made by men. The world of sexuality is no different. The prevailing cultural image of maleness supports the idea of men as dominating, powerful, and active and as the instigators of sexual interaction; the female is weak, passive, and submissive. The so-called missionary position in sexual intercourse accentuates this asymmetrical relationship.

**Dating and Rape**   A major way in which the American male is encouraged to adopt and act out the expectations associated with being a man is the institution of dating. Dating is an important social institution for both males and females. For the female it marks the conventional road to courtship and marriage and provides the opportunity to practice her "proper" role as the deferential, acquiescent, admiring, and passive partner. For the male, dating also provides the conventional road to marriage but in addition gives him the chance to demonstrate independence, masculinity, and action in this one-to-one relationship with a woman. As the expected initiator of sexual play, the male is encouraged to view his female companion as a sexual object to be won. His success is measured by how far he gets.

Of course the idea that the male will succeed in this particular demonstration of his manliness — "go all the way" — may not be shared by his female friend. When this happens, the interaction often turns sour and may result in a physical confrontation, with the male attempting to bring about precisely what is being denied him. Influenced, perhaps, by the effects of a few drinks or by what he has wrongly interpreted as sexual acquiescence by his female companion, the rejected male finds it hard to back off once he has reached that point at which, in his own mind (and, he presumes, in the minds of other males), his masculinity is put to the test (see Weis and Borges, 1973).

Certainly, most dates do not end in physical confrontations and sexual assault. However, studies indicate that rape and attempted rape during a date are by no means rare, and their occurrences are not confined to dating situations involving lower-class males. Studies on college campuses, for example, have discovered that both male and female students — in some cases as many as 25 percent of those interviewed — could recall instances in which they had committed or been the victims of sexual assault during a date (Kirkpatrick and Kanin, 1957; Kanin, 1967; Christensen and Gregg, 1970).

**Myths and Misconceptions About Rape**  Some males are quick to point out that rape can be justified. A number of convenient myths and falsehoods in our culture mark the female as a legitimate target of male sexual aggression, even violence. Some women, it is said, need to be raped; such women are "uppity"; they have stepped out of line; they are not passive or submissive and thus must be reminded of their place vis-à-vis the male. According to others, some women deserve to be raped; they have been too submissive, and thus any man can have them; or they have (heaven forbid) rejected the male as a sex partner altogether. Then again, some men say, "When a woman says no, she really means yes" or "in their hearts all women want to be raped." A survey of Minnesota men provides evidence of the prevalence of such views. Seventy-one percent of the respondents believed that women have an unconscious desire to be raped, and 48 percent felt that going braless and wearing short skirts was an invitation to rape (Hotchkiss, 1978).

A survey of Los Angeles high school students found that 54 percent of the boys and 42 percent of the girls interviewed could think of situations in which "forced sex" was justifiable (*Los Angeles Times,* September 30, 1980). Among possibly justifiable situations were

1. The girl says "yes" and then changes her mind.
2. She has "led him on."
3. The girl gets the boy "sexually excited."
4. If they have had sex before.
5. If he is "turned on."
6. If she has slept with other boys.
7. If she agrees to go to a party where she knows drinking or drugs will be.

It is small wonder that women's groups are calling for urgent and continued efforts to educate people of all ages and backgrounds in the realities of sexual violence. From the standpoint of societal reactions to crime it is crucial that the myths and confusion surrounding rape and other sexual abuse be removed. William Sanders (1983:266) points out how absurd it would seem if we used the same list of "justifications" in the case of bank robbery. Among possibly justifiable situations for bank robbery would be

1. The bank says "yes" to a loan and then changes its mind.
2. The bank has led the applicant to believe he/she will receive a loan.
3. Through advertisement, the bank has got the loan applicant "excited."
4. The bank has given the person a loan before.
5. The applicant "really needs" the money.
6. The bank has loaned other people money.
7. The loan officer goes to a party with the applicant where he knows drinking and drug use will be going on.

Even those who must deal with rape professionally share in many of the myths and help perpetuate them. Physicians and judges, it seems, are no less influenced by these misconceptions (Gager and Schurr, 1976). With assorted rationalizations to fall back on, it is not surprising that convicted rapists rarely think of themselves as criminals and usually lay the blame for their actions at the feet of their victims.

The conception of women as legitimate targets for rape fits nicely with prevailing views that the prevention of rape depends on women changing their behavior. "Don't hitchhike"; "Don't accept when a stranger or short-time acquaintance invites you to his apartment for drinks"; "Don't go out at night on your own"; "Don't wear sexy clothes"; "Don't initiate sexual play"; and, above all, "Don't promise what you won't deliver!" If you are a woman, be what you are supposed to be: vulnerable, demure, passive, dependent, and proper. And so the wheel comes full circle. Men will be men, and women should be women.

**Rape and Culture**  The reasoning just presented argues that rape is best viewed not as a manifestation of lower-class values and expectations but, rather, as a behavioral consequence of general cultural values and images. According to these values and images, the male is dominating, sexually active, and independent; the female is dependent, passive, submissive, and a legitimate target of male sexual aggression. Further, institutionalized arrangements of our society (such as dating) give males the opportunity to act out their culturally supported prerogatives and hence are conducive to rape.

Building on this view, Chappell and his colleagues (1977) have argued that more sexually permissive societies may well find themselves experiencing higher rates of rape than less permissive societies. Their reasoning is simple. In a permissive society, where casual sexual relations are more acceptable and presumed to be commonplace, the male will experience even greater threats to his image of self-worth and masculinity when his sexual advances are denied than he would in a less permissive society, in which that denial is expected and culturally valued.

Evidence in support of this view was obtained in a comparison of Boston (considered restrictive) and Los Angeles (considered permissive). In 1969, rape rates were 12.8 per 100,000 people in Boston and 25.4 per 100,000 people in Los Angeles. In a later paper Gilbert and Robley Geis (1979) present further evidence, this time from Stockholm, Sweden. The relatively high rates of rape in this city (18.9 in 1970; 22.9 in 1977) suggest support for the theory; however, the authors also found a different kind of support. In Stockholm many rapes occur after a pickup at some dance hall or bar and often involve a foreign man and a Swedish woman. After some socializing the couple ends up at one or the other's residence, the man makes sexual advances, the woman declines, and a rape follows. The more sexually liberated Swedish woman exercises her prerogative of choice in sexual matters, and that decision is an affront to the foreigner, who sees his masculinity severely challenged by the unexpected refusal. The authors conclude: "the irony is that the Swedish situation, which we think is a good thing, ends up looking bad in terms of rape rates."

**Psychological Profiles of the Rapist**  Most American males, presumably, do not commit sexual assaults, certainly not violent rapes. Hence the idea that those who do must be suffering from some sort of psychological pathology or disorder. This notion certainly fits well with the popular image of rape.

Research on the subject is inconclusive but generally does not support explanations of rape and sexual assault based on mental pathologies, brain damage, or personality disorder. Most studies show convicted rapists to be psychologically normal or, at most, suffering from some sort of neurosis (e.g., Ellis and Brancale, 1965; Gebhard et al., 1965). On the other hand, Nicholas Groth (1979: 106–109) believes that 10 percent of his sample of incarcerated rapists were psychotic at the time of the assault and that 56 percent had various personality disorders. Generalizations are always questionable when based on groups of incarcerated offenders, as most of these studies were. More than likely, such studies overestimate the occurrence of mental pathologies and disorders among rapists in general, most of whom escape official attention, in any case.

Groth's study has been widely cited for his discussion of three major types of rape: (1) *power* rape, in which sexual aggression is an assertion of control and domination; (2) *anger* rape, in which coercive sex vents anger and frustration; and (3) *sadistic* rape, in which violent sex satisfies a pathological need to inflict suffering. In Groth's view, power rape is by far the most common type, and if anything, this would tend to support the view that most rapists are similar to, rather than different from, other males.

The other element that enters the picture in discussions of offender profiles is alcohol. Three theories are popular (Rada, 1975):

**1.** The man who drinks becomes disinhibited; he loses control and judgment and acts out normally unacceptable sexual fantasies and impulses.

**2.** Men drink to feel stronger rather than to reduce their sexual inhibitions; alcohol helps them exercise power and domination, to control the situation. The finding that many rapists rarely focus on the sexual aspects of the rape is considered support for item 2 rather than for item 1.

**3.** Alcohol "may have a direct effect on either the aggressive or sexual centers in the brain, since alcohol has been shown to increase the general level of activity in some animals" (p. 62).

Rada also suggests that a third, psychobiological, theory may have merit. It has been found that particularly violent rapists have higher testosterone levels than other rapists, suggesting a connection between this male hormone and violence and sexuality (Rada, 1976). However, the research is continuing, and the fact that alcohol tends to *lower* testosterone levels makes further study important.

On balance, there is little impressive evidence that rapists are in general psychologically abnormal. Some probably are, the particularly brutal, perhaps, or serial rapists who choose many different victims, but as a general explanation of sexual assault, psychic pathology or disorder theories are of limited use. The most promising approach is one that links structural and cultural factors with situational inducements, as was the case with explanations of violence in general (see Chapter 5).

If there is a common mental attitude among rapists, then Russell (1983:123) probably captures it best in her description of the "patriarch." And when she speaks here of husbands who rape, she makes it clear the description would fit many American males:

[Patriarchs] see themselves as superior to their wives because they are men; they believe their wives are their property and that it is the duty of their wives to accommodate them sexually whenever they want; they believe they should be the boss in the marriage, and that wives who behave in an insubordinate fashion deserve punishment . . .; they subscribe to a sexual double standard in which it is acceptable for husbands to have other sexual attractions or affairs, but it is totally unacceptable for their wives to do the same. . . .

# Child Molestation

Although the most likely victims of rape appear to be the older teenager or young adult, children, including the very young, are sometimes the victims of rape and other sexual assaults. Actually, some authors claim that sexual assaults involving the physical abuse of children may even be more prevalent than nonsexual assaults such as child beating (DeFrancis, 1969). Such claims are difficult to assess, given the paucity of reliable information on either type of assault, but there is undoubtedly far more of both than is generally recognized.

As with the rapist, there is a popular image of the child molester. He is depicted as a stranger who lurks around playgrounds, parks, and other places where children wander and who lures or drags his victims into his car or home where he then sexually assaults them. This image is no more accurate than the one of rape and the rapist. For example, the child molester is not usually a stranger. In studies both here and abroad, researchers are finding that in most known cases of child molestation the offender and victim are acquainted with each other. In a New York investigation of Brooklyn and The Bronx, only 25 percent of the 250 sampled incidents involved strangers; in the remaining 75 percent of the cases, the offenders were either related to the child or were such acquaintances as neighbors, friends of the family, or baby-sitters (DeFrancis, 1969:66–68). Similarly, in a Wisconsin study of 181 convicted child molesters, 65 percent were at least casually acquainted with their victims (McCaghy, 1967:80).

Learning the details surrounding cases of child molestation is not easy. Those incidents in which very young children are victimized present the greatest difficulties for the researcher. Except when brutal physical abuses are involved, and these are a small minority of known cases, even the nature of the sexual encounter itself may be difficult to determine. From the standpoint of the criminal law, the nature and gravity of the offense hinge on the details of the encounter. Especially important when the victim is an older child, 14 or 15 years old, are the issues of resistance and consent. Did the child resist? Did the child consent to the sexual act or even encourage it? Was compliance secured by the use or threat of physical force? In dealing with these questions, both courts and researchers are often confronted with conflicting pictures of the events surrounding the incident. For one thing, the official account of the incident commonly departs from the account given by the suspect (Gebhard et al., 1965). Commenting on this discrepancy, Edward Sagarin (1974:147–148) notes:

> Both [accounts] are suspect. The child is old enough to understand that she will exonerate herself if she claims resistance or lack of encouragement in the courtroom; and since she is a prosecution witness, the prosecution encourages her in that direction in order to obtain a conviction. On the other hand, the

defendant is anxious that the court, the researcher, and even himself believe that he was led on. Indeed, some defendants denied their guilt not only to the courts, but to the investigators as well.

Bearing this in mind, many experts believe that molesters are unlikely to resort to overt physical coercion, and when a child does offer resistance it is most likely overcome by threats of deprivation (loss of love, affection, privileges) or by rewards (candy, money). Victim resistance and the offender's use of physical coercion tend more to characterize those sexual incidents involving strangers, which is what we would expect: neither the offender nor victim are bound up in affective relations with one another; hence victim compliance is problematic.

One of the important points of agreement among researchers is that child molesters do not represent a homogeneous group of people. They come from all walks of life, are of varied ages, engage in different sorts of sexual acts, choose different types of child victims, and as Donal MacNamara (1968:153) has noted, range "from senile old men, through drunken aggressors, to psychotic pedophiles, mental defectives, and adventitious offenders." About the only common characteristic is that they are most often males who choose young females (the most likely victim is 11 to 14 years old) as targets of their sexual demands. Relatively few known cases involve female offenders or male victims, although recent allegations of sexual abuse of children in day-care centers run by women suggest that there may be many more than suspected.

One promising attempt to identify types of molesters and to differentiate among them has been offered by Charles McCaghy (1967). Rather than focus simply on the characteristics of offenders (their age, social background, or psychiatric state) as some scholars have done, McCaghy's work uses information on the extent to which child molesters have interacted with children in the past and on the circumstances surrounding the offense situation. Four offense circumstances were considered important: (1) the amount of coercion used, (2) familiarity with the child victim, (3) form of sexual activity, and (4) the nature of the interaction between the offender and the child immediately before the offense. Based on his analysis, McCaghy tentatively identified six types of molesters:

1. high interaction molester [described in the next paragraph]; 2. incestuous molester (whose victim is related and living in his residence); 3. asocial molester (whose molesting offense is but one segment of a lawbreaking career); 4. senile molester (whose older age and low educational level distinguish him from other molesters); 5. career molester (whose current offense does not represent his only arrest for molesting); 6. spontaneous-aggressive molester (whose offense characteristics are opposite those of the high interaction molester). (1967:87)

Though representing only 18 of the 181 subjects studied, the *high interaction molester* category is the one McCaghy feels best meets the typological criteria of internal homogeneity and isolation from other categories. As McCaghy describes them, molesters in this category have had life patterns involving "many contacts with children outside their own home and immediate neighborhood" (p. 79). They commit their offenses against children with whom they are familiar; they do not use or threaten force; their interaction with the child begins on a nonsexual level; and the subsequent sexual activity is confined primarily to manual manipulation of their own or the child's genitals.

There is good reason to believe that the high interaction molester may be more prevalent than indicated by McCaghy's sample. First, offender–victim familiarity, coupled with the absence of physical coercion and the mildness of the sexual encounter itself, may render this offender less visible to the authorities and those engaged in research and thus is less easily discovered by them. In addition, evidence from other studies shows that the parents of child victims are less likely to press charges when the offender is a family acquaintance or friend (DeFrancis, 1969:xi).

In cases in which family members or relatives of the molester are victimized, probably the most common situations of all, the offense is often not an isolated incident but has been committed over a period of weeks, months, or even years. Given the ongoing nonsexual interaction between relatives and family members, this is not surprising. In addition, the sexual encounters themselves may have developed in an atmosphere of consensus and mutual affection. As one author has pointed out, incestuous desire on the part of both adult and child can be interpreted as a quite understandable consequence of close, personal, and satisfying relations between family members. What may begin as a loving nonsexual relationship between an adult and a child may, with the passage of time, expand to include repetitive sexual interactions (White, 1972:160–171).

Of course, cultural expectations in most societies do not extend to incest or noncoital sex acts between family members. By engaging in sex acts with any child, in fact, an adult departs from acceptable sexual roles. It is hard to imagine that molesters are, as a group, unaware that they have moved beyond culturally acceptable — not to say legal — boundaries of sexual conduct. A few may be mentally deficient or suffering from severe psychiatric disorders and therefore unaware of the normative implications of their actions. Most, however, are clearly aware of their transgressions, and like other persons who recognize that others will label them as deviant or criminal, they tend to disavow their actions or to excuse them by appealing to what they view as socially acceptable justifications.

When asked to account for their actions, child molesters commonly explain away their conduct by either blaming it on a temporary loss of sense or rationality ("I was drunk"; "I didn't know what I was doing"; "everything went blank") or by blaming it on the behavior of the victim ("she wanted me to do it"; "he started it") or on conditions of family life or other personal troubles. In his study, McCaghy found that the most common single response to the question "Why?" was to blame the offense on a temporary loss of rationality. The offenders most likely to deny their deviance in this way were those who had used force to obtain compliance and those who had molested female children.

Some molesters are quite candid about their conduct and do not attempt to deny their deviance or to justify it by appealing to external forces. Male offenders who molest boys and young men seem most likely to fall into this category. Explaining this, McCaghy (1967:82–83) argues:

> It appears that many homosexual molesters have previously accepted a homosexual role, which in itself represents a drastic departure from the sexual norms of conventional society. Being accused of molesting does not constitute a threat to their present self-concept as sexual deviants. Since deviant sexual conduct is already a way of life for them, they do not feel compelled to deny responsibility for their molesting offense. This interpretation was lent support during the author's interviews with these molesters. Many considered themselves to be first of all homosexuals. Their contact with a person under the age of fourteen was, to them, unfortunate and perhaps accidental, but only secondary to their basic sexual behavior patterns. Since they were already at odds with approved sexual norms, the molesting offense did not result in any need for serious self-examination.

We are, needless to say, far from any complete and accurate picture of child molesting and the child molester. Much research still is needed, and the greater willingness of people to talk about sensitive sexual issues will aid in that endeavor. Even so, most incidents of child molestation will remain hidden from research scrutiny, particularly those offenses in which physical force and abuse are not employed and that involve offenders and victims who are familiar with each other and are associated in continuing relationships of a nonsexual kind.

## Reactions to Rape and Child Molestation

Rape and sexual acts with minors have long been placed in the category of heinous crimes. Even when legal codes were in their formative stages, little sympathy was extended to rapists, child molesters, and those committing incest with children. The usual penalties have been death, banishment, and, in recent years, long prison sentences. Notwithstanding this tradition, public and official reactions to offenders have not been clear-cut. Rather, though generally punitive, reactions have depended on such things as who the offender is, who the victim is, and what kind of interaction the two had.

Although most state codes have at one time or another identified rape as a capital crime, for instance, those offenders most likely to receive the death penalty have been blacks. Since 1930 there have been 455 executions for rape; of those executed, nearly 90 percent were blacks. To these legal executions we must add the hundreds of blacks who were lynched for alleged sexual offenses against white women (Valantini, 1956). The feeling among some whites, particularly in the South, seems to have been that only the most severe penalty matches the outrage committed when a black man violates the social taboos surrounding white-black relations and has sex with a white woman. Whether rape was actually committed — and in numerous cases this certainly was not established — seems to have been largely beside the point. A black simply did not become "intimate" with a white, especially a white woman. The charge of rape provided a vehicle for the imposition of death, which usually matched the legal punishment for rape and, also important, exonerated the white female, who, whites could argue, would never have consented to sexual intimacies with a black. The charge and the punishment thus reinforced prevailing prejudices and discriminatory practices.

The general sense of what "true" rape is affects trial and sentencing. Important to this image are the characteristics of the victim and how she has behaved before and during the rape. If she is a virgin, a minor, or very old, and if there is circumstantial evidence that she put up resistance and was overcome by force, the offender is likely to be convicted and receive a severe sentence. In one study, for example, judges of the Philadelphia court system admitted giving considerable weight to circumstantial evidence about the alleged victim and her behavior (Bohm, 1974). These judges seemed to believe in only one kind of true rape, that fitting the popular image described earlier: the stranger leaping out of shadows in the dark alley. When perceived as a genuine victim of rape, the woman received a sympathetic hearing and the offender a severe sentence. It was different, however, when judges perceived the case to be one of "consensual intercourse" (described by some judges as "friendly rape," "felonious gallantry," "assault with failure to please," or "breach of contract") or of "female vindictiveness." Though such perceptions may have been based solely on the fact that, say, the woman had met her attacker in a bar and had allowed him to drive her home, the judicial response was typically unsympathetic to the victim and lenient or supportive to the defendant.

A glaring example of judicial bias and possibly of modern misogyny occurred in Dane County, Wisconsin, in 1977. A 15-year-old boy was convicted of assaulting a 16-year-old girl in a high school stairwell. The judge put the boy on probation, later explaining his decision as follows:

> I'm trying to say to women, stop teasing. There should be a restoration of modesty in dress and elimination from the community of sexual gratification business. . . . Whether women like it or not they are sex objects. Are we supposed to take an impressionable person 15 or 16 years of age and punish that person severely because they react to it normally? (*Time*, September 12, 1977)

The judge was subsequently removed from office through a public referendum. Other judges with similar views are doubtless sitting in some of the nation's courts today.

Another illustration of the emphasis placed on the victim's own behavior is found in two cases reported by D. A. Thomas (1967) in a review of sentencing decisions in English rape trials and appeals. In one case, a girl of 16 had been forcibly carried into a van and subsequently raped by two men. In the other case, a girl of 20 accepted a ride from two men (both of whom had previous convictions for criminal offenses), whereupon she was driven to a secluded spot and raped three times, twice by one man and once by the other. The various defendants were found guilty, but those involved in the second incident received lighter sentences than did those in the first. According to Thomas, "The difference in sentence between this case and the previous one can be explained by reference to the girl's acceptance of a lift, as opposed to being dragged forcibly into the car" (p. 515). On what grounds, one may ask, does agreement to ride with a man make his subsequent rape of the hitchhiker somehow less serious than if he had forced her into the car?

Sexual assault of children commonly provokes severe reactions. The mere attempted sexual molestation of a minor was rated eighteenth in seriousness out of 204 offenses in the recent National Crime Survey of public attitudes (Wolfgang et al., 1985). Even so, it is interesting to note that when children are the victims of sexual assault, an arrested offender is slightly *less* likely to be imprisoned for a year or more than if the victims are adults. In either case, the figure is less than 20 percent (Bureau of Justice Statistics, 1984h).

When pubescent children are involved, marked variations in official reactions have been observed. Again, much is made of the victims themselves and of their apparent role in bringing the offense about. Two more examples from England will suffice as illustrations. In one case, a young man had numerous episodes of sexual intercourse with a 14-year-old girl he had met at a dancing school. "It was accepted that the girl was a very willing participant." In another case, a married father of four children had repeated acts of sexual intercourse with his 15-year-old sister-in-law. Circumstantial evidence was entered to support the view that the girl "had been the real instigator." In both of these cases an appeals court reduced the sentences imposed by the trial judge on the major grounds of victim interest and participation (Thomas, 1967).

In general, the chances of obtaining a conviction in cases of sexual assault, especially rape, are slim. When the victims are neither very old nor very young females, the chances are reduced yet further. The fact is that rape juries, as a rule, are dominated by males, not the usual situation in other criminal trials. According to a 1972 editorial in the *Yale Law Journal:* "The existing evidence indicates that juries view rape charges with extraordinary suspicion and rarely return convictions in the absence of aggravating circumstances, such as extrinsic violence" (Anon., 1972:1380). Indeed, most states require that witness testimony be corroborated by external evidence of sexual assault (torn clothing, physical injury, weapons, and so forth). The uncorroborated testimony of the victim, no matter how compelling, cannot be the sole basis for a conviction. Although these rules are being challenged in many states, and although there have been some reforms in recent years (New York State modified the corroboration rules in 1972), there remain doubts as to how successful these challenges will be. At least two states (Georgia and Idaho) beefed up the corroboration rules, making prosecution and conviction in rape cases much more difficult.

There is no better way to sum up the tragedy of rape than from a woman's perspective. The "Missoula Rape Poem" is by Marge Piercy and is quoted by Stephen Box (1983:120):

There is no difference between being raped
and being pushed down a flight of cement steps
except that the wounds also bleed inside.

There is no difference between being raped
and being run over by a truck
except that afterward men ask if you enjoyed it.

There is no difference between being raped
and losing a hand in a mowing machine
except that doctors don't want to get involved,
the police wear a knowing smirk,
and in small towns you become a veteran whore.

There is no difference between being raped
and going head first through a windshield
except that afterward you are afraid
not of cars
but half the human race.

# CHAPTER 7

# Robbery: Theft by Violence

Activities that include the display of physical force are called "heavy" crimes in street argot. As a rule, heavy crime involves the calculated, instrumental use of violence. Typically, violence is threatened or used to deprive the victim of things of value — money, goods, or services. Examples of such crimes are armed robbery, strong-arm robbery, hijacking, piracy, and extortion.

## Heavy Crime in History and Law

Activities of the theft-by-violence type are identified as crimes in some of the oldest known legal codes. Thus we find mention of robbery in Hammurapi's Code, in Roman law, and in the laws of various Anglo-Saxon kings. These early laws were rather vague, however, and it is not always clear precisely what behavior the word *robbery* meant. Even so, in Anglo-Saxon and early Norman law robbery was quite distinct from mere theft, and those who interpreted the law paid particular attention to the violence of the offense. Indeed, one of Henry III's judges, Henry de Bracton, reminded his colleagues that whatever else robbery may be, it is still a form of theft (in Pollock and Maitland, 1968:494). Bracton's influence was substantial, and after the middle of the thirteenth century, robbery was treated in common law as *aggravated theft*.

It is interesting to note that the Anglo-Saxon and early Norman distinction between robbery and theft may have rested largely on a prevailing ethical judgment regarding the two sorts of activities and their perpetrators. Theft was considered a dishonorable activity, and the thief was accorded little respect as a person. Those who steal do so by guile, cunning, stealth, and deceitfulness. Those who rob, on the other hand, do so through direct confrontation with the victim, who, as a result of the challenge, is given an opportunity to fight in defense of his possessions. At least the robber is open and honest!

While similar views are apparently held by some robbers today, the prevailing theme expressed in dominant American culture is that robbery is one of the more heinous offenses. To explain why feudal England maintained a somewhat different view, one must look at the sociopolitical climate of the times. Physical confrontation permeated medieval England. It could be seen in the almost perpetual battles and wars being fought at home and abroad; it was encouraged as sport; and it had an integral role in the prevailing system of justice, whether in the form of self-help retaliation and feuding or trial by ordeal and official punishments. If physical confrontation is an integral part of a society's way of life, the shape in which it comes and the kind of people who indulge in it may not matter much.

**Bandits and Highwaymen** Although medieval England may have shown grudging respect for the robber and his trade, lawmakers lost little time in designating robbery as one of the more serious felony crimes, punishable by death. As far as the evidence allows, there are two reasons for this turn of events: one, concerning the frequency of offenses of the robbery type; the other, the nature of the victims.

During the thirteenth and fourteenth centuries, banditry and plundering appear to have gained in popularity as a means of subsistence for increasing numbers of oppressed and dispossessed serfs and peasants. These were hard times, made even harder by a pervasive inequality that kept the poor and lowly completely at the mercy of the rich and powerful. These were the times when tales about Robin Hood flourished, for the common people could find in his exploits solutions to their own miserable condition. Robin Hood did all the things they wanted to do but could not. But most of all, these were times of resistance and innovation: Resistance found shape in the largely unsuccessful peasant revolts; innovation found shape in banditry. Robin Hood provided the *modus operandi,* and bands of marauding robbers plied their trade around the countryside. Joined by out-of-work soldiers and men of fortune, the ranks of the robbers swelled as feudalism began to decay.

The victims were often the rich and the powerful. Though we have no way of knowing the actual distribution of robbery victims throughout the three great classes — nobility and landed gentry, churchmen, and peasantry — it is more than likely that most victims came from the first two classes. For one thing, these were the people most likely to travel from one part of the country to the next, making them easy prey for the robber whose territory was the field, the footpath, and the forest. Second, these were the people most likely to have things of value, or to have in their homes and churches possessions worth stealing. And third, these were the people at whose feet responsibility for the pervasive personal and collective troubles could be laid. What better victims could the robber find?

The growing incidence of heavy crime and the high status of its victims probably account for the severity with which robbers were handled under law. And severely handled they were: the scaffold continually felt the weight of the highwayman and bandit. By the sixteenth century, robbers who challenged their victims in dwelling houses and on public highways were denied "benefit of clergy." This simply meant that those who might previously have escaped the gallows because of birth or occupation now found it more difficult to do so. The removal of benefit of clergy may have been related to the appearance of a new category of highway robbers. During the highwayman's golden age, which stretched from the early sixteenth century until the early eighteenth century, many highwaymen were of noble birth or substantial means. Their trade permitted such people the opportunity to humiliate their peers and political adversaries and make off with plunder in the process (Pringle, n.d.). It is not surprising that those in power should have made certain that the "gentlemen robbers," as they were popularly called, did not escape full punishment for their audacity.

## THE CRIME OF ROBBERY AS DEFINED IN THE MODEL PENAL CODE

A person is guilty of robbery if, in the course of committing a theft he:

   (a) inflicts serious bodily injury upon another; or

   (b) threatens another with or purposely puts him in fear of immediate serious bodily injury. . . .

An act shall be deemed "in the course of committing a theft" if it occurs in an attempt to commit theft or in flight after the attempt or commission.

SOURCE: Excerpted from the Model Penal Code, copyright 1962 by The American Law Institute. Reprinted with the permission of The American Law Institute.

---

**Piracy**   As the era of the highwayman declined, a new form of heavy crime made its appearance, this time on the high seas: piracy. Relatively unknown before the dawn of international sea trade and exploration, "piracy emerged in the Western Hemisphere in response to a unique interaction of many natural and social events" (Inciardi, 1975:87). The exploitation of the New World provided rich cargoes, the plunder of which was made viable by the existence of well-situated islands that provided hiding and cover for the pirates, and by the increasing mastery of the sea made possible by developments in maritime technology. As navies grew, moreover, more and more seamen had sufficient knowledge of the sea to make piracy an option for the exercise of their skills.

But some of the same factors that helped piracy develop also ushered in its decline. Naval warfare, advances in technology, growth in national fleets, international maritime agreements, and the advance of civilization each helped erect insurmountable obstacles to the buccaneer. His ships became outgunned, outmanned, and out-of-date; his escape routes and hiding places were controlled by treaties and regularly patrolling fleets; his seamen were pressed into legitimate service or volunteered for it; and the maritime frontiers closed. The nineteenth century witnessed little piracy.

**Frontier Outlaws**   In nineteenth-century America, meanwhile, heavy crime was flourishing in the form of cattle rustlers, bank and train robbers, marauding bands of outlaws, and lone bandits in search of quick money. For in America, the frontier had been moving south and west, and with it went robbery, plunder, and violence. Just as robbery flourished in England during periods of social and political upheaval, so it did in America. The turbulent decades of the nineteenth century witnessed unprecedented personal and group lawlessness. First stagecoaches and then trains became the favorite targets of organized bands of outlaws and "road agents," as the highway robbers were called. Organized in gangs or operating alone, the road agents, American counterparts of the English highwayman, plied the countryside. For some of them this was a form of moonlighting. Their legitimate occupations were of all kinds, and some road agents were small-town marshals and deputies who could use their police cover to advantage: "A man skilled with a gun might serve as outlaw, sheriff, and hero of his people at various stages of his usually short-lived career as a social bandit" (Lyman and Scott, 1975:139).

The sprouting mining camps on the edges of the western frontier became the scenes of numerous battles between miners and outlaws, and among miners themselves, as people sought easy wealth by robbing companies or individuals of gold and silver. The nineteenth century was also the era of bank robberies. From Montana, the Dakotas, and Minnesota in the north, to New Mexico and Texas in the south, few banks were secure.

These developments were in part mere extensions of America's experiences when the Mississippi valley was its western frontier. As Philip Jordon (1970:102–103) describes the Mississippi situation:

> Piracy and robbery increased with the spread of settlements. Both steamboats and river towns were looted not only by individuals but also by organized groups of desperadoes. The Chicester and Morrell gangs operated on the lower river, and the Timber Wolves and the Brown gang terrorized residents in Iowa, Illinois, and Missouri. Navou, the Mormon settlement, was felt by many to be the center of Middle Border crime. The steamer *Kentuckian* was robbed of $37,000 in September 1831, and a few months later a passenger on the *Peruvian* was robbed of a trunk containing $2,500. Such thefts could be multiplied many times over. St. Louis newspapers, as the decades advanced, regularly reported steamboat robberies.

Frontier heavy crime reached its height following the conclusion of the Civil War. Thousands of discharged soldiers were left to their own devices, and many apparently found banditry a solution to their problems. Evidence shows, too, that some soldiers from the losing side organized themselves into bands of plundering outlaws whose major victims were initially "Yankee enemies." As with the gentlemen robbers of seventeenth-century England, their crimes seem to have been motivated, in part at least, by a desire to get back at and humiliate those they considered responsible for their loss of status and jobs and their financial woes.

Of the many factors that supported this era of heavy crime, probably the most important was the ready availability and common use of firearms. Even as late as 1890 few states considered the carrying or drawing of firearms a serious offense. Another influence was the natural environment itself — its geographic size and physical contours. Not only did the frontier have miles and miles of unsettled land where outlaws could roam at will, but "the successful planning and execution of their crimes were made possible by the topography of confusing ranges of high mountains, segmented by wide deserts, and creviced with inaccessible canyons (Inciardi, 1975:91). A final influence was the public sentiment of the period, one best summed up in the mystique surrounding the outlaws whose ties to the fallen Confederacy made them noble victims of tragic circumstance:

> Characteristic of the mystique surrounding the noble robber is that he begins his career not as a criminal but as a victim of injustice, that he rights wrongs, that he

robs the rich to feed the poor, that he never kills except in self-defense or just revenge, that he never deserts his people, that he is admired, aided, respected by his compatriots, that he dies because of betrayal, and, finally, that he is regarded as invulnerable. . . . No sooner is the bandit killed than popular legend restores him to life. (Lyman and Scott 1975:139)

The Younger brothers, the Dalton boys, Frank and Jesse James, Henry Starr, and Sam Bass are but a few of the outlaws eulogized in folktales and popular songs. Even while the James brothers were carrying out their most ruthless robberies, observers were ready with explanations laying the blame anywhere but at the outlaws' feet. This is certainly far from the popular sentiment regarding most robbers today.

With the dawn of the twentieth century, the era of the frontier outlaw was already on the wane. The frontier itself had disappeared as the railroads conquered the deserts, and urbanization took hold of strategic points throughout the entire country. Going, too, were some of the other conditions that had lent support to banditry. Large-scale unemployment vanished with World War I, law enforcement achieved unprecedented sophistication and professionalism, and the sociopolitical climate began to stabilize. While the depression years revived for a time some of the features of the bandit era, with John Dillinger, "Pretty Boy" Floyd, Bonnie and Clyde, and "Baby Face" Nelson playing key roles, the period from the late 1930s until the present saw the demise of frontier-style heavy crime.

## Robbery Today

In 1984, 485,008 robberies made up around 4 percent of the total index crimes reported by the FBI but accounted for 38 percent of those index offenses involving interpersonal force. Although robbery rates increased steadily during the 1960s and 1970s, the police rates have declined since 1981 by nearly 20 percent. But National Crime Survey data also show a decline in victimizations from robbery, and so we can be confident that there has been a real decline. The most likely explanation for this is that there has been a corresponding drop in the youthful population. Robbery is a crime of the young. Even though robberies take diverse forms and involve different circumstances, all FBI categories show decreases (see Figure 7.1).

Some features tend to be shared by many of the incidents on which we have information. Data compiled by the FBI, as well as those produced by a number of in-depth studies of robbery (Conklin, 1972; Normandeau, 1968; Sagalyn, 1971) indicate the following tendencies:

**1. Robbery tends to occur most frequently in the more highly populated cities of the country.** Larger cities experience higher rates than do smaller cities, and the lowest rates are found in rural areas. In 1975, for

**Figure 7.1** Trends in robbery by circumstance, 1980–1984

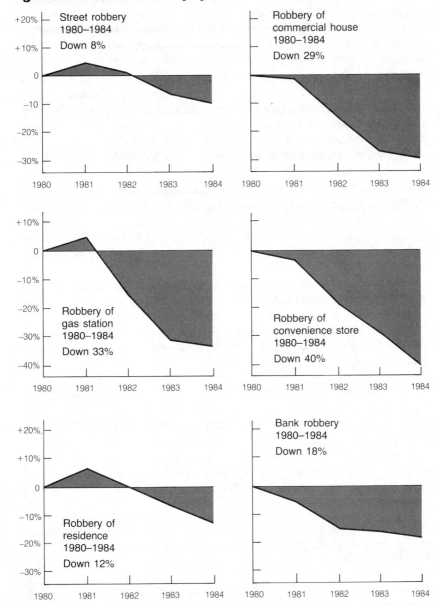

example, the fifty-eight largest American cities accounted for around two-thirds of the reported robberies.

**2. Robbery tends to involve offenders and victims who are strangers.** Although the percentages vary from city to city, estimates of the proportion of incidents involving strangers go as high as 90 percent.

**3. Robbery offenders tend to be young males.** Males between the ages of 15 and 25 predominate in arrest statistics for robbery. In addition, it seems that black males are more likely than white males to be identified as the offender in robbery incidents. Sixty percent of those arrested in 1981 were black, and 39 percent were white, according to the FBI.

**4. Robbery victims tend to be males over age 21.** Males are much more likely than females to be the victims of robbery. Whereas offenders are more likely to be blacks, the most likely victims are white males.

**5. Robbery tends to take place "on the street."** Although the percentages vary from city to city and from one part of a city to another, nationally, around 52 percent of recorded robbery incidents occur in the open — in alleys, outside bars, in streets, in parking lots, or in playgrounds.

**6. The robbery offender tends to be in possession of a weapon.** The most typical robbery is an armed robbery, with guns being used around 40 percent of the time. However, weapons are rarely used to inflict injury.

**7. The victim tends not to be injured or to be only slightly injured during the commission of a robbery.** Victimization data show seven out of ten victims are not injured.

These seven features of robberies indicate the nature of the most typical robbery in day-to-day urban living. However, as stressed at the beginning of this section, it would be misleading to think of robbery in just these terms. In recent years criminologists have drawn attention to differences in robbery and in the effort to make sense of them have suggested a number of robbery typologies or classifications. Let us then consider some of these typologies and, in doing so, draw a more complete picture of robbery and the robbery offender.

## Robbery Typologies

The two best-known typologies dealing with robbery are those by F. H. McClintock and Evelyn Gibson and by John Conklin. The first focuses on the circumstances in which the victim is attacked; the second on the robbery offender. McClintock and Gibson (1961), in their London study, offer a fivefold classification of robbery circumstances.

> **Group I: Robbery of persons who, as part of their employment, are in charge of money or goods.** This group includes robbery of shops,

banks, taxis, factories, offices, and other commercial establishments where money is likely to be handled on a regular basis by employees.

**Group II: Robbery in the open following a sudden attack.** Included here are street offenses such as mugging, yoking (putting an arm around the victim's neck from behind and pulling back on it), purse snatching, and other unprovoked, unexpected stickups.

**Group III: Robbery on private premises.** This includes robberies by persons who gained entry by force or who were disturbed by a member of the household after breaking and entering the premises.

**Group IV: Robbery after preliminary association of short duration between victim and offender.** This includes situations such as those in which the victim and offender have come together for purposes of prostitution or homosexual encounters or in which they have been drinking together in a bar or at a party. In incidents involving prostitution, whether heterosexual or homosexual, the victim may be either the prostitute or the client.

**Group V: Robbery after previous association of some duration between the victim and offender.** This includes robbery by a friend, lover, or coworker.

Some of the advantages of a classification of this sort are listed by the authors:

> There are several advantages in a classification based on the circumstances in which the victim was attacked. It is sufficiently objective to be applied in any police area; it can include all crimes recorded by the police, and not only those in which an offender has been apprehended; and it indicates the vulnerability of different classes of person to attack. (McClintock and Gibson, 1961:15)

In the London study the authors found that groups I and II accounted for around 70 percent of the robbery incidents recorded by the police in both 1950 and 1957. Over that period, however, robberies of persons in charge of money or goods (group I) had increased more than those in group II. The authors speculated that London robbery was looking more and more like the work of professionals — those who sought out lucrative targets and, among other things, made robbery a steady source of income.

**Differences Between Groups I and II**   The substantial differences between the robbery circumstances for groups I and II revolve around the robber, the victim, the method, and the losses. In robberies of persons in charge of money, the offender is likely to be older than robbers in the sudden attack situation (group II), in which juveniles and young adults predominate. The sudden attack robber is opportunistic, inexperienced, and casually involved in this form of violent theft. The victims come from all walks of life, and if women and children are the victims, they are more likely to be found in sudden attack robberies. Violence, too, is more likely to occur in sudden attack robberies than in robberies of persons in charge of money, though weapons are less likely to be carried in sudden attack robberies. (For more information on this, see pp. 188–192.) The amount stolen is likely to be greater in robberies of persons in charge of money than in sudden attack situations. Sudden attack robberies are more likely to occur during the hours of darkness and in relatively isolated spots such as parks, alleys, and dimly lit streets. Understandably, robberies of persons in charge of money are most likely to occur during business hours and involve spatial patterns reflecting the location of businesses.

**London and Philadelphia Data Compared**   To date, only one published application of the McClintock and Gibson typology has been made to robbery in America. This was done by Andre Normandeau (1970) as part of his larger study of robbery in Philadelphia. Using a 10 percent sample of robbery incidents from 1960 to 1966, Normandeau discovered that as in London, sudden attack robberies tend to involve young males who are unarmed and who strike lone victims in isolated places. However, he also found some important differences. Groups I and II accounted for over 70 percent of the robberies he investigated, as in London, but sudden attack robberies far outnumbered robberies of persons in charge of money as part of their jobs. In addition, sudden attack robberies in Philadelphia were much more likely to involve female victims than those in London.

How are we to interpret these differences? Normandeau comes to the tentative conclusion, which he admits is rather speculative, that London witnessed more organized robbery than Philadelphia. It is tentative and speculative, since the data pertain to robbery incidents rather than robbery offenders. To find out about such things as organization, planning, decision making, and professionalism we need more information about the robbers themselves. Neither the London nor the Philadelphia data really permit inferences about these dimensions of the robbery situation.

A more recent study of robbery in London suggests that sudden attack robberies have increased dramatically in that city since the McClintock–Gibson study was undertaken. The characteristics of these muggings have been detailed by Michael Pratt (1980), who argues that the increase is partly a reflection of greater opportunities to commit the crime and partly a result of greater opportunities to get away with it.

Pratt looked at a sample of muggings in London from February through August for each of the years 1971 through 1974. The following picture emerged: 80 percent of the victims were males, most of them over age 21; most of the offenders were also males, over 70 percent of those who could be identified being under age 17; 70 percent of the incidents involved no apparent weapon; the most common situation involved a single victim attacked by two assailants; 80 percent occurred in the street, and in half the cases less than $15 in cash was taken; finally, nearly 60 percent of the assailants were identified as black, whereas 80 percent of the victims were white.

## MUGGING: THE "PERFECT CRIME" FOR SOME?

The disproportionate involvement of young males, especially young black males, in both American and English muggings needs explanation. One interesting theory has been advanced by Jefferson and Clarke (1973), two British sociologists. These authors couch their explanation in terms of criminal opportunities and rationality, while calling attention to the fact that robbery is both instrumental *and* expressive for many offenders.

Opportunities for sudden attack robbery abound in urban settings. Furthermore, young black males in both England and America are disproportionately among the unemployed and the underemployed. They are also disproportionately among the undereducated and the underhoused. According to Jefferson and Clarke, these impersonal structural inequalities are made *personal* for many young blacks through racism. In England this ugly phenomenon has been directed primarily at black West Indian immigrants; in America the roots of racism go back to slavery, and remnants of that era are in evidence everywhere.

But what are the options for blacks? Jefferson and Clarke argue that in England the younger West Indians have three basic options in life: politics, crime, and drugs. Both the politics and the crime are of a self-assertive confrontational kind: the former in its ideological commitment to raising black consciousness, the latter in its victimizing character and especially its violence.

Jefferson and Clarke see mugging as a desperate solution to a desperate situation. In the eyes of many young blacks, it is the best available solution: It provides money to supplement meagre finances while also allowing for the expression of toughness and masculinity, the assertion of identity and status as a "man" and the opportunity to strike fear in native whites, the dominant class. The imagery supported by popular Reggae music, with its character, "Rudie," the "super cool hooligan who always comes out on top," may well have reinforced the defiant, aggressive behavior displayed by many young, inner-city blacks — and whites, for that matter.

Street robbery is an easy crime to commit, requiring little criminal knowledge or skill to execute, just victims with cash or valuables who are alone or unprotected. In the comparison of alternatives that rationalists presume we all make, an available, easily accessible, easily committed crime that carries the potential for quick gains at minimal risk and cost while also providing an opportunity to satisfy expressive needs must look attractive to many inner-city blacks whose motivations for crime are fueled by inequities, boredom, and racism.

If these pulls and pushes are indeed as strong as Jefferson and Clarke suggest, then it is surprising that most blacks have *not* taken to the streets to victimize the incautious who cross their path. For indeed, most young blacks are not muggers. And the racist element in the argument will not go far in explaining intraracial mugging, of which there is plenty. If race is important, it is more likely an artifact of the routine activities of whites, who go abroad more freely and are more likely to be carrying cash and credit cards, than it is a driving force in the consciousness of muggers bent on "getting even." Still, Jefferson's and Clarke's account is intriguing and, with modifications, may explain much of the street robbery in the cities of America as well as England.

## ROBBERY OFFENDERS

Do robbers plan, premeditate, and organize their robberies? Do they use weapons, and if so, why? How do they carry out their robberies? Are they "one-time losers" when convicted, or do they have a history of involvement in robbery or in other criminal offenses? What happens to them when they are arrested and go to court? Do different types of robbers exist, and if so, do they commit different types of robberies?

These questions can be answered only with information about robbers themselves. An attempt to shed light on these questions is John Conklin's (1972) study of robbery in Boston. Focusing on the robbery offender, Conklin devised a typology of robbers based on interviews with prison inmates. He then used this typology to make sense out of the data on robbery contained in police and court records.

**The Professional Robber**   Conklin describes the professional robber as

> . . . the type of offender who reflects the image of the robber in the public's mind. He is portrayed in the media as the bandit who carefully plans his robbery, executes the crime with a group of accomplices, and steals large sums of money which are used to support a hedonistic life style. He exhibits a long-term deep-seated commitment to robbery as a means of getting money and carries out his holdups with skill and planning. . . .
>
> We will here define professionals as *those who manifest a long-term commitment to crime as a source of livelihood, who plan and organize their crimes prior to committing them, and who seek money to support a particular life style that may be called hedonistic.* (1972:63)

According to Conklin, two main types of professionals are involved in robbery: those who do it almost exclusively and those who are committed to some other form of crime (such as burglary) but may occasionally commit a robbery. The professional robber is one who engages in robbery exclusively, or almost exclusively, and for whom it is the main source of income. Professional robbers are probably the least numerous.

**The Opportunist Robber**   Unlike professional robbers, opportunist robbers commit a variety of property crimes besides robbery, which is a relatively infrequent activity for them. Also in contrast with professional robbers, opportunists rarely score in a big way, and the small amounts they do obtain are generally for spur-of-the-moment needs or to maintain their life-style or peer group image. The more favored targets for the opportunist are women with purses, drunks, cabdrivers, and people who walk alone on dark streets. Opportunists tend to be young black males, relatively inexperienced in serious crime, who come from lower-class slum backgrounds. Their robberies are mostly unplanned, haphazard affairs, and the decision to rob is often a sudden thing, influenced by momentary pressures and the availability of a vulnerable victim. The opportunist is commonly involved in a sudden attack robbery and in the robbery of small shops. Conklin offers the following illustration as typical of the opportunist robber:

> One night, George and two friends stole a car. While driving around the city, one suggested that they get a little extra spending money. The driver stopped the car next to an elderly lady who was alone on the street. George got out and grabbed the lady's purse, then ran back to the car and the group drove away. (1972:70)

These youths netted seventeen dollars and were eventually caught and charged with unarmed robbery.

**The Addict Robber**   This category is a rather peculiar one, for it includes those who are addicted to drugs and commit robberies in order to support their habits, and those who simply use drugs — most notably amphetamines, psychedelics, and assorted pills — and whose robberies may or may not be motivated by need for cash to buy more drugs. Conklin brings them together in this category because they share a low level of commitment to robbery — it is often considered a last resort, a dangerous, risky business — because they seem to engage in little planning or deliberation before they rob and because they are likely to use the proceeds for drug purchases. Since they are not all addicts, the label seems a misnomer.

The relationship between drugs and robbery is difficult to assess, and most authorities are inclined to maintain that nothing about drugs as a substance leads to robbery, or to any crime for that matter. On the other hand, no one questions that those who are dependent on drug use, especially males, will rob to finance their habit when other avenues to cash appear closed off. The extent to which robbery is drug related in this way is extremely hard to establish. Evidence does suggest that other property offenses — for example, burglary, shoplifting, and larceny — are more likely than robbery is to be drug related. In any event the horror stories we hear through the media about drugs and violent property crime probably overstate the issue. (In Chapter 11 we further investigate drugs and crime.)

**The Alcoholic Robber**   This is the least convincing of Conklin's four categories of robbers. Apart from the fact that it is based on interviews with only seven inmates and relies on their claims to having been drunk at the time of their robberies, nothing definitive emerges in Conklin's descriptions of the robber who typifies this category. He is painted as part opportunist, part addict, and above all as someone who is driven to his crime by the effects of alcohol. Perhaps because alcohol affects people differently, nothing in Conklin's account provides grounds for making any predictions about such things as motivation, method, and use of violence. Some of the alcoholic robbers he describes apparently committed their robberies to gain cash for drinking purchases, two took their victims' money as an afterthought, having first beaten them up, and one robbed to recover the money he had lost in a card game. The major issue throughout seems to be that alcohol somehow induced the offender to commit his robbery, and this is the key distinction between this and the second and third categories.

Conklin's typology is useful nevertheless because it helps us understand robbery from the standpoint of those who engage in it — why and how they do it and what happens to them — and because it helps us predict patterns of robbery and societal reaction to it on the basis of the differences between them. In America there seems to be little doubt that the bulk of robbers are opportunistic; however, it is also likely that addict robbers account for the highest rates of robbery when the categories are compared.

## Violence in Robbery

Both legal and popular conceptions emphasize violence as a key feature of robbery. Whether actually used or merely threatened, physical force gives robbery its unique character as one type of criminal theft. Because force may be used, robbery is looked at with fear and apprehension. Robbery and assaultive crimes readily come to mind when people explain why they are afraid to go out alone at night, why they stay off the streets at night, and why they avoid talking to strangers. In his investigation of public conceptions of crime, Albert Biderman (1967) found that most of those interviewed in Washington, D.C., thought of crime in terms of personal attacks, and similar findings have been uncovered in other studies. Prevailing beliefs concerning robbery, particularly in its more common street forms, appear to be little different from these 1950 observations by journalist Howard Whitman.

> The hoodlum will bash in your head with a brick for a dollar and ninety-eight cents. The police records of our cities are spotted with cases of "murder for peanuts" in which the victims, both men and women, have been slugged, stabbed, hit with iron pipes, hammers or axes, and in a few cases kicked to death — the loot being no more than the carfare a woman carried in her purse or the small change in a man's pocket. (1951:5)

It is true that the kinds of things Whitman describes do occur in some robbery incidents. But how valid is this as a general description of robbery in America today? What roles does violence play in robbery incidents? Why and when does the threat of violence become actual violence? Are robbers likely to injure or kill their victims as a general rule, or is physical assault a relatively rare occurrence in robbery?

We have already seen that on the whole robbery incidents do not result in

Bank robbery by amateurs used to be rare; now it is the rule. Usually young and inexperienced, the robber has no careful plans and rarely gets away with it.

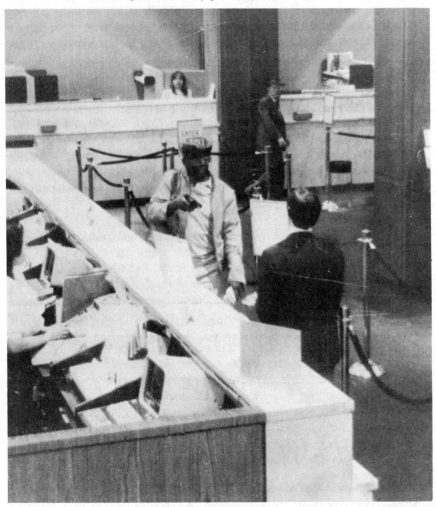

physical injury to the victims. When injury does occur, it is usually minor, requiring no hospitalization. The degrees of violence that can occur in a robbery incident range from threat alone to fatal assault. This means that the designation of robbery as a "crime of violence" tends to gloss over variations in the kind and degree of physical aggression actually found in particular robbery cases:

> There are many variations, ranging from an armed bank robbery in which several people are shot and injured to minor thefts such as purse snatching, where force or the threat of force is used. Dramatically profiling the lower end of the robbery spectrum was the report of an offense in which one of two 9-year-old

boys twisted the arm of the other in the schoolyard in order to obtain 25 cents of the latter's lunch money. Because force was used, the police correctly recorded and counted the act as "highway robbery." . . . While these less serious events should be recorded, it does not seem reasonable to include them in the same category as the more serious offenses. (Mulvihill and Tumin, 1969:25)

The FBI now distinguishes between armed and unarmed robbery. According to its reports, armed robberies outnumber unarmed robberies about three to two. But this still tells us nothing about the actual use of violence, since the presence of a weapon does not mean that it will be used to inflict injury. Indeed, evidence from the National Commission and from Conklin's Boston study show that injury is more likely to occur in cases in which the offenders are unarmed than where they are armed. In the eighteen cities covered by these studies, violence only infrequently involved shooting or stabbing; it was far more likely to amount to kicking, shoving, beating, or knocking down.

The tendency for violence to erupt in unarmed robbery incidents is not hard to explain. First, the offenders place themselves in a situation in which they have no obviously deadly weapon with which to intimidate the victim. To impress upon the victim that they mean business the robbers may therefore resort to a display of actual violence. With a gun or knife present, such a display may be unnecessary — the victim is sufficiently intimidated to offer no resistance.

Second, much unarmed robbery is of the sudden attack variety. A successful sudden attack robbery depends as much on the element of surprise and the speedy commission of the theft as it does on intimidation. The opportunist robber, bent on getting as much as possible and then making an escape uses violence in an instrumental way: it helps ensure that the victim is in no position to resist even if he or she wanted to do so, and it makes escape more likely. It may also lessen the chances that the victim will be clearheaded enough to identify the robber for the police.

Although violence is most likely to occur in situations in which the robber is unarmed, most robberies do involve the use of weapons. If weapons are present, why is force not used in most cases? We have already touched on one possible answer — the mere appearance of a weapon is sufficient to intimidate the victim and secure compliance with the robber's demands. If victim compliance is the key to use or nonuse of force in armed robberies, then we should expect to find the following two conditions in the typical armed robbery: (1) no victim resistance, or resistance so meek that a gesture with the weapon is all that is needed to secure compliance, and (2) a tendency for the robber to use force in cases in which the victim offers more than meek resistance. Some evidence indicates that both these conditions hold. For example, Conklin (1972) found in Boston that most victims did not resist (more than 80 percent in both 1964 and 1968). When the victim did resist, however, armed robbers were more likely to use force.

But this is not the end of the story. Enough cases are left to indicate that compliance per se cannot adequately account for the use or nonuse of force in armed robberies. Again using the Boston findings, more than half of those with firearms did not use force, even though their victims resisted. Conversely, around 15 percent of offenders with guns, and around a third of those with knives, used force, even with no resistance.

In such cases we must look more closely at the robber for possible explanations. What we have learned about offender types might shed some light on the issue. We know, for example, that opportunist robbers are neither continually involved in robbery nor committed to it as a career and that their robberies are often unplanned. In the usual opportunist robbery (particularly when undertaken by a group of offenders), weapons are not used. But a relatively inexperienced armed opportunist may be frightened and confused by the confrontation or perhaps carried away with it. If frightened or confused, this offender's use or nonuse of force may be a consequence of those factors likely to heighten his or her mental state — for example, the appearance of a third party, a counterthreat by the victim, an alarm going off, a weakening of resolve, or a conflict between immediate desire and pressure from significant others. The opportunist may get carried away with the exploit and use force even when the victim does not resist. This may happen when friends are looking on or participating or when the offender interprets the robbery confrontation and use of a weapon as an opportunity to display toughness.

## Doing Robbery: Management of a Mugging

Robert Lejeune (1977) has interviewed young New York City muggers, some with little experience and others claiming several hundred robberies over a six-year period. Lejeune calls mugging "a primitive form of crime . . . practiced by those too young, or otherwise too inept, to execute crimes requiring greater skill and knowledge." The mugger's success is dependent on skills and knowledge acquired on the street, where survival means being cool and tough and where interaction is often physical.

Lejeune describes how his subjects handled or "managed" their mugging activities. The *preconfrontation phase* consists of (1) managing their own fears and (2) selecting a victim. The very idea of confronting a stranger is fearful, especially to inexperienced muggers. With practice, however, young muggers learn to manage those fears by defining the activity as normal or routine. This process of "normalization" is facilitated by repeated successes, which help muggers lower their estimates of the risks and increase their estimates of the rewards, which for some muggers are intrinsic as well as extrinsic.

Muggers must contend with three threats to their safety: the police, the victim, and any witnesses. Of these, victims are seen as the least predictable and controllable. Therefore, emphasis is placed on selection of the "right" victim. They generally look for those people who are least likely to offer resistance and/or most likely to offer an acceptable payoff. However, Lejeune found little consensus on just who fit the image of the right victim. Some muggers preferred women or old people, but others did not.

During the *confrontation phase,* muggers must "denormalize" the situation for the victim and then maintain control. They accomplish the first by inducing fear, shock, and disbelief through threats and sometimes a display of actual force. A posture of toughness helps muggers maintain control, but in the event that this control weakens, they may resort to "reactive" force, a display of violence designed to counteract what the muggers interpret (perhaps erroneously) as resistance. The following is how one of Lejeune's muggers justified his use of violence (1977:144):

> I went to take off his money. But I didn't go with the intention of hurting him — because I figured he was smart enough to give up the money. But what he did when I had him in the hallway: he screamed. And I got uptight, you know. And me being uptight, I used the knife. And other times people that I went to rob, they gave me a hard time. To get the money that I wanted to get I had to stab them.

We shall see many of the same elements in the work of professional robbers, to which we now turn.

## Professional Robbers

Those who commit robbery as a steady source of income have some very special views on the use of force in their work. But first we must distinguish between the professional criminal and one who commits crime habitually. Many robbers are habitual criminals in the sense that they engage in crime repetitively. They begin their careers in crime at an early age and remain largely unsophisticated in their choice of both the crime and the methods they use. As juveniles they quickly come to the attention of authorities, mostly for minor infractions of the law or because they are repetitively tagged as delinquent and incorrigible by parents, schools, and neighbors. Some may engage in robbery repetitively — evidence is considerable that a small core of repeaters is responsible for most robberies committed by juveniles. But the robberies these repeaters commit are often of the street variety — mugging, "rolling" drunks, purse snatching — or they involve small stores and corner gas stations. They are typically opportunists, and their commitment to robbery is transitory if it exists at all. If they carry their criminal careers into adulthood, some may emerge as professionals in the long run, but most do not. The majority probably spend their early adulthood in and out of jails and in and out of opportunist crime.

George Vold (1958:225) has described the distinction between the professional and the habitual criminal:

The professional criminal must be distinguished from the merely habitual one whose activity, while repetitive and habitual, has no other element of a profession. A lawyer "habitually" practices law; a doctor is in the habit of practicing medicine. We do not, however, speak of them as habitual lawyers or doctors, but as professional men of law or medicine. Similarly, the term "habitual criminal" is descriptive of a less specific and meaningful vocational identification with crime than is true of the professional. Such a person is often a repeater in crime, but essentially a failure in the practice of crime as a vocation and a way of life. He frequently gets caught, yet wants to work at crime and associate with other criminals, but often is not good enough to be trusted with any significant assignments. Consequently he sometimes has to work at legitimate employment between "jobs" and prison sentences. The merely habitual criminal, whose only accomplishment is that he has been caught several times, has no place and no status among truly professional criminals.

Those offenders who repetitively engage in robbery sometimes develop rudimentary strategies and tactics, and may undergo some training at the hands of more experienced peers. In Clifford Shaw's classic study of the "jackroller" (a person who robs drunks and skid-row bums), "Stanley," the subject of the study, tells us about his experiences in early twentieth-century Chicago:

I went immediately to the News Alley, and there met an old pal that I had become acquainted with in St. Charles [Reformatory]. I showed him the bank roll, and that strengthened our friendship considerably. So we started to blow it in . . . and in a few days the dough was gone. I had tasted the life and found it sweet. But I was in a predicament, for I had no money, and you can't enjoy life without dough. My buddy, being an old "jackroller," suggested "jackrolling" as a way out of the dilemma. So we started out to "put the strong arm" on drunks. We sometimes stunned the drunks by "giving them the club" in a dark place near a lonely alley. It was bloody work, but necessity demanded it — we had to live (1930:84–85).

And later:

I slept like a top that night, and the next morning I met Tony. We worked out a plan for "making drunks," which was crude, although it didn't seem so to us. . . .
That night Tony and I embarked on our tour of the slums after "live ones" (bums with money), which were fairly plentiful in that district at that season. The drunks who had recently come in from the labor camps would usually have money. . . . Tony and I continued to "make drunks" and to break into apartments for about three months, and then his brother ran into him on the street. . . . Tony had to go and that left me without a pal. I was very lonely. I met many of my old friends, and one of them, knowing of my success of "making drunks" and that Tony had left me, wanted to establish a partnership with me. Realizing that I would have "cold feet" if I went out alone to steal, I considered his offer and

sized him up for the job. . . . Jack (that was his name) was a well-built, swarthy Kentucky lad of twenty-two years. I looked at his strong arms and shoulders with approval, and although he was not a polished city chap, he knew the ropes around the West Side, so I agreed to take him into partnership with me" (1930:139–141).

Although habitual offenders may skip from one type of activity to another, from legitimate enterprise to illegitimate enterprise, from burglary and shoplifting to mugging and assault, their involvement in criminal subcultures provides them with the argot (slang) and other trappings of the normative system, which help them feel at home among their fellows and offer group support for repetition in criminal activities. But to be a professional means to work at crime so that crime becomes work, a job, employment — a steady source of income. And professionalism means more than quasi membership in a criminal subculture. It means developing skills, talents, know-how, competence, viewpoints, a way of life, and assorted rationalizations and justifications. It means weighing risks, choosing among alternatives, planning, using caution, and subscribing to a code of conduct. Vold (1958:225) comments, "Any worthwhile professional man is proud of the profession he practices and is loyal to the code of conduct required of him." Professionalism in robbery means that robbery is a part of one's way of life.

Werner Einstadter (1969) investigated the social organization of professional armed robbery. His informants were convicted robbers on parole in California. All of them had committed more than one armed robbery in the company of others; the robberies had been fully planned and calculated and were not incidental to some other form of crime; and all the subjects considered themselves robbers and had spent considerable time in that line of work.

Among the features of professionalization that Einstadter discovered were the following: Proceeds are shared equally, and anyone who participates gets a share. They usually have no financial backing but meet expenses themselves or by committing a series of smaller robberies. If arrested, team members are on their own — they are under no obligation to keep quiet, nor are their colleagues under any obligation to help them. If they do "rat," however, they will lose their share. The group has little cohesion: members come in and leave the team as occasion necessitates, and leadership roles are filled more or less at will. Members of the team and other professional robbers are expected to deal honestly with one another, at least insofar as it bears on the work itself. Members have a fatalistic attitude toward events that might transpire during a robbery; this is especially true of violence and of mistakes made by the inexperienced who have not yet learned the ropes:

It's the "breaks" that count; you either have them or not. Fate is deemed to control the robber's destiny; when the cards are right, when the dice are right, when the *setup* is perfect, nothing can go wrong; but if luck is against you, "you haven't got a chance." It therefore becomes easy to excuse what would under normal circumstances be considered an unforgivable error (1969:69).

Other aspects of the professional robber's code and social organization concern cooperation, partnership consensus, planning the "hit," assigning roles (usually done on the basis of skill and knowledge), and decision making. (On pp. 209–217 we see how professionalism in robbery departs in some ways from professionalism in nonviolent theft.)

The kinds of robberies that professionals usually commit are those likely to pay large dividends, though less lucrative jobs will be taken on if financial needs are pressing. The more lucrative jobs will be well-planned robberies, usually of commercial concerns, in which the partners work as a well-oiled team. This type of planned operation, as Einstadter calls it, works only when all contingencies are evaluated beforehand (fate rules anything else), when they have rehearsals or dry runs, when the target is fully studied, perhaps over a period of weeks, and when the partners know and trust one another well. The professional is interested in banks, loan companies, drugstores, large supermarkets, and liquor stores.

Although many professional robbers confine most of their work to the robbery of commercial establishments, some apparently specialize in the robbery of individuals. Professional purse snatchers, or "cutpurses," as they are called in the trade, are an example. Though looked down upon by many of their professional colleagues, some purse snatchers are quick to claim membership in the professional ranks, and like other professionals, they distinguish themselves from the opportunists, the amateurs, and those not in robbery for a living. One such professional cutpurse tells how the profession of purse snatching had been invaded by amateurs and other characters:

Like many a once-honored trade, the traditional art of the cutpurse has fallen on evil times. The profession is now overrun with amateurs, heavy-handed louts of small talent and even smaller character who would be better employed on a rock pile. Purse-snatching has become the catch-all of crime. It's a last resort for down-at-the-heel burglars, unemployed stick-up artists, and others who have lost the professional drive and are too lazy to go straight. It's a lark for high school kids, a source of party-money for juvenile delinquents, a spur-of-the-moment thing for drunks — and for many it's the outlet for something dark and vicious inside of them. (Dale, 1974:73–74)

Today many of the forms of robbery that in the past were the primary activity of professionals are now committed as often, if not more often, by amateurs — those who are not familiar with the skills, techniques, and other professional aspects of career robbery. Bank robbery is an example. Whereas bank robbery was once a favorite of the professional, today we see growing indications that opportunists and other nonprofessionals are trying this extremely risky and difficult type of robbery. Much of the 59 percent increase in bank robberies reported by the FBI for the period between 1977 and 1981 may be attributed to the nonprofessional. The amateur status of many contemporary bank robbers is confirmed by newspaper accounts of robbers who hold up tellers while cameras take clear pictures of their undisguised faces or who try to rob drive-up facilities where the tellers are protected by bullet-proof glass and are sufficiently hidden from view that they can summon the police via silent alarm systems. According to one study of bank robbery today, most robbers do not use disguises; most do not inspect the bank before "hitting" it; and most make no long-range plans to avoid getting caught (*Justice Assistance News,* November 1984:1).

Indications of amateurism in bank robbery are also found in estimates of the amounts of money lost in such robberies and in the arrest rates of the last few years. Not only are arrest rates higher now for bank robbery than for any other felony property crime, but the average amount lost has apparently decreased over the last few decades. In 1932, the average loss was $5,583, compared with $3,654 in 1981. Of course, some of the decline is doubtless due to changes in banking procedures in the handling of cash. But a professional will know this and will not waste time on petty "scores" unless hard pressed. Considering the impact of inflation, bank robbery is certainly less lucrative than it used to be.

## Working at Robbery

We can learn more about the job of robbery by asking how professional, career robbers work. Although professional robbers are less numerous than their amateur counterparts, they have been investigated more systematically; hence far more is known about their activities, work attitudes, and organization. In addition, the professional robber is important to study for he (rarely she) steals far more than the typical amateur does and often has a lengthy career (despite concerted efforts to protect commercial establishments from him).

Since professionals make robbery their work, they cannot afford to fail or get caught; therefore they emphasize careful planning, anticipation of difficulties that might arise, assessment of risks, and teamwork. To get some idea of how career robbers pursue their work, we can look at four typical phases in the robbery attempt: going into partnership, setting up the robbery, the robbery itself, and the getaway.

### GOING INTO PARTNERSHIP

First-time robbers, and even those who have robbed before, must often get a team together before embarking on a robbery or series of robberies. For those who have not before committed armed robbery, the usual kind of professional robbery, what moves them to get involved in this particular line? It might be at the invitation of an acquaintance who has some experience in armed robbery and needs a partner; it might come up in the course of conversation among experienced thieves who are looking for a new "line"; and sometimes the decision to get involved in armed robbery comes after a careful assessment of what best serves a person's needs as he sees it:

> When my partner and I decided to go into crime, the first thing we had to decide next was just what branch of crime to go into. You've got car theft, burglary, stealing, stealing money or rolling drunks, armed robbery, other things. . . .
>
> . . . [I]n order to decide which branch we wanted to go into, since we were both inexperienced criminals at the time, we decided to do as much research as we could and find out which made the most money the fastest and that percentagewise was the safest. . . . We spent four days in the public library and we researched, and came up with armed robbery as the most likely for us. . . .
>
> We found . . . that armed robbery is by far the best as getting away with it is concerned because, unlike burglary or breaking and entering, you don't take anything that you have to convert into cash, thereby putting something in somebody else's hands, and you're not taking anything but *money*, which is spendable in any damned place. (Jackson, 1969b:20–21)

Einstadter found that partnerships might evolve as a result of casual interaction among strangers who find they have similar backgrounds and interests:

> . . . You meet some guy and you say, I like him, and he likes you, and so you start horsing around, well you don't know each other, really, you don't know anything about each other, but eventually it comes out, you know. You let slip, you ask him about something — how do you like what you're doing? — and he says — it's a whole lot better than doing time. Then I know, and I told him, yeah, and you're finally out on your backgrounds. So, we got to talking about an easier way to make money. . . . He says "I know a couple of guys, and we all got guns, and we can go out and hit a few places now and then. If we don't hit it heavy we won't get caught." So we started doing this stuff. (1969:68)

Groups of robbers who have had some experience in this line of work also formulate partnerships before going into particular jobs. Sometimes the initial impetus to engage in a series of jobs will come from a transient robber who happens to be in town and makes contact with others. Here the choice of partners will probably be made on the basis of the kinds of skills needed for whatever jobs are in the air.

## SETTING UP THE SCORE

Once a partnership is set up — and this may occur after a prospective heist has surfaced — planning consumes the partnership's time and resources. Many arrangements have to be made. Those who have been in the game for some time will make sure that they have personnel lined up for contingencies that might arise — doctors in case of injuries, lawyers in case of trouble with the police, and bondsmen to pay bail money.

The planning of the robbery may differ from one partnership to the next, but certain activities are typically involved. Among the things that must be set up are (1) the target — bank, supermarket, or liquor store; (2) role assignments for the job — someone to drive the getaway car, often called the "wheelman," someone to be the lookout, someone to be the "gunman," and someone to be his accomplice during the job; (3) stolen cars, false license plates, and routes to and from the robbery; (4) a place and time for splitting up the money; and (5) most important, "casing" the target and dry runs.

Casing the target may be done by the one who set up the robbery or by all members of the team. If done while driving around the area, attention will be paid to such factors as parking opportunities, entrances and exists, police patrols, and the movement of people into, out of, and around the target. Some groups even take special note of architectural arrangements:

> Bank robbers rely heavily on the architectural uniformity of banks. Banks are frequently located on street corners, and this is convenient for getaways. Glass doors permit the robber-doorman to see who is coming in, whereas, as a robber noted, the persons coming in have more difficulty seeing through the glass because of light reflection. The present trend toward low counters, possibly motivated by the bank officials' desire for a more personal and less prison-like atmosphere, is looked upon favorably by bank robbers. (Letkemann, 1973:94)

Quoting one of his interview subjects, Peter Letkemann continues:

> Well, sometimes you see, you might have to jump the counter. Well, if you get some of these real high counters, well, they're tough to get over. Well, you lose a few seconds by getting over the counters, and some of these banks, like, they have these gates, like with — well you can't reach over and open them because the catch is too far down, so therefore you've got to jump over this counter, you see. (p. 94)

During casing, attention is also paid to alarm systems, presence of guards, number of employees, and location of safes and cash registers. The timing of a robbery is also vital. If the job is in a small rural town, robbers are likely to have additional time to carry it out, whereas in an urban setting there is greater risk of police intervention, not to mention the coming and going of customers and employees. The extent to which some robbers go in planning their jobs is well illustrated in the memoirs of Blackie Audett (1945), who participated in nearly thirty bank robberies. He sometimes purchased specially drawn-up plans from a man who made his living supplying robbers with complete information on the target and on routes to and from it and who set up cars and other supplies for the job and any emergencies that might arise.

## THE ROBBERY

The actual procedures used during a robbery vary from one team to another and from one situation to another. If the job is in an urban area the robbers will typically do everything to avoid drawing attention to themselves, at least until the robbery is in progress. Thus they may park their cars in legal places so as to avoid the risks of police interest, or they may wait until they are inside the target before donning masks or other disguises. If the target is in a small town or village, no such restraints may be necessary:

> . . . we don't care about parking, whether or not. We drive right in front of the bank where the door is closest to it, even if it's on the sidewalk, and there's a thing that goes on the sidewalk. And if there's one there we go right on the sidewalk. Period! Because we figure that as soon as we open the door of the car, we assume that the alarm is going off right there. (Letkemann, 1973:98)

In getting to the bank or other target a common ploy is to use previously stolen vehicles whose plates have been removed or changed. These cars will then be ditched after the robbery. Often two such cars are used as security against any breakdowns or other problems. A team member whose only job is to drive will stay with the car and keep its engine running, while also being in a position to sound the horn in the event of trouble.

Once inside the target, the team will have assigned roles to which they must adhere if things are to go smoothly. "The work positions are determined by the central concern of the operation, namely speed" (Letkemann, 1973:98). One person may be assigned to watch the door and generally oversee the operation as it progresses, paying special attention to time. Another may have the sole job of keeping the employees and customers out of the way, and hence out of trouble. In smaller teams this important aspect of the job may be fulfilled by herding employees and customers into a room or vault that can be kept under surveillance but does not require the total attention of one person. In teams of four or more, two can usually be allotted the specific tasks of collecting the cash.

Letkemann notes one important aspect of the robbery situation that must be handled especially well if the attempt is to succeed with maximum payoff and minimum trouble. He calls it *victim management,* and it has two dimensions: surprise and vulnerability, and establishing authority and managing tension.

The matter of surprise is crucial. When confronted out of the blue, employees and customers are more vulnerable than when they have been forewarned in some way as to what is about to happen. Surprise, and the accompanying temporary paralysis of the victims, allows the robbers to get matters under their control and saves precious minutes. Some robbers, in fact, make a point of hitting banks and stores when employees are most likely to be sleepy and dull — early in the morning and preferably on Monday. As they see it, anything adding to surprise works in their favor.

Once things are under way the robbers must maintain their control over the situation and manage the tensions that are bound to arise. The hysterical employee, the stubborn cashier, and the glory hunter each may react differently to the stress of robbery, and all must be controlled by the robber. How this is done will differ from one situation to the next, but the tools commanded by the robber are generally limited to voice commands, appearance, and the use of force. The robbers generally want to sound and look as if they mean business. As one robber put it: "They can tell by the sound of your voice, by what you say and how you go about things, whether or not you mean business. If you're shaky, they'll know" (Letkemann, 1973:111). Masks and hoods, besides concealing identity, also have a role to play in establishing authority and managing tension. To some robbers they are important because they help to maintain the shock effect produced by the surprise entrance; to others they are useful because they conceal facial expressions and thus make it less likely that victims will detect any anxiety the robber may feel.

The use of force in professional robbery generally extends only to pushing, shoving, and, on occasion, pistol whipping. Some robbers use an overt display of force as a means to maintain their authority and keep the situation under control. One of the first things they will do is attack an employee in the expectation that this move will convince others of their purpose and resolve. According to one robber, the technique his team used was this:

> So they are froze there — their reaction is one of extreme fear and they drop on the floor and sometimes we select the strongest person — the manager especially or another teller which is very big — a six-footer, or something like that, you know. And we won't say a word, we just walk up to him and smack him right across the face, you know, and we get him down. And once he's down the people, the girls especially, they look at him and say, "My God — big Mike, he's been smashed down like that — I'd better lay down too, and stay quiet." (Letkemann, 1973:110)

The use of violence by the professional robber is apparently governed by two considerations. The first concerns getting the job done as quickly and easily as possible. The second involves escape. Typical professionals seem to have no doubt that if necessary, they will use force; if mere threat does not produce the desired results, the next step will be violence. But they will avoid using their guns if they possibly can. Studies of violence among professional robbers concur in this. Apart from the fact that weapons usually make noise and thus attract attention, robbers have no particular desire to injure seriously or kill their victims — an attitude that may stem from the widely shared view that those from whom they actually take the money are not the real victims anyway. They hold no beef against the teller, the cashier, or the customer. As Einstadter puts it:

> The employee with whom the robbery encounter is made is considered to have nothing at stake since there is no personal loss for him; at most he is conceived of

as an agent-victim. . . . [The robber] views the actual encounter as an impersonal matter for in doing so he is not robbing a person but some amorphous mass — a bank, a supermarket, a loan company. (1969:80)

It should be remembered that the robber is out for money, not blood. On those occasions when weapons are actually used, and these are rare, it is usually because the robber has been cornered or challenged by others with weapons, most notably, the police. "Although the robber will hesitate to use his gun on a civilian, confrontation by the police is seen as resulting inevitably in a 'shoot-out' " (Letkemann, 1973:115).

## THE GETAWAY

The getaway is the most important phase of any robbery, for whether or not the attempt succeeds, the robbers must still escape. Those who have carefully planned their operations will have escape routes and contingency plans already mapped out.

As with the robbery itself, speed is paramount. The longer robbers remain at or near the scene, the greater the risks of apprehension. They usually drive stolen cars, which are abandoned at a prearranged point, and then transfer to a vehicle owned by one of the team. If all goes well, the team may disperse for a time, move to a different town, or simply go underground until the "heat is off."

It is during the getaway that violence is most likely to erupt. And the violence may include shooting, running roadblocks, or taking hostages. Robbers will make every effort to clear the scene and get as far away as is necessary. Understandably, the skills of the wheelman are especially important in this phase of the operation. Not only must the getaway vehicle be in top running condition, but it must be close at hand with the engine running so that team members can hop in and clear the scene as soon as possible. Once in the car, the driver's skills and maintenance of a cool head may mean the overall success of the job (Conklin, 1972).

When robbery is studied as work, it does not look very different from many legitimate business pursuits. The popular myth depicting robbery as a senseless, violent act of plunder perpetrated by equally senseless and violent individuals can be upheld on some occasions. But a robbery is more accurately pictured as having characteristics that lie on a number of continua, of which three of the more important are *planning, organizing,* and *skill at victim management*. Those who make robbery a regular pursuit are likely to be found in robberies at the high end of these continua; those who are opportunists, or who indulge in robbery in a repetitive but sporadic and unsystematic manner, will be involved in robberies at the low end. Thus robberies committed by professionals tend to exhibit high levels of planning, organization, and victim-management skills; those committed by opportunists out for a fast buck tend to exhibit little in the way of planning and organization, and it may be in robberies committed by such individuals that we find confusion, fear, and disorder when it comes to handling their own and the victims' stresses and tensions.

## REACTIONS TO ROBBERY

Official reactions to robbery are usually severe, and to this extent parallel public sentiments. Although the police generally make arrests in only 25 percent of the incidents that come to their attention, the suspects who are arrested are almost always prosecuted. In the case of bank robbery, a federal offense, nearly 90 percent of those prosecuted are convicted (*Justice Assistance News,* November 1984). Nationwide data indicate that those arrested for any kind of robbery stand a one-in-three chance of being sent to prison (Bureau of Justice Statistics, 1985i).

More people in state prisons are serving time for robbery than for any other offense; in fact, a quarter of the nation's prisoners are convicted robbers. On the average, they are serving sentences in excess of eight years, though length of sentence differs widely around the country (Bureau of Justice Statistics, 1985i). One of the more lenient states is California (average sentence length 56 months); one of the harshest, North Carolina (135 months). Prisoners generally serve less than their maximum sentence. In the case of robbery, the average time served is just over three years (Bureau of Justice Statistics, 1984g), still longer than that of most prisoners. As we have seen, robbery is an offense of the young, a fact which is brought home in prison statistics. In 1981, half of all offenders confined in state prisons for robbery were under age 25, and nearly one-third were under age 18 (Bureau of Justice Statistics, 1984d). Robbery is heavy crime indeed for the minority who are caught and convicted.

Official and public sentiments differ when we compare the robbery of commercial establishments, such as banks and loan companies, with the robbery of private individuals. It seems that those who rob institutions are more likely to be prosecuted and to receive long prison terms than are those who rob individuals (Williams, 1976). Yet the public seems less hostile toward the robbery of institutions than the robbery of individuals. Whereas Jesse James, the Dalton gang, and the "great train robbers" in England are accorded a sympathetic hearing, the mugger is hated and feared. Robbery of institutions, like plunder in war, is more impersonal, its impact more diffuse. When the victim is also viewed in a somewhat negative light — as banks and loan companies seem to be these days — perhaps the public cares less that they are sometimes the victims of crime. Yet to the authorities these establishments are the backbone of the American economic system. To rob them is to threaten the foundations of capitalism. Perhaps this explains the more punitive official reaction in the absence of corresponding public sentiments.

# CHAPTER 8

# Varieties of
# Nonviolent Theft

Theft comes in a multitude of forms and involves countless different situations and people. Labels designating types of theft include shoplifting, pocket picking, burglary, petty larceny, grand larceny, check forgery, embezzlement, auto theft, fraud, and confidence games. Just three conditions are necessary to make a theft situation possible: some goods or service capable of being stolen, someone from whom it can be stolen, and someone to do the stealing. The box on pages 206–207 gives the Model Penal Code's definitions of some of the offenses covered in this chapter.

In industrialized nations of the West, theft is a daily occurrence. If we do not do it ourselves, then we are its victims, or we hear about thefts involving other people. Many of us may be the victims of theft without even knowing it. To put matters simply, theft is commonplace. But it would be a mistake to believe that something inherent in human beings leads them to steal; in some societies theft is almost unheard of.

As one might expect, the character of theft is not uniform throughout different societies, nor has it remained uniform throughout the history of any single society. Theft is shaped by many factors, not the least of which are those determined by the prevailing culture. If property or material possessions do not exist, people are unlikely to have any notion of stealing. What is more, the types of things that can be and are stolen, the methods used, and the kinds of people who are victims of theft all are influenced by culture, by the way people live, and by their attitudes and values.

In a society in which the acquisition and ownership of property are strongly supported, the violation of such rights meets with understandable condemnation. However, the cultural values supporting the acquisition of material wealth may also support the very behavior that is condemned. If possession of material wealth is highly valued, then people may stop at nothing to accumulate such wealth. Whether they acquire possessions through channels deemed legitimate by the dominant culture or whether they steal from others may be less important than the fact that they do acquire the possessions. If we all could acquire whatever we wanted through culturally acceptable channels, then theft might not exist. But when some people are systematically excluded from access to acceptable channels of acquisition or cannot acquire what they want even with such access, then stealing may be an alternative avenue to material wealth. Though it has remained popular to think that thieves are primarily the poor and disadvantaged, people from all walks of life, even those with all kinds of supposed advantages, may steal from others.

## Historical Developments in Criminal Theft

As a criminal activity, theft has a long and interesting history. The creation and extension of theft laws, as well as their application, have been exercises in the control of behavior in conflict with the interests of certain segments of society.

Theft in the early legal codes is a rather vague term, though few known codes did not have some laws identifying theft as punishable behavior. More interesting, perhaps, is that many of these early codes tried to distinguish among different methods of stealing and different classes of victims. On the question of methods, the Roman law of the Twelve Tables designated theft by night as a more serious offense than daylight theft. As for the victims, the Code of Hammurapi placed the interests of church and state above those of the citzenry as a whole: those who stole from temples or the king's palaces were punished by death, whereas those who stole from a private citizen merely had to pay compensation.

It is mainly in English law that we find the roots of modern criminal-law conceptions of theft. Even before the Norman conquest of 1066, theft was firmly established as an offense in Anglo-Saxon codes. We are familiar with the old adage "possession is nine points of the law," but in early English law, possession was virtually all the law. It was in terms of possession that theft was identified and the thief so labeled. Ownership was a notion quite alien to early English society. One did not own something; it was in one's posses-sion. To identify theft it was necessary to show, first, that the thief did not have lawful possession of the object in question and, second, that the person who claimed lawful possession could rightly do so. In practical terms this meant that to establish theft it was important to produce the thief, and so apprehension of the thief took on special importance in English law.

The tradition in Anglo-Saxon and early common laws was for the person who claimed lawful possession to pursue the suspected thief and challenge his or her right to possession. Akin to the "posse" of American frontier justice, the English chase was thus an integral part of the theft scene. If the suspect was caught while transporting the stolen goods from the scene of the crime, then the theft was "manifest," and justice could be meted out swiftly and severely (and often was). If the chase was unsuccessful, or the lawful possessor had failed to pursue the thief, then the theft was "secret," and justice slow and tortuous. All things considered, it was certainly in the interest of the victim to catch the thief in the act of fleeing with the loot.

Another important aspect of common law conceptions of theft was a civil law violation, *trespass.* The common legal term for theft was then, and still is, *larceny,* and larceny was but an extension of trespass. Under earlier Roman law, larceny *(latrocinium)* covered almost any type of deceit and trickery, but this was not the case in England. Larceny meant *laying hands on another's possessions without his permission,* and this was what trespass amounted to: "Simply to lay a hand on a man's thing without his permission would be trespass, therefore it was argued that there could be no larceny without trespass" (Turner, 1966:267). Larceny went beyond trespass in the notion of *animus furandi* (intent to steal), and it was argued that trespass turned into larceny when the trespasser intended to steal from the victim. The notion of trespass is still retained in many state laws dealing with theft today.

In regard to the objects of theft, the idea of "movable" possessions

## VARIETIES OF NONVIOLENT THEFT AS DEFINED BY THE MODEL PENAL CODE

### Theft by Unlawful Taking or Disposition:

(1) *Movable Property.* A person is guilty of theft if he unlawfully takes, or exercises control over, movable property of another with purpose to deprive him thereof.

(2) *Immovable Property.* A person is guilty of theft if he unlawfully transfers immovable property of another or any interest therein with purpose to benefit himself or another not entitled thereto.

**Theft by Deception:** A person is guilty of theft if he purposely obtains property of another by deception. [Deception includes creating a false impression of value, law, or intent; prevention of another from acquiring information that would affect his or her judgment of a transaction; failure to disclose lien or other legal impediment to enjoyment of transferred property; failure to correct a false impression previously created or reinforced by the deceiver.]

**Forgery:** A person is guilty of forgery if, with purpose to defraud or injure anyone, or with knowledge that he is facilitating a fraud or injury to be perpetrated by anyone, the actor:

(a) alters any writing of another without his authority; or

(b) makes . . . executes . . . or transfers any writing so that it purports to be the act of another who did not authorize that act, or to have been executed at a time or place or in a numbered sequence other than was in fact the case, or to be a copy of an original when no such copy originally existed; or

(c) utters any writing which he knows to be forged in a manner specified in paragraphs (a) or (b).

**Burglary:** A person is guilty of burglary if he enters a building or occupied structure or separately

remained central in the emerging criminal law; the old charge that the thief "stole, took, and carried away" implies as much. In medieval times the most prized movables were agricultural chattels — farm animals such as oxen, cows, horses, and pigs, which often also served as money. Not surprisingly, then, these were the movable possessions to which early theft laws most often applied. But the creators of law have never been bound by prevailing cultural definitions of what are valuable chattels. Indeed, one Anglo-Saxon king went so far as to declare: "Men shall respect everything the king wishes to be respected, and refrain from theft on pain of death and loss of all they possess" (Attenborough, 1963:137). Though this is putting the matter bluntly, the point is obvious: those who shape legal conceptions of what can be stolen are in a position to impose their own ideas about what is valuable and to determine what will and will not be deemed an object capable of being stolen. The entire history of theft laws illustrates the role of interests in the designation of objects it is possible to steal (Hall, 1952).

Once goods and services have been legally identified as possible to steal, the matter of their actual value in any given case has traditionally been irrelevant to the identification of theft. It matters little whether you steal a coat worth $5,000 or one worth only five cents — a theft has still been committed. But value clearly does matter in what happens to the thief. From at least Anglo-Saxon times, distinctions in theft have been based on the value of the property taken. Just as today many states treat theft under $50 (or some other figure) as *petty theft* and anything over that as *grand theft,* similar distinctions have been made throughout the history of theft laws. The penalties for grand theft, a felony, have traditionally been more severe. If value is an indication of seriousness, which some undoubtedly believe, then such secured or occupied portion thereof with purpose to commit a crime therein, unless the premises are at the time open to the public or the actor is licensed or privileged to enter.

**Receiving Stolen Property:** A person is guilty of theft if he purposely receives, retains, or disposes of movable property of another knowing that it has been stolen, or believing that it has probably been stolen, unless the property is received, retained, or disposed with purpose to restore it to the owner. "Receiving" means acquiring possession, control, or title, or lending on the security of the property.

**Bad Checks:** A person who issues or passes a check or similar sight order for the payment of money, knowing that it will not be honored by the drawee commits a misdemeanor. For the purposes of this section . . . an issuer is presumed to know that the check or order (other than a post-dated check or order) would not be paid, if:

(1) the issuer had no account with the drawee at the time the check or order was issued; or

(2) payment was refused by the drawee for lack of funds, upon presentation within thirty days after issue, and the issuer failed to make good within ten days after receiving notice of that refusal.

**Credit Cards:** A person commits an offense if he uses a credit card for the purpose of obtaining property or services with knowledge that:

(1) the card is stolen or forged; or

(2) the card has been revoked or cancelled; or

(3) for any other reason his use of the card is unauthorized.

SOURCE: Excerpted from the Model Penal Code, copyright 1962 by The American Law Institute. Reprinted with the permission of The American Law Institute.

---

value distinctions may be justified on the grounds that they provide a workable solution to the problem of "making the punishment fit the crime." But some authors have argued that distinctions of value merely reflect the operation of class interests and ignore that what to one person may be a great loss, to another may be a drop in the bucket. The more wealthy theft victims stand to realize more in the way of "justice" than do the poorer classes, whose individual losses will more often fall below the misdemeanor/felony cutoff point (Mannheim, 1946).

## INTERESTS AND THEFT LAWS

Criminal law is constantly changing. One reason is that existing legal formulations prove inadequate when confronted by changing social conditions and interests. Theft laws have for centuries been revised and extended, and one result is that new forms of theft and new means of committing theft have emerged from time to time. One particularly significant development in criminal theft occurred during the late 1400s, and it shows the impact on criminal law of emergent social conditions and interests (see Hall, 1952).

The "Carrier's Case" involved a man who was hired to carry some bales of merchandise to Southampton, an English port city. But instead of doing this he broke open the bales and took their contents. He was subsequently caught and charged with felony theft. As the larceny law then stood, however, his actions did not legally constitute theft: he had entered an agreement in good faith, and he thus had lawful possession of the bales. Under the possession rules he could not steal from himself (or by extension, from the merchant who hired him). After much debate a majority of the judges who handled the case finally found him guilty of felony theft and in doing so extended the law of larceny to cover cases of "breaking bulk," as it was thereafter called (though for some time a carrier was still free to steal the contents, so long as he took the bales as well!).

Most of us would probably argue that the guilty verdict and attendant legal precedent sound reasonable enough. After all, if you hire a truck driver to deliver goods, you would hardly appreciate his stealing them and would doubtless desire satisfaction. But if no laws could be applied in your particular case, then what satisfaction could you hope to receive? To judge from the Carrier's Case, successful resolution of the problem would depend on how much pressure you could bring to bear on the legal machinery to protect your interests. It so happens that at the time of the Carrier's Case, the judges were faced with a number of outside pressures:

> The most powerful forces at the time were interrelated very intimately and at many points: the New Monarchy and the *nouveau riche* — the mercantile class; the business interests of both and the consequent need for a secure carrying trade; the wool and textile industry, the most valuable by far in all the realm; wool and cloth, the most important exports; these exports and foreign trade; this trade and Southampton, chief trading city with the Latin countries for centuries; the numerous and very influential Italian merchants who brought English wool and cloth inland and shipped them from Southampton. The great forces of an emerging modern world, represented in the above phenomenon, necessitated the elimination of a formula which had outgrown its usefulness. A new set of major institutions required a new rule. (Hall, 1952:33)

And so, as William Chambliss (1975:7) puts it, "The judges deciding the Carrier Case had, then, to choose between creating a new law to protect merchants who entrusted their goods to a carrier or permitting the lack of such legal protection to undermine trade and the merchant class economic interests. The court decided to act in the interests of the merchants despite the lack of a law."

The revision and expansion of theft in law have continued to the present day. Many of the changes came about as a result of statutes designed to plug the gaps and crevices in prevailing common law standards. Embezzlement, for example, emerged in its modern form in 1799 when Parliament passed a statute to cover cases of servants misappropriating goods placed in their possession in the course of their employment. It was later extended to cover brokers, bankers, attorneys, and others in positions of trust as agents for third parties. But embezzlement statutes covered only the illegal transfer of possession. For cases of ownership fraudulently acquired — as when you sign over property to another after being tricked into doing so — the law remained inadequate until a statutory decree in 1861 created the offense of obtaining goods by false pretenses. This new offense was basically an extension of earlier common law crimes such as "larceny by trick and device," and the so-called cheats, many of which are today variations on the confidence game.

## The Prevalence and Distribution of Reported Theft

Much theft remains beyond the reach of bureaucratic data collection. Accordingly, national data on theft are extremely difficult to assess and interpret. To give some idea of the problem, recall that estimates of the true rate of burglary alone begin at more than three times the rate reported by the FBI. When we add to this the fact that only a relatively minute number of thefts are ever solved, our difficulties become obvious.

Published national data do give us some idea of the dimensions of the theft problem, at least from the standpoint of the criminal justice system. In 1984, burglary, larceny-theft, and motor vehicle theft accounted for 10,608,473 (around 90 percent) of the 11,881,755 Index offenses reported by the FBI. Arrests numbered 1,846,500, or around 80 percent of total arrests for Index offenses. All three offenses showed steady increases during the 1960s, with burglary and larceny continuing to climb, though more slowly, during the 1970s. Motor vehicle theft tapered off and remained fairly stable, with a rate of around 450 recorded incidents per 100,000 population. The published national data indicate other characteristics of these three Index offenses: (1) rural rates are substantially below those found in both cities and suburbs; (2) suburban rates have been increasing faster than have large city rates; and (3) of those offenses reported, less than 20 percent are cleared by arrest (see Figure 5.2).

The FBI data in Figures 8.1 and 8.2 show something of what police say is going on in the world of larceny-theft. Larceny-theft is a catchall category, covering a host of different forms of thievery.

## Professionalism in Theft

Professionalism in theft has a history going back at least to Elizabethan times, when "conny-catching" (a type of swindling) was a full-time profession. Over the years other varieties of theft became the focus of professionalization, with shoplifting and pocket picking two of the more common ones. Much of what we know about professional theft and the professional thief has come from firsthand accounts by thieves (both practicing and reformed), many of which are of the "as told to" sort. Among the best known are *The Professional Thief*, edited by Edwin Sutherland; Ernest Booth's *Stealing Through Life;* and the more recent accounts, *My Life in Crime*, reported by John Bartlow Martin, and *Box Man: A Professional Thief's Journey*, as told to William Chambliss. To those must be added an

**Figure 8.1** Trends in larceny-theft, 1980–1984

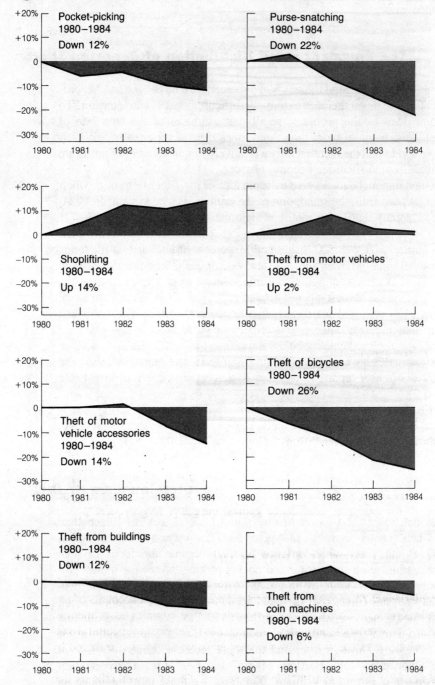

**Figure 8.2**  Larceny analysis, 1984

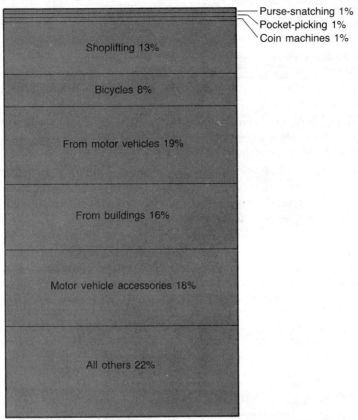

Purse-snatching 1%
Pocket-picking 1%
Coin machines 1%

Shoplifting 13%

Bicycles 8%

From motor vehicles 19%

From buildings 16%

Motor vehicle accessories 18%

All others 22%

Because of rounding, the percentages do not add to 100%. SOURCE: FBI (1985), Crime in the United States, 1984. Washington, D.C.: U.S. Government Printing Office, p. 31.

assortment of books and articles focusing on professionalism in specific types of theft — for example, confidence games, burglary, forgery, and pocket picking (e.g. Maurer, 1940).

## PROFESSIONAL THEFT AS A WAY OF LIFE

By far the most influential work on professional theft has been Sutherland's *The Professional Thief* (1937b). Sutherland used the written accounts of one professional thief ("Chic Conwell") to illustrate the complex assortment of behavior characteristics, attitudes, organizational features, subcultural patterns, and views of the world that together make up a way of life shared by professional thieves.

In describing the world to which he belonged, Chic Conwell tells us that professional thieves (1) "make a regular business of stealing"; (2) acquire their skills and professional know-how through tutelage by and association with already established professionals; (3) develop highly skilled work techniques, the most important of which is the "ability to manipulate people"; (4) carefully plan everything they do in connection with their business; (5) look upon themselves as different from amateurs and superior to them, particularly those who indulge in sex crimes; (6) have a code of ethics that "is much more binding among thieves than that among legitimate commercial firms"; (7) are "sympathetic" and "congenial" with each other; (8) view successes and failures as "largely a matter of luck"; (9) have an established vocabulary of criminal slang, the main purpose of which is to enhance "we-feeling" and promote ease of intraprofession communication; (10) rarely engage in only one specialized form of theft (the notable exception being pickpockets, or "cannons"); and (11) usually operate in gangs, "mobs," or partnerships whose life span is generally short unless they are consistently successful (pp. 2–42). Summarizing Conwell's account of professional theft, Sutherland offers this conception of the profession:

> The profession of theft is more than isolated acts of theft frequently and skillfully performed. It is a group way of life and a social institution. It has techniques, codes, status, traditions, consensus, and organization. It has an existence as real as that of the English language. It can be studied with relatively little attention to any particular thief. The profession can be understood by a description of the functions and relationships involved in this way of life. In fact, an understanding of this culture is a prerequisite to the understanding of the behavior of a particular professional thief. (pp. ix–x)

## BECOMING A PROFESSIONAL THIEF

Sutherland's work describes the behavior system of professional theft as it appeared in the first quarter of the twentieth century, viewed through the eyes of one thief. We get a more complete and up-to-date picture of professionalism in theft if we also look at some more recent contributions to the literature. Consider first how one becomes a professional thief.

There is no one way to become a professional thief, and whether or not thieves make the grade depends less on what or who they are or have been and more on how they are received by those who already make up the professional fraternity. Put bluntly, "one gets into the profession by acceptance" (Sutherland and Cressey, 1974:285). Gaining acceptance represents the pinnacle of a maturation process for the emerging professional. During the process newcomers will have learned to think, act, and be professional thieves. This means they must adopt those aspects of professionalism deemed important by those already in the fraternity, particularly those with whom they will spend much of their time.

One way aspiring professionals learn what is important is through others sharing the common store of knowledge. Although there is no formal or extensive recruiting of new members into the profession, the fraternity would die out if new members were not accepted on a fairly regular basis. It is through the process of sharing information that many take their first steps toward membership. In earlier days this sometimes took the form of systematic training and preparation, as when would-be pickpockets were formally schooled in the art, often at a young age and in groups. Today tutelage is a much more informal process, and though training in technical skills can still involve rather formal procedures, such as apprenticeships, most of what is learned comes through continued association with professionals at work and play. Things are picked up, experienced, and discussed but rarely taught. Simply by hanging around places where known professionals congregate, those interested will pick up details of the professional life-style, including many of the less tangible aspects:

> But later on . . . I started hanging around with professionals and learned from them that you didn't steal from a home or small place of business; you stole only from a big place that could afford it. (King, 1972:12)

Needless to say, association with professional thieves is governed by the life-style of the professional fraternity itself. One very important facet of this life-style is the tendency of professionals to live, "hang out," and work in particular localities. This provides the profession with a geographic and ecological identity. It also means that spending time in the same places provides a pretty good chance of forming associations with professionals, even for "straights" and the police. Just as the nineteenth-century cities boasted favored places where the criminal underworld congregated, so do most urban centers today. New York's Tenderloin, Five Points, and Satan's Circus have given way to a sixteen-block area around Times Square; London's Hoxton has been replaced by Soho. The typical urban habitat of the professional is

> . . . composed of gambling and taxi dance halls, rooming houses and cheap hotels, houses of prostitution, third-rate bars, poolrooms, second-hand stores and pawn shops, or theatre, restaurant, and penny arcade complexes. Within these districts are the girls, the gaiety, and the excitement that attract victims of the pickpocket and confidence swindler. Every city has its *line*, its *tenderloin*, its *strip*. What is found in this area of the larger cities can also be found on a proportionate level in the smaller urban centers, the satellite cities, and the provincial county seats. (Inciardi, 1975:51)

The professional crooks spend much of their time in these areas, and they often reside in them if they are not on the move or have not yet reached the pinnacle of the profession and can afford a nice place in the suburbs. The specific hangout — bar, restaurant, poolroom, or barbershop — is partly a matter of custom, partly a matter of convenience, and sometimes a matter of security (Maurer, 1964). It is in such localities that association with professionals is most likely to occur and that mutual confidences can take shape.

Most information sharing occurs when the criminals themselves can exercise some control over the process. This is contrasted with the situation in prisons, where some learning of the professional way of life also takes place. In prisons, convicted offenders are thrown together in confined spaces, and their interaction is geared to the constraints of formal prison arrangements, and so what they do with whom is not entirely a matter of choice. In prison many amateurs, opportunists, or habitual thieves are exposed to aspects of professional crime, but the exposure has less of the voluntariness and freedom of that outside prison walls.

The popular idea that more experienced cons willingly and routinely teach others the skills and know-how of professional crime is far from the truth. It seems that learning comes primarily through friendship and acquaintance with imprisoned professionals, just as it does on the outside, and frequently those who share inside information with others do so with great caution and deliberation. Much consideration is given to who receives the information — whether they can be trusted, whether they will be a useful contact after release, and whether they show promise (Inciardi, 1975). On the whole, prisons undoubtedly do provide an important information service for would-be careerists and professionals. The specifics of what is learned, however, will vary according to patterns of friendship, modes of theft (some can be more easily learned about than others), and even the prisons involved. Some prisons become known for the kinds of criminal skills and know-how that can be learned (Letkemann, 1973).

An individual becomes a professional thief not only by learning skills, argot, manners, and values but also through endeavors in the field. What is learned from others must be put into practice in a way that demonstrates that the person deserves to be considered a professional.

## STATUS AND PRESTIGE

A key feature of professionalism that Sutherland noted is the maintenance of a system that confers status and prestige. Status distinctions are based on a variety of things: type of theft engaged in, skill and technical competence, success, connections, and commitment. As in any other profession, participants confer prestige and recognition upon one another and distinguish the entire fraternity from outsiders, those who do not belong.

Within the ranks of professional thieves, certain work specialties stand out as having high status. Confidence men and "box" men (safecrackers) have traditionally been considered at the top of the pecking order. Their work involves considerable skill and ability, and the payoffs can be substantial for those who succeed. Those who become known for their expertise in these areas are usually fully integrated into the professional subculture, for their work depends heavily on group effort, trust, connections, and esprit de corps. At the other end of the status hierarchy are those whose jobs usually have a small payoff, involve more modest levels of skill and risk, and whose victims are typically individuals or small businesses. Cannons (pickpockets), "boosters" (professional shoplifters), and small-time burglars are examples of low-status thieves. Here is how two thieves view shoplifting:

> A booster is just about the lowest thief there is. Nobody has much to do with them. I mean, I seen one yesterday as a matter of fact. I saw this one, then talked to this other guy who was a meter-robber; you know, a guy who robs parking meters. They make a lot of money. I was talking to this friend and he said he saw Charlie boosting the other day. I told him: "Gee, Charlie Jay? Man, I can remember when he was a real high-classed thief." "Oh," he said, "he's down at the bottom now." In our estimation he's down dragging bottom because he's boosting. And he used to be a real high-classed thief at one time. (King, 1972:81)

Status distinctions are maintained even within theft specialties. Confidence men who operate the more sophisticated, complex games (the "big con") consider themselves and are considered by others as superior to "short con" operators who go in for quick swindles and usually a small payoff. Similarly, burglars distinguish among themselves, with high prestige going to the "good burglar," who (1) is superior in technical skills, (2) has a reputation for personal integrity, (3) tends to specialize in burglary, and (4) has been relatively successful in making money and staying out of prison (Shover, 1973).

When professionals refer to nonprofessionals — the opportunists, habitual amateurs, sex offenders, and those who use spur-of-the-moment violence — they use a variety of names to designate their inferior status. These are the "bums," "young punks," "squares," "hustlers," "small-timers," "weirdos," and "amateurs." Unlike the professionals, their involvement in crime is unsystematic and sporadic; their skills are minimal; and "anything goes." Although some make it into the ranks of the professionals as they mature in crime, most do not. They remain bums in the eyes of professionals and, for that matter, the public and the police.

## SELF-IMAGES AND WORLD VIEW

In distinguishing themselves from amateur thieves and other criminal offenders, professionals reinforce their feelings of importance and superiority and in this way bolster their self-esteem while erecting barriers against encroachment by the unworthy. Yet professionals do not conceive of themselves only in terms of other criminals and other kinds of crime. Though they recognize that their life-style often places them in conflict with the larger society, they are nevertheless products of, and participants in, that society. Like other Americans, they brush their teeth; they wear clothes; they drive on the right side of the road; they are consumers, lovers, and (from their point of view) business people; and they are concerned about prices, politics, war, the state of their country, and their own successes and failures. But unlike some others, they are committed to work that continually brings them the threat of arrest, prosecution, and punishment in the name of the larger society. Though they are committed to crime as a profession, they have trouble accepting the idea that they are deviant, immoral, or unworthy of respect.

And so, like others of us who have difficulty reconciling what we like to think of ourselves with what others appear to think of us, professional thieves negotiate a path that at once emphasizes their adherence to the "American way" and devalues their critics and oppressors. The following are some comments by professional thieves, which illustrate how the larger society is brought into focus along the path to self-respect and self-esteem:

> *A successful professional burglar:* You might laugh, but I'm for law and order. I don't hurt anyone, and anyway most of the people who lose stuff are insured, and I could tell you about the way they inflate their losses. But this mugging on the streets and rapes, and the way they have to coddle those creeps makes me sick. (Pileggi, 1968)

> *A "short con" man:* You know how it goes in this dog-eat-dog world. You got to take the other guy before he takes you. You know, the real sharpie outwits the marks [victims]. Of course, it all depends on how you get ahead. My way was no different from, say, a lawyer or businessman. You know, a lawyer has a license to steal. The cops should lay off con men. We don't hurt nobody. You can't con an honest man. . . . The cops should do their job and clear the streets of the muggers, heist men, hopheads, and the rest. Why, it's dangerous for a decent man like me to walk down the street at night. (Roebuck and Johnson, 1964:242)

And, to illustrate that "my way" is not as foolish as "your way":

> It looks so foolish to me to work for a living when I look at you. Take, like any official, any policeman, anything else, that's doing everything in the book and getting by with it, and here's you that's working your heart and soul out, if you miss three days at work you're three months behind — it looks so foolish. (Martin, 1952:279)

In sum, professional thieves can hold their heads high, knowing that they are good at what they do, successful in it, and professional in how they do it. In their view, the main thing distinguishing them from so-called upright citizens is that some supercilious, if not misguided, public servants have chosen to outlaw them.

## CONSENSUS AND PROFESSIONAL ETHICS

The survival of any profession depends in part on the maintenance of a normative system to which its members adhere and in terms of which they interpret their behavior and that of their colleagues. Professional theft is no exception. Consensual understandings are expressed as expectations about and evaluations of the conduct of one's peers. For years, because they have their rules, maxims, and codes of ethics, as well as skills, high pay, and prestige, professional thieves have likened their careers to legitimate professions. Those who violate these rules and collective expectations are subject to the derision of their colleagues and, as in other professions, are punished in various ways and with varying degrees of severity.

Professional expectations and evaluations cover a wide range of topics, probably more extensive than that of many legitimate professions. The topics include work activities, treatment of professionals and nonprofessionals, relationships with the larger society, and relationships with family and lovers. Some of the more prominent expectations for conduct among thieves are that members will deal honestly with one another, stick to their assigned roles, give aid to others in time of crisis, and pay their debts, whether it be for information, financial stakes, or other help. One of the long-standing principles of professionalism deals with informing or "snitching." A thief simply does not snitch on colleagues and expect to remain an honored and respected member of the professional fraternity, not to mention a healthy one (Inciardi, 1975). They also have the time-honored imperative, "Never grift [take] on the way out" (Sutherland, 1937b:13). This means that professional thieves will restrain their greed and take during a heist only what they have planned to take. Opportunistic plundering is the way of amateurs.

Much of the consensus among thieves can be traced directly to their isolation from the larger society and the related need for solidarity in a hostile world. The "we-feeling" among career criminals provides a sense of solidarity and helps maintain group identity and security. Argot has a special place here. The slang used and shared by thieves is an expression of togetherness and facilitates communication among members of the criminal subculture. Many of the terms used have a long history, some going back to Elizabethan days. By the adoption of an artificial language, professionals are "able to determine in only a few minutes of conversation with a stranger whether he is acquainted with the underworld, what rackets he has experience with, and whom he knows" (Inciardi, 1975:56). Needless to say, professionals are cautious in their use of criminal slang when there is a chance that it might draw attention to them. This consensus in language is especially important when thieves are on the move and are setting up "connections." With few exceptions, professionals rely on an extensive network of contacts among those within the fraternity as well as those peripheral to it. Such connections are important not only as avenues of information sharing but also as a pool of potential partners — or, if they are lawyers and bondsmen, a pool of potential help when the law strikes.

Although thieves clearly recognize the value of consensus, evidence indicates that much of the underworld code of honor among thieves may be crumbling. In his interviews with professional burglars, Shover (1973) found many spontaneous comments bemoaning the apparent decline of "the Code." In part this may be due to the fact that "the 'solid,' ethical career criminal seems to be giving way to the 'hustler,' an alert opportunist who is primarily concerned only with personal — as opposed to collective — security" (p. 512). But adherence to any code is severely tested when the chips are down, and thieves are certainly no different from the rest of us in this regard. It appears that pressures of the moment, and practical considerations generally, lie at the heart of any particular acceptance or rejection of professional codes or consensual understandings. Loyalty may have existed in the old days, but as one thief put it: "There is no loyalty among thieves today. There's no such thing at all. They have absolutely no loyalty. They'll beat one another to the money, you know, anything they can, they beat one another for their girls, or anything" (King, 1972:89). When the rules are observed, when the code is followed, honor or loyalty may have little to do with it:

> . . . honor among thieves? Well — yes and no. You do have some old pros who might talk about honor, but they're so well heeled and well connected they can afford to be honorable. But for most people, it's a question of "do unto others" — you play by the rules because you may need a favor someday, or because the guy you skip on, or the guy you rap to the cops about — you never know where he'll turn up. Maybe he's got something on you or maybe he ends up as your cellmate, or he says bad things about you — you can't tell how things could turn out. (Inciardi, 1975:70)

## The "Fix"

Most career criminals spend considerable time and energy negotiating their way around trouble with the law. For the professional, confrontations with the machinery of law are treated as normal, expected features of a thief's way of life. As a professional, however, the thief acts so as to minimize the risk that confrontations will result in conviction and confinement. Whereas amateurs seem preoccupied with avoiding detection and arrest, professionals direct their energies to avoid conviction. Letkemann found that experienced criminals "didn't particularly mind if the police 'knew' they had pulled a particular caper. The important factor for the experienced criminal was that 'they have nothing on me.' That is, there must be no evidence that will 'stand up' in court (1973:30).

The major method professionals employ to reduce the risks of conviction, and hence of confinement, is the "fix." The fix involves organization and resources, and it is the professional, as opposed to the amateur criminal, who is generally in a position to make it work. Basically, the fix works through manipulation of the judicial process. Efforts are made, therefore, to buy the help of those in a position to influence criminal proceedings. They include the police, lawyers, bondsmen, politicians, court personnel, and judges. Only one link in the chain of law enforcement need be diverted from its legally sanctioned path for the fix to work.

In most large cities, professional fixers handle many of the legal problems faced by organized thieves. These persons generally hold respectable positions within the administration of justice and are often associated with the prosecution. As holders of occupational positions within the legitimate work structure of society, fixers represent one of the more important connections between the profession of theft and the larger society. It is through this connection that organized theft helps guarantee its own survival. Without the fix, professional crime would lose one of its essential lines of defense against encroachment by organized repression. What this means, of course, is that as long as individuals who claim membership in legitimate society — and are recognized as having such membership — and engage in activities supporting acknowledged illegitimate pursuits, the distinction between what is legitimate and illegitimate itself will remain vague and contestable. It is therefore not surprising to find many thieves arguing persuasively that what they do is not that different from what respectable people do.

The perpetuation of thief-fixer relationships depends on a number of things. Obviously, if each pays off as expected, both parties will meet the immediate demands of the relationship. From the fixer's standpoint, this usually means money, but sometimes nonmonetary favors of one sort or another are involved. For the thief it means no conviction at all or the lightest possible sentence. But apart from these more obvious considerations are questions of personal security and mutual trust (which is not the same as respect!). The successful thieves and fixers are those who keep tight lips, who do not divulge confidences, and who can be relied on to fulfill their part of the bargain.

In making the most of fix possibilities, thieves display intimate knowledge of the ways of the world. They know, for example, that if it comes to a trial, court proceedings and sentence decisions may well be influenced by extraneous variables, such as the way in which their offense is handled by the media. So, some knowledgeable thieves use the fix in dealings with newspaper reporters (Gasser, 1963). By the same token, indirect methods sometimes work more productively and safely than do blatant efforts to "put the fix in":

> If you were going to pay off a judge you wouldn't offer him any money, you do it indirectly. Say you had a big case coming up. If you're any kind of businessman at all, you don't put too much faith in your lawyer. Lawyers being what they are. So you go to your state committee man who don't hold any office at all, you go to your political boss and explain what your troubles are and you'd like to be pretty sure things were going to turn out all right and it would be worth so much if you could be sure things would turn out all right. He's the guy that put the judge's name on the ballot. So about 99 times out of a hundred when you come back to his office the next day he tells you, Don't worry about it, it'll cost five thousand, everything's gonna be taken care of. (Martin, 1952:171)

Although some evidence indicates that use of the fix may be less productive and predictable than in the past, one study shows that of those professional criminals interviewed, all had employed the fix quite frequently and generally with good results. The ratio of arrests to felony convictions was 100 to 5.8 and that of arrests to imprisonment for one year or more was 100 to 3.5 (Inciardi, 1975). The fix works for those who are in a position to use it and will remain available as long as people are willing and able to manipulate the machinery of law for a price.

## "Fencing" Stolen Property

Along with the fix, the "fence" is another of the essential ties between theft and the larger social structure. Without someone to receive and dispose of stolen property, theft, particularly professional theft, would face hard times. The fence fills this role.

Despite the importance of fencing as one facet of criminal theft and its relationship with legitimate society, few criminology texts have much to say on the topic. One reason for this is the paucity of research on fencing and fences. Two authors (Chappell and Walsh, 1974) have come up with some interesting reasons for this. One reason, they suggest, is that because fencing amounts to a rational, businesslike activity, it has none of the qualities of deviance traditionally emphasized in criminological theory and research. Another reason is the intangible nature of the crime of receiving. Not only does it have low visibility, it seems to disappear on successful completion: "It is as though the conduct erases itself after execution so that, while a fundamental existence can be attested to (here, stolen property is fenced), any tangible evidence as to the conduct's independent existence is gone" (Chappell and Walsh, 1974:494). Then again, any detailed investigation of fencing is difficult because of the functional requirements of secrecy and the maintenance of a legitimate front, not to mention the probability that neither those who use fences, nor those who buy from them, have any inclination toward opening things up for research that might later be used to help put them out of business — a good thing is a good thing.

Fencing has long been a troublesome issue in criminal law. Early English common law, with its emphasis on possession and trespass, found those who received stolen property to be guilty of "receiving larcenously" — a rather nebulous concoction designed to permit the law to act against persons who could not be dealt with under prevailing conceptions of larceny. It appears that the application of this label meant different things to different judges, and though the act itself was generally considered only a misdemeanor, at least one person is known to have been hanged for it in the fourteenth century (Plucknett, 1948). After centuries of confusion, "receiving stolen goods" finally in 1707 became an independent misdemeanor by English statute and in 1827 was made a felony.

In America, as in England, there are four elements in the criminal law conception of receiving: (1) the property must have been stolen, or, as some codes put it, "feloniously taken"; (2) the property must have been received or concealed, though in most states the receiver need not actually have seen or touched it; (3) the receiver must have accepted it with the knowledge (in some states, merely the belief) that it was stolen or feloniously taken; and (4) the property must be received with fraudulent or criminal intent (Gammage and Hemphill, 1974). As you can readily see from this list of legal requirements, it is no simple matter to demonstrate an actual case of receiving.

**The "Sting"**  Recent federal efforts to combat fencing operations have led to new crime-fighting methods. The so-called sting antifencing operation was introduced in 1974 and had been tried in forty-six cities by 1979. Typically, the police set up a bogus fencing operation using undercover officers and various electronic gadgets for monitoring transactions. "Customers" include thieves as well as amateur and professional fences. The Department of Justice estimates that some $226,582,045 in stolen property had been recovered by late 1979; in its turn, the government put up some $5.95 million in "buy" money. Not a bad return by any standards.

Even more important, we are told, is the fact that some 6,654 individuals have been indicted since the sting programs began, with an astounding conviction rate of 98 percent. Many of those arrested are career thieves and professional fences with extensive criminal histories. Cities that have used the sting appear to have experienced subsequent declines in rates of robbery, burglary, larceny, and auto theft — suggesting, perhaps, that many of the "customers" have been arrested.

**Lay and Professional Fences**  A useful place to begin to understand fencing's relation to theft is with Jerome Hall's distinction between the professional and amateur, or lay, receivers. According to Hall (1952:291),

1. The professional receiver *buys for the purpose of resale,* whereas the lay receiver buys for consumption.
2. Hence the professional receiver sells stolen merchandise, whereas the lay receiver *consumes* the goods.
3. The professional receiver operates a business; he deals in stolen commodities and is apt to be *in possession of a relatively large amount of such commodities, derived from different thefts and thieves, as a stock in trade; the lay receiver does not operate a business nor does he deal in or possess a large quantity of stolen commodities.*

Lay receiving encompasses people from all walks of life and in all sorts of relationships with thieves. They are likely to be members of the family, friends, or acquaintances, and they may be plumbers, professors, or preachers. Lay receivers may be "square johns" or they may themselves be dabblers in theft or other crime (Shover, 1973). The amateur thieves, from habitual ones to sporadic opportunists, will from time to time want or need to unload stolen items. It is likely they are not familiar with professional fences or professional fencing (even if they are, professionals may not want to be involved with them) and so this leaves them little recourse but to sell or give their merchandise to friends and acquaintances. They may, of course, hock their property, in which case they get a pittance for it and take considerable risks in doing so.

The professional thief and the professional fence are better organized, better equipped, and better placed than are the amateur thief and the lay fence. Their relationship is one of mutual support and dependency. The continued rewarding existence of each depends on relations with the other. Because of their legitimate fronts, fences are in a position to provide a relatively secure outlet for stolen merchandise, but that outlet remains secure only as long as both parties maintain productive ties and respect each other's needs for secrecy and continued business. Many fences remain on the periphery of professional theft but from time to time are useful sources of tips and information for working thieves. By acting as sources of information fences can retain better control over their own enterprise, since they will know "what's coming down" and what goods will be available. Obviously, this works to both the fence's and the thief's advantage.

**Networks and Connections**  Connections are important to the fence, whose business is essentially by word-of-mouth. A variety of different networks help cement and protect these connections. Marilyn Walsh (1977) identifies three major types of networks: (1) the kinship network — dominated by family ties, with young members often supplying the stolen merchandise, which older members then sell; (2) the work-a-day network — often based on employer–employee relationships, as when a businessperson who is also a fence receives stolen property from an employee. The employee steals for the employer in the latter's capacity as fence; (3) the play network — the connections maintained by good burglars and fences whose primary activities are criminal rather than legitimate. An elite group, the play network meets socially, and information rather than business is the reason for getting together.

The major functions of these networks are described by Walsh as *association* — meeting peers, getting contacts; *risk taking* — reducing risks, increasing rewards and decreasing costs of doing business, helping other thieves and fences avoid trouble with the law; *recruitment* — providing thieves with possible partners, getting people started in thievery; *procedural ratiocination* — setting direction to theft, establishing predictability, standards, chronology, and understanding of procedures; *selective skill diffusion* — combining skills of members, raising the expertise of all, elevating burglars to the status of good burglar. Walsh points out that race, ethnicity, family, and location all affect the opportunities for maximization of skill diffusion. Finally, there is *information dissemination*. One of the major benefits of a network is the opportunity to provides for passing and withholding information.

Walsh observes that "the network serves as both an insulator and an isolator for the thief. It insulates him from the solitary, highly risky theft activities of the lone thief by offering him association with others capable of directing and enhancing his career. It provides him with information he otherwise could not generate, and it gives him working partners he may never have found on his own" (1977:145).

Apart from information, fences may also provide loans for thieves about to pull lucrative capers and can put thieves in contact with one another, as well as with bondsmen and lawyers in a time of crisis. Quite often, fences have businesses in areas where criminals hang out — taverns, poolrooms, barber-shops, and restaurants. Those fences are commonly not big money-makers in their legitimate pursuits but get their lucrative returns from fencing.

As with professional thieves, the fraternity of fences has gradations of status. One professional fence ("Morris") has outlined some of the variations in fencing practices that become sources of status distinctions (Pearl, 1974). At the top of the fencing ladder are the "master" fences, whose organization, facilities, and bankroll permit them to handle the biggest jobs. Master fences deal with all kinds of merchandise and are able at a moment's notice to arrange the disposal of a haul too big, or too general, for the more common "specialty" fence. Thieves who specialize in only certain types of merchandise — jewelry, furs, credit cards, or clothing — prefer to deal with fences who also specialize in the same goods. Morris estimates that in New York City alone there are some fifty fences who specialize in jewelry. At the bottom of the professional fence hierarchy are the neighborhood fences who are parts of the vast network of fencing operations in any large city. Their business is relatively small yet indispensable to the run-of-the-mill professional thief whose own scores are small but require regular disposal.

In line with changing methods of doing business in the American economy, fences have adapted their illegal work to the requirements of legitimate exchange. For example, whereas credit cards used to be avoided like the plague, today they are a boon to the established fence. As Morris explains:

> Years ago, if a thief picked up a credit card he would throw it away. He was afraid to use it because he didn't know how long it took before the stores found out the card had been stolen. Today it's worth anything from $50 to $200 to me, depending on when it was lifted. It takes at least five business days to get a hot sheet out on most stolen cards. My people can bang the hell out of one in three or four days. (Pearl, 1974:102)

Morris estimates his income from fencing operations to be around $250,000 a year. His work has all the earmarks of a planned, rational, business enterprise. He makes money and survives in his fencing business (only one arrest in more than twenty years) because he effectively plays off the legal and illegal sides of American economic enterprise.

## THE FENCE AS ENTREPRENEUR

Professional fencing has been studied in depth by two sociologists using vastly different data and methods. Marilyn Walsh (1977) read through police files and interviewed detectives to build her picture of the "businessman-fence," the person who straddles the worlds of legitimate business and theft as well as the criminal worlds of street crime (mainly burglary) and occupational crime (fencing itself). Carl Klockars (1974) presents a case study of one man's life in crime based on interviews with "Vincent Swaggi," the best-known fence in his city. Walsh describes the professional fence:

> The criminal receiver is a white male in his mid- to late forties who owns and operates a legitimate retail establishment; he probably has not ever been arrested, but if he has, his record is likely to show only one such encounter with the criminal justice system (and that as a traffic violator); he looks very much like the totally legitimate manager or business administrator in our society. (1977:45–51)

Both Walsh and Klockars describe professional fencing as an enterprise requiring resourcefulness, personal charisma, ingenuity, and a good grasp of market practices and the realities of economic competition. As with any other rational business enterprise, the goal is to make profits while keeping down costs and risks.

This is very much in evidence in the way fences deal with the thieves who bring them merchandise. The fence distinguishes the good burglar (see p. 215) from the young, the inexperienced, the junkies, and those known to the police. Fences vary in their prices accordingly; they will pay the junkie from 10 to 30 percent of the retail and the good burglar from 30 to 50 percent of the wholesale value. A junkie might get $65 for a $600 stereo; a good burglar will get $1,500 for a $7,500 antique lampshade (Walsh, 1977:72).

Fences are not above deceit and trickery in their dealings with thieves; in fact, Vincent Swaggi gives the impression of being proud of his tricks with quality, quantity, and price. He tells Klockars of a time he managed to get away with paying $200 for goods worth around $1,800 at retail:

> These two guys drive up to the store. They got a new Caddy, maybe a year old. Well, you wanna see it. Cartons everywhere . . . and the guy on the front seat's got one on his lap. He comes in an' asks if I'm interested, so I tell him to pull around the back an' let me see what he's got. They musta just run across an open truck, 'cause they had seven cartons, five big plus two little ones — all clothes. . . . All good stuff. So I put all the cartons in a line in my back room. Now here's somethin' to remember. You got this much stuff an' the guys bring it inside your store, they ain't gonna carry it all out. Just too much carryin'.
>
> Anyway, we start to go right down the line, just like an auction. First carton, shirts, Van Heusen. They're nice; in fact, I like 'em myself. "Whaddaya got? About three dozen? Thirty-five for this." Second carton, sweater sets . . . retail approximately eighteen dollars. "Hmmm, sweaters. Three — no. I'll make it three-fifty. Let's see, that's about fifty, hell, make it sixty." Next carton, three-dozen boxes of men's socks. "Oh-oh, socks. Can't give you more than a quarter a pair. Let's see, a quarter a pair times three dozen." I ask the thief, "A quarter a pair times three dozen, how much does that come to?" He just looks at me. "Fifteen dollars, right?" He nods. "Wait a minute," I say, "not fifteen dollars, twelve. Twelve pair, twenty-five cents a pair, that's four a dozen times three is twelve dollars." By this time I got him so confused he don't remember there's nine dozen in the carton. Next carton, more socks. "Same deal on those, OK?" Then we come to two little cartons — men's gloves. "Ok ten apiece for

these two little ones?" Then I stand up without sayin' nothin' about the next carton. I just opened the top an' sort'a hummed a little. "OK, what does all that come to? Thirty-five and a hundred for all the sweaters, that's a hundred thirty-five, plus ten apiece for the gloves, that's about a hundred fifty, plus fifteen each for the socks. Wait a minute, didn't I say twelve for the socks? Oh, make it twenty-five for both. Let's see, that's a hundred seventy-five." "Hey, wait a minute," they say, "you forgot the children's clothes here." "Oh yeh," I says, "see, I got grandchildren I was thinkin' of them for. How about you give me four for my personal use an' I'll give you two hundred for the lot. Take it or leave it." Then I start countin' out twenties. "OK now, here's a hundred for you an' another hundred for you." They took it. (Klockars, 1974:121–122)

Klockars goes on to interpret the transaction step by step. Even without his help, it is obvious that Vincent Swaggi worked his trick through a combination of fast talk and clever manipulation of numbers, all the time hiding from his thieves the true value of their merchandise.

Klockars points out that tricks are more likely to appear in Vincent's dealings when the thieves involved are of no particular consequence to him — he can do without their business. Occasionally, Vincent will con good burglars and thieves with whom he wishes to maintain good relations, but he will at other times pay them more than he needs to.

## Specialization and Varieties of Theft

Professional thieves rarely spend all or even most of their time in one particular line of theft. The common exceptions to this general rule are professional shoplifters, pickpockets, and forgers ("paper hangers"). Explaining why most thieves spread around their talents, one professional thief had this to say:

Stealing for a living isn't just being a burglar or stick-up man. You've got to be able to look around and recognize opportunities and be able to take advantage of them regardless of what the conditions are. A lot of people think once a stick-up man, always a stick-up man. Well, you can't run around stickin' up people every day of the week like a workin' man. Maybe something worthwhile sticking up only shows up every two or three months. In the meantime you're doing this and that, changing around, doing practically anything to make a dollar. (Martin, 1952:117)

Some, of course, develop interests and talents that lead them toward particular sorts of capers in preference to others. They "have a line." Some thieves express an interest in the theft of only certain types of merchandise — for example, credit cards, jewelry, or furs — and others see their talents put to the most productive (and secure) use in one line of work — picking pockets, sneak theft, forgery, or con games. On the whole, however, it seems that for both practical and social reasons, thieves are generalists rather than specialists. Some may even be adamantly opposed to specialization: it reduces the chances of remaining anonymous and increases the risks of being fingered for a caper known to be their style. Professionals do give recognition to those who can say they "have a line," but this denotes their preference and skill rather than day-to-day activity. Letkemann suggests that concern with specialization is more likely to be found among aspiring young amateurs: "It may be that they carry over to the criminal world some of the square criteria for assigning status" (1973:33).

Those varieties of theft involving high levels of skill, organization, and planning and those requiring substantial resources (some big cons) are usually outside the reach of the typical amateur. However, many types of theft attract both professionals and amateurs. Within these types, some of the major things distinguishing amateurs from professionals are arrest and conviction history, size of the heist, level of technical skill involved, and type of fencing arrangement employed. Amateurs tend to be arrested and convicted more often, to come away with smaller payoffs (or none), to employ little in the way of manipulative and technical skills, and to steal for themselves or for disposal via lay fences. Both professionals and amateurs are involved in burglary, sneak theft, forgery, and auto theft. Amateurs are rarely found in confidence swindling, counterfeiting, or extortion.

## SHOPLIFTING

When people steal from under the nose of their victims, it is commonly called *sneak theft*. Examples include shoplifting, pickpocketing, and "till tapping" (stealing from cash registers).

Of the many varieties of sneak theft not committed by employees, shoplifting has no equal. The number of shoplifting incidents that occur throughout America during a given year is unknown and unknowable, but the estimates are staggering. Baumer and Rosenbaum (1984) put the figure at over 200 million in 1979, and there is no reason to believe that the number is any smaller today. Looking back to Figure 7.1, we see that shoplifting is the only one of eight larceny offenses to have increased consistently since 1980, according to the FBI. Some of the increase could be due to higher reporting rates around the country, but just how much is a matter of conjecture. Perhaps more to the point, experts do not believe that shoplifting rates are decreasing.

The cost of it all? Around $4 billion a year to the retail industry alone, $12 billion if you include the thefts committed by retail employees (Baumer and Rosenbaum, 1984:16). The distinction is important if only because it demonstrates that those we trust are very often untrustworthy, a topic to which Chapter 9 is devoted. But more importantly, it illustrates what is true generally of crimes committed on the job, that they exact a greater financial cost than do offenses committed outside employment or by the unemployed.

Historically, shoplifting is neither new nor have its methods changed much in a hundred years. To be sure, there have been changes in the architecture of stores and in the overall character of the shopping experience, but shoplifters

Dressed just like any other shopper, the store security guard politely confronts a young woman suspected of shoplifting. Compared with the number of shoplifting offenses committed, however, arrests are rare.

still employ time-honored methods: concealing items under their clothes, hiding them in false-bottomed cases, "bad bagging" them (putting them in well-worn shopping bags), and using "booster boxes" (cartons and packages that appear sealed but in fact have an opening through which to put lifted items (see Edwards, 1958:4–15).

Shoplifting is dominated by amateurs and opportunists, and it cuts across age, sex, race, economic status, and educational distinctions. Tentative generalizations based on the studies mentioned above, as well as Mary Owen Cameron's (1964) classic *The Booster and the Snitch,* are that (1) women and children shoplift more frequently than men do; (2) most are occasional pilferers, of no particular social class; (3) the items taken rarely exceed $20 in value; and (4) the favored articles are toilet articles, clothing accessories, recreation items, food, and school supplies.

Cameron (1964) shows that professional shoplifting still thrives and is quite different from the more common amateur variety. Boosters and "heels" (thieves who exclusively shoplift) generally steal more expensive items, do so with planning and skill, and usually work in a group, sometimes with twelve to fifteen members. Professionals differ from amateur pilferers (or "snitches") in another way: they sell what they lift, usually to a fence. Between the amateurs and professionals are those who shoplift to help support a drug habit. As we shall see in Chapter 11, shoplifting is a common crime among drug users and addicts, and though not professionals, these shoplifters steal regularly and usually will try to sell their booty for cash to buy a hit.

**Reactions to Shoplifting**    Reactions to shoplifting and shoplifters reveal the most intriguing facets of this criminal activity. Time and again studies indicate that though most shoplifters are never caught, those that are often face little more than a scolding, to be sent on their way after returning or paying for the merchandise. But the shoplifter's chances of being merely "told off" depend on age, sex, ability to pay, attitude, apparent breeding, and whether or not he or she is a known or suspected professional.

Overall, it appears that the value of the items taken is the best predictor of whether the shoplifter will get by with verbal scolding or whether the police will be notified and prosecution pursued. Michael Hindelang's (1974) study of the referral behavior of a California private security agency shows that in both 1963 and 1968 those who were most likely to be referred to the police by the victim had stolen items of relatively large value. But in this same study Hindelang discovered that when the value of the item was controlled, the nature of the goods and how they were concealed also figured in the picture. The person who stole liquor, cigarettes, or fresh meat had a better chance of being referred to the police than one who did not. The person who employed a method of concealment that left little room for doubt about illegal intentions again had a better chance of being referred to the police.

Why do many offenders get little more than a scolding when caught? Because the detection and arrest of shoplifters are commonly the responsibility of store personnel, who gets arrested and what happens to them is influenced in part by the policies and attitudes held by those assuming that responsibility. Both in America and abroad, the general store policy is caution and leniency. The primary objective is to deter shoplifting while avoiding anything that might hurt store business. Store management wants to avoid scenes on the shop floor that might adversely affect the attitudes and behavior of customers; equally, it wants to minimize the time and expense involved in carrying through official prosecution of suspects; and finally, it wants to avoid unnecessary publicity that might mark the store as unfriendly, or harsh, or as a place frequented by shoplifters (Waltz, 1953). If the store can recover the items or obtain payment for them through informal and discreet means, then its interests will be at least partially met.

Other aspects of the informal approach should be born in mind. Store management knows that on the whole most pilferers are amateurs and that when confronted with their attempted theft, most are so shaken up they will do almost anything to avoid official attention. Further, they will probably refrain from stealing in that store, at least for a time. Studies have shown that typical pilferers are what the criminal subculture labels "square johns," who neither systematically involve themselves in criminal pursuits nor identify themselves as criminals but who adhere to the dominant cultural values and spend most of their time in legitimate pursuits. When caught, amateurs (particularly adults) display their commitment to dominant conceptions of right and wrong and strenuously deny that they have done anything wrong or that they are criminals. Cameron reports the following as a typical verbal response from the amateur on being apprehended:

> I didn't intend to take the dress. I just wanted to see it in the daylight. Oh! what will my husband do! I *did* intend to pay for it. It's all a mistake. Oh! my God! what will mother say! I'll be glad to pay for it. See, I've got the money with me. Oh! my children! They can't find out I've been arrested! I'd never be able to face them again. (1964:164)

Some pilferers dream up quite incredible excuses or explanations for their behavior: "The shop assistant took so long in coming"; "I thought my sister had paid for it"; "I only wanted to see whether things are properly supervised here" (Doleisch, 1960:4).

Another important reason that management may react informally rather than formally to shoplifting pertains to the legal difficulties surrounding the civilian arrest of persons suspected of misdemeanors. Since most shoplifters steal only enough to get charged with a misdemeanor, civilians are placed in a difficult situation, because many states have strict laws governing the conditions under which misdemeanor suspects may be apprehended. To arrest a misdemeanor suspect is to do so at peril because those who do may be subject to suits charging false imprisonment or false arrest (Waltz, 1953). Rather than face possible legal troubles, many stores approach a suspect discreetly and informally, playing down the fact that technically a civilian arrest is being made. Not surprisingly, retailers have in recent years brought considerable pressure to bear on legislatures to amend regulations dealing with the apprehension of suspected shoplifters. Many states now permit store personnel to detain suspects under certain broad conditions and without fear of civil suits charging false arrest or imprisonment. This may mean an increase in the official handling of pilferers, though the considerations reviewed here will continue to play an important part in management decisions.

**Consequences of Informal Reactions** The informal handling of shoplifters may have important ramifications for the way shoplifting is viewed by those apprehended as well as by the general public. The fact that many shoplifters are generally upright citizens suggests that in order to engage in shoplifting in the first place — which they recognize is wrong and illegal — they may have convinced themselves that in their case it is not really theft, certainly not crime. We have already seen that such is indeed the way many apprehended amateurs conceive of their actions. How do they arrive at this conception? How is it that what they do is not crime but what someone else does — for example, robbery and burglary — is crime?

What we view as crime is partly influenced by prevailing cultural conceptions of crime and partly by the kinds of things that happen, or at least are expected to happen, to criminals. If we do things we expect will result in our being labeled criminal, then to be so labeled will come as no surprise and will merely reinforce our conception of the act and ourselves as criminal. But if we are not sure that our actions are criminal or if we have adopted the view that they are not, we will see no reason to alter our views when reactions fail to conform with what we know, assume, or expect will happen to "real" criminals doing "real" criminal things. And so, the upright citizen who occasionally shoplifts and who when caught is treated informally and discreetly by store personnel will be under little pressure to alter his or her conception of self and behavior. The ramification of this is that informal handling of shoplifters permits upright citizens, believers in the "American way," to retain the view that what they do is not criminal and that the criminal is quite another kind of person.

Interestingly enough, American business practices may encourage amateur shoplifting in yet another way. Businesses spend billions of dollars every year on campaigns designed to convince Americans that they need and want items offered for sale. Already attuned to the values of an acquisitive society, Americans are constantly reminded to spend as much money as they can. We are continually exhorted to buy now, buy more, buy better (whatever that means), and pay later if we do not have the cash on hand. At Christmastime, when shoplifting is at its yearly peak, the glitter and the temptation are at their height. We come to learn that successful, self-respecting Americans are those who can demonstrate by consumption behavior that they have at least kept up with their peers, if not gone ahead of them. Even if we cannot really afford an item, we are discouraged from forgetting about it and instead are extolled to find a way to afford it. Continually pushed to conceive of the meaning of life in material terms, Americans have adopted standards that measure people by what they possess, what they can afford, and what they consume, rather than who they are and what they are. Among the casualties of an acquisitive society are values of fairness, dignity, decency, concern for others, and feelings of contentment and well-being, as Harry Bredemeier and Jackson Toby (1961) have argued.

**Why Shoplift?**    When faced with failing to keep up material standards (an adult rather than juvenile concern), we have two basic options. We can withdraw entirely from the battle for access to and control over material wealth, or we can try all the harder to win that battle. It is especially hard to withdraw when everything around us seems to confirm and reinforce the central place held by material things. In fact, Bredemeier and Toby argue

(1961:62), most Americans probably choose the latter option. If taken, the option of trying harder will lead us in one of three directions: (1) we can relentlessly pursue those culturally supported, institutionalized avenues to material acquisition; (2) we can reject those legitimized avenues and select alternatives; or (3) we can combine relentless pursuit of some legitimized avenues with the rejection of others. In these authors' view, the American solution to problems of acquisition revolves around three "governing principles": self-reliance (fend for yourself, "shop around"), competition (outperform or outshine those who are competing with you for rewards), and negotiated exchange (get as much as you can for as little as possible). Americans who face apparent defeat in the race for material things can be expected to frame their choice of options around these three institutionalized mechanisms. We can relentlessly pursue, or we can reject some or all of them.

Adult Americans who shoplift on an amateur basis are perhaps best understood as those who, while pursuing the solution to their acquisitive problems in the "American way," find it convenient or necessary from time to time to reject the idea of a negotiated exchange and overemphasize self-reliance — "taking care of number one". It is easier for upstanding Americans to reject the idea of bargaining for acceptable terms of exchange when they perceive that they are in fact not in a position to bargain in the first place or that no matter what they offer to negotiate, the terms are settled in the other's favor before the negotiation begins. Under these conditions the situation is itself in violation of the institutionalized principle. The feeling that retailers are to all intents and purposes "ripping us off" is simply an expression of defeat in negotiated exchange. However, when they cannot win in the exchange but still need or desire that blouse, that bottle of liquor, those earrings, that wallet, or that food, things can be worked to advantage through pursuit of self-reliance. Instead of defeat, they can claim temporary victory when they fend for themselves and rip off the store. But through all this, their interpretation of what has happened, what they have done, remains appropriately American — they were merely being self-reliant under circumstances in which the principle of negotiated exchange could not be satisfactorily followed. And so, as we saw earlier, the amateur adult shoplifters see themselves not as criminals, not as thieves, but instead as upholders of the "American way."

## BURGLARY

Though declining in recent years (Figures 8.3 and 8.4), burglary is the most common and, to many Americans, one of the more frightening of Index crimes. Victims often report that they felt as if their very person had been violated. We cherish the privacy and security of our homes and feel anger and resentment when these are breached. The victims of burglary come from all walks of life, though the poorer parts of American cities tend to bear the

**Figure 8.3** Trends in burglary, 1980–1984

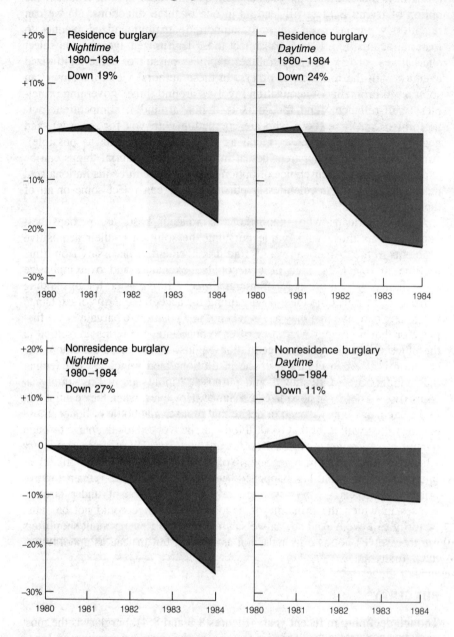

Residence burglary
*Nighttime*
1980–1984
Down 19%

Residence burglary
*Daytime*
1980–1984
Down 24%

Nonresidence burglary
*Nighttime*
1980–1984
Down 27%

Nonresidence burglary
*Daytime*
1980–1984
Down 11%

**Figure 8.4**   Household burglary rates, 1973–1982

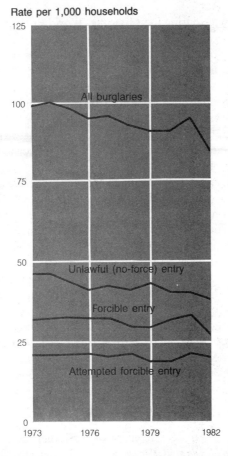

Rate per 1,000 households

SOURCE: Bureau of Justice Statistics (1985e), Household Burglary. Washington, D.C.: U.S.
Dept. of Justice, p. 2.

brunt of this assault on private property. National surveys over the period
from 1973 to 1982 show that households earning less than $7,500 per annum
averaged higher victimization rates than any other income group, blacks
averaged higher rates than whites, and the risks of being burglarized were
much higher for families living in rental property than for those who owned
their home (Bureau of Justice Statistics, 1985e). Not surprisingly, the more
valuable the property stolen was, the more likely burglary victims were to
report the incident to police.

Over the last few years the fears of middle-class homeowners have increased as suburban burglary rates have increased in relation to city rates.
Communities have organized "crime watch" groups to patrol their neighborhoods in an attempt to protect themselves from the burglar, among other

criminals. But perhaps we should be thankful we do not live in Australia: a recent Australian victimization survey shows that all Australians can expect to be burglarized twice during their lifetime (*World Press Review,* November 1984).

Whether in the suburbs, in rural areas, or in cities, most burglaries are the work of relatively unskilled amateurs. They look for cash and for items that can be readily disposed of via lay fences and pawnshops. Their methods are scorned by professionals. Professionals take pride in their ability to gain entrance without force and noise and to pull a job speedily and profitably. The unskilled, often youthful burglars are called "door shakers," "kick-it-in men," "loidmen," and "creepers" — names that reflect their amateur techniques (Pileggi, 1968).

A number of research efforts during the past decade have aimed at identifying the major contours of burglary offenses and offenders. There is considerable agreement among them as to the main characteristics. Burglary incidents tend to involve residences more frequently than commercial establishments; losses are moderate, usually well under five hundred dollars; most are burglaries of cash and cash-convertible items such as televisions, radios, and stereos; residential burglaries usually take place during the daytime, those of commercial establishments at night, often on weekends; and most involve some sort of forced entry. It is perhaps significant that the clearance rate (proportion of incidents resulting in arrest) tends to be higher for burglaries in which there is no loss at all or only a small one. Presumably these are uncompleted burglaries, and their numbers are higher than might be expected — up to 33 percent of all incidents in some studies (eg. Conklin and Bittner, 1973). They are often the work of amateurs who cannot find what they want or who are discovered or frightened away before they have had a chance to start work.

Many offenders are under 18 years of age when arrested, with blacks tending to be overrepresented. Very few are female, but when women are involved, they are more likely than men to work in partnerships or groups, although men frequently work in teams. Most adult burglars have prior arrest records, often for burglary.

When professionals work, they choose targets that have been carefully cased; they work in well-oiled teams with each member assigned a specific role based on experience and expertise; and they work with quiet speed. In search for a lucrative score, the professional must deal effectively with security systems. The ability to disarm alarms separates the good burglar from both the amateur and the aspiring professional (Letkemann, 1973).

Once inside, there is the problem of finding whatever it is the burglars are after. If they are interested in cash, as many are, finding it is not always simple. Skilled burglars apply the experience and know-how that lead them to anticipate the behavior of their victims:

In commercial establishments, he may find it in the expected places, such as safes, cash registers, or in deliberately unexpected places, such as one shoe box among several hundred others. In residential dwellings, the burglar's task may be even more difficult, since the places where cash may be found are less predictable. A home does not have a cash register, nor, necessarily, a safe. Therefore, the burglar must make quick interpretations as to the most probable location of cash. The mental activity here is really a game of wits — or operating on the basis of reciprocal expectations. He proceeds on the assumptions he has regarding routine family behavior, and he anticipates uniformities in architecture as well as in styles of placing valuables. (Letkemann, 1973:55)

In professional burglary, safecrackers are at the top of the status hierarchy, and their work makes some of the greatest demands on a thief's skill. Safecracking has been explored in detail by Letkemann. Among the basic tools and equipment are "grease" (nitroglycerine), made from a combination of sulphuric acid, nitric acid, and glycerine; soap, which must be pliable and is used for funneling the grease into the door; and "knockers and string" (detonators and fuses). The most common technique of safeblowing is the so-called jam shot, a procedure consisting of some ten coordinated steps that, if done correctly, make the door of the safe swing open on its hinges. When not done correctly, the door is blown off the safe, or worse, the door and safe buckle.

Professional safecrackers must keep up with technological advances if they are to stay in business, and those who have been long in the field recognize the importance of information sharing and connections. Safecrackers share information on jobs, on techniques, on new developments, and on any related aspects of their line. Letkemann suggests that the already fairly strong social bonds linking safecrackers have been strengthened as a result of greatly restricted access to dynamite (a ready source of grease), and the resulting need to make their own nitroglycerine: "It enabled leaders to screen new 'recruits' and necessitated the development of a stronger subculture based on mutual aid and group loyalty" (1973:88).

Today sophisticated professional burglary has been swallowed up by the growing numbers of amateur burglaries committed by those in search of immediate economic rewards. Although professional burglary is undoubtedly alive and well, it may be that increased security and decreased use of cash as a medium of exchange will help drive all but the most organized and skilled burglars into other lines of work. The one thing about a professional is that he or she will endeavor to find an alternative way to stay in business, especially if that alternative permits the retention of self-conceptions in line with professionalism.

## FORGERY

It is estimated that in any given year, losses to forgery in America run from $500 million to over $1 billion (Foldessy, 1971). By far the most common form of forgery is "paper hanging." Paper hanging is using bank checks when funds are insufficient to cover them or when the signature has been forged. Since around 90 percent of all American money transactions are made with checks, there is a ready-made climate within which forgery can flourish. Actually, it is not just the abundant use of checks that provides a supportive environment for the check forger. Public attitudes toward checks and their use, the ease with which paper hanging can be accomplished, the unwillingness of banks and stores to prosecute, and the hazy line between criminal intent and mistake all make for a supportive atmosphere. In many respects, the very things that support shoplifting also encourage check forgery.

**Naive Forgers** Checks are commonly seen as "like" money but not as "real" money; hence their misuse may escape the public censure that the loss or theft of cash receives. In addition, checks are drawn on, and supplied by, relatively impersonal institutions, which, like department stores, provide services we need in order to meet prevailing cultural standards. As institutions to which we are beholden but that are beyond our personal control, we, not they, stand as potential victims in the relationship. Those who would attempt to reverse this situation, however temporarily, may well receive a kind of quiet praise by the public, for they have bucked the institutionalized situation of dependency. Two factors help explain the seemingly pervasive public indifference to check forgery. First, it is not rare for a person inadvertently to cash or use a check without at that moment having sufficient funds to cover it. Second, check forgery does not have any of the earmarks of what we conventionally think of as a crime — it does not look like crime, so maybe it really is not (see Lemert, 1953).

Banks and stores, which provide checks and checking services, also help support forgery. Because they are in a business dependent on continued public good faith, they are unwilling to make too much of the typical case of check forgery. Rather than antagonize current or prospective clients, banks and stores are more likely to treat most paper hanging, on the surface at least, as mistakes or oversights rather than what they legally are — felonies. More privately, of course, they increase their efforts to ward off the forger. Commercial check cashers and issuers now find that insurance companies employ deductible clauses that can be invoked in cases of check forgery — another incentive for businesses to increase their vigilance (Foldessy, 1971).

These and other features of our society provide an atmosphere in which check forgery can be partly understood. Check forgery is easy (access to a check is virtually all that is needed). It can be readily explained away as a mistake or oversight. Checks are currently the major means of dealing in money, and so few of us are surprised to see checks come into our lives or are suspicious of those who use them. Paper hanging has none of the earmarks of crime. Official reaction to it by banks, stores, and police is at best ambivalent. Arrests have hardly kept pace with population increases, let alone increases in the use of checks.

The bulk of check forgers (*naive check forgers,* as Edwin Lemert calls them) do not think of themselves as criminals, cannot believe that anyone would have the audacity to call them that ("I would never hurt anyone!"), and come up with ready excuses or rationalizations for their behavior (from the more obvious, "it was a mistake," to comments such as "no one is hurt by forgery because supermarkets make great profits and don't miss a little money lost through bad checks") (Gibbons, 1973:250). Although naive forgers are found in all socioeconomic classes and include both men and women, blacks and whites, and all ethnic groups, the category of persons most often identified among forgers is that of the white male who holds a white-collar job and has little identified criminality in his history. In addition, when compared with other known felons, the convicted forger appears to have higher-than-average intelligence and to have begun in crime at a much later age — late twenties and early thirties (Lemert, 1953).

Studies of naive check forgery suggest two factors that together may help explain why some people pass hot checks. One factor is the impact of situational conditions and the importance of forgery as a psychological and behavioral mechanism for coping with stress produced in the situation. Lemert discovered that the typical instance of naive check forgery occurs when the offender is under pressure to come up with money — he or she may be out drinking, in a strange town and need cash for some contingency or other, or on a shopping spree. The pressures of the moment create a stress condition that demands resolution, or "closure," as Lemert calls it. The forger achieves closure by passing a bad check, resolving the immediate problem — getting hold of cash or buying the desired item.

But why forgery? Why not some other means of bringing the stressful situation to closure? Why not enlist the help of friends or family? The answer, it appears, is that naive forgers commonly have experienced considerable social isolation in their personal histories. Many forgers have apparently experienced stressful and unproductive relationships with others that have progressively pushed them toward a condition of isolation relative to conventional social bonds. They are often estranged from their families; many have experienced difficulties in marriage (Lemert found divorce in 40 percent of his sample); some have encountered problems in employment and military service; and some have gambling losses. As these situational pressures build, those who suffer them find themselves unwilling or unable to break the chain of personal troubles by enlisting the support and confidence of others. Instead, they seek closure of their immediate situation, but in a self-made manner (here we may again be witnessing the importance of the self-reliance principle noted in our discussion of shoplifting). Remember, however, that society has provided an exchange climate within which forgery is easily and comfortably accomplished. Therefore, the choice of forgery as a closure device must be seen as a choice directed to some extent by this supportive exchange environment. One wonders what those who now pass hot checks would do if check forgery were not available to them or if it carried the stigma of crime. If not one already, perhaps the naive forger would become a pilferer.

**Systematic Forgers**   Not all paper hangers belong to the category of naive check forger; some are professionals (Lemert (1958) prefers the term *systematic forgers*). For the systematic forger, forgery provides a steady source of income and is treated in a highly businesslike manner. Although forgery was once a well-established part of the repertoire of professional theft, evidence today is that most systematic forgers are on the periphery of the society of professional thieves. First, they most often work alone and therefore are not intimately wrapped up in the organizational facets of professionalism — they do not need connections, accomplices, financial stakes, fences, or other aspects of group support. Further, theirs is not a criminal activity requiring special skills and tutelage (although this is not true of the skilled counterfeiter) (Jackson, 1969a). In many ways, the professional forger is similar to the professional shoplifter. Moreover, some professional aspects of theft have become more vulnerable in the case of forgery because those who treat it seriously must now guard themselves against association with the more common habitual amateurs — for example, petty thieves, alcoholics, and other drug users — who cannot be trusted when the chips are down and who are not welcomed by the professionals (Lemert, 1958).

No accurate estimates have been made of the proportion of forgery efforts attributable to professionals. In all probability, professionals account for a small number of the total incidents of paper hanging. But systematic forgers stand out in the size of their rewards from forgery and in the persistence with which they pursue this line of work. Bloch and Geis (1970) tell of a female systematic forger who claims to work a forty-hour week in her line and who can expect to make around $100 an hour if things go well. One form of professional forgery requiring a little more planning and perseverance (not, according to Lemert, something many systematic forgers care for) is "check kiting":

> *Check-kiting* is a swindle related to forgery that is directed against banks. This fraudulent operation involves the covering of bad checks with other bad checks. A professional bank swindler might open a series of checking accounts at scattered banks with deposits of $25. At *Bank Z* he cashes a $100 check drawn on *Bank X*, depositing $25 and pocketing $75. He then covers the *Bank X* check with a $250 check on *Bank Y*, depositing $125 and pocketing $125. This latter check on *Bank Y* is made good with a $500 check on *Bank Z*, with $300 deposited and $200 pocketed. Manipulations of this type have been executed by both individuals and organized groups of bank swindlers, with single operations accumulating thefts in excess of half a million dollars. (Inciardi, 1975)

# CONFIDENCE GAMES

Swindlers have been around for centuries. It is said that wherever people want something for nothing, the swindler will also be found. Swindlers and confidence artists rely on the something-for-nothing attitude, and they often say "you can't cheat an honest man."

Variations on the con game are numerous: Lists of different swindles compiled over the years show as many as 250 variations (Inciardi, 1975). For at least two hundred years two of the most common con games have been "ring dropping" and "purse dropping." Both involve simple techniques of victim manipulation, and both rely on the latter's greed, gullibility, and dishonesty. In ring dropping, for example, a worthless piece of jewelry is dropped by one member of the con team (the "roper" or "steerer") near a stranger (the victim or "mark"). A second member of the team (the "inside-man") rushes forward to pick up the jewelry and, after showing it to the mark, agrees to share the proceeds if the stranger will sell it. The mark is persuaded to leave something of value with the insideman as security — a token of good faith. The climax of the game is obvious — the insideman absconds with the security, leaving the mark to discover that the jewelry is worthless.

The game just described is one variety of those swindles commonly referred to as "short cons." The aim in a short con is to fleece marks of whatever they have with them at the time, or can get hold of in a matter of minutes. In a short con, the amount of preparation needed and the size of the take are generally small — it can be put into motion at a moment's notice and the score is usually a matter of dollars and cents (Roebuck and Johnson, 1964). Another common version of the short con is the "pigeon drop," which operates along lines similar to ring dropping but requires more manipulative abilities by the confidence operator. In the typical pigeon drop, the victim is invited to share money that has supposedly been found by one member of the confidence partnership, but in order to qualify for a share the mark must first demonstrate good faith by putting up some of his or her own money.

The successful con artist must accomplish at least three things: (1) make the mark trust the con operator; (2) make the mark believe that his or her part in the enterprise will be rewarding; and, most important, (3) convince the mark to part (temporarily, of course) with some of his or her own money. Clearly, a good deal of smooth talking and friendly persuasion by the confidence team is usually necessary. This is where good con artists excel (Roebuck and Johnson, 1964:236).

Those con artists who set their sights on lucrative swindles and are able and prepared to spend considerable time and energy in preparing and performing the swindle, go after the big con. Big-con operators are at the top of the hierarchy of professional crime, and their line of work requires considerable skill and ingenuity. Big-con operators are shrewd businesspeople whose special talents lie in their acting ability and their knowledge of the limits to which people can be pushed in search of a fast buck. Big cons can reap large payoffs, as the experience of John Ernest Keely demonstrates:

> Keely, an ex-carnival pitchman, began a hoax in 1874 that reaped many fortunes and lasted for a quarter of a century. His nonexistent perpetual motion machine, "which would produce a force more powerful than steam and electricity," involved the financiers of many cities, the public of two continents, and the United States Secretary of War. Before his career ended, Keely had a 372-page volume written on his "discovery," over a million dollars in cash, a life of luxury for twenty-five years, and an international reputation. (Inciardi, 1975:24)

Most big-con operators adhere to a sequence of steps, each of which must be successfully accomplished if the con is to work. As each step is completed, it becomes more difficult for the con artists to abandon the enterprise and more likely that the swindle will succeed. Seven major steps in the sequence have been identified (Gasser, 1963: 48–51):

> Step 1: *Tying into the mark* — finding a victim, gaining his confidence, getting him ready for step two.
> Step 2: *Telling the mark the tale* — showing the victim what is at stake for him, and how he can get hold of it.
> Step 3: *Initial money gaff* — letting the mark make some money to show how easy it is.
> Step 4: *Putting the mark on the send* — sending the victim for money.
> Step 5: *Playing the mark against the store* — fleecing him of his money.
> Step 6: *Cooling out the mark* — see explanation below.
> Step 7: *Putting the mark in the door* — getting rid of the victim.

One of the most important steps in the sequence of events is "cooling out" the victim. Con artists recognize their vulnerability to the victims' passions once they have discovered that they have been duped. Accordingly, they build into their procedures a special step, the purpose of which is to reduce the chances that the mark will bring trouble down on their heads. They hope the mark will be convinced to forget the whole incident. The methods used for cooling out the mark vary, but on the whole they are based on the victims' perception of themselves and their situation. Generally, con artists avoid using violence, even if it means losing the score (Roebuck and Johnson, 1964). How, then, do they cool out the mark?

One method is to create a twist in the con artist–victim relationship whereby the victim becomes an apparent accessory to a felony (sometimes murder) and hence thinks he or she has committed a crime. From being a victim, the mark is now a criminal, facing a prison sentence if caught. Of course, the whole situation is contrived; the con artists stage a fake murder. For example, the mark in the film *The Sting,* assuming himself to be an accessory, was only too glad to forget the whole thing.

Erving Goffman (1952) has discussed a second method of cooling out the mark. This method relies on "the art of consolation." Instead of generating fear in the victims, the con artists help give them a redefinition of the situation and self so that they can feel more comfortable with the outcome. By emphasizing, for example, that it was extremely hard to con the mark or that the mark presented a real challenge, the con operators help the victim to retain a positive conception of self. Although used perhaps for higher stakes, this method is rather like the situation in which a chess opponent who has just beaten you hastily proceeds to commend you on your play and the challenge you offered. You have still lost the game, but you feel much better. Redefining the situation for the mark provides "a new set of apologies . . . [and] a new framework in which to see himself and judge himself" (p. 456).

We should remind ourselves that confidence games do not survive in our society merely because some people have the talent to pull them off. Neither do they survive simply because some of us may be dishonest and gullible. For confidence games to persist there must be values that emphasize personal acquisitiveness. As with shoplifting, forgery, and, indeed, any type of theft, the behavior itself cannot be understood solely in terms of the players or the immediate situation in which it occurs. Confidence games differ from other varieties of theft in that both offender and victim are generally after something for nothing. The con game represents a situation in which the principles of negotiated exchange and self-reliance are relentlessly pursued by all parties. And these are principles given cultural support in our society.

# CHAPTER 9

# Occupational Crime

So far, our attention has focused almost exclusively on what might be called "traditional" crime and criminality. Robbery, murder, assault, burglary, and other street property offenses are traditional crimes in a number of senses. First, they are among the activities that most readily come to mind when we think of crime. Second, they are the conventional targets of official criminalization. Third, they have long been the prime focus of law-enforcement efforts. And finally, it is primarily around these kinds of crime that criminologists have framed their theories of criminality.

To say that robbery, burglary, and interpersonal violence are traditional crimes is not to say that they are the most common forms of crime nor that they have the greatest societal impact in terms of numbers of victims, economic costs, and damage to prevailing social institutions. Having far greater impact are occupational crimes.

## What Is Occupational Crime?

As used here, the term *occupational crime* refers to illegal activities that occur in connection with a person's job. Occupational crime is preferred over the more conventional term *white-collar crime* because it makes no reference to the occupational status of the offender. When Edwin H. Sutherland (1949) coined the expression "white-collar crime," he had in mind crimes committed by persons of respectability and high social status in the course of their occupations. He observed that criminologists had virtually ignored the illegal activities of those in business, politics, and the professions, concentrating instead on the world of lower-class criminality pictured in official statistics and emphasized in the normal routine of the administration of criminal justice. Lawbreaking, he argued, goes on in all social strata. Such things as restraint of trade, misrepresentation in advertising, violations of labor laws, violations of copyright and patent laws, and financial manipulations were a part of what Sutherland called white-collar crime.

But as some authors have noted, Sutherland's emphasis on high social status excludes other occupation-related crimes that are similar to his white-collar offenses in that (1) a person's legitimate occupation provides the context and sometimes the motivation for the offense and (2) the offense (and offender) largely escapes official processing at the hands of legal authorities (Newman, 1958). The broader notion of occupational crime thus includes criminal activities committed by anyone in connection with his or her job.

## Types of Occupational Crime and Types of Offenders

Many different examples of occupational crime readily come to mind. Apart from the illegal activities already mentioned (restraint of trade, unfair labor practices, and so on), there are embezzlement, a variety of consumer frauds, thefts by computer, music and record pirating, prescription law violations, employee pilfering, food and drug law violations, corporate tax violations, housing code violations, bribery and other forms of corruption by public officials, kickbacks, bid rigging, and real estate frauds — the list could go on.

Although we bring these diverse crimes together under the umbrella of occupational crime, there are some important differences among them and among the persons who commit them. This has led some scholars to construct typologies of occupational crime that stress similarities and differences. One typology is by Herbert Edelhertz (1970), a former Justice Department official.

1. *Crimes committed by persons on an individual, ad hoc basis* [individual income tax evasions, bankruptcy frauds, credit card frauds, social security frauds, credit purchases with no intent to pay].
2. *Crimes committed in the course of their occupations by those operating inside business, government, or other establishments, in violation of their duty of loyalty and fidelity to the employer or client* [bribery and kickbacks, embezzlement, employee pilfering, payroll padding].
3. *Crimes incidental to, and in furtherance of, business operations, but not the central purpose of the business* [antitrust violations, food and drug violations, misrepresentation in advertising, prescription fraud].
4. *Crime as a business or as the central activity of a business* [medical or health fraud schemes, land and real estate frauds, securities and commodities fraud, home improvement fraud schemes, charity and religious frauds, music pirating]. (pp. 19–20; 73–75)

Although Edelhertz used what he called "general environment and motivation of the perpetrator" as the basis for his classification, there are other possibilities. One is to differentiate among occupational crimes on the basis of the victim constituency. One might, for example, distinguish among crimes that involve employers as victims and those that involve employees, the public, or the government as victims. Or we might follow Bloch and Geis (1970) and distinguish among different offenders: persons acting as individuals against other individuals (lawyers, doctors, dentists, self-employed accountants), those committing crimes against the businesses that employ them (embezzlers), those in policymaking positions who commit crimes for the corporation (antitrust violators), agents of a corporation who victimize the general public (as in advertising fraud), and merchants victimizing their customers (as in shortchanging).

Most of this chapter is concerned with those types of occupational crime thought to be most prevalent and to have the greatest impact on the nature of social life in America. The material is organized around categories 2, 3, and 4 of the Edelhertz typology. His category 1 is not discussed here, mainly because this category bears no clear connection with work, the essential criterion for separating occupational crime from other types of crime. However, some individual "moonlighting" and other "hidden economy" activities will be discussed in connection with employee fiddles, and these might properly fall in category 1.

## Work and the Historical Development of Legal Controls

Because of its close connection with the world of work, occupational crime is affected by technological advances and social change in general. Though some crimes require no special technology or social arrangements in order to exist as a form of human conduct — rape and murder are examples — such is not the case with many occupational crimes. Thus if the phonograph had never been invented, there would be no record industry and no possibility for people to engage in record pirating.

Of course, some forms of occupational crime require less sophisticated technologies and organization than others. Certain forms of commercial fraud are possible with only a simple division of labor and a rudimentary system of economic exchange. In the simplest of cases it may merely be a matter of merchants shortchanging their customers via the manipulation of weights and measures — actions that have been possible since the time people first became dependent on others for particular goods and services and the complementary roles of buyer and seller were established.

In early legal codes we find evidence of attempts to regulate occupations and the practices possible in connection with them. The Code of Hammurapi, for example, lists a variety of work-related activities for which penalties and victim compensations of one kind or another were to be assessed. Here is a sampling:

[Laws 53–54 deal with the obligations of farmers:] If a man has neglected to maintain the dike of his field, and has not kept his dike strong enough so that a break has been found in the dike and he has let the water ravage the farmland, the man in whose dike the breach was opened shall make good the grain that he caused to be lost. If he cannot make good the grain, they shall sell him and his goods for silver, and the farmers whose grain the water carried off shall divide the proceeds.

[Law 90 deals with loans and interest rates and states that those lending grain or silver will forfeit the principal lent if they charge more than 20 percent interest.

Laws 94–107 regulate commerce, the relations among business partners and the activities of salesmen. Apart from setting penalties for shortchanging customers (Law 94), these laws establish what might be called the ethics of business.

Laws 218–225 deal with physicians and veterinarians. For example, Law 218 specifies:] If a physician has performed a major operation on a patrician with a bronze knife and has caused the patrician to die, or opened up the eye-socket of a patrician with a bronzed knife and caused the destruction of the patrician's eye, they shall cut off his hand.

[Law 229 covers shoddy work in the building trade:] If a builder has constructed a house for a man, but did not make his work strong, so that the house which he built collapsed and caused the death of the owner of the house, that builder shall be put to death. [Law 230 states that if a son of the owner is so killed, the builder's son shall be put to death.

And finally, Law 253 deals with the violation of trust and employee theft:] If a man has hired someone to oversee his field, and entrusted him with feed-grain, and entrusted cattle to him, and has contracted with him to cultivate the field, if that person has stolen the seed or fodder and it has been found in his possession, they shall cut off his hand. (Gordon, 1957:7–9; 22–24)

Though by no means as extensive as Hammurapi's regulations, the laws of various Anglo-Saxon kings also assessed monetary compensation or punitive sanctions against those violating work-related regulations. Among the activities brought under legal control were withholding taxes, failing to carry out official duties, buying and selling outside designated market areas, minting coins of base metals or of insufficient purity, and bribing or being bribed by the kings' appointed officials.

Some of these early laws were clearly designed to encourage orderly, predictable, and honest relations among persons dependent on others for their livelihoods. In this sense, laws governing work in general and certain occupations in particular can be seen as efforts to stabilize and cement some of the relations binding people to one another. It requires little imagination to see how important this must have been in a time when group survival was at best doubtful.

## INTERESTS AND OCCUPATIONAL CRIME

However, the full flavor of legal inroads into the realm of occupations is lost unless we also consider the role of special interests. Besides the fact that many past laws were weighted in favor of higher-status individuals, so that the penalties for violation were less the higher one's social status, few laws formalized the obligations of masters and employers toward their servants, slaves, and employees. In addition, some laws were clearly designed to consolidate ruling-class control over economic and political activities and thus over the production and distribution of wealth and material advantages.

If we move to more recent periods in the history of laws dealing with the world of work, we have an opportunity to look more closely at the operation of special interests. Consider, for example, laws against embezzlement and criminal fraud.

**Embezzlement**    As we observed in the preceding chapter (see p. 208), embezzlement first found its way into the statute books as a modification designed to plug gaps in the existing common law that were proving an annoyance to merchants and employers. Until 1529, the criminal liability of servants did not extend to instances in which they kept for themselves valuable goods that were in their legal possession by virtue of their role as bailees for their masters. This meant that servants had committed no crime if they subsequently converted to their own use things delivered into their possession in the course of their roles as servants. Responding to the obvious risk posed for employers by this gap in the common law, Henry VIII made the "imbezilment" of such goods a felony.

Still, the new law did not cover cases in which a third party gave servants or employees cash or goods for delivery to their masters, only to have them pocketed by the servant. In cases such as these the only recourse for the employer was to institute civil proceedings against the servant, employee, or agent. And things might well have remained this way had it not been for the expansion of commerce and trade and the subsequent rise of banking, accounting, and related business pursuits. The financial interests of the business community, coupled with its growing reliance on the trusted employee and business agent roles in commerce, moved members to look for additional protection under the criminal law. Once identified as crimes, embezzlement and other types of fraudulent conversions became the targets of coercive repression, and the offenders the objects of punitive sanctions not available in civil dispositions. Their special interests at stake, businesspeople thus sought modifications in the existing legal situation that would further entrench the weapons of criminal law in their corner. So in 1799 Parliament once again extended the embezzlement provisions and later added the crimes of "false accounting" and "fraudulent conversion" to cover other features of the business relationship between employers and those working for them in positions of financial trust.

**Frauds**  When you induce someone to part with money or valuables through the use of deceit, lies, or misrepresentation, you commit *fraud*, or what was called a "cheat" in earlier times. Under English common law the possibility of fraud had long been recognized; however, criminal liability was for centuries extended only to situations in which (1) some false token or tangible device of trickery was involved and (2) the activity was such that reasonable prudence could not guard against it, and any member of the general public was its potential victim (Turner, 1966). Under the common law, a personal fraud directed against a private individual was no crime, because it was customary to assume that individuals would exercise due caution in their financial dealings with others and because when an individual was deceived, civil remedies were available.

With the extension of business and the growing complexities in commercial and industrial transactions associated with the rise of capitalism, entrepreneurs throughout the business community urged Parliament to broaden the range of criminal liability associated with fraudulent practices. In 1757 a statute was passed establishing the crime of "obtaining property by false pretenses." Subsequently adopted in the American colonies, this law has remained one of the few specifically criminal statutes dealing with fraud.

In fact, fraud can be perpetrated in many ways; its mechanics are limited only by one's imagination and ability. Sutherland and Cressey contend that fraud is probably "the most prevalent crime in America" (1974:42). The victim of fraud can be anyone, but it is likely the most commonly deceived persons are consumers — those who buy goods and services from people in the business of selling — acting on their own behalf as private individuals. This so-called consumer fraud reaches all the way from small business to immense and wealthy insurance companies, retail chains, and manufacturers of consumer goods. It costs the United States more than $25 billion a year.

Despite the extensive victimization associated with consumer fraud, the courts had until recently operated on the principle of *caveat emptor* — buyer beware. The idea was simply that in making purchases, consumers must protect themselves against deception, and since they can presumably refuse to complete the transaction, they have only themselves to blame if they get "taken." Reasonable as this may sound, it actually encourages victimization in the modern marketplace, where the complex nature of many products and services and the techniques and organization of consumer transactions are such that even knowledgeable purchasers find it well-nigh impossible to protect themselves against fraud. For example, given modern supermarket packaging practices, shoppers can rarely inspect the products they want to buy in anything more than a superficial way. And if they want to make that inspection, they are forced to pay for the privilege, since the supermarkets generally undersell the small grocery stores that still display many products without plastic wrapping and other "sanitary" devices.

Protection against consumer fraud has been slow to gain momentum largely because such efforts are not in the best interests of those in the business of selling and those in the various support industries of banking, financing, and advertising. Their interests lie in profits and dividends, and anything threatening these is heartily resisted. Still, events before the Reagan presidency demonstrated that the interests of public health and safety — if not financial well-being — were receiving some of the attention they deserve. This is best evidenced in the area of food, drugs, and cosmetics.

## PURE FOOD AND DRUG LAWS

The production, distribution, and sale of food and drug products are now regulated by a variety of laws aimed at the protection of public health and safety. Interest in the regulation of the food and drug businesses first gained prominence during the latter part of the nineteenth century, as consumers became further and further removed from agricultural producers and marketers, and the possibilities for adulteration, spoilage, exploitation, and fraud increased. Public awareness of the threats posed to their interests was enhanced partly through the changing experience of buying itself, but mostly by newspaper editorials, magazines, novels, and research findings in which the dangers of existing business practices were stressed, sometimes in lurid and frightening detail.

The first major federal legislation aimed at regulating the food and drug businesses was introduced in 1880 and soundly defeated, as were many subsequent bills. In his book, *The Therapeutic Nightmare,* Morton Mintz (1970:78–79) observes: "It and other efforts like it were defeated by a durable alliance of quacks, ruthless crooks, pious frauds, scoundrels, high-priced lawyer-lobbyists, vested interests, liars, corrupt members of Congress, venal publishers, cowards in high office, the stupid, the apathetic, and the duped." When Congress did finally pass the Federal Food and Drug Act of 1906, it was only the first step in what has turned out to be a long and hard battle between public interests and the food and drug industries.

The 1906 law declared it illegal to manufacture or introduce into an American state any adulterated or misbranded food or drug. Offenders could have their products seized, and those convicted of violating the law would be subject to criminal penalties. Thus a new area of occupational crime was born. But as Richard Quinney (1970:79) has observed:

> The need for revision of the act . . . became apparent shortly after its passage. The absence of adequate control over advertising provided an especially serious loophole for evasion of the spirit of the law, and labeling requirements of the law were such as to permit extravagant and unwarranted therapeutic claims for a product. Also, the 1906 act contained no provisions applying to cosmetics and failed to provide measures for safe and effective health devices.

Some of these inadequacies were corrected by the 1938 Food, Drug, and Cosmetic Act, passed by both houses of Congress despite heavy resistance from the industries involved. Still, by the 1960s, nearly one hundred years after public interest was first mobilized, Americans could count on one hand the number of truly significant bills designed to regulate the immense and powerful industries supplying our food, pharmaceutical products, and cosmetics. As Stuart Hills (1971:151) points out, "it has usually required a well-publicized major crisis to shock" legislatures into the passage of significant laws. Such was the case when the Kefauver–Harris Drug Act of 1962 was passed: had it not been for the thousands of deformed babies born to mothers who had taken thalidomide during pregnancy, the bill would probably have failed.

If it were not for the efforts of Ralph Nader, the American public might still be buying meat products largely unregulated by legal controls. As long ago as 1906, Upton Sinclair described the disgusting conditions of meat slaughterhouses in his highly popular novel, *The Jungle.* Writing in 1967, Ralph Nader pointed out that "we're still in the Jungle." Following his own investigation of the meat industry, Nader concluded that Americans were still buying meat products that not only were adulterated with substances ranging from water and cereals to toxic chemicals but also were prepared under unsanitary conditions, contaminated with diseased and spoiled carcass pieces — even manure and pus — and often sold in a deceptive and fraudulent manner.

The reason, in Nader's view, was partly the substantial inadequacy of existing federal and state laws and partly the pitiful efforts to enforce them.

Both the inadequacy of legal controls and their ineffective enforcement were blamed on the cozy relationship among the United States Department of Agriculture, state agriculture agencies, and the meat production and processing interests. Rather than ensure the safety of meat products and promote honesty in their packaging and sale, the interest shared by all concerned was to promote the sale of meat products. When Congress eventually passed the Wholesale Meat Act of 1968 — bringing intrastate meat processing under federal jurisdiction and establishing stricter controls — another small victory for public welfare was achieved and the range of legal penalties extended.

## Violations of Loyalty and Fidelity to Employer or Client

Violations of loyalty and fidelity to employer or client, Edelhertz's second category of occupational crime, deals primarily with crimes committed by individuals acting in their own interest and against the interests of those who employ them or who are their clients. Embezzlement, other forms of employee theft, and political corruption are included in this category.

### EMBEZZLEMENT

As we have already seen, embezzlement is the conversion to their own use of funds or property entrusted to employees or agents by others. Embezzlement is thus both theft and a violation of financial trust. It has been regarded as a serious offense since its statutory origins in 1529 and is a felony regardless of the amount embezzled. We might note, however, that the language of embezzlement statutes has not been easy to apply in the real world, and there is considerable variation from jurisdiction to jurisdiction and from court to court. Donald Cressey observed that "persons whose behavior was not adequately described by the definition of embezzlement were found to have been imprisoned for that offense, and persons whose behavior was adequately described by the definition were confined for some other offense" (1953:19). Cressey offered as his definition of embezzlement *the criminal violation of financial trust*. He further stipulated that to be called an embezzler a person must have accepted a position of trust in good faith and have violated that position by the commission of a crime.

When arrests for embezzlement are made, which is rare compared with the frequency of arrests for most other felony crimes, the suspect is usually a white, middle-class, middle-aged male, quite unlike the prevailing stereotype of the criminal. The embezzler has been called "the respectable criminal" (Cressey, 1965). Respectable or not, estimates of the frequency and costs of embezzlement are staggering. In 1967, the President's Commission on Law Enforcement and the Administration of Justice put the annual cost at more than $200 million; that figure is dwarfed by a 1974 estimate of $4 billion. Today, the figure is certainly much higher.

The respectability of embezzlers mentioned by many authors acknowledges not only the relatively high occupational status of most offenders but also the fact that they rarely have a delinquent or criminal record prior to their embezzling activities and rarely think of themselves as real criminals. According to a study of 1,001 embezzlers conducted some years ago, the typical male embezzler is the epitome of the moderately successful family man. He is ". . . thirty-five, married, has one or two children. He lives in a respectable neighborhood and is probably buying his own home. He drives a low or medium priced car and his yearly income is in the top forty percent of the nation's personal income distribution" (Jaspan and Black, 1960:24–25). The female embezzler also fits the picture of a respectable American, though her income was found to be in the bottom third of the nation's income distribution — a reflection of sex discrimination in jobs and salaries more than anything else.

Donald Cressey (1953) has conducted an in-depth study of embezzlement. In *Other People's Money,* Cressey based his analysis on interviews with 133 persons in penitentiaries in Illinois, Indiana, and California. His findings regarding the etiology of embezzlement — the factors leading up to it — show that embezzlers commit the offense after (1) coming up against a "nonshareable" financial problem; (2) recognizing that they can secretly resolve the problem by taking advantage of their positions of financial trust; and (3) gathering an assortment of rationalizations and justifications, so that they can think of their subsequent actions as noncriminal and justified and can retain a conception of self emphasizing that they are, in fact, still worthy of financial trust.

It is clear that without the possibility of violating financial trust that comes with the embezzler's occupational position, one important part of the etiological chain would be missing. But it is the presence of a nonshareable problem and the adoption of justifiable rationalizations that lie at the heart of Cressey's explanation. By a *nonshareable* problem Cressey means almost any kind of financial difficulty the individual feels cannot be resolved by enlisting the help of another. It could be some unusual family expense or gambling debts, once thought the major cause of embezzlement. It could even be linked to attempts to keep up a particular standard of living. Rationalization occurs before, or at least during, but not after, the act of embezzling. Many of Cressey's subjects, and especially those who had been independent business men, reasoned that they would be merely "borrowing" the money or that it really belonged to them anyway. The embezzlers-to-be often argued that they were merely adhering to a standard business practice, borrowing against future earnings. Looked at sequentially, then, the nonshareable problem leads to the search for a personal and secret solution; the position of financial trust provides the means to solve the problem; and the rationalization provides the final push.

Cressey's explanation of embezzlement has not been without its critics. One of the most damaging criticisms was put forward by Karl Schuessler

(1954). Schuessler noted that Cressey's generalization, based as it is on an *ex post facto* (after the fact) inductive analysis using only actual offenders, sits upon a weak methodological foundation and cannot be verified:

> The finding that all cases in the sample had a single set of circumstances in common does not, unhappily, prove that all persons in such circumstances will embezzle. The empirical validation would require an unselected group of persons having in common the hypothesized circumstances who then should all subsequently display the expected behavior. Needless to say, Cressey's proposition is impossible to test. (p. 604)

A different criticism comes from Gwynn Nettler, (1974) whose own study could not substantiate Cressey's emphasis on the nonshareable financial problem as a precondition for embezzlement. Nettler's embezzlers were apparently driven to their crimes by temptation and avarice, and their jobs provided the opportunity and the means. It does not look as if the explanation of embezzlement is a matter of consensus yet.

## "HIGH-TECH" CRIME: THE CRIMINAL AND THE COMPUTER

Technological change advances criminal opportunities as well as noncriminal ones. Nowhere is this more in evidence than in the realm of electronics. We live in an era of high technology, one in which electronic brains and silicon chips rule much of the behavior of people and machines. The more computers we have and the more things we can get them to do, the more opportunities there are for computer crime. Estimates of the annual losses from computer-related crimes go as high as $5 billion, and in all likelihood the figure will go much higher (Kolata, 1982).

The range of computer crimes is vast and growing. A few examples of what criminally motivated people can do when they have access to computer technology are shown in the box on pp. 254–255. Embezzlement, industrial espionage, theft of services (for example, using a computer that belongs to someone else for one's private business), invasion of privacy, copyright violations, destruction of information or programs, falsification of data, and a host of fraudulent transactions are just a few of the computer-related abuses that have come to light.

The potential for computer crime is staggering, and that fact is now recognized in legislative and enforcement circles. But most of the preventive work so far initiated is privately organized and paid for. Hundreds of companies have sprung up in recent years peddling advice and technology to counteract the new breed of high-tech criminal. The 1980s will be a profitable decade for both computer criminals and those in the business of prevention.

As an instrument of crime the computer may be used to victimize individuals, one's own company, competitive companies, the government, the public at large, even other countries. Criminal use of computers may be incidental to the main purpose of a business; it may be the central activity of a

"High-tech" crime is likely to spread as more homes and businesses acquire computer technology and as the potential for illicit gains continues to grow.

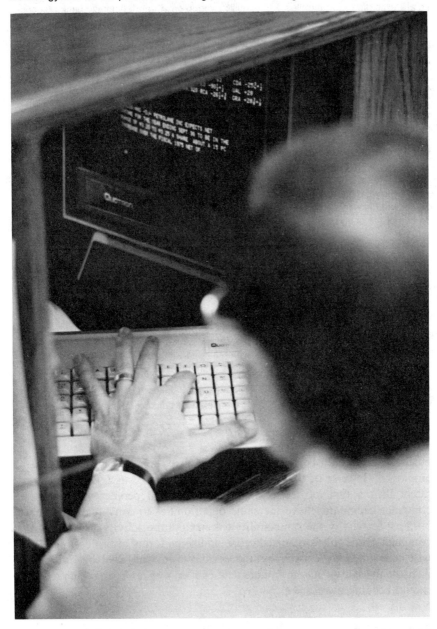

## COMPUTER-RELATED CRIME: RECENT CASES ILLUSTRATE THE RANGE OF OFFENSES

The following cases are excerpted from the files collected by the Stanford Research Institute under a grant from the Law Enforcement Assistance Administration; they represent the tip of the iceberg and were selected to illustrate the varied kinds of offenses that are committed by people with access to computer technology.

A food stamp clerk filled out and submitted a computer input form in her boyfriend's name. She was discovered only because her boyfriend's ex-girlfriend informed police about them.

A programmer in a Monterey Savings and Loan embezzled money by illegally transferring money from forty-one accounts into his wife's savings account through the use of the financial institution's computer.

An employee of Westinghouse embezzled $1,000,000 by designing an audit system that ordered the master computer to issue forged corporation drafts. Six other men were indicted for conspiracy and mail fraud.

The Securities and Exchange Commission (SEC) charged Eisco, Inc. with using a computer to understate losses and inflate profits to raise the value of stock.

In Japan, a man was arrested for stealing two million yen in cash from automatic bank dispensers by using counterfeit cards.

A man pleaded guilty to receiving stolen property after he was involved in feeding false information into a computer credit verification system, which allowed him to receive high credit ratings and thus purchase thousands of dollars of merchandise.

A police chief was indicted for tampering with government records. He was accused of having deleted a reckless driving offense from his record in the county's regional computer system.

A man pleaded guilty to one count of grand theft for stealing $15,000 of computer time.

A jury convicted a Newark, New Jersey, man of advertising and selling phony computerized diet plans through the mails. Most of the diets were similar but were supposed to be individualized by computer.

Two Blue Cross employees were indicted for a scheme to process bogus claims through one employee's computer terminal. Thirty-one others were charged with receiving and negotiating bogus claim checks.

Three persons created food stamp accounts for five nonexistent persons. One of the three was a

---

business; or it may be an activity that violates loyalty and fidelity to an employer. Because of this it is more properly viewed as a means of crime rather than a type of crime. In addition, not all people with access to computer technology have the same opportunities to convert that access to criminal activity or the same ability to carry out the activity. It is likely that computer crime, like organized crime and some forms of professional theft, will be marked by conspiracy and organization, and as it becomes more difficult for individuals to counteract security measures, this characteristic should become even more marked.

## FIDDLING AT WORK: PART OF THE HIDDEN ECONOMY

Operating within the legitimate world of work is a *hidden economy* in which goods and services are produced, stolen, or exchanged on the sly. There is no official record of this activity, and the income obtained from it is rarely, if computer terminal operator for a food stamp office. They were charged with fraud in obtaining public assistance.

A computerized scheme to launder money gained in illegal activities used genuine commodity brokerage transactions as a cover. The front was a business investment fund for doctors and other professionals in Texas. Illegal money was funneled into the legitimate trust — by mingling with clean money, dirty money was returned to Mafia front men posing as brokers. The schemers were busted by FBI undercover agents posing as potential "dirty money" clients.

In England, a British computer programmer who was fired from his job with the company stole the computer tapes containing all the company's financial planning data for the following five years. He attempted to ransom the company for approximately $470,000, as the information would have been highly valuable to competitors. The attempt was foiled and the man arrested.

An agent for the Drug Enforcement Administration (DEA) was indicted for embezzling computer printouts from the Narcotics and Dangerous Drugs Information System for use in a scheme to identify DEA informants for large-scale marijuana trafficking.

A grand jury in Illinois indicted a former police chief for selling criminal histories obtained from the state's computerized criminal information system.

A student at Queens College used the computer to tamper with his grades and those of a few other students, netting himself an unearned Phi Beta Kappa key. When a random audit picked up the discrepancy, and the student (then working for the school) was informed, he resigned immediately.

A computer operator working for the police department was angry with his wife, and so he programmed the computer to report that her car had been stolen. She got picked up; he got fired.

An employee dismissed from a small catalog sales firm retaliated by programming the computer to erase its files, resulting in $20,000 damage. Although there is circumstantial evidence (this employee was the only one with a key to log on), the firm does not think it will prosecute.

An employee at a ship-rating firm left the company and went to work for a competitor. It was found that several computer programs at the first firm had been suspiciously rerecorded, but nothing could be proved. The employer alleges they were stolen.

SOURCE: Stanford Research Institute (1979), Computer Crime: Criminal Justice Research Manual. Washington, D.C.: U.S. Department of Justice. Reprinted by permission.

---

ever, taxed. Much of the activity is itself criminal, though rarely thought of as such by the participants or the general public. Stuart Henry (1978:4–5) illustrates the range of activities that comprise the hidden economy:

A number of specific fiddles make up hidden property crime. These include . . . taking company stock home to doing jobs "on the side." . . .

Personal use of the firm's telephone, photocopying or mailing service accounts for a certain amount of the kind of fiddling which may be claimed as perks, and overestimates of petrol [gasoline], food and travel allowances that appear as inflated expense accounts might also be seen in this light. In addition, there are a number of other . . . fiddles . . . such as short-changing, overloading, overestimating, under-the-counter selling, buying off-the-back-of-a-lorry [truck] goods, fiddling time, dodging fares and smuggling duty-free goods. Nor should we neglect the numerous tax and social security fiddles involving undeclared income, falsely claimed allowances and misrepresented welfare benefits and rebate claims; nor corporate fiddles, such as computer fraud and industrial bribery.

The benefits obtained in these unofficial work-related activities may be quite modest or quite extensive, depending on the type of fiddle and the extensiveness of a person's involvement. Collectively, however, they amount to billions of dollars. In America, theft by retail employees alone costs close to $10 billion, and Gerald Mars (1983) cites estimates that 10 percent of the total U.S. gross national product is made up of unregistered production and service work, untaxed moonlighting, and other undeclared income.

In this section we shall focus on pilferage on the job. There are many forms: sometimes it is casual, sometimes systematic and repetitive; sometimes workers pilfer alone, at other times in more or less organized groups; and sometimes the pilferage victimizes the employer, sometimes the customer or client, and sometimes other workers. However, cash is rarely stolen directly, and the income obtained through fiddling at work is generally considered secondary to that obtained legitimately (Henry, 1978).

Gerald Mars (1983) argues that certain jobs are associated with certain kinds of pilfering and pilferers. He identifies four types of work situations depending on the extent to which jobs constrain and insulate workers, or foster reciprocity and competition among them, and the extent to which they give workers group support and control:

**1. Hawks** are found in jobs that stress individuality, competition, and autonomy and that value innovation. The jobs also have weak group support because the worker largely controls his or her own activities. Independent salespersons, successful journalists, small-business people, academics, and other professionals are likely to be hawks, but so too are waiters, fairground buskers, and owner-operator cabdrivers. Hawk fiddles usually involve the manipulation of time and work performance, and the scale of the fiddle increases with the status of the fiddler. Mars shows how accountants, lawyers, physicians, management consultants, and even university lecturers are able to capitalize on their status and freedom from group control. Favorite fiddles of hawks are padding expense accounts and charging for work not actually performed. The risk that hawks face is generally not that their employers or colleagues will find out — they usually know about and accept fiddles as an integral part of the business — but, rather, that the public in general will find out and react with "envy, resentment, and occasional outrage" (Mars, 1983:49).

**2. Donkeys** are in jobs characterized by isolation and relatively rigid constraints. Assembly-line workers, supermarket cashiers, and retail salespeople are good examples. "The donkey type of fiddle is an appropriate response to this minimal autonomy. Since the job isolates the worker, the worker fiddles in isolation" (Mars, 1983:71). New workers may learn of fiddling among their fellows, but there is no group support for it, nor is it practiced as a group activity. Bar stewards who give short-measured drinks and pocket the difference between what each bottle would have brought in and actually does bring in, and cashiers who fiddle change or pocket money after ringing "no sale" on the till are examples of donkey fiddlers. But Mars points out also that donkey fiddles are often not motivated by material gain but, rather, by the worker's greater measure of personal control. In addition, the absence of group controls may give rise to excessive fiddling, as when a short-order waiter skimmed $150 a day for a year before being found out (Mars, 1983:87).

**3. Wolves** operate in packs and are found in jobs in which the work is organized into crews: longshoremen, miners, prison guards, and garbage collectors are found in "wolfpack" jobs. The group comes to exercise a lot of control over the individual, and pilferage is organized and controlled by the group. Individualists are not welcome, and membership in the wolfpack is not automatic, but through acceptance by other members. Members are held together by mutual dependence and trust, with much testing of the latter.

Dock pilferage by longshoremen in Newfoundland is typical of the wolf-pack. Longshore workgangs are close-knit, with controlled membership and a ranking system based on skill and trust that effectively controls any particular member's access to cargo by allocating work responsibilities. Only through access to cargo can a dockworker pilfer, and so jobs with such access are essential. On the other hand, the nature of dockwork makes it important for those with access also to have group support in order to pull off a fiddle. Since individual workers rarely have both access and support, dock pilferage remains group centered, and there is less room for the excesses sometimes found in the pilfering of donkeys and hawks.

Donald Horning's (1970) study of pilferage in a midwestern electronics assembly plant illustrates the power of the group in wolfpack jobs. Horning interviewed eighty-eight operatives and found pilferage a common practice. However, group norms dictated what was pilferable and what was not. Three types of property were distinguished: (1) company property, consisting of buildings, fixtures, heavy machinery, power tools, and expensive electronic components; (2) personal property, consisting of anything known to belong to coworkers or marked with someone's name, such as wallets, lunch boxes, modified tools, and clothing; and (3) property of uncertain ownership, for example, unmarked clothing, nuts, bolts, scrap, waste, small tools, loose money, and so forth. These items, but not the others, were considered fair game.

Widely shared definitions of the situation gave workers their rationalizations and justifications for their pilferage: "it's a corporation. . . . It's not like taking from one person"; or "The company doesn't mind, they've got plenty . . . they're not losing anything on what I take"; or "Everyone's doing it." Although it is not clear that these rationalizations are invoked before pilfering, as Cressey argued in the case of embezzlement, a number of things point to this conclusion. First, group attitudes defining what is appropriate to steal prevail despite the arrival and departure of particular workers. Second, these attitudes are learned on the job, not brought to it, and they constitute the normative framework within which workers shape their own subsequent behavior. Third, the fact that pilferage of personal property is extremely rare, whereas that of property of uncertain ownership is pervasive, indicates that the appropriate distinctions were made before the thefts were committed. In other words, rather than rationalizations merely excusing behavior after it has occurred, the discrimination in choice of items suggests action guided by group definitions.

**4. Vultures** hold jobs that offer autonomy and freedom but are subject to overarching bureaucratic control that encourages group influence. Vulture jobs are selling jobs, postal delivery, truck driving and other traveling jobs, taxi driving, and many service jobs. Fiddling tends to be exercised individually, but mutual self-interest keeps employees tied in a bond of sometimes uneasy cooperation. The relative instability of vulture occupations means that under the surface of cooperation there is competition, and when a particular fiddle threatens others' jobs, they close ranks against the offender.

I myself experienced a vulture fiddle. Many years ago I worked for one college vacation as a delivery driver for a well-known London department store. On the first day of work I learned from my codriver that two breakfasts, a two-hour lunch period, an hour-long afternoon tea break on top of seven hours of delivering always produced a healthy overtime check. I also learned that my codriver expected me to conform to this schedule and that if I did not, it would not look good for the other drivers who were also doing the same thing. The company supposedly knew about the time fiddle, and so long as it did not become unreasonable, store management accepted it, I was told, in return for the drivers' staying nonunion.

## POLITICAL CORRUPTION

This section would certainly be incomplete if we ignored occupational crime in government and politics. We speak of political corruption when officeholders in government and politics violate the laws regulating their official conduct so as to benefit themselves or their associates, or use the power and influence associated with their office to induce others to commit crimes.

**Forms of Political Corruption**   Political corruption manifests itself in two different, though often related, forms: (1) activities designed to bring about economic gain and (2) activities designed to perpetuate or increase political power. Government officials who accept or demand monetary kickbacks in return for legislation favorable to some individual or special group are engaged in corrupt activities that promise economic gains. Politicians who arrange to have cronies stuff ballot boxes with the names of nonexistent voters are engaged in corrupt practices designed to keep them in office or to put them there. Needless to say, those who gain economically from corrupt activities may also gain political power, and those who gain political power may also gain financially. Thus it is sometimes difficult to separate the economic from the power dimension of political corruption.

It is pointless to speculate on the prevalence of corrupt practices among those in government. We simply have no way of knowing how extensive political corruption is, and we are unlikely ever to find out with any certainty. In fact, it could be that the more corruption we know about, the less there actually is, for corrupt practices thrive under a cloak of secrecy and third-party indifference. What we can say with reasonable assurance is that the opportunities for corruption are probably greater today than they have ever been. As governments have come to dominate more and more areas of social life and have expanded their roles as employers, producers, consumers, taxers, and spenders, those in political jobs have found an expanding number of opportunities to reap illicit benefits from their position in the occupational structure.

Finding out about political corruption is not easy, and this is as true for the criminologist and political scientist as it is for the general public. One reason is the insider–outsider barrier that politicians erect in their dealings with others who are not part of the political establishment. Another is the cronyism characterizing relations among politicians and their friends in business and government. This leads to a kind of "mutual protection society" and encourages a "politics is politics" attitude among insiders, who would rather look the other way than make public trouble for a colleague. During the entire history of the United States Congress, only seven senators and eighteen representatives have been censured by their colleagues.

A third reason is that the agencies responsible for policing the politicians are themselves run by politicians. If an investigation of a particular official or agency is called for, it will usually be pursued without fanfare and rarely will result in the pressing of formal charges. Even when an investigation is reliably known to be under way, heads of the responsible agencies will often deny it. Fourth, there are no official statistics on the kinds of occupational crime committed by those in politics and government. One looks in vain for "official misconduct," "high crimes and misdemeanors," "bribery," "influence peddling," and so forth, in either the Part I or Part II offense lists published by the FBI in their annual *Uniform Crime Reports*. In fact, the only specifically occupational crime listed at all is embezzlement, which victimizes the establishment.

We become aware of political corruption primarily through the efforts of journalists and those who keep watch on government in the public interest, for example, "Nader's Raiders" and Common Cause. Sometimes corruption comes to light because persons involved in it turn informer. Such was the case with the 1976 scandal involving Representative Wayne Hays and his former secretary Elizabeth Ray. The latter made public charges asserting that Hays had, among other things, put her on his office payroll because she furnished sex — not simply secretarial work.

**Crimes for Money**  The political occupational crimes that come to light are usually notable because they have been committed by high officials, have involved substantial losses to the taxpayer, or have represented a systematic and extensive violation of public trust or civil rights. During the last few years, political corruption at the national and international levels has so dominated the headlines that local scandals seem mild by comparison. Actually, the victimization brought about by local corruption may have a more far-reaching and harmful effect on the lives of Americans. When, as happened recently in a midsized Illinois city, school board officials misappropriate thousands of dollars in school funds, it may take years to overcome the damage to education, not to mention public trust.

In the course of their political careers, government officials sometimes find their past catching up with them after they have moved to national prominence. Such was the case with Vice-President Spiro Agnew and Labor Secretary Raymond Donovan. It was revealed in Agnew's case that while governor of Maryland, and earlier while a county official, he had received kickbacks from contractors doing business with the county and state governments. Upon these disclosures, Agnew resigned the vice-presidency and subsequently pleaded "no contest" to an income tax violation charge ("no contest" is not a plea of guilty but subjects the defendant to conviction). In Donovan's case, grand jury indictments charged him with fraud and grand larceny while he was in the construction business. Another case of corruption that came to light after the offender had become an official of the federal government involved Judge Otto Kerner, formerly the governor of Illinois. Kerner was tied to an Illinois scandal involving offers of racetrack stock to politicians. Subsequently he was convicted of numerous criminal offenses, including perjury, and became the first federal judge ever to spend time in prison. Kerner died in 1976, shortly after his early release from federal prison because of illness. These cases, in which bribery and kickbacks were prominent, clearly involve corruption for economic gain.

Political corruption for economic gain is encouraged by the tight links between politics and business. In addition to the fact that business provides financial support for political campaigns and governments disperse billions of dollars worth of contracts to industry, many government officials retain, while in office, a financial interest in business pursuits. Members of Congress remain active in businesses ranging from real estate and insurance to construction, law, oil, and gas. Temptations to abuse their political connections abound, particularly when proposed legislation or government contracts influence their personal finances and those of business colleagues.

The extensiveness of the connection between business and politics is illustrated by the 1976 international scandal involving payoffs to foreign government officials by multinational corporations based in the United States. Uncovered in the post-Watergate period of house cleaning, the scandal brought charges of payoffs to politicians and government officials around the world for their aid in granting lucrative government contracts to U.S.

corporations. By early 1976, forty corporations had been accused of such bribes and other questionable payoff practices, and some of the United States' largest corporations were admitting involvement. For example, Gulf Oil admitted paying $4 million to the South Korean ruling party and $460,000 to Bolivian officials; Burroughs Corporation admitted $1.5 million in improper payments to foreign officials. Aircraft companies such as Lockheed, Northrop, and McDonnell Douglas admitted by far the largest bribes, payoffs, and questionable commissions. As sellers of military and civilian aircraft, these companies stood to gain or lose billions of dollars in government contracts, and they aggressively pursued any avenue to acquisition of those contracts. Lockheed was charged with paying $202 million to foreign officials in Japan, the Netherlands, Turkey, Italy, and elsewhere. More recently McDonnell Douglas was indicted in federal court for paying $1 million in bribes to Pakistani International Airlines officials, and in 1985, General Dynamics and four other defense contractors admitted paying around $6.5 million to a South Korean general whose consulting firm helped the American corporations sell military equipment to South Korea (*St. Louis Post-Dispatch*, October 2, 1985).

**Fraud and the Defense Industry**   Companies like General Dynamics, Rockwell International, and McDonnell Douglas have prospered through government contracts. Indeed, it is from these contracts that many firms make most of their profits. For example, in 1984, Boeing made 93.7 percent of its profits from government contracts, McDonnell Douglas 97.8 percent, and General Dynamics 96.7 percent (*St. Louis Post-Dispatch*, December 15, 1985).

Because of the enormous sums of money involved — General Dynamics did $6 *billion* business with the Pentagon in 1984 alone — and the bureaucratic organization of government and large businesses, there are both the incentive and the opportunity for various types of fraud. One of the more celebrated recent cases involved the chairman of General Dynamics, David Lewis, who charged the government $320,000 for personal trips to his family farm in Georgia between 1981 and 1983. The *St. Louis Post-Dispatch* (December 15–22, 1985) investigated the business of defense fraud and found many other examples. In 1985, allegations of cost and/or labor mischarging were being investigated against McDonnell Douglas, Rockwell International, General Dynamics, Lockheed, Boeing, General Electric, United Technologies, Raytheon, Litton Industries, Grumman, Westinghouse, Ford, Northrop, Motorola, and others. It is noteworthy that despite the considerable financial cost of these crimes, the outcome for the companies involved has been minimal.

**ABSCAM**   The 1980s ushered in a new scandal involving crimes for money, this time by members of Congress. An undercover FBI operation known as ABSCAM was set in place in which one of its operatives posed as a wealthy Arab businessman seeking to obtain residency permits. Contacts were set up between the "Arab" and various congressmen to whom large sums of money were offered in exchange for help. The FBI videotaped the meetings, and when the prosecutions eventually took place, the public saw films of elected representatives gleefully filling their pockets and briefcases with money.

Although all the offenders were initially convicted, some later filed successful appeals. These were heralded by many in Washington as the fitting end to an affair in which the FBI, not members of Congress, was the culprit. Accusations of entrapment (see box on p. 20) and violation of privacy flowed from all sides, and if anyone emerged tarnished by the episode it was the FBI and the Department of Justice. Noticeably, the indignation and noise over ABSCAM are rarely heard when similar police practices are directed at drug traffickers.

**Crimes for Power**   In regard to corruption for purposes of acquiring, retaining, or increasing one's political power, the Watergate scandal immediately comes to mind. Brought to light following the uncovering of a June 1972 burglary attempt at the Democratic National Committee headquarters in the Watergate hotel and apartment complex in Washington, D.C., the Watergate affair resulted in the first resignation of a U.S. president and touched people in all areas of national politics. Due in part to vigorous investigative journalism by *Washington Post* reporters Carl Bernstein and Bob Woodward, the American public was given a two-year, in-depth look at political corruption at its worst. Not only had the White House been deeply involved in the scandals, but also included were a former secretary of the treasury, the attorney general of the United States, officials of the FBI, CIA, and Internal Revenue Service, persons connected with organized crime, international terrorists, and even some whose records looked little different from those of the street criminals who are the routine business of local police departments.

The central theme around which the Watergate affair revolved was clearly one of political power. The involvement of the Committee to Re-Elect the President, the activities of White House staffers, and the routine subversive manipulation of government agencies by Richard Nixon and his allies bear this out. Here was an incident, or rather a combination of incidents, in which maintaining and extending power stood as the central goal. The string of events began in early 1972, when the office of Daniel Ellsberg's psychiatrist was burglarized so that evidence from the files could be used to political advantage. During the presidential campaign of that year, Nixon's supporters and staffers committed various illegal actions: they used the United States Postal Service for fraudulent and libelous purposes, an aspect of the so-called dirty tricks used to discredit Democratic opponents; the Watergate break-in itself was for the purpose of "bugging" the Democratic National Committee headquarters and scrutinizing its files; they pressured the Internal Revenue Service to harass political opponents and Nixon's so-called enemies; they encouraged the FBI and CIA to obstruct justice so that these and other criminal activities would not come to light and, if they did come to light, would not be linked with the White House; they paid "hush money" to the Watergate burglars; and they misused public funds and solicited campaign contributions in violation of federal laws. Eventually, White House staffers were fired and government officials forced to resign in a last-ditch effort to plug the ever-widening holes in the defenses around the Oval Office.

In the summer of 1974 the House of Representatives' Judiciary Committee voted to impeach President Nixon. He was charged with obstruction of justice and failure to carry out his constitutional oath and duty to uphold the laws of the United States. He resigned on August 9, 1974. Much still remains unknown about the political corruption in Richard Nixon's administration. Nixon himself was pardoned by President Gerald Ford, thus making it unlikely that the true nature of his offenses will ever come to light. One is certainly left wondering whether anything would have come to light had it not been for the ill-fated break-in at the Watergate and the tenacity of two young reporters in search of news.

Writing in 1970, before Watergate, James Boyd noted that in American public life "there is no sense of honor, no concept of it, no expectation of it, no reward for it." This, Boyd contended, was a basic premise underlying what he called the "ritual of wiggle." The ritual is an enduring feature of political folk wisdom among public officials and consists of a series of steps or rules to follow if those in public life are confronted with charges of misconduct and expect to weather whatever storm develops. Boyd gives us some clues as to why political corruption will continue to persist even in the face of scandals such as Watergate, which have sharpened public scrutiny and distrust of politics and politicians. Corruption persists because even when confronted with exposure and the possibility of ruin, the "ritual of wiggle" helps redefine the wrong as right and guards against discovery of the "whole truth" and against punishment commensurate with the gravity of offenses. Here are the steps of the wiggle (Boyd, 1970:28–43):

**1.** Admit nothing until you know the worst; if it looks like a one-shot affair, hide till it blows over.

**2.** If you must speak out — confess to what is known, evade what is unknown, and cry.

**3.** If at all possible, give the money (if money is involved) back — or at least give it to someone else.

**4.** If partial confession and restitution fail to stem the headlines, arrange a quickie exoneration from a semirespected source (e.g., the House Speaker, the respective chairmen of the Senate and House Ethics Committees, the attorney general).

**5.** If the unpleasantness persists, use the "stranger in paradise" routine: You can't help it if goodhearted friends have an urge to shower you with gifts or if lucky fate strews your path with roses.

6. Insist that you would have done the same favor for any constituent.

7. At the moment of deepest personal disgrace, announce for reelection.

8. Set up a series of endorsements by prominent churchmen.

9. It's time to pick a scapegoat.

10. If the newsmen persist, bolder moves are advisable: issue a statement requesting an official investigation.

11. Threaten a multimillion-dollar libel suit against your accusers but don't file it; if you must file it for tactical reasons, withdraw it before it gets to trial.

12. When judicial proceedings become inevitable, claim constitutional immunity.

13. During trial or impeachment proceedings, observe the traditional formalities [some of which are listed below]:

    a. Never appear in public without your wife; be sure that your entire family, including preschool children, attend every court session.

    b. Feign illness and a sort of stunned vacuity, as if the indignity of it all is too much for your sensitive nature.

    c. When questioned by the press in the hallways, emphasize how you welcome the chance to clear your name, how you asked for this trial, how the only thing that bothers you is the suffering it's inflicting on your family.

    d. If convicted, abandon all dignity and beg for mercy.

# Crimes Incidental to, and in Furtherance of, Business Operations

Some occupational crimes arise in connection with business pursuits but are not the central purpose of the business. They are committed on behalf of business interests, sometimes by individuals, sometimes by groups; they surface among the self-employed and among executives of companies large and small. We shall concentrate on corporate activities that violate laws governing commerce and trade.

## RESTRAINT OF TRADE

Among the occupational crimes committed by corporate decision makers on behalf of their organizations are those violating state and federal laws dealing with restraint of trade. The first relevent federal statute was the Sherman Antitrust Act of 1890. Designed to curb the threat to a competitive, free-enterprise economy posed by the nineteenth-century spread of trusts and monopolies, this act made it a criminal misdemeanor for individuals or organizations to engage in restraint of trade by combining or forming monopolies to that end.

There are three principal methods of restraint of trade: (1) consolidation so as to obtain a monopoly position, (2) price fixing to achieve price uniformity, and (3) price discriminations, in which higher prices are charged to some customers and lower ones to others (Sutherland, 1949). From the standpoint of those engaging in these practices, they make sense: the less the competition and the greater the control over prices, the larger the profits. But the small and independent businesses will lose business, and the public at large will face higher prices and lose its discretionary buying power.

The most common violations of restraint-of-trade laws are price fixing and price discrimination. In Sutherland's investigation of seventy of the largest American corporations over a fifty-year period, violations of this sort (including the illegal use of rebates) were the most prevalent restraint-of-trade activities. Interestingly, many of the suits charging restraint of trade through price fixing and discrimination were brought by private interests rather than by the Federal Trade Commission or the Department of Justice, the two agencies given primary responsibility for enforcing restraint-of-trade provisions. In this as well as in other areas of occupational crime, in which corporate decision makers break the law on behalf of their organizations, officialdom has not been at its most aggressive in ferreting out violations and bringing charges. But this should hardly come as a surprise, given the close relationship between business and politics.

**The Sears–Goodyear Case**  The following account given by Sutherland (1949:81–82) describes a case of price discrimination that, though typical of the pattern followed in other cases, ended in a dismissal of the suit brought against the companies involved:

> The discrimination favoring the large purchaser is shown in the suit against Goodyear Tire and Rubber Co., and Sears, Roebuck and Co., which was finally dismissed on a technicality although the facts of discrimination seemed to be adequately proved. Goodyear made a contract with Sears Roebuck to furnish tires under a special brand at cost plus six percent; these tires, except in the brand name, were identical with the tires sold under Goodyear's name. From 1926 to 1933 Sears Roebuck bought approximately 200,000,000 casings and 17,500,000 tubes at a price $42,000,000 lower than the figure at which the same tires would have been sold to independent tire dealers. . . . Goodyear sold 18 percent of its entire output of tires to Sears Roebuck under these contracts and received in payment only 11 percent of its income from the sale of tires. Because of this preferential price, Sears Roebuck cut the retail price of tires by approximately 25 percent and still had a profit of approximately 40 percent. The independent tire dealers appealed to Goodyear for assistance in meeting the competition of Sears Roebuck, since the contracts between Goodyear and Sears Roebuck were not known to outsiders [i.e., the dealers were unaware of Sears' preferential position]. Goodyear produced a new tire to meet the competition but it was inferior in quality and proved inadequate. The consequence was that approximately half of the independent tire dealers in the United States in 1926 had abandoned this business by 1931. . . .
>
> The price discrimination not only gave Sears Roebuck a monopolistic position

in the sale of tires but also gave it a great control over Goodyear. Sears Roebuck exercised its right to inspect the Goodyear books as to costs, and during the life of these contracts disallowed from half a million to one million dollars a year claimed by Goodyear as costs. When the first contract terminated in 1928, Sears Roebuck claimed that other tire manufacturers were prepared to make better offers than Goodyear had made, and insisted that Goodyear build a new plant in the South in order to reduce the freight charges for the southern trade of Sears Roebuck. Although the president of Goodyear asserted that this additional capacity was not needed, he was forced, in order to secure a renewal of the contract, to build a plant at Gadsden, Alabama, at a cost of $9,000,000. While the renewal of that contract was under consideration, Sears Roebuck forced additional concessions in the form of a gift by Goodyear of 18,000 shares of common stock of the Goodyear corporation plus $800,000 cash with which to purchase 32,000 additional shares, making a total of 50,000 shares with an approximate market value of $2,250,000.

Reading this, one might imagine that Goodyear suffered, Sears Roebuck got rich, and the public was blessed with an opportunity to buy good tires at lower prices. While Sears certainly benefited financially from the deal, Goodyear did not suffer, for 18 percent was a healthy chunk of its business. But the public did not really benefit from the arrangement, at least in the long run. Unchecked, practices such as these inevitably lead to higher, not lower, prices for the consumer, not to mention a decline in purchasing discretion.

**"The Great Electrical Conspiracy"**   In 1961, twenty-one corporations and forty-five high-ranking executives in the heavy electrical equipment industry were successfully prosecuted for criminal violations of the Sherman Antitrust Act. They had been involved in a price-fixing and bid-rigging scheme that, over nearly a decade, had bilked local, state, and federal governments (and the taxpayer) out of millions of dollars on purchases averaging nearly $2 billion a year.

In carrying out their scheme — called by the trial judge, "the most serious violations of the antitrust laws since the time of their passage at the turn of the century" — executives of the conspiring companies would meet secretly under fictitious names in hotel rooms around the country. Referring to those in attendance as "the Christmas card list," and to the meetings as "choir practice," the conspirators arranged prices for equipment, allocated markets and territories, and agreed on which companies would supply the low bids on pending government contracts. The participants covered their tracks well and were discovered only because officials of the Tennessee Valley Authority had received identical sealed bids on highly technical equipment. The companies involved in the conspiracy ranged from such giants in the electrical equipment business as General Electric, Westinghouse, and Allis-Chalmers, to such smaller firms as the Carrier Corporation, the I.T.E. Circuit Breaker Company, and Federal Pacific.

**Some Other Price Conspiracies**   At least three other large-scale price-fixing conspiracies have come to light in the years since the electrical equipment conspiracy. Though significant primarily because of their overall economic impact and the extensiveness of the conspiracies, they doubtless represent but a small portion of all price-fixing activities.

In 1967, the Senate Antitrust Subcommittee found evidence of an international scheme to corner the market and inflate the price of a chemical derivative of quinine. Directly involved were British, American, and Dutch companies, and complicity was discovered by officials in the State Department and General Services Administration of the United States. In regard to the financial aspects of the conspiracy, the international cartel was able to sell for three dollars an ounce what cost them twenty-one cents to produce. The public, of course, paid more; among those relying on the drug are elderly persons with heart problems.

In another case involving drugs, American Cyanamid, Charles Pfizer, Bristol Myers, and other major pharmaceutical companies were convicted of price fixing and monopolistic practices in their distribution and sale of certain antibiotics. In the case of one drug, tetracycline, the conspirators guaranteed a markup of 3,350 percent! For example, one hundred 250-milligram capsules were produced for $1.52, sold to druggists for $20.60, and then to customers for $51. In 1971, after the conspiracy ended, these same hundred capsules sold for $5 at the retail level. Once again, the victims of this conspiracy included noninvolved competitors and the general public, especially those in need of the particular antibiotics.

The third major price conspiracy involved a four-year period of price fixing and illegal market manipulation by fifteen plumbing fixture manufacturers and eight executives. With total sales over $1 billion a year, American Standard and its fourteen coconspirators cheated wholesale and retail customers by setting artificially high prices and by stifling competition — together they controlled nearly 100 percent of total American sales of enameled cast-iron plumbing fixtures and 80 percent of vitreous china fixture sales (Hills, 1971). All conspirators pleaded guilty or "no contest" in 1969.

**Corporate Fraud: The E. F. Hutton Scheme**  Many Americans periodically write checks on bank deposits that have not yet "cleared," that is, during the time lag from when money is deposited in the bank to when it is credited to the individual's account. Technically, these new checks are worthless until the corresponding deposits have cleared. When a check occasionally bounces, at worst the individual may receive a note from the bank, and perhaps a returned check with an overdraft charge. But what if someone knowingly and repeatedly wrote checks in this manner in order to obtain what in effect would be interest-free loans until the deposits cleared? Such a scheme would constitute fraud. A federal investigation determined that this is exactly what officials at E. F. Hutton had been doing at over 400 banks around the country from July 1980 through February 1982 (*Business Week,* May 20 and September 23, 1985). The scheme took advantage of normal delays in check clearing, and as a result the banks gave Hutton the use of billions of dollars in interest-free funds. Significantly, this was a period when interest rates were high, at 18 to 20 percent.

Prosecutors alleged that 20 to 25 people were involved. In the end a plea bargain resulted in no individual prosecutions; however, the company was fined $2 million for 2,000 counts of fraud and was assessed $750,000 for investigation costs. A subsequent internal investigation by former U.S. Attorney General Griffin Bell resulted in the suspension and fine of fourteen mid-level executives. Of more significance for the company was the effect of the adverse publicity. For a while profits fell, and the company's stock tumbled. In seeking to regain public confidence, the company hired respected comedian Bill Cosby for its 1986 advertising campaign. It is likely that the adverse publicity eventually will be forgotten by the public, and those in the financial community will modify their rules of cash management and otherwise go about business as usual.

## CONSUMER FRAUD: MISREPRESENTATION IN ADVERTISING AND SALES PROMOTION

Consumers become the victims of fraud in many different ways, including misrepresentation in advertising and sales. Misrepresentation in advertising means that what prospective buyers are told about a product is untrue, deceptive, or misleading. Sometimes the misrepresentation is in regard to the quantity of a product or the actual contents of a package or container; sometimes it concerns the effectiveness of a product; and sometimes it is a lack of information or insufficient information regarding a product or service such that buyers are misled.

The fact that a fine line divides fraudulent and nonfraudulent sales promotion will become evident as we consider a problem faced by nearly all businesses: creating a need for their products and services. Many of the things we consider necessities today — canned foods, refrigerators, automobiles, insurance policies — either did not exist a few decades ago or were thought of as luxuries, certainly not necessities. We have come to think of them as necessities largely because the companies selling them have convinced us to do so. When things are necessities, people want to purchase them.

In their efforts to convince us that we need their goods and services, businesses use a variety of different ploys. To use a fraudulent ploy is to make false claims as to the effectiveness of a product in doing what it is supposed to do. Those who believe the claims will see a need for the product. An example is the advertising plan followed some time ago by the makers of Listerine. In their campaign, the makers sought to create a need for Listerine as a mouthwash, a fairly new idea at the time, and to establish that need, they presented fake claims as to the germ-killing powers of the mixture.

Less clearly fraudulent, though possibly more dangerous to health, were the sales promotions of vaginal deodorants, discussed here by Burton Leiser:

> The creation of a need is best exemplified by a new line of products that is just emerging. The advertisers have been going all out to convince women of the need for vaginal deodorants. Full-page advertisements have appeared in women's magazines recently, and on television as well, designed to convince women of the need for these deodorants and of the effectiveness of particular brands. A typical ad says:
>
> "Some sprays hide it. Some sprays mask it. But Vespre actually prevents intimate odor.
>    *"Made especially for the external vaginal area.* Unlike sprays that only hide odor, Vespre feminine hygiene deodorant stops odor-causing bacteria. Contains twice the active odor-fighter of other leading sprays.
>    *"Tested by gynecologists.* Vespre was tested in leading hospitals. It's so effective it works all day, every day of the month. . . ." (1973:39)

What makes these sprays potentially dangerous is that when used regularly they may mask vaginal odor, which can be a sign of infection or disease. Also, they can themselves contribute to skin irritations and other troublesome reactions. Leiser continues:

> Vespre, Easy Day, and similar preparations are totally unnecessary and may be harmful. But a demand is being created for them by extensive advertising campaigns designed to market products that would never have been missed if they had not been produced. . . .
>    We may suppose that nothing false has been stated in these advertisements. But lying behind each of them there is a suppressed premise — one that the reader is expected to supply for herself — namely, the assumption that women need vaginal deodorants. But this suppressed premise is false. To be sure, every woman can consult her physician to find out whether she really needs these products, but few will ever do so. Many, worried about their attractiveness, and insecure, perhaps, over a fear that they may have an unappealing odor that they themselves cannot perceive, will accept the suppressed premise uncritically and, in the process, make the marketers of Vespre and Easy Day and similar products rich. (1973:269–270)

As noted, sales promotion strategies such as that just described may not be fraudulent — in the criminal sense. But it is only a short step from these strategies to those the common swindler uses. As an example of clearly fraudulent attempts to create needs, consider the activities of the Holland Furnace Company. This company was in the business of selling home heating furnaces. With some five hundred offices and a sales force in the thousands, the company put its resources to work on a fraudulent sales promotion involving misrepresentation, destruction of property, and, in some cases, what amounted to extortion:

Salesmen, misrepresenting themselves as "furnace engineers" and "safety inspectors," gained entry into their victims' homes, dismantled their furnaces, and condemned them as hazardous. They then refused to reassemble them, on the ground that they did not want to be "accessories to murder." Using scare tactics, claiming that the furnaces they "inspected" were emitting carbon monoxide and other dangerous gases, they created, in the homeowners' minds, a need for a new furnace — and proceeded to sell their own product at a handsome profit. They were so ruthless that they sold one elderly woman nine new furnaces in six years for a total of $18,000. The FTC finally forced the company to close in 1965, but in the meantime, it had done some $30 million worth of business per year for many years. (Leiser, 1973:270)

Though blatant and outright swindles, the activities of Holland Furnace Company salesmen and other purveyors of consumer fraud differ, in Leiser's view, only marginally from those of the sellers of mouthwash, vaginal deodorants, and a host of other "necessary" products:

The difference between the cosmetic manufacturer who is trying to persuade women that they need vaginal deodorants and the exterminator who brings his own termites to display to customers whose homes he has inspected, claiming that he found them in the foundation of the home, is one of degree only. To be sure, the advertiser does not victimize any one person to the same degree. He gets rich by extracting a little money from multitudes of women, rather than by taking a lot from a very few gullible people. He has not pulled bricks from his victim's home or dismantled her furnace. But he has produced a pocketful of termites that weren't there when he arrived. (1973:271)

With more than $20 billion spent annually on advertising, businesses are making an enormous investment in the art of persuasion. Given such an investment it should come as no surprise that those making it seek all possible avenues to a healthy payoff. If it were simply a matter of meeting their investment, they would have no reason to spend the money in the first place, but companies expect to make a considerable profit out of the enterprise. To make that expectation a reality the emphasis inevitably comes down on the side of persuasion, rather than honesty and concern that prospective consumers be told all that would be beneficial to them. It hardly bodes well for the future when young business students hold the opinion that forms of deception in advertising can be acceptable business practice and are not immoral.

Misrepresentation, deception, and falsehood in sales promotion surface in all advertising media, and it is not just the large corporations, with their immense advertising budgets, that find themselves charged with this kind of occupational crime. Small concerns advertising in local newspapers and on billboards are just as prone to the practice as are their wealthier business colleagues. A sense of the range and extensiveness of misrepresentation in advertising is provided by the box on pages 272–273.

## FRAUD IN THE MAINTENANCE AND REPAIR BUSINESS

When it comes to the maintenance and repair of their property, consumers inevitably depend on the services of others. Those in the business of providing maintenance and repair services thrive on this consumer dependence, and some, if not many, are quick to take advantage of the many opportunities for fraud that that dependence generates.

Maintenance and repair attracts swindlers and opens up avenues for consumer fraud precisely because typical consumers find it necessary to maintain or repair things that they own but do not usually have the time, resources, or know-how to do themselves. But even if we could fix or service our property, we are induced not to. Inducements may take the form of warranty specifications threatening us with lapse of the product guarantee if we do not use manufacturer-approved personnel or parts. Or they may be less blatant, such as the purposive withholding by the manufacturer of important information about the product and its repair, lengthy delays in the supply of replacement parts, or the use of special techniques and devices that are meant to guard against work by "amateurs" and may even cause further damage when not handled by those "in the know."

The best opportunities for fraud arise in the maintenance and repair of expensive products and those so sophisticated or specialized as to be beyond the technical expertise of most consumers. Automobiles, electrical appliances of every sort, heating and air-conditioning systems, motorized garden equipment, and a multitude of home maintenance items can be included here. The area of home improvements bristles with opportunities for fraud: (1) because of its attractiveness to consumers — there is a ready-made, or easily encouraged, demand for improvement services; (2) because consumers expect that costs will be relatively high — meaning the swindler can pad the cost of the work or offer a deal that is hard to refuse because it costs far less than the victim had expected; and (3) because even costly home improvements are readily financed through second mortgages and are tax deductible.

Fraudulent activities in the maintenance and repair business have been found not only among fly-by-night operators who descend on a town and swindle as many customers as they can before disappearing but also among businesses with an established clientele, a permanent address, and even a respectable name in the repair field. The fly-by-nighters use a variety of techniques ranging from the offer of special discounts, prizes, and free services to tricky financial plans, the use of inferior products and parts, and promises of work that is never done. By the time the customer realizes that he or she has been duped, the swindlers have long since disappeared.

One study demonstrates the widespread occurrence of fraudulent repair practices even among supposedly reputable businesses. In 1941, investigators working for *Reader's Digest* disconnected a coil wire in the

**Acne:** July 17: Better Business Bureau (BBB) ad division halts probe of alleged misleading ad for Oxy-10 acne medication, after Norcliff Thayer cancels ads.

**Antacids:** July 17: BBB ad division halts probe of alleged misleading ad for Gaviscon antacid tablets after Marion Laboratories cancels ad.

**Beer:** July 23: FTC probes whether ads for Löwenbrau mislead consumers into thinking beer is brewed according to original formula.

**Blood Pressure:** July 27: FDA charges Searle with misleading ad for antihypertensive drugs Aldactone and Aldactazine; charges hazard warnings are not adequately represented.

**Cereals:** April 18: Ralston-Purina drops ad for Moonstones cereal following probe by BBB national advertising division.

**Comic Books:** April 23: FTC announces its plan to investigate comic book industry to deter-mine whether the ad it carries is deceptive or unfair.

**Education:** July 16: Education Commission of the U.S. and U.S. Education Office recommends that HEW suspend or terminate federal assistance to institutions that misrepresent their academic programs.

**Electrical Appliances:** April 18: GE drops ad for major appliances that was challenged before national ad division of the council of BBB.

**Encyclopedia:** April 5: FTC rules that Grolier, publisher of *Encyclopedia Americana,* made deceptive pricing claims and used unfair sales practices.

**Eyeglasses:** May 26: NYC commissioners have received numerous consumer complaints of misleading ads.

**Floor Covering:** July 17: Earl Grissmer Co., division of Liggett Group, drops ad campaign for Rins-

---

engine compartment of an automobile and then took the car to a garage for repair. In all, 347 garages in forty-eight states were contacted; of these 63 percent (218) either overcharged, did unnecessary work, charged for work not done or for unneeded parts, or perpetrated similar swindles. In a similar study, investigators took a radio in which a tube had been loosened to 304 repair shops. Once again, nearly two-thirds of the shops visited swindled the customer. In another study, a watch was taken to jewelry stores throughout the country. The investigators had simply loosened the small screw that holds the winding wheel to the internal spring of the watch. Nearly half of the repair shops visited deliberately cheated the investigators (Riis and Patric, 1942).

Though the *Reader's Digest* study was completed nearly fifty years ago, there is no good reason to believe that the situation has changed significantly since then. Though the extent of fraudulent activities among maintenance and repair businesses is unknown and unknowable — just as is the true rate of most other forms of crime — the meager data that do surface from time to time suggest that the problem is pervasive. One estimate places the costs of home improvement rackets alone at more than $1 billion a year (Rosefsky, 1973).

Although no one kind of repair business has a monopoly on fraud, the ease with which the typical motorist can be duped into paying for unnecessary repairs and services makes fraud an attractive option for auto dealers and service stations. As Leonard and Weber (1970) have shown, the major auto dealers are financially dependent on the auto manufacturers, who control the

N-Vac carpet cleaning system; BBB had been investigating the ad.

**Food:** Sept. 30: Feingold Assn. spokeswoman calls for more complete listing of additives on labels.

**Food Prices:** Mar. 27: NYC Consumer Affairs Commission says A & P chain continues to sell items at prices higher than ads despite previous fines and warnings.

**Mail Order Companies:** Nov. 24: Famous Cosmetics, offering "famous brand-name cosmetics" and "fine and unique jewelry" at reduced prices, is barred by New York State attorney general from making unsubstantiated ad claims and ordered to make restitution to dissatisfied customers.

**Mouthwashes:** April 4: U.S. Supreme Court declines to reverse lower court ruling that Warner-Lambert must include in future ads disclaimer of past claims that product can prevent ailments or lessen their severity.

**Oil:** Feb. 10: STP agrees to stop making some ad claims for its motor oil, gasoline additives, and oil filters.

**Pain Relieving Drugs:** Sept. 17: FTC administrative judge rules American Home Products falsely advertised Anacin as a tension reliever and should correct impression.

**Retail Stores:** June 22: Many stores offering close-out sales in NYC midtown area have been issued summonses for misleading sales ads.

**TV Programs:** Nov. 15: Coalition of forty-six national consumer, professional, and labor organizations contend that most TV ads aimed at children are deceptive.

**Toiletries:** August 5: Helene Curtis is sued by S. C. Johnson & Son on charges of false and misleading advertising.

**Wines:** Nov. 18: Taylor denies that its ads for new wines are misleading, urges Bureau of Alcohol, Tobacco, and Firearms to establish guidelines for taste-test ad.

SOURCE: *New York Times,* dates as given, 1978.

---

purse strings and determine the framework within which dealers will operate. The dealer is expected to meet sales quotas, to push the sale of service parts, and to minimize expenses incurred by the manufacturer under new-car warranties. The "big brother" position of the manufacturers is strengthened by the fact that most dealers are in debt to the manufacturer for the physical plant, equipment, and facilities of the dealership. Dealers are thus under considerable pressure to make profits any way they can. The situation is similar for those service station owners who sell name-brand gasoline under lease arrangements with the major oil companies.

An American unfortunate enough to take a car to a really disreputable dealer or service station could become the victim of tire "honking" (puncturing the tire in order to sell new ones), the "white smoke trick" (spraying chemicals into a hot engine to produce a cloud of smoke), "short sticking" (not putting the oil dip stick all the way down, so that it looks as if more oil is needed), and a host of other practices designed to sell unneeded parts and services (Rosefsky, 1973).

An effort to collect systematic data on consumer fraud was initiated by the George Washington University National Law Center. Though focusing only on complaints received from persons in the Washington, D.C., area, a data-gathering computer center was established in 1974, and since that time many thousands of complaints have been processed. While some complaints prove minor and without legal import, many illustrate just the kinds of fraud we have been discussing. Here are a few examples of complaints about maintenance, repair, and home improvements:

Consumer purchased a used car with "25% discount on repairs" as a warranty. The auto failed inspection shortly thereafter, was returned to the dealer who sent it on to a repair shop retained by the dealer for repairing its cars. After unspecified repairs were completed at this shop, the dealer removed the car to the shop of his dealership, where two new tires were installed at a cost of $38, also under the 25% warranty described above. The consumer refused to pay, since he had not authorized and did not want the tires, but eventually capitulated in order to get his car back, paying 75% of the total repair bill on his car. . . .

Consumer, new owner of an American-made subcompact, received a recall letter from the manufacturer indicating a serious problem and representing that the manufacturer would cover the cost of any defect-related repairs at its authorized dealer. The dealer reaffirmed this representation and took the car for repair, estimating that the cost would be $200, but that the consumer would not be charged. The actual cost of repairs turned out to be $564 and the dealer refused to honor the prior representation as to the manufacturer absorbing the cost because "the engine had been tampered with." The consumer denied this, claiming that only the dealer himself had ever worked on the car, but to no avail. The consumer paid for the repair. . . .

Consumer took a piece of furniture to be reupholstered at a shop specializing in such work. The shop was unable to get the material ordered, for which the consumer had paid $150, and refused return of the furniture or the money. . . .

Consumer ordered patio awnings on 5/10/74, giving $200 deposit. Nothing was ever delivered or installed and vendor does not answer phone. . . .

Complainant took sewing machine in to shop in response to advertisement offering "free estimate" of work needed. Repairman took machine apart in course of examination, even though no work was authorized. He then refused to release machine back to consumer until paid for $12.50 charge for reassembly of machine. No repairs were made. Repairman then threatened to sell machine and charge for storage in the meantime if not picked up and paid for. Repairman was willing to drop all outstanding charges for reassembly and storage if repair work was authorized. (Sears, 1975:45–46)

## CRIMES IN THE HEALTH FIELDS

Physicians, lawyers, accountants, architects, dentists, pharmacists, and others in respected professions are not above illegal activities. Opportunities for fraud and other illegal activities are especially abundant in the various health fields. Because our culture strongly emphasizes health and physical well-being and because most Americans learn to rely on experts when confronted with health problems, those in the business of health find a vast clientele for their services, and the unscrupulous among them have little difficulty taking advantage of this favorable position. Medical quackery thrives on customer fears, lack of medical knowledge, and promises of expert help. A good example of quackery is Harry M. Hoxsey, a midwesterner who claimed to have found a cure for cancer. Hoxsey, who was not a physician, got himself listed with an Illinois chamber of commerce and set up "cancer clinics" around the Midwest to which the ill could come for his miracle cure. Though more than once convicted for practicing medicine without a license, Hoxsey pursued his quackery for nearly forty years and in one year alone is estimated to have seen eight thousand patients and grossed more than $1.5 million! Needless to say, his cure was no cure at all, but it was not until the 1960s that the Food and Drug Administration and the American Medical Association finally succeeded in putting him out of business (see Young, 1967).

Some unscrupulous practices take special advantage of the organization of legitimate medicine and the bureaucratic context within which most health care services are administered throughout the country. As C. Wright Mills observed some years ago:

> Medical technology has of necessity been centralized in hospital and clinic; the private practitioner must depend upon expensive equipment as well as upon specialists and technicians for diagnosis and treatment. He must also depend upon good relations with other doctors, variously located in the medical hierarchy, to get started in practice and to keep up his clientele. For as medicine has become technically specialized, some way of getting those who are ill in contact with those who can help them is needed. In the absence of a formal means of referral, informal cliques of doctors, in and out of hospitals, have come to perform this function. (1956:115–116)

The informal organization of medical referrals and the clique system provide a means by which less scrupulous physicians and dentists can take advantage of their patients. One well-known scheme is called "ghost surgery." A patient is led to believe that the surgeon will perform a needed operation. In fact, another surgeon (the ghost) performs the operation. The patient ends up paying an inflated price for the surgery because the original surgeon must pay the accomplice. Another practice made easier by the informal networks among physicians and dentists is fee splitting. Though illegal in most states, fee splitting is reckoned to be a fairly common practice. It involves kickbacks from specialists to the general practitioner who refers patients to them. Again, the patient is overcharged to accommodate the payoff.

With the extension of government involvement in medicine that has emerged along with the Medicare and Medicaid programs, many health services now operate in a complicated bureaucratic atmosphere that makes control of these services extremely difficult. Physicians, dentists, and those in such support services as lab testing and retail pharmacy sometimes take advantage of the unwieldy bureaucracy by claiming payment for services and products that were never provided, by issuing prescriptions in violation of federal regulations, and by performing unnecessary services, such as surgery, hospitalization, and lab tests.

One of the most alarming facets of medical fraud is the performance of unnecessary surgery. Although we have no accurate way of knowing how much surgery is unnecessary — even the most qualified physicians may not agree as to the need for a particular operation — evidence compiled over the past few years suggests that many physicians are quick with the knife and not always because the patient needs it. One study found that of 6,248 hysterectomies performed in West Coast hospitals, 40 percent of the operations could be questioned for one reason or another, and 13 percent could not be supported by any available evidence (Doyle, 1953). Similar findings have been recorded for appendectomies, gall bladder operations, tonsillectomies, and other common surgical treatments.

Unnecessary surgery is sometimes linked to declining occupancy levels in the hospitals and clinics to which the offending doctors are attached. When the occupancy level in a hospital declines there is considerable pressure to reverse the situation, otherwise income declines while operating costs remain the same or increase. Economic decline is viewed with alarm not only because jobs are at stake but also because important support services may have to be curtailed or dropped, thus damaging health care delivery, not to mention public trust. From the standpoint of modern medical organization, anything threatening the hospital threatens the entire field of professional health care. From the standpoint of some doctors there is also the threat of personal financial troubles as their hospital investments turn sour.

In his study of prescription violations by retail pharmacists, Richard Quinney (1963) showed how the existence of conflicting occupational roles can result in job-related crime. The organization of retail pharmacy is such that the pharmacist must fill two occupational roles: the business role and the professional role. The values and expectations embodied in the business role emphasize profit making: those in the professional role emphasize the correct procedures for such things as compounding and dispensing prescriptions and the proper relationship between pharmacist and doctor and pharmacist and customer. Quinney found that pharmacists tended to overcome the strains posed by these different roles by orienting themselves toward one role more than the other. Those who had adopted an "occupational role organization" stressing the business role were more likely to violate prescription laws than those with a professional role orientation.

It appears that occupational crime in the professions is inadequately accounted for by economic factors alone. Certainly, economic pressures can and do enter into the picture; yet economic pressures may just as well lead other professionals to pursue legitimate avenues of gain — working longer hours, improving one's skills, or writing books (Bloch and Geis, 1970). It seems that a more adequate explanation of occupational crimes among professionals is one that takes account of social structure; for example, the way occupations are organized, the interrelationships among them, and the normative contexts of work.

# Crime as the Central Activity of a Business

The fly-by-night operators who defraud the American consumer by promising work they have no intention of doing, by charging exorbitant prices for shoddy and inferior services, by creating needs for a new furnace, a new roof, pest control, or aluminum siding where no need existed, or by selling products that do not exist are little different from the short-con operators we encountered in Chapter 8. They commit fraud as their business. It is their work.

It is not, however, only fly-by-nighters who make fraud and deception their business. Over the years some businesses have made fraud their major purpose and yet retain all the trappings of established respectability. They have permanent addresses, they are listed with chambers of commerce, they have boards of directors, they provide annual financial statements, and they may even issue stock for public purchase. The products and services these companies offer range from vacuum cleaners to swimming pools, from real estate to insurance.

## THE EQUITY FUNDING CORPORATION OF AMERICA

One of America's most incredible corporate frauds came to light in 1973. It involved the Equity Funding Corporation of America (EFCA) and centered on life insurance, the major business of the company and its subsidiaries (Dirks and Gross, 1974).

Established in the early 1960s, EFCA began as a new member of the legitimate life insurance business. For a while its business dealings appear to have remained on the right side of the law, though some of its operations would be illegal today. Yet by the mid-1960s, the company's top executives were not content to stay within the law. Instead they embarked on an ambitious program of fraudulent financial manipulations. On the surface EFCA remained, until its fall in 1973, a respectable company with growing assets and growing prestige in the world of high finance. In reality, however, the company's major business turned out to be fraud.

In November 1973, a federal grand jury in Los Angeles handed down criminal indictments charging twenty-two of the company's executives, including a number of its original founders, with 105 counts of criminal conspiracy for such illegal activities as securities fraud, mail fraud, bank fraud, interstate transportation of counterfeit securities and other securities obtained by fraud, electronic eavesdropping, and the filing of false documents with the Securities and Exchange Commission (Dirks and Gross, 1974:229).

At the heart of EFCA's fraudulent activities was a scheme involving the creation of fictitious insurance policies for the purpose of resale, in order to make the company seem worth far more than it actually was. Using the information contained in the files of their real policyholders, the company issued 64,000 phony policies, which were then sold to other insurance companies for cash. The companies that purchased the phony policies thought they were reinsuring bona fide policies with a total face value of $5 billion. In fact, they were buying nothing. In addition to this scheme, EFCA routinely faked its assets and earnings in its annual reports and in 1972 began printing counterfeit bonds with a face value of more than $100 million. The executives behind this last operation even established a "mail drop" in Chicago for their counterfeit bank bonds.

## THE SHADY LAND-DEVELOPMENT BUSINESS

Land, it is said, is the best investment. Some Americans have found it quite the opposite, however: Land they have purchased has turned out to be worthless, nonexistent, under water, or already owned by someone else. Even when the land has been worth something, purchasers have found that worth to be far less than its price and that the purposes for which it was bought (as a nest egg, for a vacation home, as a place for retirement) cannot be realized without extraordinary expense and inconvenience.

Disclosures in the popular press have left little doubt that fraud has been booming in the land development and investment business in recent decades. Shady land sale and development schemes have cashed in on the supposed value of land as an investment and on the dreams of many Americans to own a vacation or retirement home away from urban areas. The picture that emerges from the popular press and the few government investigations suggests that land fraud may well be tied to organized crime. The initial purchase of large slices of land, the national advertising and promotion campaigns, the construction or rental of sales facilities, and the appearance of respectability and financial success require the kind of funding and organization that organized crime has at its disposal.

Rich and poor alike can be the victims of land fraud schemes. For the poor victims, it often means the loss of life savings or a future of substantial indebtedness; for the rich, it means a bad investment that could reduce not only financial worth but also respect in the financial community, and hence access to investment credit and services in the future.

Land fraud businesses look just like their legitimate counterparts. They employ advertising agencies, maintain a sales force, keep up offices around the country (often in tourist and resort towns), and are listed in business directories and with chambers of commerce. They put together impressive brochures and they advertise in respectable newspapers and magazines. For investors who think themselves knowledgeable and cautious, the sales people have ready answers for critical questions and can show financial statements, company investment portfolios, and othe official-looking documents to underscore their legitimacy and the sound financial status of the operation. The investors discover too late that they have thrown their money down the drain and, like the victim of the con artist (see Chapter 8), vow never to be taken again. But things are heavily weighted in favor of the shady land dealers.

In 1969 Congress passed the Interstate Land Sales Act, a law designed to protect prospective purchasers. It required land developers operating on an interstate basis to register their subdivisions with the Office of Interstate Land Sales and to make a property report disclosing certain features of the land offered for sale or development. Although the new regulations may help the prospective land purchaser avoid a bad investment, developers can take advantage of numerous loopholes. The major responsibility for seeing that things are in order still rests with the buyer. The government does not endorse or recommend what is offered for sale, it does not substantiate the accuracy of the registration or the company's disclosures, and it does not protect the customer against developers who sell only within the boundaries of one state or who take advantage of legal loopholes. As Rosefsky points out, it is possible "for an unscrupulous developer to fit his program within one of the legal exemptions, such as limiting the size of an interstate subdivision to 49 parcels [lots of land], then when that's all sold out open up another one nearby of 49 parcels" (1973:155). The law exempts subdivisions under fifty lots.

# The Costs of Occupational Crime

Let us return to a matter raised in the opening paragraphs of this chapter: the costs to individuals and to society associated with occupational crime. A brief look at some of these costs should help us maintain a balanced view of the impact of crime in America and will serve to remind us that societal reactions to a particular form of crime are not necessarily an accurate reflection of its impact on people's lives, their communities, and their institutions.

## FINANCIAL COSTS

The financial costs of occupational crime far exceed those resulting from traditional crimes. The reason is partly the greater frequency with which occupational crimes are committed but, more important, the fact that a single offense can result in losses running into the millions of dollars. Recent estimates place the losses resulting from traditional crimes such as burglary and robbery at $4 to $5 billion (Michalowski, 1985:363). By contrast, losses attributed to occupational crimes are estimated at $40 to $100 billion per year, figures that do not include the costs of price fixing and other restraint-of-trade practices, industrial espionage, or violations of health and safety regulations. These offenses cost the public billions more. The overall costs of occupational crime may reach as high as $231 billion (Kramer, 1984:19).

## DAMAGE TO INSTITUTIONS AND MORAL CLIMATE

Deception, fraud, price fixing and other monopoly practices, bribery, kick-backs, payoffs, and violations of trust not only undermine the basic principles on which the American economy and policy have long been ostensibly based, but also they foster a moral climate in which lawlessness provokes little indignation — especially when its victims are vague entities such as "the public," "the consumer," "the corporation," and "the government" — and occurs largely free from any sense of guilt on the part of offenders. In particular, when those in positions of wealth, power, and prestige violate the law with relative impunity, their activities serve as a model for the rest of us, for they are the people to whom we look for leadership in our own efforts to get ahead. Looking out for number one, beating the system, getting something for nothing, or doing a favor for a price have become not disreputable approaches to life but, rather, the accepted and expected approaches for all social strata. "The businessman may pad his expense account, inflate his deductions on his income-tax return, exaggerate insurance claims, and over-charge when he can. The worker may goldbrick on his job, take as many breaks as possible, feign illness, and use other methods available to him to cheat his employer" (Haskell and Yablonsky, 1974:149). Armed with the knowledge of pervasive and unpunished thievery and corruption among those we have been brought up to respect or, at least, emulate — businesspeople, physicians, government officials — those who commit traditional crimes find handy and powerful rationalizations for their own illegal conduct. Their betters turn out to be surprisingly like themselves.

## PERSONAL HEALTH AND SAFETY

Finally, there are the costs to personal health and safety. Occupational crimes of various sorts pose health and safety hazards in numerous ways. Landlords and builders who violate building code regulations may expose their tenants to the threat of fire, building collapse, and serious disease; companies violating safety standards for their products (cars, tires, electrical appliances, toys, nightclothes, Christmas tree lights, or whatever) expose their customers to possible injury or death; physicians who do unnecessary surgery expose their patients to the risk of surgical complications; pharmaceutical companies conspiring to fix high prices threaten the well-being of those who need, but cannot afford, their products; mine and factory bosses who violate health and safety regulations expose their workers to injury, disease, and death; and companies manufacturing or selling contaminated food products or mis-labeled drugs expose their customers to unnecessary health hazards. All of these activities may, of course, result in severe psychological stresses and strains for the victims.

There can be little doubt that when the health and safety of the population as a whole are considered, the threat posed by occupational crime far exceeds that posed by traditional crimes. This is not to minimize the physical dangers associated with violence, rape, robbery, and the like but, rather, to place the two broad categories of crime in proper perspective vis-à-vis these particular costs. It is easy to overlook the physical dangers posed by occupational crime precisely because these are often less visible, less direct, and appear less concrete than those of, say, robbery and interpersonal assault. Yet they exist and are extensive. Take, for instance, the physical dangers associated with environmental pollution in the air, water, soil, work place, and home. Millions of Americans are exposed every day to known carcinogens and other potentially lethal substances, often because corporations and businesses fail to meet environmental standards or find legal ways to circumvent them.

In Missouri, the entire population of Times Beach has been forced to evacuate because dioxin-tainted waste oil was sprayed on the roads to keep the dust down. Times Beach is now a modern ghost town, its people suffering the delayed effects of dioxin (called "Agent Orange" during the Vietnam War). Among industrial workers alone, many thousands will become diseased or die because they must work under conditions that needlessly expose them to the very real threat of cancer and severe respiratory ailments. Those in the rubber, steel, asbestos, coal, and chemical industries are especially vulnerable to such diseases. One of the most costly industrial disasters of all time has been tied to "unlawful, willful, malicious and wanton" disregard for human safety — the December 1984 gas leak at the Union Carbide pesticide plant in Bhopal, India, which claimed 2,000 lives and injured 150,000 to 200,000 more. In its recent judicial inquiry, the Indian government charged Union Carbide with moral responsibility and legal liability for the leak. For its part, the company has accepted moral responsibility but denies any criminal negligence (*St. Louis Post-Dispatch,* November 29 and December 1, 1985). It remains to be seen what the courts will decide.

## Reactions to Occupational Crime

One of Sutherland's (1949) major contentions regarding white-collar crime was that offenders generally escape the punitive action and criminal stigmatization evoked by other forms of crime. In the unlikely event that corporate crooks are brought before a judge, they rarely receive a prison term upon conviction. This situation has not changed much over the years. Between 1940 and 1970 there actually was a decline in the proportion of antitrust cases resulting in criminal prosecution: from 59 percent between 1940 and 1949 to only 9 percent in 1970 (Nader and Green, 1972). From 1940 to 1961 only twenty executives and businessmen actually served jail sentences for antitrust violations (Dershowitz, 1961). More recently, the Joseph Schlitz Brewing Company was convicted of bribery to the tune of more than $3 million; its criminal punishment was $11,000 following a reduction of charges to two misdemeanors (*Newsweek,* December 3, 1979).

Marshall Clinard estimates that when convicted the corporate crook spends an average of 2.8 *days* in prison. In most cases, Clinard shows, offending corporations are merely issued warnings (Clinard et al., 1979).

There are signs that things might be changing. *Newsweek* (December 3, 1979) reported that during 1978 twenty-nine executives were imprisoned, compared with only six during 1976; fines for the two years totaled $12 million (1978), versus $3.7 million (1976). John Conklin (1977) noted that substantial fines have recently been levied by the Environmental Protection Agency against automobile manufacturers who falsified pollution control data. Thus in 1973 Ford Motor Company was fined $7 million, and in 1976 American Motors Corporation was fined $4.2 million.

Although lenient sentences for occupational crimes of all sorts appear to be the rule, the offender's social status clearly has a bearing on punishment. It is fashionable to refer to the pardon of ex-President Nixon and the prison terms given his aides following Watergate as an illustration of the link between status and punishment. It is also true that the twenty antitrust offenders mentioned earlier who received jail terms were not giants of the corporate world, but small timers and lower-level executives. In fact, of the forty-eight jail terms handed down in antitrust cases from 1890 to 1959, few involved higher-level executives of large corporations. The large defense contractors also manage to avoid strict enforcement and severe penalties, whereas smaller firms are fined and debarred into bancruptcy (*St. Louis Post-Dispatch*, December 18, 1985).

We also find a link between status and punishment in the case of employee theft. In a study of 1,631 employee-thieves, Gerald Robin (1967) found that whereas most of the thieves were fired by their employers (99.5 percent), only 17 percent were dismissed and prosecuted. However, regardless of length of service and size of theft, a significantly larger proportion of lower-level employees than higher-level employees were prosecuted. Since 99 percent of those prosecuted were convicted, the act of prosecution virtually ensured conviction and a criminal record for the offender.

## REASONS FOR LENIENCY FOR OCCUPATIONAL CRIMINALS

The relatively low probability of criminal sanctions being imposed, and the relatively high probability that they will be mild when they are imposed, is enjoyed not only by corporate offenders who violate regulatory laws, but also by those who steal from their employers, by those who defraud the public, and by those who violate public trust while holding political office. Compared with "traditional" criminals — robbers, burglars, heroin pushers, rapists — occupational criminals generally face little in the way of organized efforts to enforce the law. When exposed they are ignored, handled informally and unofficially, ordered to "cease and desist," forced to pay a nominal fine, or placed on probation.

There are a number of reasons for the general absence of a rigorous and punitive reaction to occupational crimes and those who commit them. First, many of those who violate the law in connection with their work are simply not thought of as criminals. Not only are their crimes not the kinds of activities to which that label is culturally, or even legally, applied; they also do not often look like real criminals. They are not poor, transient, unemployed, black, inner-city, uneducated, lower-class people with a history of involvement in delinquency and street crimes. They are, instead, people with all the trappings of respectability, and some are wealthy and powerful to boot.

Those occupational offenders with relatively high social status avoid criminal stigmatization, not only because they do not look like real criminals, but also because their wealth, prestige, and power — and the interests they hold in common with those who create our laws and pass out sentences — help defend against organized repression and the legal identification of their activities as criminal. The history of legislation and resource allocation for the enforcement of legal controls in the realm of business, politics, and the professions attests to the success of these defenses. Whenever new or more repressive legislation is under consideration in state or federal legislatures, it is remarkable how quickly it dies in committee, how easily it is held over to the next session, or how often it is amended into a completely different animal with plenty of loopholes.

When it is decided to prosecute upperworld crime, it is often the organization that is convicted rather than the executives who run it but are able to pass the blame to someone else. John Braithwaite (1982) points out that when individuals are prosecuted, it is often those least deserving of punishment who take the rap. And he claims to know of at least three transnational pharmaceutical companies with "vice-presidents responsible for going to jail" (p. 755). These people take a few risks in exchange for promotion to vice-president and, after a sufficient time in that position, are moved laterally to a safer vice-presidential position.

Another reason for the absence of a rigorous and punitive reaction to occupational crime in general is the "relatively unorganized resentment of the public toward" occupational crime (Sutherland, 1949:49). It is difficult to generate organized public resentment toward occupational crime when the effects of much of this crime are diffused rather than simple and direct and when the acts themselves occur within a complex, often technically sophisticated economic or political context. As members of a Ralph Nader study group put it: "When one person is robbed face to face, the injustice and indignity are obvious. But when millions are deceived in a complex economic structure, when pinpointing the blame is difficult if not impossible, when crime grows so impersonal that it becomes 'technical' — then we lose our perception of the criminal act" (Green et al., 1976:554).

Then again, organized public resentment is unlikely when value priorities strongly support self-reliance, free enterprise, individual initiative, and the drive for profits and power. When the public learns that someone's financial achievements or political successes were the result, in whole or in part, of deceit, fraud, bribery, influence peddling, embezzlement, and the like, the inclination is to applaud the obvious commitment to American success values and to play down the dishonesty. John Hagan (1985:171–173) argues that exactly this sort of rationalization helps foster a climate of moral neutrality. Upperworld indiscretions such as Watergate are thus regarded as worthwhile risks.

A climate of moral neutrality may not extend to all occupational crimes, however. Opinion studies reviewed by Braithwaite (1982) show that the public is often quite intolerant of corporate crimes that produce demonstrable harms such as pollution and government frauds. The National Crime Survey's ratings of offenses lists pollution resulting in multiple deaths as seventh in seriousness out of 204 crimes (Wolfgang et al., 1985). We must emphasize again, however, that the existence of such feelings is one thing but their effective organization is quite another.

When large, impersonal organizations are the victims of crime, public disapproval and indignation are well hidden, if they exist at all. Employee theft, embezzlement, tax evasion, and other activities victimizing corporations and government bureaucracies are considered excusable, if they are not actively condoned, in part because the victims are themselves unpopular and in part because history has not provided strong ethical guidelines for relationships between large organizations and their employees and customers. Different individuals may have different reasons for disliking large organizations, but on the whole it seems that their unpopularity results from their impersonality, their power and influence, their wealth, and their emphasis on rule following as opposed to the personal attributes of initiative and creativity. The unpopularity of organizations and lack of strong ethics governing the relationship between individuals and organizations not only make it unlikely that public reactions to crimes such as employee theft will be hostile, but they also serve as powerful justifications in the event that the crimes against them are under consideration. Erwin O. Smigel (1956) found that when a sample of 212 adults in Indiana were asked what type of organization they would steal from if forced by necessity to do so, 155 respondents indicated they would prefer to steal from a large business (102) or government (53) than from a small business. But perhaps the last laugh is had by the large corporation: Hagan (1982a) found in Canada that when such corporations are victimized, they get more justice (if they want it) than individuals do, and they are more likely to be satisfied with the outcome.

Occupational crime is likely to flourish for a long time to come. Even if there were organized public resentment, there are major obstacles to its prevention. One is the nature of work itself. Constant changes in the organization and technology of work provide new opportunities for crime. The inventive mind is able to take advantage of these opportunities and can often stay ahead of the law and its enforcement. This has happened with computer technology and now threatens to occur — with greater potential for injury — in the area of nuclear power (Bequai, 1978; Edelhertz and Walsh, 1978).

Prevention efforts are also frustrated by the close ties between business and politics mentioned earlier. The crimes likely to victimize most people, at greatest cost, are those dreamed up in corporate suites, in the offices of highly skilled professionals, and in the back rooms where political deals are often made. These high-status criminals are the people best able to capitalize on their occupational position. If they are caught they can hire the best lawyers, arrange the longest court delays, and manufacture the most compelling justifications for their actions. But usually it does not come to that: mutual protection serves mutual interests, and all parties (except the public at large) benefit when things are kept quiet and policing takes place from within.

There may be some public advantages to keeping corporations out of the criminal court and pursuing enforcement in nonlitigious or even extralegal ways. Braithwaite (1982:749–751) suggests that may unsafe practices are not covered under law, especially as rapid technological change far exceeds the ability of lawmakers to keep pace, and that even when laws exist, the enforcement apparatus often does not. If we want to stop these practices, voluntary cooperation from the offending corporation may be the best avenue, and for this there needs to be a climate of goodwill. If laws do exist, it is easy for the corporation to exercise costly delays and to exploit the complexities of the situation so that prosecution costs become prohibitive. To avoid these problems it may be in the public advantage to use threats, revoke licenses, and give adverse publicity, rather than formal punishment, to secure compliance.

Incidents like Bhopal and Times Beach, financial schemes such as those perpetrated by General Dynamics and E. F. Hutton, and the recurring incidence of political corruption may strain the public's patience, for if there is a collective conscience, it is probably getting uneasy. But for every highly publicized affair there are thousands of little crimes occurring on the job every day. The hidden economy (see Henry, 1978) thrives, and our consciences must deal with this as well.

# CHAPTER 10

# Organized Crime

Few Americans do not recognize the term *organized crime*. However, it is unlikely that many of us know much about the phenomenon. Certainly we have heard of Al Capone, Vito Genovese, Joe Bonnano, Joe Valachi, and Charlie "Lucky" Luciano. We may also have heard of Eliot Ness, the Justice Department agent assigned to break up Capone's bootlegging operations during Prohibition. And it is common knowledge that Chicago and the New York–New Jersey area are two of the major centers of organized crime activities. But what most of us have learned about organized crime has come from the more sensational portrayals presented by the mass media. Apart from periodic news items, which are usually colorful and designed to demonstrate some special kind of inside knowledge, the entertainment industry has been our major window on organized crime. The success of *The Godfather* and "Miami Vice" shows that we have enjoyed the view.

At best, the information available to the public via the mass media is fragmentary, superficial, and of questionable accuracy; at worst, it is patently false and purely titillating. And yet over the years many of us have come to believe that there is in America a national alliance or cartel composed of organized groups of criminals, dominated by Sicilian and Italian Americans, and involved in an extensive range of illicit, often violent activities. Whether we call it the Mafia, the Mob, the Syndicate, the Organization, or the Cosa Nostra, we simply know that it exists. But does it really? Is there, in fact, a national alliance or structure linking local crime groups, "families," or syndicates? Equally important, just how organized is organized crime?

## The Case for a National Cartel of Corporate Crime Groups

In 1951 and then again in 1969, highly credible sources appeared to confirm that a national crime cartel does exist in America. First, the so-called Kefauver Committee of the Senate reported that

1. There is a nation-wide crime syndicate known as the Mafia, whose tentacles are found in many large cities. . . .
2. Its leaders are usually found in control of the most lucrative rackets in their cities.
3. There are indications of a centralized direction and control of these rackets, but leadership appears to be in a group rather than in a single individual.
4. The Mafia is the cement that helps bind the Costello-Adonis-Lansky syndicate of New York and the Accardo-Guzik-Fischetti syndicate of Chicago as well as smaller criminal gangs and individual criminals throughout the country. . . .
5. The domination of the Mafia is based fundamentally on "muscle" and "murder." The Mafia is a secret conspiracy against law and order which will ruthlessly eliminate anyone who stands in the way of its success in any criminal enterprise in which it is interested. It will destroy anyone who betrays its secrets. It will use any means available — political influence,

## ORGANIZED CRIME AS DEFINED BY THE OMNIBUS CRIME CONTROL ACT

Organized crime means the unlawful activities of the members of a highly organized, disciplined association engaged in supplying illegal goods and services, including but not limited to gambling, prostitution, loan sharking, narcotics, labor racketeering, and other unlawful activities of members of such organizations.

[Note that this definition is uninformed by the wealth of scholarly work that has been undertaken in the past twenty years and reflects the rather stereotypi-cal views held in many academic and legal circles. Note also that the definition is vague and would be difficult to apply in practice. What, for example, do "highly organized" and "disciplined" mean? For further discussion of definitional problems, see Howard Abadinsky, *Organized Crime* (Boston: Allyn & Bacon, 1981), pp. 1–6].

SOURCE: Section 601(b) of The Omnibus Crime Control and Safe Streets Act of 1968. United States Code, Section 3701.

---

bribery, intimidation, etc., to defeat any attempt on the part of law-enforcement to touch its top figures or to interfere with its operations. (Tyler, 1962:343–344)

The findings of the Kefauver committee were based on information supplied mainly by police officials and informants. Using basically the same kinds of information, Donald Cressey summarized his investigation on behalf of the President's Commission on Law Enforcement and the Administration of Justice as follows:

1. A nationwide alliance of at least twenty-four tightly knit "families" of criminals exists in the United States (because the "families" are fictive, in the sense that the members are not all relatives, it is necessary to refer to them in quotation marks).
2. The members of these "families" are all Italians and Sicilians, or of Italian or Sicilian descent, and those on the Eastern seaboard, especially, call the entire system "Cosa Nostra." Each member thinks of himself as a "member" of a specific "family" and of Cosa Nostra (or some equivalent term).
3. The names, criminal records, and principal criminal activities of about five thousand of the participants have been assembled.
4. The persons occupying key positions in the skeletal structure of each "family" — consisting of positions for boss, underboss, lieutenants (also called "captains"), counselor, and for low-ranking members called "soldiers" or "button men" — are well known to law-enforcement officials having access to informants. Names of persons who permanently or temporarily occupy other positions, such as "buffer," "money mover," "enforcer," and "executioner," also are well known.
5. The "families" are linked to each other, and to non–Cosa Nostra syndicates, by understandings, agreements, and "treaties," and by mutual deference to a "Commission" made up of the leaders of the most powerful of the "families."
6. The boss of each "family" directs the activities, especially the illegal activities, of the members of his "family."
7. The members of this organization control all but a tiny part of the illegal

gambling in the United States. They are the principal loan sharks. They are the principal importers and wholesalers of narcotics. They have infiltrated certain labor unions, where they extort money from employers and, at the same time, cheat the members of the union. The members have a virtual monopoly on some legitimate enterprises. . . . Until recently, they owned a large proportion of Las Vegas. They own several state legislators and federal congressmen and other officials in the legislative, executive, and judicial branches of government at the local, state, and federal levels. Some government officials (including judges) are considered, and consider themselves, members.

8. The information about the Commissions, the "families," and the activities of members has come from detailed reports made by a wide variety of police observers, informants, wire taps, and electronic bugs. (1969:x–xi)

In Cressey's view, these crime families are organized along the lines of what sociologists call "formal organization." In this structure, the labor is divided so that tasks and responsibilities are assigned primarily on the basis of special skills and abilities; there is a strict hierarchy of authority; rules and regulations govern the activities of members and the relationships among them and with the outside world; and recruitment and entrance are carefully regulated. In short, the crime families are, like other formal organizations, rationally designed for the purposes of achieving specified objectives.

## An Alternative View

Not all authorities on organized crime agree entirely with Cressey. Some, for example, deny the existence of any national organization or structure linking and coordinating the activities of organized crime groups. The alternative view, suggested by Daniel Bell (1965), John Conklin (1973), and Francis Ianni (1973), among others, emphasizes more or less organized local criminal gangs, some of whose activities inevitably bring them into working contact with groups operating elsewhere. These authors see no real evidence of any centralized direction or domination of these localized syndicates.

Peter Reuter (1983) also rejects the notion of a formally organized, centrally directed, national alliance of Mafia families. He does not dispute the existence of Mafia families — most have continued in the same recognizable form for at least fifty years. Rather, Reuter believes that the relations among them are the result of occasional venture partnerships, occasional exchange of services, and attempts to reduce the uncertainty that arises when business takes a family into unfamiliar territory. Reuter (1983:158) also suggests that many of the connections among organized crime gangs — Mafia and other — resulted from Prohibition and from associations made while members served time in federal prisons.

Another point of contention concerns the degree and nature of organization. Some authors reject the idea that organized crime groups fit the formal organization model. Basing his argument on his own in-depth study of one Italian-American crime family, Francis Ianni (1973:120–24) notes:

> Secret criminal organizations like the Italian-American or Sicilian *Mafia* families are not formal organizations like governments or business corporations. They are not rationally structured into statuses and functions in order to "maximize profits" and carry out tasks efficiently. Rather, they are traditional social systems, organized by action and by cultural values which have nothing to do with modern bureaucratic virtues. Like all social systems, they have no structure apart from their functioning; nor . . . do they have structure independent of their current "personnel." . . . Describing the various positions in Italian-American syndicates as "like" those in bureaucracies gives the impression that they are, in fact, formal organizations. But they are not.

Perhaps the best way to approach the issue of organization is to recognize that there are degrees of organization. Although some crime families or syndicates exhibit many of the elements found in highly rationalized bureaucratic structures, as Cressey showed, others do not. This distinction is important when we consider the growing organized crime involvement of blacks, Puerto Ricans, and Cubans. Many of these groups display only rudimentary organization, mostly operating in loosely connected networks.

**The Consequences of Product Illegality**  Reuter's (1983) study of loan sharking, gambling, and the numbers racket in New York City shows how the illegality of products and services affects the organization of an economic market, keeping some enterprises localized and relatively small scale. The illegal market differs from its legal counterpart in various ways: (1) contracts cannot be enforced in a court of law; (2) the assets associated with illegal operations may be seized at any time; and (3) participants risk arrest and imprisonment. These problems differ in significance from one illegal market to another, however; heroin trafficking carries more risk than operating a numbers game.

These problems call for control over the flow of information about the operation, and those who participate are at different risk and pose different levels of threat to others. The *entrepreneurs* who control operations are at greatest risk from their *agents* or *employees,* who know most about the business, but those risks are reduced by dividing up the tasks and responsibilities, by offering employees economic incentives, by ensuring that they are not employed elsewhere, by intimidation, and by recruitment methods that rely on family ties or the incorporation of employees into the family through rite or marriage. Risks to the employees come largely from other employees, thus encouraging entrepreneurs to keep operations small scale and/or dispersed in time and space (Reuter, 1983).

Another problem faced by illegal enterprise is financing. Reuter (1983:120) found that credit works differently in illegal markets: (1) there are no accurately audited books; (2) the lender is unable to control any assets placed as collateral against a loan because the borrower is likely to demand secrecy and, in any case, lacks court protection (as a financer of criminal activities); and (3) the loan is to the individual entrepreneur and not to the enterprise, which has no legal existence apart from its owner. Therefore, the lender would have difficulty collecting from any successor.

These problems also constrain the growth of illegal enterprises, especially those in loan sharking and gambling: "Without smoothly working capital markets, the growth must be internally financed . . . out of profits. In the heroin importing business, where each successful transaction may double the capital of the enterprise, this may be a minor restriction. For the numbers bank, with a relatively modest cash flow and a need for maintenance of a substantial cash reserve, this may be a very important constraint" (Reuter, 1983:121).

## Distinguishing Characteristics of Organized Crime

It is unlikely that criminologists will soon reach a consensus on the issues we have been discussing. Even if detailed and dependable information were forthcoming, how complete a picture could be drawn from it? When we deal with people who place a premium on secrecy and engage in criminal activities, we are rarely able to learn everything we need to know. And even those in a position to know more than most — a participant who turns informant, such as Joe Valachi — may only know the facts about some aspects of their own organization and thus cannot be considered authoritative sources of information on other aspects or other organizations (see Maas, 1968). Even so, criminologists generally agree on some important features of organized crime, which, when taken together, distinguish this type of criminal activity from others.

First, organized crime is _instrumental_ crime, the purpose of which is to make money. To accomplish this, participants _organize_ in more or less complex networks. Third, most organized crime activities offer _illegal goods and services._ This does not mean, however, that those in organized crime have nothing to do with "traditional" crimes such as burglary or robbery. As Stuart Hills points out:

> It is the syndicate that has mostly controlled the importation and wholesale distribution of narcotics that, together with prohibitionist laws and police activity, compel most addicts to engage in burglary, robbery, and larceny to pay the exorbitant black-market prices. And it is the "fences," aligned with organized criminal groups, who allow thieves to convert their booty into cash. Organized crime has also been known to promote bank robbery, cargo hijacking, arson, and burglaries, sometimes in cooperation with individual professional thieves. (1971:138–139)

A fourth important characteristic of organized crime is its connections with the world of government and politics. Organized crime makes political *corruption an integral part of its business.* Indeed, political corruption is not merely a distinguishing feature of organized crime; it is critical to its survival.

The fifth feature of organized crime is its *generational persistence.* The syndicates or families comprising organized crime continue to operate despite the comings and goings of their members. Although the death or retirement of persons in leadership positions may result in significant changes of one sort or another, organized crime does not disappear, and individual organizations usually do not cease to exist. The persistence of organized crime despite the inevitable disappearance of its human participants can be explained in part by a final important feature of the phenomenon: *sanctioned rules of conduct* (sometimes called "the code"). The survival of any group or organization is problematic if the behavior of members neither is predictable nor conforms to the evaluations of at least some other members of the group. Rules of conduct help establish conformity and predictability; sanctions for violations of the rules help ensure that conformity and predictability persist over time.

## RULES OF CONDUCT

It should be stressed that there is no conclusive evidence that one particular code is shared by the various criminal organizations. Investigators have found numerous obstacles to a definitive statement of what the code (or codes) might be, the most important being the veil of secrecy that surrounds organized crime and the difficulty of gaining access to its participants.

Cressey (1969:175–178) combined snippets of information from informants with clues deduced from an analysis of the social structure of Cosa Nostra and was able to suggest the following as the code of organized crime:

1. *Be loyal to members of the organization. Do not interfere with each other's interests. Do not be an informer.* This directive, with its correlated admonitions, is basic to the internal operations of the Cosa Nostra confederation. It is a call for unity, for peace, for maintenance of the *status quo.* . . .
2. *Be rational. Be a member of the team. Don't engage in battle if you can't win.* What is demanded here is a corporate rationality necessary to conducting illicit businesses in a quiet, safe, profitable manner. . . .
3. *Be a man of honor. Always do right. Respect womanhood and your elders. Don't rock the boat.* This emphasis on "honor" and "respect" helps determine who obeys whom, who attends what funerals and weddings, who opens the door for whom, . . . and functions to enable despots to exploit their underlings. . . .
4. *Be a stand-up guy. Keep your eyes and ears open and your mouth shut. Don't sell out.* A "family" member, like a prisoner, must be able to withstand frustrating and threatening situations without complaining or resorting to subservience. The "stand-up guy" shows courage and "heart." . . .
5. *Have class. Be independent. Know your way around the world.* . . . A man who is committed to regular work and submission to duly constituted author-

ity is a sucker. . . . Second, the world seen by organized criminals is a world of graft, fraud, and corruption, and they are concerned with their own honesty and manliness as compared with the hypocrisy of corrupt policemen and corrupt political figures.

In discussing the code, Cressey pointed out that it is similar to the codes adopted by professional thieves, prisoners, and other groups whose activities bring them into confrontation with official authority and generate the need for "private" government as a means of controlling the membership's conduct.

Ralph Salerno and John Tompkins (1969:105–148) describe the "law" governing what they call "the crime confederation." Among the unwritten rules and directives are to maintain secrecy, keep the organization before the individual, keep other members' families sacred, reveal nothing to your wife, do not kidnap, do not strike another member, do not disobey orders, and always be a stand-up guy. Again, the authors' information came mainly from police intelligence and organized crime informants. Also like Cressey, Salerno and Tompkins imply that all organized crime groups subscribe to their code.

Taking exception to this position, Ianni (1973:150–155) proposes that different syndicates may well follow different codes, that the presumption of a shared code is based on the questionable belief that there is a single national organization, and that each individual organized crime group has achieved similar levels of organizational sophistication and has shared similar experiences. In Ianni's view, clues to organized crime codes are best discovered by the direct observation of members' behavior. His method "was to observe and record behavior and then seek regularities that had enough frequency to suggest that the behavior resulted from the pressures of the shared social system rather than from idiosyncratic behavior" (pp. 154–155). Family members were also asked why they and other participants behaved in a certain way.

From his two-year participant observation of one Italian-American crime family operating in New York (the "Lupollo" family) and his later research on black and Hispanic groups in organized crime, Ianni found evidence of different codes for different groups. In the case of the Lupollo family, there were three basic rules for behavior:

> . . . (1) primary loyalty is vested in "family" rather than in individual lineages or nuclear families, (2) each member of the family must "act like a man" and do nothing which brings disgrace on the family, and (3) family business is privileged matter and must not be reported or discussed outside the group. (Ianni with Reuss-Ianni, 1973:155)

Ianni found that in some respects black and Hispanic organized crime codes differed from the Lupollo rules, as well as from each other. For example, whereas the black and Hispanic groups emphasized loyalty and secrecy (as did the Lupollo family), some of these organized crime networks also stressed the rules "Don't be a coward" and "Don't be a creep" (in other words, the member's attitudes and actions must "fit in" with the group). Some stressed the rule "Be smart" (know when to obey but also when to beat the system). And some stressed the rules "Don't tell the police," "Don't cheat your partner or other people in the network," and "Don't be incompetent" (Ianni, 1975:301–305).

Ianni discovered that which rules were stressed depended in large part on how the gangs came together in the first place. Those gangs with shared family roots placed a premium on rules supporting kinship ties. On the other hand, gangs with origins in youthful street associations and partnerships tended to stress rules underscoring personal qualities ("Don't be a coward"). Those originating in strictly business or entrepreneurial associations tended to stress rules emphasizing more impersonal, activity-oriented obligations ("Don't be incompetent"). The code adopted by any one criminal organization reflects far more than the mere fact that it is a secret association engaged in regular criminal activities. How and why the participants came together in the first place, how long the organization has been operating, the cultural heritage of its major participants, and the nature and range of its activities all influence the rules of conduct adopted and maintained.

## The History of Organized Crime in America

One of the most important factors likely to influence the activities, structure, and code of an organized crime syndicate is the length of time it has been in the business of crime. The crime syndicates we read about most often — those identified as Italian-American and operating primarily in the Midwest and East — have been around for half a century; others are relative newcomers, and some are just emerging. To understand organized crime today we must understand how it was in the past.

The origins of organized crime can be traced to the gangs of thugs that roamed the streets of New York and other cities and followed the frontier west during the nineteenth century. In New York City the earliest gangs were made up of the sons of immigrant Irish families. These immigrants constituted the core of poor people and were also deprived of political power and were the routine object of discrimination. In the eyes of many of the youths growing up during the period, their survival and their path out of the ghetto lay in muscle and the willingness to use it. As Gus Tyler (1962:92) has observed, "the story of the early gangs — whether in New York, San Francisco, or the frontier — is told against a background of conflict; ethnic, economic, and political. It is the tale of men making their own law, legislating with their fists, striking out against real or imagined enemies."

From loafing and brawling the New York gangs moved into extortion and the instrumental use of force. They soon discovered that money was easily made through the intimidation of brothel owners, gambling proprietors, and others in the business of providing illicit services. More money came, and with it power, when it was discovered that politicians and businessmen would pay for their muscle. Gangs were hired to break up picket lines, to intimidate voters, to stuff ballot boxes, and to protect establishments from harassment by other gangs, not to mention the authorities. By the 1850s the gangs were the muscle behind Tammany Hall, the Democratic headquarters and the political heart of the city. With this new power, the gangs were able to open doors that formerly had been closed to the Irish. The docks were under their control, and this meant work for Irishmen; city hall felt their power, and this meant city jobs for their fathers, brothers, and cousins.

**Rags to Riches and the Quest for Respectability** The history of organized crime in America is to some extent the history of people seeking riches and respectability, and of the social, legal, and political conditions providing both the incentive and means to attain them. Whether we look at the nineteenth-century Irish gang, the Italian-American crime family, or the emergent black, Puerto Rican, and Cuban crime networks, the picture is essentially the same. We see migration and the herding of newcomers into ghettos, with few legitimate avenues of escape; we see poverty, discrimination, and degradation; we see corruption in politics and government; we see laws rendering criminal many goods and services in public demand; and we see material things held up as the legitimate symbols of success and respectability but the means to them denied the newcomers. Identifying the ghetto as the social setting in which organized crime is spawned, Ianni (1975:89–90) writes:

> The social history of American urban ghettos documents how ghetto dwellers were forced to seek escape from underclass status into the dominant society through the interrelated and interdependent routes of crime and politics. The corrupt political structures of major American cities and organized crime have always enjoyed a symbiotic relationship in which success in one is dependent on the right connections in the other. In this relationship, the aspiring ethnic, blocked from legitimate access to wealth and power, is permitted to produce and provide those illicit goods and services that society publicly condemns but privately demands — gambling, stolen goods, illegal alcohol, sex and drugs — but not without paying tribute to the political establishment. The gangsters and racketeers paid heavily into the coffers of political machines and in return received immunity from prosecution. The ghetto became a safe haven in which crime syndicates could grow and prosper. Two factors — immigrant slum dwellers' alienation from the political process and society's characteristic attitude that so long as "they" do it to each other, crime in the ghetto is not an American problem — kept the police indifferent and absent and added to that prosperity. The immigrant and his children found organized crime a quick means of escaping the poverty and powerlessness of the slums. The successful gangster like the successful politician was seen as a model who demonstrated to the masses of lower-class co-ethnics that anyone could achieve success and power in the greater society. And if they did this while defying the police and other oppressors, so much the better. Then, when political power came to the group,

partly as a result of these same illegal activities, access to legitimate opportunities became enlarged and assimilation was facilitated. The tradition became one of up and out.

## ITALIAN AMERICANS IN ORGANIZED CRIME

Over the years virtually all ethnic groups have been involved in organized crime. The Irish were followed by Eastern European Jews, the Jews by Italian and Sicilian immigrants, and in recent years this ethnic succession has encompassed Cuban immigrants, Puerto Rican immigrants, and blacks. Even the Chinese immigrants who settled on the West Coast made a place for themselves in organized crime.

Of all these groups, the Italian-American immigrants made the most lasting impression on the organized crime scene and achieved, over the years, a dominating role in it. Let us, then, examine the involvement of Italian Americans in organized crime.

**Immigration and Ghetto Residency**  Between 1820 and 1930 an estimated 4.7 million Italians arrived in the United States. Many of the early immigrants traveled to the West and South and became farmers, fishermen, tradesmen, and craftsmen. Over 2 million Italians arrived between 1900 and 1910, 80 percent coming from southern Italy and Sicily. Poor, illiterate, and lacking occupational skills, many soon returned to Italy, but the majority remained in the East and congregated in the "Little Italy" ghettos found in most urban centers, especially New York City. Like the Irish before them, they were desperate for the chance to improve their lot and achieve success and respectability in their new country. Also like the Irish, many found crime the easiest and quickest way up and out.

Unable to speak English, unfamiliar with American ways and big-city life, and dependent on one another for guidance and help, many Italian immigrants fell prey to those among them who were ready and willing to exploit their neighbors. Apparently, crime among the Little Italy residents was first of all crime against Italians: extortion, vendettas, and the kidnapping of brides. It was not, at first, organized crime, nor did the Italian criminal often venture beyond the boundaries of the ghetto. As a member of the "Lupollo" family related to Ianni:

> Can you imagine my father going uptown to commit a robbery or a mugging? He would have had to take an interpreter with him to read the street signs and say "stick 'em up" for him. The only time he ever committed a crime outside Mulberry Street was when he went over to the Irish section to steal some milk so that my mother could heat it up and put in my kid brother's ear to stop an earache. (Ianni with Reuss-Ianni, 1973:55)

Yet this was the beginning of Italian involvement in organized crime. By using muscle and by cashing in on ghetto conditions and police indifference to what went on in Little Italy, some immigrants became rich and powerful. They began to extend their illicit activities and hired other men to help them.

One key to wealth and power was extortion. Sometimes alone, sometimes with others, the extortionist would select victims from among newly arrived neighbors. Some extortionists associated themselves with the infamous "Black Hand," a loosely connected band that terrorized the vulnerable immigrant. A favorite tactic was to send a letter demanding money, the letter being signed with a drawing of a black hand. Other letters would follow, each successively more blatant in its threats of physical violence if the money was not paid. The fearful victim would search for help, which often came in the form of a man who was himself associated with the Black Hand. Sometimes the victim was able to secure a loan from a local source, thus helping enrich not only the extortionist but also the creditor. In this way, "respectable" members of the community grew wealthy from the activities of criminals. In either case, the victim went into debt, becoming more dependent and more vulnerable.

**The Mafia Connection**   The Italian immigrants brought their traditions with them. During the years of adjustment following their immigration, many naturally came to rely on their social and cultural heritage to help them, and the tendency to cling to old ways was heightened by the ethnic homogeneity of Little Italy. To understand Italian involvement in organized crime and the form it has taken, we must recognize the role played by the immigrant heritage itself.

Important to that heritage were the secret organizations that had flourished for years in southern Italy — among them, the Mafia and the Camorra. The origins of the Mafia and the Camorra are generally traced to the early nineteenth century; the Camorra was centered in Naples, the Mafia in Sicily. Though their actual beginnings are unknown, they both flourished in large part because of the widespread political and social unrest characterizing the southern Italian and Sicilian societies during the nineteenth century (Block, 1974; Ianni with Reuss-Ianni, 1973:30–40).

The concept of *mafia* was also important to the heritage. It refers not to the organization but, rather, to "a state of mind, a sense of pride, a philosophy of life, and a style of behavior which Sicilians recognize immediately" (Ianni with Reuss-Ianni, 1973:26). To describe someone as a *mafioso* does not necessarily mean that he is a member of the Mafia; it may simply mean that he is a man who is respected and held in awe. He is a man who seeks protection not through the law but by his own devices; he is a man who commands fear; he is a man who has dignity and bearing; he is a man who gets things done; he is a man to whom people come when in need; he is a man with "friends."

Though not all Italian immigrants were familiar with either the organization or the concept, those from southern Italy, especially western Sicily, undoubtedly were. Some of the immigrants themselves may have been mafiosi, in either meaning. In short, there is good reason to believe that Little Italy residents were familiar with Mafia ways and the spirit of mafia and that their behavior was affected by them. For example, Ianni noted that in the Italian ghettos, people went for protection or a redress of grievances to informal "courts" held by real or reputed mafiosi. In his testimony before the 1963 McClellan Committee of the Senate, Joe Valachi made much of the ties between the American Cosa Nostra and the secret organizations of southern Italy. One clear tie is the oath-taking ritual that changed little from that used in the early nineteenth century by both the Camorra and Mafia organizations:

> Flanked by the boss and his lieutenants, the initiate and his sponsor may stand in front of a table on which are placed a gun and, on occasion, a knife. The boss picks up the gun and intones in the Sicilian dialect: "Niatri representam La Costa Nostra. Sta famigghia è La Cosa Nostra. (We represent La Cosa Nostra. This family is Our Thing.)" The sponsor then pricks his trigger finger and the trigger finger of the new member, holding both together to symbolize the mixing of blood. After swearing to hold the family above his religion, his country, and his wife and children, the inductee finished the ritual. A picture of a saint or a religious card is placed in his cupped hands and ignited. As the paper burns, the inductee, together with his sponsor, proclaims: "If I ever violate this oath, may I burn as this paper." (*Time*, August 22, 1969:19)

This is not to say that Italian immigrants imported wholesale the Mafia or the Camorra. Rather, they imported a knowledge of the ways of secret societies and the spirit of mafia. This spirit seems to have been particularly important during early ghetto life, for those who grew rich — whether through crime or by essentially legal means such as loaning money in exchange for a part interest in a business — were able to cash in on the mafia idea. These men became the mafiosi and, like those back home, were feared while at the same time respected and upheld as models for emulation by the young. Ianni suggests that it was in the role of mafioso that Giuseppe Lupollo, grandfather of the crime family he studied, gained much of his strength.

**The Impact of Prohibition**   Lupollo and other Little Italy residents grew rich and powerful through a combination of criminal and legal activities. Usually they worked alone or with other members of their families. No secret organization tied them together, and the immigrants did not form a new Mafia or Camorra on American soil. Ianni (1973:61) gives three reasons why, until the 1920s at least, a Mafia-style organization did not emerge. First, they had not had enough time. The southern Italian immigrants were newcomers, and twenty years was hardly enough time to establish what had taken decades at home. Second, the Italian immigrants had come mostly as individuals; hence they had to establish new patterns of organization and new sources of power and profit. Third, the traditional pattern of father–son respect and obedience was not reinforced in American schools and in church; especially in school, the lessons stressed individualism, not family loyalty.

The onset of Prohibition, however, added two of the missing ingredients. Prohibition provided the incentive and means to move outside the ghetto and offered substantial rewards to those who ventured into bootlegging and other liquor-related activities. The illegal market for alcohol provided the incentive for mafiosi to work together and establish contacts outside the ghetto. Prohibition also supplied new organizational models that replaced the traditional family model that the older immigrants stressed but their American-born sons tended to reject. The organizational model was that of the American crime gang of Irish and Jewish thugs, which offered lower-echelon positions to Italian youths who had gained criminal experience in ghetto street gangs. A working relationship with non-Italians, frowned on by the older generation immigrants — called "Old Moustaches" or "Moustache Petes" by the youngsters — became an important feature of the new Italian-American involvement in organized crime.

What emerged was an Italian-American participation in organized crime that combined aspects of the old Mafia and the mafia spirit with strictly American contributions. Unlike the Italian Mafia, the new crime syndicates operated beyond the boundaries of the local community and employed non-Italians. Yet strong ethnic bonds persisted and became especially important as Italians began to secure positions within legitimate government as councilmen, judges, and police officers. Slowly, the domination of the older mafiosi was weakened as ambitious second-generation Italian Americans sought leadership roles and lucrative fields of operation (drugs, for example) over the objections of their elders.

Toward the end of Prohibition, internal dissension threatened the power and profits of the Italian-American crime syndicates, as the Old Moustaches fought for authority with their younger Americanized counterparts. The so-called Castellammarese War of 1930–1931 marked the height of the conflict. Originating in New York between the older Salvatore Maranzano faction and the second-generation gangs under Giuseppe Masseria, the feud spread to Chicago and other cities. Although Maranzano was the victor, many of the Old Moustaches were killed, and it was the Americanized gangsters such as Joe Adonis, Vito Genovese, Charlie Luciano, and Frank Costello who subsequently emerged as the powerful figures in the Italian-American syndicates.

Since Prohibition, Italian-American crime families have continued to flourish and have achieved a dominant place in organized crime. This was due to a number of events and conditions: the massive influx of Italian immigrants during the early decades of this century; the conditions of ghetto life to which they were subject; the indifference of the authorities to what went on inside the ghettos; the immigrants' familiarity with, and fear of, the Mafia and mafiosi; the attempt by Mussolini to crush the Mafia and other secret societies, thus forcing the mafiosi to seek shelter in America; the existence and successes of the semiorganized American crime gangs; and the widespread political corruption in urban areas. But most of all, it was due to Prohibition itself. Prohibition promised a quick and easy path to riches and provided the impetus for the mafiosi and other Italian Americans to organize and venture outside the ghetto. Prohibition showed the criminal gangs in the ghetto how to increase their money and power. In short, Prohibition helped organized crime come of age.

## The Money-making Enterprises of Organized Crime

During Prohibition, crime syndicates made the manufacture, distribution, and sale of alcoholic beverages their major business. Although extortion, blackmail, robbery, prostitution, gambling, and the sale of protection had been lucrative enterprises, bootlegging outweighed them all. Suddenly the law had made illegal what was much in demand by all segments of the population. Fortunes could be made by those who cared to break the law and could organize to do it.

When Prohibition came to an end in 1933 the black market quickly fell apart. This did not mean, however, that no money was to be made by dealing in booze; only that much less was to be made from it. Actually, organized crime continues to dabble in the liquor business. Some jurisdictions are still "dry," and others permit only beer or only certain labels to be sold. But even where liquor of any sort is legal, money can still be made. With the right connections, profitable liquor licenses can be bought on behalf of the syndicate; through control of bottling, warehousing, and distributing, syndicate liquor finds its way into legitimate outlets, sometimes hiding behind the label of a legal competitor (Dorman, 1972:129).

As Stuart Hills (1971:106) points out, organized crime is not restricted to any one kind of activity, legal or otherwise, and, like any entrepreneur, must keep up with changing times or go out of business. To fill the void created by the repeal of Prohibition, organized crime turned its attention to new avenues of profit and has continued to branch out ever since.

### CRIMINAL ENTERPRISES

The major enterprises providing illicit profits have been gambling, usury (loan sharking), drug trafficking, theft, and racketeering. In all these areas the money to be made is enormous. Though we can only guess, it is generally held that profits from each one of these areas run into billions of dollars every year. Estimates of the annual gross from gambling enterprises go as high as $50 billion; drug trafficking is estimated to be a $75 billion business; and a conservative estimate of the gross from loan sharking is $10 billion. Even the sale of sex, not one of the big money-makers, is estimated to gross $2 billion a year (Abadinsky, 1981; Pace and Styles, 1983). When we remember that organized crime avoids most, if not all, of the overhead and taxes legitimate businesses have to absorb, these gross figures indicate tremendous incomes for organized crime — a conservative estimate of the net profits would be 30 percent of the gross.

**Gambling** Though some speculate that the money-making possibilities of illegal gambling may be on the decline following the spread of state lotteries, gambling remains one of the principal sources of income for organized crime. Most of the money is made from the policy, or numbers, racket. Legend has it that the term *policy* originated from the nineteenth-century practice among the poor of gambling with money set aside for insurance policy premiums; Cressey, however, suggests that the term came from the Italian word for lottery ticket, *polizza*. Whatever the truth, one fact is clear: policy, or numbers, betting is predominantly a feature of urban slum life. Nationally, the numbers racket is said to take in over $1 billion a year, with $200 million spent in New York alone (Reuter, 1983).

Numbers betting is a simple concept and easy to do. The gambler simply picks any three-digit number and bets that this number will correspond to the winning number, selected in accordance with some predetermined procedure. Over the years the winning numbers have been computed from the number of shares traded on a stock exchange, the daily cash balance in the United States Treasury, and the payoffs at local pari-mutuel racetracks. At one time, the number was simply drawn from a revolving drum. The odds are 1,000 to 1 against the bettor, whereas payoff never exceeds 600 to 1.

The numbers racket attracted organized crime not only because of the immense profits to be made from it but also because the game requires organization, money, and a good deal of corruption in the right places — things only organized crime had. Although small-scale games, involving small bets and a small betting clientele, have existed in the past, they were neither very profitable nor very secure for those who ran them. To work, the numbers racket needs organized crime. The boss of a New Jersey crime network explains why:

> Everybody needs the organization — the banker, the controllers, the runners, even the customers. Here's why. Only a big organization can pay up when the bank gets hit very hard. Suppose a lot of people play the same number one day. For example, when Willie Mays hit his 599th home run, a lot of black people played "600" the next day, figuring Willie was going to make it and so were they. If that number had come up, the banker would have been wiped out, and not only that, a lot of customers would have gone without their payoffs. The whole system would have collapsed. . . .
>
> There was another reason why they needed the organization. Only the organization had the money and the muscle to keep the cops and politicians from breaking up the game and shaking down the players and operators. (Ianni, 1975:59–60)

Reuter (1983) found that New York City numbers games were not highly coordinated, though some apparently independent banks may have been branches of a single owner.

Though the specifics vary from place to place and from syndicate to syndicate, the numbers operation is organized along the following lines: The bets are picked up by "runners" from "numbers drops" in shops, factories, office buildings, and bars, or simply on the street. The runners pass the money and betting slips on to local "collectors," or "route men," in charge of their neighborhoods. The collectors pass the money and numbers tickets on to the "controller," who sends it on to the "district controller," who works for the "policy operator." The policy operator actually runs the enterprise and sometimes is known as the "banker" or "owner." He or she is usually one of a number of operators, all of whom pay a commission to the crime syndicate under whose overall supervision and control and in whose territory the racket operates. These policy operators may or may not be actual members of the crime family. At payoff time, the money simply follows the reverse route, usually starting at the "branch" or "district bank" run by the policy operator.

**Loan Sharking**   Loan sharking thrives because some people who need loans are unable or unwilling to secure them through legitimate lending institutions. Loan sharks will lend them the money, for a price. To make loans you need money; organized crime has it. To ensure that the money is repaid, with interest, you need organization and the ability to make collections; organized crime has them. Because usury is illegal, you must be able to collect without resorting to legal channels and without the interference of the law; organized crime accomplishes this through muscle and corruption.

Borrowers who come to a loan shark usually want quick loans with no questions asked. They may be gamblers in need of money to pay off debts or finance further play; they may be businesspeople faced with bankruptcy or wanting to invest in risky, perhaps illegal, ventures; they may simply be poor and in need of small loans but lack the credit or collateral required by licensed lending institutions. The interest they will pay depends on how much they borrow, the intended use of the loan, their repayment potential, and what they are worth to the mob if they cannot make their payments. Generally, the interest runs anywhere from 1 to 150 percent per week, with most smaller loans at 20 percent per week — the "six for five" loan, in which each five dollars borrowed requires six to be paid back at the end of a week. Usually a set time is established for payments, and if the required payment is not made on or before that exact time the borrower will owe another week's interest, computed from the principal plus the interest already accrued.

When payments cannot be made, intimidation and physical violence may result. Collectors employed by the loan shark use a variety of techniques, from thinly veiled threats to outright violence, to stir the borrower into meeting the terms of the loan. It is unusual for a borrower to be killed, however, for death means the money is lost forever. Though a killing may be committed occasionally to make the victim an example to others, the loan shark wants the money first and foremost, and if this cannot be secured with threats, the loan shark will look for other ways to get it. Indeed, loans are sometimes made — at very high interest rates — not in the expectation that they will be repaid but for the purpose of making the borrower a pawn in the hands of the syndicate. The mob may be looking to garner a controlling interest in a borrower's business, and when loan payments falter, this provides the leverage necessary to bring this goal about. The borrower simply turns over all or a part of the business in exchange for a temporary delay of the payments. This is one of the ways that organized crime secures a footing in legitimate business enterprises, though Reuter (1983:101) thinks it is rare among the small-time loan sharks, most of whom would not know how to carry out profitable fraud schemes involving legitimate businesses.

**Drug Trafficking**  Organized crime is involved in drug trafficking at all levels, but especially in importation and wholesale distribution. The need for organization, contacts, and large sums of money puts the business outside the reach of most individuals and small criminal groups. This does not mean, however, that organized crime is not interested in what goes on at the

Those in the higher echelons of organized crime are as likely to be removed by their own kind as by the authorities. With millions of dollars at stake, life becomes cheap.

neighborhood and street levels of the drug scene. Since its own profits depend on a healthy drug traffic, it observes the street closely and helps keep open the channels through which the drugs flow. The syndicate will also supply loans to dealers — at least the bigger, more successful ones — and through loan sharking and fencing on the street endeavors to ensure that money circulates so that buys can be made. Today much of the local heroin trade is controlled by black and Hispanic criminal groups, and this has been one of the avenues giving these groups access to the world of organized crime.

In 1984 the so-called Pizza Connection was uncovered when Italian and American police arrested over two hundred suspected Mafia members, including twenty-eight in America, after a high-ranking Mafioso named Tommaso Buscetta turned informant. Buscetto had extensive operations in Italy and Brazil, and he detailed the existence of a Sicilian-based organized crime network operating outside the established American Mafia families. This network is reputed to have imported over 1,600 pounds of heroin since 1979, with a street value of $1.65 billion. Its American members were mostly pizza parlor operators — hence the name — located in rural parts of Wisconsin, Michigan, Oregon, and Illinois, and with connections in New York and Switzerland.

The world of illicit drugs is discussed in detail in chapter 11.

**Theft**  Organized crime has been interested in theft since its earliest days. Today most organized crime efforts are directed at the kinds of thievery that promise high returns while avoiding high risks, such as truck hijacking, car-theft rings, thefts from warehouses and docks, securities theft, and fencing. Once again the organization, money, muscle, and contacts of organized crime are major factors in explaining syndicate activity in these areas.

Much has been made of syndicate involvement in securities theft and manipulation. Millions of dollars in securities disappear every year from the vaults of major brokerage houses. The lost bonds are not always stolen, but theft seems to be the major reason for their disappearance. Testimony before the Senate Committee on Banking, Housing, and Urban Affairs indicated that securities theft is a major problem these days and that behind much of the thievery lie organized crime syndicates. While estimates of the actual amounts stolen are difficult to make, the yearly totals are generally thought to exceed $2 billion and may be much higher when we include thefts from the mails and manipulations during securities transfers (Conklin, 1973:121–127; Metz, 1971).

To accomplish the theft and manipulation of stocks and bonds, organized crime needs insiders, persons employed by brokerage firms who have access to vaults or who routinely handle securities. Sometimes these important contacts are indebted to loan sharks and steal securities in exchange for a respite from their payments; sometimes extortion and intimidation are used to frighten employees into working with the underworld; and sometimes the mob manages to place one of its own into a position of trust within a brokerage firm. Once in syndicate hands, the stocks and bonds are often converted into cash. This can be accomplished by using the stolen securities as collateral for loans, as part of a company's portfolio of assets, or merely by reselling them through brokers here or abroad.

## LABOR RACKETEERING

During the nineteenth century, organized criminal groups learned that money could be made in the fields of industrial organization and management– worker relations. Faced with the prospects of strikes and unionization, companies called on criminal gangs to help them combat these threats to their power and profits. The companies paid well for the gangs' muscle, and the gangs, in turn, were happy to oblige. The infiltration of the union movement by organized crime soon followed, and with it came money and power for leaders of the fledgling unions. First the building trades and then service industries fell under the influence and domination of corrupt officials backed by gangsters with their connections and muscle. Money was collected from both employers and employees, organized crime playing off each side against the other (Hutchinson, 1969).

Racketeering is explained not merely by the corruption of union and company officials nor by the fact that organized crime is in the business of making money any way it can. Rather, the spread of racketeering stems from a combination of conditions. Some are economic, for example, excessive entrepreneurial competition and an excess supply of labor. As Walter Lippmann (1931:61) observed many years ago:

> Given an oversupply of labor and an industry in which no considerable amount of capital or skill is required to enter it, the conditions exist under which racketeering can flourish. The effort to unionize in the face of a surplus of labor invites the use of violence and terror to maintain a monopoly of labor and thus to preserve the workers' standard of living. Labor unionism in such trades tends to fall into the control of dictators who are often corrupt and not often finical about enlisting gangsters to enforce the closed shop. The employers, on the other hand, faced with the constant threat of cutthroat competition, are subject to the easy temptation to pay gangsters for protection against competitors. The protection consists in driving the competition from the field.

Identifying additional conditions that support organized crime infiltration into unions, John Hutchinson (1969:143) includes (1) the traditions of frontier violence, (2) cultural values stressing individualism, (3) an entrenched philosophy of acquisition, (4) an admiration for sharp practices, (5) a tolerance of the fix, and (6) a legacy stressing politics as a source of personal profit. Companies and unions went along with the spread of racketeering because both saw the benefits outweighing the costs and because the conditions and temperament of the times presented no great obstacles. Actually, of course, both company officials and union leaders risk becoming pawns in the hands of organized crime syndicates. This is precisely what has happened over the years, with the costs born not only by the rank-and-file union membership but also by members of the general public who hold company stock or who are simply consumers of the companies' goods and services.

Nobody knows for sure how much organized crime syndicates make from labor racketeering. In 1958, the Senate Select Committee on Improper Activities in the Labor or Management Field found that $10 million in Teamsters Union funds had been siphoned off into the pockets of union officials and their gangster friends (Salerno and Tompkins, 1969:295). Today, the Teamsters Coastal States Pension Fund is widely acknowledged to have been under the control of syndicate figures. It has been alleged that the mob helped pick Teamster presidents Jackie Presser and Roy Williams. Police informants have tied both men to organized crime groups in Chicago, New York, Kansas City, and Cleveland (*Los Angeles Times,* September 25, 1985). The fund is worth billions of dollars, and millions have apparently been spent without the knowledge of the rank-and-file membership, whose money it really is.

## PSEUDOLEGITIMATE ENTERPRISES

Apart from their patently illegal enterprises, organized crime groups have infiltrated the world of legitimate business. Though any complete list of the different businesses in which organized crime is involved would be impossible to compile, the following have been specifically identified: banking, hotels and motels, real estate, garbage collection, vending machines, construction, delivery and long-distance hauling, garment manufacture, insurance, stocks and bonds, vacation resorts, funeral parlors, bakeries, sausage manufacture and processing of other meat products, paving, tobacco, dairy products, demolition, warehousing, auto sales and leasing, meat packing, janitorial services, beauty and health salons, lumber, horse breeding, nightclubs, bars, restaurants, linen supply, laundries, and dry cleaning (National Council on Crime and Delinquency, 1969). There may well be no legitimate business enterprise in which organized crime does not have a direct financial interest.

Organized crime has sought involvement in legitimate businesses for a number of reasons. First is the obvious economic incentive: legitimate businesses can and do make profits, hence are additional sources of income. Second, legitimate businesses can provide a front for illegal activities; owning a trucking firm, for example, gives a crime syndicate the means of transporting stolen property or a cover for bootlegging. Third, legitimate businesses can serve as an important outlet for monies earned through criminal activities. Profits from the latter invested in businesses under syndicate control appear to be "clean"; also, syndicate members can receive legitimate-looking salary payments from those companies with which they are associated. These salaries constitute the members' visible sources of income, and they declare this income on tax returns in the continuing effort to keep federal agencies off their backs. Needless to say, those receiving such salaries may have contributed little or nothing to the actual day-to-day operations of the companies concerned.

A final reason that organized crime has sought holdings in legitimate enterprises is respectability. Crime is not respectable work, and the profits from it are dirty money. A long-standing interest among higher-echelon mobsters, especially Italian Americans with their traditions of family honor, has been the acquisition of respectability for their children and grandchildren, if not for themselves. Legitimate businesses provide a route to just this respectability. Instead of following in the footsteps of their elders, the younger generation is able to acquire the trappings of respectability by working in enterprises with no apparent connection to crime.

Peter Lupsha (1981) suggests that the pull of respectability may have been overstated. He sees organized crime as rational choice behavior selected not so much as a last economic resort but because it fits "one perverse aspect of our values: namely, that only 'suckers' work, and that in our society, one is at liberty to take 'suckers' and seek easy money, just as one is at liberty to be one" (p. 22). Organized crime families are not leaving the business in droves, nor are the children of members all leading exemplary lives: "a sufficient number of family members and relatives do stay in the business so that family control is maintained" (p. 20). Penetration of legitimate businesses is guided more by economic motives than any interest in respectability, in Lupsha's view.

Certainly, the legitimate enterprises are rarely, if ever, completely divorced from a syndicate's illegal enterprises, and for this reason it seems more appropriate to call them "pseudolegitimate" enterprises. A certain real estate company may appear quite legal and aboveboard; if organized crime has anything to do with it, however, all is not what it appears to be.

Organized crime moves into its pseudolegitimate enterprises in various ways. Some use intimidation and force, and others seem more like the normal avenues of business acquisition. When interested in a particular business, it is common for the syndicate to use the carrot-and-stick approach — in Don Corleone's words, "I'll make him an offer he can't refuse." Such a case was reported in the New York Court of Appeals a few years ago. An executive of several successful vending machine companies was simply told that he was to pass over to a certain family of interested persons a 25 percent share of his business interests. The request was backed up by assaults on his wife and various other forms of intimidation (Cressey, 1969:103). Another way to infiltrate businesses is to arrange, through extortion or bribes, to have syndicate associates placed in executive positions, so that eventually the company is controlled by the syndicate. Yet another way is to purchase large blocks of company stock through legitimate trading channels, though under the cover of fictitious names and companies.

One of the most common ways to acquire part or all of a business is to take advantage of a borrower's indebtedness to the syndicate loan shark and his or her inability to repay as agreed. Sometimes the indebtedness and the inability to pay are merely fortuitous, in the sense that a businessperson is in that position because of factors unconnected with any particular design on the part of syndicate loan sharks. The borrower may have asked for the loan and was simply unable to meet the payments; had he or she met the terms of the loan, things would have turned out differently. At other times, however, the syndicate has an interest in the business all along. On such occasions the syndicate creates both indebtedness and inability to pay, thus placing the borrower in a position from which he or she can escape only by turning over part or all of the business (Grutzner, 1970). To create indebtedness and the inability to pay, the syndicate actively uses its loan-sharking services — it may begin by forcing a company into bad financial straits through any number of underhanded means — and then sets ridiculously high interest rates or arranges things so that the borrower conveniently misses one or more payment deadlines. No matter how the two important conditions arise, the end result is always the same: the mob secures an interest in the business in lieu of loan repayment.

## The Survival of Organized Crime

Why does organized crime persist? The answer to this important question lies beyond the more obvious defenses that secret societies and groups erect against outsiders — secrecy, codes of conduct, mutual protection among members, and the like. We must look within the organization of crime syndicates at survival mechanisms that come into play whenever these more obvious defenses are threatened. We must look at survival mechanisms brought into play in interactions between organized crime and the larger society. We must also look at the roles played by public attitudes and behavior and at the attitudes and behavior of those ostensibly responsible for combating organized crime. We must look at the nature of criminal law itself, especially as it focuses on moral choices and private behavior.

### ROLE IMPERATIVES IN ORGANIZED CRIME

Two of the most important internal survival mechanisms appear to be the roles of "enforcer" and "buffer." These roles, assumed by select individuals in crime organizations, might well be called *role imperatives*, for without them (or something very similar) the survival of any crime organization would be threatened.

Donald Cressey (1969) goes so far as to argue that unless the division of labor provides for at least one enforcer, the organization in question is not a part of true organized crime. Yet Ianni (1973) found only weak evidence of enforcer positions in the established division of labor and authority structure of the crime family he extensively studied. Even so, internal discipline and security must be maintained if the crime organization is to survive and prosper, and even if it has no specifically identified position for an enforcer, the organization will enforce its rules and the directives of those in authority. It is imperative that enforcement be undertaken by at least one member when necessary. The methods of enforcement range from verbal warnings all the way to maiming or murder. A set of rules is not enough: from time to time they must be enforced, and organized crime sees to it that they are. Organized crime has been likened to government in this sense: not only do syndicates create their own rules, but like states, they also have their own machinery for enforcing them and their own methods of doing it.

The "buffer" role identified by Cressey and others also enhances the organization's survival possibilities. The buffer is akin to the corporate "assistant to the president," his tasks being primarily centered on internal communications and the flow of decisions in the hierarchy of authority. The buffer may also be likened to a spy, for he keeps tabs on what lower-level members do and say and reports back to his superiors. Without the buffer role, the smooth functioning of the organization would be impaired, and the decision-making process undermined. It is the buffer who keeps open lines of communication between leaders and followers, who passes down important messages from the top, who forewarns of internal dissensions and problems with operations at the street level, and who helps smooth out disagreements and conflicts.

Another role imperative is the "corrupter." Since organized crime syndicates are in the business of crime, its survival greatly depends on the fix. To put the fix in and maintain important connections with those in government and law, organized crime groups typically have one or more members assigned to corrupt officials in order to preserve good relations with them. The corrupter may be found anywhere in the organizational hierarchy, and his job is to bribe, buy, intimidate, negotiate, persuade, and sweet-talk "himself into a relationship with police, public officials, and anyone else who might help 'family' members maintain immunity from arrest, prosecution, and punishment" (Cressey, 1969:251–252).

Cressey (1969:248) calls the political objective the "nullification of government," and it is sought at two different levels:

> At the lower level are the agencies for law enforcement and the administration of justice. When a Cosa Nostra soldier bribes a policeman, a police chief, a prosecutor, a judge, or a license administrator, he does so in an attempt to nullify the law-enforcement process. At the upper level are legislative agencies, including federal and state legislatures as well as city councils and county boards of supervisors. When a "family" boss supports a candidate for political office, he does so in an attempt to deprive honest citizens of their democratic voice, thus nullifying the democratic process.

In his study of organized crime in Seattle during the sixties, William Chambliss (1978) describes a crime network that extended from street hustlers, bookmakers, pimps, drug dealers, and gamblers to businesspersons, politicians, and law-enforcement officials. Hotel, restaurant, club, and bingo-parlor operators were fronts for gambling and vice; police officers and prosecutors took bribes and offered protection, falsified reports, and covered up investigations; and politicians took campaign contributions of "dirty money" and exercised their licensing and legislative powers in support of the rackets, "one of the largest industries in the state" (Chambliss, 1978:54). This crime network depended for its survival on corruption at all levels of government, and for many years it got it.

Nullification of government is thus an important survival mechanism in organized crime. For nullification to work there must be officials willing or able to be corrupted. We already know that some persons are willing to be corrupted, but even if there were no willing corruptees, organized crime's muscle and its willingness to use it would probably ensure viable corrupter–corruptee relationships.

The truth is, however, that organized crime rarely has to use muscle to nullify government, no matter what level. The nature of politics and government is such that those acting in violation of the law and those ostensibly responsible for its creation and enforcement readily enter into mutually beneficial relationships. An associate of Louisiana mobster Carlos Marcello explains how easy and inevitable it was that those on the legitimate side of the fence would join in working relationships with those on the illegitimate side:

> You have to remember that when Carlos and I were starting out in the rackets, just about the only money available for political campaigns in Louisiana and other Southern states was rackets money. These were poor states. There were no "fat cats" around to finance political campaigns. If a guy wanted to run for any important office, the only place he could get enough money was from us. So we got control of the political machinery. We picked the candidates; we paid for their campaigns; we paid them off; we told them what to do. (Dorman, 1972:11)

Just how successful and important these connections are is evidenced by the fact that since its very beginning, organized crime has made one of its first tasks the establishment of working relationships with those in politics, government, and law enforcement. Because it pays off in security, organized crime will continue to pursue the nullification of government.

## THE LEGISLATION OF MORALITY

Organized crime will continue to flourish if lawmakers continue to enact legislation rendering illegal any activities, products, and services demanded by significant numbers of the population. Organized crime makes the bulk of its profits in supplying illegal commodities and services. Drugs, gambling, sex, and other so-called vices are profitable precisely because there are criminal laws, which have the effect of driving the activities underground and into the hands of those willing and able to carry out illicit business. In this way, criminal laws create the very conditions conducive to the emergence and spread of organized criminal activities.

The legislation of morality is, then, yet another factor in the survival of organized crime. But apart from encouraging the emergence of black marketeering, laws designed to repress what some people think of as vices also help give "a kind of franchise to those who are willing to break the law" (Schelling, 1967:117). This is what Herbert Packer (1964) called "the crime tariff"; it serves to protect those among us who will break the law by supplying drugs or gambling opportunities to those who are unwilling to do so but who will take advantage of their availability. Journalist and social commentator Walter Lippmann (1931:65ff) first drew attention to this unintended consequence of moral legislation when he noted more than forty years ago that

> . . . we have a code of laws which prohibit all the weaknesses of the flesh. This code of laws is effective up to a point. That point is the unwillingness of respectable people to engage in the prohibited services as sellers of prohibited commodities. . . . The high level of lawlessness is maintained by the fact that Americans desire to do so many things which they also desire to prohibit. . . . [They] have made laws which act like a protective tariff — to encourage the business of the underworld. Their prohibitions have turned over to the underworld the services from which it profits. Their prejudice in favor of weak governments has deprived them of the power to cope with the vast lawbreaking industries which their laws have called into question.

## THE ATTITUDES AND BEHAVIOR OF THE PUBLIC

If few among us took advantage of the illegal goods and services provided by organized crime, an important ingredient in its survival would be missing: organized crime depends for its profits and power on the widespread demand for its services. By demanding its products and services, the public helps organized crime survive and prosper.

In addition to public behavior, public attitudes and perceptions also help organized crime survive. How Americans view crime and criminals helps shape the crime scene itself. In the case of organized crime, public perceptions and attitudes are probably more fuzzy and mixed than anything else, but so far no evidence has been presented to indicate that the public perceives organized crime as a real problem deserving stringent control.

The lack of attitudinal opposition to organized crime reflects in part the fact that some of us have used its services and that many others are not convinced of the harmfulness of the services it provides. Moreover, many of us probably have only a vague idea of what organized crime really is, and, when we go in droves to films like *The Godfather,* the picture we see hardly fits in with our day-to-day experiences or our images of the world. Indeed, the mystery surrounding organized crime gives it a certain charm and appeal.

Then again, even when we consume the products and services supplied by organized crime, we rarely come in contact with persons who represent themselves as members of a crime family or syndicate, and those whom we do encounter have no distinguishing marks about them to suggest that they are part of organized crime. Stuart Hills (1971:130) points out: "Many of the customers who place a friendly bet with that nice old man in the corner bar do not perceive, in fact, that this criminal bookmaker is a businessman — not an unorganized individual gambler."

Perhaps the most important reason that public perceptions and attitudes are sketchy, stereotypical, and ambivalent is that those to whom we customarily look for clues and guidance in our thinking about crime have themselves presented a fragmented and warped picture. Government officials and law-enforcement agencies have tended to stress the individual character of crime and criminality and to downplay its organizational features. Beyond this, the stereotype of the dangerous criminal fostered by the authorities fits the mugger, rapist, burglar, and dope pusher, not Vito Genovese, Carlo Gambino, or Sam Giancana. Whether government officials purposely play down organized crime and systematically keep information about it from the public is hard to say. Salerno and Tompkins (1969:271) think that might be the case: "Too much effort spent exposing organized crime could be damaging in future elections."

## Future Trends

Organized crime is undoubtedly here to stay, at least for the foreseeable future. But changes are afoot, just as changes occurred in the past. Today there is evidence of further ethnic succession. Blacks, Chicanos, Puerto Ricans, and Cuban Americans have established a footing in organized crime, especially in the highly populated Northeast and in Chicago and Miami.

Ianni (1975) studied these recent entrants in the field. As yet they are neither as well organized nor as far-reaching in their activities as are Italian-American crime syndicates. But the die seems to be cast: in the next decade or so members of these groups should increase their participation in organized crime, and the Italian-American domination of vice should decline in the urban centers where large populations of blacks and Hispanics are concentrated.

According to Ianni, the same ghetto conditions that spawned early organized crime helped produce the contemporary ethnic succession. In addition, the Italian-American crime syndicates themselves may have helped bring about change. For one thing, established organized crime groups inevitably came to employ ghetto residents as soldiers, lower-echelon pushers, and numbers runners in their own neighborhoods. Streetwise blacks, Chicanos, Puerto Ricans, and Cubans became the vital link between the organization and the street-level buyers of commodities and services. With involvement came knowledge, contacts, and, for some, wealth. With involvement also came efforts to control the business in one's territory. An added incentive for Cuban involvement came with the establishment of a cocaine and heroin connection from South America through Cuba and Miami. Ianni (1975:235) points out the significance of this connection for the future:

> If our information is accurate, and I am confident that it is, this new route for drugs from South America should have some important effects on the drug scene in the United States. The most important effect will be the continued displacement of Italian-American syndicates from the international drug traffic as this new connection replaces the older one that came through Europe. The "street" implications of this are enormous. It not only means that new patterns of wholesaling will be established, changing the ethnic balance of power in organized crime, but it also means that cocaine may very well displace heroin as *the* street drug.

Although mainly restricted to their own ethnic neighborhoods, the crime networks of blacks and Hispanics are emerging as the new forces in the organized delivery of drugs and sex and are gaining more control over the numbers racket and loan sharking in the ghetto. Yet in order to extend and expand, these newcomers will have to accomplish what the Italian Americans did before them: "(1) greater control over sectors of organized crime outside as well as inside the ghetto; (2) some organizing principle which will serve as kinship did among the Italians to bring the disparate networks together into larger criminally monopolistic organizations; and (3) better access to political power and the ability to corrupt it" (Ianni, 1974:36).

Although the first requirement may well be the easiest to meet because of their growing control over the drug traffic, much will depend on the willingness of established crime syndicates to allow a blossoming competition from these newcomers.

Peter Reuter (1983:136–137) believes that Mafia families are responding to the recent challenges to their power and profits with accommodation rather than conflict. He speculates this is because violence would bring even more police surveillance than is currently the case, dramatically pushing up the costs of doing business.

We can expect to continue hearing about organized crime. It should be apparent that organized crime is a consequence of numerous social, cultural, political, legal, and economic conditions, many of which seem destined to remain with us. Viewed from a rationality–opportunity perspective, organized crime will continue to flourish as long as illicit goods and services are demanded and people are willing and able to organize so as to supply them for a profit. As new opportunities for criminal enterprise appear, they will be grasped by criminally motivated individuals in a position to prosper from them.

Like American values, organized crime is flexible, practical, and adaptive. It is an American institution, not a Sicilian by-product. It has moved from prostitution to pornography in film and home video cassettes as smoothly as our technology and corporations. Like corporate evolution it has evolved into a diversified multi-national conglomerate, franchising criminal markets and firms. In a society that has always had a place for lawlessness, sharp practice, easy money, a disdain for suckers, and an idolatry of mammon and lucre, organized crime is as American as McDonald's. (Lupsha, 1981:22)

# CHAPTER 11

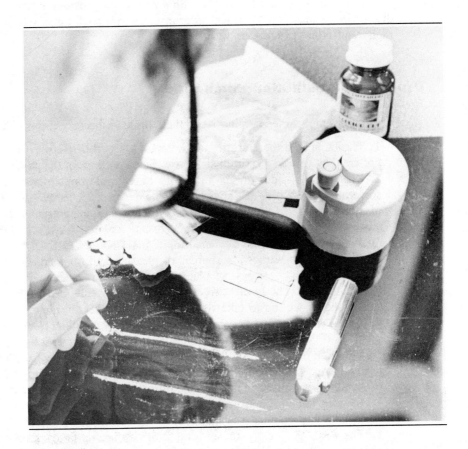

# Public Order Crime: Drugs and Prostitution

Nothing inherent in an act makes it a crime, though some crimes carry the stigma of "sin" as well as illegality. Over the centuries, societies have grappled with the problem of what to do about activities that many regard as sinful and yet many also engage in. As long as these behaviors are kept from public view, the problem is less pressing, for it is easy to deny that they really exist. However, such things as prostitution, pornography, drunkenness, and drug addiction are rarely hidden from the public eye and for that reason are often considered threats to public morality and order and so are made illegal. In this chapter we shall deal mainly with drug use and prostitution, but in our discussion of reactions to public order offenses, we shall touch on pornography and homosexuality as well.

## Drugs and Prostitution: Similarities

There are some marked similarities in the criminal aspects of drugs and sex:

**1.** Participants in these crimes often do not view themselves as criminal, nor are they viewed as criminals by significant portions of the population.

**2.** The criminal sides of sex and drugs have legal counterparts that are sometimes difficult to distinguish from them except for their legality. For example, it is legal to buy and sell alcohol and caffeine but not heroin or marijuana. It is legal (in most places) to buy and sell *Hustler* and *Penthouse* magazines but not to dance topless and bottomless in a bar.

**3.** Illegal sex and drugs are sources of pleasure and tremendous profits. The profits, more than the pleasures, are a direct consequence of criminalization. The black market drives up both prices and profits, and entrepreneurs willing to take risks will not pay taxes on their returns.

**4.** Illegal sex and drugs are prime targets of organized crime, with all three feeding off one another. For example, many prostitutes are drug addicts; most female drug addicts — at least in the ghetto — engage in prostitution; and organized crime controls large segments of both criminal drug use and criminal sex, and through the profits it makes there and elsewhere is able to extend its control, protect itself from enforcement, and increase the availability of illicit sex and drugs.

**5.** The laws that apply to sex and drugs reflect both consensus and conflict, with special interests prominent in both their substance and enforcement.

**6.** The enforcement of laws dealing with drugs and sex requires a special type of policing: the use of informants and undercover detectives. It is also a major area of graft and corruption in the criminal justice system.

**7.** Much of the behavior that is criminalized in both areas is considered to be "victimless," in that participants consider themselves willingly involved rather than being offended against.

**8.** Both areas of crime are prime targets of moral entrepreneurs, who see the behavior involved as evidence of declining morals and unreasonable permissiveness and who are continually organizing campaigns to broaden the laws and increase the penalties.

These, then, are some of the similarities. Now we shall turn to a more detailed, individual examination of these public order crimes.

## Sex and the Criminal Law

Historically, criminal labels have been applied to sex on the basis of four considerations: (1) the nature of the act, (2) the nature of the sex object, (3) the social setting in which sex occurs, and (4) the existence of consent.

In regard to the sex act itself, some sexual behaviors are considered criminal regardless of the people and circumstances involved. In most states it is illegal to engage in anal intercourse or analingus (oral stimulation of the anus), and in many states oral sex of any sort is prohibited. However, the nature of the sex act itself is often coupled with other considerations in designating the behavior as criminal.

Most criminal codes limit legal sex to interactions between partners who are both human, adults, and not members of the same family except as marital partners. Many states outlaw sex when the partners are not married (fornication) are or married but not to each other (adultery). But even when the act itself and the partners are legal, a crime may still be committed if the act is performed in public: sex in parks, restaurants, theaters, automobiles, trains, or anywhere else where it could reasonably be witnessed is usually an offense.

Last there is the important question of consent. No matter what is done, with whom or where, a crime may be committed if a partner withholds consent or is legally considered incapable of giving it (he or she is mentally ill, for example, or drugged, or a child). However, as we saw in Chapter 6, it is not a crime in many jurisdictions for a husband to force sex upon his wife.

### THE SHAPING OF MODERN SEX LAWS

In the earliest legal codes, relatively few sexual activities were singled out for legal repression. Concern seems to have focused on those sexual activities and relations that violated prevailing mores. Incest, adultery, fornication, and the defilement of virgins were common prohibitions.

With the spread of Christianity, an ever-increasing collection of sexual prohibitions emerged in law. As the church spread its gospel and increased its power in law and public policy, the foundations of modern sex laws were set in place. In England, for example, the church was quick to impose severe restrictions on sexual freedoms. At the heart of the church's stand was "a definite and detailed code of behavior regarded as obligatory [for] all Christian believers. At the center of the code was the fixed principle that pleasure in sex was evil and damnable. It was not the sex act itself which was condemned, but the pleasure which was connected with it" (Wright, 1968:20–21).

The church viewed sex in extremely narrow terms. Heterosexual copulation for the strict purposes of procreation was the rule, and then only within the framework of marriage. Any sexual activity or relationship not meeting these criteria was viewed as inherently wrong and evil. If the sex act was not "straight" intercourse, furthermore, it was considered "unnatural," "perverted" behavior.

All this does not mean the church was successful in suppressing sexual expression. On the contrary, by all accounts it was a dismal failure. Even priests themselves found it hard to abide by church rulings on sexual matters, and there are accounts of monks murdering their superiors when the latter sought to deprive them of heterosexual or homosexual outlets (Taylor, 1965). Even as late as the sixteenth century, the papal heads of the Roman Catholic church were notorious for their debauchery, incestuous conduct, and sexual adventures.

In England, the developing common law left sexual matters pretty much in the hands of the church. Despite certain exceptions — for example, rape, sexual assault on children, and sexual acts in public — sex was not a concern of criminal law. Morris Ploscowe (1951:138) describes the pre-sixteenth-century situation:

> The common law of crimes took a comparatively liberal attitude toward sex expression. A great deal of illicit sexual activity, both non-marital and extra-marital, was outside the domain of the common law and common-law courts. Fornication was no crime. Single men and women could copulate in secret without violating any penal provisions of the common law. Adultery was not a punishable offense. A man could two-time his wife or a wife cuckold her husband without having to fear the jailor or hangman. Men could masturbate each other in secret without running the risk of landing in jail.

Two things, however, seem to have provoked civil interest in sexual matters. First, the church and its ecclesiastical courts had failed to control sexual expression, and this failure left religious leaders searching for alternative ways to control sex. They turned to the state for help, reasoning, perhaps, that the criminal law and its enforcement machinery would succeed where they had failed. Second, civil leaders grew less content to give the church sanctioning power over any area of human conduct, including sex. They saw punishment as the proper domain of the state, and besides, why allow the church to levy fines when these could be paid into the royal treasury?

Henry VIII was one of the first English kings to enact specific sexual legislation. His buggery statute of 1533 made it a felony for a male to have anal intercourse with another male or for a female to have intercourse with an animal. Urged on by Protestant and later by Puritan leaders — and quite in keeping with their statutory expansion of the criminal law — Henry's successors continued to enact sex laws, and so by the eighteenth century almost every conceivable sexual activity and relationship could be made to fit common law or statutory provisions.

## VAGUENESS IN SEX LAWS

Henry VIII's buggery statute was vague, leaving unclear whether anal intercourse with a female was included or whether male sex relations with an animal was a crime. Unfortunately, we still find today that many of our sex laws are unclear regarding what exactly constitutes a crime.

Part of the problem unquestionably derives from the reluctance of legal authorities to describe in plain language what have always been sensitive matters. Writing in the late sixteenth century, Sir Edward Coke found it hard to break with that tradition and may himself have contributed to its perpetuation. His attitude is well summed up in his now famous reference to buggery as that "detestable and abominable sin, among Christians not to be named." And in regard to a description of the penetration of the vagina during intercourse — an essential element in legal conceptions of carnal knowledge — he could only bring himself to say, in Latin, "the thing in the thing" (Gigeroff, 1968:11).

The U.S. Supreme Court has not improved matters much. Consider on the one hand its 1973 ruling in *Wainwright v. Stone*. In this case the Court supported the continued enforcement of a Florida statute outlawing sodomy, defined only as "an abominable and detestable crime against nature." On the other hand, there is the matter of obscenity. Here, in *Miller v. California* (1973), the Court appeared to have washed its hands of the matter, leaving things largely up to "the average person," applying "contemporary community standards." From one perspective this might be hailed as progressive, since it allows for variations in community standards. From another it places considerable enforcement discretion in the hands of local authorities, does not reduce the likelihood of breaches of First Amendment freedoms, and encourages the activities of so-called moral entrepreneurs, those who work for the enactment and enforcement of moral prohibitions (see Becker, 1963).

Just what violates community standards depends, of course, on the standards themselves — and this is by and large a matter of conjecture and disagreement. Certainly, one sees few attempts made to poll the moral views of the electorate, especially those pertaining to sex. Generally, all that is needed for a public morality law to appear on the books is pressure on legislators from those segments of the population that officialdom feels obliged to woo. Whether it is prostitution, homosexuality, massage parlors, or pornography matters little; the important point is that legal officials can generally accommodate moral entrepreneurs. The reason: laws exist that are so worded (or interpreted) that almost anything can be brought under them. The best examples are vagrancy laws and those dealing with "disorderly conduct" and "public nuisances." Though often invoked in situations that have nothing remotely sexual about them, they are also used in cases in which the conduct is, or appears to be, of a sexual nature. X-rated movies and movie theaters, strip joints, public nudity, homosexual encounters of one sort or another, and massage parlors all have been the object of criminalization under such laws. Today even zoning ordinances are being used in some jurisdictions as a means to suppress "undesirable" sexual activities. One example is Boston's "Combat Zone," where pornography, x-rated movies, massage parlors, and other sex-oriented commercial activities have been allowed to flourish in one small downtown area but are illegal elsewhere. More commonly, zoning laws are being used to force all commercialized sex out of town.

## Consensual Sex: Prostitution

Some sex offenses are victimless in the sense that they are between consenting adults who voluntarily engage in an activity that happens to be illegal. Homosexual encounters, adultery, fornication, the sale and purchase of pornographic literature, and prostitution are examples. This section focuses on prostitution.

One author estimated that as many as 600,000 full-time and 600,000 part-time male and female prostitutes are working at any given time in the United States (Esselzstyn, 1968). These figures may be high — other estimates have placed the total number of prostitutes at around 250,000 (Sheehy, 1973). The United States undoubtedly has the largest prostitute population of any Western nation. Yet prostitution is in violation of criminal codes in all states except Nevada, which lets its various county governments decide on legality.

Prostitution has not always been illegal in the United States, and in some Western societies it is tolerated today. In Germany, Holland, and Denmark, for instance, female prostitutes are pretty much left alone as long as they ply their trade in designated areas and fulfill other requirements such as licensing and payment of taxes. Describing the situation in Hamburg, Germany, Walter Reckless (1973:175) tells us:

> On one enclosed small street (a block in length) of the Reeperbahn, the prostitutes are permitted to display themselves in the nude at every window of the houses on the narrow street. The entrance way at each end of the street has a sort of privacy screen which shields the prostitutes from view of pedestrians not entering the special section. The two privacy screens have posted notices indicating that only males over twenty-one years of age may enter the street. In addition, solicitation by prostitutes is permitted in certain cafes, especially around the central railroad station of Hamburg (the Hauptbahnhof). On the side wall of each "booth" table is an "in-house" telephone. When male customers are seated in their booth, the phone rings and the woman at the other end asks for an invitation to join the party.

Some American laws have been so designed that they may actually encourage prostitution, even though the prostitute herself breaks the law. In many states today, for example, the male client commits no offense when he agrees to buy sexual intimacies from the prostitute. Thus the risks of arrest are born solely by the woman, and men in search of sexual fun can feel free to pursue their goal without fear of criminalization. Even in those states that have made it a crime to patronize a prostitute, the designated penalties are often greater for the prostitute than her client. In Victorian England, prostitution was encouraged because the existing laws left untouched the activities of those who stood to gain financially from prostitution and were in a position to recruit and protect the women. Although appearing on the surface to be a time of moral respectability, the period was one in which prostitution flourished and the exploitation of females continued (Wright, 1968:29).

We see, then, that even though prostitution is illegal, it may be outlawed in such a way that it is actually encouraged to persist. Why? Most obviously, because those responsible for creating laws are usually male and are potential clients. While paying lip service to precepts of moral decency, our lawmakers remember that "men will be men," and that women are there to fulfill their every desire. In this sense, prostitution is, as feminists point out, yet another manifestation of the male exploitation of females. It should come as no surprise that most inquiries into prostitution have focused not on the male client but on the prostitute herself. She, after all, is the deviant, the criminal.

## SELLING SEX: THE PROSTITUTE AT WORK

Prostitutes work in various ways (see Rolph, 1955; Winick and Kinsie, 1971; Sheehy, 1973). At one end of the spectrum are the *streetwalkers,* or *street hookers.* These women may be readily encountered on the street, particularly in those sections of cities where cheap hotels, bars, and mass transportation terminals are to be found. The streetwalker is at the bottom of the pecking order among prostitutes. She works where the risks are greatest, she has little or no control over what clients she takes, she must put up with all kinds of weather, she must generally give a good portion of her earnings away for "protection," and she must usually work long hours to make enough from her "tricks" (paying customers, sometimes called "johns") to keep abreast of her financial obligations. Even the classiest streetwalkers — those working office buildings or conventions during the day or early evening hours — rarely gross more than $200 or $300 a day. The streetwalker does well to stay in business for more than a few years, and her earning capacity declines rapidly after she passes her twenty-second or twenty-third birthday.

Next up the social ladder are those prostitutes who work in *brothels* (also called *bordellos, cathouses,* or *whorehouses*). Until World War II, brothels were the major outlet for prostitution in the United States. In major cities, brothels numbered in the hundreds, and they were usually located close together in areas that came to be known as "red light districts." Run (though not necessarily owned) by *madams*, who themselves might have been working prostitutes at one time, these brothels sometimes had a "stable" of twenty or thirty women working in shifts. Since World War II, however, the brothel has declined in importance, mostly as a result of cleanup operations by city councils pressured by local citizen groups. Brothels still operate as the major context of prostitution in Nevada (the state frowns upon the streetwalker), and most large cities in the United States have brothels that maintain themselves solely through a system of informal referrals. But gone are the days when a visitor could simply appear on the doorstep of any of a string of houses and buy himself sexual pleasure.

Toward the top of the pecking order are the *call girls*. Though the operating methods differ, the established call girl usually secures her clients through individual referrals by customers or trusted friends (Bryan, 1965). She conducts the sexual transaction in her own apartment or in the office, home, or hotel room of her client. Many call girls work independently and exercise considerable discretion in their choice of clients. Topflight call girls are generally from middle-class backgrounds, some have a college education, and most are in their early twenties. The successful call girl is physically attractive, well groomed, and articulate, and she makes a pleasant date for those men who can afford the $300 or $400 it takes to purchase her company for an evening.

With the advent some years ago of publications such as *Screw*, a New York–based national magazine whose subject is sex, some call girls and male prostitutes began advertising. In *Screw* you will find scores of ads from men and women offering to sell or buy sexual intimacies. Though not all such ads are linked with the prostitute business, many clearly are. Sometimes the ads are so worded that only those familiar with the language of commercialized sex will understand them. Here, for example, are two ads that might well have appeared in *Screw* magazine:

> If your interests run to English, French, or Greek arts, call . . . between 4 P.M. and 11 P.M. for an appointment. Our international staff of experts eagerly await your patronage.

> Hi! I'm Debbie. I'm new in town and am eager to meet a strong, well-endowed man for mutual fun. I am 19, beautifully curved, and have long silky-blonde hair with which to tickle your fancy. My friends never forget me. Please, males only; no S/M.

## THE BAR AND MASSAGE PARLOR AS PLACES OF PROSTITUTION

Public bars and nightclubs have long been frequented by prostitutes. Sometimes called *bar-girls* (or, simply, *b-girls*), these women often operate along with the bar management. Not all b-girls are prostitutes — some are merely in the game of enticing customers to spend time, and thus money, in the hope of later sex (Cavan, 1966). But those who are prostitutes find the bar a good place for hustling. For one thing, they can work indoors; in addition, they have a constant flow of prospective clients, they can mingle with the crowd and thus not be so obvious, there are people around who can come to their rescue if trouble should arise, and they can choose their clients.

During the last few years, the massage parlor has emerged as a new, lucrative setting for prostitution. Though some establishments provide only therapeutic massages by trained personnel, many of the hundreds of parlors from coast to coast cater to one thing: sex. The range of sexual activities purchased extends from simple "hand-jobs" — which are permissible in some jurisdictions — to "blow-jobs," "straight" sexual intercourse, and anything else the customer may desire and the "masseuse" is willing to do (see Bryant and Palmer, 1975; Velarde and Warlick, 1973).

The massage parlor is a good front for prostitution because it provides a legal setting for customer contacts. The women need not solicit business; it comes to them. The typical customer is looking for more than merely a massage. Furthermore, the masseuses are not dependent on the customers' purchase of sex because they will receive a commission (usually 30 to 35 percent) on any legal massage they give — and these can cost the customer $100 an hour if he wants frills such as nude masseuses, champagne, and special baths. Other advantages to prostitution in this setting include a comfortable work environment, a potentially speedy turnover in customers, and some protection against police arrest and a criminal conviction for prostitution. The massage parlor prostitute is protected from arrest and conviction partly by the semiprivate character of the parlor and partly because by leaving it up to the customer to do the soliciting, she can minimize the chances of a legal arrest. An undercover cop who first solicits sex and then arrests the masseuse may well be acting illegally under the rules of entrapment. These rules generally are interpreted as follows: The police may not entice a person into committing a crime and then use the offense and evidence of it to bring about a criminal conviction if the person would not normally have voluntarily committed the offense in question.

## THE PIMP

A key position in the world of prostitution is held by the *pimp* (see Milner and Milner, 1972; Hill and Edelman, 1972). Though we have no way of knowing exactly what proportion of prostitutes works under the control of pimps, it probably runs to over 70 percent. For the pimp, prostitution is the road to considerable financial success; he, not his "girls," reaps the real profits from the billion-dollar business. Even so, without the pimp, many prostitutes would quickly fail in business.

The pimp's importance comes partly from the nature of prostitution itself and partly from his own business acumen and ability to manipulate people. Because prostitution is illegal, those in the game are constantly threatened by arrest. A pimp can help protect prostitutes from legal troubles as well as provide financial and other assistance should the law strike. Since big money can be made in meeting the persistent demand for this illegal service, competition is stiff. The pimp helps defend against the competition by establishing and maintaining control over a particular territory. An independent prostitute does not have that kind of security. Then, too, the pimp offers protection against the physical or financial threat posed by drunks, toughs, and customers who want something for nothing. Most prostitutes have little control over male access to them — indeed, they must make that access as free as possible — and when confronted by a trouble-maker it is nice to have someone in the wings who can deal with the problem.

These features of prostitution open up a role for the pimp. Even so, his place in the business also hinges on his own abilities, particularly his adeptness in establishing and maintaining the prostitute's dependence on him and his control over her. Control and dependence are the central features of what is, at its heart, a relationship of exploitation. To establish that relationship the pimp demonstrates that the practicing or would-be prostitute needs him for both material and emotional reasons. He shows his importance in the realm of material things by taking care of room and board, clothing, medical and other expenses and by running the business profitably. On the emotional level, the pimp is at once father, brother, lover, and friend. He is there when the woman needs affection, advice, and love, but he also disciplines her when she falters. Once caught up in his grip, the prostitute quickly learns the extent of her dependence on him and the risks of attempting to leave the fold. If she does decide to leave she risks not only her financial security but also her physical safety. It is by no means uncommon for a pimp to maim or even kill a defecting or "retiring" prostitute (McCaghy, 1976: 353–354).

Today pimps are predominantly blacks, at least at the street level. It is not clear just how blacks have come to dominate the pimping business, but the potential for financial success and status in an acquisitive society as well as a certain perspective on American society and women in particular suggest two explanations. In terms of money, a successful pimp can earn as much as $500 a day. With that kind of money he is tempted to feel that he can do what he wants, when he wants, how he wants. He is successful by the very standards that white society has set. In addition, the pimping role permits the black male the kind of domination normally reserved for those in the white-dominated world of legitimate business and the professions. Instead of a subservient, dependent role, he assumes a role in which he pulls the strings and others dance. Furthermore, he can bolster his own sense of manly pride by virtue of his relationship with his women and the fact that white men must pay him for their sexual pleasure. In the view of some black pimps, American society as a whole reeks of exploitation, in which one person pimps another. They are merely cashing in, in the tradition of free enterprise and individual initiative (Milner and Milner, 1972:242–244).

Prostitution will continue to flourish as long as there are willing customers. Although it is a consensual crime and in this sense victimless, prostitution involves many elements of exploitation, most of which are suffered by the prostitute.

## ENTERING THE "PROFESSION"

Those who become prostitutes risk not only police arrest and criminal punishment but also condemnation by society at large and such work-related hazards as disease, injury, theft, and exploitation. Why, then, do some women become prostitutes? A conventional and long-standing explanation is that they are forced into the role of prostitute by unsavory characters who use devices of compulsion ranging from kidnapping, blackmail, and forced heroin addiction, to the powers of love and dependency. One example of recruitment by force and deceit was reported in *Time* magazine some years ago and is summarized by Walter Reckless (1973:169):

> The report claimed that the ring of procurers had operated for ten years and that at least 35 murders of recruited girls had taken place. The girls were lured from poor families by the promise of domestic jobs with upper-class families. The girls were first raped and then sent to a training brothel. It was estimated that at least 2,000 girls had passed through the hands of the ring since 1954 (ten years before the report). The "sick" recruits were sent to [a "concentration" camp] at Leon [Mexico] to die, while the rebellious ones were also sent there for taming.

Doubtless some women are forcibly introduced to prostitution. But the current thinking on the subject places less emphasis on the role of force and more on the voluntary decision to enter prostitution and the circumstances surrounding that decision. It seems likely that when considered as a whole, only a small minority of prostitutes are forced into the profession.

Still, the women themselves may feel that they have no real choice in the matter, and some look upon their entrance into prostitution as something forced upon them by circumstances beyond their control. One circumstance often mentioned by prostitutes and researchers alike is financial insecurity. Simply stated, the belief is that some women (perhaps most) enter prostitution because they need the money. They may have a child to support; they may be out of work and unable to find a full-time job; or they may have pressing financial obligations, such as paying medical bills or financing a drug addiction, which they cannot hope to meet through conventional, legal kinds of work. But Ronald Akers (1973:166) warns us not to misinterpret the nature of the financial incentives in prostitution:

> This may sound trite or overly simplistic, but the nature of the monetary incentive in prostitution is often misunderstood. The woman need not be in dire or desperate economic straits; escape from poverty is only one way (and probably not the most frequent way) in which prostitution is economically inspired.

The choice, Akers argues, is not often between starving or becoming a prostitute but is more commonly between a low-paying, low-status but respectable job and a relatively high-paying job that happens to be illegal and unrespectable. The loss of respectability and the risks of arrest and criminal punishment are offset by the economic rewards believed to accrue from prostitution.

Even so, most people to whom prostitution would offer financial attractions do not become prostitutes. For those few who do, it seems that additional considerations facilitate their entry into the prostitute role. Based on the evidence, one factor appears to be experience in sex at a relatively early age, and another is a set of verbalized opinions favorable to prostitution. Those women who have had early sexual experiences will presumably have less difficulty accepting the idea of sex as a normal facet of male–female relationships, even among strangers. Opinions favorable to prostitution are bound to vary, but some notable ones are "prostitution is no worse than any other kind of job"; "people don't really look down on the prostitute"; "the prostitute is necessary, for without her marriages would fail, some men would have to commit rape to get laid"; and "the prostitute gives men what their wives and lovers won't" (Jackman et al., 1963; Bryan, 1966).

Actually, it is not easy to become a prostitute — at least a successful one. Not only must the novice learn how and where to find customers, she must also learn how to protect herself from disease, the police, the competition, and the customer, and how to stay in business. In his study of call girls in the Los Angeles area, James Bryan (1965) found that most went through a kind of apprenticeship. Their initial entrance into prostitution was facilitated through personal contacts with an established call girl or a pimp, and from then on they learned the ropes under the direction of other call girls, some of whom ran "classes" in their apartments. Though there was apparently little training in sexual techniques as such, the new recruits were taught the "dos and don'ts" of the game and were helped in building an initial set of customer contacts. Among the rules learned were get the money first; don't enjoy the trick or fall for the customer; don't be pleasant with the customer unless he has paid; don't engage in unnecessary interaction with him; get him "off " as soon as possible; and stay in good physical and mental health.

Surprising though it may seem to some of us, there is an art to prostitution. It is the art of the confidence game. The customer is treated to a pretense, and he pays through the nose for it. As it was graphically put by one author: "A whore is a woman who fucks for money. If you pay her enough she pretends to come" (Douglas, 1970:66). A good prostitute is a good actor and the director as well.

> There's some of them lies still as stones, they think it's more ladylike or something, but I say they don't know which side their bread's buttered. Listen, if you lie still the bloke may take half the night sweating away. But if you bash it about a bit he'll come all the quicker and get out and away and leave you in peace. Stupid to spin it out longer than you need, isn't it? I learned that from Margaret. Wonderful actress, that girl. (Douglas, 1970:66)

## Reactions to Consensual Sex Offenses

The prostitute is generally looked upon with mild intolerance by society and its legal officials. Unless community pressure to do something about prostitution builds up, the police and courts rarely go out of their way to make life difficult for prostitutes. It seems that when the police do take the trouble to arrest streetwalkers or to raid local brothels and illegal massage parlors, they do so more to harass them and get some "action" than to enforce the law. When prostitutes are hauled up before a judge, they typically pay a small fine and are back on the street within hours.

There is a similar tolerance of pornography. The Supreme Court's 1973 ruling in *Miller v. California* left the problem of defining obscenity largely in the hands of juries applying "contemporary community standards," and there seems to be little agreement as to what those standards are. But apart from this, a recent Gallup poll found that a majority of 1,020 Americans sampled favor being able to go to x-rated movies (60 percent), to buy magazines that show sexual relations (53 percent), and to buy or rent x-rated videotapes (68 percent). Yet a majority of those interviewed also believe that the depiction of sexual violence leads some people to commit sexual assault (76 percent) and that the law should prohibit pornographic violence (*Newsweek,* March 18, 1985).

The explosion in sales and rentals of pornographic videotapes and the success of sex-oriented cable and satellite channels indicate that many Americans want to view sexually explicit material, at least in the privacy of their homes. Middle-class people can now do in private what before necessitated a trip to the seamier parts of town, thereby protecting a public front of decency.

One major exception to this tolerance should be noted, and that is "kiddy porn," the depiction of children engaging in sexual activities with each other or with adults. In recent years severe penalties have been introduced by most states for offenses of this sort, and in *Ferber v. New York* (1982) the Supreme Court ruled in favor of state and local laws banning sexually explicit materials involving children.

The fight against pornography is continuing in some circles, and it has brought together strange bedfellows: on the one hand are such moral entrepreneurs as Citizens for Decency Through Law, who see pornography as a reflection of a larger moral decay (*National Decency Reporter,* October 22, 1985), and on the other are feminists who see pornography as a manifestation (and perpetuation) of sexual stereotyping, in which women are seen as "vile whores" who deserve, and probably want, to be sexually abused by men (Lederer, 1980; Dworkin, 1981). Both groups argue that at its least, contemporary pornography, with its "sexualization of violence" (Ashley and Ashley, 1984), trivializes male sexual aggression and at its worst actually encourages crimes of sexual assault. It remains to be seen whether the war against pornography waged by these groups will succeed; the cards are stacked against them, however, because commercial sex is big business and growing bigger, and because America is a patriarchal society.

## REACTIONS TO HOMOSEXUALITY

The public, police, and courts have traditionally displayed greater intolerance of and have made a more systematic effort to do something about homosexuality. With the exception of Illinois, Connecticut, and a handful of other states, homosexual acts, even in private and between consenting adults, violate state criminal codes and sometimes carry penalties placing them on a par with felonious assault, armed robbery, burglary, and even rape and murder. Compared with heterosexual offenses, the consequences of indulging in homosexual conduct are by and large more demeaning, more punitive, and longer lasting. And when there are victims, as in the case of child molesting, the chances are that life will be made more miserable for the homosexual offender. In one follow-up study of convicted child molesters, homosexual offenders served much longer prison sentences than did heterosexual offenders for the same offense (Fitch, 1962).

Studies in Los Angeles, St. Louis, and elsewhere show that the police often routinely harass suspected gays and lesbians on the street and in bars, nightclubs, and dance halls catering to the gay community. The public restroom in parks, railroad stations, and bus terminals has been the setting for more perverse police practices. These have included the use of male decoys whose job is to lure other males into making sexual advances (sometimes accomplished by the decoy making a show of fondling his own penis), the use of peepholes drilled in walls and ceilings, and the use of still and movie cameras hidden behind two-way mirrors or ventilation screens (see Gallo, 1966; Humphreys, 1970). A recent police operation at a highway rest area in Michigan resulted in the arrest of forty-two men whose sexual activities had been secretly videotaped during a ten-day surveillance period (UPI, March 20, 1986).

In their study of male homosexuality in the United States, Denmark, and the Netherlands, Martin Weinberg and Colin Williams (1975) point out that despite the availability of felony statutes (the so-called sodomy laws) providing for severe penalties upon conviction, the common practice in the United States is to charge homosexual offenders with misdemeanors. At first glance one might think that this practice reflects an attitude of leniency and tolerance. On the contrary, these authors argue, the use of misdemeanor charges is preferred because these laws are easier to apply and give a greater likelihood of conviction.

Many of those arrested for homosexual acts are first offenders, in the legal sense, and hence are inexperienced in matters of procedural law and the routine workings of the judicial process. This, coupled with their fears regarding the effects of publicity on their family, work, and social life, makes them easy prey for the disreputable and greedy among our legal officials. Sometimes they are blackmailed by corrupt police; sometimes they become patsies in a scheme of kickbacks involving the police, bonding services, and corrupt attorneys. But more often they find themselves in the hands of lawyers who make their living off the fearful and inexperienced who daily get in trouble with the law. Such lawyers, often called "courthouse regulars," get business by referrals from bondsmen, police, or court officials or by hanging around police stations and misdemeanor courts and will routinely charge upwards of $500 just to plead their client guilty. Under a hard sell and promises of no publicity, no conviction, and the like (false-hoods, or in any case not under the lawyer's control), the suspect finds it hard to refuse the "help" offered by a seemingly sympathetic, knowledgeable, and experienced attorney.

There is evidence that public and official attitudes toward homosexuality have moved in a more tolerant and permissive direction (see McCaghy, 1976:366). The National Crime Survey on offense severity ranks consensual homosexual conduct fourteenth from the bottom out of 204 crimes. Opinions, however, may well be changing again, and new laws have already been passed restricting homosexual conduct. The reason is AIDS: Acquired Immunological Deficiency Syndrome.

By the end of 1985, AIDS had been clinically diagnosed in over sixteen thousand Americans and in many more worldwide, The *Morbidity and Mortality Weekly Report* published by the Centers for Disease Control in Atlanta keeps tabs on AIDS cases, and by the time this text is published, the figures for the United States will have doubled. In addition, there are an estimated one to two million Americans who have been exposed to the virus but who have not developed clinical symptoms. An estimated 5 to 10 percent of them will develop AIDS, and many more will suffer from ARC (AIDS-Related Condition).

Among diagnosed AIDS patients, homosexual males are the largest group, consistently around 73 percent of the total. This fact, together with the death of actor Rock Hudson, has brought considerable attention to homosexual life-styles. Studies in New York and San Francisco, where around half of all American AIDS cases are located (Centers for Disease Control, 1985), show that homosexuals at the highest risk of being infected with the AIDS virus are those who engage in anonymous sex with many different partners and those whose sexual activities include anal-receptive intercourse without a condom and the ingestion of semen (Darrow et al., 1983; Jaffee et al., 1985).

Many of these high-risk activities take place in gay baths and clubs, leading authorities in New York to empower city health officials to investigate and close them down if sexual activities are observed. In Texas, the state health commissioner asked for the power to quarantine AIDS patients who refuse to discontinue their high-risk sexual activities (Associated Press, December 16, 1985). In October 1985, the U.S. Defense Department established a mandatory screening of all recruits and active duty members of the armed forces, and prison officials around the country are considering similar programs for inmates (United Press International, October 29, 1985).

Most authorities agree that the transmission of AIDS will continue unless there are drastic changes in sexual life-styles, especially among homosexual men. The evidence collected so far indicates that there have been changes but also that these have been selective and nonuniform. A follow-up study of 301 gay males found that the proportion reporting unsafe sexual practices had decreased, but even so 36 percent said they had had more than one sexual partner during the past thirty days, and 7 percent had exchanged semen (Centers for Disease Control, 1985). A survey of 655 gay males in San Francisco found that men who considered themselves monogamous were unlikely to change their high-risk sexual activities and that other men showed more significant reductions in oral-genital contact than in unprotected anal intercourse (McKusick et al., 1985). The conclusion reached by the authors of this study was that knowledge of the risks was not sufficient to produce significant changes in the sexual behavior of their subjects.

Without evidence of voluntary changes in sexual life-styles, the authorities are likely to rely more and more on the law as a weapon in the fight against AIDS. Public health and criminal justice officials will no longer treat anonymous homosexual encounters as victimless offenses because it is now clear that the risk of being infected with the AIDS virus is a real danger to the participants and that each new case of infection increases the risks for the heterosexual population. It is also likely that drug addicts and prostitutes will be subject to more rigorous surveillance and prosecution, because they, too, are in high-risk groups.

In a controversial 1986 ruling, the U.S. Supreme Court upheld a Georgia law that prohibits consenting adults from engaging in oral or anal sex and makes the offense punishable by 20 years in prison. The case in question involved two men arrested by a policeman who entered their bedroom with a warrant on an unrelated matter and saw them engaged in oral sex. The constitutional issue concerned the right to privacy, and by its 5 to 4 decision the high court ruled in effect that no such right extends to homosexual acts. Many gays interpret the decision as clear support for renewed repression of homosexuals. Others fear that the reasoning of the court in the Georgia case could be extended to the private sexual practices of consenting heterosexuals. Currently, twenty-four states and the District of Columbia have laws regulating consensual sex between adults, with penalties ranging from 30 days in jail to 20 years in prison (*Newsweek*, July 14, 1986). The Supreme Court decision may encourage some states to join the list, and others to increase their penalties.

The weight of historical evidence leaves little room for doubt that the legal repression of human sexuality is doomed to failure. Hard as it is to curb male sexual aggression toward females, it is even harder to control consensual sex. Even so, there seems to be no end to legislative and enforcement efforts to criminalize those who seek sexual pleasures in ways publicly (much less often privately) denounced. In 1976, efforts to enforce sexual morality reached new heights when actor Harry Reems was prosecuted and convicted under federal obscenity statutes for his part in the widely seen x-rated movie *Deep Throat*. Though the conviction was subsequently reversed, the entire affair extended the scope of legal repression of essentially personal matters of moral choice. If pursued, this attack will produce more criminals, but is unlikely to reduce the incidence of the behavior in question.

# Drugs and Crime

We have argued that nothing inherent in any activity makes it a crime. Rather, activities and those who engage in them become criminal when they are so labeled by persons with the authority to do so. Sometimes acts similar in substance are labeled differently — some are called crimes, others are not. This is especially true of drug-related acts. Most Americans are consumers of drugs, but some of us do nothing illegal, whereas others do. The world of drugs, then, has two sides, the legal and criminal. Although this is a criminology text and as such focuses on crime, we cannot hope to grasp the realities of the criminal side of drugs and their use if we do not at the same time consider the legal side. Indeed, it is through understanding the legal use of legal drugs that we find insights into the illegal use of drugs and drug-related crime.

**Defining Terms**  Published works on drugs frequently contain terms that are unfamiliar to many readers. We will use the word *drug* to refer to any psychoactive substance. A *psychoactive substance* is one having the capacity to alter mental states and hence influence human activity. Identifying an "altered mental state" requires a subjective assessment by the drug user, which sometimes complicates the identification of a substance as a drug. However, the evidence consistently indicates that some of the major examples of currently available drugs are alcohol, nicotine, caffeine, opiates, hallucinogens (LSD, DMT), cocaine, barbiturates ("downers"), amphetamines ("speed"), marijuana, tranquilizers, and analgesics (pain killers).

One of the most confusing of all drug-related terms is addiction. Since this term will crop up from time to time throughout our discussion, it will help if we can agree on what we mean by it. To define addiction we must confront two issues. One is the direct physical effects of a drug on the biochemistry of the human body, and the other is the mental and physical reactions to it by those using it. When people habitually take a drug, we might be inclined to say that they are addicted to its effects — they cannot do without them. But the problem is that some drugs create a bodily craving and others do not. That is, some drugs have specific effects on the cells of the body so that the cells in question "adjust" to the drug's presence and assume stable functions only when the effects of the drugs are working. The body needs the drug. Other drugs have no such effects, yet people habitually use them.

The term *addiction* is best reserved for situations in which a particular drug produces bodily dependence. The term *habituation* can then be used to describe those situations in which a person regularly uses a drug even though his or her body exhibits no physical dependence. Habituation has much to do with personality and situational factors, whereas addiction has much to do with the substance itself.

A corollary of addiction is *withdrawal*. When individuals either cease to take a drug to which they are addicted or reduce the dosage, their body cells respond to its withdrawal. The resulting adjustment can take several hours or several days. In most cases the withdrawal process is extremely distressing, and in some situations it can be fatal; alcohol, heroin, and barbiturate withdrawal are extremely dangerous. Drugs like alcohol and heroin also are known to produce *tolerance;* that is, greater amounts of the drug are required to bring about a constant level of effect.

Those drugs that are potentially addicting are alcohol, nicotine, opiates, and barbiturates. Marijuana, the psychedelics such as LSD, amphetamines, and cocaine are not addicting, though users of amphetamines and psychedelics find they build up tolerance. Though not addicted to such drugs, some users are habituated to them in that they use them on a regular, frequent basis.

## Drug Use and the Law

Psychoactive substances have been a part of American life since the founding of the country, but only in this century have drugs become a significant aspect of the crime scene. To understand the picture today we need to know something about our recent past.

The history of drug use in America is a history of politics, big business, prejudice, and hedonism. Consider the narcotics: opium, heroin, and morphine. Opium use steadily increased from colonial days to the late 1800s, by which time morphine had been extracted, and both were readily used for a variety of medicinal purposes. Morphine addiction came to be known as the "soldier's disease," as a result of its use with the Civil War wounded, and opium-based medicines were widely available both by prescription and over the counter. Nineteenth-century America was, in the words of Edwin Brecher (1972), a "dope-fiend's paradise." The sale of opiates was big business.

Whether or not the general public realized it, opiates were everywhere at hand, and many thousands became addicted. By the last quarter of the nineteenth century, as many as 1.25 million Americans were regularly using opiates in one form or another (Terry and Pellens, 1970). Although we do not know how many were addicts, there would have to be as many as 8 million opiate users today for an equivalent usage rate. This is more than eight times most current estimates.

Sanctions against opiate users first appeared in local ordinances forbidding the smoking of opium in so-called opium dens. San Francisco adopted the prohibition in 1875, and other cities soon followed suit. But opium smoking was outlawed not so much for the drug itself as for the circumstances surrounding its use. In San Francisco, for example, opium smoking was primarily a pastime of the Chinese immigrants used to build the railroads. Being immigrants and non-English-speaking, the Chinese were treated differently almost as a matter of course. When settled in San Francisco their visibility increased, and their strange life-style and willingness to work for a pittance soon drew hostility from many townsfolk around them. When white Americans, especially women and persons of "respectable" background, began visiting Chinese opium dens, officials of the city succumbed to the cries of outrage and outlawed the dens.

By the first decade of the twentieth century, the legal importation of opium had grown to more than 14,000 pounds per year, and countless more was smuggled in (Brecher, 1972). The various prohibitions seemed to have little effect. At the same time, there was considerable pressure on Congress to join other nations in an effort to curtail the opium trade. But this pressure seems to have had more to do with international politics than with morality or fears about the drug itself. The Hague Convention of 1912 culminated a series of international conferences regarding trade and political cooperation among states, and American participation had been strongly advocated by opponents of isolationism (Lindesmith, 1967). In Congress, the Harrison Narcotics Act of 1914 was heralded as a way to implement the Hague Convention while also demonstrating America's willingness to fulfill its international obligations.

**Alcohol Prohibition**   Five years after the Harrison act, Congress ratified the Volstead act, and national Prohibition, the "great experiment" had begun. Unlike narcotics prohibition, the new federal laws restricting alcohol were the culmination of over a hundred years of crusading by temperance groups with roots in Methodist and Quaker teachings. By 1869 the Prohibition party had become a powerful force in American politics (Sinclair, 1964).

There were pragmatic as well as moral concerns behind the Prohibition movement. Excessive drinking had a demonstrably negative impact on family life, on work, and on the quality of interpersonal relations generally. Besides, scientific research showed damage to nerve cells, impairment of mental functions, weakening of blood vessels, lowered resistance to illness and disease, adverse effects on digestion, and impaired judgment and reaction time. More recent research catalogues an even longer list of medical dangers (Brodie, 1973). All the medical and social ills associated with alcohol became a potent weapon in the hands of the Prohibition party and helped bring about the 1919 Prohibition victory.

## EFFECTS OF EARLY DRUG LEGISLATION

The immediate consequence of the Harrison and Volstead acts was to create a new set of crimes, and although neither law specifically criminalized the act of consumption itself, the end result was to turn users into criminals because getting the drugs meant breaking the law.

The use of the drugs apparently fell off for a while, partly because the customary sources of supply dried up, partly because the risks of being labeled criminal were simply too great for some people to accept, and partly because some people believed in obeying the law. But more striking were the effects of the laws on the social context of drug use, on the population of users, on public attitudes, and on economic interests. In the case of alcohol, these effects culminated in the repeal of Prohibition in 1933; in the case of the narcotics, they produced new ills and an expanding repression.

The repeal of Prohibition provides a good illustration of the role of special interests in the decriminalization of behavior. There was considerable public demand for alcohol, and many people continued to drink and were willing to pay inflated prices for their pleasures. This was incentive enough for the black marketers, and as we saw in the preceding chapter, Prohibition was a major factor in the development of organized crime. This in turn fostered corruption and gang warfare, hardly anticipated by the temperance lobby.

All this played into the hands of the liquor interests, those who before Prohibition were legally producing and selling billions of gallons annually (Benson, 1927). For them, even a month of Prohibition was too much. Armed with evidence of the evils of Prohibition, supported by politicians clamoring for states' rights and by a growing public opinion that the experiment had failed and probably would never work, the liquor interests got their way.

Narcotics, on the other hand, remained outlawed, and the laws were even tightened during this period. The pharmaceutical industry was able to produce and market alternative drugs, which physicians were happy to dispense in light of the increasing risks of arrest they faced in supplying patients, particularly addicts, with opiates. Erich Goode (1972) estimates that between 1914 and 1938 as many as 25,000 physicians were charged with violations of drug laws.

Many previous opiate users now became heavy users of, if not addicted to, barbiturates. Middle-class, middle-aged white women had been the largest group of opiate users before the Harrison act, primarily because opiates were widely dispensed for so-called female problems. After the act, they became the largest group of sedative users, and they remain so today (Goode, 1972: 193). But in the meantime a new class of opiate addicts began to emerge: inner-city blacks and Hispanics. A relatively small black market demand grew along with inner-city decay and the emergence of a subculture of intravenous heroin use. The tightening laws and subsequent refusal of physicians to dispense opiates to addicts pushed narcotic distribution into the ghetto, where an anonymous and concentrated population, ravaged by the Depression, became a new, profitable market for the unscrupulous. The illicit use of "hard drugs" was seen as a growing problem by the very same people who had urged the repeal of Prohibition. But the interests at work in the case of alcohol were missing here.

## Marijuana and the Drugging of America

There are two trends in America that together explain much of the current drug problem, in particular its criminological aspects. First there has been a growing recreational use of drugs, especially among the young, and second, there has been marked growth in the production and marketing of *legal* drugs. In the opinion of many experts, the former has been helped along by the latter.

## IN SEARCH OF SELF: MARIJUANA

The preeminent *illegal* youth drug is marijuana. The U.S. government estimates that from 8 to 9 thousand metric tons were consumed in 1984 (National Narcotics Intelligence Consumers Committee, 1985:8). According to national surveys of use among high school students, 27 percent of high school seniors in 1983 claimed to have used the drug during the thirty days before being interviewed (see Table 11.1). Around 7 percent of the seniors were classified as daily users. After 1969, marijuana use grew steadily among all segments of the U.S. population, reaching a peak in 1979 of over 22 million people who considered themselves current users (see Table 11.2). There is evidence of a decline in use among youth over the past decade, and the most likely reasons are the current American "health craze" and a decline in peer group support for any kind of smoking (National Institute on Drug Abuse, 1983:113).

Marijuana comes from the Indian hemp plant *(Cannabis sativa)* and has been used for centuries. The resin, called *charas* by Hindus and known as *hashish* today, was used for spiritual purposes by the Indians and as a medicine by the ancient Chinese. When the top leaves of the hemp plant are cut and dried, they may be eaten or smoked. The mixture is less potent than hashish, and the Indians called it *bhang;* we call it marijuana, grass, or pot, among other things. Today, over half the marijuana supply in the United States comes form Colombia (National Narcotics Intelligence Consumers Committee, 1985).

Hemp was used by the American pioneers in the manufacture of rope, and a number of authors have suggested that it was grown for the psychoactive resin as well (see Andrews, 1967). By the mid-nineteenth century, marijuana was used freely as a medicinal preparation, and many home medicine chests contained some. Around the same time, marijuana and hashish became a popular recreational drug, and "hashish houses" sprang up in many larger cities.

Prohibition gave marijuana a boost as a substitute for alcohol. By the late 1930s New York City claimed five hundred known marijuana peddlers, and in Harlem alone there were an estimated five hundred "teapads" operating where people gathered to smoke pot (Mayor of New York's Committee, 1944). Many accounts of marijuana use linked the drug to those whose life-styles were already considered deviant by mainstream America: musicians, sailors, artists, prostitutes, delinquents, criminals, and minority groups. The evils of marijuana use were widely reported in the press, and a "new menace" was born (Walton, 1938).

State and local governments began passing legislation outlawing the drug,

**Table 11.1** Self-reported drug use among national samples, various years

A. Percent of High School Seniors Using Drug "During last 30 Days"

| TYPE OF DRUG | CLASS OF 1980 | CLASS OF 1981 | CLASS OF 1982 | CLASS OF 1983 |
|---|---|---|---|---|
| Marijuana/hashish | 33.7 | 31.6 | 28.5 | 27.0 |
| LSD | 2.3 | 2.5 | 2.4 | 1.9 |
| Cocaine | 5.2 | 5.8 | 5.0 | 4.9 |
| Heroin | 0.2 | .2 | 0.2 | .2 |
| Stimulants | 12.1 | 15.8 | 10.7 | 12.4 |
| Sedatives | 4.8 | 4.6 | 3.4 | 3.0 |
| Alcohol | 72.0 | 70.7 | 69.7 | 69.4 |
| Cigarettes | 30.5 | 29.4 | 30.0 | 30.3 |

B. Cocaine Use Among High School Seniors, 1976–1982 (Percent Used Drug)

| FREQUENCY OF USE | 1976 | 1977 | 1978 | 1979 | 1980 | 1982 |
|---|---|---|---|---|---|---|
| Ever used | 9.7 | 10.8 | 12.9 | 15.4 | 15.7 | 16.0 |
| Used in last 12 months but not last 30 days | 4.0 | 4.3 | 5.1 | 6.3 | 7.1 | 6.5 |
| Used in last 30 days | 2.0 | 2.9 | 3.9 | 5.7 | 5.2 | 5.0 |

C. Reported Drug Use by Age Group[a] — Percent "Ever Used" Drug, 1976, 1979, 1982

| TYPE OF DRUG | ADULTS | | | YOUNG ADULTS | | | YOUTH | | |
|---|---|---|---|---|---|---|---|---|---|
| | 1976 | 1979 | 1982 | 1976 | 1979 | 1982 | 1976 | 1979 | 1982 |
| Marijuana | 12.9 | 19.6 | 23.0 | 52.9 | 68.2 | 64.2 | 22.4 | 30.9 | 26.7 |
| Cocaine | 1.6 | 4.3 | 8.5 | 13.4 | 27.5 | 28.3 | 3.4 | 5.4 | 6.5 |
| Heroin | 0.5 | 1.0 | 1.1 | 3.9 | 3.5 | 1.2 | 0.5 | 0.5 | 0.5[c] |
| Alcohol | 74.7[b] | 91.5 | 88.2 | 83.6[b] | 95.3 | 94.6 | 53.6[b] | 70.3 | 65.2 |

SOURCE: National Institute on Drug Abuse (1983), Student Drug Use, Attitudes, and Beliefs: National Trends, 1975–1983; National Institute on Drug Abuse (1985), Highlights from Drugs and American High School Students, 1975–1983. Washington, D.C.: U.S. Government Printing Office.

a. Adults are 25 years of age and older; young adults are 18 to 25; youth are 12 to 17.
b. Data are for 1974.
c. Less than.

and their efforts were spurred on by officials of the newly established Federal Bureau of Narcotics, under the directorship of Harry J. Anslinger. In 1937 Congress passed the Marijuana Tax Act, modeled after the Harrison act, and by the 1950s all states had adopted severe penalties for the cultivation, purchase, sale, or possession of marijuana. People spoke widely of marijuana addiction and marijuana-induced sex and violence.

How, then, did marijuana emerge as America's most popular illicit drug? The answer lies partly with the growth of countercultures during the late fifties and subsequent confrontations with the Establishment on college

**Table 11.2** Estimates of nonmedicinal drug use in America, 1979 survey

| TYPE OF DRUG | ESTIMATED NUMBER "EVER USED" | PERCENT OF POPULATION[a] | ESTIMATED NUMBER OF CURRENT USERS[b] | PERCENT OF POPULATION[a] |
|---|---|---|---|---|
| Marijuana | 53,800,490 | 29.9% | 22,613,220 | 12.6% |
| Inhalants[c] | 12,406,793 | 6.9 | 1,471,970 | 0.8 |
| Hallucinogens[d] | 15,213,510 | 8.5 | 2,367,550 | 1.3 |
| Cocaine | 14,924,985 | 8.3 | 4,228,426 | 2.4 |
| Heroin | 2,476,110 | 1.4 | 896,790 | 0.5[h] |
| Stimulants[e] | 13,742,878 | 7.7 | 2,020,273 | 1.1 |
| Sedatives[f] | 10,525,248 | 5.9 | 1,772,959 | 1.0 |
| Tranquilizers[g] | 6,028,816 | 3.4 | 1,431,969 | 0.8 |
| Alcohol | 160,820,730 | 89.7 | 106,585,570 | 59.4 |
| Cigarettes | 142,075,630 | 79.2 | 62,298,870 | 34.7 |

SOURCE: Compiled from various tables in National Institute on Drug Abuse (1980), National Survey on Drug Abuse: Main Findings, 1979. Washington, D.C.: U.S. Government Printing Office. Based on face-to-face interviews with a nationwide sample of Americans, aged 12 and over. Estimates presented here are based on extrapolations from the 7,224 persons interviewed.

a. Estimated population age 12 and over is 179,358,000.
b. "Current Users" are persons who admitted using a drug during the 30 days prior to the interview.
c. Inhalants include gasoline, lighter fluid, aerosol sprays, amyl nitrite ("poppers"), nitrous oxide, and other anesthetics.
d. Hallucinogens include LSD, PCP, mescaline, peyote, psilocybin, and DMT.
e. Stimulants are amphetamines, nonamphetamines, anoretics, Ritalin, and Cylert. (Examples are Dexedrine, Dexamyl, Tepanil, Benzedrine, Pre-sate, and Methedrine.)
f. Sedatives include barbiturates, nonbarbiturates, and Dalmine. (Examples are Butisol, Amytal, Phenobarbital, Doriden, Quaalude, Nembutal, Seconal and Tuinal.)
g. Tranquilizers include benzodiazepines, Meprobamate, hydroxyzine, and Benedryl. (Examples are Valium Librium, Miltown, Equanil, Serax, and Vistaril.)
h. Less than.

campuses during the sixties. The "beat" generation that emerged in the New York and San Francisco in the fifties emphasized an alternative life-style of autonomy, drugs (especially pot), music, free sexual expression, aversion to routine employment and politics, and disregard for the law (Polsky, 1967). The hippies succeeded the beats and made famous the Haight-Ashbury district of San Francisco. They claimed a similar life-style, though jazz was replaced with acid- or folk-rock, and marijuana was joined by LSD. The hippies also took pains to show off their life-style, and they enjoyed "putting on straights" and "blowing their minds" with their rejection of all that was valued by the dominant, middle-class culture.

By the end of the 1960s, the hippie culture, if not its ideology, had spread to all parts of the country, and rock music was one of its major vehicles. The other was the growing disenchantment among young people, especially college students, with the policies and practice of American government. The use of illegal drugs became a way of underscoring their opposition to the

Establishment. In addition, marijuana and the psychedelics were touted as a way to "expand the mind," to "trip," to "get your head right." They were perfect for the "now" generation, those who searched for meaning and heightened self-awareness, not the superficialities of conspicuous consumption (Carey, 1968).

## DRUGS ARE US

The second trend that has encouraged illicit drug use is the growth of drug use in general. In America, drugs have become a way of life for the healthy as well as for the sick. Beer, wine, liquor, tea, nicotine, coffee, and myriad pills and potions are daily fare for many respectable Americans. Even children are targets: aspirins are named after saints, vitamins are made to look like the Flintstones, and beer that is not really beer is marketed as if it were beer.

Table 11.2 gives some estimates of nonmedicinal drug use in America. Alcohol and tobacco far outstrip the other drugs listed. Not listed in the table, however, is caffeine, a stimulant that is found in coffee, tea, hot chocolate, cola beverages, and in over-the-counter pills for dieting and preventing sleep. The per-capita consumption of coffee is around 10 pounds per year, tea just under 1 pound, and soft drinks, most of which contain some caffeine, nearly 40 gallons. Americans drink an average of between three and four cups of coffee a day (U.S. Department of Agriculture, 1983).

Even though most other legal drugs are intended for medicinal uses, Table 11.2 shows that stimulants, sedatives, and tranquilizers are widely used for nonmedicinal purposes. The National Commission on Marijuana and Drug Abuse (1973:57) concluded that "the preponderant use of sedatives is for experimentation and enjoyment," whereas tranquilizers are used as "coping" mechanisms, and stimulants often to stay awake or "just to see how they work." A study of New York State households found that more than 70 percent of those using such drugs obtained them by prescription. The typical user is a white, middle-class female between 25 and 45, precisely the same class of people who regularly used opiates before 1914 (Chambers, 1971).

Drugs are big business. Over a decade ago, Richard Blum and Associates (1972) estimated that $25 billion a year was spent on over-the-counter-drugs, including aspirin, tobacco, and alcohol. Today the figure is certainly higher. In addition to this, Americans spent $19.6 billion on prescription medicines in 1983, a figure that does not include government and hospital purchases (Medical Economics Company, n.d.). Another measure of the economics of drugs in America are the expenditures on advertising. In 1983 the following amounts were spent in the various media (Bureau of the Census, 1985, Tables 945, 946, 968):

Magazine advertising: $243,000,000 on beer, wine, and liquor
104,000,000 on drugs and remedies
398,000,000 on tobacco products

Television ads:         $358,000,000 on beer and wine
                  575,000,000 on proprietary medicines
                    8,000,000 on tobacco products
Newspaper ads (1981): $175,000,000 on alcoholic beverages
                  24,000,000 on medical products and drugs
             391,300,000 on tobacco products

The message conveyed by advertisers is that drugs are normal, natural, and good for you. Often, they are shown making problems and difficulties go away. Drugs bring "the good things in life" and even confer respectability, we are told. You will feel better and look younger and fit in with others if you use our drug, though the word *drug* is rarely used, of course.

With so many drugs around, with so many respectable people selling and using them, it is small wonder that we have a drug problem. We grow up anticipating a place for them in our lives. That first cigarette, puffed courageously in some secluded spot, that first can of beer, downed with much bravado in a friend's car, are milestones along the road to adulthood. Most youthful experimenters know they are breaking the law, but that merely adds to the adventure. What is "cool" about doing something that children are supposed to do? Anyway, there must be something to smoking, drinking, popping pills, for why else would parents and other adults spend so much time and money doing it, and why would all those advertisements encourage it? According to Erich Goode (1972:126–128), "The legitimate drug industry is, both directly and indirectly, responsible for much of the illegal drug use taking place today. The "pusher" should be sought not only on the street but in the physician's office, the pharmacy, the tavern — and the home."

Those likely to turn on to illegal drugs are precisely those who have grown up in a social environment in which legal drugs are commonly used. No matter whether it is cocaine, heroin, marijuana, or the psychedelics, studies consistently show generational continuity in drug use and in the progression from legal to illegal drugs (see Goode, 1972:34–35; also Brecher, 1972). Of course, thousands of those who use legal drugs do not "progress" to illegal ones, and many who do usually discontinue their use after one or two episodes. But they do tend to remain consumers of legal drugs such as alcohol. The important lesson is that illegal drug use is most likely to be found in a climate favorable to drug use in general. In fact, the most significant correlate of illegal drug use is the consumption of legal drugs.

## COCAINE

By most accounts cocaine is America's new drug problem. But it is not a new drug. Cocaine is extracted from the leaves of the plant *Erythroxylon Coca*, which is found in South America. Coca leaves have been chewed for at least three thousand years by South American Indians. Cocaine use in America is not well documented but does not seem to have been particularly extensive until recently. It is now said to be a popular yuppie drug, and its street use appears to be growing (Grabowski, 1984). In fact, cocaine use has been rising among all age groups (see Table 11.1). There are fears that the cheap, smokeable form of cocaine known as "crack" will encourage many more young people to try the drug. As yet confined mainly to major east and west coast cities, crack will undoubtedly spread throughout the country as it becomes available in greater quantities.

The major site of coca cultivation continues to be Peru, but trafficking is dominated by Colombia, where the raw paste or cocaine base is converted into cocaine hydrochloride (HCI) for distribution to the United States. Generally, cocaine HCI is 90 percent pure when imported. Between 55 and 76 metric tons of cocaine were consumed in the United States during 1984, up from an estimated 33 to 60 tons in 1981 (National Narcotics Intelligence Consumers Committee, 1985:26–27). At the retail level, one gram of cocaine sells for around $100.

Cocaine use has been controlled since the Harrison Narcotic Act of 1914 restricted its manufacture, distribution, and sale. It is now illegal in all states. Cocaine is not, in fact, a narcotic; it is a stimulant that acts directly on the "pleasure" or "reward" centers of the brain. It is so powerful that it undermines the brain's ability to regulate such functional necessities as sleeping, eating, and handling stress. Users describe the "high" as elation, warmth, vigor, friendliness, and arousal (Grabowski, 1984). Because the subjective effects are so pleasant, cocaine is considered a prime target for abuse, though it is not physiologically addictive.

# Heroin: "Tragic Magic"

The millions of Americans who routinely consume psychoactive substances with little thought that they are addicts, or even drug users, stand in stark contrast with the estimated 500,000 heroin addicts. Heroin bears the brunt of public and legal intolerance, and the world of most heroin addicts is quite different from that of other, "respectable" drug users. It is a world in which getting the "shit" (or "horse," "smack," "Hi," "junk," "tragic magic") and staying alive and out of jail consume much of every waking day (see box, p. 342–343). In this section we shall explore the world of heroin addiction, with particular attention to its criminal aspects.

## HEROIN SUPPLY AND DISTRIBUTION

Before the addict gets heroin it has often traveled thousands of miles and passed across numerous links in a complex underground chain of importation and distribution. Over the past decades, the primary foreign sources of heroin have been the Middle East, Afghanistan, Pakistan, India, the Far East, and Mexico. During the 1970s, Mexico emerged as the major foreign source, with an estimated 80 percent (10 tons) of the 1975 domestic supply origina-

## A DAY IN THE LIFE OF AN INNER-CITY HEROIN ADDICT

The scene is the "marketplace" where heroin deals are struck: a dilapidated inner-city black neighborhood with a few shops and perhaps a take-out restaurant or two run by immigrants from the Far East or Latin America. People come there to buy marijuana, cocaine, Dilaudid, Quaaludes, amphetamines, barbiturates, Valium, and heroin (or "tragic magic," as some call it). The trafficking itself takes place at the curbside "copping corner," and some users then go to "shooting galleries" — nearby houses or abandoned stores where they shoot up with others, sharing needles and the other "works."

*Early morning.* For users careful to save some heroin from the day before there is first the wake-up fix, "just to get straight." For most, however, the day begins with reefer. Those with jobs follow the routines of conventional society; those without head for the marketplace, many to team up with other

addicts, find out what has been going on (i.e., who got busted, who is dealing, who has the best drugs), and plan the day's hustles.

*Midmorning.* After teaming up with other junkies, addicts look for ways to earn enough money to buy a day's supply later in the afternoon. They will try begging, borrowing, conning, and stealing; they are flexible. Many have legitimate jobs for at least a few hours a day, running errands, fetching and carrying, washing dishes, and the like.

*Noon.* The marketplace becomes a bustling street as workers come to make purchases during their lunch hours. Many whites come into the area to buy, feeling it safe to do so. A hierarchy of marketplace participants is evident: "Vultures" or dope fiends are at the bottom — dirty, unkempt, strung out and sick, mostly relying on handouts. Hustling users take care to look more casual and present-

ting there. Today, Pakistan and Afghanistan are competing with Mexico and the "Golden Triangle" (Burma, Laos, and Thailand) as the major U.S. sources (Pace and Styles, 1983). In 1984, an estimated 6 metric tons of heroin were consumed in the United States, about the same as the preceding two years (National Narcotics Intelligence Consumers Committee, 1985:45).

The mechanics of importation vary according to the location and availability of raw opium — Mexico became an important source only after America withdrew from Vietnam, and the Turkish government cracked down on opium production. But the local dealers and vendors always remain the important final links in the chain and effectively control dealing at the street level. It is the pusher, the small-time vendor, who provides the addict and user with heroin. Pushers are usually addicts themselves; they finance their own drug purchases through sales to others (Preble and Casey, 1969).

## The Money Angle

Big money can be made in every corner of the drug world. In the criminal drug scene, a drug's illegality increases its potential for profits and its costs to the user. If the substance is also addicting, profit possibilities increase even more. Addicts *need* the drug; they do not merely desire it as a person might desire a new car or a color television.

The price users pay reflects, of course, the availability of the drug. When supplies dry up the price goes up. But the bulk of profits is explained by the fact that drugs can be manufactured, distributed, and sold free from many of able, mainly because they do not want to draw attention to themselves. Those in the dealing hierarchy are stylishly dressed, with designer jeans and lots and lots of fine jewelry.

*Midafternoon.* By early afternoon most addicts have acquired enough money for their day's purchase and are trying to connect quickly with a dealer they know personally. As soon as possible after they have scored, they will shoot up. Most will avoid shooting galleries as too risky and noisy; they want to relax, enjoy the effects of heroin, and perhaps listen to music. They will head for a friendly bar or go home or to a friend's pad.

*Evening.* The evening hours are spent back on the street. Straights come home from work, change, and are on the street to join the action. Hookers appear, "johns" start driving through, and the police come out, too. The heroin trade continues, with clusters of people conversing, dealing, negotiating, and sometimes arguing, but always alert to the police. James Walters (1985:47) describes the closing of the day:

As the evening nears midnight, most [of the addicts interviewed] . . . look back on a full, even rewarding day. Once again they have met the challenges of poverty and addiction. They have parlayed their wake-up dollars into enough money to satisfy their "jones" (habit) one more day. For one more day they have avoided being burned, busted, or spasmed by withdrawal. And along the way they have had adventures, high times and maybe even some loving.

SOURCE: Compiled from Breschner, George M., and William Brower, "The scene"; and from James M. Walters, " 'Taking care of business' updated," in Bill Hanson et al., eds. (1985), Life with Heroin. Lexington, MA: Lexington Books.

the constraints that operate in the legitimate business world and free from the merchandising costs that must be met by retailers. Most businesses would be proud to list sales in the hundreds of millions of dollars. Most of this, however, would not be profits. Yet with heroin, to take just one illegal drug, sales are mostly profits. And the sales figures are staggering: Donald Cressey (1969:91) estimated 1963 heroin sales in the United States at $350 million; Richard Blum and associates (1972:5) cited a 1970 figure of $463 million for New York City alone, meaning that the total United States sales of this drug probably ran close to $1 billion that year. An estimated $20 billion a year is spent on cocaine alone.

A pusher can make over $1,000 a week by selling small amounts of heroin and cocaine to a small circle of buyers. And neither the pusher nor others in the drug trade pay income tax on their illicit business. Those who have studied the economics of the drug trade point out that the rate of return on investment far exceeds that found in legitimate business. Howard Abadinsky (1981:145) describes the enormous profits possible in drug trafficking:

A kilo of almost pure heroin (2.2046 pounds) purchased in Bangkok for about $12,000, when prepared for street sale, 3.5 percent purity, has a gross sale value of more than $2 million in the United States. Mexican heroin sells for about $45,000 a kilo and also reaches a value of more than $2 million when cut for street sale. Cocaine, selling for about $2800 a pound in Colombia, brings anywhere from $900 to $1800 an ounce in the United States. Street level purity is about 12.5 percent. Marijuana selling for about $175 a pound in Colombia can be sold for more than $500 a pound in the United States.

## HOW ADDICTS FINANCE THEIR ADDICTION

Heroin can cost an addict as much as $100 a day, though most probably spend around $25 a day on their habit (Walters, 1985). This is nearly $10,000 a year and does not include food, rent, clothing, utilities, and other essential living expenses. So where do addicts get the money?

Most addicts get their money through a combination of legitimate work and various sorts of hustles: begging, borrowing, stealing, drug pushing, and (if women) prostitution. In a Florida study, selling drugs ranked first, followed by (for men) burglary, shoplifting, and robbery and (for women) prostitution, shoplifting, and prostitute theft from johns (Inciardi, 1979). It was estimated that in one year alone, the sample of 356 Florida addicts committed a total of 118,134 offenses.

A study of the life-styles of 124 black, male, inner-city heroin addicts in Chicago, New York, Washington D.C., and Philadelphia (see box on pp. 342–343) presents the most up-to-date information on the economics of heroin addiction, at least for blacks (Hanson et al., 1985). Most of the addicts interviewed were unskilled opportunists who rarely began the day with any money. Their "overwhelming preference" was to get money in the quickest, least violent, and least risky way (Beschner and Brower, 1985:36). As with the Florida addicts, legitimate work was an important, but usually insufficient, source of income. To supplement it, most addicts engaged in a variety of hustles, some legal, some not. For half the addicts the main hustle consisted of thefts, robberies, or con games; most would also try to borrow money from family and friends.

The Hanson study (1985) distinguished four types of addict hustlers:

**1. Opportunistic hustlers** will take any opportunity, legal or not, that comes along. They will start early in the morning so as not to miss any opportunity, but beyond that they do little planning. Versatility is their hallmark, and the target is open.

**2. Legitimate hustlers** seldom engage in crimes, raising money by offering goods and services in the neighborhood to people they know. No job is rejected, no matter how menial, and their day is dictated by the routine activities of the neighborhood. They are also versatile and prepared to take drugs in exchange for services. However, those they deal with are generally not strangers.

**3. Skilled hustlers** engage in crimes and hustles that require more skill and risk but are also more lucrative: picking pockets, specialized shoplifting, burglary. Targets are selected for vulnerability, the addicts usually works with a partner, and hustles will be planned.

**4. Dope hustlers** raise money through drug trafficking. They are usually lower-echelon participants, getting drugs on consignment and selling them to fellow addicts in their own neighborhood. They may also offer services to others in exchange for dope:

Like sometimes there are people that don't know where to cop. We get their money and cop for them and get a taste. My biggest advantage is that I know, uh, I am real tight with most of the people that get in big quantity. I always know when the [good] stuff is comin' through. I always have people who want me to get it for 'em. I'm like the middleman, I got a credit line with most guys. (Fields and Walters, 1985:64)

Besides "copping," dope hustlers may also "steer" customers to sources or "route" them to a particular dealer in exchange for drugs or cash (Johnson et al., 1985).

## ADDICTION AS A CAREER

Many drug users appear to have a career of use during which they are initiated into a drug's use, become regular users, and then "mature" out of using it. Trevor Bennett (1985) analyzed heroin addiction according to these career stages and the decisions that users and addicts make. His approach is predicated on the assumption that people are self-determining, deliberate, and responsible and that their behavior is goal directed, episodic, self-limiting, and mundane.

**Initiation** Bennett discusses three popular theories: (1) Hard drug use is preceded by and may be the result of using other drugs — the escalation or stepping-stone view. Research does not support this view, Bennett claims, and though it is true that many heroin users also use marijuana or other drugs, few users of other drugs go on to use heroin. (2) Heroin users are initiated through pressures brought by pushers. This view also finds little support in the literature. (3) Initial use occurs among friends and under the influence of a normative structure providing justification and support for its use. This theory is the preferred view, and Bennett correctly points out that some of the normative supports may exist before the drug is ever taken. Bennett's own study of six groups of addicts from 1982 to 1984 found that 90 percent were introduced to the drug by friends or acquaintances, and many had made a conscious decision to try heroin some time before they actually did so.

**Continuation** Heroin users generally progress slowly toward addiction, some taking many months to reach that point. The majority of Bennett's subjects took over a year from first use to the point where they were using heroin daily, and many reported long gaps without use in between. "One addict reported that he usually gave up opioids during the summer months so that he could pursue his favourite sports. During the winter months he injected heroin on a daily basis" (1985:25). Bennett also found considerable variation in the amount consumed from day to day, suggesting purposive decision making.

**Cessation** Other studies (e.g., Winick, 1962) have shown that addicts can mature out of addiction, quitting heroin for a variety of reasons: because of a new job, family responsibilities, or an effort to change life-styles. In Bennett's Cambridge study, all the subjects were current users, and half said they had no interest in quitting permanently. The others were confident they would quit within ten years, but only if certain other things occurred, for example, if they moved away from their associates and contacts or if their lives changed dramatically in some other way.

Bennett's study indicates that the behavior of heroin users can be self-regulated and manageable. Furthermore, they are not slaves to their addiction in the sense of having lost all self-determination. A similar position was taken by Fields and Walters (1985:71–72) in a study of black heroin addicts in America. Other, more rewarding, things may temporarily supplant an addict's use of drugs, may lead to reduced levels of use, or may lead the addict to quit altogether. Unfortunately, studies of ghetto use indicate that many of the things most likely to result in cessation — a good job, a stable family life, involvement in "straight" society — are out of reach of many inner-city addicts (Hanson et al., 1985). This problem is exacerbated by, and is partly the result of, the criminal involvements of many ghetto addicts. Submerged in crime, an addict's horizons rarely extend beyond the neighborhood and a small group of drug-using friends.

## Criminal Drug Use and the Police

The existence of drug laws calls for a police response to people who violate them. A number of things, however, work to make the enforcement of drug laws extremely difficult. For one thing, the possession, sale, and use of illegal drugs are in essence *victimless crimes;* that is, they usually involve willing participants. The police, then, will usually not have an aggrieved person who will complain that he or she has been the victim of a crime. The police must typically discover drug law violations on their own. To make enforcement more difficult, an individual can violate a drug law with no one any the wiser. Who is to know that a person carries two or three joints, some illegal pills, or a day's supply of heroin?

### THE "NARC" AND THE INFORMANT

Because illicit drug offenses are mostly consensual crimes and because they are not readily observed, police enforcement strategies place a premium on infiltration and the cultivation of police informants. Through infiltration into the ranks of users, the undercover drug agent is able to develop trusting relationships with users, addicts, and pushers and thus keep tabs on the people, events, and places having to do with illegal drugs. To maintain a cover, the "narc" must learn and adopt street ways — the rules, language, and nuances of the criminal drug scene. Narcs must virtually live among those they are charged with catching. Following his investigation of the junkie's world in New York, Houston, Austin, and Los Angeles, Bruce Jackson (1969b) concluded that narcs found it hard to separate themselves from that world, even though they may despise it and their purpose is to destroy it.

Helping the police are the informants. Usually active participants in criminal drug activities, informants are cultivated by the police, who rely heavily on the information they pass and on the contribution they can make to "good busts," arrests that hold up in court. Informants' own crimes are often used as the means to induce them to work for the police. Under the threat of arrest and a jail sentence, prospective informants find their options limited and unattractive. Besides, the police can always threaten to let the word get around that they are informants (whether true or not). If the threat of jail is not enough, this will be an added inducement to go along with the police.

A common feature of the drug enforcement strategy is for undercover agents to spend months developing information on drug use and traffic so that when they are ready, the police can pounce on a large number of suspects at the same time. These dragnet raids usually take place in the early morning hours and not uncommonly produce upward of fifty arrests. Usually out of uniform, police from federal, state, and local agencies get together for the raid and systematically root out those on a list of suspects. Sometimes these raids have had their bizarre sides, as in the notorious "Collinsville Raid," when officers barged in on the wrong houses, causing havoc and terror for the families involved (Percy, 1974). Apart from producing relatively large numbers of simultaneous arrests, there is no real evidence that raids of this kind greatly reduce the availability, sale, and use of illegal drugs. They do, however, result in much local publicity, and the public is reassured that the police are working hard in their fight against the drug criminal.

In their efforts to reduce the availability of drugs such as heroin, marijuana, and cocaine, the police have met with little success. The drug pipeline is not easily breached, not only because the major importers, wholesalers, and distributors are well organized and equipped, but also because the profitability of small quantities of these drugs make large shipments unnecessary. It is like looking for the proverbial needle in the haystack.

One line of attack against the illicit drug scene is to crack down on "head shops," places where drug paraphernalia are sold. The drug paraphernalia industry is big business, estimated at several hundred million dollars annually (*Newsweek*, November 26, 1979). This law-enforcement effort may help reduce the chances of any respectability rubbing off on illicit drug use, but it is doubtful it will greatly curb it. In fact, it will probably add to the social problem of drug use, for business will once again move underground, bolstering the black market as well as the profits to organized crime.

Many states have recently passed forfeiture laws that enable officials to confiscate various types of property if these have been used in drug trafficking or manufacture or are the fruits of such activities. In some states (e.g., Alabama, Arkansas, Kansas, Nevada, New York, Oregon, and fourteen others), confiscated property may be kept for law-enforcement use. When this is not done the property is sold, with the proceeds usually going to local or state governments (Stellwagen, 1985). It remains to be seen whether forfeiture laws will have any material effect on illegal drug trafficking, though they may be beneficial to the police. In all probability, the risk of forfeiture will merely become another of the costs of doing business, unfortunate but accommodated.

The major obstacle to effective control of drug trafficking at home and abroad is the simplest to identify and the hardest to overcome: illicit drugs are in high demand, and people are willing to pay the price. The lure of high profits means there will always be plenty of people willing to pit themselves against the authorities. Even as the authorities become more organized and sophisticated in their enforcement efforts, so do the traffickers.

## DRUG ARRESTS

Notwithstanding the overall failure of drug enforcement efforts, the police do make a lot of drug arrests. In fact, if we combine all such arrests, in any given year more arrests are made for drug-related offenses than for any other broad type of criminal offense, major or minor. Table 11.3 shows that in 1979, 34 percent of all criminal arrests were drug related. In 1983, the percentage was virtually the same.

The figures in Table 11.3 include arrests on charges relating to alcohol. In fact, alcohol-related arrests far outnumber other drug arrests. Over 80 percent of all drug arrests can be linked to alcohol, whether the offense involves public drunkenness the violation of liquor laws governing sale and consumption, or driving while intoxicated (now the number-one alcohol offense). And in terms of police arrests, alcohol-related offenses are America's number-one crime problem.

Most drug-related arrests occur among the larger urban populations. Easy accessibility to drugs, concentrated user populations, and more extensive and sophisticated police surveillance all contribute to the higher arrest rates found in larger cities and their suburbs. In the case of alcohol-related arrests, especially those for drunkenness, the typical arrestee is an adult over 30 years of age. In regard to heroin, marijuana, and other illegal drugs, the typical arrestee is under age 30. Over the past few years the number of young people arrested on illegal drug charges has risen considerably. According to available FBI figures, in 1960 there were 1,458 non-alcohol-related drug arrests of persons under age 18. By 1975 the number had increased by 4,417.4 percent to 65,864 and by 1981 to 79,601 — an increase far exceeding the corresponding increase in the proportion of persons under 18. (These figures, it should be noted, are lower than the actual number of arrests, for they are based on the records of only those police departments reporting such arrests in both years.)

Arrests for nonalcohol offenses usually are for marijuana. In 1983, for

**Table 11.3**  Drug-related arrests as a percentage of all arrests

|  | 1977 | 1979 | 1981 | 1983 |
|---|---|---|---|---|
| Total arrests | 10,189,900 | 10,205,800 | 10,840,000 | 11,700,500 |
| Drug-related arrests |  |  |  |  |
|   Number | 3,632,100 | 3,472,300 | 3,730,200 | 4,196,000 |
|   As percentage of all arrests | 35% | 34% | 34% | 35.9% |

SOURCE: FBI (1978, 1980, 1982, 1984), Crime in the United States, 1977, 1979, 1981, 1983. Washington, D.C.: U.S. Government Printing Office.

example, of the 661,400 "drug abuse" arrests, over 60 percent were marijuana related. Interestingly, those 406,900 marijuana arrests were almost twice the number reported in 1971, despite the trend toward the liberalization of marijuana laws that surfaced in the early 1970s (FBI, 1985).

## THE LINK BETWEEN DRUGS AND CRIME

We have seen that where there is illicit drug use, there is often other crime, usually to finance the drug use. This *instrumental* crime is most likely to be found among people who are poor, unemployed, or unemployable and among those who are heavy users. Many inner-city heroin addicts belong to both groups.

Recent studies in Baltimore and Harlem confirm that heroin addicts who are frequent users commit crimes at a much greater rate than lower-level users. In Harlem, addicts participated heavily in drug distribution, with daily users averaging 316 drug sales per year plus 564 episodes of copping, steering, or routing. In all, daily users generated an average of $11,000 in *cash* per year from crimes of all sorts (Johnson et al., 1985). In Baltimore, a sample of 354 known users drawn from 7,510 users arrested or identified by the police between 1952 and 1976 committed four to six times the amount of crime when frequently using than when not using or using occasionally (Ball et al., 1983). Over the course of 9.5 years the Baltimore addicts admitted to nearly 750,000 offenses, mostly thefts, drug sales, and various cons.

There is little argument that illicit drug use generates other crime. However, drug use is not the only factor in many addicts' criminal histories, for criminal activity often began before the use of hard drugs, and some of the crime committed during addiction cannot be explained by it (Ball, 1982). What concerns many people, of course, is the idea that illicit drug use "causes" crime that is both instrumental and expressive, and often violent.

We have already seen that crimes of violence are relatively rare among the addicts studied by Hanson and colleagues (1985), and that finding is confirmed in the studies just cited. But what of the idea that crimes are committed because people are high, not just to get them there? News reports surface from time to time about rapes and killings induced by PCP ("angel dust"), and over the years virtually all popular, but illegal, drugs have been alleged to cause users to commit heinous crimes.

No drug directly causes a person to rob, rape, or murder. However, some drugs do produce psychoactive changes that may alter a person's capacity to make decisions, and some are believed to stimulate the aggression centers of the brain, although others have the opposite effect. The most interesting and, to many, the most alarming fact that keeps surfacing, however, is that of all popular drugs, it is alcohol that is most consistently and strongly linked with crime. Alcohol turns up again and again in cases of homicide, child abuse, wife abuse, and rape. Alcohol is linked with more than 50 percent of all traffic fatalities. A survey of middle-aged prisoners shows that most have experienced problems with alcohol (Bureau of Justice Statistics, 1983d).

There seems to be little doubt that alcohol affects the central nervous system so as to lower reaction time as well as inhibitions, while at the same time it stimulates feelings of power but reduces motor coordination. A dangerous combination, sufficient to account for most vehicular accidents, perhaps, but still not a sufficient cause of most crimes. The missing ingredients are culture, social structure, personality, and a variety of situational factors that turn behavioral predispositions into criminal events.

There are various reasons that people cling to the idea of a causal connection between drugs and antisocial behavior. One is that the idea helps us account for criminal behavior without imputing criminal intent. If the person were not "under the influence," the crime would not have happened. The drug becomes an excuse, a rationalization and justification. Another reason pertains to enforcement: it is because we believe that (mostly) illegal drugs cause terrible crimes that we accept and support the severe penalties and secretive police tactics used against drug offenders. Ordinarily, people abhor snitches and distrust those who go about in disguise, pretending to be what they are not.

## Public Opinion and the Punitive Reaction to Illegal Drug Use

When we learn, correctly or incorrectly, that a certain substance is linked with crime, we are encouraged in our condemnation of it. However, if that substance happens to be widely used and is considered legal and socially acceptable, our fears and condemnation will be appropriately toned down. Thus although alcohol shows the strongest links with crime, we remain less concerned about its availability and use than we are about illegal and socially unacceptable drugs such as heroin and LSD. We do not want to believe that alcohol is as bad as these drugs, no matter what the evidence.

Drunk driving stands as a constant reminder of the dangers of complacency toward alcohol. The majority of all auto fatalities and accidents are attributed to drinking before or while driving. The carnage on our roads has stirred some citizens to outrage, especially when courts hand down lenient sentences to those convicted of vehicular manslaughter. Recent years have seen a nationwide mobilization of public and private resources to combat drunk driving. Private efforts such as MADD (Mothers Against Drunk Drivers) and SADD (Students Against Driving Drunk); and government-sponsored campaigns such as RID (Remove Intoxicated Drivers) have combined to pressure lawmakers into revising drunk driving laws. In 1983 twenty-seven states passed new laws or toughened existing statutes (*St. Louis Globe-Democrat*, June 28, 1983). But as with all legislative efforts, success will depend on the reactions of both the public and those who enforce the laws on the street and in the courtroom. Judging from the experience in other countries, the deterrent effect of such laws is likely to be temporary, if there is any at all (Ross, 1982).

National surveys show Americans to be most concerned about illegal drugs and much less concerned about alcohol. In one survey, far more of those interviewed (more than 90 percent) thought that heroin and the psychedelics were "harmful even in small amounts" than thought the same thing about alcohol (60 percent) (National Commission, 1973). And, in a survey of high school seniors, *all* commonly used illicit drugs were rated as more dangerous than alcohol (Johnston et al., 1981). Not surprisingly, the public supports punitive reactions to their sale and use. In one Gallup poll, 80 percent of those interviewed thought that heroin vendors should receive prison terms, and nearly 70 percent felt the same way about users. In another survey, 70 percent thought that police informants should be rewarded for turning in sellers of hard drugs (Hindelang et al., 1975).

Given this climate of opinion, we are likely to see a continuation of repressive drug enforcement and severe penalties for illegal drug sale and use. In our federal prisons, violators of laws dealing with narcotics, primarily heroin and cocaine, serve more time than most other offenders, an average of 35.5 months in 1979. In some states, the penalties for possession and sale of illegal drugs, including marijuana, are equaled or surpassed only by those for murder, rape, and kidnapping. And in Georgia, Indiana, and New Jersey, extended prison terms are now provided for certain drug offenses (Bradley, 1984).

As long as we continue to view the use of heroin, psychedelics, marijuana, cocaine, and other such drugs as the proper object of legal repression, our reactions will continue to be punitive, as they are with street crime generally. Those features of drug use linked with criminalization will therefore persist. The user will be labeled and treated as a criminal; black market supplies and high prices will flourish; fear, illness, suspicion, and instrumental crime will fill the user's life; and the user will be an outcast in a society of drug users.

# PART III

# Doing Something About Crime

# CHAPTER 12

# Policing Society

The modern state places its police force in the front line of the confrontation with those who violate its laws or otherwise threaten the social order. Whereas other agencies of the state create its laws, fashion its legal priorities, and hand down official penalties, the job of uncovering law violations, apprehending violators, and seeing to it that order is maintained rests squarely with the police. As a practical matter, the police must assume the burden of routinely translating law on the books into law in action.

To the civilian the police officer is the law. Not only are police officers expected to interpret, investigate, and take action in matters of law and order, but they are also the typical citizen's most common and direct contact with the social control aspect of government. Whether or not they are invited into a situation, once officers are present the situation takes on new meaning — the "long arm of the law" has entered, and attached to that arm is the enforcement machinery of government. Police officers carry symbols of the law and confirm for us in no uncertain terms what it represents. Their uniforms and badges symbolize their authority to take action in the name of the state; their weapons symbolize the availability of coercive force to back up their commands; their handcuffs symbolize the state's power of detention.

What the police do and do not do carries more weight in the legal process than the actions of any other single agency of criminal law — perhaps more than all others put together. It is *whether* and *how* laws are enforced that most directly and completely shapes the working character of the legal process. The police are clearly at the heart of the criminal process.

When we consider the police impact on the legal process, we must not forget that the police are usually the first officials to confront the crime — or, more important perhaps, the criminal. The police, in their capacity as "first-line enforcers," make the important decision to take official action when confronted by situations in which acts legally defined as criminal have occurred (Turk, 1971:67). If they choose not to identify an act as a crime, if they choose not to label a person as a suspect, or if they choose not to take official action even when they have applied the legally appropriate labels, then for all practical purposes the act or person will escape further processing at the hands of official agencies of criminal law. By their decisions not to invoke the legal process, the police effectively determine the outer boundaries of law in action (Goldstein, 1960:543). As a rule, the police are the first to apply the *official* labels crime and criminal and in doing so start the wheels of the criminal process turning. Whatever might happen at subsequent stages in the legal process can happen only after that crucial action has been taken.

Police not only merit serious attention in criminology as part of the official machinery of law, but they also shape the crime scene itself. In their roles as crime detectors, crime investigators, and crime preventers, the police make crime a part of their work, just as does the professional thief. This is not to say that the police commit crimes (although such acts do occur from time to time) but, rather, to draw attention to their work in dealing with criminal matters, complainants, witnesses, suspects, and victims and the impact this has on the character of crime within their jurisdictions. It is in how they perceive and do their jobs that we find the unique contribution police make to the overall shape of crime. Aspects of police work such as patrolling practices and techniques, discretion, use of force, training, departmental norms and policies, and the operation of specialty details (vice, traffic, or intelligence) all have a direct impact on the reality of crime as both an aspect and a product of social life.

# Origins and Growth of Modern Police

Although most of us assume police were always present in society, the police force as we know it today is of relatively recent origin. Most students of the police trace its modern origins to the rapid industrial expansion and population growth in the late eighteenth and early nineteenth centuries in western Europe, particularly England.

For centuries, England relied for law enforcement on the services of generally unpaid, though not necessarily unrewarded, volunteers and patronage appointees. Together with the military, these early constables and sheriffs saw to it that the interests of landowner, nobility, and monarchy were protected. Considerable time and energy were spent collecting taxes and making sure that villagers and townspeople ran their personal and community affairs on behalf of the wealthy and powerful. Since the tradition of self-help justice was slow to die away, the essential responsibility for doing something about crime was placed on the shoulders of the citizenry. Individual towns and villages were held accountable for the enforcement of laws and prohibitions, and enforcement, such as it was, was largely a collective affair. As towns grew, able-bodied men (especially property owners) were expected to volunteer for nighttime duty as watchmen. These unpaid citizens were to look out for disruptions of public order or threats to property and were to guard the moral standards of the day, which covered an incredible array of "sins." The constables worked at upholding law and order during the day; the watchmen took their turns at night.

## IMPACT OF THE INDUSTRIAL REVOLUTION

Though the constables and watchmen were accorded the powers of arrest and in some towns were armed, little public protection and crime control was apparently expected of them, and little was delivered. The job seems to have been treated as a big chore, and as time passed many property owners who had participated as watchmen found ways to escape the responsibility, whereas those who stayed on the job made the most of it through a variety of corrupt and unlawful practices. Over the centuries, public and corporate faith in the reliability of the constable and watchman system steadily deteriorated.

Even though the watch system was long held in low esteem, substantial changes were not introduced until the Industrial Revolution was in full swing and cities were beginning to swell with population. The rise of capitalism and the attendant Industrial Revolution changed economic and social conditions dramatically and in many ways extremely painfully. The migration of countless thousands of hopeful workers into already crowded towns and cities added new tensions to the hardships suffered by the masses. Brutal living conditions, small wages and long hours for those lucky enough to have jobs, growing poverty in the midst of growing affluence, and the ideology of laissez-faire all helped contribute to social disorder. Add to this periodic waves of assaultive and property crimes, vagrants and beggars by the thousands, and an extremely punitive system of laws, and the scene was set for a breakdown in the existing police system, which cried for reassessment and innovation.

Matters came to a head with a series of militant demonstrations and riots in which the disadvantaged and disaffected citizenry sought to improve their lot. Those reaping the benefits of industrialization, the property owners and emerging middle class, saw opposition and resistance and felt that the very foundations of the new industrial era were under attack. It became popular to refer to the poorer classes — the unemployed, the disadvantaged, the menial factory workers — as social scum or the dross of society, and these unfortunates found themselves lumped together with petty criminals under the title "dangerous classes." It was to contain and suppress these dangerous classes that many advocated police reforms and innovations (Critchley, 1972:38–42; Silver, 1967).

The English were reluctant to accept the notion of an organized, professional, paramilitary police force, feeling it would seriously threaten traditionally prized liberties (Banton, 1973:18). Despite this opposition, the reform proposals of men such as Patrick Colquhoun eventually gained widespread support. Colquhoun (1806) proposed that a well-regulated, full-time, centrally administered police organization be set up to prevent crime by patrolling the streets of London. Its officers would be salaried men under the direction of commissioners accountable directly to the government. In 1829, Parliament, under the leadership of Home Secretary Robert Peel, enacted the Metropolitan Police Act. This act followed the model for police organization and strategy long advocated by Colquhoun. So was born the forerunner of the modern police force.

In America, meanwhile, the larger cities were facing some of the same problems that so alarmed English politicians and businessmen. Though industrialization and modern capitalism were slower to appear on the American scene, by the early 1800s many American cities were experiencing rising rates of poverty, unemployment, migration, and crime and were feeling signs of growing urban unrest. Riots and demonstrations erupted in Boston, New York, and elsewhere, and the police came under attack for ineffectiveness in controlling the dangerous classes (Bacon, 1935; Lane, 1967).

During the early colonial period, American towns and cities had relied on the constable and watchman. The protection of life, property, and public order was considered a civic responsibility, as it had been in England, and able-bodied property owners were expected to assume constable and watchman duties on a rotating basis. But these policing methods soon acquired a dubious reputation; as towns grew and abuses of duty became commonplace, city fathers sought to beef up crime control efforts. In 1772, Williamsburg, Virginia, instituted one of the first municipal night patrols, composed of four "sober and discreet people" who were its permanent, paid members. Their job was "to patrol the streets of this city from ten o'clock every night until daylight the next morning, to cry the hours, and use their best endeavors to preserve peace and good order, by apprehending and bringing to justice all disorderly people (Weston and Wells, 1972:6). Boston and New York soon followed suit, and the new patrols were given authority to enforce all laws and to stop and question anyone suspected of criminal designs (see Bacon, 1935).

Yet these moderate reforms failed to satisfy the demands for order and crime control voiced in many quarters. American city officials looked to England for help. The London "New Police," as they were called, seemed to be doing a good job, so why not try the same system in America? In New York, an 1845 ordinance established a police force with around-the-clock patrol and law-enforcement duties. The police force was administered by a board of police commissioners (composed of the mayor, the recorder, and a city judge), a model soon after adopted by New Orleans in 1853, Cincinnati and San Francisco in 1859, Detroit, St. Louis, and Kansas City in 1861, and Buffalo and Cleveland in 1866.

It became patently clear, however, that the police commissions were little more than political tools in the hands of the parties in power. Further, they proved ineffective in managing the administrative affairs of their departments, with the result that they quickly fell into disfavor. By the early 1900s many cities had abandoned them in favor of a single public official acting as police executive.

One marked difference between the organization of the English and American police has been the "home rule" jurisdictional structure in America. Although local and regional hierarchies do administer the day-to-day operations of English police forces, the English police nevertheless retain a national character, in that Parliament and the Home Office oversee operations and the police have jurisdiction in what here would be called federal matters. In America, the Constitution reserves the bulk of criminal law matters for state control and makes a clear distinction between federal and state laws and their enforcement. However, law enforcement in America operates under a complicated system of jurisdictional controls, with local, county, state, and federal political units exercising varying degrees of authority and retaining varying amounts of autonomy in police affairs.

One consequence of this division of authority is the *politicization* of law enforcement. Police operations are not divorced from politics in England; but in America, they are firmly entrenched in politics, and day-to-day political interference at all levels is the risk, if not the inevitable consequence. The association between machine politics and police work has been well documented in the case of Chicago. At the turn of the century, when Chicago was experiencing unprecedented growth and industrial development, the law enforcement apparatus was an indispensable part of machine politics. Police promotions as well as judgeships were dependent on the demonstration of party loyalty. All police employees paid a portion of their salaries into the party treasury and were required to do its bidding, even if this meant occasionally breaking the law. Today the connection between politics and police may no longer be so blatant, but it is there nonetheless.

## EXPANSION OF POLICE SERVICES UNDER THE FEDERAL GOVERNMENT

Over the past few decades, American crime control agencies have mushroomed in number, personnel, and budgets. Today more than forty thousand federal, state, and local police agencies employ over half a million officers and operate with a combined budget in excess of $27 billion (Flanagan et al., 1982:7, 19). These figures do not include the more than one million people working in private police agencies (such as Pinkerton's) and in the various inspection services employed by public authorities (such as game wardens or bank examiners). If past trends indicate what the future holds, we can expect a continuing rise in the proportion of government expenditures on police operations, as well as in the ratio of law-enforcement personnel (including civilians employed by police agencies) to total population (Cobern, 1973:198).

One of the most noteworthy aspects of the growth in American police services has been the expansion of federal involvement in crime control. Although the Constitution reserves the bulk of general criminal law matters for the states, congressional action over the past seventy-five years or so has made extensive federal participation in law enforcement inevitable. Today, approximately fifty thousand criminal cases enter the federal system each year (Bureau of Justice Statistics, 1982b).

The first federal inroads into crime control came with the establishment of the Revenue Cutter Service (later the Coast Guard) under the Treasury Department in 1790. This agency was mainly concerned with smuggling and the collection of maritime revenues. It was quickly followed by creation of the Customs Service, also under the Treasury, in 1799. The establishment of regular land patrols at the borders followed, and national Prohibition in 1920 brought two special enforcement agencies for border surveillance and enforcement of federal laws, the Border Patrol and the Customs Patrol.

Other early federal enforcement agencies included the Postal Inspection Unit under the Post Office, whose agents were in 1880 given responsibility for the detection and arrest of postal law violators. The Bureau of Internal Revenue (now known as the IRS) was put in charge of enforcing general revenue laws and in 1868 received authority to employ special agents to uncover and pursue arrest and prosecution of tax evasions and frauds. With Prohibition, the Internal Revenue Intelligence Unit was established, and the bureau was placed in charge of enforcement of the new alcohol laws. The Harrison "Narcotics" Act of 1914 and the Volstead Act of 1919 created new federal crimes, requiring more federal enforcement services, and "federal functions . . . now involved a vastly increased amount of pure police work — patrolling, detection, searches and seizures, pursuit and arrest" (Millspaugh, 1972:71).

Though the Department of Justice was formally established in 1879, it did not become actively involved in crime control until 1908. In the interim one of its primary tasks was the collection of information on federal crimes and criminals, and heavy use was made of agents attached to other federal agencies. In 1908, however, the Justice Department received authorization from Congress to establish its own enforcement agency. First called the Bureau of Investigation, its name was changed to the FBI in 1935.

Originally sold to Congress as an agency mainly concerned with interstate commerce and the enforcement of the Sherman Antitrust Act, the bureau soon acquired jurisdiction over a whole range of federal laws, from vice (under the Mann Act of 1910), to violations of copyright, espionage, and radical political activism. A continued expansion of responsibilities and the leadership of J. Edgar Hoover (appointed director in 1924) provide some clues to understanding the phenomenal role this police agency has come to play in crime control and law enforcement.

From 1910 on, federal legislation added crime after crime to the enforcement responsibilities assumed by the bureau. Following the Mann Act — outlawing transportation of females across state lines for immoral purposes, but long used as a basis for investigation and arrest in sundry other vice matters — the new legislation covered, among other activities, the interstate transportation of motor vehicles (the Dyer Act of 1919), kidnapping and the use of mails to send threatening letters (the so-called Lindbergh Act of 1932), escape across state lines to avoid prosecution for felony crimes (the Fugitive Act of 1934), and bank robbery. Throughout this period, Hoover fashioned the bureau into one of the best-equipped, best-trained, and best-financed police bureaucracies in the world. Under his leadership, the FBI sponsored numerous innovations in law-enforcement techniques, developed a training academy unsurpassed anywhere for its instructional sophistication and depth, and garnered considerable acclaim for programs such as its uniform crime reporting, its "ten most wanted" list of fugitives, and its comprehensive crime information gathering.

The bureau also received considerable criticism over the years. Whatever Hoover's motives, he guided the agency into activities and policies that upset members of Congress, union leaders, journalists, fellow police officers, and even some of his own agents (whom the director could dismiss at will). Some of the strongest criticisms have concerned the bureau's involvement in the suppression of political activists, especially those of the left; its interference in management–worker conflicts; its extensive files on thousands of citizens, many of whom have never been convicted of a crime; and its participation in activities that were clearly criminal. The extent of the FBI's fall from grace in the early 1970s is evidenced by public opinion polls showing a considerable decline in the proportion of respondents holding "highly favorable" attitudes toward the agency. In 1965, 84 percent of those polled held highly favorable attitudes toward the FBI; by 1975, that figure had dropped to 37 percent (Hindelang et al., 1977:321). As Watergate fades, and memories of covert criminal activities dull, the reputation of the FBI will probably improve.

## The Police at Work

Before investigating the police at work, we should make a number of observations. First, *not all police agencies are alike*. They differ in the scope of their routine enforcement responsibilities; in the territorial and population size of their jurisdictions; in the composition of the populations they serve; in their size, training, and salaries; and in their internal organization. Second, *not all police officers are alike*. They differ in background, personality, experience, attitudes, behavior on the job, qualifications, and interests. Third, though collectively referred to as the police, the occupational demands placed on any one officer differ from those placed on another. *There is no one type of police work*. A division of labor, or occupational specialization, exists in police work just as it does in most other work organizations. Finally, it must be remembered that policing in America is different from that found in many other countries. Therefore, what is described here may not necessarily apply elsewhere (see Archambeault and Fenwick, 1983). For at least these three reasons, then, we should remember that when speaking of the police we are not dealing with a collection of homogeneous organizations, people, or activities. We are dealing with people and agencies that share a common occupational responsibility, the enforcement of laws and the preservation of domestic order.

### JOINING THE FORCE

Much police work is "dirty work" (Hughes, 1964:23–36). Dirty work is work that respectable or good people shun, prefer not to have to think about, and leave for others to perform. It is work that is at once demanded and rejected; it is work that is both disgusting and indispensable; it is work that garners relatively little prestige and recognition for its practitioners, while at the same time it is touted as essential to maintaining the "proper" moral and social standards of the community; it is work that protects the in-group from the out-group, but those who consider themselves "in" hire outsiders to perform it.

The dirty aspects of police work — handling drunks, dead bodies, accident victims; dealing with family squabbles, prostitutes, homosexuals, muggers, and other "deviants"; and sometimes using violence to achieve control — merely reinforce the view that such work is not for us (Harris, 1973:5–6). To most respectable citizens it is precisely this facet of police work that identifies the real job of the police. How often do police officers hear: "Instead of bothering me, why don't you go and arrest real criminals like we're paying you to?" or "Why don't you clean up the streets so that respectable people like me can walk safely at night?"

In view of the dirty work of the job it is reasonable to wonder whether there is anything particularly striking about those who enter the occupation. Is there a pool or supply of individuals who are ready candidates for police work? Do they share social and personality characteristics that make them somehow different from other citizens? Are only certain types of people actively recruited by police agencies?

There are few indications that police recruits are particularly different from those who enter other occupations. It is true that they show a fair degree of homogeneity in their educational, occupational, and family backgrounds. The recruit typically comes from a lower-middle- or working-class background, has no more than a high school education, and has previously worked in clerical, sales, or manual jobs (McNamara, 1967). For many, police work represents a step up the occupational status ladder. But this is true for millions of other American workers.

The evidence on personality traits again offers no sound basis for distinguishing recruits from their peers. Some have argued that the police recruit exhibits traits associated with the "authoritarian personality." Among these traits are conventionalism (rigid adherence to middle-class values), cynicism (a view that "things are going to pot"), aggression, and stereotypical thinking. Administering the F-scale (designed to measure authoritarianism) to 116 New York City police recruits, Arthur Niederhoffer and John H. McNamara found a relatively high mean score of 4.15 (the highest possible score is 7.0). But this score was almost identical with previous scores for general working-class samples, indicating nothing exceptional about the recruits, considering their predominantly working-class backgrounds. In summarizing his discussion of the issue, Niederhoffer concluded that although police officers may well develop strong authoritarian personalities, once they have been exposed to training and the demands of the job, nothing suggests "self-selection among authoritarian personalities prior to appointment" (Niederhoffer, 1967:159).

Why, then, do people enter police work? Niederhoffer suggests they do so for reasons such as security, decent working conditions, adventure, and relatively good pay, which make the job attractive to those with little formal education, few marketable skills, and lower-class backgrounds. David

Bayley and Harold Mendelsohn (1968:32–33), investigating Denver police entrants, echo this interpretation:

> One does not need a special theory to explain why men go into police work. . . . One explains recruitment to the police force as one explains recruitment to any occupation, namely, in terms of its status, rewards, minimal educational requirements, and conditions of service. . . . Recruits bring to police work the same kinds of evaluations of the police made by people generally. They are neither more starry-eyed nor more cynical. They choose to be policemen because it fits their potentialities and promises the kinds of rewards considered by them commensurate with their background and training. By and large, it represents an advance over what their parents obtained. One understands police recruitment, then, in terms of a practical upward step in social mobility as well as an improvement in life prospects.

When questioned about their reasons for joining the force, officers voice many of the same reasons that move people to seek nonpolice jobs. Among the most often cited reasons are security and retirement benefits. Few officers speak of excitement, action, or the dirty facets of police work as reasons for joining, and few recruits are drawn to police work for idealistic reasons, such as helping rid society of criminals or contributing to law and order. These findings reinforce the view that those who enter police work are in no way a special category of people and are no different from others with similar backgrounds.

Most police agencies exercise considerable control over who is accepted for police work. The days when departments were willing to take just about anyone are over. The typical police agency now requires applicants to pass a standard civil service exam, undergo a battery of other tests and examinations (sometimes including lie-detector tests), and pass checks on health, background, and character. Many agencies place considerable weight on these last checks, and a good portion of recruits never make it past one or another of these hurdles (Harris, 1973:16–17).

Interviews are especially important as a means of weeding out "undesirables." The interview is usually conducted by senior officers, and it permits recruiters to reject applicants who might otherwise be acceptable (Bent, 1974:16). In this way, recruits who possess undesirable value systems or whose political attitudes and ethnic backgrounds conflict with those dominant in the force can also be weeded out. This tends to perpetuate the class, ethnic, and value characteristics of those already employed. Such homogeneity in personnel makes it easier for departments to retain already fashioned policies and practices, to reduce potential internal disruptions, and to maintain more complete control over their policing operations. From the standpoint of the officers themselves, it cements distinctions between the in-group and out-group and aids in the development of predictability, solidarity, and secrecy. These three important dimensions of organization and work are further emphasized as the recruit becomes a full-fledged police officer.

## TRAINING AND THE ACQUISITION OF POLICE PERSPECTIVES

Most police officers will tell you that the only way to learn about police work is by doing it; experience counts for all. Although this view is by no means unique to police officers, many features of police work not found in most other occupations underscore the importance of experience. The police carry guns and other weapons that can be used with deadly results. They are subject to other people's aggressions and hostilities just because they are police officers. They are given the authority to act in situations in which other citizens must stand back. In many jurisdictions, they are expected to be police officers twenty-four hours a day. And if they make mistakes, they may be subject to criminal and civil suits.

Because most recruits are ill prepared for the demands of police work and also because there are insistent pleas for professionalization of the police, many police agencies offer quite extensive training courses for their new recruits. If they have no police academy, they send them to universities and colleges with special law-enforcement curricula. These training programs introduce the newcomer to the legal, ethical, organizational, and operational facets of police work. It is while enrolled in the programs that the recruit gets a first taste of what it means to be a police officer. It is also during this period of formal training that an intensive socialization process begins and the "cord binding the rookie to the civilian world is cut" (Niederhoffer, 1967:43).

In training by police instructors, rookies see for the first time something of the ambiguities and conflicts inherent in police work. They learn that they are expected to enforce all criminal laws but that in practice they must be selective. They learn that the public is something akin to an enemy — they are told to be suspicious, always on the lookout for a setup, and never to rely on any help from citizens — but that they must serve and protect its members. They learn that although the powers that be demand that they combat crime and arrest criminals, those powers also insist that police officers follow procedures, even if that sometimes means the escape of a criminal, the commission of a crime, or perhaps injury and death. They learn that police work is also public relations work and that valued attributes such as zeal and honesty may get them into trouble with their superiors. Most important of all, perhaps, they learn that what they are told in class often differs markedly from what they know from experience as private citizens. Whatever idealism they brought with them is soon forgotten — perhaps temporarily but most likely permanently.

**Defensiveness, Professionalism, Depersonalization**   A study of a police training academy suggests that one of the primary goals of formal police training is the development of uniform behavior among officers so that there is less room for personal judgment and individualized behavior (Harris, 1973). Recruits must be stripped of their identity and taught to assume a police identity; to think, act, and be a police officer. Richard Harris suggests that three themes emerge during training to help generate in recruits a proper police perspective. The first, perhaps most important, is *defensiveness* — to be alert to the many dangers of police work and to build defenses against them. These dangers are not merely physical. They include the dangers of procedural violations that can lead to criminal charges, civil suits, reprimands, lost cases, and dismissal. They include the dangers of corruption, inefficiency, and emotional involvement in police–citizen encounters as well as the danger of provoking hostile and punitive reactions by members of the public who are in a position to make trouble for the department.

The second theme is *professionalization* — the development of a professional image, techniques, esprit de corps, service ideals, and a sense of "us" as opposed to "them." The third theme is *depersonalization,* which has two sides. On the one hand, recruits must realize that those with whom they come in contact, the public and their own supervisors, often treat them as faceless, lacking an individual identity; they are less persons than things. They also learn that some occupational demands necessitate the denial of personal qualities — police officers dare not personalize their official relationships with the public and must beware of those who try to personalize that relationship. The other side of depersonalization involves the officer's own adoption of stereotypes, black-and-white distinctions, and intolerance of out-groups, whose members, in turn, become faceless.

In Harris's view, one important product of defensiveness, professionalization, and depersonalization is the cultivation of solidarity among recruits: "a subjective feeling of belongingness and implication in each other's lives" (Harris, 1973:163). This solidarity, the we-feeling that comes with group identity and belonging, firms up and helps preserve the police identity fostered during training.

**Danger, Authority, Efficiency**  In a study of city police at work, Jerome Skolnick argued that police officers typically develop a distinctive "working personality" (1975:42–70). A unique combination of work elements foster in the police a particular way of looking at the world and responding to it. The key elements identified by Skolnick are *danger, authority,* and *efficiency.* Together they encourage the development of suspicion, social isolation, and solidarity — central characteristics of the police officers' relations with the world in which they work. They become suspicious of the events, persons, and things they learn to associate with danger, and the defensive posture caused by this suspicion moves them to erect barriers between themselves and the world. Even if they might not wish to erect barriers — as in their relations with neighbors, family acquaintances, civilian friends, and members of the opposite sex — they find that barriers may be erected for them, because their work makes them less desirable as a friend.

This social isolation is enhanced by the police role as an enforcer of public order and public morality: "Typically, the policeman is required to enforce laws representing puritanical morality, such as those prohibiting drunkenness, and also laws regulating the flow of public activity, such as traffic laws. In these situations, the policeman directs the citizenry, whose typical response denies recognition of his authority and stresses his obligation to respond to danger" (Skolnick, 1975:44). Expected to enforce laws that they may not support or that are resented by large segments of the population, the police officers' official authority once again encourages erection of barriers and contributes to social isolation.

Added to the effects of authority and danger is a persistent pressure to be efficient, to produce, to demonstrate that they are living up to the expectations of their superiors. Sometimes required to fill quotas for such things as traffic tickets (Skolnick reports that motorcycle patrol officers were required to write two tickets an hour) and vice arrests (a "rigidly enforced" expectation in some cities), police officers find themselves further alienating the public as they seek to meet demands for efficiency.

With barriers erected between themselves and the general public the police seek support and reciprocity in their relations with colleagues. To counteract the threat of danger and the effects of public hostility and to fulfill the persistent demands that they produce, the police are drawn together in relationships of mutual dependence and aid (see Manning, 1977). The solidarity thus encouraged becomes a central facet of police working relationships and officers draw on their we-feeling as they act out their roles. Sensing that they can rely on neither the public nor their higher-echelon superiors, they turn to one another, further separating themselves from the world around them.

## STEREOTYPING AND THE EXERCISE OF POLICE AUTHORITY

Modern police officers must reduce the complexities of a heterogeneous world to manageable proportions. In this respect they are no different from the rest of us. So that we can handle the task of living amidst a vast array of life-styles, living arrangements, value systems, and behavior patterns, we resort to simplification, distortion, and, inevitably, stereotypes.

A stereotypical view of the world means that we treat others not on the basis of complete, impartial knowledge about them, but, rather, according to what "box" we can readily place them in. Obviously, the result need not always be injurious to the person so categorized, but often it is. When the police stereotype, the potential for injury is clearly accentuated, for they are in a position to take the kind of actions prohibited to the rest of us. In their official roles they can search, seize, command, arrest, wound, and even kill, often on no firmer ground than suspicion or probable cause. In other words, if events, persons, or things are defined by the police as requiring authoritative and coercive action, then whether or not they deserve it, they are subject to that action.

All this means that authority can be invoked in situations that would not warrant such action if all the facts were known. From the standpoint of the police, however, the possible undesirable consequences of this are outweighed by the benefits of stereotyping. From the first day of training through the rest of their careers, the police find little reason to find out all the facts first, nor can they afford to. If anything, they learn that the facts are less important than initial appearances and that the best way to approach appearances is to have ready a set of categories for them.

As noted already, suspicion is central to the police officers' approach to their work. It is toward people, objects, places, and events labeled suspicious that the police direct much of their attention. Perceptual categorization and simplification are important devices in defining what is suspicious — police cannot suspect everything and everyone. It has been suggested that the police arrive at their categorization of persons and things as suspicious through *pragmatic induction*:

> Past experience leads them to conclude that more crimes are committed in the poorer sections of town than in the wealthier areas, that Negroes are more likely to cause public disturbances than whites, and that adolescents are a greater source of trouble than other categories of the citizenry. On the basis of these conclusions, the police divide the population and physical territory under surveillance into a variety of categories, make some initial assumptions about the moral character of the people and places in these categories, and then focus attention on those categories of persons and places felt to have the shadiest moral characteristics. (Werthman and Piliavin, 1967:68–69)

In this way the police create a self-fulfilling prophecy: the official criminals come from precisely those areas and groups that fit the stereotype. On the other hand, those areas and groups that do not fit the stereotype retain their "clean" look and continue to receive modest police scrutiny.

English sociologist Dennis Chapman (1968) provides a number of illustrations of the impact and perpetuation of police stereotypes and their attendant enforcement patterns. Chapman tells of a case in which for six months residents of an upper-middle-class neighborhood removed building materials from a construction site:

> Each evening and every weekend, after the workmen had departed, the site was visited by between five and fifteen men with motor-cars or wheelbarrows. They removed bricks, tiles, paving slabs, timber, mortar, and other building materials systematically, and often in large quantities. (Chapman, 1968:56)

When asked by an observer why he did not intervene, a police officer who happened to witness one evening's thievery replied that he assumed they all had permission! Neither the thieves nor the circumstances fit the prevailing stereotypes of suspicious persons and activities. Had they done so, Chapman does not doubt that police action would have been taken.

Contrast this case with an incident Alan Bent (1974) observed during his investigation of the Memphis police at work. Some police officers were under pressure to produce following an uneventful evening. Their categorization of adolescents as suspicious persons directed their subsequent activity and paid off in a pinch. Officers in four cars descended on an area adjoining a converted warehouse in which a dance was being held. The officers made numerous attempts to uncover evidence of illegal activity by teenagers moving around the area or parked in their cars. Eventually four adolescents were discovered with a couple of joints, and a bust was made. The stereotype linking young people, play, and crime (in this case illegal drugs) had worked, thus providing fuel for its further use.

The fact that considerable energy and resources are spent dealing with members of selected segments of the population — usually the poor, the inner-city residents, the young, and the black — should not be taken to mean that police-enforcement practices reflect only *police* prejudice, stereotypes, and decisions. On the contrary, the police are conforming to dominant American stereotypes, prejudices, and policies rather than deviating from them, and as such we must look beyond the police for an explanation of resource and energy allocation and police-enforcement patterns. The police operate in a sociopolitical climate that generally rewards those who conform to the dominant culture. In America the white middle class looks not to itself for the criminal and the disorderly but, rather, to those believed to pose threats to order, stability, and the preservation of traditional values.

Some evidence of police conformity with prevailing middle-class standards comes from Bent's study in Memphis. Bent found much agreement in self-appraisals and attitudes toward others between the police and white middle-class samples, despite the disparate backgrounds of the two groups. Though police views of some subjects differed from those of the white middle-class sample, their views differed most consistently from those held by blacks and students. Both the police and the typical white middle-class respondents held to an "order-stability" value structure, stressing crime control, improved police efficiency and production, and enforcement patterns aimed at preserving order and stability. This value system is contrasted with the "democratic-active," which emphasizes service responsibilities, social needs, due process, justice, human dignity, and respect for human differences. The order-stability group — represented by the white, middle-aged person with at least a high school education who earns over $15,000 a year — held "warm feelings" toward the military, conservatives, Republicans, the police, whites, and the National Guard. So did the police sample. The group held "cold feelings" toward liberals, blacks, feminists, and other persons and groups most closely associated with social innovation. So did the police. Since white, middle-class individuals typically are in the best position to influence the activities of governments and their agencies, it should come as no surprise that the police share a similar set of values and engage in behavior in support of them.

It is interesting to note that programs of higher education have been advocated as a means of broadening police attitudes, of reducing prejudice, authoritarianism, stereotyping, and hostility toward those with whom they come into contact as enforcers. In 1966, 184 colleges and universities offered degree programs in criminal justice; in 1978, there were 816 such programs (Kobetz, 1978:1). Yet it appears far from conclusive that higher education for police greatly changes their attitudes and behavior. Indeed, "there is strong evidence that the value of police education may be nullified by the realities of the police role as it is now constituted" (Weiner, 1974:323). The nature of police work, especially the need to be suspicious and to pattern enforcement in terms of arrest-productive stereotypes, coupled with pressure from middle-class law-and-order interests, seem to be blocking any real liberalization of police attitudes and behavior.

## Police Exercise of Discretion

In their daily work, the police are faced with two related decisions whenever they enter a situation. The first is whether or not to take any action at all, and the second is what kind of action to take. It is in making these decisions that the police invoke their awesome discretionary powers. The exercise of discretion lies at the heart of real police work, and its ramifications touch the entire legal process, not to mention the people immediately involved.

Discretion is, of course, exercised at all levels of the legal process:

> Police officers decide what "suspicious" persons to "stop and frisk," to round up in a "dragnet raid," to warn, or to arrest. Judges pass on the guilt of suspected offenders, make decisions on whom to release and whom to hold for further hearings (in jail or on bail), and determine the kind and length of sentence. Prosecuting attorneys exercise considerable latitude in what cases to prosecute and when to negotiate with the defense attorney over pleas, charges, and dispositions. A sifting and sorting operation occurs in which certain persons are processed through the legal machinery, with a steadily increasing attrition as suspected offenders move through the various procedural stages of the criminal justice system. At each of these stages, decisions made by certain legal officials will limit the alternatives for those operating in subsequent stages. (Hills, 1971:22)

Since the police are typically the first legal reactors to exercise discretion, their decisions are crucial to determining law in action and the official character of the crime scene.

### CONSTRAINTS ON THE EXERCISE OF DISCRETION

Discretionary decisions are available to the police in all police operations. Some scholars have argued that the most important discretionary decisions are the negative ones, such as not to arrest, not to investigate, or not to bargain. When the police do take action, their decisions are often subject to review and examination, but this is seldom the case for decisions not to invoke the legal process, for these decisions are usually of low visibility. Negative decisions, then, can remain largely free from scrutiny by interested

The manner of an arrest has both practical and symbolic value. The suspect is rendered harmless, and witnesses are reminded of the power of the state.

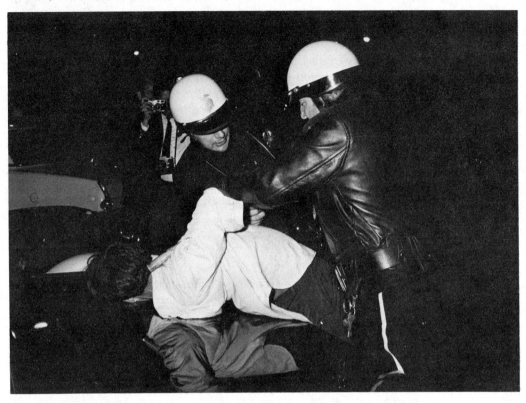

nonpolice parties and by other police officers, particularly superiors. This promotes secrecy in police operations while lessening both internal and external control.

Given the low visibility of police decisions not to invoke the criminal process, conclusive evidence regarding such discretionary actions is hard to find. However, both insider and outsider observations provide some clues to why and when nonenforcement decisions are made. We can frame the discussion around seven observations made by Mortimer and Sanford Kadish (1973:74–75).

First, the police may believe that the legislative purpose behind a particular law "would not be served by arresting all persons who engage in the prohibited conduct" (Kadish and Kadish, 1973:74). Examples are gambling laws, various sexual prohibitions (those concerning consenting adults), and laws considered obsolete. Second, some enforcement selectivity is inevitable given the limitations of police resources. These resource limitations involve more than police time, money, personnel, or equipment: if there is not enough jail space, police arrests and bookings may decline. In her study of skid-row alcoholics, Wiseman (1970:71) found a negative relationship between the number of people that the police arrest and the jail's level of occupancy.

Third, the police may be aware that some laws prohibit behavior that is acceptable and expected in some subcultures of society and thus treat violators selectively on that basis. Fourth, in some situations, victims are more interested in restitution than criminal sanctions (recall the discussion of shoplifting on pp. 226–231), and the police go along with victim interests. Fifth, the police shape their enforcement patterns to some extent on the basis of community preferences. An excellent illustration of this by Ernest Alix (1969:332–339) describes police enforcement practices in a run-down river and railroad town. Rather than bust taverns and other commercial violators of liquor and vice laws on each violation, the police responded to community pressures by rotating their raids, thus keeping the offending businesses open and the revenue flowing into the town's meager bank account. Sixth, the police routinely make use of informants, and many of these informants are known offenders whom the police decide not to arrest or charge in view of their potential usefulness:

> [The police officer's] steadiest source of information is what he collects as rent for allowing people to operate without arresting them. "Prostitutes and faggots are good. If you treat 'em right, they will give you what you want. They don't want to get locked up, and you can trade that off for information. If you rap 'em around," a very skilled patrolman said, "the way some guys used to, or lock 'em up, you don't get nothing." At a lunch counter another officer said, looking at the waitress who was getting his order, "She thinks I don't know she's hustling the truck drivers. She'll find out tomorrow. I don't care if she makes a few bucks on her back, but she is gonna tell me what I want to know." (Rubinstein, 1973:207)

Finally, there are some occasions when officers do not invoke the criminal process because "the personal harm the offender would suffer on being arrested outweighs the law enforcement gains . . . achieved by arresting." Such decisions usually have to do with the status of the offender (age, occupation, and community standing) and are most likely to be invoked for nonstreet crimes such as shoplifting. They are unlikely, therefore, to be invoked in dealings with those segments of society stereotypically linked with serious crime, namely, the poor and relatively powerless.

To these seven clues concerning discretionary nonenforcement practices we should add the impact of relationships between the police and other agents of the legal process. What the police do in their daily work cannot be divorced from what goes on among prosecutors, judges, and other legal reactors. If the decision is whether or not to arrest or charge a suspect, a negative decision may well be influenced by police expectations regarding how the case will be handled at subsequent stages in the criminal process: "Whatever their own views of the importance of particular crimes might be, if it is common knowledge that local magistrates take a very different view which is reflected in their sentencing decisions, the police will often not wish to 'waste' time on arresting individuals who may subsequently be given a merely nominal sentence by the court" (Bottomley, 1973a:41).

Steven Box (1981:162–163) argues that police discretion is further constrained by *interpretational* issues, by ideological and theoretical considerations, and by *occupational* and career worries.

Interpretational issues are important because police officers must impute meaning to behavior brought to their attention. But what meaning should they assign? Witnesses, victims, suspects, and other officers all may see a given situation differently, and as long as ambiguity exists, the investigating officer's decision will likely be influenced most by those actors most skilled at creating believable impressions of the "true" picture.

Ideological and theoretical considerations come in because what an officer decides to do (or not do) is "frequently coloured by his ideological values, his moral standards, his beliefs about the causes of criminal behavior and his stereotypical conceptions of criminals" (Box, 1981:163). Police are human beings, after all, and it is senseless to imagine that they are somehow immune from bias.

Worries about personal safety may lead an officer to withdraw from a situation, but a more general influence, Box suggests, is the *symbolic* threat posed by certain citizens. These are the ones who police believe will go over their heads and appeal to higher-ups if street decisions are not to their liking. Denver police interviewed by Bayley and Mendelsohn (1968:102) held a clear image of who those citizens are: the wealthy, the connected, those in professional jobs.

## POLICE USE OF DEADLY FORCE

Police exercise of discretion is inevitable and desirable. It also carries with it enormous responsibility. Exercised humanely, cautiously, and in the service of all the people, discretion makes for law enforcement that is just and responsive to social needs. Exercised inhumanely, incautiously, or in the service of prejudice or special interest, discretion becomes intolerable and must be curbed.

Nowhere is the problem of discretion more acute than in the decision to use deadly force against a civilian. Police in America and in many other (but not all) countries are armed with guns and are prepared to use them under various conditions. The law in most states requires that one of the following conditions be met for the police to legitimately use deadly force: (1) a suspect is engaged in a felony; (2) a suspect is fleeing the scene of a felony; or (3) a suspect is resisting arrest and has placed the officer or a civilian in mortal danger. Recent legislative decisions in some states have resulted in a narrowing of police discretion by limiting the first two conditions to forcible felonies only.

Research on police use of deadly force has generally supported three conclusions. First, rates of police shootings vary considerably from one jurisdiction to the next. In one comparison of nine American cities, a 1,500 percent variation was found even after taking account of the level of community violence and the number of arrest incidents involving violent felonies and, therefore, some risk to arresting officers. Another study found police shootings to be twice as high per 1,000 police officers in Memphis as in New York (Fyfe, 1982:707–722; see also Knoohuizen et al., 1972).

Second, the percentage of shooting incidents involving black suspects is disproportionately high. In the case of fatal shootings, blacks are anywhere from five to thirteen times more likely than whites are to be killed by police action. And when we look at the young (10 to 14 years) and the elderly (65 and over), the disproportionate representation of blacks is even more stark: Paul Takagi (1979:34) found that "black youngsters and old men have been killed by the police at a rate 15 to 30 times greater than that of whites at the same age."

The third finding drawn from some studies describes the most likely shooting situation among urban police forces:

> The most common shooting of a civilian by a police officer in urban America is one in which an on-duty, uniformed, white officer shoots an armed black male between the ages of 17 and 30 at night in a public location, in connection with an armed robbery. Typically, the shooting is subsequently deemed justifiable by the police department following an internal investigation. Even if the officer is criminally prosecuted, a jury is unlikely to convict. (Geller and Karales, 1981:1818)

Two caveats must be held in mind when we consider these findings. First, they are based on data and methodologies that in most cases cannot be compared. To mention one important variation, there are different ways to compute rates of police shootings: (1) in terms of population, such as the number of shootings per 100,000 residents; (2) in terms of police personnel, such as the number of shootings per 1,000 police officers; or (3) in terms of police–citizen encounters involving risk, such as the number of shootings per 1,000 violent felony arrests. Studies using different measures of shooting rates should not be lumped together. Another important difference among studies is the source of information on police shootings. Some studies rely only on official police accounts, whereas others have sought to include recollections of witnesses and survivors.

Second, many studies have not really tapped the situational component in police shootings. It is probably safe to say that no two shooting situations are ever the same, and decisions are often made on split-second judgment with all sorts of influences crowding in on the officer's thoughts, affecting the officer's actions, and pushing the event in perhaps unpredictable directions. The same can be said of other participants in the encounter, and since it is an *inter*action, what one person does materially affects what others will do.

Jurisdictional variations and racial issues in police shootings cannot properly be evaluated in the absence of detailed incident-by-incident information, both on situations in which officers fire and on those in which they do not fire their weapons. Needless to say, most police officers never do fire their weapons at a civilian, and yet many of them find themselves in encounters in which different decisions could well have been made. In fact, different police departments may experience similar rates of shootings but vary considerably in terms of the situations in which those shootings occurred.

James Fyfe suggests that an important distinction can be made between police–citizen encounters in which use of deadly force is *elective* and those in which it is *nonelective*. Elective shootings are "those in which the officer involved may elect to shoot or not to shoot at little or no risk to himself or others." Nonelective shootings are "those in which the officer has little real choice but to shoot or to risk death or serious injury to himself or others." Fyfe calls elective shootings "real exercises in discretion" (1982:710).

Any shooting situation will fall somewhere along a continuum from nonelective to elective. By hindsight an officer may put an encounter closer to the elective end than he or she actually did when in the situation; similarly, observers may later define a situation differently from how they did at the time; finally, persons who later hear the "facts" may interpret a situation differently from either the officer involved or any witnesses. All this merely shows how difficult it is to construct a picture of an encounter that does justice to both the subjective interpretations of participants and the objective characteristics of the situation. Nowhere is this more germane than in the not untypical situation in which an officer shoots a suspect who is actually unarmed and could not in fact have placed either the officer or any other party in personal jeopardy. Second-guessing is a luxury that only those not involved in an encounter can afford.

With this in mind, Fyfe believes that incidents falling close to the elective end of the continuum are more likely to be influenced by such things as departmental rules and policies, the attitudes and prejudices of officers, and their level of training in firearms, methods of nonlethal control of suspects, and human relations. These factors are *internal* to police organization and work. On the other hand, incidents falling close to the nonelective end are more likely to be influenced by factors *external* to police work and organization, such as the amount and type of crime in a jurisdiction and the participation rates of different population groups in activities likely to precipitate shootings.

What this means, among other things, is that when a city experiences high rates of *elective* shootings, they may reflect *police* norms, values, and competences rather than the behavior of the criminals. This would be a significant clue to the direction that control strategies should take (assuming, of course, that police shootings are something that should be brought under control). The changes we would look for would be internal rather than external. On the other hand, a city with many nonelective shootings would want to consider ways of reducing the frequency and seriousness of threats to the police or others. This does not mean that control efforts in the second case would ignore changes in police work or organization, for police behavior may itself contribute to levels of violence in a community. Rather, the focus is on changing values, norms, and opportunities that support violence in the broader community, of which the police are one part.

In comparing New York and Memphis shootings, Fyfe found that the elective-nonelective distinction was very useful in contrasting the two cities. In New York, over 60 percent of the shootings that occurred between 1971 and 1975 were interpreted by officers to have been in "defend life" (nonelective) situations; in contrast, over 50 percent of the incidents in Memphis from 1969 to 1974 occurred in situations in which officers were seeking to apprehend suspects in property crimes, not violent crimes (which in Memphis were classified as "defend life" situations). The data showed that police in Memphis were fourteen times as likely to shoot at property crime suspects than officers in New York. That difference was explained mainly by the much more liberal shooting rules in effect at the time in the Memphis police department.

On the racial question, further analysis of the Memphis situation showed that 85.7 percent of those shot at were black and 14.3 percent white. Rates of shooting per one thousand officers showed that blacks were six times as likely as whites to have been shot at and *missed*, thirteen times as likely to have been shot at and *wounded*, and over three times as likely to have been shot at and *killed*. Rate differences by race remained when calculated in terms of population and by felony arrests. Notably, the disproportionate representation of black victims in police shootings in Memphis was greatest in the case of elective shootings. In addition, between 1969 and 1976, 50 percent of those killed who were black were killed in nonassaultive situations, versus only 12.5 percent in the case of whites (Fyfe, 1982:712–721).

**Shooting in Chicago** The Memphis findings leave little room for doubt that internal influences — in that city's case department policies and racial attitudes among police — are a major factor accounting for the frequency and character of police shootings. However, this is only one city in one state and until further comparable data are secured, Memphis should certainly not be used as a basis for generalizing about police attitudes and conduct.

A very detailed study of Chicago police shootings (Geller and Karales, 1981;1982) tells us interesting things about that city's experience and warns once again about judging events on the basis of gross impressions. The Chicago study is especially significant because it represents the first time a major American city opened up its shooting investigation files to public scrutiny.

Some of the major findings from that study are as follows: (1) The most common shooting situation was one in which a suspect used or threatened to use a gun (51 percent), followed by flight without other resistance (17 percent), and use or threat of force other than with a gun (14 percent). Notably, 10 percent of the incidents (52 cases) involved accidents and 3 percent stray bullets. (2) When calculated in terms of population figures, blacks were from 3.8 to 6.6 times more likely to be shot than whites, but when calculated in terms of forcible felony arrests, blacks were only slightly more likely to be shot. (3) Blacks were more likely than whites to be involved in gun use and threat situations, and almost 3 times *less* likely to have been shot accidentally. (4) Although 70 percent of all shootings involved white officers, the rate per 1,000 officers was higher for blacks, and blacks were much more likely to shoot black suspects than were white officers. (5) Black officers were more likely than white officers to shoot while *off* duty and 29 times more likely to shoot civilians in high-crime areas than off-duty white officers.

These findings point to two conclusions. First, most of the shootings in Chicago appear to be nonelective, at least according to police accounts. Second, the disproportionate involvement of black victims and off-duty black police officers suggests that many Chicago police shootings may be patterned according to the residency of black officers in areas where opportunities for and risks of violent crime are highest. In short, the authors show no evidence of a significant racist factor in police shootings in Chicago.

It is possible that with many police shootings we are seeing the clash of two violent subcultures. On the one hand we have the subculture of police violence — a legitimized subculture associated with rule enforcement — and on the other, an inner-city subculture of the ghetto — an outlawed subculture at odds with the Establishment and deemed a threat to it. Many inner-city black youths expect violence in their daily lives and come prepared for it. Police who live in or enter these same areas also expect and come prepared for violence. And we have every reason to believe that violence reinforces violence. Surveys have shown that respondents who would accept relatively high levels of police violence are themselves likely to have been involved in violence and accept it in a variety of interpersonal situations (Blumenthal et al., 1972).

Public support for police use of violence in dealing with the "criminal element" is bound up with the catch-the-criminal-at-all-costs theme. Pushed by television and movie portrayals of cops and robbers, the theme has a cherished image: the police hero firing a .45 caliber revolver at some fast-disappearing crook, felling the crook with one shot. The fact that most police do not carry forty-fives is only one of the things wrong with the image. What may be especially dangerous about it, however, is its impact on impressionable youth, especially those who have come to see themselves as having trouble with the law one way or another. "Be prepared for violence," television tells them, "because the police are!" When all is said and done, "catch the criminal at all costs" is not a sound doctrine for either the police or the public to support. One consequence is police fatalities and injury, the subject of the next section.

## SHOOTINGS OF POLICE

Ninety-one law enforcement officers were killed in 1981 (see Table 12.1), and many more were shot at and wounded. From 1976 to 1983, just over half the 903 police officers killed were shot (Schmidt, 1985:6). The shooting *of* police officers is the other side of the police violence coin, and from the police standpoint it is the most important side. The police may come prepared for violence, they may even expect it, but when it happens to one of their own they all share in the hurt and resentment. That, above all, is at the heart of the police personality.

One of the few good studies of police shootings by civilians is by Geller and Karales (1982), the authors who investigated shootings by police in Chicago. In that city they found that nearly half of all police shot between 1974 and 1978 (187) were off duty; 27 percent shot themselves, mostly by accident but 11 were suicides, a rate higher than that for the general population. Twenty officers (11 percent) were shot by fellow officers, mostly accidentally. More than half of the off-duty officers shot were black (compared with 17.5 percent representation on the Chicago Police Department as a whole); 91 percent of the black off-duty officers shot were shot in medium- and high-crime districts where they lived. Black officers off duty were 13 times more likely to be shot in high crime areas than off-duty white officers; by contrast, off-duty black officers were only twice as likely to be shot in low-crime areas as white officers. These findings reflect the residency pattern and routine activities of black and white officers.

In Chicago, black officers who were shot were ten times more likely to survive than be killed; among white officers the difference was half as much.

**Table 12.1**  Situations in Which Law Enforcement Officers Were Killed, 1981

| CIRCUMSTANCES AT SCENE OF INCIDENT | NO. OF INCIDENTS |
| --- | --- |
| Disturbance calls (family quarrels, man with gun) | 19 |
| Burglaries in progress or pursuing burglary suspects | 6 |
| Robberies in progress or pursuing robbery suspects | 17 |
| Attempting other arrests | 15 |
| Civil disorders (mass disobedience, riot, etc.) | 0 |
| Handling, transporting, custody of prisoners | 1 |
| Investigating suspicious persons and circumstances | 10 |
| Ambush (entrapment and premeditation) | 5 |
| Ambush (unprovoked attack) | 4 |
| Mentally deranged | 2 |
| Traffic pursuits and stops | 12 |
| Total | 91 |

SOURCE: FBI (1982), Crime in the United States, 1981. Washington, D.C.: U.S. Government Printing Office.

On the whole, officers shot by civilians stand a better chance of surviving than civilians shot by police (an 86 percent survival rate versus a 74 percent rate for civilians). This is probably due to factors such as caliber of weapon, marksmanship, number of shots fired (more by police), and the type of ammunition used (police in Chicago used hollow point bullets, a very lethal form of ammunition).

Shootings of police in the Chicago study were primarily intraracial: black civilians shoot black police officers, white civilians shoot white officers. Interestingly, during the period of the study *no* Hispanic or black officer was shot by a white civilian. Yearly variations in shootings show that what happens one year is not a good predictor of the next year. This applies to both shootings of and by police. This helps demonstrate the importance of situational factors in violence, a matter discussed in Chapters 3 and 5. As a matter of fact, in 1976 Chicago police "actually were placed in greater jeopardy by themselves and their colleagues than by armed criminal suspects" (Geller and Karales, 1982:353).

Geller and Karales were particularly concerned with off-duty shootings, both of and by police. They concluded their long and detailed investigation of both types of violence with the following recommendations:

1. Off-duty officers should generally be prohibited from carrying guns when they anticipate consuming alcohol beverages.
2. Greater restrictions should be imposed on the types of weapons that may be carried by officers, and consideration should be given to tightening the minimum standards of proficiency required of officers with these weapons.
3. Police officers may need additional guidance in the kinds of incidents to which they should respond when off duty and special reminders about the dangers of resolving their own disputes by taking police action. The unavailability to off-duty officers of police radios with which they could instantly summon assistance and check information . . . may make it inadvisable for off-duty police to intervene in situations which do not obviously require immediate police attention. (pp. 373–374)

Geller and Karales were perhaps too cautious in their recommendations (they made others as well). The goal in police shooting situations, for both police and suspects, is *outcome*. If we persist in holding the view that we must catch the criminal at all costs, then that outcome is almost inevitably going to include injuries and deaths. Unless someone is directly and immediately put in mortal danger by the actions of a suspect, "it would seem more prudent to allow them to escape [temporarily at least], as many criminals do anyway" (Rubin, 1965:528).

## CRIME VICTIMS AND POLICE DISCRETION

Most police work is "reactive" rather than "proactive." That is, police-enforcement action is usually taken when a member of the public acts as a complainant. In practical terms, this means that the police are usually not the first to exercise discretion in enforcement matters. The citizenry has enormous discretionary power, for the citizen's decision whether or not to bring events and people to the attention of the police in most cases determines whether the police will be in a position to exercise their discretionary judgments.

The relationship between citizens' complaints and the police's use of discretion has only recently come under scrutiny, and much work still needs to be done. We have found, however, that police decision making is influenced not only by the presence of a complaint and the circumstances surrounding it but also by its absence. Police decisions are influenced by a variety of things that have little or nothing to do with legal issues; for example, the complainant's demeanor, preference, and relational ties with the suspect (see p. 91). But another important set of factors concerns victim decisions to appear as prosecution witnesses and to sign formal complaints when these are needed. Those reluctant to follow their complaints with further actions present police with a dilemma, and the police may refuse to pursue a complaint from those they know or believe will back away from these responsibilities. Offenders are rarely arrested or charged in family disturbance calls. Often this is because the police anticipate no further enforcement action from the complainant.

When citizen complaints come in on police switchboards, the responsibility for directing the police reaction rests squarely on the police dispatcher. Because police communication systems lie at the heart of mobilization procedures, operators are in a position of considerable power and responsibility. Their decisions determine whether or not official action will be taken, the initial nature of that action, and the time lag between call and response. Their discretion has a profound effect on enforcement efforts. Because police departments typically take steps to monitor incoming and outgoing communications, dispatchers have less discretionary leeway than their colleagues working the streets. Even so, discretionary decisions are made, and sometimes with results clearly in violation of victim interests. Here is a complainant–dispatcher conversation reported in a study by Brian Grossman (1974:67):

> "Hello, is this the police?"
> "Yes, Madame, what is the problem?"
> "He is coming up to get me."
> "Where are you, Madame?"
> "At home."
> "Where?"
> "230 Sutton Avenue."
> "Who's coming to get you?"
> "George."
> "How do you know?"
> "He just telephoned and said he would take the kid."
> "Is it his child, Madame?"

"Yes."
"Is he living with you?"
"Yes."
"When is he coming?"
"Now."
"Why would he want to kill you?"
"I don't know."
"Does he have a weapon?"
"I don't know."
Pause by dispatcher. "Madame, if George arrives and causes any trouble, you call the station and we will send a car."
Dispatcher hangs up.

It turned out that the police might have been able to prevent a crime, for the caller was subsequently assaulted by George. Why did the dispatcher decide not to activate an official police response? Apparently, so Grossman tells us, because available cars in the area were tied up and also because in the dispatcher's opinion the caller sounded as if she came from a particular ethnic group known for its disproportionate use of police resources, and previous experience suggested that a response would probably tie up police resources to no useful end.

The unresponsiveness of police in situations like these is not adequately accounted for by their lack of resources. True, if the police were to respond to every call for assistance — even those coming in on emergency numbers — there would be absolute chaos. There are simply too many calls, and many of these turn out not to be emergencies. The police are asked to deal with barking dogs, lost cats, personal problems of a noncriminal nature, and a host of other things (Cumming et al., 1965). These are support services that, though of importance to callers, are often considered by police as a drain on resources and a hindrance to their crime-fighting mission.

Another view held by some police officers is that certain groups do not deserve their attention and continued support. In a paper presented at the 1979 annual meeting of the American Sociological Association, Clifford Shearing (1979) reported on a six-month study of the communications center of a large Canadian police department. After observing and recording thousands of communications between citizens and the police and among police officers themselves, Shearing found that police officers "made a fundamental distinction between 'the public' on the one hand, and 'third- and fourth-class citizens,' 'the dregs,' or more expressively, 'the scum,' on the other. . . . The public were people the police felt duty-bound to serve and protect" (p. 6). The scum, on the other hand, were troublemakers; they needed police control and hence were viewed as an enemy of the police. Armed with this view the police are unlikely to respond energetically to calls for assistance by persons identified as scum or those who, because of their "stupidity" or "ignorance" about what the police should really be doing, are only marginally part of the "public."

# Corruption and Abuses of Police Authority

Police discretionary practices need not result in misuse of police authority, but in some cases they do. Abuse of police authority occurs when decisions are based not on legal considerations or other matters over which the police officer has no real control (such as resources or departmental policies), but instead on personal whim or fancy or in consideration of personal gain.

The sensitive and controversial issue of police corruption has followed the police from their earliest origins. An 1816 report to England's House of Commons described corruption among constables and sheriffs' deputies:

> [The] deputies in many instances are characters of the worst and lowest descriptions; the fine they receive from the person who appoints them varies from ten shillings to five pounds; having some expense and no salary they live by extortion, by countenancing all species of vice, by an understanding with the keepers of brothels and disorderly ale-houses, by attending courts of justice, and giving there false evidence to ensure conviction when their expenses are paid, and by all the various means by which artful and designing men can entrap the weak and prey upon the unwary. (Pike, 1968:464)

The practices referred to in this report — extortion, perjury, protection, and more — are merely a few of the activities included under the rubric of police corruption. To these have been added brutality, neglect of duty, nepotism, racism, and bribery.

Depending on whose opinion we accept, almost any police activity can find its way onto the list of things identified as corrupt police practices. Historically, much of the concern about corruption has focused on blatant abuses of police authority such as the misuse of force, extortion, the taking of bribes, and perjury, but some authors now include many common police practices. Examples are "police perks" such as free meals and discounts at certain stores; the use of abusive or profane language; stopping and questioning citizens; and intraorganizational practices such as payoffs for favors granted by police colleagues. In 1972, the Knapp Commission report to the mayor of New York added another dimension of corruption in arguing that "even those who themselves engage in no corrupt activities are involved in corruption in the sense that they take no steps to prevent what they know or suspect is going on about them" (p. 3).

The following definition of police corruption is not intended to resolve the probably endless debate over what constitutes corruption. It is offered instead as a guide, so that readers can better identify the common threads linking the police activities discussed below. It is, therefore, necessarily broad. Police practices are corrupt if they violate either legal or official departmental rules covering police conduct, if they violate any of the criminal laws operative in the jurisdiction in which the police hold authority, or if they result in activities that involve the use of legitimate police authority and organization for personal or collective gain. The term *practices* means regular patterns of police action rather than idiosyncratic activities on the part of this or that police officer.

One of the most promising typologies of police corruption is that by Roebuck and Barker (1974:118–127). These authors attempt to distinguish types of police corruption on the basis of (1) the kinds of norms violated, (2) the amount of peer group support, (3) the extent of organization needed to put the practices into effect, (4) who is involved in the corruption apart from the police, and (5) departmental reaction. Eight types of police corruption were identified.

**1. Corruption of authority** means receiving unauthorized, unearned material gains by virtue of status as police officer. This includes free liquor, meals, discounts, and payments by merchants for more police protection. The corrupters are respectable citizens, there is considerable peer group support, there is little adevrse departmental reaction, little organization is required, and the violation involved is primarily that of departmental regulations.

**2. Kickbacks** involve receipt of goods and services in return for referring business to a variety of patrons (doctors, lawyers, bondsmen, garages, taxicab companies, service stations, and so on). Corrupters are usually respectable persons who stand to gain from the scheme. Departments tend to ignore it, or actually condone it, depending on the respectability of the corrupter, though the practice is usually in violation of formal departmental rules. Peer group support is often substantial, though its degree may depend on the reputation and trustworthiness of the patron. The organization involved is relatively simple and "inheres in the collusion between businessmen and policemen."

**3. Opportunist theft** is the illegal taking of goods from arrestees, victims, crime scenes, or unprotected property. It involves no corrupter and is clearly in violation of criminal laws as well as departmental rules. Reaction from departments is usually negative but may depend on value of goods or cash taken, public knowledge, and willingness of the victim to prosecute. Peer group support depends on informal norms governing distinctions between "clean" and "dirty" money. Little organization is involved; the activities result from situational decisions.

**4. Shakedowns** are opportunistic behaviors that occur when the police know about a crime but accept money or services from suspects in exchange for doing nothing. The corrupter may be respectable or known to be habitually involved in criminal activities. Shakedowns violate legal and departmental norms, and though peer group support is necessary for the routinization of shakedown operations, that support is often contingent on what the suspect is known to be engaged in — bribes from narcotics pushers and robbers are apparently frowned upon. Secrecy in peer group relations is a prime element of shakedowns.

**5. Protection of illegal activities** refers to corrupters who seek to continue their illegal operations free from police harassment. The corrupters can be respectable or nonrespectable; in either case they are doing something illegal, which makes protection important. Protection violates criminal and departmental rules and involves considerable collusion, peer group support, and organization to pull it off (for one thing, officers have to know which businesses are protected). Though departmental reaction is often severe (suspension, dismissal, or criminal charges), the severity and consistency of negative reactions may depend on the degree of community support of the illegal activities being protected.

**6. The fix** refers to either quashing legal proceedings or "taking up" traffic tickets. Corrupters are arrestees attempting to avoid police action that would probably embarrass them in one way or another. The fixer is often not a patrol officer but someone with access to the investigative aspects of police work. The fix, of course, violates legal and departmental rules, and reaction is usually severe when cases are brought to light. The authors suggest that in departments where the fix occurs frequently and with considerable regularity it is a highly organized activity.

**7. Direct criminal activities** involve no corrupter, as the police alone are parties to the corruption. Direct criminal activities include crimes by police officers against suspects, victims, pedestrians, or whomever, and against property. Lack of peer group support and severe departmental reactions generally underscore the blatant criminal character of these practices. For these activities to continue some organization is necessary, and therefore they are unlikely to persist as opportunist efforts by individuals or teams.

**8. Internal payoffs** involve bribes within the police department for such things as assignments, hours, promotions, control of evidence, arrests, and so forth. Some officers are in a particularly advantageous position to take payoffs, as Jonathan Rubinstein's (1973:85) comment on the police dispatcher shows:

> He has numerous little favors he can grant a man that will ease the burdens of the tour. For instance, the patrolman can go to "lunch" (policeman [in Philadelphia, at least] refer to all their meal breaks as lunch, regardless of the hour) only with the dispatcher's permission. If the dispatcher wants a man to remain in service, he simply tells him that he cannot go. The men are not supposed to eat together and the dispatcher is responsible for seeing that they do not gather. A sympathetic dispatcher will allow several men to share their lunchtime by permitting one man to give a location where the dispatcher knows the police do not eat.

The internal payoff system is usually highly organized, particularly in those departments under pressure to produce and in those departments in which lucrative and corrupt practices such as shakedowns and protection are regular aspects of police work. Peer group support is usually considerable. Departmental reaction is tolerant if it means a more satisfied work force, and if officers involved in the payoff system are not in violation of high priority regulations or the criminal law.

The value of Roebuck's and Barker's typology lies in its applicability across departments, jurisdictions, and cultures, and in its attempt to specify some of the dimensions in terms of which corruptions can be analyzed. This brief review of one typology shows that police corruption is hardly to be understood only by reference to what the police do. The roots of and supports for corruption lie not in the police per se, but in the larger social, cultural, economic, and political climates in which they operate (Chambliss, 1971).

## BRUTALITY AND MISUSE OF FORCE

One aspect of police operations continually appears in discussions of corruption and abuse of police authority — the use of coercive force. Police are charged from time to time with brutality and abuses of their authority to employ coercive force.

What is meant by brutality and misuse of force when these are applied to police operations? As you might have guessed, there is hardly consensus on their meaning. Albert Reiss (1970) suggests that almost any routine police action will be interpreted by someone as an instance of police brutality. He argues, further, that if brutality is the actual use of force, the police themselves have no clear-cut legal or normative statements on the issue. Police training films, such as Motorola's *Shoot, Don't Shoot,* endeavor to instruct the police in the matter of using deadly force, but most officers are rarely, if ever, faced with situations in which such force is authorized or used. At lesser levels of violence, the police rely on the notion of reasonable force, but what constitutes reasonable force? A rule of thumb adopted by most police agencies, and supported by judicial actions, is that *reasonable force* means that force necessary to secure a legal goal without endangering innocent citizens. Any unnecessary force is unreasonable and may be illegal. But these are difficult distinctions to apply in practice, particularly under pressure.

In any police–citizen encounter the actors may hold different conceptions of brutality, depending on their status (police or suspect); their ability to use force (handcuffed or free to move); the weapons available (guns, knives, or fists); their sex, age, physical condition, and race; their prior experiences; and their expectations and evaluations of what will happen and what ought to. Some people apply the term *brutality* only to those situations involving force, but others include situations involving psychic manipulations, when there is loss of self-respect and threats to a positive self-concept. Although we no longer see the routine use of "third degree" techniques among our police forces, other practices associated with the questioning of suspects may be seen as unnecessarily brutal. Many no doubt would question the claim that "in dealing with criminal offenders, and consequently also with criminal suspects who may actually be innocent, the interrogator must of necessity employ less refined methods than are considered appropriate for the transaction of ordinary, everyday affairs by and between law-abiding citizens" (Inbau, 1962:150). And some might have little trepidation about denouncing as brutality police use of trickery, deceit, and other psychological devices designed to maximize psychic tension and emotional insecurity: procedures quite acceptable to the author of the statement just quoted.

The line between brutality and misuse of force is hazy. Though all brutality may well be a misuse of authorized force, not all misuse of force is brutality. An officer who fires at a fleeing felon (a legal action in most jurisdictions) and hits instead an innocent bystander would probably be considered to have used deadly force inappropriately, but is this action also properly identified as an instance of police brutality? To draw the line, we need to know something about police motives, experiences, intentions, and knowledge. *Brutality* may perhaps best be used in reference to those situations in which police knowingly and intentionally use force in order to satisfy personal or group whims, prejudices, and interests. *Misuse of force,* then, can be applied to those situations in which the police use force in a manner that goes beyond that required for the satisfaction of legal obligations, though the intent is to meet those obligations and not personal whims.

We can reasonably imagine situations in which brutality is more likely to be at issue than is misuse of force. We are more likely to be looking at brutality, for instance, if the police assault others who offer no resistance, are in no position to offer any resistance (if they are handcuffed), or if a number of officers join in the assault of a lone citizen who clearly can be subdued with less forceful means (Reiss, 1970). A clear example of brutality is the following account of an incident in Philadelphia. A man suspected of sexually molesting a child was treated to the following at the hands of his police captors:

> Any squad member who wished was allowed to beat the suspect from the ankles to the armpits with his stick. Men came in off the street to participate in the beating and then returned to patrol. Before he was taken downtown, the suspect had been severely battered, although he had no broken bones. At no time did he utter a complaint, ask for mercy, or curse the police. Without a murmur he absorbed a brutal beating, which caused him to foul himself and drew the admiring comments of several men who admitted he could "really take it." (Rubinstein, 1973:183)

A less shocking situation, but nevertheless in line with our definition of brutality, is the following, again reported by Rubinstein. Suspects who are arrested are often transported in wagons. They are handcuffed and sit on benches with no handrails or other devices on which to rely for support during the ride. The driver of the wagon can give prisoners a very uncomfortable ride merely by swerving and braking unpredictably. As Rubinstein (1973:329) describes it: "Rarely is a prisoner injured by any of these methods, but anyone who runs when he is told to halt, swears or spits at a policeman, or threatens him in any way may find himself chastened by these methods."

Police misuse of force is likely to surface if the police are under relatively extreme pressure, if they are acting overzealously, or if they have mis-interpreted the events or actions they have witnessed. In addition, poorly trained and inexperienced police officers are probably more apt to use excessive force than the more experienced. Firing warning shots in the air or shooting at fleeing suspects, practices not officially condoned by most police agencies, may have been triggered by one of these factors.

Misuse of force and, on occasion, police brutality can be linked to the police officer's desire, if not obligation, to gain control in encounters. A number of authors point out that police efforts to gain the upper hand in their dealings with suspects, witnesses, victims, and others are given high priority in police operations, for understandable reasons (Bottomley, 1973a:51). But in the effort to gain control, the police may sometimes misuse or abuse their authority to employ coercive force. Also, if police control is threatened, it is likely to be perceived by officers as a challenge to their authority, an issue to which the police are particularly sensitive. It is not too surprising, then, that excessive use of force tends to surface if police control of a situation is threatened.

**The "Stop"**   Police authority to use coercive force is most often invoked when an arrest is taking place. But in addition to actual arrests, the police exercise this authority whenever they make a routine "stop," that is, stop a citizen for questioning. Subjects may not know that failure to heed an officer's command to stop makes them liable for arrest on charges of refusing to obey a lawful command by a police officer. Behind the officer's authority to make the stop lies the authority to use force if need be.

Brutality is most likely to erupt when stop situations are contrived events bearing no relationship to legal objectives, but designed instead for purposes of harassment and to satisfy personal whim. Bent (1974:17–18) identifies a desire for "action" as one factor leading to such stops:

> With some police officers, an unrequited need for activity resulted in prankish behavior that did little to elevate the esteem of law enforcement in the eyes of the public. Occupants of a police car actively looked for "deviants" on their beat to break the monotony of a quiet evening. To these officers, deviants included anyone whose clothes, hair length, mannerisms, or race did not conform with officer's standards of acceptability. Thus, youths with long hair or garish dress — "hippies," as defined by the policemen — transvestites, and blacks were stopped and questioned at the pleasure of the patrolmen:
>
> A typical scenario in a two-man squad car during periods of prolonged inactivity went something like this: Patrolmen Harry and Jack have had an uneventful evening when a car driven by some teenagers goes by. One of the youths stares (or smiles, or grimaces, or sneers, etc.) at the police car. Patrolman Jack turns to his partner and says, "Harry, let's pull that car over. Those kids are guilty of 'contempt of cop'!" Or one of the officers spots a pedestrian who appears likely to provide some "activity" and turns to his partner saying, "Jack, let's stop the fag (or hippie, or whore, or nigger, etc.) and ask him a few questions. That ought to liven things up."

**Weapons and Brutality**   The police are encouraged to misuse and abuse their authority to employ force in a multitude of different ways. Two sources of encouragement come from traditions within police departments that support the use of nonregulation weapons and advertisers who are trying to sell police equipment.

The use of nonregulation weaponry is no longer as widespread as it used to be. According to Rubinstein (1973:288–289), for example, large city forces have had some success in outlawing such practices. Nevertheless, Rubinstein goes on, a significant number of officers still carry with them weapons that look as if their sole purpose is the infliction of great pain and suffering. Among these weapons are lead-loaded saps, some of which come in the form of an innocent-looking glove with built-in lead; hollowed-out nightsticks filled with lead; ax handles; and sticks fitted with a metal ball on their knob. Officers have also been known to carry two or even three guns. The so-called dumdum bullets that blow apart on impact are routinely used in many state, local, and federal agencies, although they are outlawed in international warfare. Armed in these various ways, officers are not encouraged to use force defensively, and a clear means, if not an incentive, exists for abuse of police power.

Advertisers' interests lie in making sales, and they will go to some extraordinary lengths to interest the police in their wares. One flier, sent out by the manufacturers of Second Chance bulletproof vests and clothing, contains various "comic strips" depicting police officers in life-or-death situations. Many include bizarre references to the police officer's uphill fight against procedural requirements of due process and Supreme Court liberalism. One even depicts a smiling policeman dreaming about two hoodlums who are stabbing the judge who gave them probation for shooting at a cop. The advertisers end their twenty-page flier with the following "editorial":

> Every time a policeman is killed, public figures will make a big show about how sorry they are. Yet, even if the killer is somehow convicted, they will refuse to enforce Capital Punishment. So-called "life imprisonment" usually means parole in five or ten years. It seems that the majority of cop killers eventually go free, thus giving no deterrent to future killers.
>
>   Due to recent court decisions and a prevailing social attitude of permissiveness, there exists only one way to give Capital Punishment to cop killers. You must survive his attack to do it. ("Second Chance," September 1973)

The last paragraph leaves little doubt that the makers of Second Chance vests support the view that the police should be executioners.

**How Much Police Corruption and Abuse of Force?**   The extent of police corruption and abuse of force is unknown and unknowable. To remove the cloak of secrecy surrounding police operations, particularly their unlawful ones, requires powers beyond the control of even congressional committees and those who head up police agencies. Serious investigations into these matters are also hampered because the time and money required for in-depth research are beyond the grasp of most criminologists, assuming they could raise the veil of secrecy. Even police officers themselves find it difficult, if not dangerous, to bring corrupt practices to light. The movie *Serpico,* which dealt with corruption in New York and was based in part on the Knapp Commission investigations, brought some of these difficulties and dangers to wide public attention. Some evidence shows that those who try to remain aloof from corruption are placed under considerable pressure to conform with the practices of their colleagues (Stoddard, 1968).

All in all, what meager evidence we do have suggests two things. First, as the Knapp Commission concluded, corruption is widespread and is likely to remain so given prevailing stereotypes of the criminal, long-standing traditions in police work, and the demand that the police enforce laws over which there is considerable disagreement and no little resentment. Second, the excessive use of force by police seems to be less prevalent than many appear to think. Albert Reiss (1970:142) found that out of 5,012 police–citizen encounters around 10 percent involved what was considered police misconduct, and in most of these cases abusive language and ridicule constituted the misconduct. He did discover one very alarming fact, however. Around 33 percent of the incidents in which excessive force was used occurred while the suspect was in police custody, under physical control. Just how much violence occurs behind closed doors is impossible to ascertain. The fact that it occurs at all raises the specter of rule by terror rather than by law.

# CHAPTER 13

# The Judicial Process

Once arrested by the police, an individual becomes eligible for further processing at the hands of official agents of the state. With the arrest, the police are in effect asserting that the individual is no longer to be treated as a law-abiding citizen but, rather, as a criminal. The change in status that arrest confirms is symbolized not only by physical detention but also by the warning that "anything you say can and will be used against you in a court of law." Law-abiding citizens are given no such warning in their dealings with the police.

The judicial process can be thought of as a series of decision stages through which some, but not all, suspects will pass. Figure 13.1 shows the various stages in detail. Notice that there is considerable attrition as defendants pass from arrest to sentencing and implementation of punishment. Of course, jurisdictions differ in their rates of attrition, but even in felony cases it is not unusual to find dropout rates after arrest of 40 or 50 percent, and even higher (Brosi, 1979:14). In this chapter we shall review the factors that influence this and other aspects of the criminal process after arrest.

## Overview of the Judicial Process

Different jurisdictions may use various procedures and terminologies in the handling of criminal suspects, but a general sense of the major decision stages in the American judicial process can be grasped from the following overview. It mainly applies to adult felony offenders, but significant differences in the judicial handling of persons suspected of misdemeanors and petty crimes are noted. Juvenile proceedings are discussed in Chapter 16.

**Initial Appearance Before a Magistrate**  Within a reasonable time after arrest (usually 48 hours), suspects must be brought before a court official, usually a magistrate, for consideration of bail. In minor cases such as drunkenness, disorderly conduct, vagrancy, traffic offenses, and violations of local ordinances, this initial appearance may also be a time when suspects can plead guilty to whatever charges the police have brought against them, and if they do so, a summary disposition is entered by the court. For those arrested on more serious charges, no plea or consideration of evidence is involved at this stage.

**Determination of Charges**  Following the initial appearance, assuming that the charges have not been dropped or dismissed, the prosecution must decide what charges to pursue. Initial determination of charges is made in the light of police reports regarding the circumstances of the case. If the decision is made to prosecute, formal charges must be lodged against the suspect. Sometimes this is done through *grand jury* proceedings, in which the prosecution (only) presents evidence in support of the case to a jury of twelve to twenty-three citizens. If the grand jury agrees with the prosecution, it will hand down an *indictment* specifying the charges, or it may reduce or alter the

**Figure 13.1** A general view of the criminal justice system

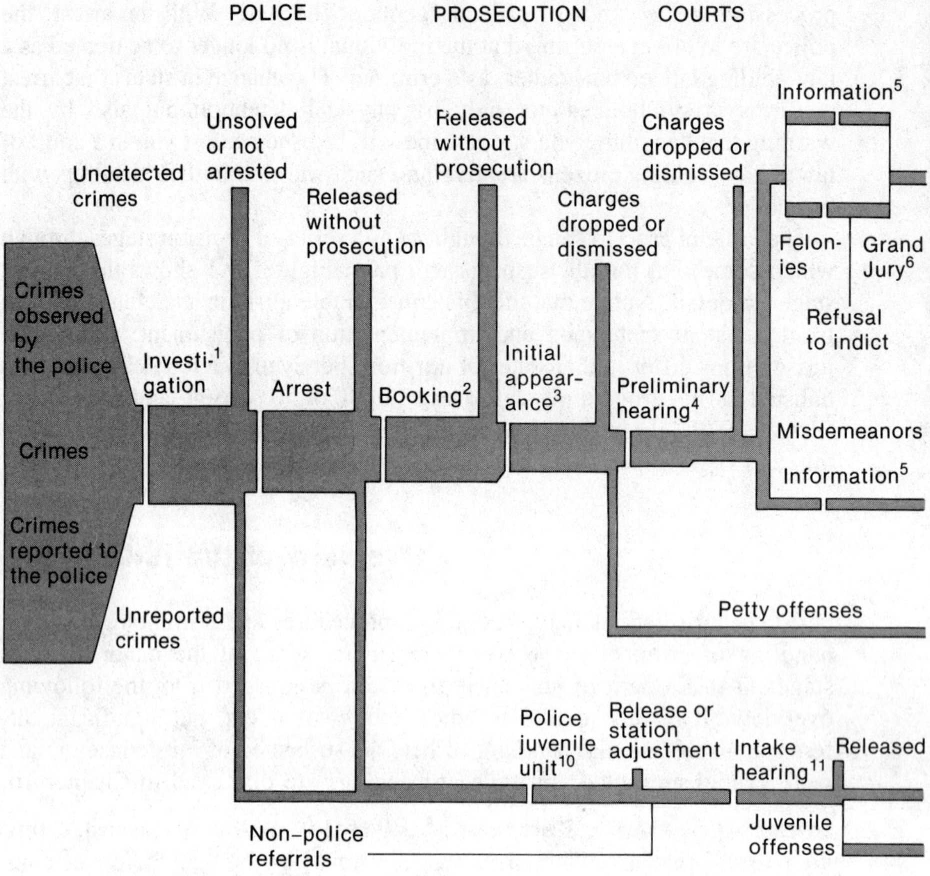

POLICE          PROSECUTION          COURTS

Information[5]

Undetected crimes | Unsolved or not arrested | Released without prosecution | Charges dropped or dismissed

Released without prosecution | Charges dropped or dismissed

Felonies | Grand Jury[6]

Crimes observed by the police | Investigation[1] | Arrest | Booking[2] | Initial appearance[3] | Preliminary hearing[4]

Refusal to indict

Crimes

Misdemeanors

Information[5]

Crimes reported to the police

Petty offenses

Unreported crimes

Police juvenile unit[10] | Release or station adjustment | Intake hearing[11] | Released

Non-police referrals

Juvenile offenses

[1]May continue until trial.
[2]Administrative record of arrest. First step at which temporary release on bail may be available.
[3]Before magistrate, commissioner, or justice of the peace. Formal notice of charge, advice of rights. Bail set. Summary trials for petty offenses usually conducted here without further processing.
[4]Preliminary testing of evidence against defendant. Charge may be reduced. No separate preliminary hearing for misdemeanors in some systems.
[5]Charge filed by prosecuter on basis of information submitted by police or citizens. Alternative to grand jury indictment; often used in felonies, almost always in misdemeanors.
[6]Reviews whether government evidence sufficient to justify trial. Some states

SOURCE: President's Commission on Law Enforcement and Administration of Justice (1967), The Challenge of Crime, in a Free Society. Washington, D.C.: U.S. Government Printing Office, pp. 8–9.

## CORRECTIONS

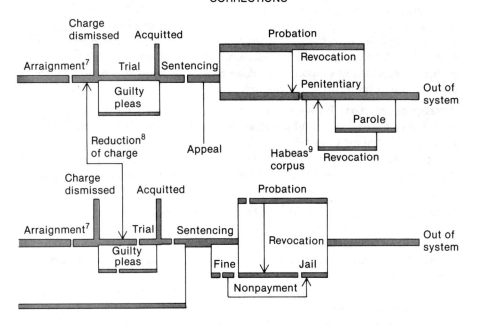

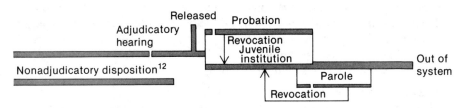

have no grand jury system; others seldom use it.

[7]Appearance for plea; defendant elects trial by judge or jury (if available); counsel for indigent usually appointed here in felonies. Often not at all on other cases.

[8]Charge may be reduced at any time prior to trial in return for plea of guilty or for other reasons.

[9]Challenge on constitutional grounds to legality of detention. May be sought at any point in process.

[10]Police often hold informal hearings, dismiss or adjust many cases without further processing.

[11]Probation officer decides desirability of further court action.

[12]Welfare agency, social services, counseling, medical care, etc., for cases where adjudicatory handling not needed.

charges or grant no formal indictment. However, a grand jury rarely disagrees with the recommendations of the prosecution.

In states without a grand jury system, and in offenses not requiring grand jury proceedings, the prosecution formally presents charges before a magistrate or judge in a *preliminary hearing,* sometimes called an *information* proceeding. Unlike the grand jury situation, the defendant may challenge the evidence presented in support of the charges and, in some jurisdictions, may elect to waive the hearings altogether.

**Arraignment and Plea**   Upon indictment, or when the defendant is bound over for trial on an information, a time is usually set for formal plea making. A judge asks the defendant for a plea, and if the judge accepts it, a trial or sentencing date will be set. A judge is not bound to accept a plea of guilty or *nolo contendere* (no contest); however, a judge *must* accept a plea of not guilty.

**Trial**   For those who have formally entered not-guilty pleas, guilt or innocence is usually decided in a court trial. All defendants are entitled to a jury trial, though this right may be waived for most offenses in most states. Trial procedures, however, are basically the same, regardless of whether or not a jury is sitting.

The trial is an *adversary* proceeding during which the prosecution and defense seek to convince the judge and jury that their presentation of the facts surrounding the case best accords with the truth. The onus of proof lies with the prosecution, who must demonstrate that the evidence implicates the defendant *beyond a reasonable doubt.* Although trial proceedings are acted out within a fairly rigid set of rules, the presiding judge may rule on matters of procedure, evidence, testimony, and trial conduct. The judge cannot, however, overrule a jury's finding of not guilty.

**Appeals**   Upon conviction, the defendant has the right to appeal the case to a higher court. If an appeals court refuses to consider the case or makes a negative ruling, the defendant may appeal to even higher courts. The end of the appeals road is the United States Supreme Court. The basis for an appeal may be procedural or evidentiary or may involve basic questions of substantive law, such as the constitutionality of a particular criminal statute. In most jurisdictions, defendants also have the right to appeal their sentences.

In its disposition of a case, an appellate court may (1) uphold ("affirm") the lower court's ruling; (2) change ("modify") part of the ruling; (3) set aside ("reverse") the lower court's ruling, without requiring any further action; (4) overturn the lower court's ruling and require further action from the lower court ("reverse and remand"), for example, a new trial; or (5) send it back ("remand") to the lower court without overturning it but requiring proceedings such as a new trial. The activity of state appellate courts grew an average of 107 percent from 1973 to 1983, with more than 400 percent growth in Alaska, Connecticut, Hawaii, and Louisiana (Bureau of Justice Statistics, 1985d).

**Sentencing**   After conviction, the defendant faces sentencing. In some states, and for some offenses, a jury may set the sentence, while in other circumstances sentencing may be decided by a panel of judges. Usually, however, the trial judge decides the offender's fate. In most felony cases a time interval between conviction and sentencing is provided so that the defendant's background, present circumstances, and criminal record can be investigated. These investigations are intended as aids for the judge in deliberating sentencing alternatives, if these are available.

These are the major decision stages in the American judicial process. The decisions made at any one stage determine whether and how criminal suspects will move to the next one. Most suspects do not go through all the stages that are available to them. How and why the decisions are made, then, become central issues in determining what actually happens to those who enter the judicial process.

## BAIL AND PRETRIAL DETENTION

Within a reasonable time after arrest, suspects must be accorded the opportunity to gain their release from custody, pending future proceedings against them. In Anglo-American law, the traditional route to freedom is posting a money bond. Those "bailed out" in this manner forfeit the amount of bail if they fail to appear at a specified later date. However, many states and countries permit the use of releases based merely on the promise to reappear, called *release on recognizance*. This is usually reserved for suspects charged with less serious offenses.

To give someone the opportunity to post bail does not guarantee that he or she will be released. First, the suspect must raise the necessary money. The actual amount of bail, whether $500 or $50,000, is beyond the reach of many arrested suspects. Those who cannot raise the bail themselves can turn to bondsmen and bonding agencies. For a fee, usually 10 to 20 percent of the bail, these bonding services guarantee the full amount of bail, permitting the release of those who hire them. The fee is not returnable, which means that suspects are out of pocket whether or not they appear in court as scheduled. Only some states permit bondsmen to operate, and in those that do not, the defendant is usually required to put up only 5 to 10 percent of the bail amount.

It might appear that bonding services make it easier for arrested suspects to secure their release. Indeed, this is true for some suspects. But it also happens that many people cannot raise even the bonding fee. Caleb Foote's (1958:633) pioneering study of bail practices in New York showed that 25 percent of all defendants failed to make bail at $500, 45 percent failed at $1,500, and 63 percent failed at $2,500. Another study (Silverstein, 1966:621–631) found that the percentage of felony suspects who could not pay bonding fees differed across the country, but in some areas it was as high as 80 to 90 percent.

Those who cannot afford bail are punished for their lack of financial resources in a variety of ways. First, they are deprived of their freedom. Second, they are often placed in overcrowded and understaffed jail facilities, which provide few modest comforts, and which are dangerous places, especially for young inmates. Third, because they are incarcerated, they are deprived of those significant personal and social relationships on which they rely for support and emotional sustenance. Fourth, they lose some of the advantages that freedom brings when they seek legal services and prepare for the judicial proceedings ahead. Fifth, they are often forced to spend hours, days, and even months in the company of people they might normally have nothing to do with. Sixth, they are subject to a regimented daily routine that strips them of ordinary decision-making opportunities and undermines their identity. And seventh, they are deprived of privacy in dealing with personal affairs and suffer forced exposure to the personal activities of others. In sum, jailed suspects suffer innumerable deprivations, even though they have not yet been legally declared criminal.

**Bail Decision Making**  Although some jurisdictions have predetermined limits governing the setting of bail, bail proceedings are generally characterized by on-the-spot decisions wherein considerable discretion is exercised. Police, prosecutors, and magistrates all influence bail decisions, and the amount of bail in any given case depends heavily on the factors influencing these legal authorities. A study of bail decisions in federal courts found that three major factors influenced the amount of bail, in this order: (1) seriousness of the offense, (2) the district in which bail is imposed, and (3) the suspect's criminal record (Bureau of Justice Statistics, 1985f).

In Anglo-American procedural law, the fundamental consideration in setting bail is the question of nonappearance: Will the defendant abscond once freed? But a judicial tradition has emerged over the years emphasizing other issues as well. For example, weight is given to the nature of the charges and the suspect's known criminal record. Further, bail decisions are often influenced by extralegal considerations that have no foundation in law, such as whether or not the suspect's freedom will impede further police inquiries and whether or not the prosecution feels that the accused is obviously guilty. In only 33 percent of the bail deliberations observed by one author did the prosecution mention the question of nonappearance (Bottomley, 1970:59–73).

The recommendations of the prosecutor are not to be ignored, for when they go against the defendant, the judge usually agrees. By agreeing with prosecution recommendations, the judge may hope to defuse potential criticism and can argue that others must share in the responsibility for the decision. Of course, if the matter of bail is to be decided strictly on the basis of nonappearance, then the task is no simple one, and we should recognize the difficulties that magistrates face. Martin Friedland (1965:176) argues, "A system which requires security in advance produces an insoluble dilemma. In most cases it is impossible to pick a figure which is high enough to ensure the accused's appearance in court and yet low enough for him to raise; the two seldom, if ever, overlap." On the other hand, recent evidence shows that few suspects flee or "willfully" fail to appear in court. Neither the likelihood of a severe punishment nor a high bond appears to have much effect on court appearances.

## PREVENTIVE DETENTION AND THE DANGEROUS OFFENDER

Over the years, considerable attention has been paid to the widespread European practice of refusing bail on the grounds that suspects pose a threat to the community if released. In American federal courts, preventive detention has generally been authorized when the accused is charged with a capital crime, is insane, or is an alien awaiting deportation proceedings (Altman and Cunningham, 1967:178). In addition, federal judicial approval has been extended to bail denial in cases in which there is a threat to witnesses or some other obstruction of justice. State courts, however, have generally assumed greater leeway in the denial of bail; judicial opinion has consistently held that defendants in state courts have no automatic right to bail.

Whatever the legal and constitutional dilemmas posed by the bail issue, and there are many, judges who see fit to keep suspects in custody may do so indirectly by setting extremely high bail. In this way, the accused is typically prevented from securing release because he or she is unable to raise bail. This practice is inherently discriminatory: "If the dangerous defendant can raise the bail sum, he goes free. By its nature, therefore, the system succeeds in retaining only the 'dangerous poor.' The 'dangerous rich' post bond and are released" (Altman and Cunningham, 1967:179).

Advocates of preventive detention are concerned that dangerous offenders will jeopardize the lives and property of members of the community. Certainly, some suspects will commit crimes they could not have committed if detained. Some may commit crimes during the period between arrest and trial to pay off the bonding fees they have incurred in obtaining pretrial release. There is also evidence that the probability of crime increases with the length of time that suspects are on bail, with the extensiveness of their criminal records, and with their involvement with drugs (Bureau of Justice Statistics, 1985f).

Some might argue that if pretrial detention can prevent even one predatory or violent act, preventive detention will have served a useful purpose. Against this view, however, is the specter of a judicial process operating on the basis of fear, speculation, and stereotypes. This problem arises because criminal justice authorities have so far been unable to accurately predict which suspects will in fact commit crimes upon release (Angel, 1971; Monahan, 1981). Failing this ability, suspects are released if they "look right" and detained if they do not. In fact, bail has been made more difficult in most states over the past decade (Bradley, 1984).

# Becoming a Legal Criminal

Legal confirmation of a suspect's criminality comes with his or her conviction in a court of law. Upon conviction, defendants officially lose their status as law-abiding citizens and are subject to punishment at the hands of the state. A conviction justifies the efforts of those who sought legal confirmation of guilt, most notably the police and prosecution:

> The policeman's triumph comes when the court vindicates his judgment by a conviction. . . . At any rate, a conviction reassures him of his own competence and at the same time of the worth of his job. . . . It provides for him a reassurance as to the correctness of his judgments. (Westley, 1970:81)

In America, all criminal defendants have the right to plead not guilty and to ask for trial by a jury of their peers. The trial provides the setting for the adversary proceedings that, in theory, are the heart of the Anglo-American judicial process. The trial is also the setting for review of previous actions against criminal suspects. It is the place where justice supposedly reigns; where fairness, impartiality, and due process guide our judgments of others. As William Chambliss and Robert Seidman (1971:398–399) describe it:

> It is the courtroom, at the trial itself, that the majestic rights enshrined in the Constitution are upheld; it is there that evidence illegally obtained will be suppressed; it is there that the prosecution will be required to keep the high standard to which it is held; and it is there that the presence of counsel and judge will prevent oppression or overreaching by police or prosecution, however weak, humble, or lowly the accused may be.

Fans of Perry Mason and other television counselors may be surprised to learn that most criminal defendants never go to trial. Instead, they plead guilty, virtually ensuring their own conviction. In fact, around 90 percent of all convictions are the result of guilty pleas, though the actual percentage varies from place to place (see Table 13.1). This means that only about 10 percent of criminal convictions occur in the adversary setting of a public trial. To understand how criminal convictions usually come about and to understand how one becomes a legal criminal, we must focus on those pretrial phases of judicial decision making in which charges and pleas are considered.

## THE DECISION TO PROSECUTE

The decision to prosecute is perhaps the most crucial in the entire criminal process. For defendants an unfavorable decision here often guarantees conviction; the only remaining question is whether something can be done to reduce the negative consequences that are likely to follow. For the police the decision to prosecute vindicates their judgment and efforts, though it may put their methods on the line. If there is no prosecution, there can be no

**Table 13.1** Percent of Convictions that Were Guilty Pleas in 1979, Fourteen Jurisdictions

| | |
|---|---|
| Louisville | 81% |
| Indianapalis | 85 |
| New Orleans | 87 |
| Washington, D.C. | 89 |
| Milwaukee | 89 |
| Salt Lake County | 90 |
| Los Angeles | 91 |
| Kalamazoo | 94 |
| Geneva, Ill. | 95 |
| Golden, Colo. | 95 |
| St. Louis | 95 |
| Manhattan | 96 |
| Cobb County, Ga. | 96 |
| Rhode Island | 97 |

SOURCE: Bureau of Justice Statistics (1983), Special Report: Career Patterns in Crime. Washington, D.C.: U.S. Department of Justice, p. 12.

adjudication of guilt or innocence, and certainly no official criminal punishment.

Many criminal cases that come before prosecutors are screened out at an early stage or end up being dismissed. Table 13.2 shows some recent figures from five American jurisdictions. In some cases there were more dismissals following arrests than either guilty pleas or trials.

**Table 13.2** Felony Attrition Rates in Five Jurisdictions, 1977

| JURISDICTION | REJECTED AT SCREENING (%) | DROPPED OR DISMISSED AFTER FILING (%) | TOTAL ATTRITION RATE (%) |
|---|---|---|---|
| Cobb County, Georgia | 18 | 11 | 29 |
| District of Columbia | 22 | 27 | 49 |
| Salt Lake County, Utah | 19 | 25 | 44 |
| New Orleans | 48 | 7 | 55 |
| Los Angeles | 40 | 12 | 52 |

SOURCE: Brosi, Kathleen B. (1979), A Cross-City Comparison of Felony Case Processing. Washington, D.C.: U.S. Government Printing Office, p. 7.

The decision not to prosecute is often made at an initial prosecution screening. Two reasons for rejection appear most often: problems with the evidence and problems with the witnesses. Evidence problems are most likely to be either insufficient testimonial corroboration — willing witnesses could not substantiate the charges — or lack of physical evidence, such as stolen property or weapons. Recent comparisons across jurisdictions have found that relatively few cases are dropped because of due-process "technicalities," such as suspected violations of the rules governing police searches and seizures. One author writes: "While these issues may be substantial in terms of legal theory, they appear to have little impact on the overall flow of criminal cases after arrest. [In this study,] due process reasons accounted for only a small portion of the rejections at screening — from 1 to 9 percent" (Brosi, 1979:18–19). When due process is an issue, it is most likely to surface in drug offense situations. The violation of due process here may be a consequence of negative attitudes toward drug offenders generally, coupled with the pressing need to secure physical evidence of possession or delivery.

Criminal charges may be dropped after cases have passed initial screening and after official charges have been filed. When this happens the major reasons are again either evidence or witness related. In many cities the failure of witnesses to appear in court or to make themselves available to the prosecution accounts for most of the dismissals and refusals to prosecute that arise after filing of charges (Brosi, 1979). However, the impact of witness and evidence problems seems to vary by offense and from jurisdiction to jurisdiction according to a 1979 study. For example, in murder cases, witnesses were more of a problem in St. Louis than in Los Angeles or New Orleans. In drug cases, witness problems were cited as the reason for 80 percent of dismissals in Washington, D.C., but for less than 10 percent in most other jurisdictions (Bureau of Justice Statistics, 1983c).

On the matter of witness cooperation it should be noted that designation of witnesses as "uncooperative" may be a result of prevailing offense stereotypes. That is, it may be that prosecutors associate certain offense situations with uncooperative witnesses and decide not to prosecute a given case because it fits the stereotype. An example that comes to mind is interpersonal assault. Here victims often consider the problem a personal matter, especially if it involves relatives or friends. Many victims are unlikely to follow through with official complaints or appear as witnesses for that reason. Both police and prosecutors know this, and it colors their handling of assault cases. It is easy for them to ignore or drop such cases, citing lack of witness cooperation even when no attempt was actually made to establish that prospective witnesses would in fact be uncooperative if given the chance to testify.

Is there evidence of such a gap between prosecutor perceptions and witness intentions? Frank Cannavale (1976:50) sought to find out in a study of witness cooperation in Washington, D.C. His conclusion was that "prosecutors were apparently unable to cut through to the true intentions of 23 percent or more of those they regarded as uncooperative and, therefore, recorded the existence of witness problems when these were premature judgments at best and incorrect decisions at worst."

The decision to prosecute is sometimes influenced by private individuals and groups who are able to put pressure on the district attorney's office. In his study of prosecutors in King County, Washington, George Cole (1970) found that staff members routinely took steps to protect the district attorney from public criticism. These steps included manipulations of the bail system as well as the vigorous prosecution of certain forms of crime — for example, child molestation. Prosecutors' charging practices can be expected to reflect community influences in those areas of enforcement where they are in substantial agreement.

## BARGAIN JUSTICE

Many guilty pleas, perhaps most, are entered as a result of an agreement between the prosecutor and defense counsel. The agreement means that both sides see themselves as better off with the plea than they would have been without it. Unfortunately, this view is sometimes not shared by either the defendant or the victim.

A number of different "bargains" are possible: a guilty plea may be exchanged for (1) a reduction in the charge(s); (2) a promise of leniency in sentencing; (3) in exchange for concurrent consideration of multiple charges — the defendant serves one sentence for a number of different crimes; or (4) in exchange for dropped charges — the defendant pleads guilty to (usually) the major charge, and other lesser charges are dismissed.

In addition to these bargains, the defendant might exchange a guilty plea for release on bail or in order to avoid some future problem. For example, a prosecutor in one jurisdiction will sometimes offer a deal to a defendant who is also wanted in another jurisdiction, using the threat of returning the defendant to that jurisdiction to induce a guilty plea (Newman, 1966:85). Finally, there is what Arnold Enker (1967) called the "tacit bargain." Though no explicit negotiation is involved, defendants may plead guilty because they believe the court will show greater leniency if they do. A guilty plea saves the state time and money and indicates that the defendant is prepared to pay for the crime. There is evidence that prosecutors and judges agree that guilty pleas should be rewarded (Mendelsohn, 1956; Vetri, 1964; Bottomley, 1970:120–122).

Defendants may feel pressure to "deal" for other reasons: (1) they want to avoid the publicity of a trial — a likely concern for offenders who are employed or with families — (2) they want to avoid the unknowns of adversarial proceedings; the outcome of a trial is influenced by many factors often beyond the defendant's control, and so why take the risk of things going wrong? And (3) a guilty plea usually gets things over with more quickly than a trial does, and some defendants may feel this is important.

**The Prosecution and Guilty Pleas**   The advantages and pressures considered by defendants are well known to prosecutors, who often use them as the carrot in negotiations. One particularly effective method used to encourage guilty pleas is to bring up the defendant on as many charges as possible. These "multiple-count" indictments include the major offense(s) and all the so-called lesser-included offenses as well. For example, an armed robbery indictment might include various assault, larceny, and weapons charges as well as the major offense. An offer to drop the lesser charges could save the defendant many years in prison, a deal hard to refuse.

If a guilty plea favors the defendant, why would the prosecutor be interested, as is usually the case? One obvious explanation is that with the current budgets and personnel, it would be virtually impossible to prosecute and try every case the police brought in. Most of the time court calendars are full, with cases set months in advance. Under such conditions prosecutors have little choice but to divert cases from the courtroom (McIntyre and Lippman, 1970).

The judicial enterprise itself brings pressures to deal. Organizational demands go beyond time and money, and they include *productivity* and *reciprocity*. Convictions are a measure of how productive one is as a prosecutor, and a good track record is important. Henry Pontell (1984:35) writes:

> Because prosecutors are elected to their positions, their "track" records (convicted defendants), which reflect how well they are protecting the public, strongly influence their future careers. They must produce conviction statistics that place their activities in the best possible light. This is likely to take precedence over other concerns of due process, social justice, and deterrence. Prosecutors strive for high rates of conviction, and correspondingly low rates of acquittal and dismissal, once cases are accepted. This is, in part, accomplished through the semi-official practice of plea bargaining.

Reciprocity is important in any group or organization, for it helps bind members and ensure that goals are met. The organization of criminal justice consists of interdependent roles connected by obligations and expectations. Reciprocity is high when these obligations and expectations are met. When the police produce arrests that hold up in court — and many do not (Bureau of Justice Statistics, 1983c:11) — the prosecutor's job is made easier. When the prosecutor speeds cases through the system so that the police are not tied up in court, the work of the police is made easier.

**The Defense Attorney and Guilty Pleas**   Defense attorneys are often the first to suggest that their client plead guilty and in many cases convince the defendant to change an initial not-guilty plea to guilty. Though this means a client's conviction, the defense counsel recognizes a professional obligation to do what is best for the defendant, and if this can be accomplished by copping a plea, then so be it. The plea bargain is attractive, if not obligatory, when the client is guilty and the case is strong enough to produce a conviction at trial. If a lighter sentence can be achieved through a deal, then this is the route any responsible defense attorney will take.

Yet this is not the whole picture. Defense attorneys are subject to some of the same organizational demands as prosecutors. Whether a public defender or a private attorney, the defense counsel's career is dependent on good relations with other actors in the system. Everyday aspects of lawyering depend for success on courthouse support and information sharing, and "legal officials are apt to follow the line of least resistance: to device policies and practices which hold the greatest promise of rewarding the legal agencies and officials involved without undue organizational stress and strain" (Hills, 1971:27). The result is that defendants are often manipulated to serve the professional interests of those within the organization.

Defense attorneys must play the game or risk losing insider status and the rewards that meeting reciprocal obligations brings. If they persist in bucking the system, sanctions will be applied. Attorneys may be excluded from information sharing and from conferences of one sort or another. Chambliss and Siedman (1971:402) recount an occasion in which a young public defender was "read the riot act" by the chief justice of his state because he refused to plea an unusually large proportion of his cases. He was warned of the necessity of cooperating with the prosecution and the bench.

There are also economic advantages to pleading a client guilty. George Cole (1970:340) argues that the criminal attorney's salable product is influence rather than technical proficiency in the law: "[King County, Washington attorneys] hold the belief that clients are attracted partially on the basis of the attorney's reputation as a fixer, or as a shrewd bargainer." In addition, private criminal attorneys usually make money in their offices, on the phone, or in the prosecutor's office, but rarely in the courtroom. Time is money, and the time spent in court is the least profitable. The more clients one can handle in a given day, the more money one can make and the wider one's contacts will become.

Criminal law is generally not a profitable business for private attorneys, nor are most lawyers that well trained in it (Downie, 1972). There is also evidence that criminal law attracts the less competent and less ethical lawyers (Carlin, 1968), many of whom become so-called lawyer regulars, who are

> highly visible in the major urban centers of the nation; their offices — at times shared with bondsmen — line the backstreets near courthouses. They are also visible politically, with club house ties reaching into judicial chambers and the prosecutor's office. The regulars make no effort to conceal their dependence upon police, bondsmen, jail personnel, as well as bailiffs, stenographers, prosecutors, and judges. (Blumberg, 1967:18)

In the hands of these attorneys, the interests of the client may be subordinated to self-interest, and the bargain actually struck may be no bargain at all.

## JUDGES AND BARGAINED JUSTICE

Judges are by no means outsiders to the processes resulting in negotiated justice. Indeed, judges quite often take an active part in the bargaining. Newman (1966: Chaps. 7 and 8) provides numerous illustrations of judiciary involvement in bargained justice, although the extent of that involvement may vary according to the character of the bargain itself (whether it is for charge reduction or sentence leniency) and the jurisdiction in which the court operates. For its part, the U.S. Supreme Court has consistently supported plea bargaining as an important element in American criminal procedure (see box on p. 405).

It should come as no surprise that judges are routinely involved in bargained justice. After all, they, with the prosecution and defense, are actors in the same play. What is more, judges are subject to direct pressures from

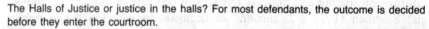
The Halls of Justice or justice in the halls? For most defendants, the outcome is decided before they enter the courtroom.

## SUPREME COURT DECISIONS SUPPORTING PLEA BARGAINING

The following U.S. Supreme Court decisions during the 1970s clearly illustrate the justices' support for the institution of bargained justice.

*Brady v. U.S.* 397 U.S. 742 (1970), held that a guilty plea is not invalid merely because it was entered into out of fear that a trial conviction would result in the death penalty.

*North Carolina v. Alford* 400 U.S. 25 (1970), held that guilty pleas entered together with protestations of innocence are not necessarily involuntary and coerced (which would be grounds for reversal).

*Santobello v. New York* 404 U.S. 257 (1971), held that the prosecution should not make promises to defendants that cannot be adhered to. When pleas rest on promises that are subsequently broken, the Court argued, this is grounds for reversal.

*Blackledge v. Allison* 431 U.S. 63 (1977), reaffirmed that guilty plea negotiations are central to the criminal process.

*Bordenkircher v. Hayes* 434 U.S. 357 (1977), held that prosecutors may carry out threats made during the course of plea negotiations if the defendant rejects the bargain and provided the threats are legal.

---

outside the immediate court organization. Their continued appointment or reelection depends on how well the court's business flows. When things get bogged down, pressure from the media, their political bosses, and the higher judiciary weighs heavily on their shoulders. Like the roles of prosecutor and defense attorney, the judge's role in the judicial process often leads to an administration of the law best characterized as a cooperative endeavor aimed at the speedy, predictable confirmation of a suspect's guilt.

## THE FUTURE OF BARGAINED JUSTICE

In recent years there has been more and more criticism of plea bargaining, both inside and outside legal circles. In one recent criminal justice text (Robin, 1980:250) sixteen different criticisms are listed, and one could probably find more. The author of that text concluded:

> There is something deeply disturbing about a criminal justice system in which lawyers avoid the due process model like the plague, in which the outcome of cases depends on the personal interests and administrative convenience of the practitioners, and in which sentences are unrelated to the crimes committed or to the defendant's genuine correctional needs.

On the heels of increasing criticism of the system, some jurisdictions moved to abolish plea bargaining. Alaska was one of the first, with a complete ban in 1975. Other jurisdictions adopted partial restrictions, for example, banning its use in cases involving career criminals, repeaters, and serious violators, or in cases involving specific heinous crimes such as rape or the killing of law enforcement personnel.

It appears that the effects of reduced bargaining were not exactly as expected, at least in Alaska (Rubinstein et al., 1980). After the prohibition went into effect the number of court trials remained small, the court docket did not bog down (actually, cases were processed faster than before), and the proportion of defendants pleading guilty remained pretty much the same as before the ban. The overwhelming modes of disposition continued to be dismissal and guilty plea. "In the final analysis, most guilty pleas and dismissals were entered because the parties simply did not perceive any better alternative" (p. 223).

If these findings were unexpected, so were the ones dealing with the severity of sentences. True, the sentences for some classes of offenders did increase drastically — 237 percent for drug offenses; 117 percent for fraud. But in the case of burglary, larceny, and receiving stolen property, sentences actually declined for experienced, older offenders charged with more serious offenses and increased for young first offenders whose charges were the least serious in this group. Furthermore, the sentences given to violent offenders remained basically unchanged.

These findings suggest caution in anticipating the consequences of reduced plea bargaining. Certainly, it appears from the Alaska experience that the response of the judicial system cannot be taken for granted. Even so, doubts and cautions should not prevent the contemplation and testing of alternatives to the present system, however far-fetched they might seem. John Griffiths (1970:397) has demanded: "What is so inconceivable about a process which includes a trial (perhaps a shorter and neater trial) for *every* defendant?" One thing a full return to the adversary system might promote is a redefinition by participants of the purpose of their activity. Instead of productivity, efficiency, and organizational self-perpetuation, the goals might bear some resemblance to the ideals of justice. Perhaps, too, the judicial process would look less like a con game to the many defendants whose fortunes are decided after a five-minute discussion with a public defender in some courthouse hallway or bullpen. Jonathan Casper (1972:18) expressed well the view held by many defendants — and undoubtedly many victims, too:

> The system as it operates in practice is seen by defendants in this study as an example of their life on the street. Outcomes do not seem to be determined by principles or careful consideration of persons, but by hustling, conning, manipulation, luck, fortitude, waiting them out, and the like. . . .
>
> How well you do in this world depends upon what you've got and how well you use it. The criminal justice system, like the streets, is a game of resource exploitation. The defendant typically has little in the way of resources and doesn't win. He can, though, with luck and skill, lose less than he might. In this way . . . the system has no real moral component in the eyes of the defendant. It is an extension of life on the street and the other participants — the police, defense attorney, the prosecutor, the judge — are themselves playing a game that is perceived as existing on the same moral level as that of the defendant.

## Sentencing

All offenders who are convicted of a crime face sentencing. In this section we shall look at the behavior of judges and at the constraints within which they operate. But a word of caution is necessary. Although officially, it is the magistrate or judge who decides what sentence the convicted criminal must serve, in reality it is often the prosecutor who largely determines the sentence. This is so because the prosecutor is in control of the charges. A suspect who is arrested for armed robbery may, after plea negotiations, be formally charged with some other, lesser, offense. In this way the prosecutor has reduced the possible sentence.

**Sentencing Disparities** Sentencing decisions in felony cases must address three questions: (1) should the defendant be incarcerated? If yes, then (2) in a local jail or in a prison? and (3) for how long? There is little consistency from jurisdiction to jurisdiction and from judge to judge in the answers to these questions, even when the offense is essentially the same. There is, in short, considerable sentencing disparity in America.

The extent of the problem is only now being fully documented, though it has been recognized for years. One study of judges in New York, Connecticut, and Vermont (the U.S. Court of Appeals for the Second Circuit) used actual presentence reports by probation officers and asked each judge to assign a sentence in twenty different cases. The range of sentences among the fifty judges interviewed was considerable, and the sentences for identical cases could not be predicted (see Robin, 1980:297–298). In a similar study, forty-seven Virginia judges were given identical descriptions of five criminal cases (Austin and Williams, 1977). They were asked to determine a verdict and assign a sentence as if the situation were real. There were high rates of agreement on the verdicts but wide variation in the sentences. Using different methods, other studies have produced similar results.

A comparison of average prison terms in four jurisdictions with similar sentencing structures, that is, with similar rules governing judicial discretion, found wide variation for the same offense categories (see Table 13.3). Furthermore, the likelihood of being sent to prison in the first place shows considerable variation around the country for similar offenses. In robbery cases, for example, 100 percent of those convicted were sent to prison in

**Table 13.3** Average Minimum and Maximum Sentence Lengths (in Months), Circa 1980

|  | ILLINOIS | | NEW YORK | | PENNSYLVANIA | | WYOMING | |
|---|---|---|---|---|---|---|---|---|
|  | MIN | MAX | MIN | MAX | MIN | MAX | MIN | MAX |
| Homicide | 346 | 743 | 130 | 156 | 42 | 112 | 146 | 195 |
| Rape | 125 | 154 | 67 | 156 | 53 | 136 | 70 | 127 |
| Robbery | 55 | 108 | 38 | 91 | 24 | 68 | 56 | 99 |
| Burglary | 21 | 60 | 25 | 61 | 19 | 52 | 28 | 58 |
| Larceny | 16 | 40 | 18 | 42 | 7 | 25 | 21 | 47 |

SOURCE: Bureau of Justice Statistics (1984), Special Report: Sentencing Practices in 13 States. Washington, D.C.: U.S. Department of Justice.

**Table 13.4** Percentage of Convictions Resulting in Imprisonment, Circa 1980

| | IOWA | NEW YORK | OKLAHOMA | PENNSYLVANIA | WYOMING |
|---|---|---|---|---|---|
| Homicide | 86.4 | 90.6 | 78.1 | 73.3 | 88.9 |
| Rape | 92.9 | 97.8 | 71.0 | 77.3 | 68.6 |
| Robbery | 100.0 | 67.4 | 79.2 | 73.4 | 57.7 |
| Assault | 50.7 | 41.5 | 37.2 | 39.1 | 34.8 |
| Burglary | 36.5 | 38.8 | 43.6 | 61.3 | 37.4 |
| Larceny | 25.4 | 24.8 | 25.1 | 33.7 | 28.1 |
| Auto theft | 33.7 | a | 46.9 | 41.6 | 42.1 |
| Arson | 36.8 | 40.7 | 37.6 | 53.2 | 31.1 |

SOURCE: Bureau of Justice Statistics (1984), Special Report: Sentencing Practices in 13 States. Washington, D.C.: U.S. Department of Justice.

a. Auto thefts in New York are included in the figure for larceny.

Iowa, versus only 57.7 percent in Wyoming — and both states are predominantly rural (see Table 13.4).

## THE PRESENTENCE INVESTIGATION

In both Europe and America, more and more attention is being given to the use of presentence investigations as an aid to sentencing. Though rarely used in dealing with misdemeanants, presentence reports are intended to help the judge choose a sentence more appropriate to the particular case. In some states, a presentence investigation is mandatory; in others it is available at the request of the judge.

A presentence report contains information about the convicted offender considered relevant to guiding the judge toward an appropriate sentence within the jurisdiction's statutory framework. The information is usually collected by probation officers or other trained social workers employed by the state. What is contained in the report will depend in part on the jurisdiction, in part on administrative policies, and in part on the experience, talents, hard work, competence, and perspectives of the investigators. "In theory [the report] is a neutral document, its purpose being neither adverse nor favorable to the sentencing fate of the defendant" (Remington et al., 1969:696). It is intended to provide accurate and relevant information on those aspects of an offender's personal and family history — police record, prior convictions, employment history, and family situation — that are thought to make a difference in sentencing alternatives.

In practice, presentence reports may be neither neutral and accurate nor filled with only relevant information. According to one study, reports often contain misinformation, prejudicial statements, and "facts" based on hearsay and rumor. Here are some illustrations, taken from presentence reports:

1. "While [the defendant] apparently never engaged in any serious criminal conduct before, and while he has never shown any tendency to use violence, it is rumored in the factory, and evidently widely believed, that about two years ago he murdered his boss's wife."
2. "His wife reports that he is given to murderous rages."
3. "In my opinion [as an experienced, graduate-trained probation and parole agent], he is the type of person who, if not checked soon, will kill somebody someday."
4. "There is a broad, deep base of sexual psychopathy in this boy. His offense may technically be burglary but he is basically a sex deviate."
5. "He is a loser, plain and simple. He is sexually inadequate, vocationally inadequate, and mentally inadequate. He has failed in everything — school, jobs, military service, with his family, and with his wife. He has even failed as a crook. There is absolutely no reason to think he can make it on probation and probably prison won't help him much. The only thing I can recommend is incarceration for as long as possible and then hope for the best." (Remington et al., 1969:697–698)

There is no reason to believe that all investigators go well beyond factual, objective, and relevant information. However, many probably do, for three reasons. First, many jurisdictions and administrative policies require or encourage investigators to recount feelings and attitudes, either their own or other people's, and to present opinions and recommendations. Second, those who write the reports sooner or later look upon themselves as experts, professionals whose opinions are learned and should be taken seriously. Third, investigators are subject to organizational pressures and they try to avoid rocking the boat. If the police are particularly anxious for a certain disposition, for example, investigators may feel obliged to tilt their reports accordingly. Remember, participants in the judicial process work together, not in opposition.

Ralph Blankenship (1974) shows how special meanings are attached to language used in the case records that accompany individuals throughout their official careers as deviants. Presentence reports, probation records, prison records, and mental hospital records are put together by professionals who share language "registers," words and phrases having special meaning for them. When compiling case records, they present an image of the subject that fits *their* perception of the criminal, psychotic, or delinquent reality: "the professional does not use his register to describe, but as a means of constructing his social reality" (1974:255). Blankenship points out how direct quotations from labeled deviants give the appearance of letting the deviant tell the story, but to those in the know they serve to discredit the story at the same time. What is quoted is, of course, under the control of the person constructing the report.

**Confidentiality**  For many years, presentence reports were for the judge's eyes only. Though the situation has changed somewhat in recent years, many jurisdictions retain the traditional approach.

The issue of confidentiality has sparked considerable debate, with little chance that it will be resolved one way or the other in the near future. On one side are those who claim that disclosure will invite retaliation by the defendant, will cause information sources to dry up, and will produce prolonged litigation as the defense seeks to challenge and cross-examine those who have collected or supplied the contents of the report. On the other are those who believe that any information to be used in sentence decision making must be subject to defense scrutiny, that confidentiality promotes backroom justice, and that the defendant must be assured of impartial and fair treatment by the state (see Remington et al., 1969:702–710).

**Impact of Reports on Sentencing**    All this matters little if presentence reports have no impact on the actual sentences handed down. At least, it matters little from a pragmatic standpoint, though fundamental ethical and constitutional issues are involved, which do matter if justice is to be met. The question is, then, are judges influenced by presentence reports and, if so, to what extent?

Data dealing with the impact of presentence reports provide few conclusive answers. Some studies show that presentence reports are influential in the sentencing process. Thus Carter and Wilkins (1967) found in California that judges and probation officials were in broad agreement on major sentencing criteria and that judges accepted 86 percent of investigators' recommendations. Other studies have found similar evidence of strong correlations between sentencing recommendations and actual sentences (e.g., Frazier and Bock, 1982).

On the other hand, Hogarth (1971) reports that Canadian magistrates are likely to use reports and other sources of information in a selective manner, when it is consistent with their own philosophy, attitudes, and preconceptions regarding the individual case. However, presentence reports tended to be requested and used when judges already considered a case difficult, when they saw themselves likely to give sentences out of keeping with their normal practice. Hogarth speculates that the presentence report gives judges the opportunity to justify a decision already made, rather than to direct them in coming to a decision.

Hogarth observed an important difference in the use and impact of presentence reports. He found that urban magistrates tended to react negatively to probation officers' recommendations, whereas rural judges appeared more likely to accept the reports. He explains the difference by referring to the rural judge's easier work load, greater self-esteem and community status, greater informality, less punitive orientation, and the closer ties between court and probation services in rural areas. In summing up the value of presentence reports, Hogarth (1971:262) concludes:

> . . . if the presentence report is to have the impact on sentencing that was originally intended, and indeed often assumed, certain favourable conditions for its proper use must exist. Magistrates must have the time to read reports

carefully. They must also have the opportunity, when the need arises, to discuss their contents informally with probation officers. Most important, they must have a set of attitudes and beliefs which are consistent with the rationale underlying the use of the presentence report, namely, the individualization of justice.

## EXTRALEGAL FACTORS IN SENTENCING

The existence of sentencing disparities would probably not be of so much concern were it not for the fact that much of the variation is thought to be the result of the judge's beliefs and feelings, rather than of the objective features of the offense and offender as recognized in law. The widely divergent sentences imposed for essentially the same crime cannot be adequately accounted for by differences in the law, in the circumstances of the offense, or in the criminality of the offender. What, then, are some of the extralegal factors thought to influence the sentencing decisions of judges?

**Race and Class** The evidence shows that sentencing decisions are influenced by social class and race. Reviewing years of American research, Wolfgang and Cohen (1970:80) found that "blacks usually receive longer prison terms than whites for most criminal offenses." Sellin (1935) also found much evidence of racial bias in sentencing practices. In England, Chapman (1968) found numerous examples of clearly preferential treatment in the case of middle-class offenders, whereas Hood (1972) found that middle-class judges gave more punitive sentences than did those with working-class backgrounds.

In many cases these differences appear to hold for offenses in general as well as for specific crimes. The impact of race and class has also been found in the sentences given juvenile offenders. In one study the records of 9,601 juvenile court dispositions in Philadelphia were analyzed. It was discovered that even when legal variables such as severity of offense and prior record were taken into account, blacks were more likely than whites to be prosecuted and institutionalized, and lower socioeconomic offenders were more severely penalized than others (Thornberry, 1973).

In a study of early releases from prison under a "shock probation" program* in Ohio, Peterson and Friday (1975) found race to be the most important factor in determining releases in certain situations. For example, when the probation department had recommended against early release, whites were twice as likely as blacks to be released, even after controlling for a variety of legal variables.

Much of the research on judicial disposition of cases seems to support the view that race and class are often taken into account in sentencing. Even so, in a review of recent studies, Steven Box (1981) found ten showing no

---

*Shock probation allows an incarcerated offender to appeal to the court of conviction for early release from prison as a form of probation. The offender must appeal within sixty days of the original sentencing date.

association between class and disposition and seventeen studies showing no association between race and disposition.

Many of the studies dealing with judicial disposition of criminal cases employed different methods. Caution must therefore be exercised in any attempt to arrive at general conclusions regarding the impact of social status on sentencing. When the data in some earlier studies have been reanalyzed and controls for such "legal" variables as prior record introduced, different conclusions have been reached. After his reanalysis of twenty studies purporting to show race and class effects, John Hagan (1974:379) concluded that "while there may be evidence of differential sentencing, knowledge of extralegal offender characteristics contributes relatively little to our ability to predict judicial dispositions."

Gary Kleck (1981) also reevaluated published research on criminal sentencing. He focused on racial bias in both capital and noncapital cases and reviewed over fifty-five studies, mostly from the 1960s and 1970s. He concluded that there was little evidence of any general, overt racial discrimination in noncapital cases, but strong evidence of discrimination in capital cases in the South when the offense was rape. However, Kleck also observed that black defendants sometimes are treated more *leniently* than whites, and especially so when their victims are also black. Kleck offers various explanations of this: (1) that blacks are devalued crime victims, hence offenses against them are deemed less serious; (2) that there exists a sort of white paternalism; and (3) that some judges may feel guilty about past discrimination or may be compensating for institutionalized racism or for any prejudice they might have. These hypotheses remain to be tested, however.

A number of authors have pointed out that prior criminal record is itself a product of previous discretionary judgments, which may themselves have been influenced by social considerations. Furthermore, when introduced as a factor in court deliberations, a prior record influences outcome indirectly by affecting a defendant's ability to secure bail and competent private counsel and to negotiate a reduction in charge. In sum, the finding reported in many studies that legal variables account for most of the variation may actually reflect the accumulated disadvantages of being black and lower class (Box, 1971:194; Kleck, 1981:799).

The evidence on status discrimination in sentencing permits no firm conclusions. Yet even if there were incontestable evidence against the conventional wisdom that there is discrimination, the fact is that the penalties assigned by law to predominantly lower-class crimes (robbery, burglary, assault, heroin pushing) are, in general, higher than those for predominantly upper-class crime (corporate fraud, misrepresentation in advertising, restraint of trade, environmental crimes). This indicates built-in bias against lower-class offenders and raises the likelihood that lower-class offenders will receive harsher penalties than higher-class criminals will, even if the crimes are similar in consequence or, worse, even if occupational crimes have more serious consequences.

**Community Characteristics** A person's attitudes and beliefs are shaped by a variety of influences. Some of the more important ones derive from the immediate social environment in which the person lives and works. Studies of judicial sentencing behavior bear this out. Almost all such studies show that it makes a great deal of difference where a judge lives and works. Hood (1962) found that judges in rural, or small town, communities were more inclined to sentence offenders to prison, this policy fitting in well with community sentiments and the "peaceful" life-style of rural communities. Emile Durkheim (1964a:102–108) argued long ago that deviance stands out like a sore thumb in small, homogeneous, tradition-bound communities, and the collective sentiments that it threatens require immediate and forceful reaffirmation:

> We have only to note what happens, particularly in a small town, when some moral scandal has just been committed. They stop each other on the street, they visit each other, they seek to come together to talk of the event and wax indignant in common. . . .

> It is necessary that [solidarity] be affirmed at the very moment that it is contradicted, and the only means of affirming it is to express the unanimous aversion which crime continues to inspire, by an authentic act which can consist only in suffering inflicted upon the agent.

The relationship between community characteristics and sentencing may be more complex than Hood and Durkheim would lead us to believe. Indeed, Hogarth (1971) showed that sentencing in rural areas is less, not more, severe than that found in urban areas. But Nagel (1967) found that sentences in rural areas are not less punitive for all offenses — rural courts were less punitive in assault cases but more so than urban and northern courts in cases involving larceny.

The different authors do agree, however, that, community characteristics cannot be ignored as influences on the sentencing behavior of judges. Since most judges in this country are appointed or elected in a decidedly political atmosphere, they cannot afford to antagonize those who have given them their jobs. Although some judges are able to isolate themselves from public opinion and other pressures (Hogarth, 1971), most probably cannot or find it unrewarding to do so. In this respect, judges are little different from other participants in the judicial process.

It is Hogarth's view that sentencing behavior largely boils down to a judge's particular judicial attitudes and penal philosophies. How judges define their role, what they see as the purpose of punishment, how they perceive the various social and legal constraints to which they are subjected, and how they view the relative merits of different sentencing options, all are subjective elements brought to sentencing decisions. If we allow wide judicial discretion, we can expect to find more room for the impact of attitude and philosophy. Within the boundaries of legal constraint, judges will attempt to organize their sentencing behavior in congruence with their perceptions of legal, situational, and social realities (Hogarth, 1971:209–210).

## CURBING JUDICIAL DISCRETION

No one argues that sentencing is easy or expects judges to behave like robots. Judges are human, and there is nothing that adequately prepares them for the awesome responsibility of deciding the fate of criminals. Whereas most experts acknowledge the need for some judicial discretion, they nevertheless support efforts to curtail it in the hope of reducing sentencing disparities and excesses.

Directed mostly toward the sentencing of felony offenders, whose crimes carry statutory prison terms of more than a year, these efforts have resulted in a variety of sentencing reforms. In some states juries are empowered to decide sentences; in others a panel of judges (often called a "sentencing council") is formed to consider penalties; in yet others a sentencing board, composed of lawyers, social workers, psychiatrists, and others with professional interest in the legal process, meets to decide sentences. The value of the last two methods lies mainly in the opportunities they provide for sharing views, philosophies, and knowledge regarding sentencing, thereby promoting greater uniformity than is found when judges act individually.

**Sentencing Guidelines**   One promising reform is to give judges guidelines based on a jurisdiction's actual sentencing practices so as to give structure to the individual exercise of discretion. Leslie Wilkins and colleagues (1978) favor this approach and have devised reference tables that can be used to determine the average, or model, sentence given by area judges in cases of similar offense and offender circumstances (see Table 13.5).

Using information about the seriousness of the offense and the prior record and "social stability" of the offender, judges can determine scores for offense and offender according to a prearranged formula. To find the model sentence for any particular combination of offense/offender scores, the judge simply finds the cell that lines up with the two scores in the table. Suppose an offender in Colorado has committed a Class 4 felony (say, a robbery) and is given an offense score of 6 and an offender score of 10. What would be the model sentence?

Wilkins considers the plan to be a middle course between the current lack of consistent policy and the much more restrictive system of mandatory flat sentencing described below. The model, or guideline, sentence is to be considered advisory, but judges are required to give written reasons if they decide to go outside the guidelines in a particular case. Wilkins and his coauthors see the plan "as a means to guide and structure — not eliminate — judicial discretion, so as to aid judges in reaching a fair and equitable sentencing decision" (Wilkins et al., 1978:vii).

**Table 13.5** Sentencing guidelines, Felony 4, Denver

| | OFFENDER SCORE | | | | |
|---|---|---|---|---|---|
| OFFENSE SCORE | −1 −7 | 0 2 | 3 8 | 9 12 | 13+ |
| 10–12 | Indeterminate minimum 4–5 year maximum | Indeterminate minimum 8–10 year maximum | Indeterminate minimum 8–10 year maximum | Indeterminate minimum 8–10 year maximum | Indeterminate minimum 8–10 year maximum |
| 8–9 | Out | 3–5 month work project | Indeterminate minimum 3–4 year maximum | Indeterminate minimum 8–10 year maximum | Indeterminate minimum 8–10 year maximum |
| 6–7 | Out | Out | Indeterminate minimum 3–4 year maximum | Indeterminate minimum 6–8 year maximum | Indeterminate minimum 8–10 year maximum |
| 3–5 | Out | Out | Out | Indeterminate minimum 4–5 year maximum | Indeterminate minimum 4–5 year maximum |
| 1–2 | Out | Out | Out | Out | Indeterminate minimum 3–4 year maximum |

SOURCE: Wilkins, Leslie T., Jack M. Kress, Don M. Gottfredson, Joseph C. Calpin, and Arthur M. Gelman (1978), Sentencing Guidelines: Structuring Judicial Discretion. Washington, D.C.: U.S. Government Printing Office, p. xv.

Note: Colorado uses a penal code that contains five levels of felonies (with Felony 1 being the most serious and Felony 5 the least serious) and three levels of misdemeanors. Typical crimes that fall within the Felony 4 category are manslaughter, robbery, and second degree burglary. The statutory designated maximum incarcerative sentence for a Felony 4 offense is 10 years. No minimum period of confinement is to be set by the court. The term "out" refers to a nonincarcerative type of sentence such as probation, deferred judgment, or deferred prosecution.

**Determinate Sentencing**  Statutory changes in favor of determinate sentencing (sometimes called "flat" or "fixed-term" sentencing) have been one of the more notable products of concern over sentencing practices. The first state to enact fixed-term sentencing was Maine, in 1975. California, Illinois, Indiana, New Mexico, and Washington (in its 1977 juvenile code) soon followed suit.

Determinate sentencing is advocated in many quarters as a solution to unfair (that is, excessively lenient or harsh) and disparate sentencing. It is supposed to eliminate judicial discretion but in some cases does so only after the judge has decided on a particular type of penalty (usually imprisonment). In other words, a judge is free to decide whether or not an offender should receive probation or some other penalty, but once the judge decides on prison, the law sets the term of imprisonment. The defendant serves a specified term with time off for good behavior; however, parole is abolished.

Slightly different is the *mandatory* sentencing system. Here a minimum sentence is required for certain offenses, usually those involving armed, violent, repeat, or drug offenders. By 1983 all but two states had instituted some form of mandatory sentencing. Maine and Illinois have combined mandatory and fixed-term sentencing. Other states have retained combinations of mandatory and indeterminate sentencing or have made sentences fixed-term but not mandatory (Bureau of Justice Statistics, 1983d:3).

As with any reform, this approach to sentencing has its critics. Some claim that discretion is not really curbed but is simply shifted from the judge to the prosecutor. Indeed, the California determinate-sentencing laws have been called a plea-bargainer's paradise, for they give prosecutors all kinds of leverage in securing guilty pleas (Alschuler, 1978:73). Rather than receiving the sentences intended by the reformers, offenders escape them through the bargaining process. In addition, some critics argue that the mandatory sentences are uniformly too high and, despite rhetoric to the contrary, will be avoided by prosecutors and judges because correctional resources are inadequate to handle the influx of new prisoners (Foote, 1978:133–141).

A study of the Indiana experience with determinate sentencing is instructive. The 1977 penal code provides for certain specific terms of imprisonment for seven classes of offense, with enhancement for aggravation (such as use of a weapon or brutality) and reduction for mitigation (such as victim precipitation). Under the code, for example, the maximum possible sentence for a Class A felony such as armed robbery or forcible rape would be thirty years *plus* twenty years in enhancement for aggravation; the minimum would be thirty years *minus* ten years in mitigation. Once in prison, the offender would be able to build up credit toward future release in the form of "good time," thus reducing the actual time served (Clear et al., 1978).

The authors of the study point out that the code increases sentencing discretion in two ways. First, the enhancement and mitigation rules greatly extend the bargaining flexibility of prosecutors who can play the carrot-and-stick game while pressuring for a plea. Under this system a lesser charge or fewer elements of aggravation add up to years off the sentence. Second, the use of credit time as the only way a sentence can be reduced once it is being served gives sentencing discretion to prison authorities. "Thus, a great deal of effective control over the inmate's sentence has been placed directly in the hands of the correctional officer who watches over him" (Clear et al., 1978:440).

"In fact," the authors go on, "that control has been formalized by the new law, and, even assuming the best intentions on the part of all concerned, the result may be a more repressive atmosphere for inmates" (p. 440). Not only that, the authors show what could happen to first offenders under the new code as compared with the old. Even assuming the offenders had earned all the available credit time, they would still end up serving an estimated 47.4 percent *more* prison time if sentenced under the new penal code. In the case of some offenses the percentage difference is more, in others less. In two cases — negligent homicide and check forgery — offenders would serve less time under the new system.

The authors' own conclusion best summarizes this study. Although the evidence may look different in other jurisdictions, the case in favor of determinate sentencing is probably not helped, and we should probably be extremely cautious in advocating wholesale changes in the law, as some have done. For all its well-documented drawbacks, the indeterminate sentencing system, with its emphasis on judicial discretion and parole, may not have been improved:

> The new Indiana Penal Code provides such wide discretion, coupled with untenably heavy penalties, that a most likely result will be the creation and solidification of a formal system of decisions and rules that barely conceals a low-visibility, busy, and pragmatic system of informal decisions regulating the actual sentence, largely in the control of prosecutors, judges, and correctional officials. The new sentencing scheme may come to bear a strange resemblance to what reformers hoped to eliminate. (Clear et al., 1978:443)

## SELECTIVE INCAPACITATION

The decision to send a felon to prison may be taken out of a judge's hands by statute, as may the length of the sentence. However, whether by statute or judicial discretion, many experts believe that these decisions should be guided by a formal policy. One policy that has attracted considerable attention has been recommended by Peter Greenwood and Allan Abrahams (1982). It is called *selective incapacitation.*

As we shall see in the next chapter, one of the ways in which punishment may prevent crime is to incapacitate the offenders, that is, to take them out of circulation. Imprisonment does this. Greenwood believes sentencing policies can be constructed so as to maximize this function of imprisonment for whom it is most needed: offenders who are most likely to commit crimes if released. Incapacitation would therefore be selective: "some offenders would be imprisoned for a longer period than others convicted of the same offense, because of predictions about their *future* criminality" (J. Cohen, 1983:3).

Greenwood (1984; Greenwood and Abrahams, 1982) studied robbery and burglary inmates in California on behalf of the Rand Corporation. He found that robbers who had *four or more* of the following characteristics committed an average of thirty-one robberies per year while on the street, compared with an average of two robberies per year for inmates with only one of these characteristics:

1. Prior convictions for robbery or burglary.
2. Being incarcerated for more than half of the preceding 2 years.
3. Juvenile conviction prior to age 16.
4. Commitment to a State or Federal juvenile facility.
5. Current heroin or barbiturate use.
6. Heroin or barbiturate use as a juvenile.
7. Employed less than half of the preceding two years, excluding jail time. (1984:6)

Selective incapacitation policy would use this seven-item "scale" as the basis for setting prison terms at sentencing.

Advocates of selective incapacitation believe one of its major advantages is that judges will be able to base their sentencing decisions on information most relevant to the crime proneness of convicted offenders rather than on a hodge-podge of information and opinion, much of it irrelevant to gauging the risk of sending them to prison for short terms, or not at all. By incarcerating the "right" offenders, the community will be spared the large number of crimes that would have been otherwise have been committed; at the same time, those offenders identified as low risk will benefit by avoiding long-term imprisonment.

Opponents of selective incapacitation have both pragmatic and moral objections (J. Cohen, 1983; von Hirsch, 1984). A common ethical objection is that two persons convicted of the same offense, say armed robbery, deserve a similar punishment. Another questions whether it is fair to send a person to prison for crimes not yet committed. On the practical side, there are serious doubts whether accurate predictions of future criminality can be made. Indeed, the errors that have shown up in past efforts suggest that around half the offenders evaluated as high risk in fact are not. A methodological objection to the Greenwood approach helps explain why many experts lack confidence in it: he studied only incarcerated offenders and based his predictions largely on self-reported information. It has not been established whether the same results would hold with offenders at large, and as Jacqueline Cohen (1984) points out: "At sentencing, one could not confidently rely on information provided by the offender."

Samuel Walker (1985:62–63) makes a rather different criticism of selective incapacitation. He observes that according to the proposed seven-point scale, unemployment carries the same weight as prior conviction offense and all the other items. It is therefore possible for a person's unemployment to make the difference between jail or prison. He goes on:

> It is outrageous that anyone could seriously recommend imposing criminal penalties for unemployment. But that is precisely what the Rand formula does. The policy would take us back 300 years to the days of imprisonment for debt
> . . . . The Rand data are undoubtedly correct: unemployment does correlate with criminal activity. The way to deal with that problem — the rational, effective, and humane way — is to provide employment.

The controversy over selective incapacitation rages on, all the more so because it has received considerable publicity. As with all efforts to curb judicial discretion, there will be some judges who welcome the assistance in a most difficult task and others who reject it as unwarranted infringement on their role. In the last analysis, the daily sentencing decision may be more influenced by the system's capacity to handle its criminals than by any formal policy (Pontell, 1984).

**CHAPTER 14**

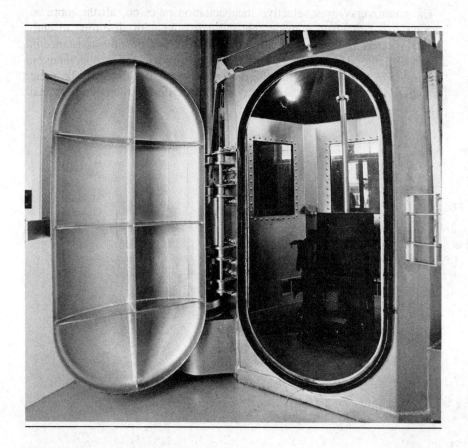

# Punishing the Criminal Offender

To do justice to the subject of criminal punishment would require an entire text. Since our space is limited, in this chapter we shall look at the meanings, objectives, and justifications of criminal punishment, as well as its major types. In Chapter 15 we shall explore in more detail the nature and impact of imprisonment and the important problems of reformation and deterrence.

# The Definition of Punishment

*Punishment* can be defined as any action designed to deprive a person or persons of things of value because of something that person is thought to have done. Examples include "liberty, civil rights, skills, opportunities, material objects, less tangible forms of wealth, health, identity, life, and — perhaps most crucial — significant personal relationships" (Turk, 1969:19).

## CRIMINAL PUNISHMENT

There are three major categories of criminal punishment. The first category, *official criminal penalties,* consists of legal punishments, punishments provided for by law and imposed by lawful representatives of a state, community, or group according to the directives of law. Examples of official criminal penalties are fines, prison terms, and probation.

The second category of criminal punishment can be designated as *extralegal penalties*. These punishments, though not illegal, are not provided for by law nor designated as punishments to be applied by officials of the state. Extralegal criminal penalties are diverse; examples are refusal to marry someone because of his or her criminality and harassment of a prisoner by a guard.

The third category consists of *illegal penalties*. These are punishments that are themselves illegal (such as torture) or that are applied illegally (such as the lynching of a convicted murderer).

## THE RELATIVITY OF PUNISHMENT

Punishment is relative, first, in the sense that what is a deprivation for one person or group may not be for another. For example, although most of us would probably consider a stay in jail as a significant deprivation, this view may not be held by everyone or by members of other societies. Second, it is relative in the sense that different people may have different views regarding which deprivations are more severe than others. Although most of us would probably consider a jail sentence a more severe penalty than a fine, this view is apparently not shared by skid-row drunks. It is not uncommon for skid-row drunks to see fines as far more punitive than workhouse or jail terms (Lovald and Stub, 1968:525 – 530). For one thing, they see a jail sentence as an opportunity to recuperate from the ravages of their life; a fine, on the other hand, means giving up drinking money.

Punishment is also relative in terms of its imposition and the sorts of deprivations involved. At different times, and in different places, certain types of deprivations have been imposed to the exclusion of others. Similarly, there are variations in the degree to which certain punishments are used. Some are used more frequently than others, and there are likely to be variations in the amount of deprivation depending on time, place, and situation. Like crime, punishment is affected by law, politics, culture, social structure, and situation.

## Legal Punishment: Justification and Aims

When convicted criminals are punished today, they are punished by the state in the name of its people. Crimes are conceived of as public wrongs, and in criminal law the state is the victim. The real injury to the real victim of a crime is formally ignored. The state prosecutes, the state adjudicates, and the state determines the possible penalties. The result, Bittner and Platt (1966:81) suggest, is that punishment has become "an abstract measure of justice," in that the penalty for a crime is not assessed in terms of the real harm experienced by its immediate victims.

This situation raises the need for a moral justification of punishment that goes beyond the notion of victim compensation. Over the years, two major arguments have been offered in support of legal punishment. The first stresses the ideas of moral responsibility and just deserts, and is favored by the *retributivists*. The second stresses the justification of punishment in terms of its capacity to deter or to reform. This view gained wide popularity through the efforts of the *utilitarians,* particularly Cesare Beccaria and Jeremy Bentham. Both perspectives seek to justify legal punishment in general and in its particular application.

### RETRIBUTION

It is a mistake to believe, as many people apparently do, that retribution is synonymous with revenge. Retributivists point out that their view of legal punishment emphasizes the principles of justice and due process, not the subjective passions of punishers seeking vengeance. Punishment is deserved when morally responsible persons are guilty of willfully violating the moral order according to the laws of the society in which they claim membership. For its part, society has the moral right, and the duty, to punish the guilty. It has the right to punish because the integrity of its moral order has been violated; it has the duty to punish because not to do so negates the very idea of crime and renders moral responsibility meaningless. All of this does not mean that penalties will necessarily be severe. A distinguished panel of educators and lawyers, which recently concluded that the only just system of punishment is one based on retribution, proposed a maximum penalty for all crimes but murder of five years imprisonment (von Hirsch, 1976:136).

Retributivists see only one possible basis for justifying specific penalties for specific crimes. A specific penalty is justified when the guilty person has received a punishment reflecting the gravity of the offense. The two issues of guilt and making the punishment fit the crime provide the grounds for arguing that any particular legal punishment is a "just desert."

But how do we make the punishment fit the crime? Various possibilities have been offered: (1) make the punishment mirror the crime itself (*lex talionis,* an eye for an eye); (2) adjust the severity of penalties according to the social harm resulting from different offenses; and (3) link the penalties to the moral outrage or indignation felt by a majority of citizens.

From a practical standpoint, none of these possibilities offers much hope of realization. Even if all agreed that one particular possibility, or combination of possibilities, offered the best approach, translating the ideas into practice meets formidable difficulties. What kinds of penalties would accurately mirror robbing a bank of $20,000 or possessing 2 grams of heroin? On what basis are things considered socially harmful, and who makes the relevant judgments? Moral outrage may offer more hope, in that public sentiments can be tapped. In one attempt, wide agreement was found in rating the seriousness of 140 offenses (see pages 9–11). Even so, a problem arises in determining the actual penalties for actual crimes. Depending on the circumstances surrounding two identical acts, the sense of moral outrage might well differ. Are we to expect judicial authorities to poll the public every time a criminal conviction is handed down? Surely this would be the only just way to deal with the problem of moral indignation.

## PREVENTION, REFORM, AND DETERRENCE

Today few people in the public eye speak of retribution when addressing the problem of punishment. This is certainly due in part to the popular misconception that retribution stands for revenge. The emphasis today is almost always on punishment as a means of preventing or reducing crime.

One of the first to outline this view was the Italian philosopher Cesare Beccaria (1963) writing in the second half of the eighteenth century. In his monumental *Essay on Crimes and Punishments,* Beccaria argued that punishment can be justified as a legal device to prevent crimes provided it is applied fairly and openly. Beccaria was extremely concerned about the rampant injustices and unimaginable terrors characteristic of eighteenth-century law enforcement and penal practice. Yet he saw, too, that crime was apparently escalating and that something had to be done. Punishment, applied fairly and properly, he thought, had to be the answer.

A just punishment, in Beccaria's view, is one that is proportionate to the offense *and* sufficient to outweigh the pleasure derived from it. The second part is important, for it lies at the heart of the *utilitarian* doctrine, which Beccaria espoused, and helps explain how punishment prevents crime.

Simply put, the utilitarians argued in favor of a guiding principle: the greatest happiness of the greatest number. Any action can produce pleasure or happiness for someone, just as it can also produce pain. In seeking their pleasures people may cause others pleasure or pain; hence others' lives are often affected by their actions, and it behooves them to consider the impact of an action on the group as a whole. Whereas crime produces pleasure for its perpetrator, it produces pain for others — considered a bad or evil thing by utilitarians. Punishment also brings pain, and so it, too, is a bad thing. Yet if by punishing the criminal we prevent crime, we give more pleasure to the group as a whole at the expense of those whose behavior is bad in the first place. We can justify the use of punishment along utilitarian lines, then, if the group as a whole is better off.

This brings us to the ways in which punishment is conventionally thought to prevent crime. First, punishment is a way to *reform* criminals so that they will not commit crimes in the future. The original penitentiary was an early application of the idea that punishment reforms. Second, punishment is a way to prevent crime by *incapacitating* offenders so that they are in no position to engage in criminal activity. Death, banishment, and other penalties that remove an individual from access to opportunities to commit crimes are incapacitating penalties.

Third, there is the question of *deterrence*. The early utilitarians, especially Beccaria and Jeremy Bentham (1948), believed that punishment could be made to deter individuals from committing crime. Like Beccaria, Bentham believed that punishment was justifiable if it prevented crime. The important remaining question is How? The answer, they believed, was obvious: since people seek pleasure and avoid pain, they will tend to avoid those things that bring pain, especially if the pain outweighs the pleasure. Accordingly, punishment can prevent crime by its threat of pain. Simply put, people are scared away from crime by fear of punishment. We shall return to a more detailed analysis of the deterrence doctrine in Chapter 15.

## Official Criminal Penalties

The range of legal punishments throughout history has been vast. Whereas in most Western societies today there are three basic penalty types — physical detention, fines, and probation — not so long ago the list included all sorts of things: torture, branding and other public humiliations, maiming, deportation, banishment, loss of property corporal punishment, forced labor, coerced penitence, self-denial, and, of course, death.

Official criminal penalties can best be approached as *types* of legal punishment. Sutherland and Cressey (1974:303) have enumerated four types of punishment: (1) removal from the group, (2) physical torture, (3) social degradation, and (4) financial loss.

## REMOVAL FROM THE GROUP: DEATH

Death, banishment, transportation, and imprisonment are examples of removal penalties. At the least, these punishments remove individuals from familiar everyday social interactions with family, friends, and acquaintances.

Death has been called "probably the most ancient of all forms of formal punishment," and "the pivotal criminal punishment in Western society from ancient times until the nineteenth century" (Newman, 1978:27). In early criminal codes, death was the penalty for a wide range of offenses. Both the ancient Mosaic code and that of Hammurapi prescribed death for witchcraft, incest, kidnapping, certain forms of theft, and negligence resulting in death. In Greece, Rome, and among the Germanic tribes governed by the laws of Tacitus, death was also a common penalty, and Durkheim noted its extensive use by the ancient Egyptians, Assyrians, and Hindus (1900:65–93).

It has been said that during the reign of Henry VIII, 72,000 people were executed, many of them for trivial offenses (Calvert, 1971:4). We can never know if this figure is accurate since complete records have not survived, but it is certainly true that the medieval period saw an upsurge in the use of the death penalty in most of Europe. The popularity of this penalty seems to have reached a peak during the sixteenth century, when it dropped off only to rise again by the end of the eighteenth century. At that time England had more than 200 capital offenses (some authors claim around 350). The list of capital crimes included arson, rape, sodomy, murder, forgery, highway robbery, pocket picking, shoplifting, burglary at night, stealing horses, cattle, and sheep, setting fire to coal mines, cutting down trees in a public avenue, destroying silk or velvet in the loom, sacrilege, mutiny, desertion, concealing the death of a bastard child, sending threatening letters, and returning from exile (Blackstone, 1962). Until well into the nineteenth century, it was not uncommon for children to be hanged. By the 1840s, however, things took a turn away from death as the principal penalty. "Only" twenty offenses were designated as capital crimes, and the execution of children was abolished.

In America, capital punishment has traditionally been reserved for a mere handful of crimes in comparison with England. But even so, it was not limited to violent and heinous offenses, for one of its earliest uses was as a punishment for sacrilege and witchcraft.

Until recent times executions were generally carried out in public. As if it were not enough to die, often miserably, the condemned were made a public spectacle, which often had all the trappings of a family picnic, a fair, and even a wedding (see Hay et al., 1975:114). Yet the often cruel and public aspects of capital punishment were conditioned by history and culture and based on what authorities felt were both reasonable and practical. Given the different kinds of offenses for which death could be imposed, the manner of execution could be varied to mirror in some way the nature and gravity of an offense. A particularly heinous crime would bring its perpetrator a crueler death than would, say, a simple case of robbery. An effort to make the execution reflect the nature of the crime is illustrated by Graeme Newman: "Ploughing off of the head was a very early form of beheading for a person who trespassed across a boundary line. The offender was buried at the place of trespass up to the neck, and then a circular plough was driven over him, thus striking off the head" (1978:31–32). Later this method was used for persons who illegally cut off the tops of trees.

Why execute in public? Here again there was reason behind the procedure. The issue was framed in terms of *deterrence* and *moral education*. The idea was that witnessing executions would deter observers from committing capital crimes by exploiting their fear of death, and further, it would reinforce in them the belief that the acts for which the condemned suffered were indeed wrong, sinful, and damnable.

John Lofland (1977) suggests that the contemporary Western way of executing personifies the art of concealment, thereby losing any deterrent effect it might otherwise have, besides depriving the condemned the opportunity to display publicly courage and dignity at the time of death. In America, the condemned are permitted few visitors; the time of execution is inconspicuous (for example, five o'clock in the morning); the place of execution is secluded; few witnesses are allowed; the technique is reliable, fast, and relatively quiet; the executioner is anonymous and impersonal; the announcement is terse; and the body is removed quickly.

**Executions in America**  As Table 14.1 shows, many countries have abolished the death penalty altogether. In 1972, it looked as if the United States might never execute again: the last execution had been in 1967, and then in 1972 the Supreme Court ruled in *Furman v. Georgia* that the death penalty violated the Eighth Amendment's prohibition of "cruel and unusual punishment." However, a majority of the judges did not object to the death penalty per se but to the arbitrary and often discriminatory way that it was applied. This left the door open for legislatures to enact new statutes to meet the Court's objections. By 1984, thirty-eight states and the federal government had done just that. In January 1977, Gary Gilmore was killed by firing squad in a shed outside the Utah State Prison, the first execution in ten years. By January 1985, thirty-two executions had taken place (all but three in the South), and over 1,400 inmates are currently on death row (Bureau of Justice Statistics, 1985b).

Of the 3,870 executions between 1930 and 1984, just under 90 percent were for murder, with rape accounting for most of the remainder. Just over 2,300 executions occurred in the South, as did all but 12 of the 455 executions for rape. Overall, more blacks than whites have been executed, and nearly 90 percent of those who died for rape were blacks.

These data clearly raise the question of racial discrimination. The charge of racial discrimination has been the main issue in the National Association for the Advancement of Colored People's (NAACP) long fight to have the death

**Table 14.1** Abolition of the Death Penalty in the World Community

| JURISDICTION | DATE OF ABOLITION | JURISDICTION | DATE OF ABOLITION |
|---|---|---|---|
| San Marino | 1848 | Iceland | 1940 |
| Venezuela | 1863 | Switzerland[a] | 1942 |
| Mozambique | 1867 | India, Travencore | 1944 |
| Portugal | 1867 | Italy[a] | 1944 |
| Costa Rica | 1880 | Brazil[a] | 1946 |
| Netherlands[a] | 1886[b] | West Germany | 1949 |
| Equador | 1897 | Finland[a] | 1949 |
| Norway[a] | 1905[b] | Greenland | 1954 |
| Uruguay | 1907 | Honduras | 1957 |
| Colombia | 1910 | Netherlands, Antilles[a] | 1957 |
| Panama | 1915 | Bolivia | 1961 |
| Sweden[a] | 1921 | Monaco | 1962 |
| Argentina | 1922 | Great Britain | 1965 |
| Dominican Republic | 1924 | Northern Ireland | 1966 |
| Denmark[a] | 1930 | Austria | 1968 |
| Mexico[c] | 1931 | | |

SOURCE: Compiled from Table 7.3 in Bowers, William J. (1974), Executions in America. Lexington, MA: D.C. Heath. Original source: Legal Defense Fund Brief for *Aikens v. California*, 406 U.S. 813:92 S. Ct. 1931 (1972).

a. Permits the death penalty during time of war or under military law.
b. Executed Nazi collaborators after World War II.
c. Twenty-nine of thirty-two states in Mexico abolished the death penalty between 1931 and 1970.

penalty abolished. Evidence accumulated during the period 1930 to 1960 seemed to support its contention (see Wolfgang and Riedel, 1973:119–33). William Bowers (1974:102) has added new evidence in support of the charge. Following careful analysis of data going back as far as 1890, Bowers believes that the findings point "unmistakably to a pattern of racial discrimination in the administration of capital punishment in America." That discrimination has been concentrated in the South, he argues, where blacks have been executed for less serious crimes, as well as for crimes less often punished by death (such as rape), when committed by whites. Further, the blacks who have been executed were generally younger than their white counterparts and were more often executed without appeals.

The picture from the northern and western regions of America shows considerably less evidence of racial discrimination in the imposition of the death penalty, but those who are executed are characteristically of low social status. Robert M. Carter (1965) has drawn a composite sketch of the men executed in California over the years, and it shows us a person who from early childhood has had little going for him. Thirty-four years old when executed, the death penalty victim comes from a rural background of poverty and alcoholism. He will have been tagged delinquent at an early age, will drop out of school by age 14, and leave a broken home by 17. With few occupational skills he will drift from job to job and will soon be arrested for some unsophisticated, unplanned property crime. When he is convicted of the crime, his young marriage will break up and he will again be in and out of jobs and jail. Back to crime, this time with a partner, he will be arrested again, this time getting five years in prison. Out in two years and on parole with no marketable skills, he will work intermittently, drink more, and begin to think of himself as worthless, a no-good bum. The culmination of a life devoid of love and security comes quickly, as we find our frustrated criminal pulling a robbery for fast money, killing the gas station operator in the process. Caught three days later, he is sentenced to death and executed two years, eight months, and twenty-eight days after his arrest.

**Public Opinion and the Death Penalty**  Public opinion surveys show that a majority of Americans favor the death penalty for some crimes in which the victims are killed. Since 1969, in fact, support of capital punishment has steadily grown. Joseph Rankin (1979) believes the change reflects the emergence of a "law-and-order syndrome," resulting from heightened concern about violent crime. There was much publicity during the 1970s about rising rates of violent crime, and periodic reports of mass murderers in our midst hardly ease a worried public's fears.

Some people favor mandatory death sentences for certain offenses, for example, the killing of police officers, and others argue as well that such an approach would prevent discrimination in the administration of the death penalty. However, William Bowers (1974:104) reports that mandatory sentencing probably will not stop discrimination. First, both the spirit and the intent of such laws can be easily circumvented through the discretionary charging that rests in the hands of prosecutors. The question is moot, in any case, for the U.S. Supreme Court ruled in *Woodson v. North Carolina* (1976) and again in *Roberts v. Louisiana* (1979) that mandatory death sentences violate the Eighth Amendment.

In 1986, the U.S. Supreme Court furthered the cause of death penalty advocates by ruling that "death qualified" juries are not unconstitutional; that is, opponents of the death penalty may be excluded from juries hearing capital cases. Since juries composed of people who support the death penalty are considered more prone to convict, this step is seen as increasing the likelihood that more convicted criminals will find themselves on death row.

## REMOVAL FROM THE GROUP: EXILE PENALTIES

Exile penalties such as transportation and banishment are rarely used today, though the deportation of aliens is a modern form of banishment. In more primitive times, banishment of wrongdoers from the tribal group or village community was a simple and effective means of ridding the group of undesirables. Often used as a substitute for death, it usually meant the same thing, for without the support and security of the group, an individual soon fell prey to a hostile environment. Significantly, banishment rendered the offender an outcast not simply in territorial terms, but also in a normative sense. Those banished were considered outside the prevailing moral order, and as such, members of the group were under no obligation to treat them as they would one another. The banished could be slain on sight, and such action required no moral justification (Bittner and Platt, 1966:85).

As distant lands were opened to exploration and colonization, transportation emerged as a new criminal penalty. By the beginning of the seventeenth century, England and other colonial powers were making systematic use of transportation as they sought to achieve two goals by one means. While the home country could be rid of its dangerous classes, the developing colonies could benefit from a continuing supply of new laborers to tame the land. Hundreds of thousands of convicts were transported from England alone, first to America and then to Australia. It was not until the second half of the nineteenth century that transportation was finally abolished (see Babbington, 1968, for more on exile penalties).

## REMOVAL FROM THE GROUP: IMPRISONMENT

Today imprisonment is one of the principal official criminal penalties; however, its use as a specific punishment upon conviction of an offense is of relatively recent origin. Ancient societies rarely used physical detention, and when they did it was not as a punishment in itself but, rather, (1) as a means of pretrial detention and surveillance, (2) because offenders had not paid their fines, or (3) because secure physical confinement was necessary if certain kinds of penalties (torture, execution, banishment) were to be imposed.

According to Durkheim (1900), prisons first gained a notable place in the punishment of criminals with the emergence of cities and a technology capable of constructing buildings large, private, and secure enough to operate as detention facilities on a regular basis. Early prisons were found in, or attached to, royal palaces, temples and churches, city walls, and even the private homes of court officials, members of the nobility, and others in positions of wealth and privilege.

Once established, prisons soon took on a directly punitive role. Inmates were subjected to abominable degradations and deprivations. Forced to live with filth and vermin, the prisoners were fed hardly enough to keep them alive, and they were often held in shackles, iron collars, and other restraining devices. As Europe moved into the medieval period, prisons were admirably suited to the growing use of physical torture.

Today the essential accomplishment and ostensible raison d'être of prisons is to remove offenders from their normal habitat, to deprive them of their freedom. This modern conception of imprisonment gained ground during the eighteenth century, as penal reforms took shape both here and abroad.

**Prison Developments in America**    The Walnut Street Jail in Philadelphia is usually identified as America's first state prison and its first penitentiary. Opened in 1773, the jail received its first state prisoner in 1790. This historic occasion rewarded the hard work and dedication of a group of Pennsylvania citizens, many of them Quakers. These citizens abhorred the cruelty and degradation of existing punishments and felt that an alternative could be devised that was both humane and reformative. The group embraced the Quaker view that criminals should be made to contemplate the evil of their ways in unrelieved solitude. Under conditions of solitary confinement day and night, inmates would immerse themselves in self-reflection and penitence — or so they asserted. Work, necessary for regeneration of the spirit, would be performed alone in one's cell.

Built inside the existing jail structure, the new penitentiary was an awesome place. Crude efforts were made to segregate women, capital offenders, and debtors, vagrants, and other petty criminals. The inmates were housed individually in tiny whitewashed cells measuring 6 feet wide, 8 feet long, and 9 feet high. A small grated window could be seen high up on the outside wall, and the toilet amenities consisted of a lead pipe in the corner of each cell. The convicts were preached to on a regular basis but were denied any form of recreation. For their part, the guards were forbidden to use chains or irons, weapons, or canes.

Ten other states soon constructed prisons along the lines of Philadelphia's Walnut Street Jail. Although particular procedures varied somewhat from state to state (in Massachusetts, for example, the guards were issued guns, bayonets, and cutlasses), the basic architectural design was the same, as was the emphasis on enforced solitude. Eventually, overcrowding in most of these early prisons forced administrators to give up on the idea of solitary confinement for all. Instead, it was used more and more for those who had violated prison rules.

Support for a penitentiary system embodying solitary confinement was reaffirmed in the 1820s when the Pennsylvania legislature authorized two new prisons — Western Penitentiary in Pittsburgh and Eastern Penitentiary in Philadelphia. The structures were monolithic, the cells small and ranged along the outside walls, and the solitude, for all intents and purposes, was total. Charles Dickens, on visiting Eastern Penitentiary, wrote of the inmate: "He sees the prison officer, but with that exception he never looks upon a human countenance or hears a human voice. He is a man buried alive; to be dug out in the slow round of years; and in the meantime dead to everything but torturing anxieties and horrible despair" (cited in Goldfarb and Singer, 1973:26).

The "Pennsylvania System" was tried and soon abandoned in New Jersey and Rhode Island. These states turned instead to what is known as the "Auburn System," after Auburn Prison in New York. In that prison, opened in 1817 but enlarged and modified by 1823, inmates were locked in separate cells at night but worked together in small groups during the day. Complete silence was maintained both day and night, however, and regimentation was complete. The prison contained tiered blocks of tiny cells with narrow galleries encircling them. All was surrounded by an outside wall of stone over 2½ feet thick. Almost all early American prisons were fashioned after Auburn. In contrast, most European and South American countries adopted the Pennsylvania system.

Another example of early prison design, this time from England, was the Panopticon Plan created by Jeremy Bentham. Called a "dinosaur of the penal world" by Goldfarb and Singer (1973:32), there are nevertheless some living examples, one at Joliet, Illinois. Basically, the panopticon consists of tiers of cells arranged along the outside of a larger circular structure. Besides the innovative architecture, Bentham had plans for heating, care of prisoners, health and educational services, and food and clothing as well. As it turned out, however, Bentham found few takers.

**The Reformatory Movement**  From around 1870 to the early twentieth century, the so-called reformatory movement held sway in American corrections. The movement's principles were outlined at the first meeting of the American Prison Congress, in 1870, and included the idea that *reformation rather than suffering* should be the cornerstone of penal practice and that *indeterminate sentences* should be adopted to enable authorities to release early, or keep longer, those inmates who had succeeded, or failed, in demonstrating their rehabilitation. Inmates were to be put into three classes, depending on their achievements and conduct: (1) First Grade, meaning that they had earned sufficient "marks" to make them eligible for parole; (2) Second Grade, mostly for new entrants yet to show their true colors; and (3) Third Grade, for those whose disobedience and lack of improvement suggested the need for sterner measures.

The first prison organized to apply these principles was the Elmira Reformatory in New York, opened in 1876. Elmira was primarily designed for young first offenders, 16 to 30 years old. Its superintendent was Zebulon Brockway, a confident and determined administrator who left no stone unturned in his efforts to prove the success of this new penology (Brockway, [1912] 1969). Encouraged by early results and the prospect of succeeding in the battle against crime, other states soon followed suit, and by 1913 some eighteen state reformatories had been organized around the country.

Yet the old style of harsh prison discipline, hard labor, and strict regimentation continued to dominate prison life. At least sixteen major state prisons of the Auburn variety — including Menard in Illinois, Folsom in California, Walla Walla in Washington State, and Brushy Mountain in Tennessee, all in operation today — were opened between 1870 and 1900. By the 1900s the reformatory movement was on the decline. It failed for a number of reasons: (1) lack of high quality leadership and staff, especially in the key area of education; (2) continued acceptance, despite the rhetoric, of the idea that the prison experience should be punishing; (3) lack of recognition that reformation and architecture might somehow be related — the reformatories were by and large monolithic stone fortresses; (4) overcrowding, which led to a breakdown in the already clumsy efforts at classification, grading, and behavior modification; (5) overemphasis on the custodial functions of prison by administrators; and perhaps most important, (6) lack of official commitment to the movement in the form of supporting policy and resources.

**Prisons Today** In America today we see an agglomeration of prison philosophies, goals, and architectures. There has, in fact, been little consequential innovation over the last fifty years. With the exception of so-called community corrections, discussed in the following chapter, the form and character of incarceration are pretty much what they were decades ago.

There are some 250 prisons housing adult offenders and administered by either state governments or the Federal Bureau of Prisons. In 1969 an attempt at classification was made. At that time, about 70 percent of the 214,000 inmates were housed in "work-oriented" prisons, about 23 percent in "rehabilitation-oriented" institutions, and about 7 percent in "special-function" institutions such as prison hospitals. Thirty-one of the rehabilitation prisons housed women, 58 housed men. Of the 77 maximum security prisons in 1969, 12 were built before 1850, 33 between 1850 and 1899, and 32 since 1900 (Goldfarb and Singer, 1973:49). In 1976, some 50,000 adult felons were serving time in maximum security prisons built before 1900. That figure represents almost one-fifth of all adult inmates in state and federal prisons on any day that year (Hawkins, 1976:42).

Today, of 100 "typical" felony offenders arrested, 29 will go to jail or prison. Looked at another way, of 100 felony offenders sentenced, 71 will be incarcerated, with 45 going to prison and 26 to jail (Bureau of Justice Statistics, 1985i:2). At year's end in 1984, there were 463,866 state and federal prisoners (Bureau of Justice Statistics, 1985g). This represents an overall growth rate of 40 percent since 1980 and is more than double the number incarcerated in 1974. The South shows the highest rates of imprisonment, with 231 inmates per 100,000 population, compared with 136 in the Northeast. There is also considerable variation from state to state. The rates for Minnesota, North Dakota, and New Hampshire were under 60; at the other extreme were South Carolina (284), Maryland (289), Louisiana (310), Nevada (380), and Washington, D.C. (649).

It has been estimated that the lifetime probability of any particular American between the ages of 13 and 84 serving time in a state prison is from one chance in seventy-seven to one chance in forty-eight. However, the risks are not born equally, as Table 14.2 shows. The highest probabilities are for black males, the lowest for white females. Joan Petersilia (1985a) found in California that a strong predictor of going to prison is the number of prior adult crime convictions. Offenders with *three or more* of the following characteristics had an 80 percent chance of going to prison:

**Table 14.2** Lifetime Probabilities of Being Imprisoned

| | ESTIMATED CHANCE FROM | | | |
|---|---|---|---|---|
| Males | 1 in 40 | to | 1 in 25 | |
| Females | 1 in 588 | to | 1 in 370 | |
| White Males | 1 in 67 | to | 1 in 42 | |
| White Females | 1 in 556 | to | 1 in 409 | |
| Black Males | 1 in 10 | to | 1 in 6 | |
| Black Females | 1 in 167 | to | 1 in 100 | |

SOURCE: Bureau of Justice Statistics (1985j), Special Report: The Prevalence of Imprisonment. Washington, D.C.: U.S. Department of Justice.

Current conviction on two or more counts.
Two or more prior adult convictions.
Being on parole or probation when arrested.
Being a drug addict.
Being armed in the current case.
Using a weapon in the current case.
Seriously injuring the victim.

Around the nation, males account for roughly 97 percent of prison inmates, blacks for nearly 50 percent. Most are under age 30, and a majority have not graduated from high school. Although a majority of inmates were employed during the month before their arrest, their jobs were nearly always manual or lower-skill service work, with wages rarely above the minimum. Nearly half America's prison inmates have never been married. This profile of the inmate population has not changed materially since the first comprehensive survey in 1974 (Bureau of Justice Statistics, 1982c).

Most inmates in state prisons are serving time for robbery, burglary, or homicide. In the federal system, bank robbery and drug offenses account for 50 percent of the prison population (Federal Bureau of Prisons, 1986). The difference reflects that (1) most street crimes are handled in state courts, whereas bank robbery is a federal crime, and (2) intense federal law-enforcement effort is currently directed at drug trafficking.

The prison terms handed down in court are quite misleading as a measure of the punitiveness of American penal practice. First, the experience in prison varies considerably from prison to prison and in any case cannot be predicted merely by knowing the sentence. Second, the actual time served by most offenders is much shorter than the length of their sentence. A survey of eleven states showed that the average time served for serious violent crime (e.g., homicide, rape, robbery, and aggravated assault) is less than three and one-half years, and for serious property crime (e.g., burglary, larceny, auto theft, and arson) is less than two years (Bureau of Justice Statistics, 1984g).

One penologist, John Conrad (1975), sees the rise in inmate populations as stemming from a new "hard line" in the administration of justice. He believes that the hard line reflects various things: first, an escalation in public anger at the criminal; second, an increase in public disenchantment with social meliorism, represented in part by the widespread use of probation and parole and in the recent advocacy of community corrections; and finally, rising crime rates in urban areas have helped exacerbate already high levels of social conflict in the cities. Once again, perhaps, we are seeing a manifestation of the law-and-order syndrome noted earlier with respect to the death penalty.

**Juvenile Detention**   Adults are not the only ones who can be imprisoned for violating the law. Children, in most states as young as 13, can be incarcerated in detention facilities for periods up to a year or more.

There are 993 publicly operated institutions for juvenile custody. Almost

A young member of the Disciples gang signals his allegiance from behind jailhouse bars while awaiting trial. Jails provide few amenities and are usually overcrowded. Most, like this one, are also old.

half are regarded as "open," which is to say there are minimal in-house physical and staff controls, and there is a good deal of accessibility to the surrounding community. Even so, 290 institutions are classified as "strict," or maximum security, and more than 400 reported allowing no community access at all (U.S. Department of Justice, 1981b).

A recent comprehensive survey of juvenile detention practices found substantial variations from state to state during the 1970s. Although annually somewhere around 520,000 juveniles are admitted to detention centers, some states (Wyoming, Montana) admitted none because they had no facilities, and one state (California) admitted fully 35 percent of the juveniles detained throughout the entire nation. The rate of juvenile detention per 100,000 juveniles aged 5 to 17 is about 100 times higher in California than it is in North Dakota (4,734 versus 45). It seems to be the policy of California courts to incarcerate juvenile offenders in *secure* facilities rather than in facilities where children are more or less free to come and go and are monitored much less closely. The guideline issued by the National Probation and Parole Association in 1958 was that 20 percent of children handled by juvenile courts should probably end up in secure facilities; few states meet this recommendation, but California puts 90 percent of its court-referred juveniles into such centers (U.S. Department of Justice, 1980).

Over the past decade many states have experienced a decline in the number of juveniles held in public facilities. This reflects recent efforts to divert juvenile offenders from detention, especially those charged with noncriminal offenses. Yet we must be careful in judging this apparent decline in juvenile incarcerations. It now appears that there has been a rise in the housing of juveniles, especially boys, in the nation's 558 private facilities (ranches, boardinghouses, group homes, shelters, and so forth). Of course, many of these private facilities have none of the characteristics we associate with prisons or reformatories, but some do. Andrew Scull (1977:53) tells us that in Massachusetts during the early 1970s, when efforts were being made to close all state reform schools, some of the juveniles handed over to private agencies were eventually housed in the very state facilities that had been newly vacated!

The decarceration trend may continue, but the odds are against it. The law-and-order syndrome that has apparently led to reaffirmation of the death penalty and to increased rates of adult incarceration is likely to touch the juvenile offender, who after all is responsible for a sizable portion of the nation's street crime. It is possible that the construction of new detention facilities will be delayed, as calls for cuts in government spending are heeded in state and federal legislatures. In the long run, however, there will almost certainly be new construction to alleviate overcrowding and to satisfy the law-and-order advocates.

**Jail as Punishment**  Jail time is generally used as punishment only for those convicted of misdemeanors and petty offenses. Sometimes a judge will allow time spent in jail while awaiting trial and sentencing to be counted toward the eventual sentence. If less than a year is left for a felony offender, that time will usually be served in a county jail.

A 1983 census of jail populations discovered that 223,551 people were being held in the nation's 3,493 jails. This represents a 41 percent increase over the figure in 1978 (Bureau of Justice Statistics, 1984c). Of these, 52 percent had not been convicted of a crime. These inmates were awaiting formal adjudication proceedings; most had simply been unable to make bail. The remaining 48 percent were serving out sentences, awaiting transfer to prison or other correctional facility, or involved in postconviction proceedings of one sort or another. The majority of jail inmates are young men in their early twenties. Most have not completed high school. Slightly less than half are black, and only 7 percent are women.

Urban jails in general are overcrowded places lacking even modest amenities. Critics contend that jail time is generally more punitive, dangerous, and degrading than time in a maximum security prison. There is, in addition, the mixing of technically innocent people with convicted offenders, not to mention petty offenders with hardened criminals. Experienced convicts say they would rather do their time in prison than in jail.

## Physical Torture

At one time or another most societies have used torture as a criminal punishment. Often, however, torture was an addition to some other punishment, such as removal from the group. The physical aggravation often attached to the death penalty is one good example, and the mutilation used for branding is another.

As a penalty alone, not in addition to another, physical torture has mainly taken the form of flogging or whipping. A variety of instruments have been used, ranging from the cat-o'-nine-tails to the birch. Flogging is probably one of the oldest criminal penalties. It is known to have been practiced by the ancient Jews, and it was a common feature of Roman and Greek punishment. In England, flogging was long considered the accepted penalty for vagrants, vagabonds, and beggars. Under the Anglo-Saxon kings, the lash was sometimes an alternative to monetary compensation and was prescribed mainly for slaves who worked, traveled, or ate on forbidden days. Around the world, flogging continued to be an official criminal penalty until well into the twentieth century, though many jurisdictions have now abolished it.

Physical torture became a fixture of Western penal law during the fifteenth century and remained so until well into the eighteenth century. In England, torture was always held to be illegal as a penalty for crime, but this did not stop its use. On the contrary, torture was used extensively, both as a punishment for crimes committed and as a device for extracting guilty pleas and confessions. Torture as a punishment mainly took the form of mutilation.

As a device for obtaining confessions and pleas, it involved all the trappings of a chamber of horrors.

The torture devices of medieval Europe ranged from thumbscrews to such monstrous devices as the rack and the "scavenger's daughter." The rack, as Vincent Price fans well know, stretches its victims; the scavenger's daughter rolls them up into a ball:

> On the rack the prisoner seemed in danger of having the fingers torn from his hands, the toes from his feet, the hands from the arms, the feet from the legs, the forearms from the upper arms, the legs from the trunk. Every ligament was strained, every joint loosened in its socket; and if the sufferer remained obstinate when released, he was brought back to undergo the same cruelties with the added horror of past experience and with a diminished fortitude and physical power. In the Scavenger's Daughter, on the other hand, the pain was caused by an ingenious process of compression. The legs were forced back to the thighs, the thighs were pressed onto the belly, and the whole body was placed within two iron bands which the torturers drew together with all their strength until the miserable human being lost all form but that of a globe. Blood was forced out of the tips of the fingers and toes, the nostrils and mouth; and the ribs and breastbone were commonly broken in by the pressure. (Pike, 1968:87–88)

In colonial America and in England, another form of torture widely used to exact confessions and pleas was the so-called *peine forte et dure* (the strong and hard pain). Heavy weights were placed on the suspect's chest so as to make every breath excruciatingly painful. Usually the torture was used on those who stood mute at their trials, and at least one American colonist is known to have died under the presses during the Salem witch hunt (Erickson, 1966:149).

Though such physical tortures have been outlawed in Anglo-American law for at least 150 years, recent disclosures indicate that cruel and vicious physical abuse has not disappeared from our prison systems. Apart from the frequently cited beatings and floggings administered in the name of discipline, we now know that in at least one state prison system, physical atrocities were common for recalcitrant inmates. In the late 1960s, Tom Murton, then head of the Arkansas prison system, revealed case after case of physical torture. Perhaps the most startling of all the atrocities was the systematic use of a device named after an Arkansas prison farm, the "Tucker telephone." This was an electrical device capable of inflicting excruciating pain on its victims. Wires from the "telephone" were attached to the genitals and feet of inmates, who were then "rung up" with an electrical charge (Murton and Hyams, 1969).

## Social Degradation

The humiliation and shame that often accompany disclosure of a person's criminal status have been explicitly promoted in some legal punishments. Penalties designed to degrade the offender have taken various forms, but all operate on the principle that those punished should suffer the additional torment of humiliation.

Some forms of degradation also incorporate elements of physical torture, such as mutilation and branding. Branding and mutilation flourished during the medieval period and remained important legal punishments until the end of the eighteenth century. Mutilations included dismemberment, loss of ears, eyes, tongue, nose, and lips, and a multitude of other disfigurements. However, there seems to have been little specification as to which offenses were to be punished by mutilation or branding, it being largely a matter of judicial discretion. In colonial America, maiming and branding were used quite frequently for a variety of offenses, including burglary, robbery, religious crimes, and hog stealing (Earle, 1969).

Less permanent degradations were suffered in the pillory and stocks, though they were not always less painful. Designed to maximize exposure to public ridicule, these devices were in use at least as early as the thirteenth century. In 1406, the English Parliament made it mandatory for each village and town to erect a set of stocks. The only difference between the two devices, both of which were placed in some prominent public place, was that in the pillory prisoners stood with their arms and head protruding from the crosslike apparatus, but in the stocks they sat so that their feet protruded as well. Any offender so punished was left to the mercy of onlookers. Often the offender had to undergo the additional embarrassment of having his or her hair cut off.

The stocks and pillory were used extensively in England and America for those convicted of minor crimes such as drunkenness, disorderly conduct, prostitution, petty theft, blasphemy, cheating, lying, swearing, and threatening. Sometimes offenders were flogged while locked in the device, and sometimes they were left in it for days. Although not a pleasant experience by any standard, what was worse for many was the outright cruelty of the crowds gathered about them. During the seventeenth and eighteenth centuries in England, violence toward the offenders became commonplace. On one occasion, "The mob no sooner saw the prisoners exposed in the pillory than they pelted them with stones, brickbats, dead dogs and cats, and other things" (Babbington, 1968:13). Some punished in the stocks and pillories died as a result of crowd violence, one reason these penalties were abolished in the early nineteenth century.

Variations on the pillory have appeared over the years. In Sweden, for example, those convicted of misdemeanors were sometimes tied on a wooden horse and left to the derision of the locals (James, 1817:236–239). In both England and colonial America the "ducking (or cucking) stool" was often used to punish those who made a nuisance of themselves by gossiping, spreading rumors, and so forth. The ducking stool was a chairlike device the offender sat in while he — or as was most often the case, she — was lowered into a pool of stagnant water.

Although we no longer brand, maim, or duck criminal offenders, many nations continue to include social degradation penalties among their legal punishments. Usually, these modern degradations involve the removal of civil or other rights, and they are specified in law as *automatic penalties on conviction for certain offenses*. They are imposed regardless of the other punishments handled down by the courts. In some jurisdictions, the deprivations extend into the areas of employment, citizenship, inheritance, other property rights, and even marriage (Damaska, 1968). In America, most states give these automatic penalties to felony offenders, who usually lose, at least temporarily, their right to vote and their right to hold public office or work in certain occupations.

## HIDDEN DEGRADATIONS

Criminal punishments often contain less visible degradations — less visible, that is, to the general public. The shame and humiliation suffered by their victims, however, are nonetheless an important aspect of the experience.

Probation is one such penalty — and it *is* a penalty, despite what many people think. The American Bar Association (1970:9) defines probation as "a sentence not involving confinement which imposes conditions and retains authority in the sentencing court to modify the conditions of sentence or to re-sentence the offender if he violates the conditions." More and more criminal offenders are being placed on probation, often as an alternative to fines or incarceration. Joan Petersilia (1985b) points out that from 1974 to 1983 the probation population grew by 63 percent. She explains "Probation sentences for adult felons have become so common that a new term has emerged in criminal justice circles, *felony probation*" (p. 2).

Use of probation varies considerably from state to state. Although the 1983 rate per 100,000 adult residents was 897 for the United States as a whole, the rates for Washington, Arkansas, and West Virginia were less than 220. Those for Georgia and Washington were over 1,900 (Bureau of Justice Statistics, 1984e). The reasons for the variation include statutory differences, variations in judicial practice, availability of prison space, and differences in prosecutors' charging practices.

When placed on supervised probation (the usual case), the probationer is often required to fulfill a variety of demeaning stipulations or conditions. The conditions of probation are often left to the discretion of courts and probation services, though they have in some cases been legislated and thus made part of the official criminal code. The degradations lie in these conditions. Probationers have been told they must attend church; must not marry without permission; must not drive a car, even if needed for work; must spend their evenings and days in ways dictated by probation officers; must spend their earnings only in certain ways; must not travel certain distances or to certain places; must dress in ways that conform to community standards; or must not smoke or drink (Imlay and Glasheen, 1971; Czajkoski, 1973).

Social degradation is incorporated in yet another experience that many criminal offenders face: *parole*. Parole is a conditional release from a prison or other correctional facility. It is granted by parole agencies at some point before the maximum term of a prison sentence is served. In 1983 over a quarter of a million Americans were on parole. Though people might not think that parole is a punishment, that view is not shared by many parolees. They are subject to all kinds of deprivations, some of which are felt to be extremely degrading. Parolees are often required to lead an exemplary life, much more so than we expect of ordinary citizens, while at the same time many of the important elements of a productive, successful, responsible, and meaningful social existence are denied them. Parolees are not free to move around. They cannot choose their friends, associates, or even employment. They have little privacy. They can make few substantive decisions without first getting permission. They have no effective control over their daily lives and yet are required to demonstrate that they can in fact control their lives. Rather than encourage the development of a favorable self-image, the conditions of parole often undermine parolees' sense of worth, reduce their status in the eyes of those they care about, and lock them into a condition of dependency (see Erickson et al., 1973).

Critics of the parole system point to the parole decisions themselves as the cause of many problems. Who gets parole is often in the hands of political appointees who look for evidence that the inmate has fulfilled the expectations of prison administrators. Parole applicants who can show that they have been model prisoners often have the advantage over others, some of whom may in fact have made a serious commitment to go straight but nevertheless have failed to impress prison officials that they held the right attitudes and were rule abiding while incarcerated (Bottomley, 1973b). For inmates facing long prison terms, a favorable parole decision is so desirable that it puts considerable pressure on them to hustle and con their way through the prison experience in the hope of selling their "new decency" to officials.

The manner in which parole hearings are carried out differs from state to state. One survey of American parole practices found that twenty-nine states denied the inmate legal representation, and thirty generally allowed no witnesses. In addition, twenty-eight states keep no verbatim record of the proceedings, twenty-eight do not allow any appeal, and five provide no written explanation of their decision (O'Leary and Hanrahan, 1977).

## PUBLIC REACTIONS AND DEGRADATION

The stigmatization of people as criminals has a degrading effect, and this is an extra legal punishment resulting from trouble with the law. Arrest, conviction, and sentencing are authoritative actions that mark people as different from, and inferior to, those recognized as straight, law-abiding, upright, and thoroughly decent citizens. Tagged as suspects, criminals, ex-cons, or ex-offenders, those officially processed as criminals must contend with the stigma such labels carry. They are now outsiders, persons perceived as untrustworthy, suspicious, and threatening. Others may respond to them in punitive ways precisely because of their redefined social identity, an identity that emphasizes their criminality to the exclusion of other personal attributes (Goffman, 1963; Shoham, 1970).

In addition to official criminal penalties, then, convicted persons often face the hostility and fear of those who know about their troubles and redefine their identity accordingly. In effect, the punishments imposed by family, friends, acquaintances, workmates, employers, landlords, and a host of others degrade people identified as criminals. They are no longer worthy of marriage, friendship, a job, or a place in the community.

The likelihood of extralegal punishments being imposed on criminal offenders depends on many factors. Most important are the nature of the alleged offense, the offender's reputation in the community, and the severity of the legal punishments meted out. If an offense is regarded as serious, if the offender has low preconviction status in the community, and if the authorities have punished the offender severely, further punishment at the hands of the community is likely. Offenders' social images are redefined downward, since they have little going for them, and everything fits neatly into place. Things may be different when people are convicted of offenses generally regarded as minor, if they had high status in the community before conviction, and if the authorities treat them lightly, for then the public may be reluctant even to label them criminals, let alone subject them to further deprivations. According to Shlomo Shoham (1970:61–64), the people least likely to be stigmatized by the criminal process and to suffer punitive consequences are those in business, politics, and the professions who commit occupational crimes. Those mostly likely to suffer deprivations at the hands of the public are those who fit the prevailing stereotype of the criminal, and a mere arrest record, with no subsequent conviction, may prompt punitive reactions from the community (Hess and Poole, 1967).

## Financial Penalties

Today fines are the most commonly imposed criminal penalties. Although no accurate national data exist, estimates usually place fines at around 75 percent of all criminal convictions. In other countries, too, the fine is the most widely used criminal penalty (Davidson, 1965).

The fine has existed in penal law for centuries. The Anglo-Saxons first systematically used financial penalties. Monetary payments in the form of damages or compensation were made to the victims of wrongs. Monetary compensation replaced the long-standing tradition of self-help justice that allowed victims to retaliate directly against those who wronged them, often with disruptive and bloody consequences. The threat to group life and property posed by victim retaliation was an important factor in the development and initial popularity of financial penalties.

As time passed and a distinction between criminal law and civil law emerged along with centralized political authority and the state, the use of monetary penalties increased. By the thirteenth century, the king received the payments in criminal cases, and victims of wrongs could receive compensation only through civil courts. The growing popularity of the fine is partly explained by the fact that financial penalties were an important source of revenue for the royal treasury. More recently, fines have been supported on similar grounds, though it is now the state and local governments that benefit from the added income. Fines are regarded with favor because they are inexpensive to impose, can be paid back if wrongly imposed, can be readily adjusted according to the gravity of the offense and the financial capacity of the offenders, and can be substituted for more stigmatizing and incapacitating punishments such as imprisonment.

The use of the fine as a legal punishment has not escaped criticism. Much of the current criticism focuses on the use of jail and prison terms as penalties imposed for nonpayment of fines and on the built-in inequities that characterize monetary punishments. Studies show, for example, that around 50 percent of those fined end up in jail or prison for nonpayment. These are usually the poor. In effect, the imposition of fines discriminates against those with low incomes and insecure financial status. Further, nonpayment often entails additional suffering avoided by those who can pay their fines. A jail term may mean loss of job and loss of housing, not to mention the multitude of other deprivations incurred through incarceration. By contrast, fines are a relative boon to those who can afford them and thus avoid these alternative punishments. Fines are imposed extensively in cases involving consumer fraud, antitrust violations, and a host of other occupational crimes. For the middle-class offender or the corporation a fine is often akin to a slap on the wrist and, in light of prevailing criminal stereotypes, merely reinforces the view that it is the "dross of society," the "dangerous classes," who belong in jail. Not surprisingly, those who are imprisoned, whether for nonpayment of fines or for other reasons, are indeed from the lower status levels. In 1978, for example, out of 158,000 adult jail inmates, around two-thirds had not graduated from high school, and well over half had incomes under $4,000. Before their arrest, 25 percent of inmates had been financially dependent on the state, their families, or friends (U.S. Department of Justice, 1981b).

# CHAPTER 15

# Consequences of
# Punishment

When we punish someone, our action signifies disapproval of both the offending act and the person who commits it. If we are staunch retributivists, we are uninterested in the consequences of the punishment; our concern lies with questions of guilt and just deserts. We want the guilty to suffer a punishment commensurate with the severity of the offense — no more, no less. If, on the other hand, we are advocates of the view that punishment can prevent crime, then the consequences of punishment will be uppermost in our minds. We want the punishment to *work,* that is, to prevent further crime. This is the focus of most American penal efforts.

The consequences of punishment merit serious thought because it is by no means established that punishment prevents crime, and there are those who believe that it may even produce a more committed criminal (see Chapter 2, pp. 51–53). In this chapter we examine the consequences of punishment, keeping in mind that although it may prevent some people from committing crimes, it may also encourage the commission of crimes by others.

## How Punishment Can Prevent Crime

In his important contribution to the literature on criminal punishment, Jack Gibbs (1975:57–93) identifies ten different ways that punishment can prevent crimes. First, certain forms of punishment incapacitate potential offenders by removing or diminishing their opportunities to commit crimes. Incapacitation is absolute when an offender is executed but is relative for other forms of punishment. Consider imprisonment: although putting someone behind bars reduces the opportunity to commit crimes, it does not rule out all manner of offenses and may actually encourage some, for example, homosexual rape.

Second, some punishments can prevent crimes because they place offenders under surveillance. The conditions of probation and parole often have this effect. Surveillance can prevent crimes simply because it increases the visibility of an offender's behavior. Gibbs acknowledges, however, that surveillance of probationers and parolees probably does not prevent a substantial amount of crime. However, recent experimentation with electronic monitoring of probationers and parolees is heralded by some as a breakthrough in preventive surveillance. Transmitters are strapped to offenders' ankles, and they emit a signal that warns officials that the wearer has moved outside permissable territory or has removed the device (see Ford and Schmidt, 1985). A device is illustrated in the photo on page 478.

Enculturation is the third preventive mechanism associated with punishment. The idea is that people acquire knowledge that a certain behavior is illegal by experiencing, witnessing, reading about, or being told of the punishment for doing it, and this knowledge furthers their respect for the law. Simply put, people refrain from committing a criminal act because they have learned that it is wrong or bad through the punitive response to it.

The fourth crime-preventive mechanism of punishment is reformation, the idea that the experience of punishment alters an offender's behavior: he or she "no longer contemplates criminal acts." Essentially, the argument is that punishment conveys to some offenders a sense of shame and remorse, and this promotes subsequent conformity. Even an arrest, Gibbs notes, may produce a "moral jolt," as we saw in the case of amateur shoplifters (see p. 228).

In his discussion of reformation, Gibbs notes that the terms *reformation* and *rehabilitation* have usually been considered interchangeable. He argues that "the meanings of the terms should be distinguished. Criminal rehabilitation is the alteration of an offender's behavior by nonpunitive means, so that he or she no longer violates laws. Criminal reformation is the alteration of an offender's behavior *through punishment,* so that he or she no longer violates laws" (p. 72). As discussed in the preceding chapter, early American prison systems clearly emphasized reformation of offenders. Modern correctional practice tends to favor the rehabilitation of offenders; work release programs, halfway houses, and other features are efforts in this direction. Later in this chapter we shall return to the issue of rehabilitation.

The fifth way in which punishment can prevent crime is through normative validation. This notion echoes an argument advanced many years ago by Emile Durkheim (1964a, 1964b). He saw in punishment the opportunity to reaffirm, and possibly intensify, condemnation of an act. Indeed, this is a "function" of punishment, according to Durkheim. When we punish, we remind people that the rule of law is valid, that the violation of it continues to be condemned.

Sixth is retribution. This may come as a surprise, especially since our discussion in Chapter 14 specifically distinguished between punishment as retribution and punishment as crime prevention. Gibbs asserts that where there exists a demand that the guilty be punished, not to do so would encourage private vengeance, the extreme form of which is armed vigilantism. The "subway vigilante," Bernard Goetz, exemplifies what Gibbs has in mind.

> Even in societies with "law," the certainty and severity of punishment could become so negligible that the citizens would seek personal retribution; and what the injured party would take to be justifiable vengeance could be criminal assault, criminal homicide, robbery, extortion, kidnapping, or theft. So no imagination is required to see that retribution "outside the law" generates crimes. Hence, retribution through legal punishments may prevent crimes. (Gibbs, 1975:83)

Stigmatization is Gibbs's seventh crime-preventive mechanism in punishment. Because it identifies a perpetrator as "criminal" — often publicly and dramatically — punishment "thereby becomes a *criterion* for subsequent social condemnation" (1975:84). An individual may refrain from crime not because of the punishment itself but, rather, because of the anticipated stigmatization. Presumably, the stigmatizing impact of public punishment is greater than that of private or secretive punishment. Another important issue is that stigmatizing effects may be linked to class or ethnic status: blacks, Hispanics, and low-income people "are less prone to view punishment as a stigma than are upper-class Anglos," Gibbs (1975:85) suggests.

The eighth preventive mechanism in punishment is normative insulation. Recall for a moment Sutherland's theory of differential association: that people may learn attitudes and values favorable to law violation in their intimate associations with others. Presumably, the more we associate intimately with persons who are not law-abiding, the more we are likely to adopt their normative orientation (see Chapter 2, pp. 42–45). If we could somehow escape their influence, perhaps our own normative orientations would be more law-abiding. In Gibb's view, at least three punishments have the effect of insulating us from the normative influence of offenders: execution, imprisonment, and banishment.

Habituation, the ninth way in which punishment is thought to prevent crime, has been discussed by Zimring and Hawkins (1973:85), among others. These authors argue that people develop the habit of conforming to the law; apparently they conform quite uncritically. Punishment comes in because it contributes to both the development and maintenance of habits. Efforts to reduce the speed at which Americans drive on the nation's highways are examples of the effects of habituation. By all accounts, many drivers are not abiding by the 55-mile-per-hour speed limit, but driving *is* slower than it was before the change in law took place, especially in states with systematic enforcement. Though it is difficult to separate habituation from deterrence, habituation is implied when drivers tend to follow speed limits in the absence of patrolling police or after enforcement has abruptly ended for some reason.

Deterrence is the tenth way in which punishment can prevent crime. Before discussing this preventive mechanism, it is appropriate to ask whether any of the preceding nine mechanisms have been shown to work effectively. Gibbs's presentation is rather discouraging here, for it is clear that there has been little research on any of them. Gibbs also makes it clear that research to establish if and how they do work is obstructed by conceptual and methodological problems, especially when efforts are made to separate out the effects, if any, of deterrence.

Obviously, if we think only of individual offenders who are caught and convicted, then incapacitation through execution would be a sure way to prevent *their* further criminality. It is preposterous to suggest this remedy for all types of offenses, and it would certainly be rejected by some even for premeditated murder. For any other type of punishment, incapacitation is a matter of degree. Among the other conventional penalties that are imposed in the Western world, only imprisonment can be considered incapacitating, and then only temporarily in most cases. Indeed, it is possible that in some instances a prison sentence provides opportunities to acquire additional skills and abilities that may be put to criminal use upon release. It is doubtful that this is a major consequence of imprisonment, but the idea is part of the conventional wisdom, and we shall return to it again for further consideration.

Some scholars consider stigmatization to be among the most important effects of conviction and punishment. Shlomo Shoham (1970:9) writes:

> . . . the social stigma of conviction is probably the most potent deterrent to potential offenders. A person who is not a professional or habitual criminal or a lawyer is rarely aware of the exact or even the approximate penalty he is likely to suffer for the offense he is about to commit, though he is, of course, aware of the possibility of detection and punishment. The fear of stigma is probably much stronger than the fear of punishment for the average law-abiding citizen. He is afraid of losing his job, of being ostracized by his business associates and friends, of the possible alienation of members of his family, of having to leave his neighborhood or even his town.

Gibbs (1975:85–86) warns that "stigmatization may generate secondary deviance or result in definitions favorable to crime through differential association. In the case of secondary deviance, the offender identifies himself as a criminal not only because of punishment but also because of subsequent stigmatization." In the case of differential association, stigmatization may bar offenders from "normal" social relations, forcing them to "turn to those who attach no stigma to punishment, and they are likely to be sources of definitions favorable to crime."

One of the ways that teachers, judges, and other authorities attempt to explain their choice of punishment is: "I'm going to make an example out of you!" This remark may be thought of as an attempt to raise fear in others who are potential offenders; in this case we would correctly think of deterrence. There is more to the remark, however, for the speaker is alerting others to the fact that punishments such as this *will be* applied to violations such as that. The intended audience — a class of schoolchildren, workers in a factory, people in general — are reminded both how they ought to behave and what the appropriate reaction will be if they do not. This is normative validation.

In the minds of many, normative validation is the hidden agenda in punishment. If we can reinforce and perhaps intensify conformity to the law, then we will see less violation of it. Yet strangely enough, a vital ingredient is often missing from the punishment of crime: publicity. Gibbs (1975:82) argues:

> If punishments validate laws and thereby reduce the crime rate, they do so only to the extent that they are publicized. But in the United States and many other countries, actual punishments are not publicized systematically, and the citizenry is informed only at the whim of the news media. The situation is all the more remarkable because publicizing punishments might further both normative validation and deterrence.

One might well ask, Have we really given normative validation a chance? The answer is probably no.

# A Closer Look at Deterrence

In the preceding chapter we spoke rather generally about deterrence, the tenth way in which punishment can prevent crime. A more detailed discussion is in order for two reasons: (1) there appears to be widespread belief that it works, a view held by many experts as well as by members of the public; and (2) deterrence has become a major research focus in criminology, giving it not only scientific standing as a cause célèbre, but also a tremendous amount of empirical scrutiny, which is not the case with the other nine preventive mechanisms.

The emergence of deterrence as an object of considerable research interest over the last decade or so shows how topics once put aside as dead issues can reemerge to claim the limelight. By the 1950s many social scientists clearly viewed deterrence as passé. After all, study after study had purported to demonstrate a lack of evidence that fear of punishment deters potential criminals. This was argued even for the ultimate punishment, death and is again confirmed in a study of capital punishment in fourteen countries (Archer and Gartner, 1984:118–139; see also Parker and Smith, 1979; Beyleveld, 1980). It was easy for some to say, "If fear of death does not deter people, how can we expect lesser penalties to act as deterrents to crime?"

The reemergence of deterrence as a major issue also illustrates the intimate connection between theory and research. As we saw in Chapter 2, the late 1950s and early 1960s witnessed growing theoretical interest in reactions to crime and deviance. The so-called labeling perspective grew up around the idea that reactions might somehow contribute to crime. Thus reactions to crime and deviance received a new lease on life, this time as independent variables in the analysis of crime. Far from deterring crime, perhaps punishment helps cause it.

This issue could not be resolved by reference to previous research partly because that research focused primarily on one type of punishment (death) and one type of crime (homicide). Even if the death penalty does not in some way deter homicide, perhaps other kinds of punishment deter (or help cause) other kinds of crime. So, careful analysis of questions pertaining to the relationship (if any) between crime and its punishment required new research ventures. These, it turned out, gave rise to new theoretical issues, among them conceptual distinctions dealing with types of deterrence, types of crime and criminals, and various dimensions of punishment.

## TYPES OF DETERRENCE

It has become conventional to distinguish between *specific* (or *individual,* or *special*) deterrence and *general* deterrence (Andenaes, 1974). The distinction recognizes two classes of potential offenders who may refrain from crime because they fear punitive sanctions: (1) those who have directly experienced punishment for a crime or crimes they committed in the past — specific deterrence; and (2) those who have not experienced punishment but are deterred from crime by the threat of punishment — general deterrence.

The distinction is important because the deterrent effect of experienced punishments may be quite different from that of threatened punishments. Even so, not all authors agree with this conventional distinction between specific and general deterrence, and it in no way exhausts the typological possibilities. For example, Jack Gibbs (1975) distinguishes between *absolute* and *restrictive* deterrence. Some people refrain from a particular criminal activity throughout their lives because they fear punishment (absolute deterrence), whereas others may modify or curtail their criminal activities for a period of time because they see a growing risk of punishment if they persist (restrictive deterrence). Typological refinements of this sort not only reveal the complexities of deterrence but also serve to guide theory and research into new, possibly fruitful directions.

## TYPES OF CRIMES AND TYPES OF OFFENDERS

Criminologists have recognized that punishment may deter only some offenders who commit only certain crimes. Regarding type of crimes, William Chambliss (1967) believes an important distinction can be made between instrumental crimes and expressive crimes. *Instrumental crimes* are those directed toward some material end: burglary, occupational crimes, tax evasion, parking violations, robbery, and so on. *Expressive crimes* constitute ends in themselves; they articulate desires: most murders and assaults, drunkenness, most sex offenses, consumption of illicit drugs, and so forth. In Chambliss's view, the deterrent effect of punishment may be greater for instrumental crimes, since these activities typically involve some degree of planning and risk assessment (though sometimes not much). Expressive crimes, on the other hand, are often impulsive and emotional; people about to commit them respond to pressures of the moment, not to what might happen to them in the future.

Andenaes (1966) presents another effort to distinguish types of offenses. He adopts the classic dichotomy of *mala in se* crimes and *mala prohibita* crimes. This distinction recognizes that some offenses are "evil in themselves" or inherently immoral, whereas others are "evil because prohibited." Examples of *mala prohibita* crimes are robbery, murder, rape, and arson; examples of *mala prohibita* crimes are drug offenses, traffic violations, and many occupational crimes. Andenaes's argument is that *mala in se* crimes support and are supported by the moral codes of society, whereas crimes that are simply illegal stand on the law alone. Accordingly, if people conform to *mala in se* prohibitions, it is more likely a result of fear of punishment rather than of any moral imperative, as would be expected in the case of crimes that are evil in themselves. Needless to say, Chambliss and Andenaes cannot both be right, for some offenses, such as burglary and robbery, would appear in the "less deterrable" column for Andenaes but in the "more deterrable" column for Chambliss. Nevertheless, some combination of properties might yet work. It is possible, for example, that crimes that are both instrumental and *mala prohibita* are more deterrable and that offenses that are both expressive and *mala in se* are less deterrable. There appears to have been no research examining this issue.

When all is said and done, we may need to know a lot more about the offender when organizing our ideas about deterrence. After all, it is people who are deterred and not the acts they commit. Perhaps some people are more amenable to deterrence than others. Chambliss (1967) offers some insights here, too. He suggests that we distinguish between persons who have a relatively high commitment to crime as a way of life and those with a relatively low commitment. Those involved in crime on a regular, perhaps even professional, basis are usually caught up in subcultures providing group support for their activities, and so crime is for them a way of life. Such offenders are less likely to be deterred, for criminal penalties are something they have learned to live with, and the threat of them may be offset by the supportive role played by peers. The typical shoplifter, naive check forger, tax evader, or other occasional offender, on the other hand, does not think of himself or herself as a criminal and receives little direct group support for criminal activity. Fear of punishment may well prove an important factor in turning such low-commitment individuals away from crime, especially if they have already experienced punishment (for other views, see Wilson and Herrnstein, 1985:397–401).

If we put all three distinctions together, then, the following predictions could serve as objects of further investigation:

**1.** Fear of punishment is most likely to deter low-commitment individuals who engage in *mala prohibita* crimes that are also instrumental crimes.
**2.** Fear of punishment is least likely to deter high-commitment individuals who engage in *mala in se* crimes that are also expressive crimes.

## THE NORMATIVE, ACTUAL, AND COGNITIVE SIDES OF PUNISHMENT

Turning to punishment itself, there are at least three sides to criminal penalties (Clark and Gibbs, 1965). The *normative* side specifies what is supposed to happen according to law when various offenses are committed. The *actual* side deals with what really happens to convicted criminals. The *cognitive* side includes people's perceptions of what happens to criminals.

The deterrence doctrine presumes an inverse correlation between punishment and criminal activity: the more severe the punishment for a crime, the lower will be the rate of that crime. But what side of punishment are we talking about? Early deterrence research focused primarily on statutory provisions (e.g., whether or not the death penalty is prescribed for certain offenses), ignoring the important possibility that it is not punishment on the books that people fear, but experiences with actual punishment.

Criminologists are slowly making up for the earlier lack of attention to actual punishments, but we have not yet corrected the imbalance concerning perceptions of punishment (see Minor, 1978). This neglect is something of a mystery, since the essential mechanisms presumed to motivate potential offenders to refrain from crime are threat, fear, and risk. These are subjective matters, based on knowledge and beliefs about punishment. It is evidence of the long-standing neglect of this side of punishment when readers have to be reminded as recently as 1977 that the deterrence doctrine is a psychological theory, properly tested only with evidence on perceptions (Erickson, Gibbs, and Jensen, 1977:305).

## PROPERTIES OF PUNISHMENT: SEVERITY, CERTAINTY, CELERITY

In their early work, Beccaria (1963) and Bentham (1948) made a significant contribution to the development of ideas about deterrence when they focused on three properties of punishment. They recognized that criminal penalties can be more or less *certain,* more or less *severe,* and more or less *swift* in their imposition. They believed that the deterrent impact of punishment will be greater the more certain, severe, and swift the penalties. Of the three properties, severity of punishment was considered less important than the others, and this idea fit the growing view in the late eighteenth century that penalties were too harsh, while suggesting an alternative policy focus on certainty and swiftness.

Except for one or two recent efforts, there has been hardly any research on the issue of swiftness (see Blumstein et al., 1978). This is sad, for it was a problem close to Beccaria's heart. Not only did he denounce the Italian practice of detaining criminal defendants for months, sometimes years, before adjudication and sentencing, but he also considered it vital to impose penalties as soon as possible so that the connection between offense and penalty was not weakened or obscured by the passage of time.

**The Problem of Causality**   A number of writers on deterrence have alerted their readers to the fact that a negative (or inverse) relationship between punishment and crime does not necessarily support the deterrence argument. Far from crime being influenced by punishment, it might be that things are the other way around.

David Greenberg (1977:286) points out that "when crime rates are high relative to police and court resources, law enforcement resources might stretch thin, reducing the chances of a crime leading to arrest or conviction." Such a "system overload" (Pontell, 1984:6) produces a negative relationship between crime rates and properties of punishment, but the direction of causality is the opposite of deterrence theory.

This problem also extends to research on the relationship between perceptions of punishment and self-reported criminality. Although some recent research attempts to place the variables in the "right" order, that is, when perceptions influence behavior rather than the other way around, the fact that this is accomplished by asking people to recall their past perceptions, or predict their future behavior, raises the likelihood of distortions. Indeed, William Minor (1978) reports one study that shows that perceptions do not remain stable over time. This raises doubts about tests of deterrence that ask people to recall earlier conduct and then relate those reports to current perceptions as if they have remained the same since the earlier behavior.

## DOES FEAR OF PUNISHMENT REALLY PREVENT CRIME?

Where does all this leave us? Certainly, deterrence is a complex matter, far too complicated for us to do it justice in a few pages. Nevertheless, one is tempted to hope that with the hundreds of studies completed during the past few years some answers to the question, Does punishment deter crime? can be given with confidence.

Regrettably, this is not the case. Although most authors agree that any rejection of the deterrence doctrine is premature, few are willing to accept it. We are confronted by a vast array of conflicting findings. This results in part from differing research methodologies, but it is also due to problems with the nature of the data and their interpretation, as well as to the complexities inherent in the subject.

To the layperson, the inability of the scientific community to substantiate or reject the conventional wisdom that punishment deters — especially if it is swift, certain, and severe — must be difficult to understand. In the minds of most people the issue is simple and must therefore be simple to resolve; people either are or are not influenced by fear of punishment. Each of us can surely come up with our own illustrations of deterrence at work, but researchers have found the going very rough indeed. In fact, the further they delve into the subject, the more complex it seems to become. Whereas thirty years ago reputable scientists were willing to fling aside the deterrence doctrine as disproved, none would do so today. All of this makes the subject an exciting and challenging area of research in criminology.

It would be misleading, however, to conclude this brief discussion of deterrence without noticing one ray of light that keeps breaking through the inconclusive haze. It concerns the certainty of punishment. Although there are (of course!) exceptions to this, it appears on balance that the more certain the imposition of punishment is perceived to be, the lower the level of crime. But when all is said and done, the most difficult and pressing task for criminology is to separate deterrence effects from the nine other preventive possibilities of punishment.

## Reformation and Rehabilitation: Do They Work?

It has become conventional to speak of "corrections" when referring to the organized efforts of governments to deal with convicted offenders whose sentences involve incarceration or some form of direct supervision. Hence the American Correctional Association is primarily composed of professionals in prison, parole, probation, or community treatment jobs. The word *corrections* means just what you would expect: to put right someone who has gone wrong.

Needless to say, if you are trying to change someone it helps if you have a firm idea of what "right" looks like. In primitive societies, or in those headed by totalitarian regimes, it is relatively easy to assert what is right and wrong, for attitudes and behaviors tend to be cast in the same mold and are confined within narrow limits. In modern complex democracies, definitions of right and wrong, of what is and is not desirable, are harder to pin down and consensus is less likely. When there is no strongly entrenched sense of what right is, the goal of corrections is largely what those in charge of it say it is. When correctional decision makers support parole applications, for example, it is because the applicant conforms to their image of a "corrected" person.

Despite these difficulties, it is conventional to use recidivism as a way of evaluating correctional outcomes. The word *recidivism* means "relapse into crime"; hence recidivists are those who once again commit crime. The *rate of recidivism* is the proportion of offenders in a population who relapse into crime after having been "corrected." Hence recidivism rates can be used to measure the success of correctional programs.

Before examining recidivism, we should point out that no one has yet managed to isolate the effects of correctional efforts from other forces that affect the behavior of criminal offenders. Apart from the other possible consequences of punishment (incapacitation, deterrence, stigmatization, and the like), there are many things likely to influence a person's behavior after release from a correctional institution. And these are often beyond the control of correctional authorities: there is nothing they can do about an offender's past record of crimes, age at first offense, race or sex, job history, marital status, or any precorrectional experience. It is extremely difficult, therefore, to demonstrate any direct causal link between an offender's experiences with reformation or rehabilitation and his or her subsequent recidivism.

## RECIDIVISM

Recidivism is a relative matter, but this fact is hardly ever recognized. Offenders may relapse into more or less serious crimes than were committed before imprisonment; they may relapse into more or less frequent criminal activity; they may relapse almost immediately after they are released or only after a considerable time has elapsed. Visualizing recidivism in this way, as a matter of kind and degree, may help in the construction of specific programs of rehabilitation and reform. Although the total eradication of recidivism is an impossibility, more reasonable designs might stress reduction in only certain forms of criminality (say, violence) or in the probability that offenders will "graduate" to more serious crimes than those for which they have been punished.

Most studies of recidivism look at the proportion of offenders released from prison who are subsequently rearrested and/or returned to prison. Needless to say, this approach uncovers only those offenders who have been unfortunate enough to get caught. Two problems should also be mentioned. First, reimprisonment does not necessarily indicate that a person has committed a new crime. From a national sample of male parolees, David Greenberg found that "many of the returnees were sent back to prison for behavior that is not forbidden to the general public, for suspicion of an offense where guilt was not proved in court, and at least sometimes when the parolee had already been tried and acquitted" (1975:551). Only 25 percent of those returned to prison during their first year of release were reimprisoned for new felony offenses.

Second, low recidivism rates do not mean that inmates are "corrected." Even if we exclude problems of discovery, that is, of establishing whether or not they have committed new crimes, we cannot be sure that ex-inmates would have committed new crimes had they not been subjected to correction. Remember, correction is not the same as incapacitation, though it is usually attempted while offenders are incapacitated. The belief that much crime is prevented through incapacitation is strengthened by recent studies showing that nearly half of those reentering prison for new offenses would still have been in prison had they fully served out their last sentence and therefore unable to commit the new crime (Bureau of Justice Statistics, 1985h). But again, this is the incapacitative effect of imprisonment, not the corrective effect.

The figures on recidivism are not encouraging. An Illinois study of 1983 prison releases found that 48 percent were rearrested within eighteen to twenty months after release, and 37 percent of those people were rearrested more than once. New property crimes accounted for 34 percent of the arrests, and violent crimes for 21 percent. Offenders with the longest criminal histories were those most likely to be rearrested (Illinois Criminal Justice Information Authority, 1985). A national survey of prison readmissions estimated that 29 to 38 percent of prisoners released for the first time would return to serve another term. Second-time prisoners had a 40 to 46 percent chance of returning, and third-time prisoners a 42 to 53 percent chance (Bureau of Justice Statistics, 1985h).

## PRISONS AND REHABILITATION

There are several schools of thought concerning the connection between correctional efforts and recidivism. There are those who argue that reform and rehabilitation simply will not work in a prison setting. Part of the problem relates to prison organization and management: "Wardens are paid for running quiet prisons, not for reforming inmates. Any attempt to establish rehabilitation programs in prison are opposed by both staff and inmates because it makes life more difficult for all concerned" (Jeffery, 1977:88).

Gordon Hawkins (1976:48) reminds us that, "the actual experience of imprisonment for most persons imprisoned in this country in this century has been simply punitive." Furthermore, prisons isolate inmates from the communities into which they will later return, often by hundreds of miles. A 1971 survey by William Nagel (1973) found even the newest correctional facilities for men located in sparsely populated areas, far from the largest cities in their states. Prison construction is largely a matter of politics — it means money and jobs for some, danger and deviance to others — almost never a matter of what is best for correctional efforts.

In the early 1970s Badillo and Haynes (1972:178–179) observed that New York State could boast the highest concentration of psychologists and psychiatrists in the world. Yet the state's penal system had none on its regular staff, and there were only sixty for the entire American prison system. Further, of the nation's correctional budget, only five cents of every dollar was actually spent on "correcting" inmates. Badillo and Haynes concluded: "We do not have in America, and never have had, any rehabilitation program on a significant scale for a significant length of time." This is the "we haven't done enough" argument, and it has many adherents. The solution, they suggest, "is simply a more full-hearted commitment to the strategy of treatment" (Martinson, 1974:49).

From another side comes the view that physical confinement breeds its own version of tyranny, expressed in the relationship between guards and prisoners and among the prisoners themselves. Philip Zimbardo's well-known experiment in the basement of a Stanford University building has helped document what he calls the *pathology of imprisonment* (see box on pp. 456–458). One manifestation of the tyranny has been the use of prisoners in research involving drugs, shock therapy, and even psychosurgery. In "Clockwork Orange in a California Prison," R. T. Trotter (1972) describes three brain operations performed in 1968 on inmates of Vacaville State Penitentiary. Richard Speiglman (1976) has documented the use in the California prison system of powerful depressants such as Thorazine, Prolixin, and Acetine. Whether in this form or in day-to-day prison life, the tyranny of confinement is viewed by many as antithetical to reform and rehabilitation. No amount of behavior modification, drug therapy, group counseling, or correctional techniques can overcome the pathology of imprisonment. *"Prisoners adjust to the environment of the prison, not to the environment of free men,"* C. Ray Jeffery (1977:86) claims; like many others he advocates the community, not the prison, as the key to rehabilitation.

**Halfway Houses** One outgrowth of interest in community-based alternatives to prison has been the *halfway house* movement. Although it began over a hundred years ago with the purpose of providing temporary shelter, food, clothing, and counsel to ex-offenders, the movement really got going in the 1950s and early 1960s. Today no single description adequately conveys the myriad forms the nation's halfway houses have taken. Sometimes called

## PATHOLOGY OF IMPRISONMENT

*"I was recently released from solitary confinement after being held therein for 37 months [months!]. A silent system was imposed upon me and to even whisper to the man in the next cell resulted in being beaten by guards, sprayed with chemical mace, blackjacked, stomped, and thrown into a strip-cell naked to sleep on a concrete floor without bedding, covering, wash basin or even a toilet. The floor served as toilet and bed, and even there the silent system was enforced. To let a moan escape your lips because of the pain and discomfort . . . resulted in another beating. I spent not days, but months there during my 37 months in solitary. . . . I have filed every writ possible against the administrative acts of brutality. The state courts have all denied the petitions. Because of my refusal to let the things die down and forget all that happened during my 37 months in solitary . . . I am the most hated prisoner in [this] penitentiary and called a 'hard-core incorrigible'.*

*"Maybe I am an incorrigible, but if true, it's because I would rather die than to accept being treated as less than a human being. I have never complained of my prison sentence as being unjustified except through legal means of appeals. I have never put a knife on a guard's throat and demanded my release. I know that thieves must be punished and I don't justify stealing, even though I am a thief myself. But now I don't think I will be a thief when I am released. No, I'm not rehabilitated.*

*It's just that I no longer think of becoming wealthy by stealing. I now only think of killing — killing those who have beaten me and treated me as if I were a dog. I hope and pray for the sake of my own soul and future life of freedom that I am able to overcome the bitterness and hatred which eats daily at my soul, but I know that to overcome it will not be easy."*

This eloquent plea for prison reform — for humane treatment of human beings, for the basic dignity that is the right of every American — came to me secretly in a letter from a prisoner who cannot be identified because he is still in a state correctional institution. He sent it to me because he read of an experiment I recently conducted at Stanford University. In an attempt to understand just what it means psychologically to be a prisoner or a prison guard, Craig Haney, Curt Banks, Dave Jaffe, and I created our own prison. We carefully screened over 70 volunteers who answered an ad in a Palo Alto city newspaper and ended up with about two dozen young men who were selected to be part of this study. They were mature, emotionally stable, normal, intelligent college students from middle-class homes throughout the United States and Canada. They appeared to represent the cream of the crop of this generation. None had any criminal record and all were relatively homogeneous on many dimensions initially.

Half were arbitrarily designated as prisoners by a flip of a coin, the others as guards. These were the

community treatment centers, the facilities provide housing for psychiatric patients, delinquent children, alcoholics and other problem drug users, neglected children, homeless adults, the mentally retarded, as well as criminal offenders.

Early halfway houses were not really part of the correctional system, but today there are close ties between the two, for these reasons: (1) recognition among those involved in community corrections that their very survival and success depend in large part on a close association with mainstream corrections and (2) increasing state and federal involvement in community corrections (McCartt and Mangogna, 1976:554–555). The correctional bureaucracy is vast and now encompasses the community as well as the more traditional institutions.

The idea that the best rehabilitative possibilities lie in the community has been challenged by at least one penologist. Nora Klapmuts (1977:439) writes:

roles they were to play in our simulated prison. The guards were made aware of the potential seriousness and danger of the situation and their own vulnerability. They made up their own formal rules for maintaining law, order, and respect, and were generally free to improvise new ones during their eight-hour, three-man shifts. The prisoners were unexpectedly picked up at their homes by a city policeman in a squad car, searched, handcuffed, fingerprinted, booked at the Palo Alto station house and taken blindfolded to our jail. There they were stripped, deloused, put into a uniform, given a number and put into a cell with two other prisoners where they expected to live for the next two weeks. The pay was good ($15 a day) and their motivation was to make money.

We observed and recorded on videotape the events that occurred in the prison, and we interviewed and tested the prisoners and guards at various points throughout the study. Some of the videotapes of the actual encounters between the prisoners and guards were seen on the NBC News feature "Chronolog" on November 26, 1971.

At the end of only six days we had to close down our mock prison because what we saw was frightening. It was no longer apparent to most of the subjects (or to us) where reality ended and their roles began. The majority had indeed become prisoners or guards, no longer able to clearly differentiate between role playing and self. There were dramatic changes in virtually every aspect of their behavior, thinking, and feeling. In less than a week the experience of imprisonment undid (temporarily) a lifetime of learning; human values were suspended, self-concepts were challenged and the ugliest, most base, pathological side of human nature surfaced. We were horrified because we saw some boys (guards) treat others as if they were despicable animals, taking pleasure in cruelty, while other boys (prisoners) became servile, dehumanized robots who thought only of escape, of their own individual survival and of their mounting hatred for the guards.

We had to release three prisoners in the first four days because they had such acute situational traumatic reactions as hysterical crying, confusion in thinking, and severe depression. Others begged to be paroled, and all but three were willing to forfeit all the money they had earned if they could be paroled. By then (the fifth day) they had been so programmed to think of themselves as prisoners that when their request for parole was denied, they returned docilely to their cells. Now, had they been thinking as college students acting in an oppressive environment, they would have quit once they no longer wanted the $15 a day we used as our only incentive. However, the reality was not quitting an experiment but "being paroled by the parole board from the Stanford County Jail." By the last days, the earlier solidarity among the prisoners (systematically broken by the guards) dissolved into "each man for himself." Finally, when one of their fellows was put in solitary confinement (a small closet) for refusing

If prisons do not rehabilitate, and if the goal of correction is to reduce recidivism through integration of offender and community, it seems axiomatic that treating the offender without removing him from society will be more effective. Unfortunately, while one may express the opinion that, since prisons are not effective (a validated observation) then one *might as well* retain offenders in the community, one cannot assume without the support of adequate research that the best rehabilitative possibilities are to be found in the community. The most rigorous research designs generally have found that offenders eligible for supervision in the community in lieu of incarceration do *as well* in the community as they do in prison or training school. When intervening variables are controlled, recidivism rates usually appear to be about the same.

Where community correction clearly has the edge over imprisonment is in the opportunity it provides for an offender's continuation of many of the social relationships that free people take for granted. Another particularly damaging aspect of imprisonment is that the removal of individuals from

# PATHOLOGY OF IMPRISONMENT
(continued)

to eat, the prisoners were given a choice by one of the guards: give up their blankets and the incorrigible prisoner would be let out, or keep their blankets and he would be kept in all night. They voted to keep their blankets and to abandon their brother.

About a third of the guards became tyrannical in their arbitrary use of power, in enjoying their control over other people. They were corrupted by the power of their roles and became quite inventive in their techniques of breaking the spirit of the prisoners and making them feel they were worthless. Some of the guards merely did their jobs as tough but fair correctional officers, and several were good guards from the prisoners' point of view since they did them small favors and were friendly. However, no good guard ever interfered with a command by any of the bad guards; they never intervened on the side of the prisoners, they never told the others to ease off because it was only an experiment, and they never even came to me as prison superintendent or experimenter in charge to complain. In part, they were good because the others were bad; they needed the others to help establish their own egos in a positive light. In a sense, the good guards perpetuated the prison more than the other guards because their own needs to be liked prevented them from disobeying or violating the implicit guards' code. At the same time, the act of befriending the prisoners created a social reality which made the prisoners less likely to rebel.

By the end of the week the experiment had become a reality, as if it were a Pirandello play directed by Kafka that just keeps going after the audience has left. The consultant for our prison, Carlo Prescott, an ex-convict with 16 years of imprisonment in California's jails, would get so depressed and furious each time he visited our prison, because of its psychological similarity to his experiences, that he would have to leave. A Catholic priest who was a former prison chaplain in Washington, D.C., talked to our prisoners after four days and said they were just like the other first-timers he had seen.

But in the end, I called off the experiment not because of the horror I saw out there in the prison yard, but because of the horror of realizing that I could have easily traded places with the most brutal guard or become the weakest prisoner full of hatred at being so powerless that I could not eat, sleep, or go to the toilet without permission of the authorities. I could have become Calley at My Lai, George Jackson at San Quentin, one of the men at Attica, or the prisoner quoted at the beginning of this article.

SOURCE: Excerpted from Zimbardo, Philip G. (1972), The pathology of imprisonment. Society 9:4–8. Published by permission of Transaction, Inc.

---

society interrupts their normal or expected progress through the cycles of life, especially those pertaining to work. Most inmates are young and would normally be embarking on a series of important economic and social "moves" in life to ensure their "making it." It is not the prison regimen or efforts at rehabilitation that really affect recidivism rates but, rather, the degree to which those important moves are interrupted. It does not take long to be left behind in a highly technological age.

A measure of this nation's failure to take seriously the challenge of rehabilitation is the vast number of criminal offenders with whom virtually nothing constructive is done. We saw in the last chapter that each year millions of offenders are placed on probation, and although this may be suitable and sensible in many cases, especially for minor miscreants, there is growing sentiment, and some evidence, that the widespread use of felony probation poses serious threats to public safety. Joan Petersilia's (1985a) study of California felony probationers shows that during a forty-month period after sentencing, 65 percent were rearrested and 53 percent were formally charged with new crimes. Those most likely to recidivate were property offenders, suggesting that correctional specialists would do well to take criminal histories into account when developing crime-prevention strategies.

# The Effects of Imprisonment: A Closer Look

As we observed in the preceding chapter, America's prison population has been increasing over the past few years. Whatever the merits of decarceration and community corrections, it is clear that prisons remain an important feature of this country's reaction to at least some crimes and some criminals. In fact, America's imprisonment rates are highest among industrialized democracies (see Table 15.1).

What of the charge that far from "correcting" criminals and preventing crime, prisons may actually be contributing to the rate of crime through their effects on inmates? In an age and country in which rationality is thought to rule, it would certainly be ironic if one of our major forms of punishment helped produce precisely what it was thought to prevent. The problem boils down to evaluating what really goes on in prison.

## THE "PAINS OF IMPRISONMENT"

In a study of life in a maximum security prison, Gresham Sykes (1958) wrote about the "pains of imprisonment." He observed, as others had before him, that prison means much more than mere deprivation of freedom. First, there

**Table 15.1**  Imprisonment Rates of Industrialized Democracies

| | | | |
|---|---|---|---|
| United States | 21.5 | Denmark | 5.4 |
| (average rate; figures vary from | | France | 5.2 |
| 4.3 in Vermont to 25.0 in Louisiana) | | Italy | 5.1 |
| New Zealand | 9.7 | Sweden | 4.3 |
| Canada | 9.0 | Norway | 4.0 |
| England and Wales | 8.15 | Holland | 1.8 |
| West Germany | 8.1 | | |
| Australia | 6.65 | | |
| (average rate; figures vary from | | | |
| 4.09 in Victoria to 8.5 in Western | | | |
| Australia) | | | |

SOURCE: Corrections Compendium xi (February–March 1978), p. 12. Reprinted by permission.

Note: Rate represents number of prisoners per 10,000 population (1976).

is a deep sense of rejection by the free community. Every day the inmate remains cut off from society, he or she is reminded of this rejection, and the psychological toll is heavy. Second, prisons are not hotels, as some seem to think, but are places of involuntary confinement that lack most of the amenities that Americans take for granted. The prisoner lives under extreme material deprivation. In the larger society the possession and use of myriad goods and services is taken as a sign of one's status; not to have them, or not to be able to control their use, marks the individual as a loser, an incompetent, a person lacking worth.

Deprivation of heterosexual relationships is a third pain of imprisonment. The inmate is "figuratively castrated by involuntary celibacy" (Sykes, 1978:523). Apart from physical pleasures there is the psychic pleasure that sex involves; both are officially denied the inmate of most prisons.

Fourth, there is the deprivation of autonomy, the lack of independence that is typical of "total institutions" such as prisons, mental hospitals, and military installations. There are rules and regulations to cover virtually everything. Seemingly, the inmate's most trivial actions are brought under the control of someone else.

The fifth pain of imprisonment Sykes identified is forced association with other criminals, often for long periods of time and always under conditions of deprivation. This involuntary association has many aspects, but those likely to be most threatening are those that undermine an inmate's sense of physical security. In an analysis of prison violence, Hans Toch (1977:53) draws a stark picture of this facet of prison life:

> Jails and prisons . . . have a climate of violence which has no free-world counterpart. Inmates are terrorized by other inmates, and spend years in fear of harm. Some inmates request segregation, others lock themselves in, and some are hermits by choice. Many inmates injure themselves.
>
> The "testing out" of new arrivals by their peers leaves many a first offender feeling vulnerable. Rumors of danger are rife. In jails, inmates who have already spent time in the "pen," or who claim to know what happens there, spread horrifying tales about brutality. Recipients of such accounts arrive in prison expecting to struggle for their survival. Such fears cause problems beyond the immediately obvious ones. In prison, fear is a stigma of weakness, and it marks men as fair game for exploitation. . . . Inmate norms contain implicit threats of violence. Unpaid debts call for violence; group loyalties prescribe retaliation for slights to group members. There is also the norm of "fight or flight": Beleaguered inmates are told (by both fellow inmates and staff) to do battle unless they wish to seek refuge in segregation.

Toch warns of the probability that prison violence will increase as a result of recent trends in criminal justice. The emphasis on decarceration has resulted in primarily the violent and hard-core offenders' receiving prison terms. Hence prisons are being filled with inmates who are aggressive, tough, or bitter. By the same token, determinate sentences and tougher parole policies have reduced the stakes that inmates have in remaining nonviolent. Being passive, quiet, obedient, and nonaggressive is no longer good for an early release.

## VICTIMIZATION OF PRISONERS

Sociologist Lee Bowker (1978:1–2) has depicted the inmate experience as one of *victimization*, "a continuous process extending through all hours of the day and the night." Any transaction is seen as victimizing when "a relatively more powerful individual receives more goods, services, or other advantages from a relatively less powerful individual through the coercive exercise of superior strength, skill, or other power resources." Victimization of prisoners involves four systems, according to Bowker: the biological, the psychological, the economic, and the social. A brief look at these levels of victimization will provide further insights into the prison experience.

**Biological Victimization**   Included in biological victimization are murder, rape, and assault. These are more likely to characterize relationships between inmates than guard–inmate relationships. However, recent discussions of prison life have spoken of a "trench warfare climate" and have taken special note of the physical intimidation of guards by inmates (see box on pp. 462–463). Inmates are often prepared for violence, as evidenced by the routine carrying of assaultive devices such as knives and iron bars, called "headknockers" (Guenther, 1975).

Homosexual rape and other sexual assaults have long been associated with prison life, and the reasons are not hard to find. Both the satisfaction of physiological need and the display of power and domination that such behavior exhibits can be linked to the pains of imprisonment. Although there are no accurate data on the frequency of sexual assaults in prison, most authorities consider the behavior widespread and repetitive. The problem may be even worse in jails. In one study of sexual assaults in the sheriff's vans and jails of Philadelphia, Alan Davis (1968) estimated that two thousand rapes had occurred in a twenty-six-month period in the late 1960s. The exchange of sex for protection has been widely documented both here and abroad. In a twist to this common theme, Davis discovered that many of the aggressors he interviewed felt they had to continue participating in gang rapes to avoid becoming victims themselves. As for women's prisons, it appears that sex is probably more widespread than in men's prisons, but it is less directly related to demonstrations of power and domination (Giallombardo, 1966; Heffernan, 1972; N. Wilson, 1978).

Bowker suggests that there may be even more violence in juvenile institutions than in adult ones. If true, one explanation could be that youths are still in that period of life when proving oneself, especially one's masculinity, is important. Life in the detention home and reformatory is an extension of life on the street, but a more intense one. The opportunities for asserting one's manliness are probably more frequent, and the constant surveillance by adult keepers merely increases the likelihood that demonstrations of "cool-

## A GUARD'S FIRST NIGHT ON THE JOB

... When I arrived for my first shift, 3 to 11 P.M., I had not had a minute of training except for a one-hour orientation lecture the previous day. I was a "fish," a rookie guard, and very much out of my depth.

A veteran officer welcomed the "fish" and told us: "Remember, these guys don't have anything to do all day, 24 hours a day, but think of ways to make you mad. No matter what happens, don't lose your cool. Don't lose your cool!"

I had been assigned to the segregation unit, containing 215 inmates who are the most trouble. It was an assignment nobody wanted.

To get there, I passed through seven sets of bars. My uniform was my only ticket through each of them. Even on my first day, I was not asked for any identification, searched, or sent through a metal detector. I could have been carrying weapons, drugs, or any other contraband. I couldn't believe this was what's meant by a maximum-security institution. In the week I worked at Pontiac, I was subjected to only one check, and that one was cursory.

The segregation unit consists of five tiers, or galleries. Each is about 300 feet long and has 44 cells. The walkways are about 3½ feet wide, with the cells on one side and a rail and cyclone fencing on the other. As I walked along one gallery, I noticed that my elbows could touch cell bars and fencing at the same time. That made me easy pickings for anybody reaching out of a cell.

The first thing [they] told me was that a guard must never go out on a gallery by himself. You've got no weapons with which to defend yourself, not even a radio to summon help. All you've got is the man with whom you're working.

My partner that first night was Bill Hill, a soft-spoken six-year veteran who immediately told me to take the cigarettes out of my shirt pocket because the inmates would steal them. Same for my pen, he said — or "They'll grab it and stab you."

We were told to serve dinner on the third tier, and Hill quickly tried to fill me in on the facts of prison life. That's when I learned about cookies and the importance they have to the inmates.

"They're going to try and grab them, they're going to try and steal them any way they can," he said. "Remember, you only have enough cookies for the gallery, and if you let them get away, you'll have to explain to the guys at the end why there weren't any for them."

Hill then checked out the meal, groaning when he saw the drippy ravioli and stewed tomatoes. "We're going to be wearing this," he remarked, before deciding to simply discard the tomatoes. We served nothing to drink. In my first six days at Pontiac, I never saw an inmate served a beverage.

Hill instructed me to put on plastic gloves before we served the meal. In view of the trash and waste through which we'd be wheeling the food cart, I thought he was joking. He wasn't.

"Some inmates don't like white hands touching their food," he explained.

Everything went routinely as we served the first 20 cells, and I wasn't surprised when every inmate asked for extra cookies.

Suddenly, a huge arm shot through the bars of one cell and began swinging a metal rod at Hill. As he ducked away, the inmate snared the cookie box.

---

ness," "toughness," and independence will be highly valued in interpersonal relationships.

**Psychological Victimization**   Combined with other forms of victimization, psychological victimization primarily consists of manipulation and intimidation for the purposes of achieving status, prestige, authority, and power. The new prisoner (often called a "fish") is likely to be scared, confused, and vulnerable to demands made by more experienced cons. Among the types of psychological victimization described in one study of a juvenile institution are "threat-gestures," "ranking," and "scapegoating" (Polsky, 1962). Bowker (1978:7) describes them in this way:

> In threat-gestures, threatening verbal commands and denigrating gestures are used to keep lower status boys in a constant state of psychological turmoil.

From the other side of the cart, I lunged to grab the cookies — and was grabbed in turn. A powerful hand from the cell behind me was pulling my arm. As I jerked away, objects began crashing about, and a metal can struck me in the back.

Until that moment I had been apprehensive. Now I was scared. The food cart virtually trapped me, blocking my retreat.

Whirling around, I noticed that mirrors were being held out of every cell so the inmates could watch the ruckus. I didn't realize the mirrors were plastic and became terrified that the inmates would start smashing them to cut me up.

The ordinary din of the cell house had turned into a deafening roar. For the length of the tier, arms stretched into the walkway, making grabbing motions. Some of the inmates swung brooms about.

"Let's get out of here — now!" Hill barked. Wheeling the food cart between us, we made a hasty retreat.

Downstairs, we reported what had happened. My heart was thumping; my legs felt weak. Inside the plastic gloves, my hands were soaked with sweat. Yet the attack on us wasn't considered unusual by the other guards, especially in segregation. That was strictly routine, and we didn't even file a report.

What was more shocking was to be sent immediately back to the same tier to pass out medication. But as I passed the cells from which we'd been attacked, the men in them simply requested their medicine. It was as if what had happened minutes before was already ancient history. From another cell, however, an inmate began raging at us. "Get my medication," he said. "Get it now, or I'm going to kill you." I was learning that whatever

you're handing out, everybody wants it, and those who don't get it frequently respond by threatening to kill or maim you. Another fact of prison life.

Passing cell No. 632, I saw that a prisoner I had helped take to the hospital before dinner was back in his cell. When we took him out, he had been disabled by mace and was very wobbly. Hill and I had been extremely gentle, handcuffing him carefully, then practically carrying him down the stairs. As we went by his cell this time, he tossed a cup of liquid on us.

Back downstairs, I learned I would be going back to that tier for a third time, to finish serving dinner. This time, we planned to slip in the other side of the tier so we wouldn't have to pass the trouble cells. The plates were already prepared.

"Just get in there and give them their food and get out," Hill said. I could see he was nervous, which made me even more so. "Don't stop for anything. If you get hit, just back off, 'cause if they snare you or hook you some way and get you against the bars, they'll hurt you real bad."

Everything went smoothly. Inmates in the three most troublesome cells were not getting dinner, so they hurled some garbage at us. But that's something else I had learned: Getting no worse than garbage thrown at you is the prison equivalent of everything going smoothly.

SOURCE: Excerpted from an article by William Recktenwald, St. Louis Globe-Democrat, Nov. 13, 1978. Reprinted by permission of the Chicago Tribune Company Syndicate, Inc.

Ranking is the use of verbal insults to remind weak boys of their social inferiority. Scapegoating combines threat-gestures, ranking, and physical aggression toward certain individuals who have come to permanently occupy positions at the bottom of the social hierarchy. Once a boy has been manipulated into the scapegoat role, it is very unlikely that he will be able to reestablish himself as a viable member of the community of prisoners.

There are various ways in which guards and other staff members victimize prisoners through manipulation and intimidation. It is the guards who control the flow of information and materials inside the prison. They are in an excellent position to intimidate and disrupt the psychic equilibrium of prisoners. Refusing to allow inmates to shower, make telephone calls, receive mail when it comes, and eat certain foods are deprivations that take on added significance in a prison setting. Similarly, purposely deceiving and exploiting inmates by breaking promises and using information against them intensify the pains of imprisonment.

**Economic Victimization**   Material deprivation leads to the development of a "hidden economy." Economic transactions between inmates and between inmates and guards involve all sorts of goods and services, from sex to drugs to books to wages. We earlier mentioned the use of inmates for drug research as an aspect of the tyranny of imprisonment; Bowker sees it as an example of economic victimization.

In addition, there is constant thievery of personal possessions whenever inmates' backs are turned, and simply getting commissary purchases back to one's cell may entail running a gauntlet of would-be robbers. Those inmates who give up any attempt to protect their economic rights become fair game for exploitation and harassment.

The prison bureaucracy is not above blatant forms of economic victimization. The idea that prisons could be a source of productive labor goes back a long way. In the seventeenth century the English geared their jails and workhouses to convict labor. Georg Rusche and Otto Kirchheimer ([1938], 1968) have argued that prison labor grew in popularity during the early period of capitalistic expansion, when the supply of free labor was unstable and at times dwindled to precarious levels. In their view, it was one further example of the exploitative nature of early capitalism. In America, both private and public enterprises have taken advantage of the cheap labor afforded by the prison system.

The question of economic exploitation looms when we consider the material benefits accruing from the work, regardless of its purpose. Who gets what? Who really benefits? There can be no doubt that there is a tremendous labor potential in our prisons — one author estimates its value at over $1 billion (Singer, 1973) — but there must surely be justice in its development and use. Today many prisoners are paid no wages for their work, and those that are receive little more than a pittance. Perhaps if work in prison helped inmates secure valuable work skills, habits, attitudes, and future jobs on the outside, wages would seem less important, but these are considered only remote possibilities by most authorities. Hawkins (1976:121) reminds us that real learning can take place only in settings approximating those in the outside world.

Even so, it is worth pointing out that economic victimization through the prison labor system is not inevitable. An assessment of Scandanavian prison labor programs offers hope for the future (Wickman, 1978). In Finland, for example, efforts are directed at making prison as much like the outside as possible. Though they emerged in the late 1940s in response to labor shortages — further support for Rusche and Kirchheimer — the Finnish labor colonies have apparently lost the taint of exploitation. There are no guards as such, no bars, no outer walls; inmates wear civilian clothes, are referred to as workers, and are allowed family visits on weekends. They are paid the minimum trade union rates, sometimes more, from which the prison deducts 25 percent to pay for their keep and whatever special items (like saunas) they use. Only about 10 percent of Finland's prison population can be found in the labor colonies, however. And these "lucky" offenders are usually misdemeanants or first-timers.

In Sweden, inmates are transferred from a more traditional closed prison to a modern one at Tillberga. Resembling a modern factory (though it has a thirty-foot fence around it), Tillberga has single-story dormitories housing twenty-four inmates, each in his own room with his own key. A strong work ethic is mixed with economic reward. Pay is set at the minimum wage, with about one-third deducted for expenses; however, the inmates do get wage increases, as would workers on the outside. The results of all this must await further research. Both Finnish and Swedish efforts are encouraging, if for no other reason than they appear to reduce the impact of economic victimization in prison settings.

**Social Victimization**  By social victimization Bowker (1978:14) means the victimization of prisoner groups rather than specific individuals. He identifies three bases for the victimization: race and ethnicity, religion and ideology, and nature of offense.

In Bowker's view, racial and ethnic group victimization is the most significant and widespread. It used to be that the minority black inmates were the object of victimization, but now it appears that in many prisons it is the whites, especially the middle-class whites, who are victimized by black inmates. Leo Carroll's (1974) research at a New England state prison confirms the direction of interracial aggression, as does a more recent study of Stateville, the Illinois penitentiary at Joliet. In Stateville, James Jacobs (1977) found four highly cohesive gangs whose reputation and power dominated interracial contacts and radiated throughout the prison. The Black P. Stone Nation, the Devil's Disciples, and the Vicelords are black gangs; the Latin Kings is made up of Hispanic inmates. Their exploitation of other prisoners is extensive.

Certain offenders are singled out for special victimization by other inmates. In particular, child molesters, child rapists, and homosexuals are at the bottom of the pecking order and consequently come in for the most systematic victimization by other inmates as well as guards. In contrast, violent offenders who commit murder, adult rape, and robbery stand at the top of the hierarchy; unless they subsequently demonstrate otherwise, their reputations for being tough and cool are valuable in this world dominated by streetwise felons. As for the victimization of particular religious or ideological groups, which Bowker calls commonplace, Black Muslims and members of the Native American Church are the most likely sufferers. Until recently, when "court decisions forced some degree of religious freedom, minority group religions were . . . outlawed by prison administrators on the grounds that they were both illegitimate and a danger to the custody operations of the institutions" (Bowker, 1978:15; see also Jacobs, 1976).

## POWER AND THE PRISON GUARD

Prison guards have been called "forgotten men" (Hawkins, 1976), and little is known about how they perceive prison life. With few exceptions (one is Jacobs and Retsky, 1975), prison research has tended to focus on the inmates or on organizational structure rather than on the values and attitudes of the guards.

This oversight is now being rectified, and one recent paper examines the important question of power. John Hepburn (1985) distinguishes five types of power, each with a different basis of obedience. *Legitimate* power is obeyed because the guards' position in the authority structure gives them the right to expect obedience. *Coercive* power is obeyed because prisoners perceive that guards have the ability to punish disobedience. *Reward* power is obeyed because the prisoners recognize that guards are in a position to reward them, sometimes formally, as in committee or program assignments, and sometimes informally, with friendship or by overlooking petty violations of the rules.

*Expert* power is obeyed because guards are recognized as having special skills, knowledge, or expertise and can make professional judgments of the prisoners' needs. Finally, *referent* power is obeyed because prisoners respect or admire the guards' performance of their duties.

In order to assess which sort of power guards perceived themselves as exercising, Hepburn had 360 guards at five male prisons fill out self-administered questionnaires. He found that the guards were most likely to mention legitimate and expert power as the reason that prisoners obeyed them and that they were least likely to mention reward or coercive power: "Prison guards believe their control over prisoners to be based largely on their position as guards and on their reputation for competence and good judgment" (Hepburn, 1985:154). This appeared true for all five prisons. However, those guards more likely to see their job as custody oriented were also more likely to emphasize coercive power.

Research like this helps provide a more complete picture of the dynamics of prison life and may lead to the creation of more stable, productive, and humane conditions in our prisons. It may also help lessen the effects of *prisonization,* our final subject in this discussion of imprisonment.

## PRISON SUBCULTURES AND PRISONIZATION

Most maximum security prisons in this country and in Europe are monolithic, forbidding structures, primarily housing those offenders who are considered dangerous to others and who have extensive histories of criminal involve-

The 1980 riot at New Mexico State Penitentiary left thirty-three prisoners dead at the hands of their fellow inmates. Is there a solution to the pains and pathology of imprisonment?

ment. It is in precisely such prisons that we would expect to find the most brutalizing effects of incarceration.

Those who have investigated prison life speak of the adaptations that inmates make to the pains of imprisonment. Among these is the development of *inmate subcultures*, consisting of particular values, social roles, and norms. Studies have found different subcultural characteristics from one prison to the next, but there is little argument about their existence in and importance to prison life (Irwin, 1970; Bowker, 1977).

There *is* extensive debate among authorities over so-called prisonization.

Donald Clemmer (1940) was the first to use the term. He defined *prisonization* as "the taking on in greater or lesser degree of the folkways, mores, customs, and general culture of the penitentiary." It is a process of assimilation, in which newcomers come to adopt, and are adopted into, the subcultural elements of prison existence. Most important to Clemmer, prisonization implies a *change* in the attitudes, values, and behaviors of those who are imprisoned: they become more antisocial, more criminal. It is a variation of the "prisons as schools of crime" argument, and Clemmer thought that one of the most important determinants of prisonization is length of sentence: the longer the sentence is, the more complete the prisonization will be.

Gordon Hawkins (1976:63–80) has identified three lines of criticism. First, there is the assumption that prisonization is directly related to the time spent in prison. A number of authors have found a "U-shaped" pattern or curve, in which prisonization apparently fades as time passes. From being antisocial and nonconformist during the bulk of their stay, inmates become more social and conformist in the months before their release (Garabedian, 1963). Other studies have found little evidence of any increase in prisonization as time passes (Wellford, 1967; Atchley and McCabe, 1968). There are, as always, conflicting findings, but Clemmer's prisonization hypothesis is placed in doubt.

Second, the prisonization hypothesis does not sufficiently emphasize the variations in prison organization. A number of studies have shown that inmate attitudes and behaviors are much more positive in treatment-oriented prisons than in custody-oriented institutions (Street, 1965; Berk, 1966). A comparison of twenty-five prisons in five countries (the United States, Mexico, Spain, West Germany, and Great Britain) found substantial variation in prisonization (measured by adherence to inmate codes). The nonpunitive, humanitarian milieu of treatment prisons was less conducive to prisonization than was the degrading, punitive milieu of custody prisons; however, a majority of inmates in all but two prisons saw a prisonized subculture within the institutional population, though this perception was more likely, the more prisonized the respondent. Whereas this might be interpreted as evidence of inmate consensus and solidarity, it was apparent that in all prisons the inmate respondents *overestimated* the other inmates' adherence to the inmate subculture (Akers et al., 1978:90–115). In fact, some studies have shown little actual solidarity among prison inmates (see Mathieson, 1965).

Finally, there is the criticism that, far from being indigenous (a functional adaptation to prison life itself), inmate subcultures may in fact be largely imported from outside. The importation view has been advocated by John Irwin and Donald Cressey (1962; also Thomas, 1977), and received support in the cross-cultural study mentioned in the previous paragraph. In that study it was found that inexperienced prison newcomers tended to resist prisonization and held the least antisocial attitudes when in maximum security prisons. Jacob's (1974, 1977) study of inmate gangs at Stateville penitentiary in

Illinois also supports the importation model. Here the prison served not only to preserve the street norms and organization of the gangs but also to strengthen them. When incarcerated, gang members brought with them the essential features of the parent gangs; the same people who were the leaders on Chicago streets were the leaders in prison.

Hawkins (1976:72–73) concludes his analysis of the prisonization question with a great deal of pessimism and no little skepticism regarding the benefits of imprisonment. Prisons, he argues, probably do not have a lasting impact on convicts; they merely provide a setting in which earlier-acquired predispositions can be acted out:

> One starts with doubt about the reformative effects of imprisonment on the ground that inmates are being prisonized and in effect criminalized. One concludes with doubt about the crimogenic effects of imprisonment on grounds which imply not merely that inmates are not being corrupted but rather that neither their attitudes nor their behavior are being affected in any significant fashion by the experience of imprisonment.

The view that prisons neither reform nor criminalize most inmates is reiterated by John Irwin (1980:21), himself an ex-convict. Speaking of the "Big House" — those monolithic, maximum security prisons whose heyday stretched over sixty years through the 1940s — Irwin concludes that the experience "did not reform prisoners or teach many persons crime. It embittered many. It stupefied thousands."

By all accounts the correctional future looks bleak. There may be more prison disorder and rioting such as that which occurred in New Mexico in 1980 and in Oklahoma in 1985. According to Irwin, two factors helped promote the prison unrest that culminated in the earlier revolts at the Missouri State Penitentiary and at Attica, New York, and that set the scene for the turmoil of the 1970s. First, prisons began housing more and more blacks, who by the 1960s were becoming more assertive, and finally militant. This fueled white fears and prejudices, stirring up more tension between the races. Second, many inmates grew disenchanted with rehabilitation and its promise: "After years of embracing rehabilitation's basic tenets, submitting themselves to treatment strategies, and then leaving prison with new hope for a better future, they discovered and reported back that their outside lives had not changed" (Irwin, 1980:63). Prisoners, educated by the very programs they came to despise, spread their indictment of rehabilitation and taught themselves to "see through things" and to fight "the system."

Today, Irwin (1980:195) believes, a new prison hero has emerged: the "convict."

> The convict or hog stands ready to kill to protect himself, maintains strong loyalties to some small groups of other convicts (invariably of his own race), and will rob and attack or at least tolerate his friends' robbing and attacking other weak independents or their foes. He openly and stubbornly opposes the administration, even if this results in harsh punishment. Finally, he is extremely

assertive of his masculine sexuality, even though he may occasionally make use of the prison homosexuals or, less often, enter into more permanent sexual alliance with a kid. . . . To circulate in this world, the convict world, one must act like a convict and, with few exceptions, have some type of affiliation with a powerful racial clique or gang."

Prisons today are full of hate, with "dope fiends, pimps, bikers, [and] street gang members" competing for power and respect. It is hard to imagine that anyone can emerge from prison and "go straight."

# CHAPTER 16

# Crime and Public Policy

In this text we have seen abundant evidence of the close connection between crime and politics. This connection is seen in the fact that "the criminal law, courts, and prisons are instruments of government, created and funded by government, and administered by government functionaries" (Allen, 1974:4). Passing laws, deciding about law-enforcement practices, adopting modes of punishment, and deploying money and resources to deal with crime all are political actions. In this final chapter we look more closely at the politics of crime as manifested in public policy — the decisions and practices adopted by those in or employed by government. Public policy impinges on all aspects of the crime scene. Its impact begins with official decisions about what and whom to identify as criminal, and continues through all phases of the criminal process.

## The Underpinnings of Public Policy

Many things shape public policy, whether on crime or anything else. Not least among these influences are the attitudes, beliefs, ideas, and assumptions about crime of those in positions of political power and influence. These attitudes and beliefs constitute the ideological underpinnings of policy and shape the positions taken on specific issues. The particular ideology underlying public policy is not always obvious, but it is there nonetheless and actual policy decisions cannot be divorced from it. As Walter Miller observed, "ideology is the permanent hidden agenda of criminal justice" (1973:142).

The same ideology is not, of course, shared by everyone, nor does a particular ideology necessarily retain its influence over time. Policies will change as time passes. We can also expect that the policies created, adopted, and implemented at any particular time will not meet with the approval of all who have an opinion on crime.

Different assumptions and beliefs about criminal matters have achieved prominence throughout history and across cultures. The ideologies embodying these assumptions and beliefs have sometimes stimulated policy change and sometimes reinforced existing policies; sometimes they have had little or no effect on public policy. Whether or not a particular ideology does influence policy depends on many things, and most important are the power and influence of those subscribing to it.

There have been few attempts to identify and classify beliefs and assumptions about crime. Walter Miller (1973) offers one of the most detailed statements on major ideological positions. He used as his data source public statements (verbal or written) on criminal matters made by a variety of Americans, including novelists, sociologists, journalists, legislators, other government officials, lawyers, police, clergy, historians, and labor leaders. Though we do not hear so much these days from the radical left, the distinctions that Miller presents provide a useful starting point in thinking about ideology and public policy on crime.

Miller placed the different ideological positions he was able to identify on a one-dimensional scale:

| | Leftist | | | | Centrist | | | | Rightist | |
|---|---|---|---|---|---|---|---|---|---|---|
| 5 | 4 | 3 | 2 | 1 | 0 | 1 | 2 | 3 | 4 | 5 |
| | radical | | | | | | | conservative | | |

The most extreme ideological positions were given the value 5. More moderate ones ranged between the extreme left and extreme right positions. The ideological position left 3 is more leftist than position left 1 but less leftist than position left 5. Each ideological position Miller identified concerns a specific crime issue and is made up of assumptions and beliefs about that issue. (See box on pp. 474–475.)

Miller observes that there are convergences and divergences, consistencies and inconsistencies, among and within the various ideological positions. He also notes that although the statements might reflect the gist of someone's ideology, that person is unlikely to feel comfortable with all the statements exactly as phrased. But most interesting is Miller's (1973:148) observation that both left and right can be reduced to basic governing principles or values and that few Americans would quarrel with them, since they are "intrinsic aspects of our national ideals":

> For the right, the paramount value is order — an ordered society based on a pervasive and binding morality — and the paramount danger is disorder — social, moral and political. For the left, the paramount value is justice — a just society based on a fair and equitable distribution of power, wealth, prestige, and privilege — and the paramount evil is injustice — the concentration of valued social resources in the hands of a privileged minority. . . .
>
> Stripped of the passion of ideological conflict, the issue between the two sides could be viewed as a disagreement over the relative priority of two valuable conditions: whether *order with justice,* or *justice with order* should be the guiding principle of the criminal justice enterprise.

## The Impact of Ideology on Crime Policy

The expectation that ideology influences public policy is based on the assumption that our views or theories about an issue guide us in structuring our subsequent actions toward it (Stoll, 1968:121). But in the realm of policy it all depends on whose ideology we are talking about.

Those whose views and theories about criminal matters are most likely to be articulated in policy are persons in occupations dealing directly with such matters — legislators, government officials, judges, police officials, lawyers, prison officials, and others whose work routinely brings them into contact with law, crime, and criminals. Also included are persons with acknowledged expertise in the study of criminality and law — psychologists, psychiatrists, criminologists, sociologists, and economists.

# IDEOLOGICAL POSITIONS ON CRIMINAL JUSTICE ISSUES

## 1. Opinions on the causes of crime and the locus of responsibility for it:

**Left 5.** Behavior designated as "crime" by the ruling classes is an inevitable product of a fundamentally corrupt and unjust society. True crime is the behavior of those who perpetuate, control, and profit from an exploitative and brutalizing system . . . . [Those labeled "criminals" by the establishment] bear no responsibility for what the state defines as crime; they are forced into such actions as justifiable responses to deliberate policies of oppression, discrimination, and exploitation.

**Right 5.** Crime and violence are a direct product of a massive conspiracy by highly organized and well-financed radical forces seeking deliberately to overthrow the society. Their basic method is an intensive and unrelenting attack on the fundamental moral values of the society, and their vehicle is that sector of the populace sufficiently low in intelligence, moral virtue, self-control, and judgment as to serve readily as their puppets by constantly engaging in those violent and predatory crimes best calculated to destroy the social order. . . .

**Left 3.** Public officials and agencies with responsibility for crime and criminals must share with damaging social conditions major blame for criminality. By allocating pitifully inadequate resources to criminal justice agencies the government virtually assures that they will be manned by poorly qualified, punitive, moralistic personnel who are granted vast amounts of arbitrary coercive power. These persons use this power to stigmatize, degrade and brutalize those who come under their jurisdiction, thus permitting them few options other than continued criminality. Society also manifests enormous reluctance to allocate the resources necessary to ameliorate the root causes of crime — poverty, urban deterioration, blocked educational and job opportunities — and further enhances crime by maintaining widespread systems of segregation. . . .

**Right 3.** The root cause of crime is a massive erosion of the fundamental values which traditionally have served to deter criminality, and a concomitant flouting of the established authority which has traditionally served to constrain it. The most extreme manifestations of this phenomenon are found among . . . the young, minorities, and the poor. Among these groups and elsewhere there have arisen special sets of alternative values or "countercultures" which actually provide direct support for the violation of the legal and moral norms of law-abiding society. A major role in the alarming increase in crime and violence is played by certain elitist groups of left-oriented media writers, educators, jurists, lawyers, and others who contribute directly to criminality by publicizing, disseminating, and supporting these crime-engendering values.

Ideological positions are likely to reflect actual work experiences and the effects of the socialization process normally associated with entering an occupation. We saw the importance of these experiences in our discussion of the police "working personality" (pp. 366–367). Since these experiences are not the same for all crime-related occupations or for all persons in a particular occupation and since the backgrounds, current status, and prior experiences of those entering various occupations will be different, there are likely to be ideological differences among persons working in the field of crime. There will also be differences in the intensity of particular ideological positions and the emotional commitment to them. Miller's impressions of four crime-related professions — the police, the judiciary, corrections, and academic criminology — support these expectations. For example, the police are not only rightist, but substantially so; academic criminologists, on the other hand, lean toward the left.

Miller also found ideological differences in the *same* crime-related pro-

## 2. Assumptions and beliefs concerning the proper methods of dealing with offenders:

**Left 4.** All but a very small proportion of those who come under the jurisdiction of criminal justice agencies pose no real danger to society, and are entitled to full and unconditional freedom in the community at all stages of the criminal justice process. . . . Criminal justice processing as currently conducted is essentially brutalizing — particularly institutional incarceration, which should be entirely abolished. "Rehabilitation" under institutional auspices is a complete illusion; it has not worked, never will work, and must be abandoned as a policy objective. Accused persons, prisoners, and members of the general public subject to the arbitrary and punitive policies of police and other officials must be provided full rights and resources to protect their interests — including citizen control of police operations, full access to legal resources, fully developed grievance mechanisms, and the like.

**Right 4.** Dangerous or habitual criminals should be subject to genuine punishment of maximum severity, including capital punishment where called for, and extended prison terms (including life imprisonment) with airtight guarantees that these be fully served. Probation and parole defeat the purposes of public protection and should be eliminated. . . . To speak of "rights" of persons who have chosen deliberately to forfeit them by engaging in crime is a travesty, and malefactors should receive the punishment they deserve without interference by leftists working to obstruct the processes of justice. "Rehabilitation" as a policy is simply a weakly disguised method of pampering criminals, and has no place whatever in a proper system of criminal justice. Fully adequate facilities for detection, apprehension, and effective restraint of criminals should be granted those police and other criminal justice personnel who realize that their principal mission is swift and unequivocal retribution against wrongdoers and their permanent removal from society to secure the full protection of the law-abiding.

**Left 2.** Since the behavior of most of those who commit crimes is symptomatic of social or psychological forces over which they have little control, ameliorative efforts must be conducted within the framework of a comprehensive strategy of services which combines individually oriented clinical services and beneficial social programs. . . . Institutional programs organized around the concept of the therapeutic community can be most effective in helping certain kinds of persons, such as drug users, for whom external constraints can be a useful part of the rehabilitative process. Rehabilitation rather than punishment must be the major objective in dealing with offenders. . . . Where imprisonment is indicated, sentences should be as short as possible, and inmates should be accorded the rights and respect due all human beings.

**Right 2.** Lawbreakers should be subject to fair but firm penalties based on the protection of society,

fessions: "Judges show enormous variation in ideological predilections, probably covering the full range from right five to left four" (1973:150). (Remember the earlier discussion of factors influencing sentencing and the important effect of differences in penal philosophy and the personal attitudes of judges toward crime issues — see pp. 413–414.) This means that in policy we are likely to find strains, as competing ideological positions are more or less articulated.

In the last hundred years or so, public policy on criminal matters has indeed incorporated competing crime strategies. Two "ideal type" models of organized reactions to crime and criminals have been identified. One rests heavily on *order with justice*, the other on *justice with order*. Although neither model is meant to portray reality in all its detail and complexity, both are drawn from criminal justice in action and emphasize what are thought to be fundamental divergences in assumptions and beliefs about the correct way to deal with criminals. The models were first suggested by Herbert L. Packer but taking into account as well the future of the offender. Successful rehabilitation is an important objective since a reformed criminal no longer presents a threat to society. Rehabilitation should center on the moral reeducation of the offender, and instill in him the respect for authority and basic moral values which are the best safeguards against continued crime. These aims can be furthered by prison programs which demand hard work and strict discipline. . . . Sentences should be sufficiently long as to both adequately penalize the offender and insure sufficient time for effective rehabilitation. . . .

## 3. Positions regarding the proper operating policies of criminal justice agencies:

**Left 5.** The whole apparatus of so-called "law-enforcement" is in fact simply the domestic military apparatus used by the ruling classes to maintain themselves in power, and to inflict harassment, confinement, injury or death on those who protest injustice by challenging the arbitrary regulations devised by the militarists and monopolists to protect their interests. To talk of "reforming" such a system is farcical; the only conceivable method of eliminating the intolerable injustices inherent in this kind of society is the total and forceful overthrow of the entire system, including its so-called "law-enforcement" arm. All acts which serve this end, including elimina-

tion of members of the oppressor police force, serve to hasten the inevitable collapse of the system and the victory of progressive forces.

**Right 5.** Maximum possible resources must be provided those law enforcement officials who realize that their basic mission is the protection of society and maintenance of security for the law-abiding citizen. In addition to increases in manpower, law-enforcement personnel must be provided with the most modern, efficient and lethal weaponry available, and the technological capacity (communications, computerization, electronic surveillance, aerial pursuit capability) to deliver maximum force and facilities possible to points of need — the detection, pursuit, and arrest of criminals, and in particular the control of terrorism and violence conducted or incited by radical forces.

**Left 3.** The more efficiency gained by law enforcement agencies through improvements in technology, communications, management, and so on, the greater the likelihood of harassment, intimidation, and discrimination directed against the poor and minorities. Improvements in police services . . . should be achieved by abandoning antiquated selection and recruitment policies which are designed to obtain secure employment for low-quality personnel and which systematically discriminate against the minorities and culturally disadvantaged. . . . The outmoded military model with its rigid hierarchical distinctions found among the police and

---

(1964, 1968), who calls them the *crime control model* and the *due process model*.

**Order with Justice: The Crime Control Model**   According to Packer (1968:158), the ideology underlying the crime control model emphasizes repression of conduct defined as criminal as the most important function of the criminal process:

> The failure of law enforcement to bring criminal conduct under tight control is viewed as leading to the breakdown of public order and thence to the disappearance of an important condition of human freedom. If the laws go unenforced — which is to say, if it is perceived that there is a high percentage of failure to apprehend and convict in the criminal process — a general disregard for legal controls tends to develop. The law-abiding citizen then becomes the victim of all sorts of unjustifiable invasions of his interests. His security of person and property is sharply diminished, and, therefore, so is his liberty to

other agencies should be eliminated, and a democratic organizational model put in its place. The police must see their proper function as service to the community. . . . [L]aw enforcement agencies should stringently limit access to information concerning offenders, especially younger ones, and much of such information should be destroyed. . . . The major burden of corrections should be removed from the institutions, which are crime-breeding and dehumanizing, and placed directly in the communities, to which all offenders must at some point return.

**Right 3.** Law enforcement agencies must be provided all the resources necessary to deal promptly and decisively with crime and violence. . . . The right of the police to stringently and effectively enforce the law must be protected from misguided legalistic interference. . . . The scope of the criminal law must be expanded rather than reduced; there is no such thing as "victimless" crime; the welfare of all law-abiding people and the moral basis of society itself are victimized by crimes such as pornography, prostitution, homosexuality, and drug use, and offenders must be vigorously pursued, prosecuted, and penalized. Attempts to prevent crime by pouring massive amounts of tax dollars into slum communities are worse than useless, since such people can absorb limitless welfare "benefits" with no appreciable effect on their criminal propensities. Communities must resist attempts to open up their streets and homes to hardened criminals through halfway houses and other forms of "community corrections."

**Left 1.** There must be better coordination of existing criminal justice facilities and functions so as to better focus available services on the whole individual. . . . Coordination and liaison must also increase between the criminal justice agencies and the general welfare services of the community, which have much to contribute both in the way of crime prevention and rehabilitation of criminals. Local politicians often frustrate the purposes of reform by consuming resources in patronage, graft, and the financial support of entrenched local interests, so the federal government must take the lead in financing and overseeing criminal justice reform efforts. . . .

**Right 1.** The operations of the police should be made more efficient, in part through increased use of modern managerial principles and information processing techniques. Police protection should focus more directly on the local community. . . . Prison reform is important, but innovations should be instituted gradually and with great caution, and the old should not be discarded until the new is fully proven to be adequate. . . . The federal government must assume a major role in providing the leadership and financial resources necessary to effective law-enforcement and crime control.

SOURCE: Miller, Walter B. (1973), Appendix to "Ideology and criminal justice policy: Some current issues." Journal of Criminal Law and Criminology 64:155–162.

function as a member of society. The claim ultimately is that the criminal process is a positive guarantor of social freedom.

To support this ideology the crime control model pays the most attention to the capacity of the criminal justice system to catch, prosecute, convict, and dispose of a high proportion of criminal offenders. With its emphasis on a high rate of apprehension and conviction, and given limited resources, the crime control model places a premium on speed and finality. Speed is enhanced when cases can be processed informally and when procedure is uniform or standardized; finality is secured when the occasions for challenge are minimized. To ensure that challenges are kept to a minimum, the model also demands that those who work in criminal justice presume that the apprehended are in fact guilty. This places heavy emphasis on the quality of administrative fact finding and the coordination of agency tasks and role responsibilities. Success is gauged by how expeditiously nonoffenders are

Incapacitation outside prison? A new penal technique uses home incarceration with electronic monitoring. Officials are automatically alerted if the wearer removes the device or moves beyond a predetermined distance from the telephone.

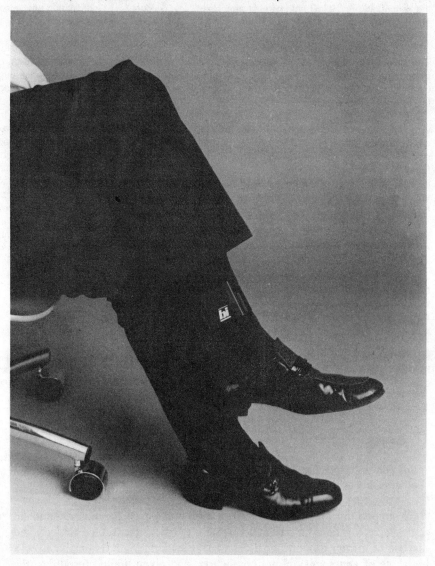

screened out of the process and offenders are passed through to final disposition. Packer likens the crime control model to an assembly-line conveyer belt, down which an endless stream of cases flows, to be processed by workers performing routinized, but essential, tasks.

**Justice with Order: The Due Process Model**  Whereas the crime control model resembles an assembly line, Packer (1968:163) visualizes the due process model as an obstacle course: "Each of its successive stages is designed to present formidable obstacles to carrying the accused any further along in the process." The ideology underlying the due process model is not diametrically opposed to that of the crime control model — it does not rest, for instance, on the view that the repression of crime is undesirable. Rather, it emphasizes a different set of concerns.

The due process model sees the crime control function as subordinate to ideals of justice. This model emphasizes ensuring that the facts about the accused are subjected to formal scrutiny; ensuring that the accused is afforded an impartial hearing under adversary procedures; ensuring that coercive and stigmatizing powers are not abused by those in an official position to exercise them; maintaining the presumption of innocence until guilt is legally proven; ensuring that all defendants are given equal protection under the law, including the chance to defend themselves adequately; and ensuring that suspects and convicted offenders are accorded the kind of treatment that supports their dignity and autonomy as human beings. The emphasis, then, is on justice first.

# The First Priority Is Order

American public policy on criminal matters today, as it has been for decades, is dominated by the ideology and practices of the crime control model. Over the years we have seen the proliferation of public and private police forces whose primary goal is the detection and apprehension of criminals and the defense of order. We have seen continued efforts to create and enforce laws dealing with moral questions and essentially private behavior. We have seen the increasing efforts to unite and coordinate crime control at the federal, state, and local levels. We have seen a growing emphasis on informality in the criminal process, best exemplified in the extensive use of plea bargaining. We have seen continued efforts to promote efficiency, productivity, and professionalism in the activities and personnel of our law enforcement agencies. We have seen, conversely, a paucity of judicial decisions supporting due process values and few serious efforts to organize and fund programs to ensure equal protection under the law and to guarantee the dignity and autonomy of all who come into contact with the enforcement agencies of government.

The dominant crime control model with its emphasis on establishing order through efficient legal repression had its roots in events of the 1950s and 1960s and in the way those in positions of power and influence interpreted them. Early in the 1950s, America entered a phase of domestic conflict against a background of cold-war tensions. Many Americans visualized a communist (or black) subversive under every bed. The McCarthy era, coupled with large-scale migration from rural to urban areas and growing racial tensions as blacks moved closer to full civil rights, presented the image that a breakdown of public order was imminent or had already arrived. Published reports of increased social disorganization in the cities and rising crime rates helped complete the picture.

In the 1960s, public order was given new shocks. President John F. Kennedy was assassinated in 1963. The "American way" was mocked by strange people, among them hippies and long-haired rock and folk musicians. Suddenly the universities — previously bastions of middle-class morality and purpose — seemed to be overrun by pot-smoking, acid-dropping weirdos who preferred free love and the words of Timothy Leary to fraternities and respectable careers. Riots erupted in Watts, followed by more riots in nearly every major city. Then came more assassinations, more riots, the Black Panthers, the Students for a Democratic Society, campus demonstrations and sit-ins, violence at the Democratic National Convention in Chicago, and new evidence of sharply rising rates of street crime.

Some thought America was under siege. Crime became the number-one problem in the minds of many, if not most, citizens. In 1965 President Lyndon Johnson encouraged people to think this way: he launched the war on crime, asserting that Americans "must arrest and reverse the trend toward lawlessness." He called for urgent steps toward more and better law enforcement, with increased federal involvement in crime control. To get the ball rolling and to lend force to the sense of urgency, Johnson established the President's Commission on Law Enforcement and the Administration of Justice, a commission to be "composed of men and women of distinction who share my belief that we need to know more about the prevention and control of crime" (in Quinney, 1974:60).

This commission, and later ones dealing with crime and public order, confirmed that urgent steps toward more efficient crime control were necessary to win the war on crime and reestablish order. Priority was given to the repression of threats to public order and middle-class morality. This came as no surprise to some authors, who pointed out that commission members were overwhelmingly drawn from the established business, political, legal, and religious elites, constituencies with a large stake in the preservation of order and the existing political, legal, and economic structure of American society (Platt, 1971:20; Quinney, 1974:60–75).

A contemporary advocate of the crime control model is James Q. Wilson, a political scientist at Harvard University and the author of many works dealing with crime. Wilson (1984) argues that a "mature" crime control policy for the 1980s will include an increase in the swiftness and certainty of punishment for "serious offenders," which Wilson sees in the conventional sense of the street criminal. Wilson believes that control efforts should be focused on what happens before (i.e., the police and prosecution) and after (i.e., corrections) sentencing, in order to get and keep high-rate offenders off the streets.

Legislative support for emphasizing order through crime control came in 1968 when Congress passed the Omnibus Crime Control and Safe Streets Act. The act has subsequently been revised and extended, but its basic purpose has remained the same: to channel federal resources and efforts into a massive campaign against lawlessness, particularly the lawlessness of the street criminal, the political activist, and the military dissenter. Under Title 1 of the act, Congress established the Law Enforcement Assistance Administration (LEAA) under the Department of Justice. Through this move, Congress extended federal involvement in the enforcement activities of state and local governments, and helped establish what were to become the primary crime strategies throughout the nation. Although the Constitution specifically places the major responsibility for criminal matters in the hands of the states, the federal government was able to assume considerable power and influence in such matters.

## LEAA AND OJARS

When it was established in 1968, the rationale and purpose of the LEAA was expressed as follows (note how well this mandate fits the crime control model and its underlying ideology):

> Congress finds that the high incidence of crime in the United States threatens the peace, security and general welfare of the Nation and its citizens. To prevent crime and to insure the greater safety of the people, law enforcement efforts must be better coordinated, intensified, and made more effective at all levels of government. . . .
>
> It is the purpose of this Title to (1) encourage States and units of general local government to prepare and adopt comprehensive plans based on their evaluation of State and local problems of law enforcement; (2) authorize grants to States and units of local government in order to improve and strengthen law enforcement; and (3) encourage research and development directed toward the improvement of law enforcement and the development of new methods for the prevention and reduction of crime and the detection and apprehension of criminals. (cited in Quinney, 1974:101)

To help LEAA carry out its mandalte, Congress allocated just over $60 million for its operations in 1969. Over the next few years, the LEAA was one of the fastest growing federal agencies; its annual budget quickly reached half a billion dollars (in 1971), then climbed over $800 million, and by 1976 it stood at $1.015 billion (U.S. Department of Justice, 1976:42).

As a result of numerous criticisms of agency practices during the 1970s, however, Congress voted LEAA only $486 million for 1980 and then scrapped the agency altogether. The Justice System Improvement Act of 1979 established as its successor agency OJARS, the Office of Justice Assistance, Research and Statistics. Its budget for fiscal 1981 was $144,397,000 and, after a couple of leaner years, grew to $197.3 million in 1984 (McGarrell and Flanagan, 1985:25).

Most earlier LEAA money went to programs and research projects designed to upgrade the efficiency, productivity, and organization of police agencies. LEAA funds have been used to purchase new and sophisticated police equipment (from weapons and ammunition to vehicles, computers, and bulletproof clothing); to train officers and reorganize police departments; to finance management training programs and operations research; to fund research at universities and private institutes into scientific and technological innovations to aid the war on crime; and to plan future policy throughout the various levels of the legal process. Insofar as government funded research reflects and supports government policy, one can see in criminal justice research further evidence of the conservative bent of national crime policy (Glaser, 1977; Reckless and Allen, 1979). High-priority areas for future research are deterrence, career criminals, prosecution, and sentencing.

As noted, most LEAA money found its way to police agencies. When LEAA was scrapped, however, there were no substantial cutbacks in general police funding. True, educational and research outlays for state and local agencies were significantly curtailed, but federal enforcement budgets remained in pretty good shape. Indeed, the Justice Department's budget requests for the period 1984 to 1987 are expected to average $3–5 billion (McGarrell and Flanagan, 1985:24). Included in the 1984 budget request was the FBI's first billion dollar budget, an increase of nine hundred agents for the Drug Enforcement Agency and the FBI, $184 million more for twelve regional task forces to combat drugs and organized crime, $106 million for expanding the federal prison system, and $800,000 for a new twenty-five-member federal SWAT team (St. Louis Globe-Democrat, February 3, 1983, p. 1a).

Henry Pontell (1984:51–55) shows that state expenditures mirror the federal outlays on crime control. In California, for example, police budgets increased 126 percent over the period between 1968 and 1974, compared with only a 50 percent for the courts, which also suffered a *decrease* in per-capita personnel. Pontell warns that this sort of funding policy gives rise to a "structural imbalance" in the criminal justice system, reducing the capacity of certain agencies to sanction violators and thereby undermining the crime control capacity of the system as a whole (1984:35).

## SCIENCE, TECHNOLOGY, AND THE MILITARY

One of LEAA's major contributions to the crime control effort was the funding of programs designed to advance the application of science and technology to law-enforcement problems. LEAA's predecessor, the Office of

Law Enforcement Assistance, had funded a special task force to report on science and technology. As part of the 1967 President's Crime Commission, the task force reviewed and evaluated the past and potential contributions to crime control from science and technology. The task force concluded that these areas should be exploited to the fullest extent possible, with the federal government assuming leadership and the major fiscal role.

Congress responded to the task force recommendations by including within the 1968 Omnibus Crime Control Act provisions for a research institute, under the authority of LEAA, that would sponsor and fund scientific research and technological development. Thus was established the National Institute of Law Enforcement and Criminal Justice. The money for research and development, coupled with the much larger funds of LEAA's grant programs and those available from other federal agencies (such as the National Institute of Mental Health), gave the federal government considerable power and influence in the application of science and technology to crime control. Also, enforcement agencies previously too poor to attempt serious rationalization of their crime control activities were able to pursue more directly and vigorously the strategies of order through crime control.

**Information Systems**   The development of sophisticated systems to handle information about crime has been one of the federal government's major contributions to crime control. Most of these systems center on computers, and all have been designed with one central aim — to improve detection, apprehension, and conviction rates.

Today computers are a fact of life in America. Few, if any, of us have escaped them. The value of computers in law enforcement was recognized early in their development, but the high cost of running them put them beyond the reach of most agencies. But the federal government could afford them, and the FBI was one of the first agencies to put them to use. Today the FBI's National Crime Information Center (NCIC) is hooked up to teleprinters in most of the nation's law-enforcement agencies. Computers, and the electronic technology that goes with them, now provide immediate access to millions of bits of information about crime, suspects, and offenders, and this information can be stored, manipulated, retrieved, and passed on at a moment's notice.

**SWAT — A Military Offshoot**   The threats to order posed by riots, demonstrations, hijackings, and acts of terrorism during the 1960s were met in the government by calls for the application of military technology and tactics to domestic crime problems. These calls were supported by the task force report on science and technology, which urged the same line. One well-known product of this concern has been SWAT, Special Weapons and Tactics. SWAT became familiar to Americans when ABC ran an adventure series of the same name, based on the Los Angeles Police Department's SWAT teams.

SWAT was initiated in Los Angeles in late 1967 "in response to the increased incidence of urban violence, and in particular the emergence of the sniper as a threat to police operations, the appearance of the political assassin, and the threat of guerrilla warfare" (Center for Research on Criminal Justice, 1975:48). In Los Angeles, and later elsewhere, SWAT teams of five- or six-member squads were assembled for intensive training in the precise and lethal operations of guerrilla combat. Each team member was expected to handle a wide range of tasks and to use effectively the many devices and weapons with which the teams were equipped, including "automatic rifles, semiautomatic shotguns, gas masks, gas canisters, smoke devices, ropes, pry bars, manhole hooks, and walkie talkies" (Center for Research on Criminal Justice, 1975:48).

Most SWAT activities center on the protection of police and fire personnel, the rescue of hostages, the nonviolent apprehension of barricaded suspects, and the protection of public officials. The notorious May 14, 1974, shootout in Los Angeles, involving twenty-nine SWAT members and resulting in the deaths of six suspected Symbionese Liberation Army members, obscured the fact that before that time SWAT teams had fired weapons on only a handful of occasions. Even so, the proliferation of military-style police units in the name of order underscores the policy emphasis on order.

Heavy funding of crime control research and technological developments is likely to continue through the next decade. Yet at least one evaluation expert questions whether new technology will significantly improve crime prevention and control. George Kelling (1978:182–183) notes that with the possible exception of radios and bulletproof vests, "there is no evidence that any technological devices have significantly improved the effectiveness of police service."

## Public Policy and Criminal Stereotypes

President Johnson, in calling for a war on crime, and Congress, in passing the Omnibus Crime Control and Safe Streets Act, drew attention only to certain crimes and certain criminals. Despite using such broad expressions as "lawlessness in America," they considered the real crime problem to be the overt threats to public order and prevailing institutions represented in street crimes — muggings, forcible rapes, burglaries, assaults, and armed robberies — and the activities of junkies and dope pushers, militant activists, and other so-called radicals. Except for the last two groups the bulk of those identified as the real threat to law and order are lower-class individuals living mostly in the poverty areas of the nation's cities.

Nineteenth-century officials dubbed such persons "the dangerous classes." Today, as then, policymakers focus crime control efforts on the relatively poor, uneducated, and powerless members of society. Describing the situation over the years, William Chambliss (1969:86) concludes:

The lower-class person is (1) more likely to be scrutinized and therefore to be observed in any violation of the law; (2) more likely to be arrested if discovered under suspicious circumstances; (3) more likely to spend the time between arrest and trial in jail; (4) more likely to come to trial; (5) more likely to be found guilty; and (6) if found guilty, more likely to receive harsh punishment than his middle-class counterpart. Even after the sentence is passed, the built-in biases continue — among those sentenced to death for murder, lower-class persons are more likely to be executed than are the others.

This is not a new situation, nor is it characteristic only of America or other capitalistic countries. In Nigeria, for example, the tendency has also been for law in action to single out as criminals those lacking money or influence (Chambliss, 1975). Further, the picture has been the same throughout history. Those low in status and relatively powerless have traditionally been the persons most likely to be labeled criminal and most likely to receive the coercive attention of the state.

Because current crime policies show no evidence of changing their focus, people have no incentive to alter their long-held stereotypes of the criminal. On the contrary, current policies merely reinforce these stereotypes. American citizens are encouraged to view the streets as the unsafe turf of the criminal class. They are encouraged to believe that drug pushers and heroin addicts pose a serious and constant threat to their security and well-being and to that of the nation as a whole (President Richard Nixon once remarked, "The drug problem has assumed the dimensions of a national emergency"). They are encouraged to distrust less-well-off neighbors, and to demand speedy and harsh disposition when others are charged with criminal offenses. The destruction of an entire city block in Philadelphia in 1985 when police dropped a bomb on religious deviants is testimony to the link between stereotypical images of the dangerous class and crime control policy.

The targets of crime policy, meanwhile, view themselves as subjugated and oppressed by the authorities and see their illegal actions as political crimes (Allen, 1974:75–76). They feel that they are oppressed because they lack political power and that their "crimes" are legitimate reactions to this political condition. Crime control policy further alienates and aggravates the disadvantaged segments of society when they realize that middle-class criminality escapes the serious attention of the state. That it had escaped serious attention until recently is evidenced by the paucity of government programs aimed at detecting and apprehending those who commit occupational crimes. With all of the money spent on projects and programs dealing with drugs, burglary, robbery, and street crimes generally, the government has little left over to spend on policing the middle class.

This is not to say that street crimes should receive no attention or even that they should receive less attention than they do. The issue is how much and what kind of attention they receive relative to other forms of criminality. The relative lack of attention authorities give to occupational crime is hard to justify when we consider its impact on society. This inattention reinforces prevailing stereotypes about the middle-class criminal. For when middle-class offenders are apprehended, unusual as that is, the view seems to be that they must be ill or disturbed, since real criminals do not come from this class:

> The middle-class offender does not *need* to steal and is, therefore, in a different category from the working-class offender who is assumed to *need* to steal and must, therefore, be prevented by the threat of prosecution. . . . Underlying the attitudes expressed by the police, the prosecution, and the magistrates and judges is the belief that the wealthy do not need to commit crimes, especially crimes of theft, so that if they do it is because of physical ill health, mental illness, or evil influence. (Chapman, 1968:72–75)

Since our policies make hare the detection, apprehension, and harsh punishment of occupational criminals, they confirm the belief that only the rare middle-class person turns to crime. We are encouraged to continue thinking that crime is a lower-class phenomenon.

An extreme version of this view is presented in Jeffrey Reiman's 1979 book, *The Rich Get Richer and the Poor Get Prison.* Reiman believes that the criminal justice system has failed to reduce crime and protect society precisely because that failure "serves the interests of the rich and powerful in America." How can that be? Reiman asserts that this failure performs an ideological service by funneling discontent toward those depicted as responsible for rising crime — the poor, the black, the lower classes — and away from the rich and powerful. At the same time, the system focuses on individual wrongdoing rather than the institutions that make up the social order, thus "implicitly conveying the message that the social conditions in which crime occurred are not responsible for the crime." If social conditions are not responsible for crime, then cries for fundamental change in the social order are without substance; the "radical" threat can be resisted by a united middle class urging support of prevailing government policies and practices. When crime is not lower class, it is the political crime of lower-class sympathizers.

## POLITICAL CRIME

Political crime is difficult to define, partly because there is virtually no formal recognition of it in substantive criminal law. In recent years, however, some consensus in criminological literature has emerged, and the emphasis is clearly on a definition incorporating two elements: (1) the acts have been defined by the authorities as crimes; and (2) they are interpreted (either by the perpetrators or by officialdom) as designed to bring about or influence change in the political system or its policies. Clinard and Quinney (1967:15) identify political crimes as "treason, sedition, espionage, sabotage, military draft violations, war collaboration, radicalism, and various other forms of protest which may be defined as criminal." These crimes sometimes appear no different from traditional crimes — murder, kidnapping, or theft. The true political criminal has been characterized as one whose illegal actions express a commitment to a cause going beyond personal gain or satisfaction, for example, the overthrow of a political regime (Schafer, 1971; Minor, 1975).

Over the centuries, governments everywhere have reacted vigorously to those they see as posing a threat to their control. Those in power do all they can to protect their favored position and the existing order supporting it. One thing they do is create laws proscribing subversive conduct:

> The history of attempts to outlaw certain groups and ideas that are felt to threaten the viability of the state is the history of the use of law to protect the state. All nations have such laws and use them at various times to prevent attempts to change the distribution of power in society. These laws are by their very nature repressive of free communication and have been the product of times of national crisis. American examples of such efforts include the Sedition Act of 1798, criminal anarchy laws and criminal syndicalism laws enacted in the early twentieth century, the Smith Act of 1940, the McCarren Act of 1950, and the "Rap Brown" portion of the 1968 Omnibus Bill. (Reasons, 1974:158)

Although times of national crisis, real or imagined, spur legislative action and concentrate enforcement activities, times of domestic tranquility do not normally result in the repeal of crisis legislation. In fact, the tendency is for repressive legislation to accumulate, so that as new crises occur the state has the force of old and new coercive measures. Francis Allen (1974:47–48) observes:

> Typically, laws proscribing political behavior are enacted in periods of strong public feeling, sometimes bordering on hysteria. Typically, too, such periods, although recurrent, are short-lived. Nothing is so dead as yesterday's red scare; but the veering of public attention away from the subject that earlier produced hysteria weakens the impetus to repeal or modify the legislation passed in a state of public excitement. The result is to confer a kind of immortality on such laws, making some available for continued application by an unobserved bureaucracy, and maintaining all for use in the next period of public agitation. When the next period arrives, not only are the old laws likely to be applied, but they may also stimulate new legislative adventures in repression and crime definition.

The events of the past few decades signified a time of national crisis to those in government. The result was a concerted effort on the part of the authorities to crack down on demonstrations, civil disorders, radicals, militant activists, and any individual thought, rightly or wrongly, that constituted a threat to the establishment and the validity of its laws. Old laws were reused and new ones passed. Lists of subversives were compiled in secret and circulated around various government agencies. The federal government, in particular, drew on its vast resources in the crime control field and began operations involving the FBI, the CIA, the IRS, the Justice Department, the White House, and a motley crew of informers and *agent provocateurs*. How ironic that "law and order" should have been the rallying cry of those who routinely broke the law.

# Due Process

Granted that an ideology of order through crime control has dominated public policy for many decades, yet that policy has not been totally devoid of elements furthering the cause of justice. To be sure, due process has been a poor competitor of crime control, yet significant enough for some people to assert that criminals are being "mollycoddled" and that the hands of the police and courts are tied. These comments are usually directed at those seeking due process for criminal suspects and defendants or advocating increased use of probation, pretrial release, therapy, or community-based corrections.

The doctrine of *due process of law* originated with the signing of the Magna Carta in 1215. This document set out the terms of an agreement between King John and the English barons. It was a charter of liberties and rights designed by the barons to counteract the threat that the state would abuse its coercive powers in dealing with them. The king promised that "no man shall be arrested, or imprisoned, or disseized [deprived of his lands], or outlawed, or exiled, or in any way molested; nor will we proceed against him unless by the lawful judgment of his peers or by the law of the land" (Cole, 1975:105).

In America, the legal document outlining due process of law is the Constitution, particularly the Fourth, Fifth, Sixth, Eighth, and Fourteenth amendments. The essential provisions of these amendments are

[*Fourth Amendment*] The right of the people to be secure in their persons, houses, papers, and effects, against unreasonable searches and seizures, shall not be violated, and no Warrants shall issue, but upon probable cause, supported by Oath or affirmation, and particularly describing the place to be searched, and the persons or things to be seized.

[*Fifth Amendment*] No person shall . . . be subject for the same offence to be twice put in jeopardy of life or limb; nor shall be compelled in any criminal case to be a witness against himself, nor be deprived of life, liberty, or property, without due process of law. . . .

[*Sixth Amendment*] In all criminal prosecutions, the accused shall enjoy the right to a speedy and public trial, by an impartial jury . . .; to be confronted with the witnesses against him; to have compulsory process for obtaining Witnesses in his favor, and to have the assistance of counsel for his defence.

[*Eighth Amendment*] Excessive bail shall not be required, nor excessive fines imposed, nor cruel and unusual punishments inflicted.

[*Fourteenth Amendment*] . . . No State shall make or enforce any law which shall abridge the privileges or immunities of citizens of the United States; nor shall any State deprive any person of life, liberty, or property, without due process of law; nor deny to any person within its jurisdiction the equal protection of the laws.

## THE U.S. SUPREME COURT AND DUE PROCESS

The United States Supreme Court has the responsibility to rule on constitutional matters. It reacts to requests for rulings on constitutional questions rather than initiating them, and so its decisions are always set against a backdrop of legal controversy. Also, its rulings are not fixed; it may rule one way and later rule another way on the same question. This fact explains why basic policy questions often return again and again for rulings by the Court. It also explains why the composition of the Court is such an important issue, and why, when a President makes a new appointment, the ratification process in Congress is often so heated: whoever is appointed could shift the direction of Court rulings. For this reason the Supreme Court cannot be divorced from politics and the prevailing ideologies held by those in positions of power and influence.

Rulings in support of due process values have been relatively rare in the history of the Court. Even over the last seventy years a supportive ruling has been so unlikely that when one does occur it has been greeted with considerable fuss. Should a number of such rulings come from any particular Court, the Court is honored with the reputation of being "liberal" or "radical."

Some significant due process rulings have been made, however. One was *Weeks v. United States* (1914), in which the court established the "exclusionary rule," arguing that evidence obtained illegally by the police must be excluded from subsequent criminal proceedings. In *Rochin v. California* (1952) the Court ruled that the sanctity of a person's body is inviolate and that attempts to remove from it evidence for a conviction (in this case, narcotics pumped from a suspect's stomach were used to convict him) constitute illegal search and seizure. In *Mapp v. Ohio* (1961) the Court ruled that neither state nor federal courts can accept evidence obtained in violation of the constitutional requirements of reasonable search and seizure. In *Gideon v. Wainwright* (1963) the Court ruled that any indigent defendant should be allowed free legal counsel. In *Escobedo v. Illinois* (1964), *Gideon* was extended to include right to counsel at the time of interrogation. In *Miranda v. Arizona* (1966), the Court ruled that upon arrest, the police must notify suspects of their rights during interrogation, their right to counsel, and the possible uses of evidence obtained during interrogation. In *Katz v. United States* (1967) the Court ruled that a court order is required to use electronic surveillance. In *Duncan v. Louisiana* (1968) the Court reaffirmed the right to a jury trial regardless of the legal seriousness of the offense. In *Witherspoon v. Illinois* (1968) the Court reaffirmed that the jury must be impartial. *Chimel v. California* (1969) restricted the physical vicinity subject to search without a warrant to that within the "immediate control" (reach) of a suspect. Other rulings have been mentioned in previous chapters.

Many of these significant due process decisions came out of the last few years of the Warren Court (named after its chief justice, Earl Warren).

However, the Warren Court's last major decision in the realm of criminal affairs, *Terry v. Ohio* (1968), seemed to reverse the trend in support of due process for which that Court had become famous. In this decision, eight justices agreed (only Justice William O. Douglas dissented) that a police officer may frisk (make a search of outer clothing) a suspect when the officer "observes unusual conduct which leads him reasonably to conclude in the light of his experience that criminal activity may be afoot and that the persons with whom he is dealing may be armed and presently dangerous."

However, in Justice Douglas's opinion, there was no "probable cause" to believe that a crime was being committed, had been committed, or was about to be committed in the case under consideration. With this decision the Supreme Court began chipping away at due process safeguards. The trend continued throughout the seventies and was still going strong when Chief Justice Warren Burger retired in 1986. In *U.S. v. Leon* (1984), the Supreme Court created a "good faith" exception to the exclusionary rule, establishing that illegally seized evidence may be used at trial if the illegal police action is based on mistakes by judges or magistrates and not on any intention to violate a citizen's Fourth Amendment rights. Arguing for the minority in the six-to-three decision, Justice William H. Brennan articulated a fear held by due process advocates: "When the public demands that those in government increase their efforts to combat crime, it is all too easy for . . . government officials to seek expedient solutions."

## THREE PRINCIPLES OF A MORAL CRIMINAL PROCESS

Federal Judge David Bazelon (1981:1143–1170) has questioned whether it is necessary "to compromise the most basic values of our democratic society in our desperation to fight crime." He believes that a "truly moral criminal law" will be guided by three fundamental principles:

1. "The criminal process must always remain sensitive to the social realities that underlie crime." Bazelon calls this the *reality* principle, and he draws attention to the fact that the bulk of street crime, especially violent offenses, is committed by people whose lives have been shaped by the poverty and desperation of the underclass. Muggers, rapists, pursesnatchers and burglars "turn to crime for economic survival, a sense of excitement and accomplishment, and an outlet for frustration, desperation, and rage." Our fear of street crime must not lead us to lose sight of the social inequities that help shape it.
2. The criminal process "must make meaningful the claim of 'equal justice under law.' " This is the *equality* principle, and it challenges authorities to do something about the inequities in the criminal process, to practice what they preach. Those who accept these inequities, Bazelon writes, "are only donning moral blinders."
3. The criminal process "must, through a process of constant questioning, force the community to confront the painful realities and agonizing choices

posed by social injustice." This Bazelon calls the *education* principle. He argues that the criminal justice system is in a position to encourage humane and intelligent responses to the crime problem by articulating and reaffirming fundamental moral values in its own actions with respect to the constitutional issues embedded in the Bill of Rights.

Bazelon's views are not shared by all, but they offer a challenge to those who advocate more of the same as well as a strategy for balancing due process interests with those of crime control.

## Crime Victims and Public Policy

Until recently the victim was the forgotten actor in the crime drama. There are various reasons for this, among them the fact that the real victim of crime has no legal status. The word *victim* does not even appear in many statute books, and in modern criminal law the victim is the *state,* not the individual actually injured; it is the state that prosecutes, adjudicates, and punishes criminals.

Other important reasons for the neglect of crime victims pertain to the traditional focus of scientific, professional, and popular interest in crime and its prevention. That focus has always emphasized criminals: how to explain their behavior, how to deal with them, how to prevent them from committing crimes again. Little attention has been paid to the victim, and when victims are brought in it is in the guise of precipitating factors in crime or as unofficial agents of the state who, as crime reporters and witnesses, could help "nail" the criminal.

But the picture has changed dramatically since the early 1970s. An international effort is under way to study the victimizing effects of crime (and other social ills) and to bring the real victim back into the picture. Much of this effort has been directed at changing criminal justice policy and practice to accommodate a more active role for victims who for years have been "twice victimized": first by the criminal, and then by the very system to which they have turned for help. Treated as nonentities, victims have been shuffled around, kept in the dark, had their property taken and not returned, and, worse still, been subjected to abuse and ridicule in court.

The impact of crime on victims can be devastating. Horror stories abound of victims who were horribly mutilated, killed, driven insane, or made penniless by crime. Every time a sensational murder comes to light — the "Son of Sam" killings, the Tylenol murders, the Gacy killings, the "Manson family" atrocities — our sympathies go out to the families and friends of the victims. But on a much more mundane level millions of crime victims — many not even realizing they are victims — suffer unsensationally and find that few seem to care about their plight. Estimates of the losses, damage, and personal injuries suffered by victims of theft, burglary, and unarmed robbery show the magnitude of the problem nationwide. Of 32,799,325 victimizations, only 7 percent did not result in property loss, damage, or personal injury (Harland, 1981:7).

A variety of constructive responses are now being made to the needs of crime victims. Some of these responses seek to reduce the probability of victimization and in that sense are part of crime prevention efforts. Neighborhood crime watch programs and Operation Identification are examples. Other responses seek to improve the treatment of victims by the judicial process, and others seek to redress the grievance occasioned by crime.

## VICTIM / WITNESS ASSISTANCE

Victim/witness programs are operated at local and state levels and are designed to help victims pursue their case through the criminal justice system. Many jurisdictions have assistance programs, and most were started up with LEAA funds. A typical program might provide the following services: reimbursement for persons who must give up pay while in court; transportation to and from court; counseling and moral support; lodging for out-of-town victims and witnesses; information and guidance regarding criminal procedures and outcomes; and even clothing for people who are improperly dressed for a formal courtroom appearance.

Since funds for nonpolice, noncorrectional uses have been drastically reduced in recent years, it remains to be seen whether victim/witness assistance programs will survive. As it is, many operate on a shoestring, and efforts are under way to secure private contributions through a variety of mechanisms.

There is hope that the 1984 Victims of Crime Act will help matters. Among its provisions are the collection of fines, penalties, and other assessments from those convicted of federal crimes for distribution to states for improved victim/witness services. Other legislative efforts around the country will help keep victims in the foreground, at least for a while (see Search Group, Inc., 1984b).

There is evidence that victims feel better about criminal justice proceedings if they are present when crucial decisions are made. However, victims' contacts with the police and counsel may *lessen* their opinions of the accused (Hagan, 1982). This may explain some of the dissatisfaction that many victims express with the sentencing actions of judges (Forst and Hernon, 1985). For their part, judges show less inclination than either prosecutors or police to use victims as a direct source of information about the harm to the victims resulting from crime (Forst and Hernon, 1985). Victims who seek justice may find that their participation in the process does not necessarily ease their frustration with the outcome.

One new goal of advocates of improved conditions for victims and witnesses comes in the form of proposals to reduce intimidation. A committee of the American Bar Association has written:

Intimidation of victims and witnesses . . . is a persistent problem with two unique aspects: It is the one crime in which only unsuccessful attempts are ever reported or discovered. It is also a crime which inherently thwarts the processes of the justice system itself. For that reason, intimidation can undermine public confidence in our legal processes. Further, when it is allowed to exist, our criminal justice system appears able and willing to take care of only the powerful and secure; intimidation's impact is particularly harsh on the poor and disadvantaged. It is a crime which is very common — yet one for which there is no probability of punishment. Existing state statutes are largely inadequate to deal with intimidation, as are procedures utilized by law enforcement and prosecutors. (n.d.)

Intimidation comes in three basic forms, according to the ABA report: (1) personal or property threats by or on behalf of the perpetrator against a victim or witness; (2) "cultural intimidation," where neighbors, friends, or relatives try to dissuade a victim or witness from official action (usually found in urban subcultures and small town communities); and (3) "perceived intimidation," which is fear of further victimization when no actual threat is made. The first two types of intimidation are estimated to effect 7,500 victims annually in the Brooklyn, New York court system alone.

The ABA concluded hearings on the subject and made sweeping recommendations touching all aspects of the criminal process. At the community level, the ABA advocated strengthening of victim/witness assistance efforts, and recommended that community organizations establish victim/witness "hotlines" in cooperation with the police, as well as posttrial support for those who participate in court proceedings.

To date, some legislative steps have been taken to meet the problem of victim/witness intimidation. In 1982 Congress passed the Victim and Witness Protection Act, setting new penalties and procedures for dealing with intimidation in federal cases, and a number of states now proscribe a broad range of intimidating acts, including verbal threats and harassment.

**Compensation / Restitution Programs** The other major change in the treatment of crime victims has been the establishment of mechanisms for a material redress of grievances against an offender. Two types of program are currently operative in the United States:

**1. Victim compensation.** Thirty-nine states had established compensation programs as of July 1984. These programs are funded by the state with various amounts of monetary compensation being awarded to victims. Generally, victims have to meet stringent eligibility requirements before being paid, and even then the maximum payment rarely exceeds $25,000 and is usually less. Furthermore, compensation is usually available for only a narrow range of offenses, mostly those involving violence.

**2. Victim restitution.** Restitution differs from compensation in a number of important respects. First, it involves payments of money or services to the victim by the *offender,* not the state. Second, it therefore requires that an offender be caught and convicted. Third, whereas compensation does not rest on the ability of an offender to pay or render services, restitution does. Fourth, restitution is considered by many to have a correctional goal, whereas compensation clearly does not. The idea very simply is that through making restitution the offender will gain some rehabilitative benefit. One similarity the programs share is the narrow range of offenses to which they are usually applied — in the case of restitution that means primarily crimes of theft.

Because restitution has not been approached with a unified purpose, little systematic consideration has been given to the question of whether restitution can provide meaningful benefits to victims while constructively deal with criminal offenders. Some programs strongly emphasize offender rehabilitation, and others emphasize victim satisfaction. In all, restitution programs have been established and run in a rather haphazard manner, and there has so far been little systematic evaluation of costs, benefits, and long-term utility. The importance of research and careful planning is emphasized in a report by Alan Harland (1981:25):

> Wholesale expansion of restitutive justice — before research has shown for which offenders, offenses, victims, and under what circumstances it is a viable option — could have any or all of the following consequences: inappropriate use with indigent offenders might lead to a *de facto* introduction of a situation akin to debtor's prison; meanwhile, the search for more effective alternative offender dispositions might be thwarted; introduction of an essentially civil remedy into criminal proceedings without procedural protections comparable to those afforded a civil respondent; public and legislative opinion might be misled to believe that victims are being compensated adequately, whereas much of the restitution ordered will never be paid; this in turn leads to a possible obstacle to the development of alternative victim remedies in those cases in which restitution does not materialize.

Finally, institutionalized restitution could create a special class of offenders who are penalized because they do *not* make restitution in money (because they cannot afford to) but must do so by performing menial tasks. Arbitrary and capricious practice is an ever-present danger when freedom is dependent on money or labor (Hudson and Galoway, 1975:66–67).

## The Rehabilitative Ideal and the Therapeutic State

Just as the Warren Court was accused of tying the hands of the crime control apparatus, those advocating rehabilitation and treatment rather than punishment have been accused of coddling criminals and wanting to turn prisons into country clubs. Few policy issues generate more heated debate than the question of what to do with, to, or for criminal offenders.

Historically, the established policy both here and abroad has been to emphasize punishment as the appropriate way to deal with criminals. Yet during the last seventy-five years or so, there has been a trend away from strictly punitive measures. This can be seen in the increased use of probation, parole, community-based corrections, and various programs designed to "treat" offenders. Treatment programs cover the gamut of therapeutic approaches — from psychotherapy to reality therapy, behavior modification, chemotherapy, transactional analysis, and group therapy.

The trend toward rehabilitation and treatment cannot be explained by any one cause; it seems to be rooted in a number of things. First, nineteenth-century positivism led many to view criminality as a problem amenable to scientific analysis and solution. Another factor was the growing number of scholars and practitioners who questioned the deterrent efficacy of traditional ways of dealing with criminals. Some held that crime was the result not of free will and wickedness but of "sickness" brough on by genetic or environmental conditions. Also, humanitarians condemned existing policies as harsh and cruel. Perhaps most important, practitioners and theorists in the developing fields of psychology and psychiatry saw in the criminal — a deviant — the perfect opportunity to put their theories into practice. What actually allowed the "rehabilitative ideal" to make inroads into crime policy, more than anything else, was the fact that its advocates held the view that crime was injurious to society and promised to provide new defenses against it (Allen, 1959:226–236).

## JUVENILE JUSTICE

It is by no means coincidental that at the same time governments were becoming aware of the rehabilitative promise, new approaches to the question of juvenile justice were surfacing. Juvenile courts were established under the *parens patriae* doctrine; their avowed purpose was to care for, rather than punish, the delinquent. The doctrine placed "little or no emphasis . . . upon an individual's guilt of a particular crime; but much weight is given to his physical, mental, or social shortcomings. In dealing with the deviant, under the new system, society is said to be acting in a parental role . . . seeking not to punish but to change or socialize the nonconformist through treatment or therapy" (Kittrie, 1973:3).

Illinois was the first state to establish a juvenile court (in Cook County in 1899), and by the end of World War II every state had passed legislation providing for the special handling of juveniles (usually defined as those under 17) following the *parens patriae* doctrine. As the juvenile court system unfolded, its typical features were (1) private hearings before designated officials — judge or probation officer — and parents or guardian only; (2) informal hearings, because the court trial atmosphere was considered inappropriate given the state's parental role; (3) no juries and usually no counsel, either for the prosecution or defense; (4) no cross-examination of one's accusers; (5) no sentence — the preferred term was "adjudication" or "disposition"; and (6) no punishment — the preferred expression was "treatment" or "care."

## THE THERAPEUTIC STATE

Based on *parens patriae* and individualized treatment, juvenile justice became part of the trend toward what some authors have called the "therapeutic state" — a state in which therapy is a tool that governments use to control deviants and enforce conformity to rules. Today therapy for social control purposes is found in the areas of mental health, alcoholism, drug addiction, psychotherapy, juvenile delinquency, and adult crime. In some of these areas citizens may volunteer for treatment; in all of them, however, the state may make treatment compulsory. According to Nicholas Kittrie (1973:4–8), the trend has been divestment: the criminal law has been forced to relinquish its jurisdiction over areas formerly its concern alone. Freed from the criminal law, these areas are also freed from the constraints to which the state is subject in criminal matters. In other words, the state has emerged largely unfettered in its expanding role of *parens patriae*. A considerable danger has thus been created by the trend toward rehabilitation and therapy. In its dealings with nonconformists, the state need pay no attention to due process and the rights and dignities of its citizens.

This serious danger has in fact proved real, leading some observers to demand that the rehabilitative ideal be exposed for what it has turned out to be — another tool of repression, but a more insidious one. Critical studies of juvenile justice in action and of the use of therapy in prisons and mental institutions show that whatever the original aims and expectations might have been, the "welfare and health components of the therapeutic power have served as subterfuge for circumventing traditional limitations against excesses of state power" (Kittrie, 1973:379; see also Cicourel, 1968; Mitford, 1973). Under the guise of therapy, rehabilitation, and reform, criminals of every age, sometimes only suspects, have been incarcerated under indeterminate sentences, forced to undergo treatment of all kinds, used as guinea pigs in therapeutic experiments, and even brainwashed. The fact that many of these "offenders" — particularly juveniles and those adjudged mentally ill — found themselves in therapy programs without due process of law makes the abuses all the worse.

## RECENT DEVELOPMENTS

Some recent developments have produced important reforms in juvenile justice. Many state legislatures are currently considering mandatory flat prison sentences as a replacement for indeterminate sentences. This means that offenders would have to be released upon completion of the term of their sentences and could not be held for rehabilitative purposes. A trend toward more lengthy prison terms may also be developing, and the longer a person must stay in prison the less justifiable, or useful, would be attempts at therapy. Also, the feeling is widespread that rehabilitation has no effect whatever on the overall crime rate, and with the rebirth of scholarly interest in punishment as a deterrent, this could mean a return to punishment as the cornerstone of official reactions to crime.

Some court decisions in the last twenty years have reaffirmed the importance of due process for juveniles and have also outlawed some of the commonplace abuses in the nation's jails and prisons under the guise of treatment. In *Kent v. United States* (1966), the Supreme Court argued that juveniles could not be transferred to an adult criminal court without a hearing and that they had right to counsel. Justice Abe Fortas wrote the majority opinion and observed in his preliminaries that "there may be grounds for concern that the child receives the worst of both worlds: that he gets neither the protections accorded to adults nor the solicitous care and regenerative treatment postulated for children." This decision was followed by the more significant case, *in re Gault* (1967). Here the Court extended to juvenile court proceedings the right to counsel, the right to confront one's accusers, the right to remain silent, and the right to speedy notification of the charges.

Some federal court decisions have laid down restrictions on what can be done with offenders and suspects incarcerated for therapy. After the atrocities at the Cummings and Tucker prison farms in Arkansas became known in the late 1960s, one federal court ruled that the conditions at the prisons constituted cruel and unusual punishment. Another federal court ruled in Michigan that psychosurgery could not be performed on inmates without their informed consent. These and other recent decisions may curb therapeutic abuses, but when all is said and done, some questions still must be answered, and the answers are as yet wanting. Nicholas Kittrie (1973:47–48) enumerates some of the more compelling questions:

> Foremost is the question of the basic balance between society's right to protect and improve itself in its members through preventive measures, and the individual's right to be left alone. How much of a social hazard must be demonstrated before society may step in and subject a deviant to therapy? May society seek to remedy one's status or personality over one's objections? . . .
>
> Beyond the substantive questions regarding the exercise of therapeutic sanctions looms the question of procedural due process. . . . Should there be a right to a hearing and counsel? . . . Should the state be required to disclose the medical record upon which it proceeds against an individual? Should the term of therapeutic treatment be determinate or indeterminate? Should social sanctions depend on the availability of treatment? Should the individual against whom sanctions are exercised have the legal right to demand effective treatment?

Francis Allen (1959:226) asks another important question: what are we trying to produce with our efforts at rehabilitation, and by what scale of values do we determine the ends of therapy? This question is perhaps the most important of all.

# Future Policy

What about the future? Will policy remain dominated by conservative ideology? Will more emphasis be placed on doing something about occupational crime, or will we see a continued policy bias in favor of the suppression of lower-class criminality? Will significant moves be made toward the decriminalization of victimless crimes, or will governments continue to enact and enforce laws dealing with drugs, prostitution, and the like? Will serious efforts be made to curb the discretionary powers of the police, or will we see attempts to extend them?

President Jimmy Carter promised a fresh look at crime and bemoaned the tendency of past crime policy to reinforce the traditional stereotype of the criminal. For a time, there was hope that money and resources would be channeled to improving the quality of life for all Americans, especially the poor and disadvantaged. However, President Ronald Reagan has made it clear that this is not to be the route his administration takes. He is seeking "moral or spiritual" solutions to the crime problem and looks to "truths like: right and wrong matters; individuals are responsible for their actions; retribution should be swift and sure for those who prey upon the innocent" (Justice Assistance News, November 1981:1). Summarizing his administration's first two years of criminal justice efforts, Reagan pointed with particular pride to his initiatives in making bail more difficult to secure, in making sentences stiffer, in fighting drug trafficking, and in "achieving a better balance among law enforcement, prosecutorial, and correctional resources" (St. Louis Globe-Democrat, February 1, 1983:8A). This is a far cry from the moral criminal process advocated by Judge Bazelon and incorporated in the "justice with order" perspective.

And the future? Rather than speculating on changes in policy, it is more realistic, and sobering, to consider what is unlikely to change in the foreseeable future. Some very basic conditions seem destined to remain largely unchanged. First, the demand for order will remain. Second, the state will still rely on law as its major tool in maintaining order. Third, the established elites will continue to hold the trump card in policy decision making. Fourth, officials will look toward science and technology for answers to questions about crime. Fifth, as always, organizations seek their own perpetuation, and so the criminal justice bureaucracy will continue to exist, though perhaps in different form. There is already a muddying of distinctions between public and private policing, and now private enterprise is encroaching on the prison system. And sixth, punishment will remain the cornerstone of reactions to crime. The persistence of these conditions does not bode well for any radical changes in crime policy.

Robert Bradley (1984) looked at trends in state crime control legislation during the 1980s. His list of changes is a catalogue of innovative conservatism, if I can be excused the oxymoron:

Building of new prisons.

Emergency early release because of prison overcrowding.

Community reintegration as an early release strategy.

Tougher penalties for "serious" offenses.

Mandatory and determinate sentencing.

Increased use of the death penalty.

Extended incarceration of violent and/or repeat offenders.

Abolishment or modification of insanity plea to permit incarceration of mentally ill dangerous offenders.

Easing of restrictions on trying juveniles as adults.

Increased and/or mandatory sentences for crimes committed with a handgun.

Greater use of preventive detention and stricter limits on a suspect's right to bail.

One of the most substantial impediments to any significant changes is the ways in which crime and criminals "benefit" society. Karl Marx (1969:387–388) wrote on this point:

> The criminal produces not only crimes but also criminal law and in addition to this the inevitable compendium in which [the] professor throws his lectures onto the general market as "commodities." This brings with it augmentation of national wealth. . . . The criminal, moreover, produces the whole of the police and of criminal justice, constables, judges, hangmen, juries, etc.; and all these different lines of business . . . create new needs and new ways of satisfying them. Torture alone has given rise to the most ingenious mechanical inventions, and employed many honourable craftsmen in the production of its instruments. . . . In this way . . . the criminal comes in as one of those natural "counterweights" which bring about a correct balance and open up a whole perspective of "useful" occupations.
>
> The effects of the criminal on the development of productive power can be shown in detail. Would locks ever have reached their present degree of excellence had there been no thieves? Would the making of bank-notes have reached its present perfection had there been no forgers? Would the microscope have found its way into the sphere of ordinary commerce but for trading frauds? Doesn't practical chemistry owe just as much to adulteration of commodities and the efforts to show it up as to the honest zeal for production?

Marx's point is that respectable people make a living off crime and criminals even though they condemn them. An entire industry has grown up around crime; hence change would actually undermine this industry and is likely to be resisted. Reasons and Kaplan (1975:360–372) argue that efforts to do away with prisons, for example, will be resisted because of the jobs they create, the scientific research they benefit and support, the reduction of unemployment rates they can produce, and the prison-related occupations they support. Some argue that even if a viable plan were devised to prevent or significantly reduce crime, it would be resisted by the very same people who consider crime a problem. This was the case during the witch hunts of medieval Europe. Some of the very people who heartily condemned witch-craft saw to it that the crime of witchcraft flourished rather than disappeared. They helped create witchcraft (by pointing an accusing finger at someone), so they could be witch finders, witch hunters, witch watchers, torturers, executioners, and judges (Currie, 1968:20–22). Although the crime scene in America may change in character, some people will always ensure that crime continues to be a problem — and those people will not always be the criminals.

# Appendix

Throughout the text are references to various criminal offenses. Each of the chapters in Part II deals with the historical development of relevant offenses, and an effort is made to acquaint the reader with contemporary criminal law definitions. However, the FBI maintains its own offense classification and definitional system. When FBI data are presented for certain offenses, the conception of that offense may not strictly agree with dominant criminal law definitions, and sometimes the FBI includes in its offense categories a number of discrete criminal law offenses. So that you will know exactly how the FBI defines any particular offense category, the following list of FBI offenses is presented.* Use it as a reference when you deal with FBI data.

## FBI Part I Offenses

**Criminal homicide:**   (a) Murder and nonnegligent manslaughter: all willful felonious homicide as distinguished from death caused by negligence. *Excludes* attempt to kill, suicide, accidental death, or justifiable homicide. (b) Manslaughter by negligence: any death that police investigation established was primarily attributable to gross negligence of some individual other than the victim.

**Forcible rape:**   The carnal knowledge of a female, forcibly and against her will in the categories of rape by force, assault by rape, and attempted rape. *Excludes* statutory offenses (no force used, victim under age of consent).

**Robbery:**   Stealing or taking of anything of value from the care, custody, or control of a person by force or violence or by putting in fear, such as strong-arm robbery, stickup, armed robbery, assault to rob, and attempt to rob.

*From FBI (1984), Uniform Crime Reports, 1983. Washington, D.C.: U.S. Government Printing Office.

**Burglary, breaking or entering:** Burglary, housebreaking, safecracking, or any breaking or unlawful entry of a structure with the intent to commit a felony or a theft. Includes attempted forcible entry.

**Aggravated assault:** Assault with intent to kill or for the purpose of inflicting severe bodily injury by shooting, cutting, stabbing, maiming, poisoning, scalding, or the use of acids, explosives, or other means. *Excludes* simple assault.

**Larceny-theft (except auto theft):** The unlawful taking, carrying, leading, or riding away of property from the possession or constructive possession of another. *Excludes* embezzlement, con games, forgery, worthless checks, etc.

**Auto theft:** Unlawful taking or stealing or attempted theft of a motor vehicle. Specifically excluded from this category are motor boats, construction equipment, airplanes, and farming equipment.

**Arson:** Willful or malicious burning with or without intent to defraud. Includes attempts.

## FBI Part II Offenses

**Other assaults (simple):** Assaults that are not of an aggravated nature.

**Forgery and counterfeiting:** Making, altering, uttering, or possessing, with intent to defraud; anything false that is made to appear true. Includes attempts.

**Fraud:** Fraudulent conversion and obtaining money or property by false pretenses. Includes bad checks except forgeries and counterfeiting. Also includes larceny by bailee.

**Embezzlement:** Misappropriation or misapplication of money or property entrusted to person's care, custody, or control.

**Stolen property — buying, receiving, possessing:** Buying, receiving, and possessing stolen property, and attempts.

**Vandalism:** Willful or malicious destruction, injury, disfigurement, or defacement of property without consent of owner or person having custody or control.

**Weapons — carrying, possessing, etc.:** All violations of regulations or statutes controlling the carrying, using, possession, furnishing, and manufacturing of deadly weapons or silencers. Includes attempts.

**Prostitution and commercialized vice:** Sex offenses of a commercial nature and attempts, such as prostitution, keeping a bawdy house, procuring, or transporting women for immoral purposes.

**Sex offenses (except forcible rape and last category):** Statutory rape, offenses against chastity, common decency, morals, and the like. Includes attempts.

**Narcotic drug laws:** Offenses relating to narcotic drugs, such as unlawful possession, sale, use, growing, manufacturing, and making of narcotic drugs.

**Gambling:** Promoting, permitting, or engaging in gambling.

**Offenses against the family and children:** Nonsupport, neglect, abuse, etc.

**Driving under the influence:** Driving or operating any motor vehicle while drunk or under the influence of alcohol or narcotics.

**Liquor laws:** State or local liquor law violations, except drunkenness and driving under the influence.

**Drunkenness:** Drunkenness or intoxication.

**Disorderly conduct:** Breach of the peace.

**Vagrancy:** Vagabondage, begging, loitering, etc.

**Suspicion:** Arrest for no specific offense and release without formal charges being placed. [It is interesting that the FBI considers suspicion an offense. See Chapter 12 for a discussion of police views of suspicion.]

**Curfew and loitering laws (juveniles):** Offenses relating to violation of local curfew or loitering ordinances where such laws exist.

**Runaway (juveniles):** Limited to juveniles taken into protective custody as runaways under provisions of local statutes.

# Text Acknowledgments (continued from page iv)

J. B. Martin, excerpts from *My Life in Crime*. Reprinted by permission of Harold Ober Associates, Inc. Copyright 1952 by John Bartlow Martin. Copyright renewed 1980.

Michael A. Maxfield, Dan A. Lewis, and Ron Szoc, from "Producing Official Crimes: Verified Crime Reports as Measures of Police Output," *Social Science Quarterly* 61 (1980), p. 225, Table 1. Reprinted with the permission of the publisher, The University of Texas Press.

Walter B. Miller, Appendix to "Ideology and Criminal Justice Policy: Some Current Issues," *Journal of Criminal Law and Criminology* 64 (June 1973), pp. 155–162. Reprinted by permission.

Excerpted from the Model Penal Code, copyright 1962 by The American Law Institute. Reprinted with the permission of The American Law Institute.

Marge Piercy, excerpt from "Rape Poem." Copyright © 1974 by Marge Piercy. Reprinted from *Living in The Open* by Marge Piercy, by permission of Alfred A. Knopf, Inc.

Richard Quinney, excerpted from *Criminology: Analysis and Critique of Crime in America*. Copyright © 1975, 1970 by Little, Brown and Company (Inc.). Reprinted by permission.

Walter C. Reckless, from *The Crime Problem*, 5th ed. Copyright © 1973 by Goodyear Publishing Company. Reprinted by permission.

William Recktenwald, excerpt from an article in the *St. Louis Globe-Democrat*, Nov. 13, 1978. Reprinted by permission of the Chicago Tribune Company Syndicate, Inc.

Jonathan Rubinstein, excerpts from *City Police*. Copyright © 1973 by Jonathan Rubinstein. Reprinted by permission of Farrar, Straus and Giroux, Inc.

Clifford R. Shaw, *The Jack-Roller: A Delinquent Boy's Own Story* (Chicago: University of Chicago Press, 1930), pp. 84–85, 139–141. Reprinted by permission of the University of Chicago Press. All rights reserved.

Edwin H. Sutherland and Donald R. Cressey, from *Criminology*, 9th ed. (Philadelphia: Lippincott, 1974). Reprinted by permission.

Table 5.3 from *United Nations Demographic Yearbook, 1983*, Table 21. Reprinted by permission.

Dermot Walsh, from *Break-ins: Burglary from Private Houses* (London: Constable, 1980), pp 144–145. Reprinted with permission of Constable Publishers.

Philip G. Zimbardo, "The Pathology of Imprisonment," *Society*, vol. 9, no. 6, pp. 4–8. Copyright © 1972 by Transaction, Inc. Published by permission.

# Photograph Acknowledgments

*Chapter 1,* page 3 Christopher Brown/Stock, Boston; page 20 Frank Wing/Stock, Boston.

*Chapter 2,* page 23 © Hugh D. Barlow; page 50 © George W. Gardner.

*Chapter 3,* page 57 © Hugh D. Barlow.

*Chapter 4,* page 87 Cary Wolinsky/Stock, Boston; page 99 © 1983 Tony O'Brien/Picture Group.

*Chapter 5,* page 114 courtesy of the St. Louis Police Department; page 140 Bob Adelman/Magnum Photos, Inc.

*Chapter 6,* page 151 © Jane Scherr/Jeroboam, Inc.; page 157 © Hugh D. Barlow.

*Chapter 7,* page 175 Bob Fitch/Black Star; page 189 AP/Wide World Photos.

*Chapter 8,* page 203 Gilles Peress/Magnum Photos, Inc.; page 227 © Hugh D. Barlow.

*Chapter 9,* page 242 Michel Philippot/Sygma; page 352 © Robert Eckert/The Picture Cube.

*Chapter 10,* page 286 AP/Wide World Photos; page 303 AP/Wide World Photos.

*Chapter 11,* page 315 Arthur Tress/Photo Researchers, Inc; page 325 Eric Kroll/Taurus Photos.

*Chapter 12,* page 355 © Hugh D. Barlow; page 371 William R. Ray/Time Magazine.

*Chapter 13,* page 390 Mary Ellen Mark/Archive Pictures, Inc.; page 404 Francis Miller, LIFE Magazine, © Time, Inc.

*Chapter 14,* page 420 © 1983 Bill Powers; page 434 © Hugh D. Barlow.

*Chapter 15,* page 443 Andrew Brilliant/The Picture Cube; page 467 Barbaraellen Koch/ The Santa Fe New Mexican.

*Chapter 16,* page 471 Cary Wolinsky/ Stock, Boston; page 478 courtesy of BI, Inc., Boulder, CO.

# References

Abadinsky, Howard (1981), Organized Crime. Boston: Allyn & Bacon.

ABA Section of Criminal Justice Committee on Victims (n.d.), Reducing Victim/ Witness Intimidation: A Package. Washington, D.C.: U.S. Department of Justice.

Adler, Freda (1975), Sisters in Crime: The Rise of the New Female Criminal. New York: McGraw-Hill.

Advertising Flyer (September 1973), Second Chance. Central Lake, Mich.

Agnew, Robert (1985), Social control theory and delinquency: A longitudinal test. Criminology 23:47 – 60.

Akers, Ronald L. (1973), Deviant Behavior: A Social Learning Approach. Belmont, Calif.: Wadsworth.

Akers, Ronald L., Robert L. Burgess, and Weldon I. Johnson (1968), Opiate use, addiction and relapse. Social Problems 15:459 – 469.

Akers, Ronald L., Norman S. Hayner, and Werner Gruninger (1978), Prisonization in five countries: Type of prison and inmate characteristics. In Dennis Szabo and Susan Katzenelson, eds. (1978), Offenders and Corrections. New York: Praeger.

Akers, Ronald L., and Edward Sagarin, eds. (1974), Crime Prevention and Social Control. New York: Praeger.

Alix, Ernest K. (1969), The functional interdependence of crime and community social structure. Journal of Criminal Law, Criminology, and Police Science 60:332 – 339.

Allen, Francis A. (1959), Criminal justice, legal values, and the rehabilitative ideal. Journal of Criminal Law, Criminology, and Political Science 50:226 – 236.

Allen, Francis A. (1974), The Crimes of Politics. Cambridge, Mass.: Harvard University Press.

Alschuler, Albert W. (1978), Sentencing reform and prosecutorial power: A critique of recent proposals for "fixed" and "presumptive" sentencing. In Determinate Sentencing: Reform or Regression, Proceedings of the Special Conference on Determinate Sentencing, University of California, Berkeley, June 2 – 3, 1977.

Altman, Janet R., and Richard O. Cunningham (1967), Preventive detention. George Washington University Law Review 36:178 – 189.

American Bar Association (1970), Standards Relating to Probation. New York: Institute of Judicial Administration.

Amir, Menachim (1971), Patterns in Forcible Rape. Chicago: University of Chicago Press.

Andenaes, Johannes (1966), The general preventive effects of punishment. University of Pennsylvania Law Review 114:949 – 983.

Andenaes, Johannes (1974), Punishment and Deterrence. Ann Arbor: University of Michigan Press.

Anderson, Nels (1923), The Hobo. Chicago: University of Chicago Press.

Andrews, D. A. (1980), Some experimental investigations of the principles of differential association through deliberate manipulation of the structure of service systems. American Sociological Review 45:448 – 462.

Andrews, George, ed. (1967), The Book of Grass: An Anthology of Indian Hemp. New York: Grove Press.

Angel, Arthur R. (1971), Preventive detention: An empirical analysis. Harvard Civil Rights – Civil Liberties Law Review 6:309 – 332.

Anon (1972), Editorial. Yale Law Journal 81:1380.

Archambeault, William G., and Charles R. Fenwick (1983), A comparative analysis of Japanese and American police organizational models. Police Studies (Fall):3 – 12.

Archer, Dane, and Rosemary Gartner (1984), Violence and Crime in Cross-national perspective. New Haven, Conn.: Yale University Press.

Ashley, Barbara Renchkovsky, and David Ashley (1984), Sex as violence: The body against intimacy. International Journal of Women's Studies 7:352 – 371.

Atchley, Robert M., and Patrick M. McCabe (1968), Socialization in correctional communities: A replication. American Sociological Review 33:774 – 785.

Attenborough, F. L., ed. (1963), The Laws of the Earliest English Kings. New York: Russell and Russell.

Audett, Blackie (1945), Rap Sheet: My Life Story. New York: William Sloane.

Austin, William, and Thomas A. Williams III (1977), A survey of judges' responses to legal cases: Research notes on sentencing disparity. Journal of Criminal Law and Criminology 68:306 – 310.


Babbington, Anthony (1968), The Power to Silence. London: Robert Maxwell.

Bacon, Sheldon (1935), The early development of American municipal police. Ph.D. dissertation, Yale University.

Badillo, Herman, and Milton Haynes (1972), A Bill of No Rights: Attica and the American Prison System. New York: Auterbridge and Lazard.

Bailey, Ronald H. (1976), Violence and Aggression. New York: Time–Life Books.

Ball, J., L. Chester, and R. Perrott (1978), Cops and Robbers: An Investigation into Armed Bank Robbery. London: Andre Deutsch.

Ball, J. C. (1982), Lifetime criminality of heroin addicts in the United States. Journal of Drug Issues 12:225 – 239.

Ball, J. C., J. W. Shaffer, and D. N. Nurco (1983), Day-to-day criminality of heroin addicts in Baltimore—A study of the continuity of offense rates. Drug and Alcohol Dependence 12:119 – 142.

Bandura, Albert (1973), Aggression: A Social Learning Analysis. Englewood Cliffs, N.J.: Prentice-Hall.

Banton, Michael (1973), Police Community Relations. London: William Collins.

Barlow, Hugh D. (1983), Factors affecting the lethality of criminal assaults. Paper presented at the annual meeting of the American Society of Criminology, November 12.

Barlow, Hugh D. (1985), The medical factor in homicide victimization. Presented at the Fifth International Symposium on Victimology, Zagreb, Yugoslavia.

Barlow, Hugh D. (1985), Victim injuries and the prosecution of violent offenders. Paper presented to the annual meeting of the Academy of Criminal Justice Sciences, Las Vegas.

Baumer, Terry L., and Dennis P. Rosenbaum (1984), Combatting Retail Theft: Programs and Strategies. Boston: Butterworths.

Bayley, David H., and Harold Mendelsohn (1968), Minorities and the Police: Confrontation in America. New York: Free Press.

Bazelon, David L. (1981), Foreword: The morality of criminal law: The rights of the accused. Journal of Criminal Law and Criminology 72:1143 – 1170.

Beccaria, Cesare (1963), Essay on Crimes and Punishments, trans. Henry Paolucci. Indianapolis: Bobbs-Merrill.

Becker, Gary S. (1968), Crime and punishment: An economic approach. Journal of Political Economy 76:493 – 517.

Becker, Howard S. (1963), Outsiders: Studies in the Sociology of Deviance. New York: Free Press.

Becker, Howard S., ed. (1964), The Other Side: Perspectives on Deviance. New York: Free Press.

Bell, Daniel (1965), Crime as an American way of life: A queer ladder of social mobility. In Daniel Bell, The End of Ideology, rev. ed. New York: Free Press.

Beman, Lamar T., ed. (1927), Prohibition: Modification of the Volstead Law. New York: H. W. Wilson.

Bennett, Trevor (1985), A decision-making approach to opioid addiction. Paper presented at the Home Office Conference on Criminal Decision Making, Cambridge, England.

Bennett, Trevor, and Richard Wright (1981), Burglars' choice of targets: The use of situational cues in offender decision making. Paper presented at the annual meeting of the American Society of Criminology, Washington, D.C.

Bennett, Trevor, and Richard Wright (1984), Burglars on Burglary. Aldershot, England: Gower Publishing Co.

Bensing, Robert G., and Oliver Schroeder (1960), Homicide in an Urban Community. Springfield, Ill.: Charles C Thomas.

Benson, Allen L. (1927), The propaganda against prohibition. In Lamar T. Beman, ed. (1927), Prohibition: Modification of the Volstead Law. New York: H. W. Wilson.

Bent, Alan Edward (1974), The Politics of Law Enforcement. Lexington, Mass.: Heath.

Bentham, Jeremy (1948), The Principles of Morals and Legislation. New York: Hofner.

Bequai, August (1978), White-Collar Crime: A Twentieth Century Crisis. Lexington, Mass.: Lexington Books.

Bercal, Thomas E. (1970), Calls for police assistance: Consumer demands for government service. American Behavioral Scientist 13:682.

Berk, Bernard B. (1966), Organizational goals and inmate organization. American Sociological Review 31:522 – 534.

Berk, Richard A., Kenneth J. Lenihan, and Peter H. Rossi (1980), Crime and poverty: Some experimental evidence from ex-offenders. American Sociological Review 45:766 – 786.

Berkowitz, Leonard (1962), Aggression: A Social Psychological Analysis. New York: McGraw-Hill.

Beschner, George M., and William Brower (1985), The scene. In Bill Hanson, George Beschner, James M. Walters, and Elliott Bovelle (1985), Life with Heroin. Lexington, Mass.: Lexington Books.

Beyleveld, Deryck (1980), A Bibliography on General Deterrence. London: Saxon House.

Biderman, Albert (1967), Report on a Pilot Study in the District of Columbia on Victimization and Attitudes Toward Law Enforcement, Field Survey 1. Washington, D.C.: U.S. Government Printing Office.

Bittner, Egon, and Anthony M. Platt (1966), The meaning of punishment. Issues in Criminology 2:81.

Black, Donald J. (1970), Production of crime rates. American Sociological Review 35:733 – 748.

Blackmore, John (1974), The relationship between self-reported delinquency and official conviction amongst adolescent boys. British Journal of Criminology 14:172 – 176.

Blackstone, William (1962), Commentaries on the Laws of England, vol. 4. Boston: Beacon Press.

Blanchard, W. H. (1959), The group proces in gang rape. Journal of Social Psychology 49:259 – 266.

Blankenship, Ralph L. (1974), Toward a sociolinguistic perspective on deviance labeling. Sociology and Social Research 58:253 – 261.

Bloch, Herbert A., and Gilbert Geis (1970), Man, Crime, and Society, 2nd ed.. New York: Random House.

Block, Anton (1974), The Mafia of a Sicilian Village. New York: Harper Torchbooks.

Block, Richard, and Franklin E. Zimring (1973), Homicide in Chicago; 1965 – 1970. Journal of Research in Crime and Delinquency 10:1 – 12.

Blum, Richard, and Associates (1972), The Dream Sellers. San Francisco: Jossey-Bass.

Blumberg, Abraham S. (1967), The practice of law as a confidence game: Organizational cooptation of a profession. Law and Society Review 1:15 – 39.

Blumenthal, Monica, Robert L. Kahn, Frank M. Andrews, and Kendra B. Head (1972), Justifying Violence: Attitudes of American Men. Ann Arbor, Mich.: Institute for Social Research.

Blumstein, Alfred, Jacqueline Cohen, and Daniel Nagin, eds. (1978), Deterrence and Incapacitation: Estimating the Effects of Criminal Sanctions on Crime Rates. Washington, D.C.: National Academy of Science.

Boggs, Sarah Lee (1964), The ecology of crime occurrence in St. Louis: A reconceptualization. Ph.D. dissertation, Washington University, St. Louis.

Bohannan, Paul (1960), African Homicide and Suicide. Princeton, N.J.: Princeton University Press.

Bohm, Carol (1974), Judicial attitudes toward rape victims. Judicature (Spring):303 – 307.

Bohm, Robert M. (1982), Radical criminology: An explication. Criminology 19:565 – 589.

Bonger, Willem (1916), Criminality and Economic Conditions. Boston: Little, Brown.

Bonger, Willem (1969), Criminality and Economic Conditions, abridged ed. Bloomington: Indiana University Press.

Booth, Alan (1981), The built environment as a crime deterrent: A reexamination of defensible space. Criminology 18:557 – 570.

Bordua, David, ed. (1967), The Police: Six Sociological Essays. New York: Wiley.

Boris, Steven Barnet (1979), Stereotypes and dispositions for criminal homicide. Criminology 17:139 – 158.

Bottomley, A. Keith (1970), Prison Before Trial. London: G. Bells.

Bottomley, A. Keith (1973a), Decisions in the Penal Process. London: Martin Robinson.

Bottomley, A. Keith (1973b), Parole decisions in a long-term closed prison. British Journal of Criminology 13:26 – 40.

Bowers, William J. (1974), Executions in America. Lexington, Mass.: Heath.

Bowker, Lee H. (1977), Prisoner Subcultures. Lexington, Mass.: Heath.

Bowker, Lee H. (1978), Victimization in correctional institutions: An interdisciplinary analysis. Paper presented at the annual meeting of the Academy of Criminal Justice Sciences, New Orleans, March.

Bowman, Phillip J. (1980), Toward a dual labor-market approach to black-on-black homicide. Public Health Reports 95:555 – 556.

Box, Steven (1981), Deviance, Reality and Society, 2nd ed. London: Holt, Rinehart and Winston.

Box, Steven (1983), Power, Crime, and Mystification. London: Tavistock.

Boyd, James (1970), The ritual of wiggle: From ruin to reelection. Washington Monthly 2:28 – 43.

Bradley, Robert J. (1984), Trends in state crime-control legislation. In Search Group, Inc. (1984a), Information Policy and Crime Control Strategies. Washington, D.C.: U.S. Department of Justice.

Braithwaite, John (1982), Challenging just deserts: Punishing white collar criminals. Journal of Criminal Law and Criminology 73:723 – 763.

Brantingham, Paul J., and Patricia L. Brantingham (1981), Environmental Criminology. Beverly Hills, Calif.: Sage.

Brecher, Edwin (1972), Licit and Illicit Drugs. Boston: Little, Brown.

Bredemeier, Harry C., and Jackson Toby (1961), Social Problems in America. New York: Wiley.

Brockway, Zebulon R. (1912/1969), Fifty Years of Prison Service: An Autobiography. Montclair, N.J.: Patterson Smith.

Brodie, H. Keith H. (1973), The effects of ethyl alcohol in man. In National Commission on Marijuana and Drug Abuse (1973), Patterns and Consequences of Drug Use. Washington, D.C.: U.S. Government Printing Office.

Bromberg, Walter (1961), The Mold of Murder: A Psychiatric Study of a Murder. Westport, Conn.: Greenwood Press.

Brosi, Kathleen B. (1979), A Cross-city Comparison of Felony Case Processing. Washington, D.C.: U.S. Government Printing Office.

Brown, Brenda A. (1974), Crime against women alone. Mimeographed, Memphis Police Department.

Brown, Richard Maxwell (1969), Violence in America. In Donald J. Mulvihill, Melvin Tumin, and Lynn Curtis (1969), Crimes of Violence. Washington, D.C.: U.S. Government Printing Office.

Brownmiller, Susan (1975), Against Our Will: Men, Women, and Rape. New York: Simon & Schuster.

Bryan, James H. (1965), Apprenticeships in prostitution. Social Problems 12:287 – 297.

Bryan, James H. (1966), Occupational ideologies and individual attitudes of call girls. Social Problems 13:441 – 450.

Bryant, Clifton D., and C. Eddie Palmer (1975), Massage parlors and "hand whores": Some sociological observations. Journal of Sex Research 11:227 – 241.

Bullock, Henry Allen (1961), Significance of the racial factor in length of prison sentences. Journal of Criminal Law, Criminology, and Police Science 52:411 – 417.

Bureau of the Census (1965), Statistical Abstract of the United States. Washington, D.C.: U.S. Government Printing Office.

Bureau of Justice Statistics (1980), Criminal Victimization in the United States. Washington, D.C.: U.S. Department of Justice.

Bureau of Justice Statistics (1982a), Criminal Victimization in the United States: 1979 – 1980 Changes, 1973 – 1980 Trends. Washington, D.C.: U.S. Department of Justice.

Bureau of Justice Statistics (1982b), Federal Justice Statistics. Washington, D.C.: U.S. Department of Justice.

Bureau of Justice Statistics (1982c), 1979 Survey of Prison Inmates. Washington, D.C.: U.S. Department of Justice.

Bureau of Justice Statistics (1983a), Jail Inmates, 1982. Washington, D.C.: U.S. Department of Justice.

Bureau of Justice Statistics (1983b), The Prosecution of Felony Arrests, 1979. Washington, D.C.: U.S. Department of Justice.

Bureau of Justice Statistics (1983c), Setting Prison Terms. Washington, D.C.: U.S. Department of Justice.

Bureau of Justice Statistics (1983d), Special Report: Career Patterns in Crime. Washington, D.C.: U.S. Department of Justice.

Bureau of Justice Statistics (1984a), Special Report: Electronic Fund Transfer and Crime. Washington, D.C.: U.S. Department of Justice.

Bureau of Justice Statistics (1984b), Criminal Victimization in the United States, 1982. Washington, D.C.: U.S. Department of Justice.

Bureau of Justice Statistics (1984c), The 1983 Jail Census. Washington, D.C.: U.S. Department of Justice.

Bureau of Justice Statistics (1984d), Prison Admissions and Releases, 1981. Washington, D.C.: U.S. Department of Justice.

Bureau of Justice Statistics (1984e), Probation and Parole, 1983. Washington, D.C.: U.S. Department of Justice.

Bureau of Justice Statistics (1984f), Special Report: Family Violence. Washington, D.C.: U.S. Department of Justice.

Bureau of Justice Statistics (1984g), Special Report: Time Served in Prison. Washington, D.C.: U.S. Department of Justice.

Bureau of Justice Statistics (1984h), Tracking Offenders: The Child Victim. Washington, D.C.: U.S. Department of Justice.

Bureau of Justice Statistics (1985a), Criminal Victimization in the United States, 1983. Washington, D.C.: U.S. Department of Justice.

Bureau of Justice Statistics (1985b), Capital Punishment, 1984. Washington, D.C.: U.S. Department of Justice.

Bureau of Justice Statistics (1985c), The Crime of Rape. Washington, D.C.: U.S. Department of Justice.

Bureau of Justice Statistics (1985d), The Growth of Appeals. Washington, D.C.: U.S. Department of Justice.

Bureau of Justice Statistics (1985e), Household Burglary. Washington, D.C.: U.S. Department of Justice.

Bureau of Justice Statistics (1985f), Pretrial Release and Misconduct. Washington, D.C.: U.S. Department of Justice.

Bureau of Justice Statistics (1985g), Prisoners in 1984. Washington, D.C.: U.S. Department of Justice.

Bureau of Justice Statistics (1985h), Special Report: Examining Recidivism. Washington, D.C.: U.S. Department of Justice.

Bureau of Justice Statistics (1985i), Special Report: Felony Sentencing in 18 Local Jurisdictions. Washington, D.C.: U.S. Department of Justice.

Bureau of Justice Statistics (1985j), Special Report: The Prevalence of Imprisonment. Washington, D.C.: U.S. Department of Justice.

Burgess, Robert L. (1979), Family violence: Some implications from evolutionary biology. Paper presented at the annual meeting of the American Society of Criminology.

Burgess, Robert L., and Ronald L. Akers (1966), A differential association – reinforcement theory of criminal behavior. Social Problems 14:128 – 147.

Burrows, John, and Kevin Heal (1980), Police car security campaigns. In R. V. G. Clarke and P. Mayhew, eds. (1980), Designing Out Crime. London: Her Majesty's Stationary Office.

Burt, Cyril (1925), The Young Delinquent. London: University of London Press.

Calhoun, George (1927), The Growth of Criminal Law in Ancient Greece. Berkeley and Los Angeles: University of California Press.

Calvert, E. Roy (1971), Capital Punishment in the Twentieth Century. New York: Kennikat Press.

Calvin, Allen D. (1981), Unemployment among black youths, demographics and crime. Crime and Delinquency 27:234 – 244.

Cameron, Mary Owen (1964), The Booster and the Snitch. New York: Free Press.

Cannavale, Frank J. (1976), Witness Cooperation. Lexington, Mass.: Heath.

Carey, James T. (1968), The College Drug Scene. Englewood Cliffs, N.J.: Prentice-Hall.

Carlin, Jerome E. (1968), Lawyer's Ethics. New York: Russell Sage.

Carroll, Leo (1974), Hacks, Blacks, and Cons: Race Relations in a Maximum Security Prison. Lexington, Mass.: Heath.

Carter, Robert M. (1965), The Johnny Cain story: A composite of men executed in California. Issues in Criminology 1:66 – 76.

Carter, Robert M., and Leslie T. Wilkins (1967), Some factors in sentencing policy. Journal of Criminal Law, Criminology, and Police Science 58:503 – 514.

Carter, Robert M., and Leslie T. Wilkins, eds. (1976), Probation, Parole, and Community Corrections, 2nd ed. New York: Wiley.

Carter, Ronald L., and Kim Q. Hill (1979), The Criminal's Image of the City. New York: Pergamon.

Casper, Jonathan D. (1971), Did you have a lawyer when you went to court? No I had a public defender. Yale Review of Law and Social Action 1:4 – 9.

Casper, Jonathan D. (1972), American Criminal Justice: The Defendant's Perspective. Englewood Cliffs, N.J.: Prentice-Hall.

Cavan, Sherri (1966), Liquor License: An Ethnography of Bar Behavior. Chicago: Aldine.

Center for Research on Criminal Justice (1975), The Iron Fist and the Velvet Glove. Berkeley, Calif.: Center for Research on Criminal Justice.

Centers for Disease Control (1985), Morbidity and Mortality. Weekly Report October 11, pp. 613 – 618.

Chambers, Carl D. (1971), An Assessment of Drug Use in the General Population. New York: Narcotics Addiction Control Commission.

Chambliss, William J. (1967), Types of deviance and the effectiveness of legal sanctions. Wisconsin Law Review (Summer):703 – 719.

Chambliss, William J. (1969), Crime and the Legal Process. New York: McGraw-Hill.

Chambliss, William J. (1971), Vice, corruption, bureaucracy, and power. Wisconsin Law Review (Fall):1150 – 1173.

Chambliss, William J. (1973), The saints and the roughnecks. Society 11:24 – 31.

Chambliss, William J. (1975a), Criminal Law in Action. Santa Barbara, Calif.: Hamilton.

Chambliss, William J. (1975b), The political economy of crime: A comparative study of Nigeria and the U.S.A. In Ian Taylor, Paul Walton, and Jock Young (1975), Critical Criminology. London: Routledge and Kegan Paul.

Chambliss, William J. (1978), On the Take: From Petty Crooks to Presidents. Bloomington: Indiana University Press.

Chambliss, William J., and John T. Liell (1966), The legal process in the community setting. Crime and Delinquency 12:310 – 317.

Chambliss, William J., and Robert B. Siedman (1971), Law and Order. Reading, Mass.: Addison-Wesley.

Chapman, Dennis (1968), Sociology and the Stereotype of the Criminal. London: Tavistock.

Chappell, Duncan, Robley Geis, and Gilbert Geis (1977), Forcible Rape: The Crime, the Victim, and the Offender. New York: Columbia University Press.

Chappell, Duncan, and Marilyn Walsh (1974), Receiving stolen property—The need for systematic inquiry into the fencing process. Criminology 11:484 – 497.

Chodorkoff, Bernard, and Seymour Baxter (1969), Psychiatric and psychoanalytic theories of violence and its origins. In Donald J. Mulvihill, Melvin Tumin, and Lynn Curtis (1969), Crimes of Violence. Washington, D.C.: U.S. Government Printing Office.

Christensen, Harold T., and Christina Gregg (1970), Changing sex norms in America and Scandinavia. Journal of Marriage and the Family 32:625 – 626.

Christiansen, K. O. (1977a), A preliminary study of criminality among twins. In Sarnoff A. Mednick and K. O. Christiansen (1977), Biosocial Basis of Criminal Behavior. New York: Wiley.

Christiansen, K. O. (1977b), A review of studies of criminality among twins. In Sarnoff A. Mednick and K. O. Christiansen (1977), Biosocial Basis of Criminal Behavior. New York: Wiley.

Cicourel, Aaron V. (1968), The Social Organization of Juvenile Justice. New York: Wiley.

Clark, Alexander L., and Jack P. Gibbs (1965), Social control: A reformulation. Social Problems 12:398 – 415.

Clarke, R. V. G., and P. Mayhew, eds. (1980), Designing Out Crime. London: Her Majesty's Stationary Office.

Clear, Todd R., John D. Hewitt, and Robert M. Regoli (1978), Discretion and the determinate sentence: Its distribution, control, and effect on time served. Crime and Delinquency 24:428 – 445.

Clemmer, Donald (1940), The Prison Community. New York: Holt, Rinehart and Winston.

Clinard, Marshall B., and Daniel J. Abbott (1973), Crime in Developing Countries. New York: Wiley.

Clinard, Marshall B., and Richard Quinney, eds. (1967), Criminal Behavior Systems: A Typology. New York: Holt, Rinehart and Winston.

Clinard, Marshall B., Peter C. Yeager, Jeanne Brissette, David Petrashek, and Elizabeth Hames (1979), Illegal Corporate Behavior. Washington, D.C.: Law Enforcement Assistance Administration.

Cloward, Richard A., and Lloyd E. Ohlin (1960), Delinquency and Opportunity: A Theory of Delinquent Gangs. New York: Free Press.

Coburn, Morris (1973), Some manpower aspects of the criminal justice system. Crime and Delinquency 19:198–199.

Cohen, Albert K. (1951), Juvenile Delinquency and the Social Structure. Cambridge, Mass.: Harvard University Press.

Cohen, Albert K. (1955), Delinquent Boys: The Culture of the Gang. New York: Free Press.

Cohen, Jacqueline (1983), Incapacitating criminals: Recent research findings, NIJ Reports. Washington, D.C.: National Institute of Justice.

Cohen, Jacqueline (1984), Incapacitating Criminals: Recent Research Findings. Washington, D.C.: National Institute of Justice.

Cohen, Lawrence E., David Cantor, and James R. Klugel (1981), Robbery victimization in the U.S.: Analysis of a nonrandom event. Social Science Quarterly 62:644 – 657.

Cohen, Lawrence E., and Marcus Felson (1979), Social change and crime rate trends: A routine activity approach. American Sociological Review 44:588 – 608.

Cohen, Lawrence E., Marcus Felson, and Kenneth C. Land (1980), Property crime rates in the United States: A macrodynamic analysis, 1947 – 1977, with ex-ante forecasts for the mid-1980's. American Journal of Sociology 86:90 – 118.

Cohen, Stanley, ed. (1971), Images of Deviance. Hammondsworth, England: Penguin.

Cole, George F. (1970), The decision to prosecute. Law and Society Review 4:331 – 343.

Cole, George F. (1975), The American System of Criminal Justice. North Scituate, Mass.: Duxbury Press.

Colquhoun, Patrick (1806), A Treatise on the Police of the Metropolis, 6th ed. London: Joseph Mawman.

Conklin, John E. (1972), Robbery and the Criminal Justice System. Philadelphia: Lippincott.

Conklin, John E., ed. (1973), The Crime Establishment: Organized Crime and American Society. Englewood Cliffs, N.J.: Prentice-Hall.

Conklin, John E. (1977), Illegal but Not Criminal: Business Crime in America. Englewood Cliffs, N.J.: Prentice-Hall.

Conklin, John E., and Egon Bittner (1973), Burglary in a suburb. Criminology 11:206 – 232.

Conrad, John P. (1975), We should never have promised a hospital. Federal Probation 39.

Cramer, James A., ed. (1978), Preventing Crime. Beverly Hills, Calif.: Sage.

Cressey, Donald R. (1953), Other People's Money: A Study in the Social Psychology of Embezzlement. New York: Free Press.

Cressey, Donald R. (1965), The respectable criminal. Transaction 3:12 – 15.

Cressey, Donald R. (1969), Theft of the Nation: The Structure and Operations of Organized Crime in America. New York: Harper & Row.

Critchley, T. A. (1972), A History of Police in England and Wales, 2nd ed. Montclair, N.J.: Patterson Smith.

Cullen, Francis T., and Karen E. Gilbert (1982), Reaffirming Rehabilitation. Cincinnati: Anderson Publishing Co.

Cullen, Francis T., Bruce G. Link, III, Lawrence F. Travis, and John F. Wozniack (1985), Consensus of crime seriousness: Empirical reality or methodological artifact? Criminology 23:99 – 118.

Cumming, Elaine, Ian Cumming, and Laura Edell (1965), Policeman as philosopher, guide and friend. Social Problems 12:276 – 286.

Currie, Elliot P. (1968), Crimes without criminals: Witchcraft and its control in Renaissance Europe. Law and Society Review 3:20 – 22.


Dale, Robert (1974), Memoirs of a Contemporary Cutpurse. Cambridge, Mass.: Schenkman.

Damaska, Mirjam R. (1968), Adverse legal consequences of conviction and their removal: A comparative study. Journal of Criminal Law, Criminology, and Police Science 59:347 – 360, 542 – 568.

Darrow, W., H. Jaffee, and J. Curran (1983), Passive anal intercourse as a risk factor for AIDS in homosexual men. Lancet 2:309 – 313.

Davidson, Ralph (1965), The promiscuous fine. Criminal Law Quarterly 8:74 – 76.

Davis, Alan J. (1968), Sexual assaults in the Philadelphia prison system and sheriffs' vans. Transactions 6:9 – 16.

Davis, F. James (1962), Law As a Type of Social Control. New York: Free Press.

DeFrancis, Vincent (1969), Protecting the Child Victims of Sex Crimes Committed by Adults. Denver: American Humane Society.

Dershowitz, Allen M. (1961), Increasing control over corporate crime: A problem in the law of sanctions. Yale Law Journal 71:291.

Dirks, Raymond L., and Leonard Gross (1974), The Great Wall Street Scandal. New York: McGraw-Hill.

Doerner, William G. (1983), Why does Johnny Reb die when shot? The impact of medical resources upon lethality. Social Inquiry 53:1 – 12.

Doleisch, Wolfgang (1960), Theft in department stores. Proceedings of Fourth International Criminological Congress, The Hague, vol. 2, sec. 2:4 – 7.

Dollard, John, N. Miller, L. Doob, O. H. Mowrer, and R. R. Sears (1939), Frustration and Aggression. New Haven, Conn.: Yale University Press.

Dorman, Michael (1972), Payoff: The Role of Organized Crime. New York: McKay.

Douglas, Jack D., ed. (1970), Observations of Deviance. New York: Random House.

Downie, Leonard, Jr. (1972), Justice Denied. Baltimore: Penguin.

Doyle, James C. (1953), Unnecessary hysterectomies. American Medical Association Journal 151:360 – 365.

Durkheim, Emile (1900), Deux lois de l'évolution pénale. l'Anne Sociologique 4:65 – 93.

Durkheim, Emile (1952), Suicide. London: Routledge and Kegan Paul.

Durkheim, Emile (1964a), The Division of Labor in Society. New York: Free Press.

Durkheim, Emile (1964b), The Rules of the Sociological Method. New York: Free Press.

Dworkin, Andrea (1981), Pornography: Men Possessing Women. New York: Putnam.

Earle, Alice M. (1969), Curious Punishments of By-gone Days. Montclair, N.J.: Patterson Smith.

Edelhertz, Herbert (1970), The Nature, Impact, and Prosecution of White-Collar Crime. Washington, D.C.: U.S. Government Printing Office.

Edelhertz, Herbert, and Marilyn Walsh (1978), The White-Collar Challenge to Nuclear Safeguards. Lexington, Mass.: Lexington Books.

Eder, George Jackson (1965), Urban concentration, agriculture, and agrarian reform. The Annals 360:28.

Edwards, John N. (1972), Sex and Society. Chicago: Markham.

Edwards, Loren E. (1958), Shoplifting and Shrinkage Protection for Stores. Springfield, Ill.: Thomas.

Einstadter, Werner J. (1969), The social organization of armed robbery. Social Problems 17:64 – 83.

Ellis, Albert, and Ralph Brancale (1965), The Psychology of Sex Offenders. Springfield, Ill.: Thomas.

Ellis, Lee (1982), Genetics and criminal behavior. Criminology 20:43 – 66.

Enker, Arnold (1967), Perspectives on plea bargaining. In President's Commission on Law Enforcement on the Administration of Justice (1967a), Task Force Report: The Courts. Washington, D.C.: U.S. Government Printing Office.

Erez, Edna (1980), Planning of crime and the criminal career: Official and hidden offenses. Journal of Criminal Law and Criminology 71:73 – 76.

Erickson, Kai T. (1962), Notes on the sociology of deviance. Social Problems 9:307 – 314.

Erickson, Kai T. (1966), Wayward Puritans: A Study in the Sociology of Deviance. New York: Wiley.

Erickson, Maynard L., Jack P. Gibbs, and Gary L. Jensen (1977), The deterrence doctrine and perceived certainty of legal punishments. American Sociological Review 42:305 – 317.

Erickson, Rosemary J., Waymon J. Crow, Louis A. Zurcher, and Archie V. Connett (1973), Paroled but Not Free. New York: Behavioral Publications.

Esselzstyn, C. (1968), Prostitution in the United States. The Annals 376:126 – 143.

Evans-Pritchard, E. E. (1940), The Nuer. Oxford, England: Clarendon Press.

Farley, John E. (1982), Majority – Minority Relations. Englewood Cliffs, N.J.: Prentice-Hall.

Farley, Reynolds (1980), Homicide trends in the United States. Demography 17:177 – 188.

Federal Bureau of Investigation (1965), Profile of a robber. Law Enforcement Bulletin 34:21.

Federal Bureau of Investigation (1978), Crime in the United States, 1977. Washington, D.C.: U.S. Department of Justice.

Federal Bureau of Investigation (1980), Crime in the United States, 1979. Washington, D.C.: U.S. Department of Justice.

Federal Bureau of Investigation (1981), Crime in the United States, 1980. Washington, D.C.: U.S. Department of Justice.

Federal Bureau of Investigation (1982), Crime in the United States, 1981. Washington, D.C.: U.S. Department of Justice.

Federal Bureau of Investigation (1984), Crime in the United States, 1983. Washington, D.C.: U.S. Department of Justice.

Federal Bureau of Investigation (1985), Crime in the United States, 1984. Washington, D.C.: U.S. Department of Justice.

Federal Bureau of Prisons (1986), 1985 Annual Report. Washington, D.C.: U.S. Department of Justice.

Feinberg, Stephen F., and Albert J. Reiss, eds. (1980), Indicators of Crime and Criminal Justice: Quantitative Studies. Washington, D.C.: U.S. Government Printing Office.

Ferdinand, Theodore N. (1968), Sex behavior and the American class structure: A mosaic. The Annals 376:82 – 84.

Fields, Allen, and James M. Walters (1985), Hustling: Supporting a heroin habit. In Bill Hanson, George Beschner, James M. Walters, and Elliott Bovelle (1985), Life with Heroin. Lexington, Mass.: Lexington, Mass.

Fisher, Joseph C. (1976), Homicides in Detroit: The role of firearms. Criminology 14:387 – 400.

Fitch, J. H. (1962), Men convicted of sex offenses against children: A follow-up study. British Journal of Sociology 13:18 – 37.

Flanagan, Timothy T., David J. van Alstyne, and Michael R. Gottfredson, eds. (1982), Sourcebook of Criminal Justice Statistics, 1981. Washington, D.C.: U.S. Government Printing Office.

Flynn, Edith Elizabeth, and John P. Conrad, eds. (1981), The New and the Old Criminology. New York: Praeger.

Foldessy, Edward P. (1971), The Paper Hangers. Princeton, N.J.: Dow-Jones Books.

Fooner, Michael (1971), Money and economic factors in crime and delinquency. Criminology 8:311 – 332.

Foote, Caleb (1958), A study of the administration of bail in New York City. University of Pennsylvania Law Review 106:633 – 658.

Foote, Caleb (1978), Deceptive determinate sentencing. In Proceedings of the Special Conference on Determinate Sentencing, University of California, Berkeley, June 2 – 3.

Ford, Daniel, and Amesley K. Schmidt (1985), Electronically monitored home confinement, NIJ Reports, November. Washington, D.C.: U.S. Department of Justice.

Forst, Brian E., and Jolene C. Hernon (1985), The criminal justice response to victim harm, NIJ Research in Brief. Washington, D.C.: U.S. Department of Justice.

Fort, Joel (1973), Alcohol: Our Biggest Drug Problem. New York: McGraw-Hill.

Fox, Richard G. (1971), The XYY offender: A modern myth? Journal of Criminal Law, Criminology, and Police Science 62:59 – 73.

Frazier, Charles E., and E. Wilbur Bock (1982), Effects of court officials on sentence severity. Criminology 20:257 – 272.

Friday, Paul C. (1977), Changing theory and research in criminology. International Journal of Criminology and Penology 5:159 – 170.

Friedland, Martin (1965), Detention Before Trial. Toronto: University of Toronto Press.

Fyfe, James J. (1982), Blind justice: Police shootings in Memphis. Journal of Criminal Law and Criminology 73:707 – 722.

Gager, Nancy, and Cathleen Schurr (1976), Sexual Assault: Confronting Rape in America. New York: Grosset & Dunlap.

Gallo, Jon J. (1966), The consenting adult homosexual and the law: An empirical study of enforcement and administration in Los Angeles County. UCLA Law Review 13:647 – 832.

Gammage, Allan Z., and Charles F. Hemphill (1974), Basic Criminal Law. New York: McGraw-Hill.

Garabedian, Peter (1963), Social roles and processes of socialization in the prison community. Social Problems 11:139 – 152.

Garfinkel, Harold (1949), Research note on inter- and intra-racial homicides. Social Forces 27:369 – 381.

Gartner, Michael, ed. (1971), Crime As Business. Princeton, N.J.: Dow-Jones Books.

Gasser, Robert Louis (1963), The confidence game. Federal Probation 27:47 – 54.

Gastil, Raymond (1971), Homicide and a regional culture of violence. American Sociological Review 36:412 – 427.

Gebhard, Paul, John H. Gagnon, Wardell B. Pomeroy, and Cornelia V. Christiansen (1965), Sex Offenders: An Analysis of Types. New York: Harper & Row.

Geis, Gilbert (1978a), Lord Hale, witches, and rape. British Journal of Law and Society 5:26 – 44.

Geis, Gilbert (1978b), Rape-in-marriage: Law and law reform in England, the United States, and Sweden. Adelaide Law Review 6:284 – 303.

Geis, Gilbert, and Robley Geis (1979), Rape in Stockholm. Criminology 17:311 – 322.

Geller, William A., and Kevin J. Karales (1981), Shooting of and by Chicago police: Uncommon crises, Part 1: Shootings by Chicago police. Journal of Criminal Law and Criminology 72:1813 – 1866.

Geller, William A., and Kevin J. Karales (1982), Shootings of and by Chicago police: Uncommon crises Part II: Shootings of police, shooting correlates, and control strategies. Journal of Criminal Law and Criminology 73:331 – 378.

Gelles, Richard J. (1978), Violence toward children in the U.S. American Journal of Orthopsychiatry 48:580 – 592.

Gelles, Richard J., and Murray A. Straus (1979), Violence in the American family. Journal of Social Issues 35:15 – 39.

Giallombardo, Rose (1966), Society of Women: A Study of a Women's Prison. New York: Wiley.

Gibbons, Don C. (1973), Society, Crime, and Criminal Careers, 2nd ed. Englewood Cliffs, N.J.: Prentice-Hall.

Gibbons, Don C., and Peter Garabedian (1974), Conservative, liberal and radical criminology: Some trends and observations. In Charles E. Reasons (1974), The Criminologist: Crime and the Criminal. Pacific Palisades, Calif.: Goodyear.

Gibbs, Jack P. (1966), Crime and the sociology of law. Sociology and Social Research 51:23 – 38.

Gibbs, Jack P. (1968), Definitions of law and empirical questions. Law and Society Review 2:431 – 432.

Gibbs, Jack P. (1975), Crime, Punishment and Deterrence. New York: Elsevier.

Gibbs, Jack P. (1985), Review essay. Criminology 23:381 – 388.

Gibbs, Jack P., and James F. Short (1974), Criminal differentiation and occupational differentiation. Journal of Research in Crime and Delinquency 11:89 – 100.

Gibson, Evelyn, and S. Klein (1969), Murder, 1957 – 1968. London: Her Majesty's Stationary Office.

Gigeroff, Alex K. (1968), Sexual Deviation and the Criminal Law. Toronto: University of Toronto Press.

Gil, D. G. (1970), Violence Against Children: Physical Abuse in the U.S. Cambridge, Mass.: Harvard University Press.

Glaser, Daniel (1956), Criminality theories and behavioral images. American Journal of Sociology 61:433 – 444.

Glaser, Daniel (1971), Social Deviance. Chicago: Markham.

Glaser, Daniel (1977), The federal government and criminal justice research. Federal Probation 41:9 – 14.

Glueck, Sheldon, and Eleanor Glueck (1950), Unraveling Juvenile Delinquency. New York: Commonwealth Fund.

Goffman, Erving (1963), Stigma: Notes on the Management of Spoiled Identity. Englewood Cliffs, N.J.: Prentice-Hall.

Gold, Martin (1970), Delinquent Behavior in an American City. Monterey, Calif.: Brooks/Cole.

Goldfarb, L., and Linda R. Singer (1973), After Conviction. New York: Simon & Schuster.

Goldstein, Joseph (1960), Police discretion not to invoke the criminal process: Low visibility decisions in the administration of justice. Yale Law Journal 69:543 – 570.

Goode, Erich (1972), Drugs in American Society. New York: Knopf.

Goode, William (1973), Explorations in Social Theory. New York: Oxford University Press.

Gordon, Cyrus H. (1957), The Code of Hammurapi: Quaint or Forward Looking? New York: Holt, Rinehart and Winston.

Gordon, David M. (1971), Class and the economics of crime. Review of Radical Economics 3:51 – 75.

Gordon, David M. (1973), Capitalism, class and crime in America. Crime and Delinquency 19:163 – 186.

Gould, Leroy C. (1969), The changing structure of property crime in an affluent society. Social Forces 48:50 – 59.

Grabowski, John (1984), Cocaine: Pharmacology, Effects and Treatment of Abuse. Washington, D.C.: National Institute of Drug Abuse.

Green, Mark J., with Beverly C. Moore and Bruce Wasserstein (1976), Criminal law and corporate disorder. In Jerome H. Skolnick and Elliott P. Currie (1976), Crisis in American Institutions, 3rd ed. Boston: Little, Brown.

Greenberg, David F. (1975), The incapacitative effect of imprisonment: Some estimates. Law and Society Review 9:541 – 580.

Greenberg, David F. (1977), Crime and deterrence research and social policy. In Stuart S. Nagel (1977), Modelling the Criminal Justice System. Beverly Hills, Calif.: Sage.

Greenberg, David F., ed. (1981), Crime and Capitalism. Palo Alto, Calif.: Mayfield.

Greenwood, Peter W. (1984), Selective incapacitation: A method of using our prisons more effectively, NIJ Reports. Washington, D.C.: National Institute of Justice.

Greenwood, Peter W., and Allan Abrahamse (1982), Selective Incapacitation. Santa Monica, Calif.: Rand Corporation.

Griffin, Susan (1971), Rape: The all-American crime. Ramparts 10:34 – 45.

Griffiths, John (1970), Ideology in criminal procedure, or a third "model" of the criminal process. Yale Law Journal 79:359 – 417.

Grossman, Brian (1974), The discretionary enforcement of law. In Sawyer F. Sylvester and Edward Sagarin, eds. (1974), Politics and Crime. New York: Praeger.

Groth, Nicholas (1979), Men Who Rape: The Psychology of the Offender. New York: Plenum.

Grutzner, Charles (1970), How to lock out the Mafia. Harvard Business Review 48:50 – 55.

Guenther, Anthony L. (1975), Compensations in a total institution: The forms and functions of contraband. Crime and Delinquency 21:243 – 54.

Guerry, André Michel (1833), Essai sur la Statistique Morale. Paris.

Hackney, Sheldon (1969), Southern violence. In Hugh D. Graham and Robert T. Gurr (1969), Violence in America. Washington, D.C.: U.S. Government Printing Office.

Hagan, John (1974), Extra-legal attributes and criminal sentencing: An assessment of a sociological viewpoint. Law and Society Review 8:357 – 383.

Hagan, John (1982a), The corporate advantage: The involvement of individual and organizational victims in the criminal justice process. Social Forces 60:993 – 1022.

Hagan, John, ed. (1982b), Deterrence Reconsidered: Methodological Innovations. Beverly Hills, Calif.: Sage.

Hagan, John (1982c), Victims before the law: A study of victim involvement in the criminal process. Journal of Criminal Law and Criminology 73:317 – 330.

Hagan, John (1985), Modern Criminology: Crime, Criminal Behavior and Its Control. New York: McGraw-Hill.

Hakim, Simon, and George F. Rengert, eds. (1981), Crime Spillover. Beverly Hills, Calif.: Sage.

Hall, Jerome (1952), Theft, Law, and Society, rev. ed. Indianapolis: Bobbs-Merrill.

Hall, Jerome (1960), General Principles of Criminal Law. Indianapolis: Bobbs-Merrill.

Hanson, Bill, George Beschner, James M. Walters, and Elliott Bovelle (1985), Life with Heroin. Lexington, Mass.: Lexington Books.

Harland, Alan T. (1981), Restitution to Victims of Personal and Household Crimes, Analytic Report VAD-9. Washington, D.C.: U.S. Department of Justice.

Harris, Richard N. (1973), The Police Academy: An Inside View. New York: Wiley.

Hartjen, Clayton (1974), Crime and Criminalization. New York: Praeger.

Hartogs, Renatus, and Eric Artzt (1970), Violence: Causes and Solutions. New York: Dell.

Haskell, Martin R., and Lewis Yablonsky (1974), Crime and Delinquency, 2nd ed. Chicago: Rand McNally.

Hawkins, Gordon (1976), The Prison: Policy and Practice. Chicago: University of Chicago Press.

Hay, Douglas (1975), Albion's Fatal Tree: Crime and Society in Eighteenth Century England. London: Allen Lowe.

Healy, William (1915), The Individual Delinquent: A Textbook and Prognosis for All Concerned in Understanding Offenders. Boston: Little, Brown.

Henry, Stuart (1978), The Hidden Economy. Oxford, England: Martin Robinson.

Hepburn, John R. (1985), The exercise of power in coercive organizations: A study of prison guards. Criminology 23:145 – 164.

Hess, Albert G., and Fre le Poole (1967), Abuse of the record of arrest not leading to conviction. Crime and Delinquency 13:494 – 505.

Hill, Susan, and Bob Edelman (1972), Gentleman of Leisure. New York: NAL.

Hills, Stuart L. (1971), Crime, Power, and Morality. Scranton, Pa.: Chandler.

Hindelang, Michael J. (1974), Decisions of shoplifting victims to invoke the criminal justice process. Social Problems 21:580 – 593.

Hindelang, Michael J. (1978), Race and involvement in common law personal crimes. American Sociological Review 43:93 – 109.

Hindelang, Michael J., Christopher S. Dunn, L. Paul Sutton, and Alison L. Armick (1975), Sourcebook of Criminal Justice Statistics. Washington, D.C.: U.S. Department of Justice.

Hindelang, Michael J., Michael R. Gottfredson, Christopher S. Dunn, and Nicolette Parisi (1977), Sourcebook of Criminal Justice Statistics, 1976. Washington, D.C.: U.S. Government Printing Office.

Hindelang, Michael J., Travis Hirschi, and Joseph G. Weiss (1979), Correlates of delinquency: The illusion of discrepancy between self-report and official measures. American Sociological Review 44:995 – 1014.

Hirschi, Travis (1971), Causes of Delinquency. Berkeley and Los Angeles: University of California Press.

Hirschi, Travis (1985), On the compatibility of rational choice and social control theories of crime. Paper presented at the Home Office Conference on Criminal Decision Making, Cambridge, England.

Hirschi, Travis, and Michael J. Hindelang (1977), Intelligence and delinquency: A revisionist view. American Sociological Review 42:572 – 587.

Hochstedler, Ellen, ed. (1984), Corporations As Criminals. Beverly Hills, Calif.: Sage.

Hoebel, E. Adamson (1941), The Cheyenne Way. Norman: University of Oklahoma Press.

Hoebel, E. Adamson (1954), The Law of Primitive Man. Cambridge, Mass.: Harvard University Press.

Hogarth, John (1971), Sentencing As a Human Process. Toronto: University of Toronto Press.

Holzman, Harold R. (1982), The rationalistic opportunity perspective on criminal behavior. Crime and Delinquency 28:233 – 246.

Hood, Ernest B. (1973), Behavioral implications for the xyy genotype. Science 179:130 – 150.

Hood, Roger (1962), Sentencing in Magistrates' Courts. London: Stevens.

Hood, Roger (1972), Sentencing the Motoring Offender. London: Heinemann.

Hooton, Earnest A. (1939), Crime and the Man. Cambridge, Mass.: Harvard University Press.

Horning, Donald N. M. (1970), Blue-collar theft: Conceptions of property, attitudes toward pilfering, and work group norms in a modern industrial plant. In Erwin O. Smigel and H. Laurence Ross, eds. (1970), Crimes Against Bureaucracy. New York: Van Nostrand.

Hotchkiss, Susan (1978), Realities of rape. Human Behavior, December, pp. 18 – 23.

Hough, J. M., R. V. G. Clarke, and P. Mayhew (1980), Introduction. In R. V. G. Clarke and P. Mayhew, eds. (1980), Designing Out Crime. London: Her Majesty's Stationary Office.

Hudson, Joe, and Burt Galoway (1975), Restitution in Criminal Justice. Lexington, Mass.: Lexington Press.

Huff-Corzine, Lin, Jay Corzine, and David C. Moore (1986), Southern exposure: Deciphering the South's influence on homicide rates. Social Forces 64:906–924.

Hughes, Everett C. (1964), Good people and dirty work. In Howard S. Becker, ed. (1964), The Other Side: Perspectives on Defiance. New York: Free Press.

Humphreys, Laud (1970), Tearoom Trade. Chicago: Aldine.

Hutchinson, John (1969), The anatomy of corruption in the trade unions. Industrial Relations 8:135 – 137.


Ianni, Francis A. J. (1974), New Mafia: Black, Hispanic and Italian styles. Society 11:30 – 36.

Ianni, Francis A. J. (1975), Black Mafia: Ethnic Succession in Organized Crime. New York: Pocket Books.

Ianni, Francis A. J., and Elizabeth Reuss-Ianni (1973), A Family Business: Kinship and Control in Organized Crime. New York: Russell Sage.

Illinois Criminal Justice Information Authority (1985), The Compiler, vol. 6. Chicago: ICJIA.

Imlay, Carl H., and Charles R. Glasheen (1971), See what conditions your conditions are in. Federal Probation 35:3 – 11.

Inbau, Fred (1962), Police interrogation—A practical necessity. In Claude R. Sowle, ed. (1962), Police Power and Individual Freedom. Chicago: Aldine.

Inciardi, James A. (1975), Careers in Crime. Chicago: Rand McNally.

Inciardi, James A. (1979), Heroin use and street crime. Crime and Delinquency 25:335 – 346.

Irwin, John (1970), The Felon. Englewood Cliffs, N.J.: Prentice-Hall.

Irwin, John (1980), Prisons in Turmoil. Boston: Little, Brown.

Irwin, John, and Donald R. Cressey (1962), Thieves, convicts and the inmate culture. Social Problems 10:142 – 155.


Jackman, Norman R., Richard O'Toole, and Gilbert Geis (1963), The self-image of the prostitute. Sociological Quarterly 4:150 – 161.

Jackson, Bruce (1969a), Exile from the American dream: The junkie and the cop. Atlantic Monthly 219:44 – 51.

Jackson, Bruce (1969b), A Thief's Primer. New York: Macmillan.

Jacobs, James B. (1974), Street gangs behind bars. Social Problems 21:395 – 409.

Jacobs, James B. (1976), Stratification and conflict among prison inmates. Journal of Criminal Law and Criminology 66:476 – 482.

Jacobs, James B. (1977), Stateville: The Penitentiary in Mass Society. Chicago: University of Chicago Press.

Jacobs, James B., and Harold G. Retsky (1975), Prison guard. Urban Life and Culture 4:5 – 29.

Jaffee, Harold W., William W. Darrow, and Dean F. Echenberg (1985), The acquired immunodeficiency syndrome in a cohort of homosexual men: A six-year follow-up study. Annals of Internal Medicine 103:210 – 214.

James, J. T. (1817), Journal of a Tour. London: John Murray.

Jaspan, Norman, and Hillel Black (1960), The Thief in the White Collar. New York: Lippincott.

Jefferson, T., and J. Clarke (1973), Down these mean streets: The meaning of mugging. Stencilled Occasional Paper, Centre for Contemporary Cultural Studies, University of Birmingham, England.

Jeffery, C. Ray (1957), The development of crime in early English society. Journal of Criminal Law, Criminology, and Police Science 47:533 – 552.

Jeffery, C. Ray (1959), An integrated theory of crime and criminal behavior. Journal of Criminal Law, Criminology, and Police Science 49:533 – 552.

Jeffery, C. Ray (1977), Crime Prevention Through Environmental Design. Beverly Hills, Calif.: Sage.

Jensen, A. R. (1969), How much can we boost IQ and scholastic achievement? Harvard Educational Review 39:1 – 123.

Johnson, B., P. Goldstein, E. Preble, J. Schmeidler, D. Lipton, B. Spunt, and T. Miller (1985), Taking Care of Business. Lexington, Mass.: Lexington Books.

Johnson, Elmer H. (1974), Crime, Correction, and Society. Homewood, Ill.: Dorsey Press.

Johnson, Guy B. (1941), The negro and crime. The Annals 277:93 – 104.

Johnston, Lloyd D., Patrick D. O'Malley, and Jerald G. Bachman (1981), Student Drug Use in America, 1975 – 1980. Washington, D.C.: U.S. Government Printing Office.

Jordon, Philip D. (1970), Frontier Law and Order. Lincoln: University of Nebraska Press.


Kadish, Mortimer R., and Sanford H. Kadish (1973), Discretion to Disobey. Palo Alto, Calif.: Stanford University Press.

Kanin, Eugene J. (1967), Reference groups and sex conduct norms' violation. Sociological Quarterly 8:495–504.

Kelling, George L. (1978), Police field services and crime: The presumed effects of a capacity. Crime and Delinquency 24:182–183.

King, Harry (1972), Boxman: A Professional Thief's Journey, ed. William Chambliss. New York: Harper & Row.

Kirkpatrick, Clifford, and Eugene J. Kanin (1957), Male sex aggression on a university campus. American Sociological Review 22:53–62.

Kitsuse, John I. (1962), Societal reactions to deviant behavior: Problems of theory and method. Social Problems 9:247–256.

Kittrie, Nicholas N. (1973), The Right to Be Different: Deviance and Enforced Therapy. Baltimore: Penguin.

Klapmuts, Nora (1977), Community alternatives to prison. In Robert G. Leger and John R. Stratton, eds. (1977), The Sociology of Corrections: A Book of Readings. New York: Wiley.

Klebba, Joan A. (1975), Homicide trends in the United States, 1900–1974. Public Health Reports 90:195–204.

Kleck, Gary (1981), Racial discrimination in criminal sentencing: A critical evaluation of the evidence with additional evidence on the death penalty. American Sociological Review 46:783–805.

Klockars, Carl B. (1974), The Professional Fence. New York: Free Press.

Knapp Commission Report on Police Corruption (1972), New York: Braziller.

Knoohuizen, Ralph, Richard P. Fahey, and Deborah J. Palmer (1972), The Police and Their Use of Fatal Force in Chicago. Evanston, Ill.: Chicago Law Enforcement Study Group.

Kobetz, Richard W. (1978), Criminal Justice Education Directory, 1978–1980. Gaithersburg, Md.: International Association of Chiefs of Police.

Kolata, Gina (1982), When criminals turn to computers, is anything safe? Smithsonian 13:117–126.

Korn, Richard, and Lloyd McCorkle (1957), Criminology and Penology. New York: Holt.

Kramer, Ronald C. (1984), Corporate criminality: The development of an idea. In Ellen Hochstedler, ed. (1984), Corporations As Criminals. Beverly Hills, Calif.: Sage.

LaFave, Wayne R. (1965), Arrest: The Decision to Take a Suspect into Custody. Boston: Little, Brown.

Lane, Roger (1967), Policing the City: Boston, 1821–1885. Cambridge, Mass.: Harvard University Press.

Law Enforcement Assistance Administration (1970), National Jail Census, 1970: A Report on the Nation's Local Jails and Types of Inmates. Washington, D.C.: U.S. Government Printing Office.

Law Enforcement Assistance Administration (1975a), Census of State Correctional Facilities, 1974, Advance Report. Washington, D.C.: U.S. Government Printing Office.

Law Enforcement Assistance Administration (1975b), The Nation's Jails. Washington, D.C.: U.S. Government Printing Office.

Law Enforcement Assistance Administration (1977), Forcible Rape: A National Survey of Response by Prosecutors. Washington, D.C.: U.S. Department of Justice.

Lederer, Laura, ed. (1980), Take Back the Night. New York: Bantam Books.

Leger, Robert G., and John R. Stratton, eds, (1977), The Sociology of Corrections: A Book of Readings. New York: Wiley.

Leiser, Burton M. (1973), Liberty, Justice, and Morals. New York: Macmillan.

Lejeune, Robert (1977), The management of a mugging. Urban Life 6:123–148.

Lemert, Edwin M. (1951), Social Pathology. New York: McGraw-Hill.

Lemert, Edwin M. (1953), An isolation and closure theory of naive check forgery. Journal of Criminal Law, Criminology, and Police Science 44:297–298.

Lemert, Edwin M. (1958), The behavior of the systematic check forger. Social Problems 6:141–148.

Lemert, Edwin M. (1972), Human Deviance, Social Problems and Social Control, 2nd ed. Englewood Cliffs, N.J.: Prentice-Hall.

Lemert, Edwin M. (1974), Beyond Mead: The societal reaction to deviance. Social Problems 21:457–468.

Leonard, Eileen B. (1982), Women, Crime and Society. New York: Longman.

Leonard, William N., and Marvin Glenn Weber (1970), Automakers and dealers: A study of crimogenic market forces. Law and Society Review 4:408–422.

Letkemann, Peter (1973), Crime As Work. Englewood Cliffs, N.J.: Prentice-Hall.

Lindesmith, Alfred R. (1967), The Addict and the Law. New York: Random House.

Lintott, A. W. (1968), Violence in Republican Rome. Oxford, England: Clarendon Press.

Lippmann, Walter (1931), The underworld as servant. In Gus Tyler, ed. (1962), Organized Crime in America. Ann Arbor: University of Michigan Press.

Lipsky, Michael, ed. (1970), Law and Order: Police Encounters. Chicago: Aldine.

Lizotte, Alan J., and David J. Bordua (1980), Firearms ownership for sport and protection: Two divergent models. American Sociological Review 45:229–244.

Lofland, John (1977), The Dramaturgy of State Executions. Montclair, N.J.: Patterson Smith.

Loftin, Colin, and Robert H. Hill (1974), Regional subculture and homicide: An examination of the Gastil–Hackney thesis. American Sociological Review 39:714–724.

Lombroso, Cesare (1911), Crime, Its Causes and Remedies. Boston: Little, Brown.

Lorenz, Konrad (1971), On Aggression. New York: Bantam Books.

Lovald, Keith, and Helger R. Stub (1968), The revolving door: Reactions of chronic drunkenness to court sanctions. Journal of Criminal Law, Criminology, and Police Science 59:525–530.

Luckenbill, David F. (1977), Criminal homicide as a situated transaction. Social Problems 25:176–186.

Lunde, Donald T. (1970), Murder and Madness. San Francisco: San Francisco Book Co.

Lundesgaarde, Henry P. (1977), Murder in Space City. New York: Oxford University Press.

Lupsha, Peter A. (1981), Individual choice, material culture, and organized crime. Criminology 19:3–24.

Lyman, Stanford M., and Marvin B. Scott (1975), The Drama of Social Reality. New York: Oxford University Press.


Maas, Peter (1968), The Valachi Papers. New York: Putnam.

MacDonald, John M. (1971), Rape: Offenders and Their Victims. Springfield, Ill.: Thomas.

Mack, J. A. (1964), The able criminal. British Journal of Criminology 12:45–55.

Mack, J. A. (1975), The Crime Industry. London: Saxon House.

MacNamara, Donal E. J. (1968), Sex offenses and sex offenders. The Annals 376:153–162.

Maine, Sir Henry Sumner (1905), Ancient Law, 10th ed. London: John Murray.

Malinowski, Bronislaw (1926), Crime and Custom in Savage Society. New York: Harcourt, Brace.

Mannheim, Hermann (1946), Criminal Justice and Social Reconstruction. London: Routledge and Kegan Paul.

Manning, Peter K. (1977), Police Work: The Social Organization of Policing. Cambridge, Mass.: MIT Press.

Mars, Gerald (1983), Cheats at Work: An Anthropology of Workplace Crime. London: Unwin Paperbacks.

Martin, J. B. (1952), My Life in Crime. New York: Harper & Row.

Martinson, Robert (1974), What works? Questions and answers about prison reform. The Public Interest 35:22–54.

Marx, Karl (1969), Theories of Surplus Value, vol 1. Moscow: Foreign Languages Publishing House.

Marx, Karl (1971), A Contribution to the Critique of Political Economy. London: Lawrence and Wishart.

Marx, Karl, and Frederick Engels (1947), The German Ideology. New York: International Publishers.

Mathieson, Thomas (1965), The Defenses of the Weak. London: Tavistock.

Matza, David (1964), Delinquency and Drift. New York: Wiley.

Maurer, D. W. (1940), The Big Con. Indianapolis: Bobbs-Merrill.

Maurer, D. W. (1964), Whiz Mob. New Haven, Conn.: College and University Press.

Maxfield, Michael A., Dan A. Lewis, and Ron Szoc (1980), Producing official crimes: Verified crime reports as measures of police output. Social Science Quarterly 61:221–236.

Mayhew, P., R. V. G. Clarke, J. N. Burrows, J. M. Hough, and S. W. Winchester (1979), Crime in Public Places. Home Office Research Study No. 49. London: Her Majesty's Stationary Office.

Mayor of New York's Committee on Marijuana (1944), The Marijuana Problem in the City of New York. New York: Cattell.

McCaghy, Charles H. (1967), Child molesters: A study of their careers as deviants. In Marshall B. Clinard and Richard Quinney, eds. (1967), Criminal Behavior Systems: A Typology. New York: Holt, Rinehart and Winston.

McCaghy, Charles H. (1976), Deviant Behavior: Crime, Conflict and Interest Groups. New York: Macmillan.

McCartt, John M., and Thomas J. Mangogna (1976a), The history of halfway houses in the U.S. In Robert M. Carter and Leslie T. Wilkins, eds. (1976), Probation, Parole, and Community Corrections, 2nd ed. New York: Wiley.

McCartt, John M., and Thomas J. Mangogna (1976b), Overview of issues relating to halfway houses and community treatment centers. In Robert M. Carter and Leslie T. Wilkins, eds., Probation, Parole, and Community Corrections, 2nd ed. New York: Wiley.

McClintock, F. H., and Evelyn Gibson (1961), Robbery in London. London: Macmillan.

McDermott, M. Joan (1979), Rape Victimization in 26 American Cities. Washington, D.C.: U.S. Department of Justice.

McDonald, William, ed. (1976), Criminal Justice and the Victim. Beverly Hills, Calif.: Sage.

McGarrell, Edmund F., and Timothy J. Flanagan, eds. (1985), Sourcebook of Criminal Justice Statistics. Washington, D.C.: U.S. Government Printing Office.

McIntosh, Mary (1971), Changes in the organization of thievery. In Stanley Cohen, ed. (1971), Images of Deviance. Hammondsworth, England: Penguin.

McIntyre, Donald M., and David Lippman (1970), Prosecutors and early disposition of felony cases. American Bar Association Law Journal 56:1154–1159.

McIntyre, Jennie J., and Thelma Myint (1979), Sexual assault outcomes: Completed and attempted rapes. Paper presented at the annual meeting of the American Sociological Association, Boston, August 27–31.

McIver, John P. (1981), Criminal mobility: A review of empirical studies. In Simon Hakim and George F. Rengert, eds. (1981), Crime Spillover. Beverly Hills, Calif.: Sage.

McKusick, Leon, William Horstman, and Thomas J. Coates (1985), AIDS and sexual behavior reported by gay men in San Francisco. American Journal of Public Health 75:493–496.

McNamara, John H. (1967), Uncertainties of police work: Recruits' background and training. In David Bordua, ed. (1967), The Police: Six Sociological Essays. New York: Wiley.

Medical Economics Company (n.d.), Drug Topics. Oradell, N.J.: Medical Economics Company.

Mednick, Sarnoff A., and K. O. Christiansen (1977), Biosocial Basis of Criminal Behavior. New York: Wiley.

Mednick, Sarnoff A., Jr., W. F. Garbrielli, and B. Huthings (1984), Genetic influences in criminal convictions: Evidence from an adoption cohort. Science 224:891–894.

Mendelsohn, Alan J. (1956), The influence of defendants' plea on judicial determination of sentence. Yale Law Journal 66:204–222.

Merton, Robert K. (1938), Social structure and anomie. American Sociological Review 3:672–682.

Merton, Robert K. (1957), Social Theory and Social Structure. New York: Free Press.

Messner, Steven F. (1983), Regional and racial effects on the urban homicide rate: The subculture of violence revisited. American Journal of Sociology 88:997–1007.

Metz, Tim (1971), Hot stocks. In Michael Gartner, ed. (1971), Crime As Business. Princeton, N.J.: Dow-Jones Books.

Michael, Jerome, and Mortimer Adler (1933), Crime, Law, and Social Science. New York: Harcourt, Brace.

Michalowski, Raymond J. (1985), Order, Law, and Crime. New York: Random House.

Miethe, Terance D. (1982), Public consensus on crime seriousness: Normative structure or methodological artifact? Criminology 20:513–526.

Miller, Walter B. (1958), Lower class culture as a generating milieu of gang delinquency. Journal of Social Issues 14:5–19.

Miller, Walter B. (1966), Violent crimes in city gangs. The Annals 364:109–112.

Miller, Walter B. (1973), Ideological and criminal justice policy: Some current issues. Journal of Criminal Law and Criminology 64:141–162.

Mills, C. Wright (1956), White Collar. New York: Galaxie Books.

Millspaugh, Arthur G. (1937/1972), Crime Control by the National Government. New York: Da Capo Press.

Milner, Christina, and Richard Milner (1972), Black Players: The Secret World of Black Pimps. Boston: Little, Brown.

Minor, W. William (1975), Political crime, political justice, and political prisoners. Criminology 12:385–397.

Minor, W. William (1978), Deterrence research: Problems of theory and method. In James A. Cramer, ed. (1978), Preventing Crime. Beverly Hills, Calif.: Sage.

Minor, W. William (1980), The neutralization of criminal offense. Criminology 18:103–120.

Mintz, Morton (1965), The Therapeutic Nightmare: A Report on Prescription Drugs, the Men Who Take Them, and the Agency That Controls Them. Boston: Houghton Mifflin.

Mitford, Jessica (1973), Kind and Usual Punishment. New York: Knopf.

Monahan, John (1981), Predicting Violent Behavior: An Assessment of Clinical Techniques. Beverly Hills, Calif.: Sage.

Monahan, John, and Henry J. Steadman (1983), Crime and mental disorder: An epidemiological approach. In Michael Tonry and Norval Morris, eds. (1983), Crime and Justice: An Annual Review of Research, vol. 4. Chicago: University of Chicago Press.

Moore, Wilbert E. (1964), Social Aspects of Economic Development. Chicago: Rand McNally.

Morris, Terrence (1958), The Criminal Area. New York: Humanities Press.

Mulvihill, Donald J., Melvin Tumin, and Lynn Curtis (1969), Crimes of Violence. Washington, D.C.: U.S. Government Printing Office.

Munford, Robert S., Ross J. Kazer, Roger A. Feldman, and Robert R. Strivers (1976), Homicide trends in Atlanta. Criminology 14:213–232.

Murton, Tom, and Joe Hyams (1969), Accomplices to the Crime: The Arkansas Prison Scandal. New York: Grove Press.

Nader, Ralph (1967), We're still in the jungle. New Republic July 15, 1967, pp. 11–12.

Nader, Ralph, and Mark Green (1972), Coddling the corporations: Crime in the suites. New Republic 166:18–24.

Nagel, Stuart S. (1967), Disparities in criminal procedures. UCLA Law Review 14:1296.

Nagel, Stuart S., ed. (1977), Modelling the Criminal Justice System. Beverly Hills, Calif.: Sage.

Nagel, William G. (1973), The New Red Barn: A Critical Look at the Modern American Prison. New York: Walker.

National Commission on Marijuana and Drug Abuse (1973), Patterns and Consequences of Drug Use. Washington, D.C.: U.S. Government Printing Office.

National Council on Crime and Delinquency (1969), The infiltration into legitimate business by organized crime. Washington, D.C.: National Council and Crime and Delinquency.

National Institute on Drug Abuse (1980), National Survey on Drug Abuse: Main Findings, 1979. Washington, D.C.: U.S. Government Printing Office.

National Institute on Drug Abuse (1983), Student Drug Use, Attitudes, and Beliefs: National Trends, 1975–1982. Washington, D.C.: U.S. Government Printing Office.

National Institute on Drug Abuse (1985), Highlights from Drugs and American High School Students, 1975–1983. Washington, D.C.: U.S. Government Printing Office.

National Narcotics Intelligence Consumers Committee (1985), Narcotics Intelligence Estimate 1984. Washington, D.C.: U.S. Government Printing Office.

Nettler, Gwynn (1974), Embezzlement without problems. British Journal of Criminology 14:70–77.

Newman, Donald J. (1958), White collar crime. Law and Contemporary Problems 283:735–753.

Newman, Donald J. (1966), Conviction: The Determination of Guilt or Innocence Without Trial. Boston: Little, Brown.

Newman, Graeme (1978), The Punishment Response. Philadelphia: Lippincott.

Newman, Graeme (1979), Understanding Violence. New York: Lippincott.

Newman, Graeme R., Jean C. Jester, and Donald J. Articolo (1981), A Structural Analysis of Fraud. In Edith Elizabeth Flynn and John P. Conrad, eds., 1981, The New and the Old Criminology. New York: Praeger.

Newman, Oscar (1972), Defensible Space: Crime Prevention Through Urban Design. New York: Macmillan.

Newton, George D., and Franklin E. Zimring (1969), Firearms and Violence in America. Washington, D.C.: U.S. Government Printing Office.

Niederhoffer, Arthur J. (1967), Behind the Shield: The Police in Urban Society. New York: Anchor Books.

Normandeau, André (1968), Trends and patterns in crimes of robbery. Ph.D dissertation, University of Pennsylvania.

Normandeau, André (1970), Robbery in Philadelphia and London. British Journal of Criminology 10:71–79.

O'Leary, Vincent, and Kathleen Hanrahan (1977), Law and practice in parole proceedings: A national survey. Criminal Law Bulletin 13:205–211.

Orsagh, Thomas (1980), Unemployment and crime. Journal of Criminal Law and Criminology 71:181–183.

Pace, Denny F., and Jimmie Y. Styles (1983), Organized Crime: Concepts and Control. Englewood Cliffs, N.J.: Prentice-Hall.

Packer, Herbert L. (1964), The crime tariff. American Scholar 33:551–557.

Packer, Herbert L. (1968), The Limits of the Criminal Sanction. Stanford, Calif.: Stanford University Press.

Palmer, Stuart (1968), Murder and suicide in forty non-literate societies. Journal of Criminal Law, Criminology, and Police Science 56:320–324.

Parker, Robert Nash, and M. Dwayne Smith (1979), Deterrence, poverty, and type of homicide. American Journal of Sociology 85:614–624.

Pearl, Michael (1974), The Confessions of a Master Fence. Cambridge, Mass.: Schenkman.

Pelfrey, William V. (1979), Mainstream criminology: More old than new. Criminology 17:323–329.

Percy, Senator Charles H. (1974), The legacy of no-knock: Drug enforcement abuse. Contemporary Drug Problems 3:5–8.

Petersilia, Joan (1985a), Granting Felons Probation: Public Risks and Alternatives. Santa Monica, Calif.: Rand Corporation.

Petersilia, Joan (1985b), Probation and felony offenders, NIJ Reports. Washington, D.C.: National Institute of Justice.

Peterson, David M., and Paul C. Friday (1975), Early release from incarceration: Race as a factor in the use of "shock probation." Journal of Criminal Law and Criminology 66:79–87.

Peterson, Mark A., Harriett B. Braiker, and Suzanne M. Polich (1980), Doing Crime: A Survey of California Prison Inmates. Santa Monica, Calif.: Rand Corporation.

Phillips, David P. (1983), The impact of mass media violence on homicide. American Sociological Review 48:560–568.

Pike, Luke Owen (1968), A History of Crime in England, vol. 2. Montclair, N.J.: Patterson Smith.

Pileggi, Nicholas (1968), 1968 has been the year of the burglar. New York Times Magazine, November 17.

Pittman, David J., and William Handy (1964), Patterns in criminal aggravated assault. Journal of Criminal law, Criminology, and Police Science 55:462–470.

Platt, Anthony M. (1971), The Politics of Riot Commissions. New York: Macmillan.

Platt, Anthony M. (1974), Prospects for a radical criminology in the United States. Crime and Social Justice 1:3–10.

Ploscowe, Morris (1951), Sex and the Law. Englewood Cliffs, Calif.: Prentice-Hall.

Plucknett, Theodore F. T. (1948), A Concise History of Common Law. London: Butterworths.

Pollock, Sir Frederick, and Frederick William Maitland (1968), The History of English Law, vol. 2, 2nd ed. Cambridge, England: Cambridge University Press.

Polsky, Howard W. (1962), Cottage Six. New York: Wiley.

Polsky, Ned (1967), Hustlers, Beats, and Others. Chicago: Aldine.

Pontell, Henry N. (1984), A Capacity to Punish. Bloomington: Indiana University Press.

Pope, Carl E. (1977), Crime Specific Analysis: The Characteristics of Burglary Incidents. Washington, D.C.: U.S. Government Printing Office.

Porkorny, Alex D. (1965), Human violence: A comparison of homicide, aggravated assault, and attempted suicide. Journal of Criminal Law, Criminology, and Police Science 56:488–497.

Post, James E., and Edwin Baer (1978), Demarketing infant formula: Consumer products for the developing world. Journal of Contemporary Business 7:17–37.

Pound, Roscoe (1923), Interpretations of Legal History. New York: Macmillan.

Pound, Roscoe (1943), A survey of social interests. Harvard Law Review 57:1–39.

Pound, Roscoe (1951), The development of American law and its deviation from English law. Law Quarterly Review 67:49–66.

Pratt, Michael (1980), Mugging As a Social Problem. London: Routledge and Kegan Paul.

Preble, Edward A., and John J. Casey (1969), Taking care of business—The heroin user's life on the street. International Journal of the Addictions 4:8–12.

President's Commission on Law Enforcement and the Administration of Justice (1967a), Task Force Report: The Courts. Washington, D.C.: U.S. Government Printing Office.

President's Commission on Law Enforcement and the Administration of Justice

(1967b), Task Force Report: Organized Crime. Washington, D.C.: U.S. Government Printing Office.

President's Commission on Law Enforcement and the Administration of Justice (1969), Task Force Report: Crime and Its Impact. Washington, D.C.: U.S. Government Printing Office.

Pringle, Patrick (n.d.), Stand and Deliver: The Story of the Highwayman. New York: Norton.

Pyle, Gerald F. (1976), Spatial and temporal aspects of crime in Cleveland, Ohio. American Behavioral Scientist 20:175–178.

Quetelet, Adolphe (1835), Sur l'Homme et le Dévélopment de Ses Facultés: In Essai de Physique Sociale. Paris.

Quinney, Richard (1963), Occupational structure and criminal behavior: Prescription violations by retail pharmacists. Social Problems 2:179–183.

Quinney, Richard (1970), The Problem of Crime. New York: Dodd, Mead.

Quinney, Richard (1974), Critique of Legal Order: Crime Control in Capitalistic Society. Boston: Little, Brown.

Quinney, Richard (1975), Criminology: Analysis and Critique of Crime in America. Boston: Little, Brown.

Quinney, Richard (1979), Criminology, 2nd ed. Boston: Little, Brown.

Rada, Richard (1975), Alcohol and rape. Medical Aspects of Human Sexuality 9:48–65.

Rada, Richard (1976), Testosterone levels in the rapist. Psychosomatic Medicine 38:257–268.

Radcliffe-Brown, A. R. (1948), The Andaman Islanders. New York: Free Press.

Radzinowicz, Leon (1966), Ideology and Crime. New York: Columbia University Press.

Rankin, Joseph (1979), Changing attitudes toward capital punishment. Social Forces 58:194–211.

Reasons, Charles E. (1974), The Criminologist: Crime and the Criminal. Pacific Palisades, Calif.: Goodyear.

Reasons, Charles E., and Russell L. Kaplan (1975), Tear down the walls?—Some functions of prisons. Crime and Delinquency 21:360–372.

Reckless, Walter C. (1950), The Crime Problem. New York: Appleton-Century-Crofts.

Reckless, Walter C. (1973), The Crime Problem, 5th ed. Englewood Cliffs, N.J.: Prentice-Hall.

Reckless, Walter C., and Harry E. Allen (1979), Developing a national crime policy: The impact of politics on crime in America. In Edward Sagarin (1979), Criminology: New Concerns, Beverly Hills, Calif.: Sage.

Reckless, Walter C., and Simon Dinitz (1967), Pioneering with self concept as a vulnerability factor in delinquency. Journal of Criminal Law, Criminology, and Police Science 58:515–523.

Reed, John Shelton (1971), To live . . . and die . . . in Dixie: A contribution to the study of southern violence. Political Science Quarterly 86:424–443.

Reed, John Shelton (1977), Below the Smith and Wesson line: Reflections on southern violence. Lecture to the second annual Hugo Black symposium, University of Alabama at Birmingham.

Reiman, Jeffrey H. (1979), The Rich Get Richer and the Poor Get Prison. New York: Wiley.

Reiss, Albert J., Jr. (1970), Police brutality: Answers to key questions. In Michael Lipsky ed, (1970), Law and Order: Police Encounters. Chicago: Aldine.

Remington, Frank J., Donald J. Newman, Edward L. Kimball, Marygold Melli, and Herman Goldstein (1969), Criminal Justice Administration. Indianapolis: Bobbs-Merrill.

Reppetto, Thomas A. (1974), Residential Crime. Cambridge, Mass.: Ballinger.

Reuter, Peter (1983), Disorganized Crime: Illegal Markets and the Mafia. Cambridge, Mass.: MIT Press.

Riedel, Marc, and Margaret A. Zahn (1985), The Nature and Patterns of American Homicide. Washington, D.C.: National Institute of Justice.

Riis, Roger, and John Patric (1942), The Repairman Will Get You If You Don't Watch Out. New York: Doubleday.

Riley, D. (1980), An evaluation of a campaign to reduce vandalism. In R. V. G. Clarke and P. Mayhew, eds. (1980), Designing Out Crime. London: Her Majesty's Stationary Office.

Robin, Gerald D. (1967) The corporate and judicial disposition of employee thieves. Wisconsin Law Review (Summer):635–702.

Robin, Gerald D. (1980), Introduction to the Criminal Justice System. New York: Harper & Row.

Rock, Paul (1973), Feature review symposium. Sociological Quarterly 14:595.

Roebuck, Julian B., and Thomas Barker (1974), A typology of police corruption. In Ronald L. Akers and Edward Sagarin, eds. (1974), Crime Prevention and Social Control. New York: Praeger.

Roebuck, Julian B., and Ronald C. Johnson (1964), The "short con" man. Crime and Delinquency 10:235–248.

Rolph, C. H. (1955), Women of the Streets. London: Secker and Warburg.

Roncek, Dennis W. (1981), Dangerous places: Crime and residential environment. Social Forces 60:74–96.

Rose, Harold M., and Paula McClain (1981), Black Homicide and the Urban Environment. Rockville, Md.: National Institute of Mental Health.

Rosefsky, Robert S. (1973), Frauds, Swindles, and Rackets. Chicago: Follett.

Ross, H. Laurence (1982), Interrupted time series studies of deterrence of drinking and driving. In John Hagan, ed. (1982b), Deterrence Reconsidered: Methodological Innovations. Beverly Hills, Calif.: Sage.

Rossi, Peter H., Emily Waite, Christine E. Bose, and Richard E. Berk (1974), The seriousness of crimes: Normative structure and individual differences. American Sociological Review 39:224–237.

Rowe, D. C., and D. W. Osgood (1984), Heredity and sociological theories of delinquency: A reconsideration. American Sociological Review 49:526–540.

Rubin, Sol (1965), Cops, guns, and homicides. The Nation, December 27, 1965, pp. 527–531.

Rubinstein, Jonathan (1973), City Police. New York: Farrar, Straus & Giroux.

Rubinstein, Michael L., Stevens H. Clarke, and Teresa J. White (1980), Alaska Bans Plea Bargaining. Washington, D.C.: U.S. Department of Justice.

Runkle, Gerald (1976), Is violence always wrong? Journal of Politics 38:367–389.

Rusche, George, and Otto Kirchheimer (1938), Punishment and Social Structure. New York: Russell and Russell.

Russell, Diana E. H. (1983), Rape in Marriage. New York: Collier.

Sagalyn, Arnold (1971), The Crime of Robbery in the U.S. Washington, D.C.: National Institute of Law Enforcement and Administration of Justice.

Sagarin, Edward (1979), Criminology: New Concerns. Beverly Hills, Calif.: Sage.

Salerno, Ralph, and John S. Tompkins (1969), The Crime Confederation. Garden City, N.Y.: Doubleday.

Sanders, William (1983), Criminology. Reading, Mass.: Addison-Wesley.

San Marco, Louise R. (1979), Differential sentencing patterns among criminal homicide offenders in Harris County, Texas. Ph.D. dissertation, Sam Houston State University.

Sarbin, Theodore R., and Jeffrey E. Miller (1970), Demonism revisited: The xyy chromosomal anomaly. Issues in Criminology 5:195–207.

Schafer, Stephen (1969), Theories in Criminology. New York: Random House.

Schafer, Stephen (1971), The concept of the political criminal. Journal of Criminal Law, Criminology, and Police Science 62:380–387.

Schelling, Thomas D. (1967), Economic analysis of organized crime. In President's Commission on Law Enforcement and the Administration of Justice (1967b), Task Force Report: Organized Crime. Washington, D.C.: U.S. Government Printing Office.

Schmidt, Amesley K. (1985), Deaths in the line of duty. NIJ Reports, January, 8:6.

Schuessler, Karl (1954), Review. American Journal of Sociology 49:604–610.

Schulman, Joanne (1981), State-by-state information on marital rape exemption laws. In Diana E. H. Russell (1983), Rape in Marriage. New York: Collier.

Schwartz, Michael, and Sandra S. Tangri (1965), A note on self-concept as an insulator against delinquency. American Sociological Review 30:922–926.

Scull, Andrew T. (1977), Decarceration: Community Treatment and the Deviant—A Radical View. Englewood Cliffs, N.J.: Prentice-Hall.

Search Group, Inc. (1984a), Information Policy and Crime Control Strategies. Washington, D.C.: U.S. Department of Justice.

Search Group Inc. (1984b), Victim/Witness Legislation: An Overview. Washington, D.C.: U.S. Department of Justice.

Sears, John (1975), Testimony before the Committee on Commerce, United States Senate. Serial No. 94-15 April 15, 23:33–46.

Sellin, Thorsten (1935), Race prejudice in the administration of justice. American Journal of Sociology 41:212–217.

Sellin, Thorsten (1937), The Lombrosian myth in criminology. American Journal of Sociology 42:898–899.

Sellin, Thorsten (1938), Culture Conflict and Crime. New York: Social Science Research Council.

Sellin, Thorsten, and Marvin E. Wolfgang (1964), The Measurement of Delinquency. New York: Wiley.

Selznick, Philip (1968), Sociology of law. International Encyclopedia of the Social Sciences 9:50–59.

Shaw, Clifford R. (1930), The Jack-Roller: A Delinquent Boy's Own Story. Chicago: University of Chicago Press.

Shaw, Clifford R. (1931), Delinquency Areas. Chicago: University of Chicago Press.

Shaw, Clifford R., and Henry D. McKay (1942), Juvenile Delinquency and Urban Areas. Chicago: University of Chicago Press.

Shearer, Lloyd (1979), Rape in marriage. Parade, April 22, pp. 6–9.

Shearing, Clifford D. (1979), Subterranean processes, the maintenance of power: An examination of the mechanisms coordinating police action. Paper presented at the annual meeting of the American Sociological Association, August 17–21.

Sheehy, Gail (1973), Hustling: Prostitution in Our Wide-Open Society. New York: Delacorte.

Shelley, Louise (1980), Crime and Modernization. Edwardsville: Southern Illinois University Press.

Shoham, Shlomo (1970), The Mark of Cain. Dobbs Ferry, N.Y.: Citadel.

Shover, Neal (1973), The social organization of burglary. Social Problems 20:499–514.

Silver, Allan (1967), The demand for order in civil society. In David Bordua, ed. (1967), The Police: Six Sociological Essays. New York: Wiley.

Silverstein, Lee (1966), Bail in the state courts—A field study and report. Minnesota Law Review 50:621–631.

Simon, Rita J. (1975), Women and Crime. Lexington, Mass.: Lexington Books.

Sinclair, Andrew (1964), Era of Excess: A Social History of the Prohibition Movement. New York: Harper & Row.

Singer, Neil M. (1973), The Value of Inmate Manpower. Washington, D.C.: American Bar Association.

Skogan, Wesley G. (1977), Dimensions of the dark figure of unreported crime. Crime and Delinquency 23:41–50.

Skolnick, Jerome H. (1966), Justice Without Trial: Law Enforcement in a Democratic Society. New York: Wiley.

Skolnick, Jerome H. (1975), Justice Without Trial, 2nd ed. New York: Wiley.

Skolnick, Jerome H., and Elliott P. Currie (1976), Crisis in American Institutions, 3rd ed. Boston: Little, Brown.

Smart, Carol (1979), The new female criminal: Reality or myth? British Journal of Criminology 19:50–59.

Smigel, Erwin O. (1956), Public attitudes toward stealing as related to the size of the victim organization. American Sociological Review 21:320–327.

Smigel, Erwin O., and H. Laurence Ross, eds. (1970), Crimes Against Bureaucracy. New York: Van Nostrand.

Sowle, Claude R., ed. (1962), Police Power and Individual Freedom. Chicago: Aldine.

Sparks, Richard F. (1980), Criminal opportunities and crime rates. In Stephen F. Feinberg and Albert J. Reiss eds. (1980), Indicators of Crime and Criminal Justice: Quantitative Studies. Washington, D.C.: U.S. Government Printing Office.

Speiglman, Richard (1976), Building the walls inside: Medicine, corrections and the state apparatus for repression. Ph.D. dissertation, University of California, Berkeley.

Spitzer, Steven (1975), Toward a Marxian theory of deviance. Social Problems 22:638–651.

Stellwagen, Lindsey P. (1985), Use of Forfeiture Sanctions in Drug Cases. Washington, D.C.: National Institute of Justice.

Stoddard, Ellwyn R. (1968), The informal "code" of police deviancy: A group approach to "Blue Coat Crime." Journal of Criminal Law, Criminology, and Police Science 59:201–213.

Stoll, Clarice S. (1968), Images of man and social control. Social Forces 47:119–127.

Street, David (1965), The inmate group in custodial and treatment settings. American Sociological Review 30:40–55.

Sutherland, Edwin H. (1937a), Criminology. New York: Lippincott.

Sutherland, Edwin H. (1937b), The Professional Thief. Chicago: University of Chicago Press.

Sutherland, Edwin H. (1949), White Collar Crime. New York: Dryden Press.

Sutherland, Edwin H., and Donald R. Cressey (1974), Criminology, 9th ed. Philadelphia: Lippincott.

Sykes, Gresham M. (1958), The Society of Captives. Princeton, N.J.: Princeton University Press.

Sykes, Gresham M. (1972), The future of criminality. American Behavioral Scientist 15:409–419.

Sykes, Gresham M. (1978), Criminology. New York: Harcourt Brace Jovanovich.

Sykes, Gresham M., and David Matza (1957), Techniques of neutralization: A theory of delinquency. American Sociological Review 22:664–670.

Sylvester, Sawyer F., and Edward Sagarin, eds. (1974), Politics and Crime. New York: Praegar.

Szabo, Dennis, and Susan Katzenelson, eds. (1978), Offenders and Corrections. New York: Praeger.


Takagi, Paul (1979), Death by "police intervention." In U.S. Department of Justice (1979), A Community Concern: Police Use of Deadly Force. Washington, D.C.: U.S. Government Printing Office.

Tangri, Sandra S., and Michael Schwartz (1967), Delinquency research and the self-concept variable. Journal of Criminal Law, Criminology, and Police Science 58:182–190.

Tannenbaum, Frank (1938), Crime and the Community. New York: Columbia University Press.

Tappan, Paul W. (1947), Who is the criminal? American Sociological Review 12:96–102.

Taylor, G. Rattray (1965), Sex in History. London: Panther.

Taylor, Ian, Paul Walton, and Jock Young, eds. (1975), Critical Criminology. London: Routledge and Kegan Paul.

Terry, C. E., and Mildred Pellens (1928/1970), The Opium Problem. Montclair, N.J.: Patterson Smith.

Thomas, Charles W. (1977), Theoretical perspectives on prisonization: A comparison of the importation and deprivation models. Journal of Criminal Law and Criminology 68:135–145.

Thomas, D. A. (1967), Sentencing: The basic principles. Criminal Law Review 15:514–520.

Thornberry, Terence P. (1973), Race, socioeconomic status, and sentencing in the juvenile justice system. Journal of Criminal Law and Criminology 64:90–98.

Thornberry, Terence P., and R. L. Christenson (1984), Unemployment and criminal involvement: An investigation of reciprocal causal structures. American Sociological Review 49:398–411.

Toch, Hans (1977), Police, Prisons, and the Problem of Violence. Rockville, Md.: National Institute of Mental Health.

Tonry, Michael, and Norval Morris, eds. (1983), Crime and Justice: An Annual Review of Research, vol. 4. Chicago: University of Chicago Press.

Toro-Calder, Jaime (1950), Personal crimes in Puerto Rico. Master's thesis, University of Wisconsin.

Trotter, R. T. (1972), Clockwork orange in a California prison. Science News 101:174–175.

Turk, Austin T. (1966), Conflict and criminality. American Sociological Review 31:338–352.

Turk, Austin T. (1969), Criminality and Legal Order. Chicago: Rand McNally.

Turner, J. W. Cecil, ed. (1966), Kenney's Outlines of Criminal Law, 19th ed. Cambridge, England: Cambridge University Press.

Tyler, Gus, ed. (1962), Organized Crime in America. Ann Arbor: University of Michigan Press.

United Nations (1983), Demographic Yearbook. New York: United Nations Publishing Service.

U.S. Center for Women Policy Studies (1979), Violence in the Home Is a Crime Against the Whole Family. Washington, D.C.: U.S. Government Printing Office.

U.S. Department of Agriculture (1979), Food consumption, prices, and expenditures. Statistical Bulletin 702. Washington, D.C.: U.S. Government Printing Office.

U.S. Department of Agriculture Economic Research Service (1983), Food Consumption, Prices, and Expenditures. Washington, D.C.: U.S. Government Printing Office.

U.S. Department of Justice (1975), The Nation's Jails: A Report on the Census of Jails from the 1972 Survey of Inmates of Local Jails. Washington, D.C.: U.S. Government Printing Office.

U.S. Department of Justice (1976), The LEAA: A Partnership for Crime Control. Washington, D.C.: U.S. Government Printing Office.

U.S. Department of Justice (1979), A Community Concern: Police Use of Deadly Force. Washington, D.C.: U.S. Government Printing Office.

U.S. Department of Justice (1980), Reports of the National Juvenile Justice Assessment Centers: Juveniles in Detention Centers and Jails. Washington, D.C.: U.S. Government Printing Office.

U.S. Department of Justice (1981a), Children in Custody: Advance Report on the 1979 Census of Private Juvenile Facilities. Washington, D.C.: U.S. Government Printing Office.

U.S. Department of Justice (1981b), Profile of Jail Inmates: Sociodemographic Findings from the 1928 Survey of Inmates of Local Jails. Washington, D.C.: U.S. Government Printing Office.

Valentine, Alan (1956), Vigilante Justice. New York: Reynal.

van Den Berghe, Pierre L. (1974), Bringing beasts back in: Toward a biosocial theory of aggression. American Sociological Review 39:777–778.

Vander Zanden, James W. (1970), Sociology: A Systematic Approach, 2nd ed. New York: Ronald Press.

Velarde, Albert J., and Mark Warlick (1973), Massage parlors: The sensuality business. Society 11:63–74.

Vetri, Dominick R. (1964), Guilty-plea bargaining: Compromise by prosecutors to secure guilty pleas. University of Pennsylvania Law Review 112:896–908.

Vold, George B. (1958), Theoretical Criminology. New York: Oxford University Press.

Vold, George B. (1979), Theoretical Criminology, 2nd ed. New York: Oxford University Press.

Vold, George B., and Thomas J. Bernard (1986), Theoretical Criminology. New York: Oxford University Press.

von Hentig, Hans (1948), The Criminal and His Victim. New Haven, Conn.: Yale University Press.

von Hirsch, Andrew (1976), Doing Justice: The Choice of Punishments. New York: Hill & Wang.

von Hirsch, Andrew (1984), Selective incapacitation: A critique, NIJ Reports. Washington, D.C.: National Institute of Justice.

Voss, Harwin L., and John R. Hepburn (1968), Patterns in criminal homicide in Chicago. Journal of Criminal Law, Criminology, and Police Science 59:499–508.


Walker, Nigel (1971), Crime, Courts, and Figures. Baltimore: Penguin.

Walker, Samuel (1985), Sense and Nonsense About Crime: A Policy Guide. Monterey, Calif.: Brooks/Cole.

Walsh, Dermot (1980), Break-ins: Burglary from Private Houses. London: Constable.

Walsh, Marilyn (1977), The Fence. Westport, Conn.: Greenwood Press.

Walters, James M. (1985), "Taking care of business" updated: A fresh look at the daily routine of the heroin user. In Bill Hanson, George Beschner, James M. Walters, and Elliott Bovelle (1985), Life with Heroin. Lexington, Mass.: Lexington Books.

Walton, Robert P. (1938), America's New Drug Problem. Philadelphia: Lippincott.

Waltz, Jon R. (1953), Shoplifting and the law of arrest. Yale Law Journal 62:788–805.

Ward, David A., Maurice Jackson, and Renee E. Ward (1969), Crimes of violence by women. In Donald J. Mulvihill, Melvin Tumin, and Lynn Curtis (1969), Crimes of Violence. Washington, D.C.: U.S. Government Printing Office.

Warren, E. H., Jr. (1978), The economic approach to crime. Canadian Journal of Criminology 10:437–449.

Weber, Max (1954), Law in Economy and Society. Cambridge, Mass.: Harvard University Press.

Weinberg, Martin S., and Colin J. Williams (1975), Male Homosexuals: Their Problems and Adaptations. Baltimore: Penguin.

Weiner, Norman (1974), The effect of education on police attitudes. Journal of Criminal Justice 2:323–330.

Weis, Kurt, and Sandra S. Borges (1973), Victimology and rape: The case of the legitimate victim. Issues in Criminology 8:85–89.

Wellford, Charles (1967), Factors associated with adoption of an inmate code: A study of normative socialization. Journal of Criminal Law, Criminology, and Police Science 58:197–203.

Wellford, Charles (1975), Labeling theory and criminology: An assessment. Social Problems 22:332–345.

Werthman, Carl, and Irving Piliavin (1967), Gang members and the police. In David Bordua, ed. (1967), The Police: Six Sociological Essays. New York: Wiley.

Westley, William A. (1970), Violence and the Police: A Sociological Study of Law, Custom and Morality. Cambridge, Mass.: MIT Pres.

Weston, Paul B., and Kenneth M. Wells (1972), Law Enforcement and Criminal Justice. Pacific Palisades, Calif.: Goodyear.

Wheeler, Stanton (1976), Trends and problems in the sociological study of crime. Social Problems 23:525–534.

White, Leslie T. (1972), The definitions and prohibitions of incest. In John N. Edwards (1972), Sex and Society. Chicago: Markham.

Whitman, Howard (1951), Terror in the Streets. New York: Dial Press.

Wickman, Peter (1978), Industrial wages for prisoners in Findland and Sweden. In Dennis Szabo and Susan Kalzenelson, eds. (1978), Offenders and Corrections. New York: Praeger.

Wilbanks, William (1985), Is violent crime intraracial? Crime and Delinquency 31:117–128.

Wilkins, Leslie T., Jack M. Kress, Don M. Gottfredson, Joseph C. Calpin, and Arthur M. Gelman (1978), Sentencing Guidelines: Structuring Judicial Discretion. Washington, D.C.: U.S. Government Printing Office.

Williams, Joyce E., and Karen Holmes (1981), The Second Assault: Rape and Public Attitudes. Westport, Conn.: Greenwood Press.

Williams, K. (1978), The role of victims in the prosecution of violent crimes. Washington, D.C.: Institute for Law and Social Policy.

Williams, Kirk R. (1984), Economic sources of homicide: Re-estimating the effects of poverty and inequality. American Sociological Review 49:283–289.

Williams, Kristen M. (1976), The effects of victim characteristics on the disposition of violent crimes. In William McDonald, ed. (1976), Criminal Justice and the Victim. Beverly Hills, Calif.: Sage.

Williams, Linda (1984), Sex, race, and rape: An analysis of interracial sexual violence. Paper presented at the annual meeting of the American Society of Criminology, Cincinnati.

Wilson, James Q. (1984), Problems in the creation of adequate criminal justice information systems. In Search Group, Inc. (1984a), Information Policy and Crime Control Strategies. Washington, D.C.: U.S. Department of Justice.

Wilson, James Q., and Richard J. Herrnstein (1985), Crime and Human Nature. New York: Simon & Schuster.

Wilson, Nanci Koser (1978), Styles of doing time in a co-ed prison. Masculine and feminine alternatives. In Dennis Szabo and Susan Katzenelson (1978), Offenders and Corrections. New York: Praeger.

Wilson, Sheena (1980), Vandalism and defensible space in London housing estates. In R. V. G. Clarke and P. Mayhew, eds. (1980), Designing Out Crime. London: Her Majesty's Stationary Office.

Winick, Charles (1962), Maturing out of narcotic addiction. Bulletin on Narcotics 14:1–7.

Winick, Charles, and Paul M. Kinsie (1971), The Lively Commerce: Prostitution in the United States. Chicago: Quadrangle Books.

Wiseman, Jacqueline P. (1970), Stations of the Lost: The Treatment of Skid Row Alcoholics. Englewood Cliffs, N.J.: Prentice-Hall.

Wolfgang, Marvin E. (1958), Patterns in Criminal Homicide. Philadelphia: University of Pennsylvania Press.

Wolfgang, Marvin E. (1961), Pioneers in criminology: Cesare Lombroso (1835–1909). Journal of Criminal Law, Criminology, and Police Science 52:361–391.

Wolfgang, Marvin E. (1967), Crimes of Violence. A Report to the President's Commission on Law Enforcement and the Administration of Justice. Washington, D.C.: U.S. Government Printing Office.

Wolfgang, Marvin E., and Franco Ferracuti (1967), The Subculture of Violence. London: Tavistock.

Wolfgang, Marvin E., and Bernard Cohen (1970), Crime and Race. New York: Institute of Human Relations Press.

Wolfgang, Marvin E., Robert M. Figlio, Paul E. Tracy, and Simon I. Singer (1985), The National Survey of Crime Severity. Washington, D.C.: U.S. Department of Justice.

Wolfgang, Marvin E., and Marc Riedel (1973), Law, judicial discretion, and the death penalty. The Annals 407:119–133.

Wolin, Sheldon S. (1970), Violence and the western political tradition. In Renatus Hartogs and Eric Artzt (1970), Violence: Causes and Solutions. New York: Dell.

Wright, Helena (1968), Sex and Society. London: Allen & Unwin.

Wright, James D., and Peter H. Rossi (1981), Weapons, Crime, and Violence in America. Washington, D.C.: National Institute of Justice.

Yablonsky, Lewis (1966), The Violent Gang. New York: Penguin.

Yochelson, Samuel, and Stanton E. Samenow (1976, 1977), The Criminal Personality, vols. 1 and 2. New York: Jason Aronson.

Young, James H. (1967), The Medical Messiahs. Princeton, N.J.: Princeton University Press.

Young, Wayland (1964), Eros Denied: Sex in Western Society. New York: Grove Press.

Zimbardo, Philip G. (1972), The pathology of imprisonment. Society 9:4–8

Zimring, Franklin E. (1972), The medium is the message: Firearm caliber as a determinant of death from assault. Journal of Legal Studies 15:97–123.

Zimring, Franklin E., and Gordon J. Hawkins (1973), Deterrence: The Legal Threat in Crime Control. Chicago: University of Chicago Press.

# Author Index

Warlick, Mark, 323, 535
Warren, E. H., Jr., 75, 536
Wasserstein, Bruce, 518
Weber, Marvin Glenn, 272, 523
Weber, Max, 11, 12, 536
Weinberg, Martin S., 329, 536
Weiner, Norman, 370, 536
Weis, Kurt, 164, 536
Weiss, Joseph G., 520
Wellford, Charles, 52, 468, 536
Wells, Kenneth M., 359, 536
Werthman, Carl, 368, 536
Westley, William A., 398, 536
Weston, Paul B., 359, 536
Wheeler, Stanton, 65, 537
White, Leslie T., 70, 537
White, Teresa J., 531
Whitman, Howard, 188, 537
Wickman, Peter, 464, 537
Wilbanks, William, 134, 159, 537
Wilkins, Leslie T., 410, 414, 415,
    511, 525, 537
Williams, Colin J., 329, 536
Williams, Joyce E., 152, 537
Williams, K., 148, 537
Williams, Kirk R., 140, 147, 537
Williams, Kristen M., 202, 537
Williams, Linda, 159, 537
Williams, Thomas A., III, 407, 506
Wilson, James Q., 29, 30, 31, 75, 76,
    137, 450, 480, 481, 537

Wilson, Nanci Koser, 461, 537
Wilson, Sheena, 71, 537
Winchester, S. W., 525
Winick, Charles, 321, 345, 537
Wiseman, Jacqueline P., 372, 537
Wolfgang, Marvin E., 9, 11, 28, 95,
    120, 126, 127, 129, 130, 131,
    142, 144, 145, 147, 173, 284,
    411, 427, 532, 537, 538
Wolin, Sheldon S., 121, 538
Wozniack, John F., 514
Wright, Helena, 318, 321, 538
Wright, James D., 128, 129, 538
Wright, Richard, 82, 507

Yablonsky, Lewis, 145, 280, 519, 538
Yeager, Peter C., 513
Yochelson, Samuel, 32, 538
Young, James H., 275, 538
Young, Jock, 58, 512, 534
Young, Wayland, 538

Zahn, Margaret A., 125, 127, 128,
    530
Zimbardo, Philip G., 455, 456, 457,
    458, 538
Zimring, Franklin E., 129, 446, 508,
    528, 538
Zurcher, Louis A., 515

# Subject Index

"Crack," 341
Crime(s)
 definition of, 5–9
 displacement of, 82–84
 and economic conditions, 38–39
 economic model of, 75
 as an event, 67–70
 *mala in se* and *mala prohibita,* 15, 16, 449–450
 measurement of, 88–115
 and opportunity, 67–70, 72–74
 prevention of, 423–424, 444–447
 rates of, in United States, 100, 106, 108–109, 123, 125, 159–160, 180, 209, 232
 and rationality, 74–85
 situational perspectives on, 66, 67–74, 84, 131–132
 spatial analysis of, 36, 71, 77–78
 unreported, 96–103, 156–158
 victimless, 316, 346
 *see also* Data on crime; individual crimes, e.g., Burglary
Crime control
 federal role in, 360, 481–484
 policy emphasis on, 476, 479–484
"Crime Control Model" of criminal process, 476–477
Crime rates, defined, 94–95
Crime seriousness
 national survey scores, 10–11
 public attitudes toward, 9
Crime targets, selection of, 79–82
Criminal(s)
 "able," 78–79
 biological view of, 27–33, 76, 136–137
 definition of, 19
 psychological view of, 32–33
 stereotype of, 8, 367–370, 484–486
Criminal defenses, 21–22
Criminal law
 definition of, 13
 and interests, 16–17
 origins and development of, 16–18
 procedural, 18, *see also* Due Process
 *see also* Common law; Law
Criminal lawyers, 403

Criminal opportunities, 67–70, 72–74, 230, 236
Criminal statistics, *see* Data on crime
Criminality
 and labeling process, 8, 19–21, 51–55, 484–486
 self-reported, 99, 101–103
 social process theories of, 42–54
Criminalization
 and conflict, 26, 53–55
 defined, 7
Criminology
 classical, 58–75
 conservative, 25
 critical, 26, 58–65
 development of, 24–56
 liberal-cynical, 25–26


Dangerous places, 71–72
Data on crime
 lost through nonreporting, 89, 91, 96–97
 official, United States, 105–110
 police role in production of, 91–96
 production of, 88–96
Data on criminal justice, 111–114, *see also* Arrest(s)
Dating and sexual aggression, 163–164
Death penalty, *see* Capital punishment
Defense attorney and bargained justice, 402–404
Defensible space, 71–72
Delinquency, *see* Juvenile delinquency
Delinquent subculture(s), 39–42
Determinate sentencing, 416–417
Deterrence, 424, 448–452
Differential association, 42–45, 446
Discretion
 citizen, 89, 379–381
 police, 91–92, 370–373
Displacement of crime, 82–84
Drug(s)
 American use of, 333, 334, 335–341
 public attitudes toward illegal use of, 350–351
 trafficking in, 303–304, 313, 341–342